EUROPEAN ENERGY LAW REPORT XIII

Energy & Law Series

European Energy Law Report I, Martha M. Roggenkamp and Ulf Hammer (eds.)

The Regulation of Power Exchanges in Europe, Martha M. Roggenkamp and François Boisseleau (eds.)

European Energy Law Report II, Martha M. Roggenkamp and Ulf Hammer (eds.)

European Energy Law Report III, Ulf Hammer and Martha M. Roggenkamp (eds.)

European Energy Law Report IV, Martha M. Roggenkamp and Ulf Hammer (eds.)

A Functional Legal Design for Reliable Electricity Supply, Hamilcar Knops

European Energy Law Report V, Martha M. Roggenkamp and Ulf Hammer (eds.)

European Energy Law Report VI, Martha M. Roggenkamp and Ulf Hammer (eds.)

Electricity and Gas Supply Network Unbundling in Germany, Great Britain and The Netherlands and the Law of the EU, Eckart Ehlers

Legal Design of Carbon Capture and Storage, Martha M. Roggenkamp and Edwin Woerdman (eds.)

European Energy Law Report VII, Martha M. Roggenkamp and Ulf Hammer (eds.)

European Energy Law Report VIII, Martha M. Roggenkamp and Ulf Hammer (eds.)

European Energy Law Report IX, Martha M. Roggenkamp and Olivia Woolley (eds.)

EU Regulation of Cross-Border Carbon Capture and Storage, Marijn Holwerda

The Non-Discrimination Obligation of Energy Network Operators, Hannah Kruimer

European Energy Law Report X, Martha M. Roggenkamp and Henrik Bjørnebye (eds.)

A Legal Framework for a Transnational Offshore Grid in the North Sea, Hannah Katharina Müller

Prevention and Compensation for Transboundary Damage in Relation to Cross-Border Pipelines, Mehdi Piri Damagh

Handbook of Shale Gas Law and Policy – Economics, Access, Law and Regulation in Key Jurisdictions, Tina Hunter (ed.)

European Energy Law Report XI, Martha M. Roggenkamp and Catherine Banet (eds.)

European Energy Law Report XII, Martha M. Roggenkamp and Catherine Banet (eds.)

European Energy Law Report XIII, Martha M. Roggenkamp and Catherine Banet (eds.)

EUROPEAN ENERGY LAW REPORT XIII

Edited by
Martha M. Roggenkamp
Catherine Banet

INTERSENTIA

Intersentia Ltd
8 Wellington Mews
Wellington Street | Cambridge
CB1 1HW | United Kingdom
Tel.: +44 1223 736 170
Email: mail@intersentia.co.uk
www.intersentia.com | www.intersentia.co.uk

Distribution for the UK and Ireland:
NBN International
Airport Business Centre, 10 Thornbury Road
Plymouth, PL6 7PP
United Kingdom
Tel.: +44 1752 202 301 | Fax: +44 1752 202 331
Email: orders@nbninternational.com

Distribution for Europe and all other countries:
Intersentia Publishing nv
Groenstraat 31
2640 Mortsel
Belgium
Tel.: +32 3 680 15 50 | Fax: +32 3 658 71 21
Email: mail@intersentia.be

Distribution for the USA and Canada:
Independent Publishers Group
Order Department
814 North Franklin Street
Chicago, IL 60610
USA
Tel.: +1 800 888 4741 (toll free) | Fax: +1 312 337 5985
Email: orders@ipgbook.com

The Energy & Law Series is published in parallel with the Dutch series Energie & Recht.

European Energy Law Report XIII

ISBN 978-1-78068-950-0
D/2020/7849/16
NUR 828

British Library Cataloguing in Publication Data. A catalogue record for this book is available from the British Library.

PREFACE

The editors are very pleased to present the *European Energy Law Report XIII*. The *European Energy Law Report* is an initiative taken by the organisers of the European Energy Law Seminar which has taken place on a regular basis in the Netherlands since 1989. The aim of this seminar is to present an overview of the most important legal developments in the field of international, EU and national energy and climate law. Whereas the first seminars concentrated on the developments at European Community (EC) level, which were the results of the establishment of an Internal Energy Market, the focus has now gradually switched to the developments at the national level following the implementation of the EU Directives on the internal electricity and gas markets, promoting renewable energy sources, mitigating climate change and securing energy supply. This approach can also be found in these reports.

Similar to the previous *European Energy Law Reports*, this book includes chapters based on papers presented at the preceding European Energy Law Seminar, held on an annual basis. This Report, however, covers the main contents of the European Energy Law Seminars from both 2018 and 2019. It examines some new developments following from the liberalisation of the electricity market, the hydropower sector, investments in the energy sector and the increased role of flexibility, but also the other side of the coin – the gradual closure of coal-fired power plants and nuclear plants, as well as the decommissioning of offshore oil and gas facilities. The latter is again linked to the need to reduce carbon dioxide emissions, which notably rely on the use of carbon capture and storage (CCS) technologies, and the opportunity to re-use and re-purpose installations. Renewable energy generation and CCS are climate mitigation instruments to reduce CO_2 emissions and are often considered in national climate plans and climate laws, which are examined in the last part of the book. This Report thus contains six parts: 'Newcomers in the Electricity Market: Aggregators and Storage', 'Hydropower Concessions in the EU: A Need for Liberalisation or Privatisation?', 'Investments and Disinvestments in the Energy Sector', 'Offshore Decommissioning in the North Sea', 'CCS as a Climate Tool: North Sea Practice' and 'From EU Climate Goals to National Climate Laws'.

We are grateful for the support of the speakers at the seminar and their co-operation in rewriting their papers for the purpose of this book. We also would like to thank the authors and co-authors who were not speakers at the seminar but who were willing to participate in this project so that we are able to provide you with a 'complete' picture of all the topics discussed. Finally, we would like to acknowledge the help and support of the publisher in publishing this book. We are confident that these reports will be part of an important and long-lasting tradition in this field.

Martha M. Roggenkamp and Catherine Banet
Groningen/Oslo, 30 October 2019

CONTENTS

PART I. NEWCOMERS IN THE ELECTRICITY MARKET: AGGREGATORS AND STORAGE

LIST OF ABBREVIATIONS

ACER	Agency for the Cooperation of Energy Regulators
AIB	Association of Issuing Bodies
APG	Austrian Power Grid AG
ARH	Hydrographic district administrations
ARP	Access Responsible Party
ASC	Adaptation Sub-Committee (United Kingdom)
ASN	Nuclear safety authority (France)
BEIS	Department for Business, Energy and Industrial Strategy
BMUs	Balancing Mechanism Units
BPEO	Best Practicable Environmental Option
BRP	Balance Responsible Party
BSC	Balancing and Settlement Code
BSUoS	Balancing Services Use of System
BVerfG	Federal Constitutional Court (Bundesverfasssungsgericht)
CAE	Energy Acquisition Agreements (Contratos de Aquisição de Energia)
CAISO	California ISO
CCA	Climate Change Act (United Kingdom)
CCC	Committee on Climate Change (United Kingdom)
CCS	UK Climate Change Act 2008
CCL	Climate Change Levy
CCS	Carbon capture and storage
CCUS	Carbon capture use and storage
CEER	Council of European Energy Regulators
CEN	European Committee for standardization
CETA	EU-Canada Comprehensive Economic and Trade Agreement
CfD	Contracts for Difference
CJEU	Court of Justice of the European Union
CMEC	Costs of Maintenance of the Contractual Equilibrium (Compensation Mechanism)
CO_2	Carbon dioxide
ConEd	Consolidated Edison
CREG	Commission for Electricity and Gas Regulation (Belgium)
CRPPA	Corporate Renewable Power Purchasing Agreement
CS	Continental Shelf
CSP	Curtailment service provider

CUSC	Connection and Use of System Code
DCC	Dutch Civil Code
DCO	Development consent order
DEA	Danish Energy Agency
DERs	Distributed energy resources
DERP	Distributed energy resource providers
DGEG	Directorate General of Energy and Geology (Portugal)
DKK	Danish Crown
DNO	Distribution network owners
DPO	Plan for development and operation
DR	Demand response
DSA	Decommissioning Security Agreement
DSO	Distribution system operator
DSR	Demand side response
DUC	Danish Underground Consortium
DUoS	Distribution Use of System
EAC	Energy Attribute Certificate
EBN	BV Energie Beheer Nederland
ECT	Energy Charter Treaty
ECHR	European Convention for the Protection of Human Rights and Fundamental Freedoms
ECtHR	European Court of Human Rights
EDF	Electricité de France
EDP	Energias de Portugal (formerly Electricidade de Portugal)
EEA	European Economic Area
EECS	European Energy Certificate System
EEZ	Exclusive Economic Zone
EFR	Enhanced Frequency Response
EFTA	European Free Trade Agreement
E&P	Exploration and Production
EHR	Enhanced Hydrocarbons Recovery
EOR	Enhanced Oil Recovery
EPA	Environmental Protection Agency (Sweden)
EPR	European pressurised reactor
ESA	EFTA Surveillance Authority
ESDER	Energy Storage and Distributed Energy Resource
ESR	EU Effort Sharing Regulation
ETTF	Energy Transition Task Force
EU	European Union
EU ETS	EU Emission Trading Scheme
EV	Electric vehicles
Exaa	Electricity Exhange Austria
FDI	Foreign Direct Investment

FDM	Flexibility Data Manager
FEED	Front and end engineering design
FERC	U.S. Federal Energy Regulatory Commission
FFR	Firm Frequency Response
FGC	Federal Grid Code (Belgium)
FIT	Feed in Tariffs
FOV	Fortum Oslo Varme
FPA	Federal Power Act
FPSO	Floating production storage and offloading vessels
FRIFO	Union of Outdoor Recreation Organizations
FSP	Flexibility service providers
FSR	Florence School of Regulation
FTA	Free trade agreement
GATT	General Agreement on Tariffs and Trade
GBS	Gravity base storage
GHG	Greenhouse gas
GO	Guarantee of Origin
GW	Gigawatt
HEC	High Efficiency Cogeneration
HSE	Health, Safety and Environment
ICH	Load interruptibility mechanism
ICSID	International Centre for Settlement of Investment Disputes
IDNO	Independent distribution network operators
IE	Industrial Emissions
IEA	International Energy Agency
IMF	International Monetary Fund
IMO	International Maritime Organization
INAG	National Water Institute (Instituto Nacional da Água)
INT NC	Network Code on interoperability and data exchange rules
IPCC	Intergovernmental Panel on Climate Change
ISCC	International Sustainability and Carbon Certification
ISO	independent system operators
JDA	Joint Development Agreement
JOA	Joint Operating Agreement
LCA	Life Cycle Assessment
LNG	Liquefied natural gas
LVK	Norwegian Association of Municipalities hosting Hydropower Plants
MEP	Multi-annual energy plan (Programmation Pluriannuelle de l'Energie)
MFN	Most-favoured nation treatment
MIBEL	Iberian Electricity Market
MP	Member of Parliament

MPE	Ministry of Petroleum and Energy
MS	Member State
MW	Megawatt
NCS	Norwegian Continental Shelf
NECP	National Energy and Climate Plan
NGET	National Grid Electricity Transmission plc
NGO	Non-governmental organisation
NOPR	Notice of Proposed Rulemaking
NOVI	National Environmental Strategy (Nationale Omgevingsvisie)
NPS	National policy statement
NSIP	Nationally significant infrastructure project
NT	National treatment
NTE	Not-to-Exceed values
NVE	Norwegian Energy Directorate
NWA	Non-wires alternatives
OECD	Organisation for Economic Cooperation and Development
OGA	Oil and Gas Authority
OSPAR	Convention for the Protection of the Marine Environment of the North-East Atlantic
PBL	Netherlands Environmental Assessment Agency (Planbureau voor de Leefomgeving)
PDR	Proxy Demand Resource
PNBEPH	National Program of High Hydroelectric Energetic Potential Power Plants (Programa Nacional de Barragens de Elevado Potencial Hidroeléctrico)
Porthos	Port of Rotterdam CO_2 Transport Hub & Offshore Storage
PTE	Panel of technical experts
RBMP	River Basin Management Plan
RED	Renewable Energy Directive
REN	National Electricity Grid (Portugal)
RES-E	Renewable sources
REV	Reforming the Energy Vision
RNT	National Transmission Grid (Rede Nacional de Transporte)
RO	Renewables Obligation
RTO	Regional transmission organisations
SABIMA	Norwegian Biodiversity Network
SEN	Sistema Eléctrico Nacional
SEP	Public Electricity System (Portugal)
SLC	Standard Licence Condition
SEN	National Electricity System (Portugal)
SRN	Liaison Committee of Nature Conservation
SWD	Staff Working Document
TCM	Technology Centre Mongstad

TCR	Targeted charging review
TNUoS	Transmission Network Use of System
TFEU	Treaty on the Functioning of the European Union
TPA	Third party access
TSO	Transmission system operator
UGS Tariff	Global Use of System Tariff
UKCS	United Kingdom continental shelf
UN	United Nations
UNCLOS	United Nations Convention on the Law of the Sea
UNFCCC	UN Framework Convention on Climate Change
WFD	Water Framework Directive
WTO	World Trade Organization

LIST OF CONTRIBUTORS

Inês de Abreu Régio
Trainee Lawyer, Cautrecasas law firm, Lisbon, Portugal. Email: ines.abreu.regio@cuatrecasas.com

Catherine Banet
PhD, Associate Professor, Scandinavian Institute of Maritime Law, Energy and Resources Law Department, University of Oslo, Norway. Email: catherine.banet@jus.uio.no

Jannis Bille
Associate, Herbert Smith Freehills LLP, London, United Kingdom. Email: jannis.bille@hsf.com

Lolke Braaksma
PhD candidate, Groningen Centre of Energy Law and Sustainability, University of Groningen, the Netherlands. Email: l.s.braaksma@rug.nl

Clara Greve Brett
Legal Consultant, Accura Law Firm, Copenhagen, Denmark. Email: clara.greve.brett@accura.dk

Thierry D'hoore
Head of Legal Regulated Activities, Elia System Operator, Belgium. Email: thierry.dhoore@elia.be

Elise van Dijk
Legal counsel, Authority for Consumers & Markets, the Netherlands. Email: elise.van.dijk@acm.nl

Filippo Donati
Professor of Law, University of Florence, and High Council of the Judiciary (Consiglio Superiore della Magistratura), Italy. Email: f.donati@donatilex.it

Dinand Drankier
Policy Officer, Ministry of Economic Affairs and Climate, the Netherlands. At the time of writing, Researcher, Groningen Centre of Energy Law and Sustainability, Groningen, the Netherlands. Email: d.drankier@live.nl

Joel B. Eisen
Professor of Law, University of Richmond School of Law, USA. Email: jeisen@richmond.edu

Dirk Van Evercooren
Director, Flemish Regulator for the Electricity and Gas Market (VREG), President at Association of Issuing Bodies (AIB), Brussels, Belgium. Email: dirk.vanevercooren@vreg.be

Ruven Fleming
PhD, Assistant Professor of Energy Law, Groningen Centre of Energy Law and Sustainability at the University of Groningen, the Netherlands. Email: r.c.fleming@rug.nl.

Sofie Fogstad Vold
Advisor, Climate Industry and Technology Department, Ministry of Petroleum and Energy, Oslo, Norway. Email: sofie-fogstad.vold@oed.dep.no

Kristina Forsbacka
PhD researcher, Luleå University of Technology, Sweden. Email: kristina.forsbacka@ltu.se

Silke Goldberg
Partner, Herbert Smith Freehills LLP, London, United Kingdom, and PhD researcher at the Groningen Centre of Energy Law and Sustainability, the Netherlands. Email: silke.goldberg@hsf.com

Greg Gordon
PhD, Professor of Law, University of Aberdeen, Scotland, United Kingdom. Email: g.w.gordon@abdn.ac.uk

Kars de Graaf
PhD, Professor of Public Law and Sustainability, Groningen Centre of Energy Law and Sustainability, Groningen, the Netherlands. Email: k.j.de.graaf@rug.nl

Adrien de Hauteclocque
PhD, Head of Cabinet, Chambers of the President of the General Court of the European Union, Luxembourg. Email: adrien.de_hauteclocque@curia.europa.eu

Dag Erlend Henriksen
Senior Advisor, Ministry of Petroleum and Energy, Oslo, Norway. Email: dag-erlend.henriksen@oed.dep.no

Bernard Kieffer
Hydro Consultant SAS, France. Email: bkieffer74@yahoo.fr

Gijs Kreeft
Legal Consultant, Royal HaskoningDIIV, the Netherlands. At the time of writing, Researcher at the Groningen Centre of Energy Law and Sustainability, Groningen, the Netherlands. Email: gijs.kreeft@rhdhv.com.

Knut Fredrik Kroepelien
CEO, Energy Norway (*Energi Norge*), Oslo, Norway. Email: kk@energinorge.no

Romain Mauger
PhD, Post-doctoral Researcher, Groningen Centre of Energy Law and Sustainability, University of Groningen, the Netherlands. Email: r.j.g.mauger@rug.nl

Gavin McLeod Little
PhD, Professor of Environmental & Public Law, University of Stirling, Scotland, United Kingdom. Email: gavin.mcleod.little@stir.ac.uk

Thomas L. Muinzer
PhD, Centre for Energy, Petroleum and Mineral Law and Policy, University of Dundee, Scotland, United Kingdom. Email: t.muinzer@dundee.ac.uk

John Paterson
PhD, Professor of Law, Aberdeen Centre for Energy Law, Aberdeen, Scotland, United Kingdom. Email: j.paterson@abdn.ac.uk

Martha M. Roggenkamp
PhD, Professor of Energy Law and Director of the Groningen Centre of Energy Law and Sustainability, University of Groningen, Groningen, the Netherlands. Email: m.m.roggenkamp@rug.nl

Daphne ter Telgte
Legal counsel, Authority for Consumers & Markets, the Netherlands. E-mail: daphne.ter.telgte@acm.nl

Gerrit van der Veen
PhD, Professor of Environmental Law, University of Groningen, and Partner at the law firm AKD, Rotterdam, the Netherlands. Email: g.a.van.der.veen@rug.nl

Cees Verburg
Attorney-at-Law, Pels Rijcken & Droogleever Fortuijn, and fellow of the Groningen Centre of Energy Law and Sustainability, the Netherlands. Email: cees.verburg@pelsrijcken.nl

Lourenço Vilhena de Freitas
PhD, Professor of Law, Lisbon Faculty of Law, Partner at Cuatrecasas, Gonçalves Pereira law firm, Lisbon, Portugal. Email: lourenco.freitas@cuatrecasas.com

INTRODUCTION

Martha M. Roggenkamp and Catherine Banet

The European Energy Law Report XIII presents an overview of the most important developments in the field of International, European Union (EU) and national energy and climate law as discussed at the 29th and 30th European Energy Law Seminars, which were held on 22–23 January 2018 and on 21–22 January 2019, respectively, in The Hague, the Netherlands. Although a wide range of topics and developments were discussed at the seminars, we recognise that the common thread is the liberalisation of the energy market in combination with the increased use of renewable energy sources (RES). New types of RES are being introduced and more and more often they take the form of distributed energy sources. As a result, new market parties are gradually emerging, which play an increasingly important role as providers of flexibility services. However, changes are also taking place with regard to traditional RES, i.e. hydropower. Countries like Norway, France, Italy and Portugal, where hydropower has traditionally played an important role, are currently assessing the existing legal regime and the extent to which these markets need to be further liberalised or even privatised. The energy transition process is thus faced with new investments, which can take many shapes and forms. One of them is using Guarantees of Origin (GOs), a certificate-based tracking system for electricity generation attributes. In addition, the European Commission has presented a Regulation that aims at the screening of foreign direct investments into the EU. However, the process of energy transition has also led to an opposite development: the closure of coal-fired power plants and nuclear facilities due to climate change or environmental concerns. Closely related to the latter is the issue of the decommissioning of oil and gas installations in the North Sea. Although the issue of 'decommissioning' involves the removal of disused installations, coastal states are faced with the need to balance economic and environmental interests when deciding about the extent to which installations need to be removed. The issue of decommissioning can be linked to the use of carbon capture and storage (CCS) technologies, which are one of the instruments to reduce carbon dioxide (CO_2) emissions and which may rely on the opportunity to re-use and re-purpose offshore installations. Last but not least, RES generation and CCS are climate mitigation instruments that can be used to reduce CO_2 emissions; both are often considered in national climate plans and climate laws, which are examined in the last part of the book.

Those issues are discussed successively in the six parts of this volume. As a preliminary to the abovementioned analyses, the book starts with an overview of recent EU case law with relevance for the energy sector.

In Chapter 1, Adrien de Hauteclocque, Elise van Dijk and Daphne ter Telgte offer a comprehensive review of the most notable court case decisions delivered by EU courts in 2018. The judgments have not been numerous but have concerned important points of law. Despite Brexit, the UK still generates important cases, with two notable examples for this time period. First, in *Austria v Commission* (T-356/15), the General Court confirmed the decision of the European Commission to declare aid to the nuclear energy project 'Hinckley Point C' compatible with Article 107(3)(c) of the Treaty on the Functioning of the European Union (TFEU). Second, in *Tempus Energy v Commission* (T-793/14), the General Court annulled a decision taken by the Commission not to raise objections and to declare the UK capacity mechanism compatible with the internal market, with the consequence of imposing a 'standstill period' on the UK's Capacity Market and on requiring the Commission to open a formal investigation. Both cases are currently under appeal. As pointed out by the authors, these two cases set important precedents for the assessment of state funding in favour of nuclear energy and capacity mechanisms. Another series of case concerns 'ongoing sagas' related to the Agency for the Cooperation of Energy Regulators (ACER) decision on the capacity allocation regions in Austria/Germany and the OPAL pipeline. In addition to those cases focused purely on energy, the chapter analyses other landmark cases with high significance for the wider energy sector, such as: the judgment in *Scuola Elementare Maria Montessori e.a. v Commission* (Joined Cases C-622/16 P to C-624/16 P) concerning conditions for admissibility in state aid cases; the *Achmea* judgment (C-284/16) on the legality of arbitration procedures under intra-EU bilateral investments treaties; and the judgment in *Ville de Paris e.a. v Commission* (T-339/16, T-352/16 and T-391/16) concerning the action for annulment brought by the cities of Paris, Brussels and Madrid against the emission limits for oxides of nitrogen adopted by the Commission. As a final point, the authors review the ongoing reform of the institutional framework of the CJEU.

NEWCOMERS IN THE ELECTRICITY MARKET: AGGREGATORS AND STORAGE

Aggregators have appeared as a new category of market actors in the aftermath of the electricity market liberalisation. They provide a new type of service based on the grouping of the energy consumption or generation of several consumers. The next two chapters examine two approaches to the regulation of aggregators, one from Europe and one from the United States.

In Chapter 2, Thierry D'hoore reviews the growing role of aggregators in the EU electricity market and looks more closely at their regulation in Belgium. First, the author makes the link between electricity market liberalisation and the development of aggregators, reviewing the different steps in EU liberalisation legislation, from the first liberalisation directive of 1996 to the Clean Energy Package of 2019. The author then stresses the multiple interactions between aggregators and transmission system operators (TSOs), including in terms of the balancing of the system, ancillary services such as demand responses and, more generally, market efficiency. There is also a discussion of the necessary adaptations made to the Belgian legislation in order to let aggregators operate.

In Chapter 3, Joel B. Eisen analyses aggregation of distributed energy resources (DERs) in the United States as an important part of the ongoing energy transition. The author explains how aggregation can address many of the challenges raised by the integration of DERs into the electric grid. Particular attention is given to the programs and initiatives in place to expand wholesale market participation through third-party DER aggregators. Although there is little DER aggregation beyond wholesale market demand response programs, the author makes clear that this is expected to change. Notably, there is an assessment of DER aggregation at the distribution level. The chapter reviews both state and federal regulators initiatives in order to support the further deployment of aggregated DERs to provide grid services.

The need to store electricity is becoming more and more apparent as without storage, there is a lack of flexibility and the possibility of unbalance in the grid. Following the introduction of a new Electricity Directive in January 2019, a provision on electricity storage has finally been included, thus acknowledging the need for such storage. When assessing this provision, we can note that it reflects the ongoing discussion regarding the position of storage in the market and the breadth of the definition used. One of the key issues is the extent to which storage should be considered as a flexibility tool to be applied by network operators, and thus being regulated, or as a market-based activity. The European legislator clearly prefers the latter but also recognises that market parties may not be interested in being involved. As some Member States have already introduced a storage regime or are in the process of doing so, it remains to be seen whether these national regimes coincide with the new EU regime. With regard to the second point, the European legislator has taken a very broad view on the concept of storage as it clearly also aims to include electricity conversion, i.e. from power to gas or from power to heat. This book will discuss both of these developments.

Silke Goldberg and Jannis Bille discuss in Chapter 4 the regulation of electricity storage in the UK and analyse the potential hurdles involved. The chapter discusses the concept and definition of electricity storage from a UK perspective, as well as its regulatory framework, ownership rights, subsidies and the role of TSOs and DSOs. The main obstacles identified are to be found in the existing planning regime and the financing of investments in storage facilities. Chapter 5 continues by assessing 'power-to-gas' and hydrogen for energy storage under EU energy law. Gijs Kreeft and Ruven Fleming focus in particular on the conversion of electricity from RES to hydrogen (green hydrogen). After discussing some of the available techniques, the authors examine the EU legal framework. This entails an interrogation of the concept of power-to-gas and how this fits into the definition, which has recently been included in the Electricity Directive, but also how this relates to the definition of storage in the Gas Directive. Last but not least, the chapter discusses the potential technical and safety standards that may apply to hydrogen and the injection of hydrogen into the gas system.

HYDROPOWER CONCESSIONS IN THE EU: A NEED FOR LIBERALISATION OR PRIVATISATION?

Hydropower remains the dominant source of renewable energy generation in the EU. Although exploited for a long time, hydropower is facing a series of challenges where the European Commission is questioning the compatibility of the legal regime applied in several Member States with internal market legislation and competition rules. In March 2019, the Commission sent letters of formal notice to seven Member States (Austria, France, Germany, Poland, Portugal, Sweden and the UK) and a second complementary letter of formal notice to Italy, with the objective of ensuring that public contracts in the hydroelectric power sector are awarded and renewed in conformity with EU law. The provision of hydropower is typically organised under two frameworks in the Member States, either authorisations, falling under the Services Directive 2006/123/EC, or concessions, falling under the public procurement rules of Directive 2014/23/EU. In the view of the Commission, completing the internal energy market also entails ensuring a level playing field between companies within the hydropower sector, which therefore justifies taking action to remove any barriers to this. This book presents four national case studies – Norway, France, Italy and Portugal – where the legal regime for hydropower has been challenged under EU/EEA rules.

Knut F. Kroepelin examines in Chapter 6 the main areas of influence of EU law on the Norwegian hydropower concession system through the application of the EEA Agreement. The two main issues which have arisen relate to public ownership and environmental restrictions. On the first issue, ironically, the judgment of the EFTA Court in the 'Waterfall' case against the Norwegian government (*Hjemfall*, Case E-02/06) resulted in a consolidation of the public ownership model. On the second issue, the Norwegian government has been challenged for its implementation and application of environmental protection rules as enshrined in the Water Framework Directive.

In Chapter 7, Bernard Kieffer provides an analysis of the hydroelectric licensing regime applied in France. After retracing the history of the legal framework from the 1919 Act relating to the use of hydraulic power to the latest amendments to the Energy Code following the 2015 Law on Energy Transition for Green Growth, the chapter reviews the components of the hydroelectric license – which constitutes simultaneously both a license of public works and one of public service. The chapter then examines the remaining issues related to the competitive tendering for hydroelectric licenses and the opening of competition for the award of licensing contracts.

In Chapter 8, Filippo Donati similarly retraces the evolution of the Italian legislation on hydropower concessions from a system of state monopoly to a progressive introduction of competition as a consequence of the entry into force of the First Electricity Directive. However, instead of fostering competition, the Italian government has tried to slow down the liberalisation process by extending the duration of the concessions already granted, notably through the adoption of the 1999 Bersani Decree. The chapter reviews the later influence of EU law on the Italian regime through a series of infringement procedures initiated by the European Commission which challenged both the preference granted to the outgoing concessionaire and the automatic extension of the concessions in force when the Bersani Decree came into force. As a consequence, the Bersani Decree was repealed in 2005 and new competitive rules for granting hydroelectric concessions were introduced. Despite these changes, the concessions have been further extended by the government without being subjected to competition. While the Commission has been arguing that those extensions provided an unjustified advantage to existing operators and was contrary to the freedom of establishment for other operators, the Constitutional Court has disputed the competence of the state to legislate with such detail on hydropower concessions and undermining the competence of the regions. The competence issue was later clarified in a 2012 legislative decree providing for the conditions for launching new competitive tenders for the award of new hydropower concessions. Despite this new reform, the Commission is still questioning, through infringement procedures, the alleged distortions of competition deriving from the excessive duration of Italian concessions and the lack of effective competition.

In Chapter 9, Lourenço Vilhena de Freitas and Inês de Abreu Régio offer a fourth national example of a regulatory approach to hydroelectric concessions.

Similarly to the French and Italian examples, moving from a situation of national monopoly to the opening up to competition has been the main challenge in terms of compliance with EU law. A particularity of the Portuguese model is to provide for direct capacity payment mechanisms to guarantee the availability of hydropower plants and, consequently, the security of supply.

A common reflection shared by several of the above chapters is whether the launch of separate infringement procedures outside of a more harmonised legislative framework at EU level could, paradoxically, result in greater imbalances between the countries and, in doing so, negatively impact the functioning of the internal market by creating even more distortions.

INVESTMENTS AND DISINVESTMENTS IN THE ENERGY SECTOR

The increased use of RES and the subsequent process of energy transition has led to the need for new investment in the production of electricity using RES, often through new and/or innovative technologies, and, at the same time, to the need to close down existing facilities such as coal-fired power plants and nuclear facilities due to a variety of climate change or environmental concerns. This section of the book addresses both developments.

Dirk van Evercooren examines in Chapter 10 the EU approach to the regulation of guarantees of origin (GO). The chapter starts by discussing the arguments about why electricity is such a different product from others and how this influences consumer information about the origin of the electricity supplied and consumed. It continues with a history of the GO and an analysis of the EU regulation of electricity disclosure. Indeed, the certificate-based tracking system that the GO embodies offers a reliable mechanism of compliance with the disclosure requirement and enables suppliers to inform consumers about the way they source their electricity. Therefore, there is a close correlation between the disclosure obligation and the empowerment of consumers through the free choice of suppliers. The GO system contributes to this mechanism and indirectly provides financial support to renewable energy producers. The chapter analyses the new provisions of the Clean Energy Package on GOs and questions the newly-introduced compliance obligation with CEN/CENELEC standard EN16325.

In Chapter 11, Cees Verburg focuses on the new Regulation 2019/542 that aims to 'screen' foreign direct investments into the European Union. This Regulation has been 'inspired' by Chinese attempts to acquire shares in European companies, i.e. the Belgian and Portuguese TSOs. The author discusses this new Regulation within the broader framework of the EU merger regulation, but also with other EU trade and investment agreements such as the Energy Charter Treaty (ECT) and the more recent EU-Canada trade agreement (CETA). Both the ECT and CETA provide for national security and public order considerations as a possibility for the justification of measures that restrict foreign investment. The author concludes that the new Regulation fits in seamlessly with this trend and that its effects should not be underestimated.

By contrast to the investments needed in RES, several Member States are planning to close down existing power plants. Romain Mauger, in Chapter 12, explores the developments in Germany, Sweden and France. These countries have some of the highest levels of electricity produced from nuclear energy and have either decided to completely phase out this type of generation (Germany and Sweden) or at least to reduce it significantly (France). Decisive factors are the nuclear accidents in Chernobyl, pushing for the phase-out in Sweden and Germany, and, more recently, in Fukushima, which reinforced the German commitment and led to a decision in France to reduce the share of nuclear energy in the total electricity generation. This chapter first discusses the national policies and strategies to close down these nuclear plants and, thereafter, the legal, organisational and financial consequences of these policies. The author concludes that the three countries assessed have chosen different approaches and that key factors for a stable and fiscal revenue-saving nuclear shutdown are foreseeability and legal certainty.

The need for regulatory certainty is also one of the key issues in the two countries where the closure of coal-fired power plants has been assessed: the Netherlands and Germany. Lolke Braaksma and Ruven Fleming examine the relevant procedures and legal frameworks in Chapter 13. In the Netherlands, the need to close down coal-fired power plants follows on from the need to reduce the country's CO_2 emissions, especially from the ruling in the *Urgenda* case. It therefore not only affects older coal-fired power plants but also relatively new generators, which are highly efficient. The chapter presents the background for the decision to close down these modern plants and the accompanying legal framework. Instead of introducing law that requires the closure of all coal-fired power plants, the legislator has introduced a law that forbids the use of coal in power plants. Although the government claims that de facto there is no direct interference in the property rights of companies, and thus no or limited need for financial compensation, it remains to be seen whether this will indeed be the case. The situation in Germany is slightly different as it involves older power plants and the discussion consists more of a societal debate, i.e. job security and unemployment levels. Apart from political and societal discourse about the technicalities of actually ending electricity production from coal-fired power plants, the debate is concentrating on the need for structural, monetary support for those *Länder* where the coal-fired power plants are located. Both examples show, however, that there is barely a role for the EU to play in this process and that although states try to avoid expropriation claims, this is difficult to achieve and does rely on proper legal instruments.

OFFSHORE DECOMMISSIONING IN THE NORTH SEA

The next four chapters focus on the decommissioning of oil and gas installations in the North Sea. The process of decommissioning relates to the stage at which an installation is getting to a state of disuse and a decision needs to be made about its removal. As in the case of the phase out of nuclear installations and coal-fired power plants, an EU legal framework is absent. However, there are instead provisions in international law (UNCLOS) that govern the abandonment and removal of disused installations. These are based on the concept that fixed installations may basically intervene with the freedom of navigation and fishery and should only be permitted as long as exploration and production of oil and gas are ongoing.

Dinand Drankier and Martha M. Roggenkamp present in Chapter 14, first, the relevant international legal framework and, in particular, what 'disused' means in relation to the possible re-use of installations for other purposes. Second, they analyse the situation on the Dutch continental shelf and the legal framework governing abandonment and removal. In contrast to most other North Sea states, the situation in the Netherlands is relatively clear. The Dutch part of the North Sea consists of relatively shallow waters and, therefore, the installations need to be entirely removed when they are no longer in use. Given the smaller size of the fields and installations, some experience has already been gained. The authors also note that there is uncertainty about the possible removal of disused cables and pipelines. The legal framework governing the construction and use of offshore pipelines is unclear, as are the rules on removal. The current debate focuses on the possibilities for re-use for other purposes. So long as these new uses are not related to oil and gas activities, an appropriate legal regime remains absent – though necessary.

Greg Gordon and John Paterson follow this theme on in Chapter 15 by discussing the legal regime on the UK continental shelf. The regime differs from the Dutch one given the deeper waters, larger continental shelf and bigger installations involved. Therefore, the extent to which a disused installation needs to be removed entails a difficult balancing act between economic and environmental costs of complete or partial removal. In order to set the scene, they also assess the international legal framework and the possibility for re-use as part of a rigs-to-reef option. Thereafter, they discuss the UK legal framework, which covers not only the handling of abandonment plans but also the relevant commercial and contractual issues involved (Joint Operating Agreements and

Decommissioning Security Agreements), as well as the introduction and use of a standard decommissioning contract.

Chapter 16 examines the Danish legal framework. Clara Greve Brett begins with an in-depth overview of the history of oil and gas developments in Denmark. As in the Netherlands, the activities and installations take place in relatively shallow waters and the Danish continental shelf is now also considered a 'mature province'. Nevertheless, no meaningful decommissioning activities have so far been carried out, but it is expected that this will change soon. Following a review of the applicable legal framework, the author raises the issue of which party is liable for decommissioning, for accidents during or following decommissioning and how to secure these liabilities. There is then a discussion on the need to remove offshore pipelines. Although no decommissioning has taken place as of yet, production in some fields is rapidly declining and it now remains to be seen whether the existing legal framework meets the expectations and the requirements of the international legal framework.

The last chapter of this section focuses on the legal framework that applies to the Norwegian continental shelf. Dag Erlend Henriksen presents the decommissioning practice in Norway. The situation is to some extent comparable with the UK as it involves a large continental shelf and deep waters. The situation is also challenging given the fact that more use is made of concrete platforms than elsewhere. Although some platforms have been decommissioned and the lifetime of many other platforms has been extended, it is expected that in the next few years many of them will reach end-of-life and need to be decommissioned. The author thus presents the existing legal regime and pays particular attention to the role of the decommissioning plan under the Petroleum Act, the requirements applying to a decision on disposal and the obligation to implement a disposal decision. This is followed by an analysis of the (secondary) liability of decommissioning costs and the role of the Joint Operating Agreements in the decision-making process. In contrast to other North Sea countries, a discussion of any re-use of installations has not yet started. So far the emphasis has been on the possibilities of prolonging the activities as much as possible and postponing decommissioning.

CCS AS A CLIMATE TOOL: NORTH SEA PRACTICE

One of the possibilities for re-using and/or repurposing installations is by using them for subsoil storage of CO_2. To be sure, this will depend on the choice of storage location. When using saline aquifers there are no installations in place to be re-used, but this may be possible if use is made of (almost) depleted oil and gas fields. In this part, three regimes governing CO_2 will be discussed: those of Norway, the UK and the Netherlands. In contrast to the decommissioning regime discussed above, CO_2 storage is governed by EU law (Directive 2009/31/EC on the geological storage of carbon dioxide (the CCS Directive)).

In Chapter 18, Sofie Fogstad Vold presents the main components of the Norwegian CCS policy, which, at the moment, is structured around the completion of one full-scale demonstration project to be operational by 2023/2024. The chapter gives an in-depth description of the CCS Directive before reviewing its implementation into Norwegian law. It analyses the implementation technique, the resource management principles (coinciding with the principles from the petroleum regulation), and the permit system for exploration and storage of CO_2 on the Norwegian continental shelf.

John Paterson presents in Chapter 19 the legal framework for carbon capture and storage (CCS) in the UK. In similar fashion to the directive, the focus is on the part governing storage of CO_2. Following an introduction discussing the background and need for CCS, an analysis of the EU directive and the way in which it has been implemented in UK law is put forth. The chapter then proceeds to discuss the particle impacts. Several attempts have been made to develop some demonstration projects and so far these have not been successful, primarily due to the high costs involved and lack of financial support. The author then turns to some recent developments presented in an action plan and which represent a shift from CCS to CCUS and a new model for re-use of installations, which may bring down transport and storage costs. The option of enhanced recovery is also addressed. The author notes that enhanced recovery could be considered as a type of use in the CCUS chain. The author concludes that despite some false starts, the UK appears to be in a relatively strong position in relation to the development of CCS as the legislative and regulatory regime appears to be well bedded in. However, the current uncertainty in the UK surrounding Brexit means that what will happen next is difficult to predict.

The last chapter in this section is on CCS in the Netherlands. Martha M. Roggenkamp examines in Chapter 20 the long and winding process governing CO_2 transport and storage. Interestingly, the process started around the year 2000 with the idea of using CO_2 instead of natural gas in greenhouses, thus saving the use of natural gas. This approach has encountered some problems as the CO_2 used is not permanently stored and remains (partially-)emitted, while the greenhouse growers were not accountable for the CO_2 emissions as they were not subject to the ETS. In addition, the initial idea was to store CO_2 onshore in depleted oil and gas fields; this was facilitated by the storage regime of the Mining Act of 2003. Nevertheless, onshore storage was not achieved due to large-scale opposition. Therefore, the attention shifted to carbon storage offshore. The chapter surveys the developments in the legal framework, the transposition of the EU Directive in the Mining Act and some of the attempts to permanently store CO_2 offshore. The first major attempt – the ROAD project – was successful in the sense that all permits had been awarded.

However, given the fact that a coal-fired power plant would initially be the main supplier of CO_2, there are financial uncertainties relating to government attempts to close down these plants as discussed in Chapter 13, this project was terminated. More recently, a new project has been proposed: the Porthos project. This project is being developed as an open access project. The chapter analyses these developments and concludes that a CCS project will possibly be realised in the Netherlands soon.

FROM EU CLIMATE GOALS TO NATIONAL CLIMATE LAWS

The last part of the book is dedicated to the analysis of three different approaches to climate legislation, as an increasing number of countries have adopted climate laws during the past few years.

In Chapter 21, Thomas L. Muinzer and Gavin McLeod Little provide a detailed analysis of one of the pioneering climate laws, the UK's Climate Change Act 2008 (CCA). They review the background for the adoption of the CCA as well as its main provisions. A common feature in all climate laws is that they are driven by targets. In the case of the UK, the CCA applies a 34 per cent greenhouse gas (GHG) emissions reduction target for the UK to attain by 2020, with the emissions reduction percentage based on 1990 emissions levels. It also applies an 80 per cent GHG emissions reduction target based on 1990 levels for 2050. In 2019, the UK government has legislated for a 'Net Zero' 2050 target, which means the 2050 target has increased from 80 to 100 per cent. The authors have characterised these two reduction markers as the regime's 'milestone' targets. The targets are economy-wide and cover emissions arising all over the UK. The 2020/34 per cent and 2050/100 per cent milestone targets outline an emissions reduction trajectory for a carbon budgeting scheme. This carbon budgeting scheme covers all major socio-economic sectors and activities within the UK and is divided into successive five-year periods that roll on continually, one after the other. An interesting feature of the CCA is that the primary duties and obligations under the terms of the CCA are generally borne by the Secretary of State. Another key actor in the CCA institutional framework is the Committee on Climate Change, which plays the role of an expert advisory and reporting body. The second part of the chapter is dedicated to the evaluation of the legal research base for the CCA.

Kristina Forsbacka analyses in Chapter 22 a much more recent climate legislative framework, the 'Climate Policy Framework' and the Climate Act adopted in 2017 by the Swedish Parliament. The Climate Policy Framework is a key component in fulfilling Sweden's obligations under the Paris Agreement and is, according to Forsbacka, the most significant climate reform in

Swedish history. The author systematically reviews the three main components of the Swedish Climate Policy Framework, which are: the new ambitious long-term climate targets; the Climate Act; and the Climate Policy Council.

Rounding off the Report in Chapter 23, Gerrit van der Veen and Kars de Graaf present a review of the efforts made in the Netherlands to follow up the decision in the *Urgenda* case and to develop a Dutch Climate Act. A further development analysed in the chapter relates to the efforts made by the administration, in close cooperation with industry and societal parties, to work towards an agreement on voluntary measures to reduce the emission of greenhouse gases in the Netherlands (*Klimaatakkoord*, or Climate Agreement). The Climate Agreement is an agreement between a multitude of Dutch stakeholders with the aim of devising measures to reduce global warming as a result of greenhouse gas emissions, allowing the Netherlands to meet European and international targets for 2030 and 2050 respectively. The Climate Agreement follows up on the decision in the *Urgenda* case and complements the Climate Act since the Act itself does not incorporate any measures to reduce the emission of greenhouse gases, but does impose upon the government the obligation to draft a document incorporating such measures for the purpose of achieving the targets laid down in the Act.

CHAPTER I

HOW IS THE ENERGY SECTOR FARING AT THE EU COURTS?

A Year in Review

Adrien DE HAUTECLOCQUE, Elise VAN DIJK
and Daphne TER TELGTE*

1. INTRODUCTION

The year 2018 was relatively quiet at the European Union (EU) courts on the energy and climate front, at least from a quantitative perspective. There have nonetheless been important cases in substance. Notwithstanding the Brexit context, the two most important cases undoubtedly came from the United Kingdom (UK). First, in the judgment of 12 July 2018, *Austria v Commission* (T-356/15, EU:T:2018:439, hereafter the '*Hinkley Point C* case'), the General Court confirmed the decision of the European Commission (the Commission) to declare aid to the 'giant' nuclear project compatible with the internal market on the basis of Article 107(3)(c) of the Treaty on the Functioning of the European Union (TFEU). Second, in the judgment of 15 November 2018, *Tempus Energy and Tempus Energy Technology v Commission* (T-793/14, EU:T:2018:790, hereafter the '*Tempus* case'), the General Court annulled the decision of the Commission not to raise objections and to declare the UK capacity mechanism compatible with the internal market. Both cases, which are under appeal (case C-594/18 P for the *Hinkley Point C* case and case C-57/19 P for the *Tempus* case), deserve an in-depth discussion as they may pave the way for further nuclear project[1] and capacity mechanism[2] cases. We will also observe the developments of some

* This chapter is written in the personal capacity of the authors.

1 See, in this regard, case T-101/18, *Austria v Commission*, concerning the Paks project in Hungary.

2 See, in this regard, case T-110/18, *Grange Backup Power v Commission*, concerning the Irish capacity mechanism.

ongoing sagas, the main decisions for which are yet to come. For example, there has been a series of cases concerning the Agency for the Cooperation of Energy Regulators (ACER) decision on the capacity calculation regions in Austria/ Germany, as well as numerous battles surrounding the OPAL pipeline which connects Nord Stream I in North Germany to the gas network in the Czech Republic.

As is often the case, the most important Court cases for energy companies in 2018 have not dealt directly with energy or climate issues but rather, horizontally, may have profound repercussions for energy companies. This chapter will briefly discuss: the judgment of 6 November 2018, *Scuola Elementare Maria Montessori e.a. v Commission* (Joined cases C-622/16 P to C-624/16 P, EU:C:2018:873, hereafter the '*Montessori* case') arguably opening the conditions for admissibility in State aid cases; the much-discussed judgment of 6 March 2018, *Achmea* (C-284/16, EU:C:2018:158) on the legality of arbitration procedures under intra-EU bilateral investment treaties; and the judgment of 13 December 2018, *Ville de Paris e.a. v Commission* (T-339/16, T-352/16 and T-391/16, EU:T:2018:927), which validated the importance of cities as key actors in climate change litigation at EU level (under appeal, see cases C-177 to 179/19 P).

Finally, this chapter will provide a quick overview of the ongoing reform of the institutional framework of the Court of Justice of the European Union (CJEU), which is soon to be completed.

2. SELECTED CASES: ENERGY AND ENVIRONMENT

2.1. THE *HINKLEY POINT C* CASE

In 2013, the UK notified measures in support of the construction of a nuclear power station: Hinkley Point C. In response, the Commission adopted a decision in support of the aid measure,[3] declaring the measures at issue compatible with the internal market, pursuant to Article 107(3)(c) TFEU.[4] Austria contested the Commission's greenlight before the General Court. The *Hinkley Point C* case is the first instance of a Member State initiating a case before the EU Courts against a decision of the Commission declaring a State aid granted to *another Member State* as compatible with the internal market.

3 Commission Decision (EU) 2015/658 of 8 October 2014 on the aid measure SA.34947 (2013/C) (ex 2013/N) which the United Kingdom is planning to implement for support to the Hinkley Point C nuclear power station (notified under document C(2014) 7142).

4 Under this article, State aid to facilitate the development of certain economic activities or of certain economic areas, where such aid does not adversely affect trading conditions to an extent contrary to the common interest, is permitted.

The General Court rejected the appeal and declared that the aid under review pursues an objective of common interest on the basis of Article 107(3)(c) TFEU. In the following, we will focus on the most interesting parts of the judgment.[5]

2.1.1. *Is Article 107(3)(c) TFEU Applicable?*

This case was an opportunity to clarify to some extent the interface between the Euratom and TFEU treaties. The General Court stated that, even though the Euratom Treaty constitutes a *lex specialis*, the TFEU rules on State aid still apply, as the Euratom Treaty does not contain specific rules in this regard. Since the case covers aid in the nuclear sector, the provisions and objectives of the Euratom Treaty must nevertheless be considered when applying the TFEU provisions on State aid.[6]

2.1.2. *Is Promoting Nuclear Power an Objective of Common Interest?*

One of the most interesting parts of the judgment is arguably when the General Court addresses the definition of an 'objective of common interest' within the meaning of Article 107(3)(c) TFEU. In this regard, the General Court rejected the applicant's argument that one must take into account the legitimate interests of all Member States. The Court found that it is sufficient for State aid to pursue an objective common interest that is appropriate, necessary, and proportionate for *one* Member State.[7]

The Court also rejected the applicant's arguments that the Commission had disregarded the fact that the impact on trade must be assessed from the point of view of the EU, and that the Commission had wrongfully concluded that a Member State is entitled to pursue the promotion of nuclear energy. As such, a Member State is permitted to realise an objective of common interest related to the Euratom Community's goal of facilitating investment in the nuclear field, thereby raising the standard of living of Member States.[8]

2.1.3. *Is Finding a 'Market Failure' Necessary?*

Always a difficult question – the Court decided that a finding of market failure (which State aid seeks to correct) is a relevant, but not necessary, factor for

---

5 For a full commentary, see L. Hancher, 'State Aid to the Nuclear Power Sector: The General Court's Ruling on the UK Reactor at Hinkley Point C', *Oil, Gas & Energy Law*, December 2018.

6 T-356/15, *Austria v Commission (Hinkley Point C case)*, paras 72–28.

7 T-356/15, para 85 and judgment of 15 June 2010, T-177/07, *Mediaset v Commission* (EU:T:2010:233).

8 T-356/15, paras 93–99.

declaring State aid compatible with the internal market on the grounds of Article 107(3)(c) TFEU. The Court rejected Austria's arguments that the Commission had wrongly declared the State aid to be compatible because it found that the liberalised market for the generation and supply of electrical power was failing.[9] In essence, to pass the necessity test, the relevant question is whether the objective of common interest pursued would have been reached without public intervention. State intervention can be considered necessary when market forces alone are unlikely to allow for the said common interest to be met, even though the market is not failing altogether.

2.1.4. *Was Public Intervention Necessary in the Particular Case?*

The Commission has a wide margin of discretion under Article 107(3) TFEU to declare that certain categories of State aid are compatible with the internal market. State intervention was necessary to achieve the public interest objective of the creation of new nuclear energy-generating capacity. The Court therefore confirmed that the Commission's analysis in the contested decision was correct.

The Court held that the Commission had sufficiently clarified that State aid was necessary to deliver the investment in new nuclear energy-generating capacity in sufficient time. Moreover, the aid was necessary given the lack of market-based financial instruments and other types of contracts that could hedge against such substantial risk.[10] The Court also examined the magnitude of the political risks involved with the investments in nuclear energy. It held that the Commission had explained in detail why investment in nuclear energy was subject to such substantial risks.[11] According to the Court, the Commission had correctly concluded that the investments are based on the common interest of creating new nuclear energy-generating capacity. Such large investments need to be established in sufficient time and pertain to the goal of creating low-carbon generation and remedies for the availability of electricity.[12]

2.1.5. *Determination of the Aid*

The Court established that the Commission was not obliged to quantify the precise amount of the aid. The conditions laid out in Article 107(3)(c) TFEU are commonly referred to as the 'balancing test'. A public measure will inevitably

---

9 T-356/15, paras 150–151.

10 T-356/15, paras 155 and 156.

11 The Court addressed seven considerations contested by the applicant in the Commission's decision (paras 163–221).

12 T-356/15, paras 222–226.

distort competition, albeit to a small extent. It is up to the Commission to balance the positive and negative effects of the aid.[13] If the Commission is able to conclude that an aid measure is necessary, appropriate, and proportional without precisely quantifying the precise amount of aid, it can so conclude without doing so. Neither the case law nor other legislation brought forward by the applicant were sufficient justifications as to why the Commission should be obliged to quantify the precise amount of the grant equivalent arising from the State aid so as to establish the proportionality.[14] In consequence, given the fact that it is impossible to calculate the amount compensated under the contract for differences in the future, the Commission could limit itself to look at the rate of return used to define the strike price.

2.1.6. Operating Aid or Investment Aid?

State aid control distinguishes between investment and operating aid. The Court states that operating aid intended to maintain the status quo or lower the usual ongoing operating expenditure is not considered compatible with the internal market. Other sorts of aid, including operating aid, may however be declared compatible with the internal market if the conditions laid out in Article 107(3)(c) TFEU are met.[15]

In sum, the General Court allows for Member States to intervene in nuclear energy capacities. Interestingly, the Court confirms that it is not necessary to consider the legitimate interests of *all* Member States. Nor is it necessary for there to be *new* nuclear technology, seeing as the State aid should also be assessed in the context of the Euratom Treaty. Additionally, the Commission's discretion under Article 107(3)(c)TFEU should be assessed in light of the Commission's State Aid Modernisation initiative.[16] Furthermore, the literature suggests that instead of referring to a balancing exercise, the Commission should dictate that State aid is rendered incompatible when it creates unnecessary distortions to the internal market.[17] Such a hypothesis can be illustrated in this nuclear case, where not only competition but also the energy mix of a Member State and the Euratom Treaty are taken into account.

---

13 P. Nicolaides, 'What should state aid control protect? A proposal for the next generation of state aid rules' (2019) *European Competition Law Review* 276.

14 T-356/15, *Hinkley Point C case*, paras 249–250.

15 T-356/15, paras 579–580.

16 COM/2012/0209, 'Communication from the Commission to the European Parliament, the Council, the European Economic and Social Committee and the Committee of the Regions, EU State Aid Modernisation (SAM)', Brussels, 8 May 2012.

17 Nicolaides, above n. 13.

2.2. THE *TEMPUS* CASE

One of the most important and difficult challenges for the electricity market is to deal with security of supply. In recent years, several Member States have implemented capacity mechanism schemes.[18] These are mechanisms to ensure security of electricity supply by providing a payment for reliable sources of capacity in exchange for their commitment to provide electricity or reduce or delay their electricity consumption during times of system stress. The Commission approved six of these mechanisms, namely for Great Britain, Germany, France, Belgium, Poland, Italy and Greece. The General Court recently ruled upon the capacity mechanism of Great Britain, which also might affect future schemes.[19]

In 2014, the Commission decided that the first capacity market scheme of Great Britain was in line with the EU State aid rules. However, Tempus, a company that based its business model on demand-side response technology, contested this decision. The General Court annulled the decision on procedural grounds. It did not consider the compatibility of the capacity market scheme itself but came to the conclusion that the Commission should have opened the formal investigation procedure laid down in Article 108(2) TFEU.

According to the UK and the Commission, there might soon be a shortage of electrical energy to meet the demand during moments of system stress. They pointed out that capacity suppliers encompass both electricity generators (power plants, including those using fossil fuels) and demand-side response operators.[20] Conversely, Tempus argued that the capacity market privileges generation over demand-side response (DSR) in a way that is discriminatory and disproportionate.[21]

The Court recalled that the Commission has no discretion in deciding whether or not to open the investigation procedure. If there are any doubts about the compatibility with the internal market, the Commission must start the Article 108(2) TFEU procedure.[22] For this, the Commission has to actively research whether there are doubts. The Court emphasised that the Commission is not limited to analysing the information contained in the notification of the measure. The Commission can – and, where necessary, must – seek relevant information to find all factors that can reasonably be considered sufficient and clear for the purposes of its assessment.[23]

---

18 See generally on this L. Hancher, A. de Hauteclocque and M. Sadowska (eds.), *Capacity Mechanisms in the EU Energy Markets: Law, Economics & Policy* (Oxford University Press, 2015).

19 Tempus is now also contesting the legality of the Polish scheme.

20 T-356/15, *Hinkley Point C case*, paras 55, 56.

21 T-356/15, para 56.

22 General Court 15 November 2018, T-793/14, *Tempus v Commission*, paras 62–65.

23 T-793/14, para 69.

In its assessment, the General Court found several objective and consistent indications of doubt, such as the length of the discussions between the Commission and the UK and the novelty and complexity of the measure. It did not take into account that the Commission decided to initiate a sector inquiry on capacity mechanisms,[24] since this decision was taken after the contested decision. However, the Court did take into consideration the duration of discussions and the information shared between the Commission and the UK.[25] The Court also stated that both power generation and DSR could form a solution for the capacity adequacy problem. Therefore, the Commission should have made sure that these actors were treated equally by the aid scheme. According to the Court, the Commission did not examine this sufficiently.[26] Considering the potential of DSR, the Commission should have examined if the envisaged capacity market would sufficiently take this potential into account.[27] A relevant factor that was taken into account by the Court was the report of the UK independent panel of technical experts (PTE). This panel examined the National Grid's[28] recommendations concerning the capacity to be auctioned on the capacity market. The PTE expressed its concern that generation capacity was granted a larger role than was strictly necessary.[29]

All in all, the Court concluded that from the objective and consistent indications of doubt it appeared that the Commission took the contested decision despite the existence of doubts. The Commission should have started the formal investigation procedure under Article 108(2) TFEU. A few months after this decision the Commission decided to start such procedure.[30]

2.3. T-339/16 – *PARIS AND OTHERS v COMMISSION*

On 20 April 2016, the Commission published Regulation 2016/646 concerning emissions from light passenger and commercial vehicles (Euro 6) (Regulation 2016/646).[31] The cities of Paris, Brussels and Madrid requested an action for annulment of Regulation 2016/646. The cities argued that the Commission was not permitted to adopt the Not-to-Exceed values (NTE) for emissions of oxides

---

24 Commission Decision C(2015) 2814 final of 29 April 2015 initiating an inquiry on capacity mechanisms in the electricity sector pursuant to Article 20a of Regulation No 659/1999.

25 T-793/14, *Tempus*, para 111.

26 T-793/14, paras 125, 126.

27 T-793/14, para 155.

28 The UK transmission system operator.

29 T-793/14, para 156.

30 Commission Decision C(2019) 1296 final of 21 February 2019, State Aid SA.35980 (2018/NN) – United Kingdom Electricity Market Reform: Capacity Mechanism.

31 Commission Regulation (EU) 2016/646 amending Regulation (EC) No 692/2008 as regards emissions from light passenger and commercial vehicles (Euro 6), OJ L 109, 20 April 2016.

of nitrogen applied, which are higher than the limits on those emissions laid down for the Euro 6 standard. The Commission contested the admissibility of the parties' request.

The dispute concerns the effect of Regulation 2016/646 on the rules laid out in Article 4(3) of Directive 2007/46/EC.[32] The General Court assessed the standing of the cities of Paris, Brussel and Madrid on the basis of Article 263(4) TFEU, in particular whether proceedings may be instituted against a regulatory act[33] which is *of direct concern* to those parties.[34]

Before addressing the question, the General Court initially established that the rules set out in Regulation 2016/646 do not entail implementing measures in relation to the applicants. For the General Court, measures such as the registration, sale, entry into service or circulation on the road of vehicles on the grounds of Article 4(3) Directive 2007/46 do not comprise an implementing measure in relation to the applicants on the basis of Article 263(4) TFEU.[35]

Does the contested regulatory act directly affect the legal positions of the cities? The Court addressed the question of whether Regulation 2016/646 leaves no discretionary powers to the recipients in charge of its implementation. It is settled case-law that any regulatory act which prevents an entity from exercising its competence, has a direct concern in accordance with Article 263(4) TFEU.[36] In other words, traffic regulations concerning vehicles falling under Regulation 2016/646 should not interfere with the requirements already set out in Article 4(3) Directive 2007/46.

The Court clarified that, as a result of adopting Regulation 2016/646, the parties may not limit the circulation of those vehicles that do not comply with the emission limits for oxides of nitrogen. However, there is a contradiction in the limits laid down in the Euro 6 standard, which nevertheless comply with the NTE values for emissions of oxides of nitrogen defined in Regulation 2016/646, but that are higher than the emission limits.[37] The consequences of Regulation

---

32 Directive 2007/46/EC of the European Parliament and of the Council establishing a framework for the approval of motor vehicles and their trailers, and of systems, components and separate technical units intended for such vehicles, OJ L 263, 5 September 2007. Article 4(3) of Directive 2007/46 establishes that a Member State may not 'prohibit, restrict or impede the registration, sale, entry into service or circulation on the road of vehicles, components or separate technical units, on grounds related to aspects of their construction and functioning covered by this Directive, if they satisfy the requirements of the latter.'

33 The fact that Regulation 2016/646 is a regulatory act is not contested.

34 The fourth paragraph of this provision stipulates that any natural or legal person may institute proceedings against a regulatory act which is of direct concern to them and does not entail implementing measures.

35 General Court, T-339/16, *Ville de Paris e.a. v Commission*, para 40.

36 General Court 13 December 2018, Joined cases T-339/16, T-352/16 and T-391/16, *Paris and others v Commission*, para 50.

37 T-339/16, para 76.

2016/646 are such that the applicants cannot, as they claim, implement the framework of a targeted measure taking into account the polluting emissions levels of vehicles.[38] The cities of Paris, Brussels and Madrid successfully justified that the regulatory act is of direct concern to them in this respect.[39] This follows from their competences under national law to protect the environment and public health, in particular their competences to enforce traffic regulations aimed at reducing air pollution.

The General Court made a step forward in this ruling to validate the importance of cities as key actors in climate change litigation at EU level. The Commission, however, still disagrees and the case is currently under appeal at the Court of justice.[40]

2.4. ACER SERIES OF CASES: T-146/17 – *MONDI* AND T-123/17 – *EXAA*

Not everyone can submit an appeal or request for intervention to ACER's board of appeals. As the General Court illustrates in the *Mondi v Acer* and *Exaa v Acer* cases, it is not possible to contest ACER's decisions without a truly direct interest in the resolution of the case (or sufficient motivation therefore).

On 17 November 2016, ACER published its Decision 6/2016 on the Proposal by TSOs for the Determination of Capacity Calculation Regions (Decision 6/2016).

Exaa Abwicklungstelle für Energieprodukte AG (Exaa), a company that operates on the Austrian electricity exchange market and Mondi AG (Mondi), a company in the paper packaging sector, put forward that Decision 6/2016 would negatively affect their trading positions on the Austrian and German markets.

In two separate cases, ACER rejected the request for intervention by Exaa and Mondi in support of the appeal lodged against Decision 6/2016 by Austrian Power Grid AG (APG) to ACER's board of appeals. ACER submitted that neither Mondi nor Exaa had a 'direct and current' interest in a solution in the issue at hand. Furthermore, ACER argued that both parties would not be otherwise affected if Decision 6/2016 were to be annulled.[41]

The General Court first addressed whether Exaa and Mondi had a 'direct and current interest' in the solution to the appeal brought by APG. Such an interest must be directly affected by Decision 6/2016 in as much that a solution brought

38 Ibid.

39 T-339/16, para 81.

40 For more information, see cases C-177 to 179/19 P.

41 General Court, 20 September 2018, T-146/17, *Mondi v Agency for the Cooperation of Energy Regulators (ACER)*, para 10 and General Court, 20 September 2018, T-123/17, *Exaa v ACER*, para 10.

forward by the parties would result in a change in the applicants' legal positions.[42] The Court established that Mondi and Exaa had insufficiently substantiated their interest in a resolution of the affair at hand.

The second argument submitted by the parties was an objection to ACER's alleged violation of their right to be heard. ACER presented observations on the request for intervention, without disclosing this to the parties. ACER acted in accordance with the rules of procedure for ACER's board of appeals. The General Court reiterated that ACER was not obligated to present its observations to the requesting parties. Moreover, the observations made did not form a basis for ACER's rejection of the request. As such, the Court concluded that there was no violation of Mondi's and Exaa's rights to be heard.

2.5. THE *OPAL* SAGA[43]

Time and time again, Russian gas in Europe appears to be a controversial issue. As we know, Nord Stream II led to lots of discussions and triggered an amendment to the Gas Directive.[44] Not for the first time, the position of Central and Eastern EU Member States is opposed to that of the North Western Member States. The same goes for the so-called OPAL saga. The story starts in June 2009, when the Commission adopted an exemption decision regarding the OPAL pipeline.[45] The OPAL pipeline connects Nord Stream I in North Germany to the gas network in the Czech Republic. In its exemption decision, the Commission fully exempted the OPAL pipeline from the obligation to grant third-party access (TPA) and from tariff regulation. However, it added a condition that prevented Gazprom (a company with a dominant position) from using more than 50 per cent of the capacity, unless it implemented a 'Gas Release Programme', i.e. an open, transparent and non-discriminatory sale of gas. Gazprom never implemented such a programme.[46] Since gas transiting through the OPAL pipeline could only enter through the Nord Stream I pipeline, in practice, 50 per cent of the pipeline remained unused.

---

42 T-146/17, paras 25–27 and T-123/17, paras 25–27.

43 Order of 21 July 2017, T-130/17 R, *Polskie Górnictwo Naftowe i Gazownictwo v Commission*, EU:T:2017:541; order of 9 March 2018, T-196/17, *Naftogaz of Ukraine v Commission*, not published, EU:T:2018:140 and order of 21 July 2017, T-883/16 R, *Poland v Commission*, EU:T:2017:542.

44 Directive 2009/73/EC of the European Parliament and of the Council concerning common rules for the internal market in natural gas and repealing Directive 2003/55/EC, OJ L 21, 13 July 2009.

45 European Commission 12 June 2009, Decision C(2009) 4694.

46 President of the General Court, 21 July 2017, T-130/17 R, *Polskie Górnictwo Naftowe i Gazownictwo S.A. v Commission*, para 5.

Seven years later, in October 2016, in response to a notification of the German regulatory authority, the Commission revised the exemption. It decided to liberalise the remaining 50 per cent of the OPAL capacities by making it subject to the third-party access provisions. Hereby the Commission made sure that 20 per cent of the capacity could actually be obtained by third parties, as Gazprom is only allowed to bid at the base price for that part.[47] This decision was not received well by Central and Eastern EU Member States. They were worried that an increase in use of OPAL capacities would reduce the transport of gas through the Yamal-Europe and Fraternité gas pipelines, thereby threatening the security of supply and competition.[48] Poland, especially, started legal proceedings calling for the suspension and, subsequently, the annulment of the Commission decision. The Polish State-owned gas company and its subsidiary issued similar claims.[49] Also, the Ukrainian State-owned gas company similarly issued an action for annulment concerning the revised exemption.[50]

Then a period of insecurity regarding the application of the exemption began. Firstly, in December 2016 the General Court decided to provisionally suspend the revised exemption.[51] However, the President of the General Court later rejected the stay of execution of the revised exemption, stating that the harm alleged was not immediate.[52] The President pointed out that Gazprom could still deliver gas to the Polish market based on two existing contracts. On 7 August 2017, Gazprom stated that it used the OPAL pipeline for the first time since the restriction was lifted.[53]

In March 2018, the Court decided on the Ukrainian case. It declared the action for annulment inadmissible.[54] It is therefore still in question how the Court will decide on the substance of the case. The denouement of this saga still awaits, but probably it will be given in the case *Poland v Commission*.[55]

---

47 T-130/17 R, para 9.

48 K. Yafimava, The OPAL Exemption Decision: a comment on the CJEU's ruling to reject suspension, The Oxford Institute for Energy Studies, Oxford, September 2017.

49 General Court, 18 April 2017, T-130/17, *Polskie Górnictwo Naftowe i Gazownictwo v Commission*. General Court, 6 February 2017, T-849/16, *PGNiG Supply & Trading v Commission*.

50 General Court, 9 March 2018, T-196/17, *Naftogaz of Ukraine v Commission*.

51 General Court, 23 December 2016, T-883/16 R, *Poland v Commission*.

52 President of the General Court, 21 July 2017, T-130/17 R, *Polskie Górnictwo Naftowe i Gazownictwo v Commission*, para 18. See also press release of the General Court No 83/17, 21 July 2017.

53 O. Kobzeva and O. Vukmanovic, 'UPDATE 1-Opal pipeline operating at full capacity – Gazprom', Reuters, 9 August 2017.

54 General Court, 9 March 2018, T-196/17, *Naftogaz of Ukraine v Commission*.

55 Pending Case T-883/16, *Poland v Commission*.

2.6. C-305/17 – *FENS*

The *FENS v Slovak Republic* case concerns one of the EU internal market core principles: the free movement of goods. In this case, an electricity supplier contested a specific charge based on a Slovakian government regulation. This charge was imposed on using the network for the export of electricity that was produced in Slovakia, including export to EU Member States. The reason for this charge was to ensure the security of supply, in view of the cessation of two units at the Jaslovské Bohunice nuclear power plant. According to the Court of justice, the charge is to be considered as a charge equivalent in effect to a customs duty, which is not compatible with the free movement of goods.

The Court ruled that compatibility of the charge should be examined based on Articles 28 and 30 TFEU instead of the Electricity Directive 2003/54/EC[56] and Directive 2005/54/EC on security of electricity supply and infrastructure investment. The Court of justice clarified that these Directives have not exhaustively harmonised the rules to be applied and therefore, the examination needs to be done on the basis of the Treaty.[57] Subsequently, the Court of justice ruled that the charges fall within the scope of the free movement of goods. It is settled case-law that electricity is a good and that a charge that is calculated on the basis of the number of kilowatt-hours transmitted must be treated as having been imposed on the product itself.[58] As a result, the Court of justice came to the conclusion that the charge was imposed for the sole reason that the electricity crosses the border. It did not follow the Slovakian argument that a similar charge is imposed on electricity that is produced and consumed within Slovakia. The Court of justice pointed out that these charges are not levied at the same commercial stage, since the disputed charge is imposed when the product crosses the border.[59]

Therefore, the Court of justice came to the conclusion that the charge is to be considered as having the equivalent effect to a customs duty. Such a charge is prohibited by Article 28 TFEU. This conclusion leaves no room for escape, since this prohibition is absolute; no derogation is possible.

2.7. C-561/16 – *SARAS ENERGIA*

We turn now to the 2020 targets. In March 2007, the Council emphasised the need to increase energy efficiency to meet the 2020 targets. An important legal

---

56 Now Directive 2009/72.

57 Judgment of 6 December 2018, C-305/17, *FENS spol s.r.o v Slovak Republic*, EU:C:2018:986, para 25.

58 C-305/17, para 34.

59 C-305/17, *FENS*, paras 38–41.

instrument to accomplish this is Directive 2012/27/EC on energy efficiency. The Directive reflects the reluctance of Member States to determine too much at EU level. It prescribes legally binding measures, instead of targets, to achieve the 2020 targets.[60] Moreover, the *Saras Energia* case confirms that the Directive leaves Member States with a broad margin of discretion in the choice of methods suitable for fulfilling the energy efficiency objectives.[61]

The case concerns the Spanish implementation of the Energy Efficiency Directive. Saras Energia, a Spanish energy undertaking, contested a Spanish Order by which it was obliged to contribute to the Energy Efficiency National Fund for 2015. According to Saras Energia, it follows from the Energy Efficiency Directive that Member States should allow companies to meet their energy-saving obligations by implementing effective energy-saving measures instead of contributing to the national fund. Moreover, the fact that the obligation is only imposed on retail energy sales companies and not on energy distributors would not be in line with the Directive.[62]

The relevant provision in this regard is Article 7 of the Energy Efficiency Directive. The key question of the case is whether the national measure qualifies as an energy efficiency obligation scheme in the sense of Article 7(1), or as an alternative to setting up such an energy efficiency obligation scheme, according to Article 7(9). If the former applies, it follows from Article 20(6) that the Member States need to leave a choice to the companies in the way they fulfil their obligation. In the event that the latter provision applies, it is up to the Member State to decide.[63]

Contrary to the Spanish judge who doubted the applicability of Article 7(9) in this case,[64] the Court of justice clarified that the contested measure should be considered as an 'alternative' in the sense of Article 7(9). Therefore, Spain is allowed to oblige a company to contribute to the national fund as long as the alternative leads to a result equal to that which a measure based on Article 7(1) would have led to and the conditions of Article 7(10) and (11) are met.[65]

Furthermore, the Court of justice made it clear that Member States are also allowed to only impose energy efficiency obligations on particular energy undertakings, to the exclusion of others, as long as they are based on explicitly stated, objective and non-discriminatory criteria.[66] All in all, the Court of justice

---

60 COM(2013) 762, 'Communication from the Commission to the European Parliament and the Council Implementing the Energy Efficiency Directive – Commission Guidance', Brussels, 6 November 2011.

61 CJEU 6 December 2018, C-305/17, *FENS*, para 24.

62 C-305/17, para 14.

63 C-305/17, paras 28–29.

64 C-305/17, para 18.

65 C-305/17, para 34.

66 C-305/17, paras 50–52.

respected the broad margin of discretion of the Member States and made clear that the Spanish Order as such, was not unlawful.

2.8. EXPECTED FUTURE CASE LAW

In light of the above, we can expect new cases from the EU Courts in line with the rulings set out in 2018. The Commission has filed a case pleading that the Hungarian national regulatory authority has not facilitated the possibility to take into account 'all costs actually incurred by network operators' in setting its tariffs.[67] This case concerns Article 13(1) of the Gas Regulation and Article 14(1) of the Electricity Regulation.[68]

Furthermore, the Commission submitted an application alleging the incorrect implementation of Directive 2009/72/EC and Directive 2009/73/EC by the Republic of Germany with regard to vertically integrated undertakings.[69]

Within the series of *ACER* cases, we can expect cases in the same vein as *Mondi* and *Exaa* in 2019: T-333/17, *APG and VUEN v ACER* (against decision of the Board of Appeal on Capacity Calculation Region); T-332/17, *E-Control v ACER* and T-735/18, *Acquind v ACER* (TPA exemption).

Last, but not least, as already mentioned, the CJEU is still to rule upon the substance of the cases about the OPAL pipeline. This is to be expected in the pending case T-883/16 *Poland v Commission*.

3. SELECTED CASES: NON-ENERGY

3.1. C-622/16 P – *MONTESSORI v COMMISSION*

The *Montessori* case may mean good news for third parties trying to challenge State aid decisions of the Commission before the European Courts. The Court of justice declared the claims of two competitors of the beneficiaries of an Italian State aid regime admissible.

In this decision, the Commission declared the Italian rules incompatible with Article 108(3) TFEU. Subsequently, the Commission stated that in view of the circumstances of the case, it would be absolutely impossible for Italy to

67 Pending Case C-771/18, *Commission v Hungary*.

68 Regulation (EC) No 714/2009 of the European Parliament and of the Council of 13 July 2009 on conditions for access to the network for cross-border exchanges in electricity and repealing Regulation (EC) No 1228/2003; and Regulation (EC) No 715/2009 of the European Parliament and of the Council of 13 July 2009 on conditions for access to the natural gas transmission networks and repealing Regulation (EC) No 1775/2005.

69 Pending Case C-718/18, *Commission v Germany*.

recover the unlawful aid. Therefore, the Commission did not order it to do so.[70] The latter finding is being contested by complainants, who ask annulment of this part of the Commission decision.

Similarly to *Paris and others v Commission*, a central issue in this case is the applicability of the conditions of admissibility of actions for annulment brought by natural and legal persons, as laid down in Article 263 TFEU. Importantly, in this case, the Court of justice came to the conclusion that the Commission decision is a regulatory act, thereby making it easier for companies to meet the conditions of admissibility. It firstly ruled that all non-legislative acts of general application must be considered to be regulatory acts. Then it added that it is settled case law that Commission decisions authorising or prohibiting State aid schemes are of general application.[71] Thus, it considers the contested decision to be a regulatory act. This means only two criteria have to be met: the decision must be of direct concern to the complainants and it may not comprise implementing measures. The Court of justice came to the conclusion that in this case these two conditions are met. Therefore, the two competitors have legal standing in this case.

3.2. C-284/16 – *ACHMEA*

The autonomy of EU law was put to the test in a preliminary ruling under Article 267 TFEU. The CJEU took a different view to the delivered Opinion[72] and established that a bilateral treaty between two Member States, containing an arbitration clause, is contrary to EU law.

In 1991, the former Czech and Slovak Federative Republic and the Kingdom of the Netherlands entered a bilateral agreement on the encouragement and reciprocal protection of investments (the BIT). On 1 January 1993, the Slovak Republic succeeded to the rights and obligations under the BIT, and on 1 May 2004, the State acceded to the EU.

When the Slovak Republic partly reversed liberalisation of its private health insurance market, Achmea, a Dutch undertaking which had set up a subsidiary in Slovakia, claimed to have suffered damages. Achmea brought arbitration proceedings against the Slovak Republic on the grounds of Article 8 of the BIT, which provides that disputes between the contracting parties should be settled in an arbitral tribunal of a third State – in this case Germany. The Slovak

70 Judgment of 6 November 2018, Joined cases C-622/16 P to C-624/16 P, *Scuola Elementare Maria Montessori v Commission, Commission v Scuola Elementare Maria Montessori and Commission v Ferracci*, EU:C:2018:873, para 10.

71 Judgment of 6 March 2018, C-284/16, *Slovak Republic v Achmea*, EU:C:2018:158, paras 28–31.

72 Opinion of Advocate General Wathelet in C-284/16, *Slovak Republic v Achmea*, EU:C:2017:699, paras 229–237.

Republic raised an objection of lack of jurisdiction of the arbitral tribunal. It submitted that, as a result of its accession to the European Union, recourse to an arbitral tribunal was incompatible with EU law. In essence, the referring court asked whether Articles 267 and 344 TFEU must be interpreted as precluding a provision in an international agreement concluded between Member States, such as Article 8 of the BIT, under which an investor from one of those Member States may, in the event of a dispute concerning investments in the other Member State, bring proceedings against the latter Member State before an arbitral tribunal whose jurisdiction that Member State has undertaken to accept.

The Court noted that, as EU law forms part of the law in force in every Member State, the arbitral tribunal referred to in Article 8 of the BIT may be called upon to interpret or apply EU law, in particular the fundamental freedoms. The arbitral tribunal at issue in the main proceedings, however, cannot in any event be classified as a court or tribunal 'of a Member State' within the meaning of Article 267 TFEU and it is therefore not entitled to make a reference to the Court for a preliminary ruling. In addition, it must be noted that in the case at hand, judicial review is limited to the validity of the arbitration agreement and the consistency with public policy of the recognition or enforcement of the arbitral award.[73]

Consequently, Articles 267 and 344 TFEU must be interpreted as precluding a provision in an international agreement concluded between Member States, such as Article 8 of the BIT. The ruling has far-reaching consequences for investment trade and other existing investment treaties. In consequence, the Commission published Guidance on the protection of cross-border EU investments, in order to ensure the protection of investors within the EU.[74] Moreover, this ruling has set the scene for ensuing cases concerning bilateral agreements.[75]

4. INSTITUTIONAL ISSUES: REFORM OF THE CJEU

Since 2015, the CJEU has been undergoing a profound wave of structural changes with the gradual redefinition of its judicial architecture. The need for

---

73 The Court notes that arbitration proceedings such as those referred to in Article 8 of the BIT are different from commercial arbitration proceedings. While the latter originate in the freely expressed wishes of the parties, the former derive from a treaty by which Member States agree to remove from the jurisdiction of their own courts – and hence from the system of judicial remedies which the second subparagraph of Article 19(1) TEU requires them to establish in the fields covered by EU law – disputes which may concern the application or interpretation of EU law.

74 European Commission – Fact Sheet, 'Commission provides guidance on protection of cross-border EU investments – Questions and Answers', http://europa.eu/rapid/press-release_MEMO-18-4529_en.htm, 19 July 2018.

75 See also judgment of 18 June 2019, T-624/15, T-694/15 and T-704/15, *European Food and Others v Commission*, EU:T:2019:423.

reform essentially came from the increasing caseload of the General Court and the resulting risks in terms of reasonable delay of judgment, in potential breach of Article 47 of the Charter of Fundamental Rights of the EU.[76] Unsurprisingly, the increasing number of cases mainly stemmed from the advancement of the internal market and, in parallel, the greater volume of legal acts adopted by the different agencies and institutions of the EU.

Regulation 2015/2422 of the European Parliament and of the Council of 16 December 2015 amended Protocol N° 3 on the Statute of the Court of Justice of the European Union to provide a structural solution. The option of setting up a specialised trademark court on the basis of Article 257 TFEU was not adopted. It was decided instead to double the number of judges at the General Court (hence two judges per Member State). Twelve additional judges took office in 2015. In September 2016, the Civil Service Tribunal (composed of seven judges) was transferred to the General Court, which is now hearing civil service cases at first instance. The remaining nine judges will take office in September 2019.

Article 3 of Regulation 2015/2422 foresees the production of two reports. A first report was released as planned on 14 December 2017 about possible changes in the distribution of competences between the General Court and the Court of Justice. At this stage, the Court of Justice only proposed the devolution of competences for certain infringement proceedings, which was opposed by the Commission and thus postponed. Discussions concerning the distribution of competences for preliminary rulings under Article 247 TFEU, as well as infringement proceedings, could resurface in the not-so-distant future. A second report will have to be produced by 26 December 2020. According to Article 3(1), 'that report shall focus on the efficiency of the General Court, the necessity and effectiveness of the increase to 56 Judges, the use and effectiveness of resources and the further establishment of specialised chambers and/or other structural changes'.

The reform has already had a substantial impact on the General Court. In particular, the duration of proceedings has decreased to about 20 months on average and the number of pending cases has stabilised at around 1300. Recourse to an enlarged formation of judgment of five judges, instead of three, has generalised. Ten per cent of cases are now judged by enlarged formations of judgment. In addition, the General Court vested its vice-president with a new mission concerning the coherence of the case-law.

Last, but not least, following the report of 14 December 2017, Regulation 2019/629 of the European Parliament and of the Council of 17 April 2019 amending Protocol No 3 on the Statute of the Court of Justice of the European Union, inter alia, organised a new appeal mechanism at the Court of Justice.

---

76 See, for instance, CJEU 13 December 2018, C-138/17 P and C-146/17 P, *European Union v Gascogne Sack Deutschland and Gascogne.*

This mechanism is limited to the cases which have been already considered twice, initially by an independent board of appeal and then by the General Court. This is most notably the case in trademark cases. It has been noticed that, for this category of cases, the Court of Justice very often finds appeals manifestly unfounded or inadmissible. It was therefore considered necessary, in order to allow the Court of Justice to focus on the most important cases, to allow appeals only where it raises an issue that is significant with respect to the unity, consistency or development of EU law. At this stage, this new procedure concerns decisions of the independent boards of appeal of the European Union Intellectual Property Office, the Community Plant Variety Office, the European Chemicals Agency and the European Union Aviation Safety Agency. This procedure

> shall also apply to appeals brought against decisions of the General Court concerning a decision of an independent board of appeal, set up after 1 May 2019 within any other office or agency of the Union, which has to be seised before an action can be brought before the General Court.[77]

These developments are coherent in so far as they should enable the Court of Justice to focus on its constitutional role while giving the General Court the resources it needs to deliver judgments of a high quality in a reasonable time.

5. CONCLUSION

It is hard not to see that there is a widening interface between Union law and the energy transition. This is reflected, for instance, in the interesting cases already pronounced in the course of the first semester of 2019. Suffice it to mention here the judgment of 15 May 2019, *Achema and Others v VKEKK* (C-706/17, EU:C:2019:407) concerning measures intended to compensate providers of public interest services in the electricity sector in Lithuania and, most importantly, the judgment of 28 March 2019, *Germany v Commission* (C-405/16 P, EU:C:2019:268) which annulled the judgment of the General Court confirming the Commission decision declaring the aid granted by certain provisions of the amended German law concerning renewable energy sources (EEG 2012) partially incompatible with the internal market. A number of important cases are still pending, as we have seen. It is also useful to add to the list of aforementioned pending cases,

77 Protocol No 3, Article 58a.

among others, cases T-417/16 *Achema* (aid concerning the Lithuanian LNG Terminal), C-473/17 and C-546/17 *Repsol Butano* (*Federutility* line of case law), T-705/18 *Air Liquide Industriegase v Commission* (aid to energy-intensive users in Germany), T-616/18 *Polskie Górnictwo Naftowe i Gazownictwo v Commission* (Article 102 TFEU procedure concerning Gazprom), T-328/18 *Naturgy Energy Group v Commission* (coal support scheme in Spain), T-674/18 *Vattenfall Europe Nuclear Energy v Commission* (atomic law in Germany). There will therefore be plenty of material to discuss in next year's volume.

PART I

NEWCOMERS IN THE ELECTRICITY MARKET

Aggregators and Storage

CHAPTER II

NEWCOMERS IN THE BELGIAN ELECTRICITY MARKET

Aggregators

Thierry D'HOORE*

1. INTRODUCTION

When reflecting on aggregators' role as newcomers in the Belgian electricity market, every word in the title, not to mention the interrelations between these concepts, raises questions.

In the first place, there is the electricity market, which in the end is what this is all about.[1] The electricity market today is the result of the liberalisation it experienced in recent times. Before the liberalisation of this market, the market often involved the supply of electricity by one or a few producers/suppliers, often also operating the system or part of it, even if electricity was already recognised as a product subject to the rules of free movement.[2] Customers could then get access to electricity at a negotiated or regulated price. Although electricity systems had been interconnected for a number of decades already, interconnections served the operational security requirements of the systems, whereas the markets were regulated at national level. The aim of liberalisation was to facilitate electricity trading across Europe through the adoption of harmonised rules, as this was needed for the creation of a free and

---

* This chapter presents the personal opinion of the author and does not reflect the views of Elia. The author thanks his colleagues Anna Tsiokanos, Justine Diepart and James Matthys-Donnadieu for their valuable suggestions.

1 Although the liberalisation of the energy markets concerns both the electricity and gas markets, this chapter will only examine the former. Their liberalisation is based on similar principles but the two products' technical characteristics are too different to include the gas market here.

2 Council Directive 85/374/EEC of 25 July 1985 on the approximation of the laws, regulations and administrative provisions of the Member States concerning liability for defective products.

competitive market. This liberalisation did not happen in isolation but went hand in hand with other policies, such as those relating to security of supply, promotion of renewable energy sources and energy efficiency. As a result, Belgium has become fully interconnected with its neighbouring countries and increasingly integrated into the regional market.

Secondly, we come to the aggregators, which are one kind of market player. Aggregators are a product of market liberalisation, closely related to the need to fulfil objectives of security of supply and energy efficiency. Of particular interest for this chapter is the interaction between aggregators and transmission system operators (TSOs), and the influence the latter can have on aggregators when proposing appropriate market rules for the compensation of quarter-hourly imbalances which are so vital for aggregators. As will be further explored, aggregators are becoming key players contributing to the electricity market efficiency as such as well as fulfilling TSOs' needs in terms of balancing of the system.

Finally, this chapter is an opportunity to challenge the common impression: are aggregators really newcomers? A series of changes in the market rules already gave them some room for manoeuvre a few years ago, but then some imperfections in these rules had to be eliminated. More precisely, rules had to be adapted to address the restrictions they imposed on operations such as balance responsibilities. In this respect, some major changes have been introduced into Belgian law in order to allow aggregators to operate as fully-fledged market players.

These three aspects will form the constant thread running through this chapter, which starts by reviewing the impact of liberalisation and other related policies on the development of aggregators (section 2). The chapter continues with an analysis of the transposition of the relevant European Union (EU) provisions into Belgian national law[3] (section 3). It ends with some concluding remarks (section 4)

2. THE GROWING PLACE OF AGGREGATION IN EU ELECTRICITY MARKET LEGISLATION

To understand how aggregators were established and how their roles and responsibilities have evolved until today, it is necessary to review the relevant provisions of the successive energy 'packages'.[4]

3 Please note that there is no official English translation of Belgian legislation and regulations and therefore this chapter features free translations of the official texts.

4 Please note that the use of the term 'first' and 'second' package has been introduced in an informal way after the 'third' energy package in 2009.

2.1. THE FIRST ENERGY PACKAGE

In the 1990s, when most national electricity and natural gas markets were still monopolies, the EU decided to gradually open up these markets to competition. The first liberalisation directive for the electricity market[5] was adopted under the First Energy Package in 1996 and was to be transposed into Member States' legislation by 1998. On 29 April 1999, Belgium transposed Directive 96/92/EC into national law by passing the Act on the organisation of the electricity market.[6]

Article 2 of Directive 96/92/EC provided that the market players which might have access to the system belong to one of two categories, namely customers and producers, depending on whether (in the case of offtakes) they were being supplied by or – in the case of injections – supplying the transmission or distribution system. No reference was made to aggregators.

For the organisation of access to the system, Member States could choose between two procedures: the negotiated access procedure referred to in Article 17 and/or the designation of a single buyer as provided for in Article 18.

Customers' ability to benefit from the liberalisation of the electricity market depended on eligible customers' capacity and Member States' annual publication of the criteria for the definition of eligible customers.

The First Energy Package was really a first step towards the organisation of a market based on supply and demand, where supply came from producers, who were often also transmission and/or distribution system operators (TSOs/DSOs), to meet the demand of final customers. Wholesale customers somehow fell outside the scope of these categories. This was because they were purchasing electricity not as final customers but with a view to selling it to other wholesale or final customers, without being a producer or system operator themselves. This concept has some similarities with more recent concepts of flexibility service provider and aggregator, given that the electricity purchased is not consumed but sold to another market player, and it creates an internal commercial trade[7] entailing a balance responsibility. However, it differs from them, for example, insofar as the wholesale customer has a solely commercial purpose, at least until it registers on the legislator's radar and other market players are involved. Nor was the wholesale customer at that time a typical provider of balancing services to the system operator, as it did have the appropriate generation facilities.

5 Directive 96/92/EC of the European Parliament and of the Council of 19 December 1996 concerning common rules for the internal market in electricity.

6 Hereinafter referred to as the 'Electricity Act' (Belgian Official Gazette of 11 May 1999).

7 Defined in the Belgian BRP contract as 'the transfer of energy within the Elia control area between [BRP] and another Balance Responsible Party authorised by Elia to exchange energy on a bilateral basis, for which an Internal Commercial Trade Schedule must be submitted to Elia by said Balance Responsible Parties pursuant to the BRP-Contract […].'

A key innovation in the First Energy Package was the designation, by the Member State of a system operator,[8] who was responsible for operating, ensuring the maintenance of and – if necessary – developing the transmission system.

Unless the transmission system was already independent from generation and distribution activities, in the interests of producers and their customers the system operator should be independent, at least in management terms, from other activities not related to the transmission system.

Therefore, the independence of the system operator was not considered a precondition for legal independence or ownership unbundling. The market players were protected under Belgian statutory law by general public-order principles, such as transparency and the principle of non-discrimination between system users or categories of system users, in particular avoiding any favouritism towards subsidiaries or shareholders.[9]

As regards its responsibility to manage energy flows in the system, based on exchanges with other interconnected systems, the system operator was also responsible for ensuring a secure, reliable and efficient electricity system and, in that context, for ensuring the availability of all the appropriate ancillary services.[10] Ancillary services are all the services required for the operation of a system, such as primary, secondary and tertiary reserve services. Directive 96/92/EC did not describe how the system operator was meant to ensure the availability of these services.

2.2. THE SECOND ENERGY PACKAGE

The Second Directive[11] was adopted in 2003 and had to be transposed into national law by Member States by 2004, with some provisions entering into force only in 2007.

Through the implementation of the Directive, Member States had to ensure, among other things, the establishment of a system of third-party access (TPA) to the transmission and distribution systems. based on published tariffs, applicable to all eligible customers and applied objectively and without discrimination between system users. Moreover, these tariffs, or the methodologies underlying their calculation, had to be approved prior to their entry into force, and these

8 According to Article 7.1, Member States could also require undertakings owning transmission systems to designate a system operator.

9 Article 7.5 of Directive 96/92/EC.

10 Article 7.3 of Directive 96/92/EC.

11 Directive 2003/54/EC of the European Parliament and of the Council of 26 June 2003 concerning common rules for the internal market in electricity and repealing Directive 96/92/EC.

tariffs and the underlying methodologies (only in those cases where these methodologies had been approved) were published prior to their entry into force.[12]

The regulatory authorities were empowered to supervise the right of access, being given the responsibility of determining or approving, prior to their entry into force, at least those methodologies used to calculate or establish the terms and conditions for connection and access to national networks, including transmission and distribution tariffs.

Article 21 established a calendar for the gradual opening-up of the market, ensuring that as from 1 July 2007, all industrial and domestic consumers were eligible and free to choose their own electricity suppliers from a wider range of competitors.

To ensure efficient and non-discriminatory network access, the distribution and transmission systems need to be operated by legally separate entities, where vertically-integrated undertakings exist.[13] This legal separation of distribution and transmissions systems did not require ownership unbundling in cases where they were owned by a vertically-integrated undertaking, but the system had to be independent at least in terms of its legal form, organisation and decision-making from other activities not relating to transmission, so as to guarantee the effective decision-making required to independently maintain, operate and develop networks.

Where it came to ensuring the availability of ancillary services and as soon as the electricity market was sufficiently liquid,[14] TSOs had to procure the energy they used to cover energy losses and reserve capacity in their systems according to transparent, non-discriminatory and market-based procedures.[15]

Not only did the balancing rules adopted by TSOs have to be objective, transparent and non-discriminatory but the regulatory authorities also had a responsibility to determine or approve them. The same went for rules for charging system users of their networks for any energy imbalance.[16]

As such, even in the absence of a liquid market, national regulatory authorities did more than play an active role to ensure that balance tariffs were non-discriminatory and cost-reflective. They could also at the same time provide appropriate incentives to balance electricity injections and offtakes to avoid compromising the system. As this chapter will show below, the market rules for balancing the system made a significant contribution to the development of the electricity market in general.

12 Article 20 of Directive 2003/54/EC.
13 Recital (8) of Directive 2003/54/EC.
14 Recital (17) of Directive 2003/54/EC.
15 Articles 9(c) and 11.6 of Directive 2003/54/EC.
16 Article 11.7 of Directive 2003/54/EC.

The reference in recital (17) of Directive 2003/54/EC to new entrants and to appropriate incentives to balance electricity injections and offtakes could have been used as a stepping stone, so that demand-side management would be used as a resource for the balancing market. However, the Directive still considered this from just an energy-efficiency perspective,[17] with Chapter III treating it as an alternative to generation for establishing tendering or equivalent procedures for new capacity to promote security of supply.

Directive 2006/32/EC of 5 April 2006 on energy end-use efficiency and energy services took the same approach by providing for the possibility of using energy efficiency and demand-side management[18] as alternatives to new supply and for environmental protection, as well as investments, maintenance and other expenditure on equipment using energy and on energy services and other energy-efficiency improvement measures. Yet it can also be seen as a key step towards aggregation.

2.3. THE THIRD ENERGY PACKAGE

In April 2009, a Third Energy Package seeking to further liberalise the internal electricity and gas markets was adopted, amending the Second Package and providing the cornerstone for the implementation of the internal energy market.

The principles regarding access as provided for under Directive 2003/54/EC are repeated in Directive 2009/72/EC. The new measures to protect the effective functioning of the electricity market involve both increasing the TSO's independence and consolidating the independence requirements and the powers and responsibilities of the regulatory authorities.

Article 9 has fundamentally changed the status of TSOs, providing for ownership unbundling as the default mechanism, subject however to certification to check whether the ownership unbundling requirements are met. Only in cases where the transmission system was part of a vertically-integrated undertaking on 3 September 2009, could a Member State decide not to opt for

17 In accordance with Article 2.29, 'energy efficiency/demand-side management' means 'a global or integrated approach aimed at influencing the amount and timing of electricity consumption in order to reduce primary energy consumption and peak loads by giving precedence to investments in energy efficiency measures, or other measures, such as interruptible supply contracts, over investments to increase generation capacity, if the former are the most effective and economical option, taking into account the positive environmental impact of reduced energy consumption and the security of supply and distribution cost aspects related to it.'

18 Annex III of the Directive recognises demand response management (e.g. load management, peak shaving control systems) as one of the eligible energy efficiency improvement measures in the industrial sector.

the ownership unbundling. In such instances, they could instead designate an independent system operator in accordance with Article 13 or comply with the provisions of Chapter V with regard to the independent transmission operator. A third option consisted in maintaining the arrangements which were already in place and which guarantee the TSO's independence more effectively than the provisions of Chapter V.

Regulatory authorities not only had to be wholly independent from the interests of the electricity industry but also legally distinct and functionally independent from any other public or private entity. This illustrated the fact that the development of a competitive, secure, environmentally sustainable and properly functioning and efficient market – notably by eliminating restrictions on the trade in electricity, ensuring that system operators and system users were granted appropriate incentives and that customers benefited from the efficient functioning of the market – had become priorities for the regulatory authority.

TSOs were expected to facilitate the participation of final customers and the latter's aggregators[19] in reserve and balancing markets.[20] In this way, demand response was explicitly recognised as a means of providing the required ancillary services. Of course, this assumed the implementation by the Member States of intelligent metering systems that would promote the active participation of consumers in the electricity supply market.

Article 15.8 of the Directive 2012/27/EU is the real starting point for the participation of demand response:

> Member States shall ensure that national energy regulatory authorities encourage demand side resources, such as demand response, to participate alongside supply in wholesale and retail markets.
>
> Subject to technical constraints inherent in managing networks, Member States shall ensure that transmission system operators and distribution system operators, in meeting requirements for balancing and ancillary services, treat demand response providers, including aggregators, in a non-discriminatory manner, on the basis of their technical capabilities.
>
> Subject to technical constraints inherent in managing networks, Member States shall promote access to and participation of demand response in balancing, reserve and other system services markets, inter alia by requiring national energy regulatory authorities or, where their national regulatory systems so require, transmission system operators

19 It was only in Article 2(45) of the Directive 2012/27/EU of the European Parliament and the Council of 25 October 2012 on energy efficiency, amending Directives 2009/125/EC and 2010/30/EU and repealing Directives 2004/8/EC and 2006/32/EC that the term 'aggregator' was defined, namely as 'a demand service provider that combines multiple short-duration consumer loads for sale or auction in organised energy markets'.

20 Recital (35) of Directive 2009/72/EC.

> and distribution system operators in close cooperation with demand service providers and consumers, to define technical modalities for participation in these markets on the basis of the technical requirements of these markets and the capabilities of demand response. Such specifications shall include the participation of aggregators.

The definition of 'aggregator' as 'a demand service provider that combines multiple short-duration consumer loads for sale or auction in organised energy markets'[21] acknowledges the support for demand response.

Article 37.8 of the Directive 2009/72/EC is also of great importance, since it allows regulators to grant DSOs and TSOs appropriate incentives to increase efficiencies, foster market integration and security of supply, and support the related research activities. Article 15.4 of Directive 2012/27/EU also explicitly added that within the framework of Directive 2009/72/EC, 'tariffs allow suppliers to improve consumer participation in system efficiency, including demand response [...].' More generally, incentives in transmission and distribution tariffs that are detrimental to the overall efficiency (including energy efficiency) of the generation, transmission, distribution and supply of electricity or those that might hamper making demand response contribute to balancing markets and ancillary services procurement had to be removed.

2.4. THE CLEAN ENERGY PACKAGE

The Electricity Directive 2019/944 adopted as part of the Clean Energy Package confirms both the importance of the access of all customers to the electricity markets to trade their flexibility and self-generated electricity, and the importance of aggregators as intermediaries between customer groups and the market. It also recognises, however, the need of having models where imbalances are settled or where perimeter corrections are introduced.[22] It follows from Article 17.4 of the Directive that Member States may require electricity undertakings or participating final customers to pay financial compensation to other market participants or to the market participants' balance responsible parties, if those market participants or balance responsible parties are directly affected by demand response activation. These evolutions in the field of the customers' active participation in the electricity market require smart metering systems which are able to provide data.[23]

---

21 See Article 2(45) of the Directive 2012/27/EU.

22 See Recital (39); Article 15 also sets the financial responsibility for the imbalances caused in the electricity system, amongst the rights and obligations of the active customers.

23 See Recital (55) and Article 23.

3. TRANSPOSITION OF THE EU ENERGY PACKAGES INTO BELGIAN LAW

3.1. GENERAL OBSERVATIONS

On 29 April 1999, Belgium transposed Directive 96/92/EC into national law through the adoption by the federal parliament of the Act on the organisation of the electricity market. As Belgium is a federal state and most aspects of energy policy are regional powers,[24] this Directive has also been transposed into regional legislation.[25]

As part of the transposition of Directive 96/92/EC, the Belgian legislator chose to establish an independent regulatory authority, called the Commission for Electricity and Gas Regulation (CREG),[26] At the same time, an independent TSO, Elia, was designated following a nomination put forward by the grid owners, a reasoned opinion from CREG and consultation in the Federal Council of Ministers.[27] The King (in practice the Belgian federal government) has the responsibility of establishing rules to guarantee the independence of Elia management.[28] CREG was competent for, notably, approving the general terms and conditions of the regulated contracts[29] for connection and access to the grid and for balance responsibility. It was also given the power to determine tariffs.[30] The Act of 8 January 2012 extended CREG's powers in accordance with Directive 2009/72/EC. Of the other amendments made to the Electricity Act,

24 Article 6 §1 VII of the Special Act on the State Reform of 8 August 1980 regulates the division of powers on energy between the regional and federal authorities.

25 See the Ordinance of 19 July 2001 on the organisation of the electricity market in the Brussels-Capital Region, the Flemish Energy Act of 8 May 2009 and the Walloon Act of 12 April 2001 on the organisation of the regional electricity market.

26 Article 23 of the Electricity Act.

27 Article 10 of the Electricity Act. Elia was designated by the Ministerial Decree of 13 September 2002 (Belgian Official Gazette of 17 September 2002).

28 Article 9 *ter* of the Electricity Act.

29 Also see Article 6 of the Royal Decree of 19 December 2002 establishing the technical regulation for the operation of the transmission grid and the access thereto, Belgian Official Gazette, 28 December 2002 (hereinafter former 'Federal Grid Code' or 'TGC') repealed by the Royal Decree of 22 April 2019 establishing the technical regulation for the operation of the transmission grid and the access thereto, Belgian Official Gazette, 29 April 2019 (hereinafter 'new FGC') a.o. to implement the network codes established by the European Commission on the basis of Article 6 of Regulation 714/2009.

30 Article 12 of the Electricity Act; until the transposition by the Act of 8 January 2012 of Directive 2009/72/EC in the form of the Electricity Act, the Electricity Act entrusted the King with the power to fix the tariff structure. On this basis, the Royal Decree of 8 June 2007 set the rules governing the determination and control of the total income and the fair profit margin, the general tariff structure, the balance between costs and receipts and the basic principles and procedures concerning the proposal and the approval of the rates, reporting and cost control by the TSO (Belgian Official Gazette of 29 June 2007).

the ones relevant to this chapter were introduced by the Act of 28 June 2015[31] transposing Directive 2012/27/EU and the Act of 13 July 2017[32] introducing the transfer of energy.

Although the 2009 and in particular the 2012 Directives indicate that there was a need to provide access to demand response and to generation for ancillary services, and despite the fact that TSOs, in particular Elia, developed demand response products, one particular issue emerged in Europe, specifically in light of the *Voltalis* case in France.[33] There was an apparent need for compensation both for the supplier of a customer, in cases in which the customer decides not to use its energy but to sell it on the market, and for the Balance Responsible Party (BRP) for the impact of this course of action by the customer on its balancing perimeter. In 2016, the Belgian federal government commissioned CREG to conduct a study whose conclusions identified the need to amend the Belgian legal framework. This gave rise to the Electricity Act amendment of 2017 which represents a milestone in the Belgian legislation regarding demand response. Further details of the CREG study and the legislative provisions are given in section 3.4 below on energy transfers.

3.2. THE ROLE OF THE TSO WITH REGARD TO DEMAND RESPONSE

The responsibilities and roles of the TSO are laid down in Article 8 §1 of the Electricity Act, according to which, the TSO is responsible for the operation, maintenance and development of the transmission grid, including the interconnection lines to other electricity grids, in order to guarantee the continuity of energy supply. To keep the electricity system secure, reliable and efficient, the TSO must ensure the availability and activation of the requisite ancillary services, which include the services provided in demand response, through a transparent market platform.

In the Act of 8 January 2012, Article 8 of the Electricity Act was supplemented with a paragraph 1*bis*, specifying that 'in the context of the tasks referred to in §1, the system operator is primarily committed to promoting market integration'. Although market integration was not defined in the Electricity Act or the preparatory works of the Act of 8 January 2012, paragraph 1*bis* further focuses on the coordination with neighbouring and other relevant system operators

31 Belgian Official Gazette of 6 July 2015.

32 Belgian Official Gazette of 19 July 2017.

33 On 9 July 2009, the French Energy Regulatory Commission declared that Voltalis, which sells energy management devices that curb energy consumption, have to compensate the supplier for the power saved by its devices. This decision is annulled by the French State (Conseil d'État, 9ème et 10ème sous-sections réunies, 03/05/2011, 331858).

rather than on balancing mechanisms. However, this chapter will demonstrate that the latter have also contributed to market integration, notably by enabling foreign capacity to be used for balancing services and foreign energy providers to get involved in these in recent years.

The new FGC is based on Article 11 of the Electricity Act, which provides for e.g. the following:

> 2° the operational rules to which the system operator is subject in the technical management of the electricity flows and in the measures that he must take to deal with problems of overload, technical defects and defects of production units;
>
> […]
>
> 4° the support services that must be established by the system operator;
>
> […]
>
> 7° the provisions in the field of information or of prior approval by the committee of operational rules, general conditions, standard agreements, forms or procedures applicable to the system operator and, where applicable, to the users.

One of the characteristics of electricity is that it is still difficult to store on a very large scale. Electricity generated and injected into a system must be the subject of offtakes from that system for both consumption and storage at the same time, to maintain the frequency at the European standard level of 50 Hz. If the volume of injections exceeds that of offtakes, the frequency will increase, whereas it will decrease if the volume of offtakes outstrips that of injections. Due to the unbundling obligation, the TSO cannot be involved in both generation and supply activities, and supplying electricity requires balance responsibility within a portfolio of injections and offtakes. The same goes for portfolios with imports and exports and internal commercial transactions between electricity traders. According to Article 157 §1 of the former FGC, balance responsibility is a responsibility to make all reasonable resources available and to deploy them to maintain the balance on a quarter-hourly basis between injections of active power and offtakes of active power in the control area. In practice, the BRP must be in balance on introducing access programmes and must maintain this balance in real time. In Belgium, balance responsibility also includes the compensation of active losses occurring in the transmission grid.

The TSO has a responsibility to maintain the overall balance at the level of the control area[34] and must therefore, at all times, monitor, maintain or restore the balance between supply and demand of electrical power in the control area, caused inter alia by the individual imbalances of the various BRPs. To this end,

[34] According to Article 3 of the former FGC: 'The system operator monitors the compensation of the overall imbalance of the control area caused by the individual imbalances of the various access responsible parties [i.e. BRPs].'

the TSO activates the resources at its disposal during the operation of the system, in particular:

1. the activation of primary frequency control;
2. secondary control of the balance in the control area;
3. the resources made available by third parties, including the power provided by the generators in accordance with Article 159, §2, the tertiary-reserve power and adjustments to the daily access programmes in terms of load offered by the BRPs to the TSO.[35,36]

Two key principles apply to Article 157 §2 of the former FGC: (i) the system operator activates the resources according to the lowest-price criterion of the lowest price, and (ii) the market functioning rules for the compensation of quarter-hourly imbalances.[37]

Article 159 §1 of the former FGC states that these balancing rules are adopted by CREG following a proposal by the system operator and then published by the latter.

3.3. THE OPENING-UP OF ANCILLARY SERVICES TO DEMAND RESPONSE

Despite the general wording of Article 232 of the former FGC which entrusted the TSO with the procurement of ancillary services according to objective,

---

35 Article 157 §2 3° of the former FGC was amended by the Royal Decree of 3 December 2017. Previously, tertiary reserve power could only be activated after the activation of the power made available by the generators in accordance with Article 159 §2 and adjustments to the daily access programmes offered to the system operator by the balance responsible parties. This way of working was no longer sustainable as there were regular price spikes in these offers of power and they prevented the full application of the 'lowest-price' criterion, resulting in inefficient cost management for the activation of tertiary control. According to Article 159 §2, 'all the generators in the control area whose nominal power for access to the network is greater than or equal to 75 MW shall keep their power available to the system operator in accordance with Articles 222 and 223. This subscription for reserve capacity shall be accompanied by a price quote. Those generators whose nominal power for access to the network is lower than 75 MW, as well as the generators who are active in another control area insofar as the operational rules between the relevant control zones allow this, can also make available their available quarter-hourly power in accordance with objective and transparent methods determined by the system operator.' Under Articles 199 and 200 of the new FGC, the merit order is not set any more by the FTC, but by the balancing rules approved by the regulator.

36 In the (EU) Regulation 2017/2195 concerning the electricity balancing guideline, the primary, secondary and tertiary control are called, respectively, frequency containment reserve (FCR), automatic frequency restoration reserve (aFRR) and manual frequency restoration reserve (mFRR).

37 Hereinafter referred to as 'balancing rules'.

transparent and non-discriminatory procedures, based on the market rules and in accordance with the operational rules provided for in this Decree, these services were initially only designed for and offered by generators that were also BRPs. Title III Chapter I Section V of the former FGC regulating the specifications of connections and the right to supply ancillary services only applied to generation-units[38] and the grid user's right to provide ancillary services was made dependent on compliance with these specifications.[39] Furthermore, in the context of ancillary services, only conventional power plants with a capacity of more than 75 MW[40] were required to keep power available to the TSO, as stipulated in Article 159. The activation of active power as requested by the TSO in that context only resulted in a correction of the BRP's balance perimeter if that activation was requested to a producer.[41] On the other hand, there was no legal basis for a correction for activation of ancillaries from offtake. Even the public service obligation the King can impose with a view to ensuring security of supply and subject to the conditions set by Article 12 *quinquies* of the Electricity Act[42] and the volumes and prices of ancillary services, is limited to generators[43] in the Belgian control area.

In 2004, the TSO submitted for approval a load interruptibility mechanism (ICH), to be regarded as a tertiary reserve service. The ICH was limited to connected transmission grid users and was subject to several limitations in terms of volume, duration and number of activations. CREG approved this change, considering that the mechanism was no obstacle to access and did not compromise the safety, reliability or efficiency of the grid, in accordance with the general interest.[44] This was despite the lack of a legal basis for the correction of the balance perimeter. However, the perimeter of a grid user's BRP could be corrected in cases where the activation was directly requested of that grid user on an individual basis. It is also worth noting that this mechanism was introduced by a modification to the Access Responsible Party (ARP) contract on the basis of Article 6 of the former FGC, as opposed to the decisions below, which were based on Article 159 of the former FGC.

---

38 Article 76 of the former FGC.

39 Articles 119 and 135 of the former FGC.

40 According to the former FGC, any production unit that directly injects electricity into the transmission grid or the operation of which affects the safety, reliability or efficiency of the transmission grid must conclude a contract coordination of the activation of the production unit (CIPU). These production units are generally called CIPU units. Non-CIPU units are often smaller, decentralised units.

41 Article 194 of the former FGC.

42 Article 234 of the former FGC gave the Federal Minister of Energy the ability to take these measures, but there is potentially some doubt surrounding whether the King was empowered by the legislator to delegate this power to the Minister.

43 This limitation can also be found in Article 239 (for primary control), Article 246 (for secondary control) and Article 252 (for tertiary control) of the former FGC.

44 Decision 040923-CDC-352.

By the time the balancing rules based on Article 159 and described below were introduced, CREG had developed the following considerations for the approval of these rules:

- the need for the rules to enhance the transparency to better inform participants and discourage abusive behaviour, along with the importance of price signals;
- the maintenance of the balance in the control area, contributing to the safety, reliability and efficiency of the grid;
- the contribution made to the functioning of the market, taking due account of market characteristics (the increasing interest in participation with demand flexibility, the decrease of generation capacity, and the balance between reasonable compensation and regulation which remains essential when competition is limited);
- the minimisation of the imbalance compensation cost through appropriate mechanism and imbalance tariffs;
- the need for appropriate market mechanisms and tariffs to prevent ancillary services being used for parties' own needs (similarly to gaming based on arbitration in the case of the spot/intraday (ID) market);
- the flexibility of the mechanism to accommodate future adjustments;
- technology neutrality;
- the enhancement of the functioning of the market;
- the avoidance of obstacles to the integration of the European market.

In 2010, the CREG approved a mechanism aiming to open up the market for the provision of secondary control to all generators, regardless of whether or not they had signed reservation contracts under the secondary control mechanism.[45] CREG also approved a mechanism limiting the activation of ICH. Both mechanisms offered more flexibility and competition, allowing smaller market players to provide secondary and tertiary control.

A couple of years later, in 2012, this was followed by CREG's approval of a mechanism allowing the absorption of generation surplus which was forecasted for the summer period by an activation of a decremental bid triggered by an imbalance price of -€100/MWh.[46] The innovation was that non-coordinatable units could also participate in the supply of balancing services.

A subsequent development which is to be seen in the context of a decrease in the offers for reservation of control services by large generation units and which therefore aimed to promote the participation of small players, was the approval by the CREG of the mechanism allowing suppliers with 5 MW capacity to make secondary reserve contract offers for generation.[47]

---

[45] Decision 101223-CDC-1028.

[46] Decision 120621-CDC-1165.

[47] Decision 120628-CDC-1163.

In 2013,[48] short-term contracting for primary and secondary control was introduced. CREG also approved the activation of free bids per unit[49] which could be adapted up until one hour before real time, the introduction of the provision of reserved tertiary control for generation through the secondary market and a new penalty system, enhancing the security of the system (as well as attracting the participation of smaller generation units and limiting their risks). Alongside this, an initial step was taken towards aggregation with the introduction of the tertiary reserve dynamic profile (R3DP) dedicated to demand response and small generation units, known as non-CIPU units, and open also to flexibility located in the DSO grid with a view to improving the operation of demand flexibility: this product was determined by maximum duration and number of activations. The volume covered at the lowest possible global price (reservation) was intended to enhance competition with R3prod (i.e. R3 production, which was the classic tertiary reserve offered by CIPU units until then); it is also worth noting that provision was only made for R3DP to be activated at the end of the merit order and that there was no activation price and also no correction of the BRP perimeter, giving rise to imbalance fee payments to the BRP.

As more and more generators closed down or mothballed their gas-fired generation units, being out of the market following a huge upsurge in intermittent renewable generation, this scarcity of these units has been a catalyst both for demand flexibility through aggregation and for strategic reserves.[50]

In 2014, the selection criteria for short-term reservation offers were changed to allow offers as low as 1 MW (instead of 5 MW).[51] In a second decision, the minimum capacity for long-term reservation offers was reduced from 5 MW to 1 MW to increase liquidity.[52] In the meantime, due to the accumulation of knowledge, the ability of distribution system operators to monitor the impact of R3DP on their grid operation and the aggregators having the time to increase their customer base, the volume of R3DP increased from 50 MW to 100 MW, boosting competition with R3prod.

Following the success of short-term auctions for primary and secondary control and developments in Western Europe, the introduction of short-term auctions for 15 per cent of reserved capacity for tertiary control was approved by CREG.[53] It was of the opinion that involvement in low-volume offers helped increase market liquidity and that this development of 'contractualisation' was

48 Decision 130407-CDC-1252.
49 Based on the pay-as-bid principle.
50 The strategic reserve was introduced into the Electricity Act by the Act of 26 March 2014 and could also be offered by demand.
51 Decision 140228-CDC-1390.
52 Decision 140515-CDC-1331.
53 Decision 150717-CDC-1424.

a step in the right direction for tertiary control in terms of price, liquidity and integration into the Western European market.[54]

The next developments Elia has proposed, and which have been approved,[55] mainly relate to four issues:

1. the introduction of the reservation of primary control power through a shared platform from 1 August 2016 onwards, boosting liquidity;
2. the deployment of the secondary intraday market in the event of a problem with a generation unit;
3. the short-term (currently monthly rather than daily) contracting of all tertiary reserve capacity, except for ICH;[56]
4. developments relating to the integrated gasification combined cycle (IGCC),[57] which was also welcomed for its contribution to the liquidity of the market and the integration of the European market.

Decision 161013-CDC-1556 turned the products R3prod and R3DP into R3std and R3flex (offered by both CIPU and non-CIPU units) to make them more technology-neutral and bring them more into line with Elia's needs. Despite Elia's efforts, the products could not be assimilated because of the lack of a legal basis for the transfer of energy when R3 is offered by non-CIPU units (which is the case for aggregators). Therefore, during a transition period, offers by non-CIPU units could not result in the correction of the BRP perimeter or be remunerated with an activation fee. Also, during the transition period, the following merit order would apply: R3std for CIPU units, R3std for non-CIPU units, R3flex for CIPU units, R3flex for non-CIPU units, R3 for ICH. Although this posed the risk of fragmentation of the R3 market, the lack of an activation price for non-CIPU-related R3 had less impact on the price of R3 offers and was in line with product activation characteristics. Finally, new reservation and activation penalties were provided for during this transition period.

On 30 March 2017,[58] CREG approved the proposal concerning the adjustment of the balancing rules. One of the proposed developments was the opening-up of the primary reserve market to new technologies, including frequency containment reserve (FCR) provider groups, which bring together smaller resources, so that they can comply with European FCR standards. Another was the opening-up of non-reserved tertiary control power to the technical non-CIPU units. With a view to controlling this activation, for as long as there was no legal basis for the

[54] See Article 8 §1*bis* of the Electricity Act.

[55] Decision 160609-CDC-1525.

[56] This was due to the differing characteristics of the ICH product, which is based on the 'drop by' principle, while the product R3DP and the future product R3 are flexible products based on the 'drop to' principle, meaning that they could not be brought together at the same auction.

[57] Cross-border imbalance netting.

[58] Decision 30.3.2017 (B)1605.

transfer of energy[59] this product was only available to suppliers who were BRPs for all delivery points or suppliers with an agreement with their BRP and with suppliers and BRPs of delivery points participating in the offer.

Decision 19.10.2017 (B)1658 abolished the ICH product as of 2018, expanded the secondary market for reserved R1, R2 and R3, and the activation conditions for reserved R3 std and flex by non-CIPU units (including the activation of power beyond the reserved capacity) have been clarified.

A pilot project for offering R2 with non-CIPU units has also been approved by the CREG as part of a tariff incentive decision.[60]

This summary of decisions on the system operator's balancing rules shows that the opening-up of ancillary services to demand response (including through an aggregator) was a landmark development, which should, however, be considered alongside other changes. Some of them were triggered by the capacity issue, such as the involvement of smaller generation units, shorter-term reservation, and the participation of foreign capacity, and this created more competition, more diversity, and more efficient use of all the existing capacity. There have also been operational issues (e.g. the ability of the balancing rules to trigger the appropriate behaviour on the part of the participants, the merit order, the possible abuse of a dominant position, inadequate control over activation, the correction of the balance perimeter, etc.) so that new operational rules also had to be implemented. It goes without saying that these market developments also required investments to be made in IT to ensure the proper functioning of the market without compromising the security, reliability and efficiency of the system.

3.4. TRANSFER OF ENERGY

The Energy Efficiency Directive determined that system operators had to be non-discriminatory in their treatment of demand response providers, including aggregators, doing so on the basis of their technical capacity. The transposition of this Directive has empowered CREG to take all reasonable measures to encourage demand response to participate in the wholesale market in the same way as supply.[61] As long as there is no clarity about whether or not to correct the balancing perimeter and as long as there are deviations between products, the lack of legal certainty with regard to the correction of the perimeter has left the flexibility service providers (FSPs) with considerable uncertainties when developing their portfolios.

59 For the aggregator the absence of any correction of the balance perimeter for the non-CIPU R3 product created a conflict of interest between the aggregator (and also the final customer) and the BRP, forcing the product to only be activated late in the merit order, when the imbalance price was high and could therefore serve to compensate the affected BRP.

60 Decision 29.6.2017 (B) 658E/45.

61 Article 23 §1 5*bis* added to the Electricity Act by the Act of 28 June 2015 transposing Directive 2012/27/EU.

Prior to the amendment of the Electricity Act, CREG had the task of 'investigat[ing] the means to be used to facilitate access to the market for demand management'.[62] CREG observed that there were various types of obstacles in this regard (of a regulatory,[63] economic, commercial, behavioural or technical nature and obstacles related to the organisation of the markets[64]). It suggested working with a market model, covering both the general contractual flexibility connected to the market in general and the flexibility in the context of the ancillary services, based on the following principles:

- Principle 1: Every final customer is entitled to exercise flexibility without opposition from its supplier or BRP.
- Principle 2: Every final customer is entitled to choose its flexibility service provider (FSP), regardless of its electricity supplier.
- Principle 3: The FSP must take responsibility for balance issues relating to the activation of the demand flexibility it manages.
- Principle 4: The FSP must not take any action that disadvantages other parties. This has the following implications:
  - 4.1. The source BRP's balance perimeter has to be corrected;
  - 4.2. The source final customer's electricity supplier has to be subject to financial compensation.
- Principle 5: The correction of balance perimeters must be centralised and carried out by a neutral entity with the required competencies.
- Principle 6: As regards financial compensation (and also the choice of a baseline), commercial negotiations should be the preferred option. If the parties fail to come to an agreement or if an agreement is not an option, a default solution must be applicable to ensure that demand-side response offers can be taken into account.
- Principle 7: From the viewpoint of market operation, compensation is desirable for any activation blocked by a system operator.
- Principle 8: The final customer is the holder of the measuring and metering data and is free to communicate such data.
- Principle 9: The confidentiality of commercially sensitive data must be ensured.
- Principle 10: A single invoice should be sent to the final customer detailing their electricity consumption.

---

62 Study (F)160503-CDC-1459 of 5 May 2016.

63 For example, 'the lack of a definition of the role of an FSP or of the relationship between FSPs, BRPs and suppliers in terms of the transfer of energy and financial compensation, where the main stumbling block is the problem of the confidentiality of the data when the flexibility is activated by an FSP other than the source supplier.' (CREG Study (F)160503-CDC-1459, p. 15).

64 With regard to the balancing market, CREG reiterated that the lack of legal certainty surrounding the correction of the perimeter left the flexibility service providers (FSPs) with considerable uncertainties when developing their portfolios.

The model proposed by the CREG looks like this:

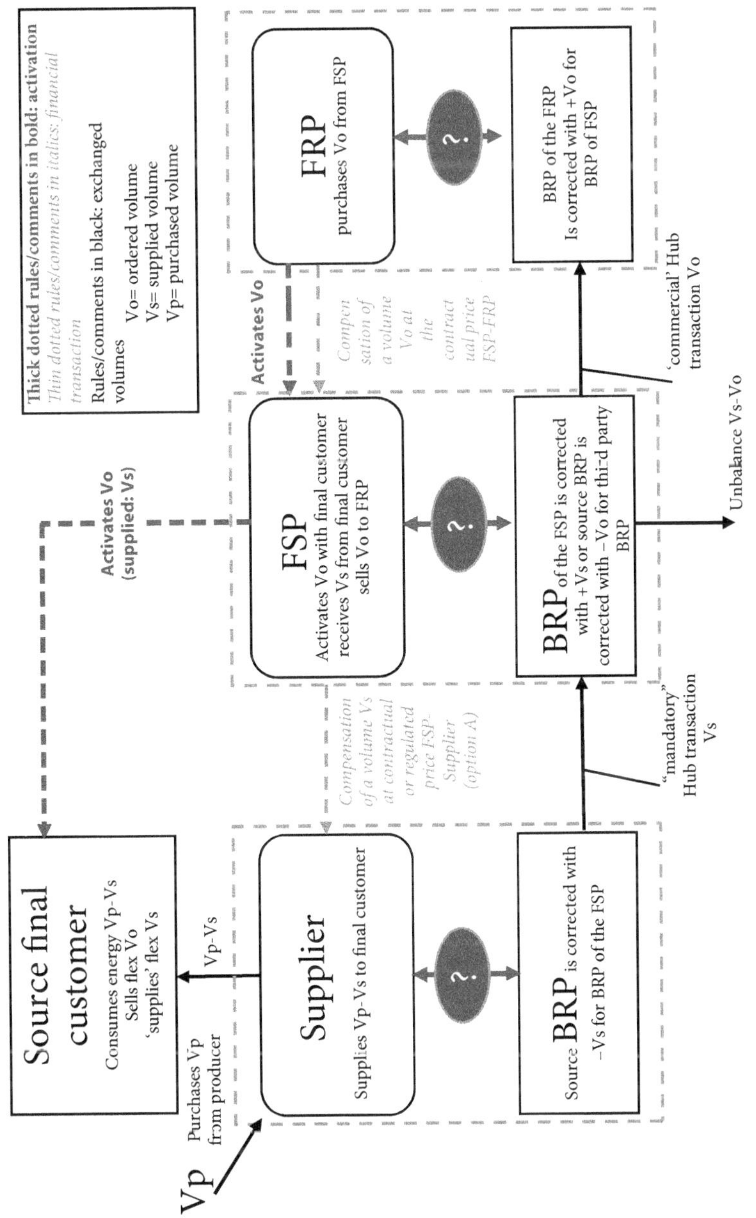

Figure 1. The market model proposed by CREG
Source: CREG.[65]

65 Free translation of scheme 3, p. 39 of the Study (F)160503-CDC-1459 of 5 May 2016.

To ensure the appropriate transposition of the Energy Efficiency Directive, CREG was of the opinion that the law should be amended to give the final customer the right to develop its flexibility regardless of its energy supplier, to define new rules for FSPs and flexibility data managers (FDMs) and the compensation of FDMs and to provide a framework for issuing Royal Decrees specifying the arrangements for any energy transfer. Due to the complexity of the subject matter, Article 159 of the former FGC did not offer a sufficient legal basis therefor.

As a result, a new Article 19 *bis* has been introduced in the Electricity Act to implement the aforementioned 10 principles for the energy transfer, which it also defines as the 'activation of demand flexibility involving a supplier and a FSP who have separate balance responsibilities and/or a FSP who is not their supplier'.[66]

Article 19 *bis* §2 entrusts the CREG, at the proposal of the TSO and, after consultation with the competent regional authorities,[67] to lay down the rules for the organisation of the energy transfer through a FSP.[68] The TSO's proposal is drawn up after consultation with the market players. The rules apply to the day-ahead market, the intraday market, the strategic reserve market and the market for compensation of quarter-hourly imbalances, with the exception of the market for activation of primary frequency control.

The rules determine in particular:

1. the principles for the determination of the activated flexibility volume;
2. the principles for the correction of the quarter-hourly imbalance created by the activation of demand flexibility by a FSP;

---

66 Act of 13 July 2017, Belgian Official Gazette of 19 July 2017.

67 The Electricity Act is a federal act. This chapter will not discuss regional electricity legislation, as the transfer of energy is a competence of the federal authorities. The Belgian federal legislator was of the opinion that energy transfers involve commercial flexibility and therefore decided it was competent. This opinion was essentially based on the distinction made by the Constitutional Court between commercial flexibility, i.e. the flexibility offered, via a third party as the case may be, involving free participation in an organised market with market-based prices or flexibility in the context of ancillary services, and technical flexibility, i.e. flexibility that is imposed by the system operator in the context of the operation of its grid, for the payment of regulated compensation as the case may be (Constitutional Court judgment 56/2016 of 28 April 2016). Also, when it comes to the operation of the flexibility data and the metering and sub-metering data of final customers connected to the distribution grid, which fall under regional powers, the federal legislator prescribed that CREG had to consult the regional authorities about the rules for the organisation of the transfer of energy via a flexibility service provider. By doing this, the federal legislator ensured it complied with the principle of federal loyalty and did not compromise the powers of the regions.

68 The term is defined in Article 2,64° Electricity Act; the aggregator is a flexibility service provider combining several consumer loads.

3. the exchange of the information and data required for the implementation of the energy transfer;
4. the phased implementation of the energy transfer in the various aforementioned markets.

Since compensation was a sensitive issue, the following details are to be determined by the CREG:

1. the rules to follow with regard to the reimbursement of the energy transferred;
2. notwithstanding Article V.2 of the Code of Economic Law, the formula(e) for determining the standard price for the transfer;
3. the mechanisms for the financial and contractual guarantees to be obtained from the FSP.

The Act also charges the CREG with setting default contractual and financial rules, in case no agreement has been reached in commercial negotiations between the market players.

The TSO has a central role with respect to the management of the flexibility data with regard to the development of the flexibility of demand entailing an energy transfer.

This legislation has been implemented gradually for part of the market segments envisaged by the Electricity Act. CREG has made various key decisions in recent years with regard to the opening-up of the energy transfer mechanism to the tertiary reserve (on a reserve and non-reserved basis): on 24 May 2018, it approved the transmission system operator's proposal for the organisation of energy transfers[69] and on 17 September 2018, a change to these rules was approved.[70] Based on the CREG's decision (B)1677 of 15 March 2018, Elia has established The Rules for Transfer of Energy for several balancing services. Changes to the general terms and conditions of the ARP contract were adopted on 19 April 2018[71] and on 8 November 2018.[72] These rules apply to both reserved and non-reserved tertiary control. In future, other changes to the rules governing energy transfers will be made to open up energy transfers to other market segments. On 11 October 2018, a draft decision[73] was made

[69] Decision (B) 1747.
[70] Decision (B) 1807.
[71] Decision (B) 1741.
[72] Decision (B) 1854.
[73] Decision (B) 1846.

(and submitted for consultation) on the proposed standard form for the bank guarantee used in case of energy transfers.

Although this chapter is too short to include a complete analysis of the provisions of the recast Electricity Directive and its forthcoming implementation in Belgium, it has to be recognised that Articles 19 *bis* and *ter* Electricity Act, even if their approval preceded the recast Directive by almost two years, are quite well aligned with the recast Directive and that, in its study (F)160503-CDC-1459, the CREG made the right analysis of the transfer of energy. The issue of the transfer of energy is generally recognised as an intrinsic aspect of aggregators.

4. CONCLUSION

The aggregator already has a few years behind it, as it was recognised and defined in Directive 2012/27/EU. The Second Energy Package also linked demand-side management to energy efficiency and security of supply. However, for the full potential of load to be realised in these objectives, service providers can combine multiple short-term consumer loads for sale or auction in organised energy markets and develop these consumers' portfolios, allowing them to better manage their consumption, offering extra capacity to the market but also to the system operator. As demand-side participation not only had to be promoted as one of the ingredients for increasing energy efficiency and security of supply, but also had to grow and develop sustainably and really compete with suppliers and producers, the balancing rules had to be adapted. These have been a key tool promoting the participation of demand response, but we must not forget that several other aspects also needed to be addressed close to real time, activation rules and the participation of all capacities, including demand response to cross-border balancing services platforms (which contributes to European market integration). Above all, transfer of energy has shown that energy needed not only to be considered in terms of sales and purchases but also in terms of its impact on each party's balance responsibility. The changes that have been made to the legislation and regulations also removed earlier obstacles, such as the conflicts of interest of certain market players. As a result, the Act of 13 July 2017 offers an all-encompassing legal framework for both the day-ahead and intraday markets and the balancing market, ensuring that the aggregator is now a mature market player contributing to energy efficiency and security of supply.

CHAPTER III

AGGREGATION OF DISTRIBUTED ENERGY RESOURCES IN THE UNITED STATES

Current Uses and Potential for More Widespread Deployment

Joel B. Eisen

1. INTRODUCTION

Aggregation of distributed energy resources (DERs) in the United States can be an important component of a revolutionary energy transition that integrates significant new quantities of DERs in the electric grid and transforms end users from energy consumers into energy producers and managers. The term 'distributed energy resources' encompasses a wide variety of small-scale distributed generation units such as rooftop solar panels, as well as electric vehicles, 'demand response', and energy storage, among others. The principal characteristic all DERs share is their location at the edge of the electric grid. This chapter uses the definition of DER from the U.S. Federal Energy Regulatory Commission (FERC), which is: '[a]ny source or sink of power that is located on the distribution system, any subpart thereof, or behind a customer meter.'[1]

DERs are connecting to the American electric grid in ever-growing numbers, and can provide significant flexibility and resilience benefits to the grid. They can serve as the equivalent of conventional power plants, providing electricity in wholesale energy, capacity and ancillary services markets. At the distribution level, they can help defer or replace more costly investments in traditional grid infrastructure. And DERs can help integrate renewable resources into the grid and decrease greenhouse gas emissions.

1 Electric Storage Participation in Markets Operated by Regional Transmission Organizations and Independent System Operators, 81 Fed. Reg. 86,522 (30 November 2016) (to be codified at 18 C.F.R. Part 35) Notice of Proposed Rulemaking (hereinafter 'FERC Storage NOPR').

DERs present new challenges to an American electric grid that until recently relied heavily on central generating stations and long-distance transmission lines to serve customers. Evolving from the grid of the past to relying on a myriad of DERs, and taking full advantage of their unique characteristics, requires new paradigms for utilities, grid operators, and regulators. As deployment grows, the operation of DERs can interact with both the bulk power system, which is managed by wholesale market operators subject to federal regulation, and the distribution system, which is managed by utilities subject to state regulation. Careful management of the impacts of thousands of new DERs on distribution systems is therefore necessary, as is development of wholesale market models to allow DERs to meet grid needs.

Some of the many challenges to full integration of DERs in the electric grid may be addressed through aggregation. 'Aggregation' means combining DERs from a diverse array of end users into a single resource through the use of systems that remotely and automatically combine and optimize generation, demand-side, and storage resources.[2] For example, a firm acting as an intermediary between end users and the wholesale electricity markets could manage the charge stored in an electric vehicle's battery, the demand reduction from residential devices such as air conditioners and water heaters in response to incentives, and the electricity generated by rooftop solar panels as an aggregated resource.[3]

Aggregation offers utilities and regional grid operators the opportunity to meet demand with an array of DERs, and to realize many benefits of DERs that would otherwise not be achievable. Aggregation also has important socioeconomic dimensions. It allows individual consumers to take part more fully in the energy transition when they would otherwise not be able to do so.[4] And it promises to encourage new business models that could promote competition with established utilities and thereby accelerate the ongoing transition away from monopoly providers of electricity.

This chapter evaluates current programs and initiatives to expand wholesale market participation through third-party DER aggregators serving as intermediaries between individual customers and the wholesale markets.[5]

---

2 Janine Migden-Ostrander, John Shenot, et al., *Regulatory Assistance Project, Enabling Third-Party Aggregation of Distributed Energy Resources* (2018), at 10.

3 As an example, one report indicates, 'For example, the DR potential of multiple industrial customers or thousands of residential air conditioners can be managed as an aggregated resource, providing significant peak demand reductions, frequency response services, etc.' *Regulatory Assistance Project*, above n 2, at 10.

4 Susan F. Tierney, *The Value of 'DER' to 'D': The Role of Distributed Energy Resources in Supporting Local Electric Distribution System Reliability* (2016) p 2.

5 For this reason, the term 'aggregator', as used in this chapter, does not include any individual electric utility or its customers.

At present, there is little DER aggregation beyond wholesale market demand response (DR) programs, but that is expected to change. Some coverage is devoted to developments involving distribution-level utilities, including 'non-wires alternatives' projects by distribution utilities that forgo traditional infrastructure upgrades for DER procurement to meet system needs, and contemplation of distribution-level markets where aggregated resources are offered to provide services. However, most discussion here, as with discussions on DER aggregation in the U.S. generally, focuses on the potential for third parties to bid aggregated resources into wholesale electricity markets, rather than on utility aggregation programs.

The present contribution describes the policies that state and federal regulators are implementing to encourage more widespread deployment of aggregated DERs to provide grid services. FERC has recognized and promoted the ability of DERs to participate in the wholesale capacity, energy, and ancillary services markets.[6] It is also considering promoting DER aggregation through a potential rulemaking process, as noted below. In addition, some states, notably New York with its 'Reforming the Energy Vision' (REV) program and California with its 'Distributed Energy Resource Provider' initiative, have sought to establish programs by which aggregated DERs can participate more fully in the grid.

This chapter addresses the forms and benefits of DER aggregation, the state and federal laws that have encouraged aggregation, and the current legal hurdles to aggregation's more widespread use. Section 2 describes aggregation and its potential benefits in the United States, within the context of the rapid transformation taking place in the electric power sector. The discussion centers on third-party aggregators seeking to take part in wholesale electricity markets, with a focus on the prevalent form of aggregation today, demand reductions bid into these markets (known as 'demand response'). Section 3 analyzes the potential for more DER aggregation programs in the wholesale markets, summarizing the recent experience in the California markets and the proposed federal rule that built, in part, on this experience. Section 4 examines DER aggregation at the distribution level, with a focus on 'non-wires alternatives' projects that have used aggregation to benefit distribution utilities. Section 5 discusses an important potential 'roadblock' to aggregation: the uncertainty regarding the extent to which state and federal regulators can assert jurisdiction over it. Finally, Section 6 concludes by summarizing the progress to date on DER aggregation and the obstacles to further progress that remain.

---

6 FERC Storage NOPR, above n 1.

2. AGGREGATION OF DERs IN THE U.S. ELECTRIC POWER SECTOR

2.1. POTENTIAL FOR AGGREGATED DERs IN THE UNITED STATES

The potential for aggregated DERs in the United States must be understood within the context of the new technologies and business models that are bringing rapid change to the electric power sector. Over the past 100 years, the model for electricity distribution has involved large power plants producing electricity, which is distributed to consumers through a centralized grid.[7] The laws that govern the grid are largely based on this one-way flow of power to consumers whose only responsibility has been to pay a monopoly utility for it. State public utility commissions regulate utilities' rates and services to guard against monopoly rent-seeking.

Today, many advances have made the U.S. electric grid more diversified. The electric power mix is transforming nationwide, with less reliance on traditional, large-scale fossil-fueled and nuclear power generation, and more natural gas, wind, solar, distributed generation, and demand response resources. Solar and wind power is being added to the grid at a rapid rate. Virtually all new capacity being added to the grid is powered by renewables or natural gas, and coal plants are facing retirement.[8] There is also increased deployment of DERs across the nation, as confirmed by recent reports showing that 2.3 GW of new distributed solar power was installed in the second quarter of 2018 alone,[9] that one million electric vehicles have been sold in the U.S.,[10] and that there is exponential growth in the energy storage market.[11]

Making the U.S. electricity system more diverse, distributed, and renewable has widely known benefits. Given the urgency to address climate change, DERs have become especially important in mitigating electricity sector greenhouse gas (GHG) emissions.[12] DERs can help the electric grid by increasing grid

---

7 Joel B. Eisen, 'Distributed Energy Resources, "Virtual Power Plants," and the Smart Grid' (2012) 7 *University of Houston Environmental and Energy Law and Policy Journal* 191, 192.

8 U.S. Energy Information Administration, *Electric Power Monthly*, August 2018, at Table 6.6 – 'Planned U.S. Electric Generating Unit Retirements'.

9 Solar Energy Industries Association, 'U.S. Solar Market Insight', September 2018, https://www.seia.org/us-solar-market-insight.

10 Paul Ruiz, 'U.S. Reaches 1 Million Electric Vehicle Sales', *Energy Fuse*, 11 October 2018, http://energyfuse.org/u-s-reaches-1-million-electric-vehicle-sales/.

11 Energy Storage Association, Facts and Figures, http://energystorage.org/energy-storage/facts-figures. One major catalyst of growth is the mandate of the California Public Utilities Commission that the state's three major investor-owned utilities procure 1.3 GW of storage by 2020. *Ibid.*

12 U.S. Department of Energy, 'Transforming the Nation's Electricity System: The Second Installment of the QER', January 2017, at page 3-1.

reliability and resilience, making the grid less vulnerable to power outages.[13] They can also reduce energy delivery losses through the closer proximity between the electricity source and the consumer that leads to less required maintenance of grid infrastructure and additional cost reductions.[14] Increased DER deployment decreases emissions of conventional pollutants. And beyond the environmental and energy advantages, there are social benefits, such as widespread decentralized ownership of DER facilities, to empower consumers.

DERs and accompanying advanced technologies allow for contemplation of a multidirectional grid. Through added deployment of residential solar photovoltaic (PV) systems, connected electric vehicles and other distributed resources, power may be added back to the grid and provide important services to it.[15] Not far off in the future, the U.S. electric grid may evolve into a fully 'transactive system'.[16] This in turn challenges incumbent utilities (one influential report mentioned a possible 'death spiral' due to competition from DERs)[17] and requires rethinking of long-held laws and policies favoring centralized infrastructure investment and rates rewarding utilities for their investments.

Recognizing the opportunities for widespread DER deployment, numerous states have begun regulatory proceedings aimed at reconsidering the roles and responsibilities of utilities, collectively known as 'grid modernization' proceedings.[18] While no two of these proceedings are the same, they typically involve deploying intelligent technologies to overhaul the electric system, and giving consumers new tools for making, using, and conserving electricity. These proceedings are often aimed (among other objectives) at DER integration into the grid and accomplishing other goals such as reducing GHG emissions and improving overall reliability. States typically contemplate new regulatory structures under which the regulated utility and a variety of third parties enable customer choice through advanced distribution system planning and networking. As discussed more fully below (see Section 4), some states envision a role for aggregation by distribution utilities that they regulate.

Capturing aggregation's benefits requires that DERs have sufficient opportunities and incentives to provide electricity and grid services. Generally speaking, there are three distinct ways in which DERs offer value to the grid. They can benefit the bulk power system, which includes (i) the facilities and control systems necessary for operating the interconnected electric energy

---

13 See, *e.g.*, GridWise Alliance, 'Improving Electric Grid Resilience and Reliability: Lessons Learned From Superstorm Sandy and Other Extreme Weather Events' (2013).

14 Tierney, above n 4, at 3–4.

15 Joel B. Eisen and Felix Mormann, 'Free Trade in Electric Power' (2018) *Utah Law Review* 50.

16 *Ibid.*

17 Peter Kind & Energy Infrastructure Advocates, 'Disruptive Challenges: Financial Implications and Strategic Responses to a Changing Retail Electric Business' (2013) p 1.

18 Joel B. Eisen and Shelley Welton, 'Clean Energy Justice: Charting An Emerging Agenda' (2019) 43 *Harvard Environmental Law Review* 307, 328.

transmission network, and (ii) the electric energy from generation facilities needed to maintain transmission system reliability.[19] They can also provide services in the wholesale electricity markets that facilitate the buying and selling of power between generators and load-serving entities (electric utility companies, and retail electric suppliers in states that have restructured their retail electricity markets). Finally, they can benefit the local distribution system, and the customers and local communities that participate in aggregation programs.[20]

To maximize revenue opportunities, DER owners can in principle provide services at all of these levels. Recognizing this, the concept of the 'value stack'[21] has recently emerged to focus on how DERs can combine multiple streams of potential revenue. New York has a value stack process/program underway at its Public Service Commission to determine appropriate levels of DER compensation,[22] and in an order in 2018, California developed a methodology for allowing storage resources to stack services in multiple markets.[23]

2.2. FORMS AND POTENTIAL BENEFITS OF AGGREGATION

Aggregating DERs into reliable grid resources raises fundamental questions about the electric grid's architecture. Addressing issues such the types of DER that can and should take part in aggregation, the conditions under which aggregated DERs may participate in the markets, the business models under which aggregators own or control DERs, and the rates paid to them for their services has enormous implications for regulation of the grid's future.[24] Most of the discussion around third-party aggregation of DERs assumes that it will take place in the wholesale electricity markets, although, as noted above, aggregators could provide grid services in the distribution system. As for the types of resources that can participate, there is no specific reason to limit them, though a variety of legal and financial barriers have thus far inhibited the potential of many DERs to take part in the markets.

There is no reason why aggregators *must* be third-party companies. Distribution utilities could do aggregation and indeed have done so for years

---

19 16 U.S.C. §824o 'Electric Reliability'.

20 Tierney, above n 4, at 3–4.

21 Zach Pollock and Chad Abbey, 'Unpacking the Value Stack: The Challenge Facing the Energy Storage Industry', *Renewable Energy World*, 13 February 2018.

22 New York Public Service Commission, VDER Resources, https://www.nyserda.ny.gov/All%20Programs/Programs/NY%20Sun/Contractors/Value%20of%20Distributed%20Energy%20Resources (website for PSC activities to establish the value stack in New York).

23 California Public Utilities Commission, Decision on Multiple-Use Application Issues, Rulemaking 15-03-011, Decision 18-01-003 (11 January 2018).

24 Tierney, above n 4.

(although it has not been labeled that way) in energy efficiency programs outsourced to private firms and DR programs focused on delivering benefits to utilities. But it is more likely that the wholesale markets will see third parties performing aggregation as their core business. A third-party aggregator has a stronger incentive than a utility to develop innovative strategies for providing the interface between DERs and the markets, providing customer service to DER owners, and tailoring product offerings specifically to the needs of individual customers.[25] Aggregators can

> specialize in certain types of DERs (e.g., DR or storage) or certain grid services (e.g., emergency load reduction or frequency response), and they can partner with (or even be) equipment manufacturers that understand DER capabilities even better than utilities do.[26]

Of course, as the types of entities providing aggregation and the services they offer become more diverse, regulation to promote this diversity can be more challenging for state utility commissions and regional grid operators.

The principal benefit of DER aggregation for a utility or regional grid operator is that DERs can provide energy, capacity, and ancillary services that have traditionally come from centralized power plants. For example, aggregated DERs could provide as much as 163 MW of frequency response in California, which would be a 'significant benefit' to that wholesale market.[27] Without aggregation, however, legal terms in wholesale market tariffs, such as requirements that resources have a minimum size of 1 MW for bidding, would preclude most DER participation. Moreover, owners of individual DERs would be hard pressed to understand and comply with complex market rules and procedures. And an owner of a single solar panel system or electric vehicle would not earn sufficient revenue from the markets to offset the costs of participation. Thus, it has been observed that, 'the transaction costs of market participation are substantial and will only be practical for large industrial and commercial customers who can afford to dedicate professional staff to this activity.'[28]

The role of aggregators in facilitating participation is critical because it would be costly for a regional grid operator to deal with an individual DER owner, and that owner would not provide a resource that would have sufficient value to the markets to warrant the transaction costs. Working with owners of multiple

---

25 Regulatory Assistance Project, above n 2, at 11.

26 Regulatory Assistance Project, above n 2, at 12.

27 North American Electric Reliability Corporation, Distributed Energy Resources: Connection Modeling and Reliability Considerations, February 2017, at 4. Frequency Response is a premium grid service and is offered to commercial and industrial clients who are able to rebalance sudden changes in supply and demand which have a negative impact on grid frequency.

28 Regulatory Assistance Project, above n 2, at 10.

small DERs as an intermediary to the markets, an aggregator can overcome the transaction costs to market participation and create resources that are substantial enough to be bid into the wholesale markets. This can also foster new business models and practices that put pressure on utilities to innovate.[29]

At the distribution level, many DERs operate in a passive mode and do not follow dispatch signals, and therefore are not visible to distribution utilities. Utilities are unlikely to have information on the 'location, type, size, configuration, interconnection characteristics, disturbance response characteristics, and date of operation' of an individual DER.[30] An aggregator can create visibility into resources located behind customers' meters with hardware and software solutions that can properly control the DERs. It can send dispatch signals when needed to provide distribution-level services. Aggregators can also develop innovative ways to properly compensate DER owners for the services they provide.

The principal benefit for DER owners is that aggregation expands the opportunities to gain economic value from DERs. Beyond revenues from market participation, customers' benefits can include improved quality of service, autonomy from utilities' dominance of their energy future, and control over energy costs.[31] At the community level, DERs provide decentralized and community-generated energy production, bringing empowerment to communities and environmental improvements in the form of lower GHG emissions and, often, employment gains.[32]

2.3. THE U.S. WHOLESALE MARKET SYSTEM AND AGGREGATION PROGRAMS

Roughly two-thirds of the U.S. falls within the footprints of independent system operators and regional transmission organizations (ISO/RTOs[33]) that manage transmission networks and operate organized wholesale markets. Although ISO/RTOs vary, they typically administer three different types of markets. In an energy market, utilities and other load-serving entities purchase electricity for delivery within the next hour or a day ahead. Some ISO/RTOs have capacity

---

[29] MIT Center for Energy and Environmental Policy Research, *The Value of Aggregators in Electricity Systems* 1 (January 2016), https://energy.mit.edu/wp-content/uploads/2016/01/CEEPR_WP_2016-001.pdf.

[30] North American Electric Reliability Corporation, above n 27, at 4.

[31] Tierney, above n 4, at 4.

[32] Shelley Welton, 'Grasping for Energy Democracy' (2018) 116 *Michigan Law Review* 581.

[33] *About the IRC*, ISO/RTO Council, https://isorto.org/#about-section. The distinction between ISOs and RTOs is not meaningful for this chapter, which will use 'ISO/RTO' to describe these entities.

markets in which participants commit to serve future demand with new generating capacity. Finally, ancillary service markets compensate providers of frequency regulation and reserve services that enable the reliable transmission of electricity. The principal form of DER aggregation in the U.S. wholesale markets today is demand response (DR), with some energy efficiency taking part in the ISO-New England markets.[34]

2.3.1. *Wholesale Market Demand Response*

DR in the wholesale markets involves the reduction in electricity usage by end-use customers. For example, an industrial user can reduce its purchases from the grid (perhaps offsetting them with backup generation) or homeowners can turn off devices such as water heaters and air conditioners. That reduction in demand is in response to reliability needs of the electric grid, or high prices on the markets.[35] Thus, FERC defines DR as

> Changes in electric usage by demand-side resources from their normal consumption patterns in response to changes in the price of electricity over time, or to incentive payments designed to induce lower electricity use at times of high wholesale market prices or when system reliability is jeopardized.[36]

In emergency-based DR programs, consumers receive an incentive (usually monetary compensation) for decreasing their electricity consumption over a specific time period in response to a signal to reduce demand. Economic DR provides an incentive to reduce consumption when electricity prices are high. At present, wholesale markets have limited economic DR activity.

These demand reductions can have significant benefits for the wholesale markets. Demand for electricity fluctuates and wholesale market prices spike in a limited number of hours each year. Therefore, even modest amounts of DR can reduce wholesale prices at those times. DR can help reduce peak demand

---

34 Gordon van Welie, ISO New England, Inc., *State of the Grid: 2018* (February 2018), https://www.iso-ne.com/static-assets/documents/2018/02/02272018_pr_presentation_state-of-the-grid_2018.pdf, at 16.

35 Joel B. Eisen, 'Demand Response's Three Generations: Market Pathways and Challenges in the Modern Electric Grid' (2017) 18 *North Carolina Journal of Law and Technology* 351, 363–364. Demand response exists in part because U.S. electricity markets are unique: wholesale costs cannot be passed directly to consumers, the vast majority of whom still have fixed electric rates set by state regulators.

36 Reports on Demand Response & Advanced Metering, Federal Energy Regulatory Commission, https://www.ferc.gov/industries/electric/indusact/demand-response/dem-res-adv-metering.asp; Joel B. Eisen, 'Demand Response's Three Generations: Market Pathways and Challenges in the Modern Electric Grid' (2017) 18 *North Carolina Journal of Law and Technology* 351, 363–364.

by substituting demand reductions for starting or using another power plant. More widespread use of DR can minimize the strain on the grid, lessen the likelihood of power outages, and reduce emissions and the need to build new power plants.[37] Increased availability of DR can also help with integrating other DERs into the grid, counterbalancing the inherent variability of renewable energy sources such as solar and wind power.

Aggregation of DR involves taking demand reductions from multiple customers and then bidding that amount of reduced electricity demand as a block – a resource in its own right – into a wholesale market. Utilities can, and do aggregate DR resources without offering the resulting resource into a wholesale market. Indeed, in states within ISO/RTO footprints, as the figure below indicates,[38] customers can often take part both in wholesale market programs through aggregators, as well as utility DR programs. Utility DR programs are a form of aggregation themselves (collecting DR resources together for the utility's benefit), but because the interaction is direct with the utility, this chapter will not focus on them.

2.3.2. *Aggregation of DR in U.S. Wholesale Markets (Curtailment Service Providers)*

RTOs' DR programs have grown and diversified since their inception in the early 2000s. The PJM RTO, for example, allows deployment of DR as a resource in four different markets that it administers: the capacity, energy, reserve and regulation markets.[39] Developments in the mid-2000s made it possible for DR to participate more extensively in the organized wholesale markets. In particular, the advent of capacity markets created a new market opportunity. By the end of the decade, capacity market DR participation skyrocketed in the PJM RTO, although it has leveled off as a result of new market rules that reserve the highest level of compensation for DR resources that can perform year-round, which DR based on seasonal reductions cannot do.[40] On the other hand, some claim that aggregated DR could experience a surge as a result of these new rules if it can be controlled year-round.

---

37 Joel B. Eisen, 'Demand Response's Three Generations: Market Pathways and Challenges in the Modern Electric Grid', above n 36, at 367–368.

38 Joel B. Eisen, 'Demand Response's Three Generations: Market Pathways and Challenges in the Modern Electric Grid', above n 36, at 385.

39 PJM Interconnection LLC, 2018 Demand Response Operations Markets Activity Report: November 2018.

40 Jeff St. John, 'Demand Response Startup Voltus Raises $10M', *Greentech Media*, 23 October 2017 (describing DR industry consolidation in the face of the new policy and other challenges); *Advanced Energy Management Alliance v. FERC*, No. 16-1234 (D.C. Circuit 2017) (upholding the new policy).

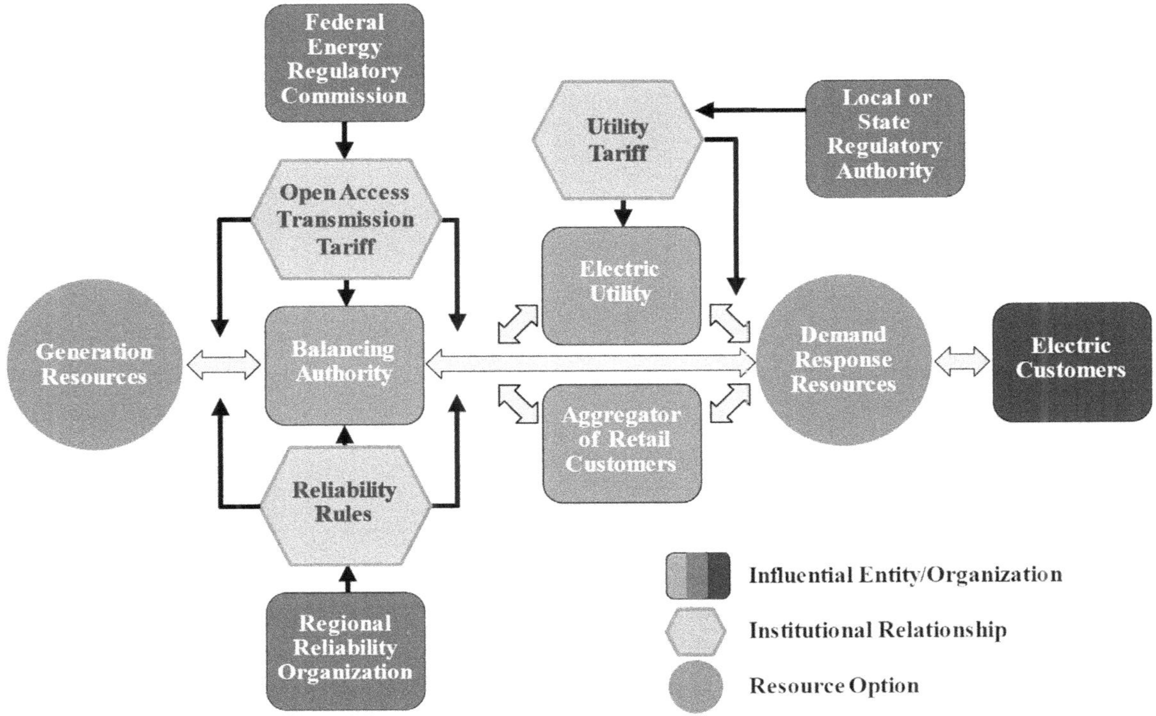

Figure 1. Entities and organizations that influence relationships between resources and the bulk power system

Source: Adapted from Cappers et al. (2012).

The intermediaries between end users providing demand reduction and the wholesale markets are known as 'curtailment service providers' (CSPs).[41] Not all DR are bid into the wholesale markets as the result of aggregation, as CSPs often bid demand reductions from individual commercial and industrial customers that meet minimum size thresholds. But the use of aggregated DER for DR is growing in some ISO/RTOs, with CSPs using sophisticated technologies to combine smaller demand reductions into one block. This arrangement allows retail customers to participate in the markets, which they could not do directly, due to minimum bid restrictions and other limitations that limit market participation to CSPs.[42]

2.3.3. *Federal Policies Encouraging Wholesale Market Demand Response*

The U.S. Congress and FERC have acted to address barriers to DR participation in the wholesale markets. The federal Energy Policy Act of 2005 declared a national policy to encourage DR and specifying that 'unnecessary barriers to demand response participation in energy, capacity and ancillary service markets shall be eliminated.'[43] FERC implemented this provision in part through its Order 719, which required ISO/RTOs to accept bids from DR resources and to allow aggregators to participate in their wholesale markets. Order 719 defined an 'aggregator of retail customers', specifying that each ISO/RTO

> must accept bids from an aggregator of retail customers that aggregates the demand response of the customers of utilities that distributed more than 4 million megawatt-hours in the previous fiscal year, and the customers of utilities that distributed 4 million megawatt-hours or less in the previous fiscal year, where the relevant electric retail regulatory authority permits such customers' demand.[44]

This state veto has been employed in some cases, particularly in the Midcontinent ISO footprint.

FERC's Order 745, promulgated in 2011, established a uniform, nationwide approach to compensating DR in wholesale markets. Order 745 concluded that DR can provide benefits similar to generation resources, and required wholesale energy markets to pay the same market price for DR as for electricity

---

41 See, *e.g.*, PJM Interconnection LLC, Curtailment Service Providers, https://www.pjm.com/markets-and-operations/demand-response/csps.aspx (listing active CSPs in the PJM RTO).

42 Joel B. Eisen, 'Demand Response's Three Generations: Market Pathways and Challenges in the Modern Electric Grid', above n 36, at 396.

43 Joel B. Eisen, 'Demand Response's Three Generations: Market Pathways and Challenges in the Modern Electric Grid', above n 36, at 401.

44 18 Code of Federal Regulations § 35.28(g)(1)(iii).

generation. The Supreme Court upheld this federal rule in its 2016 decision in *FERC v. Electric Power Supply Association*, discussed below in connection with the ongoing jurisdictional issues for DER aggregators.

While capacity market participation has increased, DR participation in ancillary services markets is still small today. And aggregated DR participation by residential customers is still in its infancy, although new technologies and market rules hold the promise of substantial expansion of this market over the next decade. In summary, there is still far less DR than its estimated potential. FERC believes DR could achieve peak demand reductions of up to 20 per cent, but only a fraction of that potential has been realized. There are many different reasons for this, including continuing economic, regulatory and technological challenges.

3. EXPANDING AGGREGATION IN WHOLESALE MARKETS

The potential for aggregation in the wholesale markets beyond DR is only beginning to be realized. The California ISO (CAISO) was the first ISO/RTO to begin to remove barriers to entry for other forms of DER aggregation, as one part of a multi-year effort known as the Energy Storage and Distributed Energy Resource (ESDER) initiative.[45] This aggregation program is still in its infancy, yet served as a foundation for the FERC proposed rule on DER aggregation, which is still pending.

3.1. THE CALIFORNIA EXPERIENCE

California's ESDER initiative has a number of different components that are aimed at lowering participation barriers and enhancing the abilities of storage and other forms of DERs to participate in the CAISO markets. The number and diversity of DERs in the state are growing – for example, the state aims to have 5 million zero-emission vehicles by 2030[46] – and DERs are an increasingly important part of the grid's future. One element of this initiative is a path-breaking experiment with changing wholesale market rules to enable DER aggregator participation

45 California ISO, Energy Storage and Distributed Energy Resource Stakeholder Initiative, http://www.caiso.com/informed/Pages/StakeholderProcesses/EnergyStorage_DistributedEnergyResources.aspx.

46 California Public Utilities Commission, Zero-Emission Vehicles, http://www.cpuc.ca.gov/zev/.

CAISO already has two demand response aggregation programs in its wholesale markets.[47] The Proxy Demand Resource (PDR) and Reliability and Demand Response Resource programs allow aggregated DR resources to participate in CAISO's wholesale energy and ancillary services markets (CAISO has no capacity market, and FERC recently rejected a proposal to establish one[48]). For example, the provider Stem, Inc. used PDR in 2017 to help reduce energy market clearing prices driven up by the need for cooling technology during a heat wave.[49] As CAISO has recognized, however, technical and other barriers such as aggregation rules imposing geographic constraints on DR have had a limiting effect on full DR participation.[50] In view of these limitations, CAISO has recently acted to change some of its requirements to promote fuller DR participation.[51]

Because these two programs involve demand reductions, they cannot be used for DERs that add power to the grid. CAISO recently adopted a program for market participation by 'distributed energy resource providers' (DERP), a new category of participant that can aggregate all types of DERs for CAISO market participation.[52] The CAISO tariff amendment for this program, which FERC approved in 2016, establishes resource aggregation rules at the ISO network level. It allows a DERP to aggregate individual DERs to meet the minimum size requirements of the CAISO markets and to avoid a direct metering relationship between individual DERs and the ISO. DERPs may submit aggregations of between 500 kW and 10 MW that can meet the requirements for CAISO's day-ahead and hourly energy markets, or its ancillary services markets.[53] DERs are defined as any resource connected to the distribution system, including generation such as rooftop solar panels, energy storage, plug-in electric vehicles, and demand response resources, regardless of size or of whether the resource is connected behind or in front of the end-use customer meter. This potentially

---

47 California ISO, Demand response and load participation, http://www.caiso.com/participate/Pages/Load/Default.aspx. CAISO also has a designation for a Non-Generator Resource such as storage that can go back and forth between producing and consuming energy.

48 Gavin Bade, 'FERC rejects generator proposal for CAISO capacity market', *Utility Dive*, 21 November 2018.

49 'Stem Energy Storage Network Delivers Emergency Grid Relief in California Heat', 26 June 2017, https://www.stem.com/stem-energy-storage-network-delivers-emergency-grid-relief-in-california-heat/.

50 California ISO, Energy Storage and Distributed Energy Resources Phase 3 Issue Paper, 29 September 2017, at p. 5.

51 California ISO, Decision on the Energy Storage and Distributed Energy Resource phase 3 Proposal, 29 August 2018.

52 California ISO, Distributed energy resource provider, http://www.caiso.com/participate/Pages/DistributedEnergyResourceProvider/Default.aspx.

53 California ISO, Distributed Energy Resource Provider Participation Guide with Checklist, http://www.caiso.com/Documents/DistributedEnergyResourceProviderParticipationGuideandChecklist.pdf.

allows DERs in California, such as the hundreds of thousands of residential solar rooftop systems, to participate in the wholesale markets. Due to their sheer number, this would be impractical if CAISO were required to communicate with each DER individually.

Participation as of now is light, as only seven aggregators are enrolled in the program,[54] and the two DR programs are more popular.[55] It has been suggested that the design of the DERP program includes market rules that do not sufficiently encourage DER participation, and that economic barriers and technical requirements make it difficult for DERPs to participate.[56] CAISO is continuing to study why DER aggregators are not making more widespread use of the DERP tariff, and to address communications and coordination issues relating to aggregation of multiple DERs to serve its wholesale markets.

3.2. SUBSEQUENT FEDERAL INITIATIVES

In 2016, FERC issued a two-part Notice of Proposed Rulemaking popularly known as the 'Storage NOPR'. The second part of the proposed rule encouraged DER aggregation and participation in the wholesale markets, based in part on the California experience with developing rules for aggregated DER participation in its wholesale markets.[57]

FERC's Notice solicited public comments on a proposed federal rule that would remove barriers to the participation of electric storage resources and DER aggregations in ISO/RTOs' wholesale electricity markets.[58] FERC promulgated the proposed rule pursuant to its authority under section 206 of the Federal Power Act, which allows it to order changes to ISO/RTO tariffs that it finds are 'unjust, unreasonable, unduly discriminatory or preferential'.[59] In the second part of the Notice, FERC defined DER aggregators as a new type of market

54 California ISO, Distributed Energy Resource Provider Market Participants, http://www.caiso.com/Documents/ListofDistributedEnergyResourceProviderMarketParticipants.pdf.

55 See, *e.g.*, Federal Energy Regulatory Commission, Participation of Distributed Energy Resource Aggregations in Markets Operated by Regional Transmission Organizations and Independent System Operators, Docket No. RM18-9-000, Comments of Sunrun Inc. in Support of Allowing DERs to Compete in Wholesale Markets, https://www.hwglaw.com/wp-content/uploads/2018/06/Sunrun-PT-Comments.pdf, at p. 12.

56 Justin Gundlach and Romany Webb, 'Distributed Energy Resource Participation in Wholesale Markets: Lessons From the California ISO' (2018) 39 *Energy Law Journal* 47, 51.

57 The first part would require RTOs/ISOs to establish a storage 'participation model' that, recognizing the unique physical and operational characteristics of storage resources, promotes the fuller participation of energy storage in the organized wholesale markets.

58 Electric Storage Participation in Markets Operated by Regional Transmission Organizations and Independent System Operators, 81 Fed. Reg. 86,522 (30 November 2016).

59 *Ibid.*, at 86,522.

participant in the organized wholesale electric markets. It also aimed to require ISO/RTOs to have a participation model for a DER 'that best accommodates the physical and operational characteristics of its distributed energy resource aggregation.'[60] As in the storage section of the Notice, the participation model would have defined certain characteristics that ISO/RTOs would be required to adopt in their tariffs to facilitate DER aggregation, but would also have left others for the individual ISO/RTOs to decide for themselves.

In the NOPR, FERC explained that the barriers to participation experienced by DER aggregators in the wholesale markets 'unnecessarily restrict competition, which could lead to unjust and unreasonable rates.'[61] To demonstrate this, FERC provided a number of examples in which current market participation models exclude DER aggregation. For example, FERC found that, in many cases, DER resources are only allowed to be used as demand response, which limits their participation.[62]

In February 2018, FERC moved forward with the storage component of its proposed rule. Its Order No. 841 directs ISO/RTOs to develop and implement market rules for energy storage to participate more fully in the wholesale energy, capacity and ancillary services markets, and to remove barriers to this participation. However, FERC chose to reserve judgement on DER aggregation due to the potential complexity of the issues involved.[63] It then convened a Technical Conference (a type of stakeholder meeting it can initiate to assist it in gathering information on a specific topic) in April 2018 to examine a wide variety of issues and gather additional information essential to making a decision.

FERC received numerous comments at the Technical Conference, which were directed to these key areas laid out in the NOPR: (1) the viability of a participation model for DER aggregation; (2) locational requirements for DER aggregators; (3) bidding parameters and other technical requirements for DER aggregations; (4) information and data requirements for aggregations, including metering and telemetry system requirements; (5) how modifications to the lists of resources in an aggregation should be handled; (6) coordination between the ISO/RTOs, the DER aggregators, and the distribution utilities; and (7) the use and content of market participation agreements for DER aggregators.

At present, FERC has not submitted a new proposed rule, and continues to study the issues associated with DER aggregation in the wholesale markets.

---

60 Electric Storage Participation in Markets Operated by Regional Transmission Organizations and Independent System Operators, 81 Fed. Reg. at 86,523–524.

61 *Ibid.*, at 86,526.

62 *Ibid.*

63 Electric Storage Participation in Markets Operated by Regional Transmission Organizations and Independent System Operators, Order No. 841, 83 Fed. Reg. 9,580 (6 March 2018).

4. DISTRIBUTION-LEVEL DEVELOPMENTS

As noted above, several states are radically reforming their regulatory processes to accelerate DER deployment. In New York, for example, the Reforming the Energy Vision (REV) program envisions a 40 per cent reduction in GHG emissions from 1990 levels and a mandate for 50 per cent of the state's electricity to be generated from renewable resources by 2030.[64] The New York Public Service Commission has issued regulatory orders that require the state's distribution utilities to transition from the historic one-way model to a dynamic model that relies increasingly on DERs. The central vehicle for effectuating this transition is transforming the state's utilities into Distributed System Platform Providers which are responsible for planning and operations, and, as discussed below, establishing market-based platforms. In the near term, the state is focusing attention on the development of structures to ensure DERs are adequately rewarded for the services they provide. The ongoing value stack regulatory proceeding aims to compensate DERs accurately, based on when and where they provide electricity to the grid.[65]

One element of the REV framework requires the state's major investor-owned distribution utilities to consider 'non-wires alternatives' (NWA) projects. While not involving third-party aggregators, NWA projects are important because they involve the procurement of DERs by utilities to enable them to defer or avoid conventional distribution-level infrastructure investments. One definition of NWA is:

> An electricity grid investment or project that uses non-traditional T&D solutions, such as distributed generation, energy storage, energy efficiency demand response, and grid software and controls, to defer or replace the need for specific equipment upgrades, such as T&D lines or transformers, by reducing load at a substation or circuit level.[66]

Traditionally, when a utility had a need to upgrade or replace substations and other distribution-level infrastructure due to aging equipment or increased load demand, it would build new infrastructure on which it could earn a regulated rate of return. Increasingly, though, utilities are turning to NWA to provide solutions using DERs at a lower cost with emissions benefits and maintained or improved

---

64 New York State, DPS – Reforming the Energy Vision, About the Initiative, http://www3.dps.ny.gov/W/PSCWeb.nsf/All/CC4F2EFA3A23551585257DEA007DCFE2?OpenDocument.

65 Above n 22; the specific proceeding is New York State, Department of Public Service, Case 15-E-0751: Value of Distributed Energy Resources (VDER), http://www3.dps.ny.gov/W/PSCWeb.nsf/All/8A5F3592472A270C8525808800517BDD?OpenDocument.

66 Brett Feldman, 'Non-Wires Alternatives: What's up next in utility business model evolution', *Utility Dive*, 12 July 2017.

system reliability. An example is the 'Brooklyn–Queens Neighborhood Program' of the New York utility Consolidated Edison (ConEd),[67] which involves energy efficiency measures, from traditional incentives for replacing inefficient light bulbs, appliances and air conditioning units to new building management systems. It also has used a new DR auction system, with 10 offers accepted totaling 22 MW of expected DR by 2018.[68]

In California, two major investor-owned utilities have conducted NWA projects. And the District of Columbia has proposed legislation that would establish the nation's first ever independent DER authority,[69] which, among other responsibilities, would oversee the development of NWA procurement. Although this bill has not yet become law, it is yet another signal of the ever-increasing attention being paid to NWA by distribution-level utilities.

New York also proposes to eventually adopt new market trading platforms that would provide greatly enhanced opportunities for DER to provide grid services. Distribution-level markets would allow for the buying and selling of products and services among a broad set of market participants. The services provided would be different from those which DERs provide on the wholesale markets, as they would address needs of the distribution system. An example of such a service would be the use of solar PV panels with smart inverters to supply voltage and reactive power regulation services on a distribution feeder line, which some believe it can do more quickly than traditional sources of power correction. New York has chosen the distribution utilities, rather than any new entity such as a distribution system operator, to serve as platform providers.

5. RESOLVING STATE/FEDERAL JURISDICTIONAL COMPLICATIONS

Relating to FERC's proposed rule, an important issue that must be addressed in promoting aggregation of DERs more widely is the question of whether state or federal regulators, or both, have authority over aggregators seeking to provide DER services in wholesale markets. A challenge at present is that both federal and state regulators can claim jurisdiction. In the United States, regulation of the electric grid is divided between the state and federal governments. Connections among end users, aggregators and the wholesale markets straddle

67 The Neighborhood Program – For Residents, https://www.coned.com/en/save-money/rebates-incentives-tax-credits/rebates-incentives-tax-credits-for-residential-customers/residential-neighborhood-program; Jan Ellen Spiegel, 'Another $1.2 Billion Substation? No Thanks, Says Utility, We'll Find a Better Way', *InsideClimate News*, 4 April 2016.

68 Gavin Bade, 'ConEd awards 22 MW of demand response contracts in Brooklyn–Queens project', *Utility Dive*, 8 August 2016.

69 Gavin Bade, 'DC Council bill would establish US's first independent DER authority', *Utility Dive*, 11 April 2018.

this jurisdictional line, and the question of who regulates DER aggregation in this divided regulatory system has no clear answer.

The basis for FERC's jurisdiction over aggregated DERs is that aggregators' sales of electricity into wholesale markets are sales at wholesale in interstate commerce, which are defined as sales of electric energy to another person for resale.[70] FERC has exclusive jurisdiction over these sales, regardless of the DERs' locations. Conversely, the states' jurisdiction extends to 'facilities used for the generation of electric energy' and 'facilities used in local distribution.'[71] Because DERs interconnect on the distribution system and provide distribution-level services, states therefore claim authority. But this authority overlaps with the federal authority. When a local distribution facility is used in a sale at wholesale, FERC has jurisdiction over that transaction.[72] An example of the complications this introduces is FERC's order from May 2019 on rehearing, which upheld Order 841. That order reaffirmed FERC's authority over energy storage, located on distribution systems, that participates in wholesale markets, but this was not a unanimous view. One Commissioner dissented, believing the states should have jurisdiction over storage located there.[73]

Untangling this complex legal puzzle is of paramount importance, as it determines which level of regulation governs, and how such matters as coordination will be established and maintained between distribution- and wholesale-level operations to ensure grid reliability and proper compensation for the services that DERs provide. As an example of the practical considerations involved, consider that distribution utilities and ISO/RTOs must collaborate on the dispatch of aggregated DER resources. There must be operational coordination and appropriate levels of visibility, monitoring, and controls for the ISO/RTO, the distribution utility, and the DER aggregator. And there must be some form of understanding that constraints on the distribution system might limit dispatch of aggregated resources. It must also make clear that visibility on the part of the ISO/RTO into distribution-level operations is necessary to ensure the smooth functioning of wholesale markets. Clarity about which level of government regulates these matters is instrumental in addressing these issues.

Unfortunately, the relevant law is unclear, as the Federal Power Act has not been amended substantially since 1935. Reimagining the state/federal jurisdictional divide for the modern era has proven challenging. The U.S. Supreme Court has issued three decisions in the past four years involving

70 See 16 U.S.C. §824(a) and §824(d). Sales are in interstate commerce if the electric energy moves from the seller to the buyer via the interconnected interstate transmission grid. *Federal Power Commission v. Florida Power & Light Co.*, 404 U.S. 452 (1972).

71 16 U.S.C. §824(b)(1).

72 See, *e.g.*, *Wisconsin-Michigan Power Co. v. FPC*, 197 F.2d 472 (7th Cir. 1952).

73 Electric Storage Participation in Markets Operated by Regional Transmission Organizations and Independent System Operators, Order on Rehearing and Clarification, 16 May 2019.

jurisdiction over the electric grid, including *ONEOK v. Learjet*,[74] *FERC v. Electric Power Supply Association*,[75] and *Hughes v. Talen Energy Marketing*.[76] As noted above, *FERC v. EPSA* upheld FERC's ability to regulate DR. In that decision the Court found that regulating DR fell comfortably within FERC's authority over 'practices' affecting wholesale rates if rates are 'directly' affected. It rejected the argument that had prevailed in a lower court that DR was exclusively within the jurisdiction of the states. The Court found that Order No. 745 was based specifically on improving the wholesale markets, and noted that DR bid into the wholesale markets directly affects wholesale rates because it changes wholesale prices.[77] The Court acknowledged that Order No. 745 has impacts on state-regulated retail rates, but concluded that those effects were not relevant to the jurisdictional inquiry.[78]

The *FERC v. EPSA* decision eroded the bright line that previously existed between 'retail' (subject to state regulation) and 'wholesale' (subject to FERC authority),[79] and resulted in a blurring of the jurisdictional divide. The question of whether regulating DER aggregations is within FERC's authority remains largely unresolved. As a practical matter, in this new and uncertain jurisdictional landscape, it is unlikely that either level of government will claim plenary authority over DER aggregation.[80] In this fluctuating regulatory environment, the greater integration of DERs into the grid through new approaches that encourage broader participation in the wholesale markets is unlikely to result from unilateral actions by federal or state regulators. Instead, a process of close collaboration is to be expected.

6. CONCLUSION

Collectively speaking, the obstacles to fuller participation by aggregated DERs in organized wholesale markets in the U.S. may be divided into six different categories:

- *threshold barriers*, such as market rules which exclude specific types of DERs from participation in particular markets;

[74] *ONEOK, Inc. v. Learjet, Inc.*, 575 U.S. (2015). The case involved the Natural Gas Act, but decisions under that Act are read *in pari materia* with those under the Federal Power Act.

[75] *FERC v. Electric Power Supply Association*, 136 S. Ct. 760 (2016).

[76] *Hughes v. Talen Energy Marketing*, 136 S. Ct. 1288 (2016).

[77] *FERC v. Electric Power Supply Association*, 136 S. Ct. at 776 (2016).

[78] *Ibid.*, at 775.

[79] Joel B. Eisen, '*FERC v. EPSA* and the Path to a Cleaner Electricity Sector', (2016) 40 *Harvard Environmental Law Review Forum* 1.

[80] Ari Peskoe, Harvard Law School, Environmental & Energy Law Program, The Case Against Direct FERC Regulation of Distributed Energy Resources, 20 September 2018.

- *performance barriers*, such as parameters defined in market rules that can make it difficult for DERs to participate;
- *technology barriers*, including the lack of standard protocols among connected devices, measurement and verification challenges, and other technical requirements that aggregators find difficult and expensive to meet;
- *economic barriers*, such as insufficient compensation in markets to provide incentives for participation;
- *procedural barriers*, such as states' vetoes on aggregators' participation or laws specifying the conditions under which aggregators can engage with customers, and RTOs' governance procedures that make market rule changes complex and difficult; and
- *non-market barriers*, including the lack of more widespread use of dynamic pricing such as time-of-use prices, and the need for education to overcome customer reluctance to give up control of some electricity consuming devices to an aggregator.[81]

In short, substantial challenges remain to using aggregated DERs to meet grid needs. A frequently cited example of a technical challenge involves more widespread deployment of advanced metering infrastructure, or 'smart meters.' For an aggregator to capitalize on the considerable potential of DERs to provide grid services, it must have the technical capability to communicate with a wide variety of DERs, such as thermostats, electric vehicles, and solar energy systems. This requires 'visibility of the capabilities and operating status of participating DERs, interval data on each participant's energy consumption (or injection), and the ability to send control signals to the customer's premises.'[82] Advanced smart electric meters and hardware and software making the connections to the aggregator are essential to facilitate these connections. Until recently, however, most electric meters did not have two-way communications capabilities and only measured the amount of electricity consumed. Today's more advanced smart meters have two-way capabilities that could support more robust interactions between aggregators and their customers.[83]

Although utilities have been installing smart meters at a rapid clip in the United States, deployment is not uniform across the nation, and less than half of residential electricity customers have them.[84] Moreover, some states have

---

81 Joel B. Eisen, 'Demand Response's Three Generations: Market Pathways and Challenges in the Modern Electric Grid', above n 36, at 395 discusses this six-part taxonomy.

82 *Regulatory Assistance Project*, above n 2, at 24.

83 *Ibid.*

84 U.S. Energy Information Administration, 'Nearly half of all U.S. electricity customers have smart meters', 6 December 2017.

rejected requests by utilities to install smart meters, disallowing cost recovery if they are not convinced of the net benefits.[85]

In sum, in the United States, federal and state regulators have taken important steps toward market participation by approving rules and conditions under which DER aggregators can participate, but fundamental questions that relate to the future of aggregation are still unresolved. A smart, connected electricity network featuring aggregated DERs is within contemplation, but many barriers remain to full participation.

85 In the American state of Kentucky, for example, regulators recently rejected a utility's request for rate recovery for smart meter installations. Robert Walton, 'As Kentucky regulators reject smart meter plans, troubling trend continues for AMI', *Utility Dive*, 30 August 2018.

CHAPTER IV

POTENTIAL HURDLES TO THE REGULATION OF ELECTRICITY STORAGE DEVELOPMENT IN THE UK

Silke Goldberg and Jannis Bille

1. INTRODUCTION

The energy sector is rapidly evolving – new market participants, an increasing share of renewably generated electricity as part of our energy mix and the increasing importance of data in the sector are but a few examples. As the industry moves generally in the direction of decentralisation (i.e., the increased tendency towards embedded generation connected to distribution grids only, without connection to the central transmission grid, and off-grid or private wire projects), digitation (via smart meters) and decarbonisation (via the slow phase-out of fossil fuels and the increase of renewable energy sources), the technological challenge for grid operators has grown. Until recently, the industrial-size storage of electricity was thought to be the stuff of science fiction rather than a possible solution to current challenges of the electricity grid.

This is not surprising as the development of more financially viable, efficient and reliable electricity storage (hereafter only referred to as "storage") is indeed so recent that in the Overarching National Policy Statement for Energy, published in July 2011 by the Department of Energy and Climate Change,[1] storage was only mentioned once. Since then, however, it has become clear that storage will be increasingly relevant for the future outlook of the UK's energy system. Underlining this trend, the Carbon Trust, a UK-based organisation advocating a transition to a low carbon energy future,[2] found that the deployment of storage in the UK "could significantly reduce the cost of a future UK electricity system"

1 Department of Energy and Climate Change, "Overarching National Policy Statement for Energy (EN-1)" (2011).

2 See: https://www.carbontrust.com/home/ for further information.

and "could save £2.4 billion a year by 2030", but identified regulatory barriers as one key hurdle for such deployment.[3] Furthermore, National Grid identified storage as a central technology for any future energy scenarios in the UK.[4]

Recognising that the UK energy system was changing and that the regulatory environment had to adapt to the deployment and development of new smart technologies, Ofgem and the UK Government published a call for evidence in November 2016, seeking views and evidence relating to existing policy and regulatory barriers to the development of smart technologies including storage. The response was published in July 2017 and was followed up by further consultation on the topic, including Ofgem's Smart Systems and Flexibility Plan. Furthermore, Ofgem began to look more specifically into the effective deployment of storage in the UK electricity system.

This chapter discusses the different developments in the context of the general approach to regulation of storage in the UK and the hurdles to the development of such storage. It should be noted that while the Government and relevant regulators have been active in this field over the past years, Parliament's recent focus on Brexit means that a number of developments are still awaiting parliamentary attention, including the transposition of the recast Renewables Directive[5] and the recast Directive on common rules for the internal market for electricity.[6]

2. STORAGE – SOME BACKGROUND INFORMATION

2.1. THE NEED FOR STORAGE

Efficient energy storage can find application in a wide array of fields, but, with regard to the electricity industry, it will be an integral building-block for the viability of key renewable energy sources such as solar and wind, which by their nature are only intermittent electricity generators. A solar plant does not produce electricity at night and a wind farm is unable to generate electricity when there is a calm period. Due to this intermittency, in order to be able to use them as reliable energy sources, electricity needs to be stored at times of generation excess so that it can be released into the system later at times of interruption, in order to smoothen out the overall output of the plant.

---

3 Carbon Trust and Imperial College London, "Energy Storage Report: Can storage help reduce the cost of a future UK electricity system?" (2016).

4 National Grid, "Future Energy Scenarios" (2018).

5 Directive (EU) 2018/2001 of the European Parliament and of the Council of 11 December 2018 on the promotion of the use of energy from renewable sources (recast), OJ, L 328/82 of 21 December 2018.

6 Directive (EU) 2019/944 of the European Parliament and of the Council of 5 June 2019 on common rules for the internal market for electricity and amending Directive 2012/27/EU (recast), OJ, L 158/125 of 14 June 2019.

Similarly, storage would generally enable network operators more easily to balance the grid when faced with a greater proportion of intermittent generation, allowing for the system to adapt better to capacity peaks and lows, avoiding potential outages and contributing to a more efficient running of the network. At the same time storage arguably allows for a more sustainable approach to energy production, as excess generation would not be lost but could be released back into the network at a later time, therefore reducing the need for additional generation. In a system where energy from fossil fuels still plays a role this could contribute to a considerable decrease in the consumption of fossil fuels and related carbon emissions.

With regard to the wider application of storage, another key area will be the transport sector and its planned transition away from combustion engines towards an electric solution. The transport sector is an important contributor to greenhouse gas emissions in the UK and Europe. It is therefore essential to decarbonise the transport sector to meet national and international emission reduction targets to combat climate change. Electric vehicles ("EVs") are an important part of the roadmap towards meeting these targets.

As of summer 2018, there were about 155,000 electric vehicles on British roads. Whilst this is currently a small minority, in the context of nearly 30 million fuel-powered cars, there is a steady growth of EVs with around 4,500 additional vehicles being registered each month. The UK Government's objective to halve non-electric vehicle sales by 2030 and providing that by 2040 all new cars and vans should be zero emission vehicles (zero carbon dioxide and other harmful tailpipe ("exhaust") emissions) gives an additional push for this growing market. Whilst it is not yet clear whether the UK will reach those numbers, it is clear that the growing fleet of EVs will require significant investment and further development of storage, which is conventionally in the form of batteries.

This large-scale rollout of battery storage will require appropriate regulation to deal with the unique features of such a mobile form of storage, including minimum standards, industry codes and specific legislation. The biggest hurdle will be the significant increase in charging infrastructure required and how this specifically will be regulated. Additionally, looking at the life-span of a battery, another big concern will be the appropriate decommissioning of batteries which have reached the end of their "lifetime".

Notwithstanding the importance of storage in the transport sector, however, this chapter will continue with a discussion of storage in terms of the electricity market.[7]

---

7 For further information on electric vehicles and their use in relation to the grid, please see the report entitled "Electric Vehicle Storage to Grid" by the Energy Networks Association of Great Britain, available at: http://www.energynetworks.org/electricity/engineering/energy-storage/vehicle-to-grid.html.

2.2. STORAGE AS A CONCEPT

There is a wide variety of different storage technologies available, with some being developed and others further refined and perfected. To date there has not yet been a single technology which has managed to establish itself as the perfect solution. This uncertainty with regard to "which horse to bet on" could be seen as a significant source of uncertainty and a possible deterrent for developers and financiers. Generally speaking, storage technologies can be grouped into three categories based on their scale and discharge times:

- Grid-scale: pumped hydro, compressed air energy storage and power-to-gas;
- Distributed: batteries, flow batteries and thermal storage; and
- Fast: flywheels, super-capacitors and superconducting magnetic energy storage.[8]

As set out above, there is a range of technologies available and a number of factors will inform a decision on the most appropriate technology (or combination of technologies) for a particular storage application. All of these technologies create the possibility of storing electricity by converting it into a state which allows the release or regeneration of power when this is needed. For example, for hydro storage, water is pumped to a higher elevation using excess energy, allowing the regeneration of energy by releasing this water at a later point to power a turbine with the gravitational power of the water when flowing back down. In this conversion of energy there is always a certain level of loss, but the various technologies differ in their efficiency in this regard and in their responsiveness (i.e. how quickly they can release energy to or absorb energy from the system).

In the UK, pumped hydro is the most prevalent form of existing energy storage, however, anecdotally, prospective storage project sponsors and developers are seemingly also particularly interested in the use of lithium-ion batteries.

At EU level, the concept of storage has been addressed in Article 2(59) of Directive (EU) 2019/944 of the European Parliament and of the Council of 5 June 2019 on common rules for the internal market for electricity, which provides a technologically neutral definition of "energy storage" as

> in the electricity system, deferring the final use of electricity to a moment later than when it was generated, or the conversion of electrical energy into a form of energy which can be stored, the storing of such energy, and the subsequent reconversion of such energy into electrical energy or use as another energy carrier.

[8] See also Chapter 9, Matthijs van Leeuwen and Martha Roggenkamp, *Innovation in Energy Law and Technology*, Oxford, Oxford University Press, 2018.

The EU definition emphasises the deferred use of generated electricity, which would support the classification of electricity storage as generation, as it views storage simply as the delayed usage of generated electricity (see below).

3. THE LEGAL FRAMEWORK IN GREAT BRITAIN[9]

3.1. REGULATORY CLASSIFICATION AND TREATMENT OF STORAGE AS GENERATION

The UK regulatory framework originates from a centralised model of energy generation, distribution and supply in which large-scale pumped hydro installations were the only real form of storage. While this is currently changing, with a wider array of alternative technologies being rolled out on the market, it explains why the GB national regulatory authority, Ofgem, decided to treat all electricity "storage" as generation assets for regulatory purposes. Ofgem has explained this rationale as based on the shared similar characteristics of generation and storage and the fact that the two perform similar functions in terms of generating and exporting electricity to the grid.[10] However, the variety of modern storage systems is often difficult to fit within the single and simple regulatory definition of a generation asset.

Treating an electricity storage project as a generating station may seem at odds with its underlying purpose; i.e., to store power that has already been generated from a primary source. However, there is arguably some scientific support for the Government's approach as, to take the example of batteries, even stored chemical energy must be "regenerated" before it is capable of being exported to the National Grid.

The Government and Ofgem agree that the lack of clarity on the regulatory definition of electricity storage, together with accompanying uncertainties around how storage assets will therefore be treated under the licensing and planning frameworks, are a barrier to the deployment of electricity storage assets in the UK.[11] The Government's stated aim is to legislate to define storage as

---

9 The electricity markets in the UK are organised in two separate markets: (1) the electricity market of England, Scotland and Wales (i.e., Great Britain) which is regulated by Ofgem; and (2) the electricity market of Northern Ireland which is integrated with the electricity market of the Republic of Ireland as the Integrated Single Electricity Market (iSEM) and regulated by a bilaterally appointed SEM Committee (see https://www.semcommittee.com/). This chapter addresses in the situation in Great Britain (GB) only.

10 Ofgem, "Decision on enabling the competitive deployment of storage in a flexible energy system: Changes to the electricity distribution licence" (20 December 2018), p. 4.

11 HM Government and Ofgem, "Upgrading Our Energy System Smart Systems and Flexibility Plan. Call for Evidence Question Summaries and Response from the Government and Ofgem"

a distinct subset of generation by amendment of the Electricity Act 1989, with the intention of therefore providing greater clarity for both licensing and planning purposes.[12]

Both the Government and Ofgem propose to use the Electricity Storage Network's definition of storage[13] as the basis for defining storage in industry codes, licences and legislation:

- "*Electricity Storage*" in the electricity system is the conversion of electrical energy into a form of energy which can be stored, the storing of that energy, and the subsequent reconversion of that energy back into electrical energy; and
- "*Electricity Storage Facility*" in the electricity system means a facility where Electricity Storage occurs.

Separately, Ofgem consulted in 2017 on the introduction of a definition for "electricity storage" and "electricity storage facility" in the electricity generation licence to clarify electricity storage as a subset of generation.[14] Following a review of the responses to this consultation, Ofgem launched a second consultation, this time concerning the definitions of "electricity storage" and "electricity storage facility" themselves. This second consultation closed in July 2019[15] and the industry now awaits a decision in relation to each consultation.

Following National Grid Electricity Transmission plc's ("NGET") proposal in 2016 to introduce appropriate Grid Code provisions for storage devices, taking note of the fact that technical requirements for storage devices have not yet been covered under the EU Network Codes, a working group was implemented and a related workgroup consultation raised in December 2018. This consultation proposes an unambiguous definition of storage in the Grid Code, a technical understanding of storage and how it can be deployed in the UK, as well as the

(July 2017) response to Question 6: https://assets.publishing.service.gov.uk/government/uploads/system/uploads/attachment_data/file/631656/smart-energy-systems-summaries-responses.pdf.

12 Ofgem Decision, 20 December 2018, p. 4.

13 Electricity: Storage: Written Question – HL1253, as answered by the Lord Prior of Brompton on 13 September 2017, accessible at: https://www.parliament.uk/business/publications/written-questions-answers-statements/written-question/Lords/2017-09-05/HL1253/.

14 Ofgem, "Clarifying the regulatory framework for electricity storage: Licensing" (2 October 2017): https://www.ofgem.gov.uk/publications-and-updates/clarifying-regulatory-framework-electricity-storage-licensing.

15 Ofgem, "Clarifying the regulatory framework for electricity storage: Statutory consultation on proposed modifications to the electricity generation licence" (26 June 2019): https://www.ofgem.gov.uk/publications-and-updates/clarifying-regulatory-framework-electricity-storage-statutory-consultation-proposed-modifications-electricity-generation-licence.

implementation of proportionate minimum technical requirements for new connections to aid the technology's flexibility.[16]

At the time of writing, the industry awaits a Final Modification Report. The Draft Final Modification Report was published on 25 June 2019 and notes that the working group concluded that the proposed amendments facilitate the Grid Code's objectives better than the current definitions.[17]

Therefore, the focus again lies on the introduction of clarity regarding the understanding of what storage means from a regulatory standpoint, in particular as to whether it ought to be regarded as an instrument for balancing, generation or a new category *sui generis*. At the same time this consultation adds the practical element of understanding the deployment of storage which will hopefully aid the effective deployment of such devices in the future and bring existing regulatory hurdles in the deployment of storage devices to the attention of the regulator. The implementation of minimum technical requirements may add further clarity to the regulatory arena for storage and introduces a certain level of quality control to this still developing sub-sector, as will the implementation of the recast Directive on the common rules of the electricity market (see above) if it is to implemented in the UK.

3.2. PROHIBITION OF GENERATION (INCLUDING STORAGE) FOR IDNOs AND DNOs

While existing unbundling rules already limited the extent to which network monopolies could own storage at transmission and distribution level,[18] Ofgem's recent review[19] of electricity distribution licences has clarified previous grey areas.

In order to avoid any potentially negative effect on competition within the energy storage market, Ofgem has introduced Licence Conditions 31D and 43B, which prohibit independent distribution network operators ("IDNOs") and distribution network owners ("DNOs") from carrying out any generation activities, including storage. This applies to all relevant storage activities, even

---

16 National Grid, Grid Code Modification, GC0096: Energy Storage (7 December 2018), pp. 4 and 5: https://www.nationalgrideso.com/sites/eso/files/documents/GC0096%20Workgroup%20Consultation%20Final%20Complete.pdf.

17 National Grid, Grid Code Modification, GC0096: Energy Storage (25 June 2019), p. 4: https://www.nationalgrideso.com/document/146266/download.

18 In relation to the unbundling regime applicable in GB, please see Articles 10A–10O of the Electricity Act 1989. The GB unbundling regime reflects the EU's full ownership unbundling regime as detailed in the Third Energy Package. An electronic version of the Electricity Act can be found here: http://www.legislation.gov.uk/ukpga/1989/29/contents.

19 For details of the review and Ofgem's final decision on the same, please see: https://www.ofgem.gov.uk/ofgem-publications/144252.

storage assets which are licence-exempt, unless an activity is captured by an exception or the licensee has been issued with a direction.[20]

Ofgem expressed the view that the operation of storage assets by network operators could present risks to the competitive deployment of storage and consequently inhibit Ofgem's plans to increase flexibility within the electricity system. Specifically, the prohibition aims to prevent de facto monopoly entities (DNOs which also control the provision of storage services) from participating in the storage market in light of their competitive advantage over third-party storage providers. Another reason for the prohibition was the possible access by network operators to information which other participants would not have, and which would therefore provide network operators with a further advantage.

Ofgem cited Article 26 of the Electricity Directive in support of its approach, clarifying that DNOs must ensure that there is operational separation between network activities and generation assets, which includes storage.[21] While Article 26 of the Electricity Directive does not explicitly prohibit the ownership of generating assets by DNOs and IDNOs, Ofgem took the view that the Electricity Directive only sets out a minimum standard for unbundling across the EU,[22] which is in line with the view that the Council of European Energy Regulations has taken on the topic.[23] However, Ofgem has further stated that in its view, and in line with the European rules on storage ownership as set out in the Recast Renewables Directive (see above), there may be need to further strengthen the unbundling regime in the future to include separate ownership of assets with generation capability.[24]

3.3. EXCEPTIONS TO THE PROHIBITION

The new licence conditions provide for three exceptions to the general prohibition, namely Category A (Standard Licence Condition 31D.1(a)/43B.1(a)), island-based networks, Category B (SLC 31D.1(b)/43B.1(b)), generation for specific authorised activities and Category C (SLC 31D.2/43B.2), generation pursuant to a direction by Ofgem.

The Category A exception allows for a licensee to operate generation assets as part of an island-based electricity system. These are defined by Ofgem in their guidance as electrical systems which serve physical islands (other than mainland Great Britain) within the jurisdiction of Ofgem, but do not include

---

20 Ofgem Decision, 20 December 2018, "Decision on enabling the competitive deployment of storage in a flexible energy system: Changes to the electricity distribution licence", p. 1.

21 Ofgem Decision, 20 December 2018 p. 2.

22 Ofgem Decision, 20 December 2018 p. 5.

23 Council of European Energy Regulators, "The Future Role of DSOs: A CEER Conclusions Paper" (July 2015).

24 Ofgem, "Draft Guidance: Prohibition on Generating Guidance (POGG)" (28 September 2018) at para. 1.7.

micro grids. An exception pursuant to category A is non-transferable. Therefore, if the asset subject to an exception is replaced by a similar asset, the asset loses its exception.[25]

The Category B exception provides for small-scale applications of licensee-operated generation assets which support continuity of supply, system resilience, or energy management. According to Ofgem, these include devices to ensure uninterrupted power supply, devices for emergency response and devices with the sole purpose to generate or store electricity produced at a licensed site for later consumption at the same site.[26]

Where a licensee operates or intends to operate generation assets which do not fulfil the requirements for a Category A or B exception it has to apply for a Category C exception. Pursuant to this, if the licensee satisfies certain criteria, Ofgem may issue a direction permitting the operation of a generation asset, attaching any conditions it considers appropriate.[27] Pursuant to SLC 31D.2 an applicant for such direction will have to set out to the satisfaction of the Authority: (a) which reasonable steps have been taken to obtain a market-based solution; (b) that a licensee-operated asset provides the most economical solution; and (c) the arrangements put in place that minimise the risk of discrimination or distortion of current and future markets.[28]

3.4. LICENSING REQUIREMENTS

As discussed above in Section 3.1, Ofgem has traditionally treated storage as a subset of generation which it has confirmed will continue to be Ofgem's policy on the matter and the approach will be codified by Parliament in an amendment to the Electricity Act 2004. Consequently, it comes as no surprise that storage falls under the generation licence regime.

Just as conventional generation assets, storage assets which are smaller than 50MW are exempt from the requirement to be licensed. Larger installations above this 50MW threshold must apply for a generation licence. However, the generation licence does not yet provide for storage, as this has not even been defined within the licence. Recognising this shortfall, Ofgem published a consultation on amending the generation licence to better adapt to storage and to provide better regulatory certainty by defining "electricity storage" within the licence as a subset of generation, using the wording as set out above at Section 3.1.[29]

---

25 POGG, paras. 2.7–2.11, p. 8.
26 POGG, paras. 2.12–2.14.
27 POGG paras. 2.15–2.16.
28 SLC 31D.2 and 43B.2 at: https://www.ofgem.gov.uk/system/files/docs/2018/12/storage_unbundling_electricity_slc_modification_dec2018_final_-_for_website.pdf.
29 Ofgem, "Clarifying the regulatory framework for electricity storage: licensing" (29 September 2017).

In addition, the amended licence introduces the requirement, that "the licensee shall not have self-consumption as the primary function when operating its storage facility."[30] In this context, it is not entirely clear what Ofgem intends to class as a "primary" function as opposed to any secondary or ancillary function.

The requirement to obtain a generation licence where a storage facility has more than 50MW capacity can represent a hurdle for developers of large-scale installations, as making an application for a licence which is not necessarily well matched to the underlying asset can be a burden for such a project. Furthermore, the requirement of a generation licence brings with it further underlying obligations, including signing up to the relevant industry codes, such as the Balancing and Settlement Code ("BSC") Framework Agreement[31] or the Connection and Use of System Code ("CUSC"),[32] the contractual framework for connection to, and use of, the GB electricity transmission grid. These added complications may discourage developers from larger projects due to the additional regulatory hurdles.

This could arguably be alleviated by the introduction of specific storage licences tailored to the specific asset class. However, the proposed definition of storage as a generation activity reaffirms the Government's approach of dealing with storage under the generation licence. Ofgem has stated in its recent decision regarding the electricity distribution licence that next steps in relation to the generation licence with regard to storage and the outcome of the consultation will be published shortly.[33]

Therefore, it will be interesting to see how stakeholders have responded to Ofgem's suggestion and to what extent Ofgem has adapted its approach regarding the appropriate treatment of power storage under the generation licence. In any event, any clarification of the regulatory regime applicable, even if imperfect, will aid the future development of storage by introducing a higher level of legal and regulatory certainty.

3.5. OWNERSHIP AND OPERATION RESTRICTIONS FOR TSOs AND DNOs

In theory, Transmission System Operators ("TSOs") and Distribution Network Operators ("DNOs") would be well placed to exploit storage solutions as they

---

30 Electricity Generation Licence Condition E1.1 (as proposed by the consultation into the electricity licence).

31 An electronic copy of the BSC can be found here: https://www.elexon.co.uk/bsc-and-codes/balancing-settlement-code/.

32 An electronic copy of the CUSC can be found here: https://www.nationalgrideso.com/codes/connection-and-use-system-code-cusc.

33 Ofgem decision, 20 December 2018, p. 4.

have the required capital and, by virtue of their general activities, potential interest in the development of storage capacity. However, these entities face two significant regulatory hurdles. As a requirement of EU unbundling rules, TSOs and DNOs must ensure full legal unbundling of the ownership of generation from operation activities. In addition, as discussed above, DNOs are generally prohibited from operating generation assets pursuant to the new Distribution Licence SLCs (as set out above at Section 3.3). However, as the prohibition is only set out in the Distribution Licence, it does not appear to apply to TSOs.

While this would suggest that TSOs, following this grey area of the unbundling regime, may own storage assets which do not require a licence (i.e. assets smaller than 50MW), Ofgem clarified that "[b]ecause the assessment of TSO unbundling looks at the activities of companies within an ownership group, and not necessarily the licences that are held, the licence exemptions for smaller generators have no bearing on the TSO unbundling rules."[34] This clearly presents a hurdle to the development of storage solutions (by TSOs), but Ofgem has reiterated its commitment to ensuring this unbundling separation continues to apply to storage assets in its recent amendment to the Distribution Licence.[35] Consequently, this hurdle will remain in place, and Ofgem may decide in the future to extend the new general prohibition on generation activity to the Transmission Licence.

In addition to the general prohibition under the Distribution Licence, DNOs are restricted from: (i) generating more than 2.5 per cent of their total annual turnover from non-distribution activities; or (ii) making investments in non-distribution activities that exceed on an aggregate basis 2.5 per cent of the total of the DNO's issued share capital, share premium and consolidated reserves. While at present, given the low levels of storage development, this does not pose an issue, it may in time present an upper limit on DNOs' storage development, provided DNOs receive relevant exceptions and directions for the operation of such storage assets in the first place.

3.6. USE OF SYSTEM CHARGES AS A BARRIER TO ENTRY FOR STORAGE UNITS

At present, the complexity of the charging regime in the electricity market may present a barrier in itself to potential investors.

Storage assets are liable to a multitude of charges which are not applied in a manner appropriate to the nature of storage, resulting in a number of instances of

---

34 Ofgem Consultation, "Enabling the competitive deployment of storage in a flexible energy system: Changes to the electricity distribution licence", 29 September 2017, at page 35, https://www.ofgem.gov.uk/ofgem-publications/122285.

35 HM Government and Ofgem, Call for evidence (n. 2 above) response to Question 4.

double-charging, and generally in an unfair treatment of storage assets compared to conventional generation assets.

Storage is subject to Transmission Network Use of System ("TNUoS")[36] charges, Balancing Services Use of System ("BSUoS")[37] charges, Distribution Use of System ("DUoS")[38] charges and residual charges which are charged by each DSO. Ofgem has expressed the view that storage may be at a relative disadvantage to other types of generation in providing the same or similar services to other providers with respect to BSUoS and residual charges.[39] Further to that, National Grid has set up a working group which is in the process of drafting two separate modifications of the CUSC, raised to address the related issues of BSUoS and TNUoS charging in relation to storage.[40]

Balancing Services Use of System charges cover the costs of the system operator (i.e. National Grid Electricity Transmission or NGET) for its internal running costs and the balancing services it provides to keep the transmission system running.

"Under the current Charging Methodology, storage providers pay BSUoS on both their import and export volumes (in addition to the BSUoS costs implicit in their 'fuel cost')"[41] and are consequently contributing more towards the cost of balancing the system than other users. This places storage providers at a competitive disadvantage when trying to compete with generators in the provision of ancillary services and effectively distorts competition in the market.

Regarding BSUoS, in its consultation Ofgem is proposing to "change the BSUoS Charging Methodology within section 14[42] of the CUSC to remove the liability of BSUoS on storage facilities import volumes."[43]

---

36 An electronic copy of the TNUoS is available here: https://www.nationalgrideso.com/charging/transmission-network-use-system-tnuos-charges.

37 An electronic copy of the BSUoS is available here: https://www.nationalgrideso.com/charging/balancing-services-use-system-bsuos-charges.

38 There is no single, nationally applicable DUoS – the charges are set by each DSO (and subject to approval by Ofgem). By way of example, the DUoS of Western Power, a DNO in the Midlands, South Wales and South West England, can be found here: https://www.westernpower.co.uk/our-network/use-of-system-charges.

39 Ofgem, CMP280 (Stage 2: Workgroup Consultation) "Targeted charging review: minded to decision and draft impact assessment" (28 November 2018) at para. 2.15.

40 CUSC modifies CMP280 "Creation of a New Generator TNUoS Demand Tariff which Removes Liability for TNUoS Demand Residual Charges from Generation and Storage Users" and CMP281 "Removal of BSUoS Charges From Energy Taken From the National Grid System by Storage Facilities". The Modification aims to remove liability from storage facilities for Balancing Services Use of System. (BSUoS) charges on imports.

41 National Grid, CMP281 (Stage 2: Workgroup Consultation) "Removal of BSUoS Charges From Energy Taken From the National Grid System by Storage Facilities" (22 October 2018), p. 4.

42 Specifically section 14.29.4.

43 National Grid, CMP281 (Stage 2) p. 4.

To do so the relevant working group suggests the application of an exemption similar to the treatment of Balancing Mechanism Units ("BMUs") and Trading Units associated with interconnectors, by defining an Exemptible Storage BMU and removing the liability to pay BSUoS on their imports of electricity from the grid.[44] As a result, storage providers would only pay the relevant BSUoS for releasing electricity back into the system but not for the import of excess capacity.

While under the current Charging Methodology, generator and storage parties both contribute to the Generation and Demand TNUoS Residual tariff elements, storage operators are potentially much more exposed to these charges because their imports typically exceed exports, whereas for generators imports are typically a small proportion of exports.

Transmission Network Use of System charges consist of the locational charge and a residual charge, such as the Transmission Generation Residual Charge. Residual charges are a form of TNUoS charge, and aim to recover the costs resulting from past investments in the transmission network infrastructure which cannot be recovered through the locational charge or by encouraging network users to change their behaviour.

This is called residual because it makes up the remainder of the overall TNUoS allocation. In total the TNUoS is meant to cover the capital cost to the Transmission Owners of the transmission network. Currently, TNUoS generation charges are only payable by generators that are connected directly to the transmission network, or by generators with a capacity over 100MW that are connected to a distribution network.

Under the current Charging Methodology, generators and storage providers contribute to both the Generation and Demand TNUoS Residual tariff element and consequently contribute more towards the residual cost of the network, which is unfair in itself. In addition, storage assets are at a competitive disadvantage compared to conventional generation assets due to their much higher exposure to TNUoS Demand Residual tariff elements, as in the case of storage, imports typically exceed exports, whereas for generators imports are typically a small proportion of exports.[45]

Similarly to their proposals with regard to the BSUoS, to rectify the double-charging practice affecting both generators and storage providers, Ofgem is suggesting amendments to the TNUoS Charging Methodology within section 14 of the CUSC to reflect the fact that generator parties and storage operators should not be liable for the TNUoS Demand Residual element of the tariff.

---

44 National Grid, CMP281 (Stage 2), p. 4.

45 National Grid, "Creation of a New Generator TNUoS Demand Tariff which Removes Liability for TNUoS Demand Residual Charges from Generation and Storage Users" (19 June 2018), p. 4.

The proposed modifications to the charging regime are part of a wider "targeted charging review" ("TCR") which was kick-started in 2017. The TCR is intended to address certain issues arising out of the current regime, as Ofgem believes that the currently applicable charging structure has the potential to distort outcomes and increase charges for some consumers. Ofgem's latest consultation on the TCR and the proposed new charging regime closed on 4 February 2019 and it is not yet clear how the future regime might affect storage units or their prospects in the GB energy market, as commentators have suggested that the impact of the new regime might have unexpected side-effects and affect some classes of generators more than others.

Aside from the proposed modification reviews above, Ofgem is also carrying out a Significant Code Review. However, Ofgem explained that in order to deliver the necessary changes as quickly as possible, amendments to network charges for storage should proceed through the usual code modification process rather than the Significant Code Review.[46]

While it is a welcome development that Ofgem appears to address some double-charging concerns in relation to storage, it is surprising that the double-charging of DUoS charges has not been addressed by Ofgem. DUoS charges apply to all distribution network users. As storage assets take electricity off the network when charging, and put electricity back onto the network when discharging, they are liable to pay DUoS charges twice. Some of the DUoS import charges can be recovered on export; however this does result in an additional cost to storage assets which does not reflect their overall contribution to network balancing. Therefore, it will be interesting to see whether, and if so when, this is addressed by Ofgem going forward.

3.7. SUBSIDIES

The UK has a number of subsidy regimes aimed at supporting the deployment of low carbon generation, specifically the Climate Change Levy ("CCL"), Renewables Obligation ("RO"), Feed in Tariffs ("FIT") and Contracts for Difference ("CfD").[47] As the original legislation for these schemes did not reference storage, it is not entirely clear how storage will interact with a project's existing or planned subsidies, and this uncertainty may present a further hurdle to overcome. The Government has therefore recently sought to clarify the position with respect to each type of subsidy.

46 Ofgem, "Targeted Charging Review – Significant Code Review launch statement" (4 August 2017).

47 For details regarding the CfD regime and its role in the reform of the GB electricity market reform, please see S. Goldberg and X. Woodhead, "Electricity Market Reform in Great Britain – a European Perspective" in *European Energy & Law Report X*, Intersentia, Cambridge 2014.

Supplies of electricity are taxed under the main rates of the CCL when consumed by business and public sector consumers. However, as the Government has clarified that it considers storage facilities to constitute electricity generation, storage facilities may be able to take advantage of the CCL exemptions for electricity generators provided they meet the relevant conditions.[48] Largely these will be limited to the supply of de minimis quantities and electricity supplied for a qualifying use, as further set out under the guidance issued by the British tax authority HMRC.[49] CCL will still need to be charged when the stored electricity is supplied to the final consumer, again subject to relevant conditions.[50]

In relation to projects benefitting from the RO and FIT support regimes, Ofgem has already reviewed and retained accreditation for a number of existing generators who have deployed storage at the same location. To clarify the regime, Ofgem published guidance on "Co-location of electricity storage facilities with renewable generation supported under the Renewables Obligation or Feed-in Tariff Scheme" in 2017 and released a revised version in 2018 following a consultation.

The general position is that accredited RO generating stations or FIT installations are required to notify Ofgem of co-located storage in the same way as they would notify changes to the generating station or installation.[51] Ofgem clarified that the RO and FIT legislation do not provide for generators to obtain assurances from Ofgem in relation to whether intended changes to co-location storage will impact a generation station's accreditation under the schemes.[52] Generally, Ofgem will consider and assess any changes notified to them on a case-by-case basis.

The main focus on such assessment will lie on whether all relevant eligibility requirements are still met by the co-located storage. It should be noted that co-locating storage with an accredited RO generating station or FIT installation may impact the level of support the generator receives under the respective scheme.[53] In respect of CfDs, the standard terms and conditions of the CfD define both "electricity storage" and "electricity storage facility". The contract states at 31.1(E) that "no Electricity Storage Facility shall be used by or otherwise

48 HMRC's Excise Notice CCL1/3 "Climate Change Levy – reliefs and special treatments for taxable commodities", updated 27 March 2018, Notice 701/19: Fuel and power, sections 3 and 5.

49 Notice 701/19 (n. 47 above), section 5.1 and 5.2.

50 HM Government and Ofgem, Call for evidence (n. 2 above) response to Question 6.

51 Ofgem, "Guidance for generators: Co-location of electricity storage facilities with renewable generation supported under the Renewables Obligation or Feed-in Tariff schemes (Version 2)" (7 December 2018) at section 1.5.

52 Ofgem, "Guidance for generators: Co-location of electricity storage facilities with renewable generation supported under the Renewables Obligation or Feed-in Tariff schemes (Version 2)" (7 December 2018) at section 1.5.

53 Guidance on Co-location (n. 21 above) at section 1.8.

associated with the generation facility." The CfD contract does, however, allow for association of a storage facility and a generation facility where the storage is registered in a separate balancing mechanism unit to the CfD generating facility. In addition the contract further permits storage to be registered in the same balancing mechanism unit as the CfD generating facility if certain conditions are met.[54]

3.8. THE ROLE OF STORAGE FOR THE BALANCING SYSTEM

In the GB electricity market, the TSO issues a tender for certain balancing services, to which generators then submit offers. The relevant contracts are awarded to the bidders pursuant to the applicable procurement rules.

There are a number of balancing services for which storage will be relevant, including, amongst others, Firm Frequency Response ("FFR") and Enhanced Frequency Response ("EFR"). The contracts for such balancing services have generally been subject to exclusivity which has presented another hurdle for developers. While, traditionally, exclusivity has been a means for system operators to ensure capacity and balancing mechanisms are available as needed on the network, exclusivity prevents contract stacking, i.e. contractors are restricted to a single contract and therefore a single revenue stream.

This means that developers of flexible storage systems are currently unable to take advantage of multiple revenue streams by contract stacking, and are thereby faced with limited revenue opportunities, which reduces the overall project viability.[55] On the other hand, smaller developers have also reported that it is expensive for them to negotiate a large number of contracts, which are often bespoke.[56]

In September 2018 a consultation letter was published to start off a review of exclusivity clauses within balancing services contracts and get industry insights on this. In particular Ofgem requested input on service and revenue stacking.[57] This is expected to further progress in 2019 and may possibly address the concerns as outlined above.

Furthermore, the short duration of many balancing services contracts has also acted as a hurdle to investment in new technologies. Some contracts by

---

54 BEIS, CFD standard terms and conditions, Clause 31.1(E)(ii).

55 HM Government and Ofgem, Call for evidence (n. 2 above) response to Question 12.

56 Parliament, POSTnote 492 (14 April 2015) Energy Storage. https://researchbriefings.parliament.uk/ResearchBriefing/Summary/POST-PN-492.

57 National Grid ESO, Consultation Letter "Review of Exclusivity Clauses within Balancing Services Contracts" (28 September 2018): https://www.nationalgrideso.com/sites/eso/files/documents/Review%20of%20Exclusivity%20Clauses%20within%20Balancing%20Services%20Contracts%20Sep%202018.pdf.

National Grid for FFR services have been limited to six months ahead of tender month only with a maximum of two years in duration.

National Grid has started to offer four-year contracts for storage services, recognising that the contract length is a crucial consideration when investing in a new technology.[58] It is anticipated that by offering longer-term contracts with more certain revenue streams, the risk profile for lenders will become more appetising, and boost confidence for debt financing of storage projects.

4. HURDLES TO INVESTMENT AND FINANCING STORAGE FACILITIES

4.1. OBTAINING PLANNING CONSENT FOR STORAGE FACILITIES

Storage differs from other emerging technologies in that it is not simply an iteration of a pre-existing type of infrastructure that has already been contemplated by the statutory code. Rather, it is an entirely new concept of development that demands bespoke treatment within the planning system.

Defining storage as a subset of generation in the Electricity Act 1989 will confirm the Government's current position that storage facilities should be treated as a form of electricity generating station for planning purposes.

Classifying storage projects as a form of electricity generation is important, principally because it is an essential consideration to establishing which consenting regime will apply to the respective development projects:

- Under Part 3 of the Planning Act 2008,[59] the construction or extension of a generating station with capacity of more than 50MW is classified as a nationally significant infrastructure project ("NSIP"). An application must be made to the Secretary of State for a development consent order ("DCO") where a storage facility exceeds the 50MW threshold.[60]
- Where a storage facility has a generating capacity of less than 50MW, a planning application must be submitted to the local planning authority as would normally be required under Part 3 of the Town and Country Planning Act 1990.[61]

---

58 National Grid, "Enhanced Frequency Response: Frequently Asked Questions" (29 March 2016), p. 14.

59 For an electronic version of the Planning Act 2008, please see: http://www.legislation.gov.uk/ukpga/2008/29/contents.

60 Planning Act 2008, section 15.

61 Town and Country Planning Act 1990, section 58.

DCO applications are usually determined in accordance with the relevant national policy statement ("NPS") which sets out the Government's objectives for granting consent in relation to NSIPs. This is perhaps less relevant for storage projects given that no NPS specifically applies to this form of infrastructure development. EN-1, which sets out the Government's strategic objectives for all nationally significant energy infrastructure projects, will be a material consideration. However, EN-1 was drafted in 2011.[62] At that time storage was not viable and national policy focussed on how electricity demand could simultaneously and continuously meet supply.

The main advantage of the DCO regime, which applies to large projects of national importance and is designed as a one-stop-shop for all relevant planning consents in relation to a project, is that it provides much greater certainty in terms of the timescales for a decision. In most cases, a decision will be made within a maximum period of 18 months of an application being submitted to the Planning Inspectorate. There is also greater certainty in terms of the outcome. The other potential advantage of the project falling under the DCO regime is that the decision will be made at national level by either the Secretary of State or an appointed Inspector. Accordingly, the application is less exposed to the politics of local decision-making.

The major drawback of the DCO process is that it is generally lengthier and involves significant additional work. This includes carrying out at least one round of consultation with the public and statutory consultees before the application is submitted to the Planning Inspectorate. This can often result in much higher costs and longer lead-in times compared to submitting a planning application to the local planning authority. For these reasons, it can be desirable for a developer to make sure that the generating capacity of its project does not exceed the 50MW threshold. Furthermore, the current system does not distinguish between stand-alone and co-located storage facilities.[63]

Recognising that an urgent update in policy is required, the Department for Business, Energy and Industrial Strategy ("BEIS") published a consultation on "the treatment of electricity storage within the planning system" in January 2019. This consultation proposed to retain the 50MW capacity threshold for generating stations in the NSIP regime that apply for stand-alone storage, as BEIS found on its initial investigation that the current threshold does not significantly distort sizing and investment decisions of storage developers, thus any change would be unjustified.[64] However, BEIS suggested an amendment of the Planning Act 2008 to establish a new capacity threshold for composite (i.e. co-located) projects which include storage and another form of generation. Under this

---

62 See n. 1 above.

63 BEIS, Consultation on Proposals regarding the planning system for electricity storage, p. 11.

64 BEIS, Consultation on Proposals regarding the planning system for electricity storage, p. 11.

proposal a composite project would fall under the NSIP regime where either its generation capacity, excluding any storage, is more than 50MW or the capacity of any storage is more than 50MW. Where the capacity threshold is not met the project would fall under the local planning regime.[65]

The consultation closed in March 2019 and, perhaps due to time pressures on the British civil service arising from Brexit-related preparations, the industry continues to await the outcome of the consultation.[66]

4.2. FINANCING INVESTMENT IN STORAGE

Due to the unbundling regime applicable to electricity storage (which prevents the TSO from developing commercial storage projects), the vast majority of storage projects will be developed by existing generators or independent project developers. Of those, the majority are likely to require third-party financing for their storage projects.

With technological developments moving at a rapid pace, many traditional lenders are reluctant to back "the wrong horse" and therefore hesitate to back projects, which, in turn, restricts access to financing for many projects.[67] However, the recent entry of more established companies into the storage market has provided a boost to investor confidence, so this hurdle may be slowly starting to dissipate.[68]

With new technologies still under development, there is not yet a set of common codes or standards which would support wider roll-out of such technologies. In time, these will be required to provide common and formal safety standards, installation practices, and allow for wider training to up-skill the potential workforce required to support such a greater number of developments. The current Grid Code consultation on storage[69] could mark a first step in that direction.

Overall, most storage technologies are more expensive than traditional back-up electricity supplies (e.g. diesel-fuelled generating units) and consequently financial viability remains an important hurdle for nearly all storage projects. Further, while solar and wind energy have been financed on a relative certainty through FIT or RO subsidies with secure revenue streams for up to 20 years,

---

65 BEIS, Consultation on Proposals regarding the planning system for electricity storage, pp. 6 and 7.

66 Updates on the consultation can be found here: https://www.gov.uk/government/consultations/the-treatment-of-electricity-storage-within-the-planning-system.

67 Bloomberg, "The Age of the Giant Battery Is Almost Upon Us", Joe Ryan and Brian Eckhouse, 21 February 2017.

68 Bloomberg, "The Age of the Giant Battery Is Almost Upon Us", Joe Ryan and Brian Eckhouse, 21 February 2017.

69 See n. 15 above and accompanying text.

this is not available to the same extent to storage facilities. Storage is much more dependent on revenue from balancing services to National Grid, which, as outlined above, is limited due to contract exclusivity. Therefore, if the consultation on exclusivity clauses and revenue stacking leads to a relaxation of the contracts, this would considerably increase the financial viability of storage facilities.

That being said, battery storage and demand-side response won over 500MW of contracts in the T-1 Capacity Market[70] auction in February 2018, i.e. those capacity market auctions in the GB electricity market which are run one year ahead of their potential utilisation year.

Whilst the Capacity Market has been suspended since the ECJ's annulment of the Commission's granting of state aid approval in November 2018, these results show that storage has been able to compete with other established technologies, and that there is a clear and increasing demand for storage in the UK from now on.

This will affect the financing available for storage projects going forward, the better established the different technologies become and the more certainty is being introduced regarding future revenue streams for storage.

5. CONCLUSION AND OUTLOOK

The storage market is fragmented due to the variety in different technologies, each of which has different characteristics and capabilities and offers developers different types of services. The industry is still exploring the best uses for each type of storage system which creates a number of hurdles.

Until recently, without a clear regulatory definition of storage, developers have been uncertain as to how their project may be treated under the regulatory and planning frameworks. Going forward, in light of the definitions in the distribution licence and the proposed amendments to the codes and the Electricity Act 2004 this uncertainty should be reduced considerably.

The Ofgem report has shown and is still applying an increased focus on identifying and rectifying regulatory shortcomings with regard to the development and deployment of storage in the UK. This is reflected in efforts to define storage on a legislative basis, the amendment of licences and numerous consultations on the different aspects of storage. It appears that a key interest of Ofgem is to finally provide for a level of regulatory certainty when it comes to storage as well as ensuring that the market provides equal

70 For further background on the GB capacity market, please refer to Julian Lang, "The Capacity Market in Great Britain" in *European Energy Law Report XII*, Intersentia, Cambridge 2018, pp. 193ff.

opportunities for storage developers. The latter is mainly reflected in the new prohibition in the distribution licence, barring DNOs from being engaged in any generation activities (including storage), to avoid DNOs from developing de facto monopolies of distribution, which would have made it more difficult for independent storage providers to penetrate the market. While this change could be seen as a hurdle for developments, having eliminated a potential investor for storage projects, it does support and protect independent providers of storage services. Other efforts by Ofgem, such as the charges reviews, ensure a fairer application of charges to storage activities, making them more financially viable in the process.

While there remain multiple hurdles to the deployment of storage it appears that the combined efforts of the regulator and the industry are going in the right direction.

However, it should be noted that most efforts are still in the development phase with multiple consultations on-going but only rather few changes actually having been implemented to date. Therefore, it will be interesting to see whether and if so, when and how these current considerations will be implemented in practice. In any event, it will be helpful for parliamentary attention to return to practical politics soon, as legislative involvement may be needed beyond Ofgem's current attention to the topic.

CHAPTER V

POWER-TO-GAS AND HYDROGEN FOR ENERGY STORAGE UNDER EU ENERGY LAW

Ruven FLEMING and Gijs KREEFT

1. INTRODUCTION

Power-to-Gas and hydrogen are becoming prominent topics in debates on the design of future energy systems. The technology is gaining popularity amongst the energy industry and energy regulators alike, as highlighted by the increasing policy research in this field.[1] The reason for this popularity is the flexible and versatile way in which the technology could facilitate the ongoing energy transition.

Power-to-Gas could be used for a number of purposes,[2] but one of the most promising is the storage of surplus electricity from renewable energy installations. In this way renewable energy could be stored and the time of use can be inferred. This would be helpful to counter the naturally intermittent production pattern of renewable energy installations, which do not produce (and thus do not feed electricity into the system) when the sun does not shine and the wind does not blow. In these situations the electricity has to be balanced, which at the moment means that coal and gas-fired power plants have to make up for temporary shortages in renewable energy generation. Storing electricity via Power-to-Gas could be a long-term option to counterbalance

---

1 Examples are the HyLAW project which identifies legal and regulatory barriers to use of hydrogen in the European Union (www.hylaw.eu) and Task 38 of the International Energy Agency 'Hydrogen Implementing Agreement' which includes an analysis of legal and regulatory conditions regarding Power-to-X (http://ieahydrogen.org/Activities/Task-38.aspx).

2 Ruven Fleming, 'Regulating Power-to-Gas in the Energy Union' (2018) *Oil, Gas & Energy Law* 11–12.

seasonal differences (strong winds in autumn, but not in summer). The current chapter will specifically focus on this promising potential of Power-to-Gas as a means to store electricity to counter this intermittence issue.

Current numbers, however, are rather sobering, as 96 per cent of hydrogen at the moment is produced from fossil fuels through methane steam reforming, according to the International Energy Agency.[3] This process generates greenhouse gases in significant quantities.[4]

By contrast, merely four per cent of hydrogen is derived from renewable sources via electrolysis.[5] This hydrogen, produced from renewable energy sources, is referred to as 'green hydrogen', while hydrogen produced from fossil fuels, is called 'grey hydrogen'.[6]

When zooming in on 'green' hydrogen, we can see that it has two main sources. First, biomass-based production and second, water-electrolysis based on electricity from renewable sources, also known under the term 'Power-to-Gas'.[7] According to Ball/Seydel/Wietschel/Stiller, offshore wind via electrolysis/ Power-to-Gas can play a very important role in hydrogen production after 2020 and become its main source.[8] This, however, will depend on technical advances as well as a clear legal framework for the technology.

This chapter focuses on the energy law framework at EU level and how it applies to storage of renewable energy via Power-to-Gas. It scrutinizes the existing legal framework of the EU and outlines the current regulatory developments for Power-to-Gas as a storage option.

As a starting point, it is important to explain that the applicable energy law framework for Power-to-Gas at the EU level is currently in transition. The European Commission created a new legal framework for the European energy system with the aim of taking technical developments like Power-to-Gas better into account. By the end of 2016 the EU Commission launched a legislative

3 International Energy Agency, 'Energy Technology Essentials Hydrogen Production & Distribution' (2007) 4, table 1, https://www.iea.org/publications/freepublications/publication/essentials5.pdf (hereinafter: IEA Hydrogen).

4 Joseph Romm, 'The Hype about Hydrogen: Fact and Fiction in the Race to Save the Climate' (2004) 3 (hereinafter: Romm).

5 Michael Ball, Werner Weindorf and Ulrich Bünger, 'Hydrogen Production' in Michael Ball and Martin Wietschel (eds.), *The Hydrogen Economy: Opportunities and Challenges* (Cambridge University Press, Cambridge 2009) 279; International Energy Agency, 'Energy Technology Essentials Hydrogen Production & Distribution' (2007) 4, table 1, https://www.iea.org/publications/freepublications/publication/essentials5.pdf.

6 Michael Ball, 'Why Hydrogen?' in Michael Ball and Martin Wietschel (eds.), *The Hydrogen Economy: Opportunities and Challenges* (Cambridge University Press, Cambridge 2009) 3839 (hereinafter: Ball).

7 Michael Ball et al. in Michael Ball and Martin Wietschel (eds.), *The Hydrogen Economy: Opportunities and Challenges* (Cambridge University Press, Cambridge, 2009) 399 (hereinafter: Ball/Seydel/Wietschel/Stiller).

8 Ball/Seydel/Wietschel/Stiller. 418.

package called 'Clean Energy for All Europeans'.[9] The package consists of a number of legislative instruments,[10] but at its heart are two recast directives, the recast Renewables Directive[11] and the recast Electricity Directive.[12] The recast Renewables Directive and the recast Electricity Directive are relevant for the storage of electricity via hydrogen.

They are contrasted with the existing regulations of a third Directive, the Gas Directive,[13] the revision of which is not part of the Clean Energy for all Europeans package.[14] A proposal for a new Gas Regulation is, however, expected by the end of 2019 or beginning of 2020. It can be expected that Power-to-Gas will be integrated better into the new Gas Directive, as the focus of the current one on natural gas raises question about its applicability to hydrogen, as will be discussed below.

After some remarks on the technical aspects in section 2, section 3 discusses the legal categorization of hydrogen as a form of renewable energy under the new recast Renewable Energy Directive and the repercussions for electricity storage via hydrogen. Section 4 will explore the extent to which current EU Electricity and Gas legislation applies to electricity storage via hydrogen and who, under EU unbundling rules, is allowed to own and/or operate these Power-to-Gas facilities for the purpose of storing electricity. Section 5 will provide the main conclusions and recommendations for further clarifications in the legal frameworks.

---

9 European Commission, 'Clean Energy for All Europeans – unlocking Europe's growth potential', http://europa.eu/rapid/press-release_IP-16-4009_en.htm.

10 European Commission, 'Commission proposes new rules for consumer centred clean energy transition', https://ec.europa.eu/energy/en/news/commission-proposes-new-rules-consumer-centred-clean-energy-transition.

11 European Commission, 'Proposal for a Directive of the European Parliament and of the Council on the promotion of the use of energy from renewable sources (recast)', COM(2016) 767 final/2 (hereinafter: proposed recast RED).

12 European Commission, 'Proposal for a Directive of the European Parliament and of the Council on common rules for the internal market in electricity (recast)', COM(2016) 864 final/2 (hereinafter: proposed recast Electricity Directive). Moreover, there are proposals for Directives and Regulations dealing with energy efficiency, but they are not discussed in this Article, as they are not directly relevant to Power-to-Gas.

13 Council Directive (EC) 2009/73 of 13 July 2009 concerning common rules for the internal market in natural gas and repealing Directive 2003/55/EC [2009] OJ L 211/94 (hereinafter: 2009 Gas Directive).

14 However, the Gas Directive is also currently being revised under the umbrella of another legislative initiative, aiming to extend the scope of the EU energy law regime to offshore pipelines coming into the EU ('Nord Stream 2'), see: European Commission, 'Proposal for a Directive of the European Parliament and of the Council amending Directive 2009/73/EC concerning common rules for the internal market in natural gas 8 November 2017', COM(2017) 660 final, available at: https://ec.europa.eu/energy/sites/ener/files/documents/act_gas_dir_adopted.pdf.

2. POWER-TO-GAS TECHNOLOGY AND APPLICATIONS

Power-to-Gas is an energy conversion technology that allows for the transfer of the energy content of electrons to molecules, thereby enabling alternative storage and usage pathways of electricity generated from renewable sources (RES-E). In a first step, electricity is used for a water-electrolysis process which decomposes a water molecule (H_2O) into hydrogen (H_2) and oxygen (O_2).[15] The resulting hydrogen can be stored and/or transported as pure hydrogen or admixed in limited volumes to natural gas flows. In case of electricity storage, a further second step is needed (Gas-to-Power) to reconvert hydrogen molecules again into electrons. This is most frequently done by using a fuel cell, which is also deployed already today for various purposes, including fuel cell vehicles.

By establishing this link between the electricity and gas sectors, Power-to-Gas is frequently linked to terms as 'sectoral integration' or 'sector-coupling'.[16] This coupling of sectors through energy conversion plays an important role for the seasonal storage of renewable energy,[17] but also enables the decarbonization of end-uses such as mobility[18] or heat.[19] Sectoral integration for storage purposes can facilitate integrated network planning and operation.[20]

In this chapter, we will take an end-use neutral approach by focusing on the Power-to-Gas energy conversion process and hydrogen storage.

---

15 See, for a techno-economic analysis of the Power-to-gas chain: Manuel Götz, Jonathan Lefebvre, Friedemann Mörs, Amy McDaniel Koch, Frank Graf, Siegfried Bajohr, Rainer Reimert and Thomas Kolb, 'Renewable Power-to-Gas: A Technological and Economic Review' (2016) 85 *Renewable Energy* 1371–1390.

16 Asset, 'Sectoral Integration- long-term perspective in the EU Energy System' (2018), https://ec.europa.eu/energy/sites/ener/files/documents/asset_study_2018.pdf; Maria Olczak and Andris Piebals, Sector Coupling: the New EU Climate and Energy Paradigm?', Florence School of Regulation Policy Brief, http://fsr.eui.eu/wp-content/uploads/QM-AX-18-017-EN-N.pdf.

17 Stephen Clegg and Pierluigi Mancarella, 'Storing Renewables in the Gas Network: Modelling of Power-to-Gas Seasonal Storage Flexibility in Low-Carbon Power Systems' (2015) 10(3) *IET Generation, Transmission & Distribution* 566–575.

18 Martin Robinius, Alexander Otto, Philipp Heuser, Lara Welder, Konstantinos Syranidis, David S. Ryberg, Thomas Grube, Peter Markewitz, Ralf Peters and Detlef Stolten, 'Linking the Power and Transport Sectors – Part 1: The Principle of Sector Coupling' (2017) 10(956) *Energies* 1–22.

19 Benedetto Nastasi and Gianluigi Lo Basso, 'Power-to-Gas Integration in the Transitions Towards Future Urban Energy Systems' (2017) 42(38) *International Journal of Hydrogen Energy* 23933–23951.

20 Stephen Clegg and Pierluigi Mancarella, 'Integrated Modeling and Assessment of the Operational Impact of Power-to-Gas (P2G) on Electrical and Gas Transmission Networks' (2015) 6(4) *IEEE Transactions on Sustainable Energy* 1234–1244 (hereinafter 'Clegg and Mancarella, P2G for Networks').

3. RENEWABLE ENERGY, HYDROGEN AND THE LAW

Although Power-to-Gas is not a 'green' technology per se, it is often associated with renewable energy. This perception is mainly rooted in the possibility to use hydrogen to store electricity that has been produced from renewable sources.[21] The 2009 Renewable Energy Directive (hereinafter: RED) already included a number of favourable conditions and privileges for renewable energy, compared to conventional energy.[22] The Renewable Energy Directive has been revised recently and from December 2018 onwards the recast Renewable Energy Directive (REDII) has been in force, which is part of the 'Clean Energy for All Europeans' package.[23] This chapter is already taking this recent development into account. Two legal aspects are crucial for the issue of Power-to-Gas as a storage option in relation to renewable energy. First, it has to be assessed whether or not hydrogen falls within the definition of 'renewable energy' under the REDII; second, renewable energy support mechanisms (broadly defined), particularly the so-called Guarantees of Origin scheme, have to be checked for applicability to hydrogen.

3.1. DEFINITION OF RENEWABLE ENERGY

Regarding the first point, hydrogen is not an energy source in itself, rather an energy carrier. Similarly to electricity, hydrogen is as green as its source, or more accurately, as green as the source of the electricity used for electrolysis to produce hydrogen for storage. This is also the logic behind the approach of the REDII (2018/2001)[24] towards hydrogen. While hydrogen is not explicitly mentioned as 'renewable energy' in its own right in article 2(1) RED, 'green' hydrogen is included indirectly in the scope of the RED.[25] This becomes

21 See Ruven Fleming, 'Regulating Power-to-Gas in the Energy Union' (2018) *Oil, Gas & Energy Law* 11–15.

22 More on that can be found at Hans Vedder, Anita Ronne, Martha Roggenkamp and Inigo del Guayo, 'EU Energy Law' in Martha M Roggenkamp et al. (eds.), *Energy Law in Europe* 3rd edition (Oxford University Press, Oxford 2016) paragraph 4.406 (hereinafter: Vedder et al., 'EU Energy Law').

23 European Commission, 'Clean energy for all Europeans' Package, available at: https://ec.europa.eu/energy/en/topics/energy-strategy-and-energy-union/clean-energy-all-europeans.

24 Directive (EU) 2018/2001 of the European Parliament and of the Council of 11 December 2018 on the promotion of the use of energy from renewable sources (recast) OJ L 328/82 (hereinafter: RED).

25 This reference includes only 'green' and not to 'grey' hydrogen, see European Parliament 'Briefing EU Legislation in Progress Promoting renewable energy sources in the EU after 2020', page 7, http://www.europarl.europa.eu/RegData/etudes/BRIE/2017/599278/EPRS_BRI(2017)599278_EN.pdf.

clear from article 7(1) second sentence, concerned with counting the share of energy from renewable sources: '... hydrogen from renewable sources shall be considered only once for the purposes of calculating the share of gross final consumption of energy from renewable sources.' The article thus works on the assumption that hydrogen from renewable sources can be considered as renewable energy.

With a view to storage, recital 60 RED establishes that the use of energy storage systems for integrated variable production of energy from renewable sources shall be supported, but no article in the body of the RED actually follows up on this. However, there is a different, yet interesting way in which hydrogen produced from renewable energy, inter alia for storage purposes, is being supported by the RED – the Guarantees of Origin scheme.

Recital 59 RED acknowledges indirectly that the term 'renewable gas' encompasses hydrogen from renewable energy sources. This means 'grey' hydrogen, derived from fossil fuels, falls outside of this definition and the applicability of the Renewable Energy Directive.

3.2. THE GUARANTEES OF ORIGIN SCHEME

As regards Guarantees of Origin, recital 59 together with Article 19(7)(b)(ii) RED establish that Guarantees of Origin shall now be issued for renewable gases, including 'green' hydrogen. According to Article 19(1) RED, each Member State must be able to guarantee the origin of energy from renewable sources.[26] Guarantees of origin have the sole function to prove to a final customer that a given share of energy was produced from renewable sources.[27]

However, a guarantee of origin can be transferred independently of the energy to which it relates, from one holder to the other – regardless of the energy to which it refers.[28] The underlying rationale is to use guarantees of origin as evidence of 'green supply' in order to allow consumers to differentiate between 'green' and 'grey' energy commodities, but do not of themselves confer a right to benefit from national support schemes.[29] This system of guarantees of origin was in place for renewable electricity and will now be extended to renewable gases like hydrogen.

---

26 In the new RED of 2018 the term 'electricity' has been altered to 'energy' to clarify that renewable gases are included.

27 Recital 59 and Article 19(1) RED.

28 Vedder et al, 'EU Energy Law' paragraph 4.400.

29 Vedder et al. 'EU Energy Law' paragraph 4.401.

4. THE CLASSIFICATION OF POWER-TO-GAS AND HYDROGEN STORAGE

The legislative archives of the EU provide no indication that Power-to-Gas and hydrogen storage were a topic of consideration during the drafting of the 2009 Third Energy Package. The Electricity Directive (2009/72/EC) and Gas Directive (2009/73/EC) both reflect that the energy system was, and is, dominated by 'traditional' actors which can be classified as either producer, system operator, gas storage operator, or consumer. It is based on these classifications that the Directives prescribe how energy markets need to be organized and what the rights and obligations of the respective entities are. Market integration of 'new' technologies such as Power-to-Gas for electricity storage via hydrogen, thus, provokes three questions. First, how does electricity storage via hydrogen fit with recent EU electricity law? Second, is electricity storage via hydrogen possible under current EU gas legislation? And third, who is actually allowed to own and/or operate a Power-to-Gas plant for electricity storage under the EU's unbundling provisions?

4.1. STORAGE THROUGH POWER-TO-GAS UNDER ELECTRICITY LEGISLATION

In the old Electricity Directive of 2009 no mention of 'electricity storage' was made.[30] That changed with the introduction of the new recast Electricity Directive (EU) 2019/944[31] (hereinafter: Electricity Directive). Article 2(59) of the Electricity Directive defines energy storage as

> (…) in the electricity system, deferring the final use of electricity to a moment later than when it was generated, or the conversion of electrical energy into a form of energy which can be stored, the storing of such energy, and the subsequent reconversion of such energy into electrical energy or use as another energy carrier.

While hydrogen and Power-to-Gas are not explicitly mentioned here, the formulation about the conversion of electrical energy into another, storable, form of energy and subsequent re-conversion to electricity, suggests that

30 Directive 2009/72/EC of the Parliament and of the Council of 13 July 2009 concerning common rules for the internal market in electricity and repealing Directive 2003/54/EC [2009] OJ L 211/55.

31 Directive (EU) 2019/944 of the European Parliament and of the Council of 5 June 2019 on common rules for the internal market for electricity and amending Directive 2012/27/EU [2019] OJ L 158/125.

Power-to-Gas plants – in which, indeed, the hydrogen is re-converted to electrical energy by a fuel cell or gas turbine – would be covered.

This interpretation of the text is bolstered by a Staff Working Document (SWD) of the European Commission, which elaborates upon an earlier proposed version of this article.[32] It explains that

> storage within the electricity system covers all power-to-power solutions, including batteries, pumped hydro and compressed air energy storage. It also covers power-to-hydrogen when the produced hydrogen is used for re-electrification (...).[33]

The wording of Article 2(59) Electricity Directive, however, is much more open than that. The last six words 'or use as another energy carrier' indicate that no re-conversion of electricity is required for a Power-to-Gas plant to be recognized as an electricity storage facility. This is a crucial point, as it means that electricity can be converted to hydrogen and stay hydrogen. Although the wording of the cited Staff Working Document (SWD) is stricter and, indeed, only covers hydrogen that is used for re-electrification, this is not a valid argument. The SWD dates from 2017 and is, thus, not actually interpreting the final law (Electricity Directive). By the time the SWD was drafted, the European Parliament as well as the European Council and the European Commission all proposed slightly different versions of a possible wording for Article 2(59). With the coming into force of the new Electricity Directive in 2019 the European legislator decided on the exact wording and, given the fact that there had been a lively discussion about the exact wording in the drafting phase, it may only be assumed that the legislator made a conscious decision here to also include Power-to-hydrogen without re-conversion to electricity in the definition of electricity storage. The will of the legislator needs to be respected during interpretation of the law.[34]

An interesting discussion for the future interpretation is the one about intention ('dolus'). In cases where hydrogen is stored and not re-converted to electricity, is there a need for an *intention* to undergo this process with the aim to store electricity? What if someone is using Power-to-Gas to produce hydrogen and wants to produce hydrogen for the sole purpose of producing hydrogen and with no intention to store electricity. This would most likely not be considered as electricity storage. Mind you, article 2(59) Electricity Directive actually does not define 'electricity storage', but instead the term

---

32 Commission Staff Working Document 'Energy storage – the role of electricity' SWD(2017) 61 final (hereinafter: SWD Energy Storage).

33 SWD Energy Storage section 4.1.

34 Günter Hager, *Rechtsmethoden in Europa* (Mohr Siebeck, Tübingen 2009) 54: Heiko Sauer, 'Juristische Methodenlehre' in Julian Krüper (ed.), *Grundlagen des Rechts*, 2nd edition (Nomos, Baden-Baden 2013) §9 paragraphs 28 et seq. and 34.

'energy storage' is used. Given that this is broader than only storing electricity, the described constellation would still be likely to fall within the definition, even without a deliberate 'storage' intention.

Moreover, there are two interesting, yet overlooked, consequences following from the wording. First, all types of Power-to-Gas plants that produce hydrogen for re-conversion are covered. That includes 'green' but also 'grey' and any other hydrogen, as long as it was produced from electrical energy and is being re-converted to that. Power-to-Gas can work perfectly well with 'conventional' electricity produced from fossil fuels and is by no means only an option to store renewable electricity. The Electricity Directive clearly applies to any source of the hydrogen, as long as it is electricity.

Second, the wording of article 2(59) Electricity Directive leaves interesting leeway for discretion and interpretation. It does not clarify what happens when the Power-to-Gas plant, the hydrogen storage and the plant for re-conversion are not all integrated and built on one premise, but rather all three are detached from each other and lone-standing plants.[35] While the wording seems to assume that all three steps are integrated, this does not have to be the case. What if a Power-to-Gas plant sells its hydrogen to a variety of customers, e.g. manufacturers of automotive fuels, refineries or to fuel-cell plants that convert the purchased hydrogen to electricity. Would the fuel-cell plant be still considered as engaging in the business of energy storage? Or the Power-to Gas plant?

Article 2(60) Electricity Directive provides some answers here. It says that 'energy storage facility' means, in the electricity system, a facility where energy storage occurs. Thus, the place where the energy is stored is considered as the storage facility. These considerations might not appear to be of much relevance at the moment, as the market for electricity storage still needs to be developed, but in the future this might change. A further point of interest is the interplay between the storage provisions of the Electricity and the Gas Directive, which will be discussed next.

4.2. POWER-TO-GAS UNDER EU GAS LEGISLATION

As Power-to-Gas is deemed to be a cross-energy vector technology which functions as a linkage between the worlds of electricity and gas, the applicable legal framework for the electricity sector only tells half of the story. When the energy is no longer carried by electrons but by hydrogen molecules in a gaseous

35 Gijs Kreeft, 'European Legislative and Regulatory Framework on Power-to-Gas' (2017), STORE&GO project, https://www.storeandgo.info/fileadmin/downloads/20171030_STOREandGO_D7.2_RUG_submitted.pdf, 33 (hereinafter: Kreeft (2017) 'EU Law on Power-to-Gas').

state, it becomes necessary to consider the extent that EU natural gas legislation equally applies. Similarly to natural gas, hydrogen is a gaseous energy carrier which can be compressed and stored in salt caverns, aquifers and depleted oil- and gasfields.[36] This similarity with natural gas makes hydrogen produced through Power-to-Gas such an attractive option for the storage of large volumes of renewable energy.[37] Against this background, we will explore in this section the extent that EU natural gas legislation applies to hydrogen and, subsequently, how Power-to-Gas and hydrogen storage can be classified from the perspective of EU gas legislation which still stems from 2009.[38]

4.2.1. *Applicability of EU Natural Gas Legislation to Hydrogen*

Our exploration of the applicability of EU natural gas legislation on the Power-to-Gas and hydrogen sector starts by asking the preliminary question whether the rules under the 2009 Gas Directive even apply to hydrogen production, storage and transportation.

Similarly to its predecessors from 1998 and 2003, the aim of the 2009 Gas Directive is the establishment of a competitive internal market in natural gas. To this end, Article 1(1) stipulates that the Directive 'establishes common rules for the transmission, distribution, supply and storage of *natural gas*' (emphasis added). This does not mean that the drafters of the Gas Directive have ignored the increased attention and demand for alternative gases such as biogas. It was the European Parliament which suggested, during the negotiations leading up to the 2003 Gas Directive, the inclusion of biogas and other gas from biomass under the scope of the Gas Directive in order to increase the share of renewable energy in gas consumption.[39] In response, the European Commission expressed its willingness to accept this proposal on the condition that a clause was added which emphasized that the Directive would only apply to such gases insofar as they can be technically and safely injected into the natural gas system.[40] Finally, it was on the instigation of the Council that the

---

36 See for a technical analysis of underground hydrogen storage: Netherlands Enterprise Agency, 'The effects of hydrogen injection in natural gas networks for the Dutch underground storages' (2017), www.rvo.nl (hereinafter: Netherlands Enterprise Agency).

37 See Hans Christian Gils and others, 'Integrated modelling of variable renewable energy-based power supply in Europe' (2017) 123 *Energy* 173–188.

38 A similar exercise in the context of power-to-synthetic natural gas (power-to-SNG) can be found in: Kreeft (2017) 'EU Law on Power-to-Gas', n. 35 above.

39 European Parliament Committee on Industry, External Trade, Research and Energy, 'Report on the proposal for a directive of the European Parliament and of the Council amending Directives 96/92/EC and 98/30/EC concerning common rules for the internal market in electricity and natural gas' (2002), Doc. A5-0077/2002, Amendments 110 and 118.

40 European Commission, 'Amended proposal for a directive of the European Parliament and of the Council amending Directives 96/92/EC and 98/30/EC concerning rules for the internal markets in electricity and natural gas' COM (2002) 304 final.

scope of the 2003 Gas Directive (2003/55/EC) also applied to 'other types of gases' than natural gas and biomass-based gases.[41] What specific 'other types of gases' the Council had in mind when it introduced this addition can, however, not be inferred from the legislative history.

A few years later, during the course of the negotiations resulting in the adoption of the 2009 Gas Directive (2009/73EC), the element of non-discrimination was added to Article 1(2) on the initiative of the European Parliament. This reference to the non-discrimination principle was justified by the statement that 'assuming the technical and chemical safety threshold for the different gases are met, the need for non-discrimination for access between the gases from different sources must be emphasized.' Article 1(2) on the scope of the 2009 Gas Directive now reads:

> [t]he rules established by this Directive for natural gas (...) shall also apply in a *non-discriminatory* way to biogas and gas from biomass or *other types of gas* in so far as such gases can technically and safely be injected into, and transported through, the *natural gas system* (emphasis added).

As it is basic chemistry that hydrogen molecules can constitute a 'gas', and as hydrogen is neither natural gas nor biogas, we can safely state that hydrogen which is produced through the Power-to-Gas process falls within the category of 'other types of gases'.[42] We thus arrive at our first conclusion on the applicability of the 2009 Gas Directive to hydrogen: the Directive applies to hydrogen in so far hydrogen can technically and safely be injected into, and transported through, the natural gas system. Importantly, the extended scope of the Gas Directive only relates to the non-discriminatory treatment of alternative gases in relation to *the natural gas system*. What this means for the classification and treatment of Power-to-Gas and hydrogen storage will be discussed next.

4.2.2. *Classification of Power-to-Gas under EU Gas Legislation*

We already discussed the possibility that a Power-to-Gas installation could fall under the definition of 'energy storage' under the 2019 Electricity Directive.[43] Now, we will perform the same exercise from the perspective of the EU gas legislation. As the Gas Directive and Regulation have not received an update

41 Council of the European Union, 'Common Position adopted by the Council on 3 February 2003 with a view to the adoption of a Directive of the European Parliament and of the Council concerning common rules for the internal market in natural gas and repealing Directive 98/30/EC' [2003] OJ C 50E/36.

42 Although hydrogen can be produced from biomass through gasification, we focus in this contribution on hydrogen produced from electricity generated from wind and solar energy.

43 See section 4.1.

simultaneously with the Electricity Directive and Regulation, the concept of 'energy storage' under Article 2(59) of the Electricity Directive has not yet been mirrored in gas legislation.[44] We may have to wait for the new EU Gas Package for this to happen, which is expected for 2020 or 2021.[45] Today's EU gas legislation, therefore, still revolves around the activities of gas production, gas storage, and the transportation of gas. As our focus in this contribution is on Power-to-Gas for the storage of electricity, we reflect on the possibility that Power-to-Gas is classified as being gas production and/or gas storage.[46] As we will illustrate, the outcome of this exercise may be different depending on the setting in which the Power-to-Gas plant and hydrogen storage are operated.

First, let's consider a Power-to-Gas facility for electricity storage which is not directly connected to the natural gas network or indirectly via a hydrogen storage facility which is connected to this network. Instead, the electricity is withdrawn from the electricity grid or generation facility, converted to hydrogen, intermediately stored as hydrogen, re-converted to electricity, and finally fed back into the electricity system. As such a 'closed' power-to-hydrogen-to-power system is not at all interacting with the natural gas system, there seems no logic in applying the rules and classifications under the Gas Directive thereto. As we expressed earlier, the subject-matter of the 2009 Gas Directive is the functioning of the internal market in *natural gas*. Alternative gases such as biogas and hydrogen only fall under the scope of this Directive in so far they are 'injected into, and transported through, the natural gas system'.[47] Where this is not the case, the 2009 Gas Directive is irrelevant to the question how a Power-to-Gas facility and hydrogen storage facility in such a closed setting should be classified. The answer should, instead, solely be found in the legal regime for energy storage under the Electricity Directive.[48]

If we consider a Power-to-Gas and hydrogen storage facility in an 'open' setting, whereby the hydrogen is injected and transported through the natural gas system, our exercise becomes more complex.[49] Looking at the Power-to-Gas process, a first question is how to classify the decomposition of water

---

44 See section the Conclusion section on an outlook to the Gas Package 2020.

45 Maria Olczak and Andris Piebalgs, 'What to Expect from the 2020 Gas Package' (2019) 7(1) *Politics and Governance* 165–169.

46 We do not reflect on Power-to-Gas as an activity or asset in the transportation context, although a Power-to-Gas facility could in the future play a role in the crossover of electricity and gas infrastructures. See, in this context, the combined 2050 outlook by the Dutch gas TSO Gasunie and electricity TSO TenneT: Gasunie and Tennet, 'Infrastructure Outlook 2050' (2019), www.tennet.nl.

47 See Article 1(2) of the 2009 Gas Directive.

48 See section 4.1.

49 See section 5 on the access and gas quality conditions for hydrogen injection into the natural gas system.

molecules by electricity into oxygen and hydrogen, a gas. Is this gas production similar to biogas production through the anaerobic digestion of biomass or the extraction of gas from natural reservoirs? Notably, the Gas Directive does not contain a definition of 'gas production'. The Oxford English Dictionary defines 'production' as: 'the action of making or manufacturing from components or raw materials, or the process of being so manufactured'. Following this definition, it can be argued that the conversion of water molecules (raw material) through electrolysis (process) into hydrogen (product) is a production process. Also from a functional perspective, Power-to-Gas can be considered as a 'production' activity, as it adds 'new' molecules to the natural gas system.

Another question is whether we can classify a hydrogen storage facility which is connected to the gas network as a gas storage facility. A gas storage facility is defined in Article 2(9) of the 2009 Gas Directive as a 'facility used for the stocking of natural gas and owned and/or operated by a natural gas undertaking (...)'.[50] The view has been put forward that hydrogen storage facilities are indeed gas storage facilities as it is technically and safely possible to inject hydrogen into salt caverns and depleted oil- and gasfields.[51] The argument is then that since storage facilities are part of the *natural gas system*,[52] this triggers the non-discriminatory treatment clause for other gases such as hydrogen under Article 1(2) of the Gas Directive, so that hydrogen storage facilities fall under the same regime as facilities for the stocking of natural gas. In so far as the hydrogen storage facility is connected to the natural gas network, it can indeed be argued that the storage facility is part of the natural gas system. However, the view that a dedicated hydrogen storage facility falls under the definition of a gas storage facility under Article 2(9) of the 2009 Gas Directive could be seen as being at odds with the function of gas storage in the natural gas system, which is to provide flexibility to the system by withdrawing and injecting natural gas. Although it would be possible to inject hydrogen from the storage facility into the natural gas system, the other way around would not be possible. Furthermore, it could be argued that a hydrogen

50 For this see Ruven Fleming and Joshua Fershee 'The "Hydrogen Economy" in the US and the EU – Regulating Innovation to Combat Climate Change' in Donald Zillmann, Lee Godden, LeRoy Paddock, Martha M. Roggenkamp (eds.), *Innovation in Energy Law and Technology: Dynamic Solutions for Energy Transitions* (Oxford University Press, Oxford 2018), pp. 150–151.

51 Fleming, 'Regulating Power-to-Gas in the Energy Union' (2018) *Oil, Gas & Energy Law* 12. With regard to the technical aspects of hydrogen storage see: Maximilian Fichtner, 'Hydrogen Storage' in Micheael Ball and Martin Wietschel, *The Hydrogen Economy* (Cambridge University Press, Cambridge 2009), p. 318; Netherlands Enterprise Agency.

52 Fleming, 'Regulating Power-to-Gas in the Energy Union' (2018) *Oil, Gas & Energy Law* 12. The author points here to the definition of 'system' under Article 2(13) of the 2009 Gas Directive as meaning 'any transmission networks, distribution networks, LNG facilities and/or storage facilities (...)'.

storage facility fulfils a similar function to storages which are operated in the context of natural gas production and which do not fall under the definition of Article 2(9) of the 2009 Gas Directive.

As is clear from the analysis in this section, there are currently more questions than answers concerning the classification of Power-to-Gas and hydrogen storage. It would, therefore, be necessary for the European Commission to take account of these issues when drafting the new Gas Package.

4.3. UNBUNDLING AND ELECTRICITY STORAGE

After assessing electricity and gas legislation for applicability to Power-to-Gas and electricity storage via hydrogen, the next question is: Who is entitled to construct and operate such an energy storage facility? We hereby focus on the 'closed' Power-to-Gas system where the hydrogen is re-converted to electricity after storage. Given the current market constellation there are four possible answers to this question: electricity customers, electricity generating companies, DSOs/TSOs[53] and independent companies.

For the first option, electricity customers as owners, a differentiation needs to be made. The normal, passive customer of electricity will not be interested in this. For a start, only really big electricity customers would even be able to build and run their own Power-to-Gas storage facilities. However, even they would have no incentive to do so, since European electricity customers are already supplied with a steady stream of electricity, generated further up the energy chain.

However, with the recent emergence of active electricity customers (a new term used by the European Commission) or 'prosumers' (as they were hitherto called in the literature),[54] this picture can change. With Article 15, the Electricity Directive now features an article dedicated to active electricity customers. Article 15(5) Electricity Directive assumes that such customers can own energy storage facilities and provides a number of legal assurances to such customers. As discussed earlier, Power-to-Gas facilities that are used to produce hydrogen for electricity storage purposes fall within the definition of 'electricity storage'. As a result an active customer would be allowed to own an energy storage facility. It should be noted that Article 15(5) Electricity Directive only speaks of 'owning' an energy storage facility, not operating it. However, as becomes clear from the four assurances provided in Article 15(5)(a)–(d) Electricity Directive, the legislator does assume that such active customers

53 The function of TSOs and DSOs is explained in Hans Vedder et al., 'EU Energy Law' in Martha M. Roggenkamp et al. (eds.), *Energy Law in Europe*, 3rd edition (2016) paragraph 4.10 (hereinafter: Vedder et al.).

54 Sharon B. Jacobs, 'The Energy Prosumer' (2017) 43(3) *Ecology Law Quarterly* 519–580.

would also often operate the storage facilities. In any case, while this might become important in the future, there are no current examples of that in the EU.

The second option would be for electricity generating companies to own and operate Power-to-Gas facilities that work with the purpose of storing electricity. Indeed, there is a real interest by renewable energy generation companies in Power-to-Gas.[55] Their aim is to generate a steady stream of electricity before it is fed into the system.[56] The aim for the future could be to receive a reward from the transmission system operator for countering the intermittent feed-in pattern of renewable energy and helping him with balancing the system.

Running an energy storage facility as an energy producer, however, can conflict with rules on the liberalization of the European energy market. Under the Gas Directive, for example, producers are not allowed to run a gas storage facility.[57] A prohibition for producers/generators to run storage facilities, similar to the one in the Gas Directive, does not feature in the Electricity Directive. In the absence of an explicit prohibition it has to be assumed that electricity generators could run those facilities. The key-point here is the categorization of hydrogen storage for electricity generation purposes. Is it storage of gas (then the Gas Directive applies and its current ambiguities as discussed above) or storage of electricity in the form of gas (which is possible under the Electricity Directive)? The European legislator should consider this interrelation between the two Directives and align them.

The third option would be TSOs and/or DSOs that could also develop an interest in running hydrogen storage facilities. In principle it could be conceivable that both kinds of system operators want to use Power-to-Gas facilities as electricity storage options to solve congestion and as an alternative to grid expansion. These, however, could only be electricity TSOs/DSOs and not gas TSOs/DSOs for the purpose of the Electricity Directive, which is dealing with electrical energy. As a starting point it has to be understood that energy storage was designed under European energy market rules as a competitive activity, which TSOs/DSOs should stay away from.[58] From the point of view of the European Commission, flexibility and ancillary services by energy storage and other technologies are primarily a market activity.[59] Usually the TSO has

55 A good example for Power-to-Gas experiments is the windturbine and electricity producer Enercon, see: Enercon Storage Technology, 'First pilot projects for energy storage realised' (2015) Issue 3 *Windblatt* 10–15, http://www.enercon.de/fileadmin/Redakteur/Medien-Portal/windblatt/pdf/en/WB_032015_GB_150dpi.pdf.

56 Ibid.

57 Only natural gas undertakings are, according to Article 2(9) Gas Directive.

58 European Commission Directorate General Energy, 'Energy Storage – Proposed policy Principles and Definitions' (June 2016), https://ec.europa.eu/energy/sites/ener/files/documents/Proposed%20definition%20and%20principles%20for%20energy%20storage.pdf.

59 European Commission Directorate General Energy, 'Energy Storage – Proposed policy Principles and Definitions' (June 2016), https://ec.europa.eu/energy/sites/ener/files/documents/Proposed%20definition%20and%20principles%20for%20energy%20storage.pdf.

contractual relationships with commercial market parties to purchase the flexibility services it needs.[60] The role of DSOs is so far limited in this context.

In line with this general rule, Articles 36(1) (dealing with DSOs) and 54(1) (dealing with TSOs) of the Electricity Directive state that neither TSOs nor DSOs shall own, develop, manage or operate energy storage facilities. There are, however, two exceptions to that rule. The Member States can allow TSOs and DSOs to engage in electricity storage activities via the Power-to-Gas technology if (alternatively)

1. the storage facility is a fully integrated network component and the regulatory authority has granted its approval or
2. the following three conditions are met cumulatively:
    (a) other parties, following an open, transparent and non-discriminatory tendering procedure that is subject to review and approval by the regulatory authority, have not been awarded a right to own, develop, manage or operate such facilities, or could not deliver those services at a reasonable cost and in a timely manner;
    (b) such facilities are necessary for the distribution system operators to fulfil their obligations under this Directive for the efficient, reliable and secure operation of the distribution system and the facilities are not used to buy or sell electricity in the electricity markets; and
    (c) the regulatory authority has assessed the necessity of such a derogation and has carried out an assessment of the tendering procedure, including the conditions of the tendering procedure, and has granted its approval.[61]

At least every five years, the relevant regulatory authority of the Member State must hold a public consultation on the existing energy storage facilities in order to assess the potential availability and interest of other parties in investing in such facilities.[62] If these consultations indicate that third parties are able to own, develop, operate or manage such facilities in a cost-effective manner, the regulatory authority shall ensure that the TSOs or DSOs' activities in this regard are phased out within 18 months.[63] This entire procedure is, thus, in the hands of Member States and includes a number of decisions that will entail leeway for discretion for the regulatory authority in charge. Just think about the interpretation of 'cost-effective manner'. Which costs are included/excluded?

---

60 Dimitrios Zafirakis, Konstantinos Chalvatzis, Giovanni Baiocchi, Georgios Daskalakis, 'The Value of Arbitrage for Energy Storage: Evidence from European Electricity Markets' (2016) 184 *Applied Energy* 971–986.

61 Articles 36(2) and [similarly worded] 54(2) Electricity Directive.

62 Articles 36(3) and [similarly worded] 54(4) Electricity Directive.

63 Ibid.

How is effectivity measured, etc.? All of this will be subject to the interpretation of regulatory authorities of Member States.

And there are even more ambiguous terms. Articles 36(4) and 54(5) Electricity Directive allow for derogations from the necessity to have consultations every five years and the 18-month period for phasing out of energy storage ownership/operation by TSOs and DSOs. These requirements shall not apply to fully integrated network components or for the usual depreciation period of new battery storage facilities with a final investment decision until 4 July 2019, provided that four further conditions are fulfilled.[64]

This wording provides two alternatives: either we are talking about a 'fully integrated network component' or a 'new battery storage facilities with a final investment decision until 4 July 2019'. These are alternatives, not cumulative pre-requisites. A Power-to-Gas plant is not a battery storage facility, so the second alternative does not apply. However, the first option could apply if the Power-to-Gas facilities are 'fully integrated network components'. According to Article 2(51) Electricity Directive,

> 'fully integrated network components' means network components that are integrated in the transmission or distribution system, including storage facilities, and that are used for the sole purpose of ensuring a secure and reliable operation of the transmission or distribution system, and not for balancing or congestion management.

As mentioned earlier, Power-to-Gas for electricity storage might be used as a congestion management tool in certain constellations. So, this section would only apply to those facilities not used for congestion management.

Moreover, the question arises what exactly demarcates a *fully* integrated from a *partly* integrated network component. This wording has been introduced into the Directive at the wish of the European Council (as opposed to the proposal of the European Parliament to use the term 'an integral part of the transmission system' instead).[65]

Finally, there is the fourth possibility that independent parties are running Power-to-Gas plants and hydrogen storage facilities with the aim of re-conversion of electricity. Under the current recast Electricity Directive there is nothing to prohibit such independent parties from engaging in storage activities and it would also fall in line with the overall rationale of energy market liberalization in Europe to have different activities assigned to independent parties.

---

64 Articles 36(4) and [similarly worded] 54(5) Electricity Directive.

65 See for a comparison of the proposals by the EU institutions: Council of the European Union, 'Proposal for a Directive of the European Parliament and of the Council on common rules for the internal market in electricity (recast)', 2016/0380(COD), 7506/4/18 REV 4.

5. ENERGY STORAGE THROUGH HYDROGEN ADMIXING TO THE NATURAL GAS GRID

The European natural gas system performs a double role in the energy system: 1) it is used for the transportation of large volumes of energy over long distances, and 2) it stores large amounts of energy as the gas travels from A to B. In contrast to the electricity system for which input and output has to be continuously balanced, the gas system has a buffer which can be used for so-called 'linepack storage'.[66] Similarly, the hydrogen produced through Power-to-Gas can be stored in the natural gas system by admixing to the natural gas in the European gas system.[67] In this section, we therefore focus on the gas system access regime relevant for the admixing of hydrogen to natural gas.

5.1. TECHNICAL AND SAFETY ISSUES OF ADMIXING HYDROGEN

It was concluded under section 4.2 that hydrogen is only entitled to the same treatment as natural gas under the 2009 Gas Directive when it can 'technically and safely be injected into, and transported through, the natural gas system'.[68] The question is then whether this is the case.[69]

Concerns related to hydrogen injection exist because of the different physical properties of hydrogen (H_2) compared to those of methane (CH_4), which is the main component of natural gas.[70] First, due to what is known as 'hydrogen embrittlement', hydrogen volumes of more than 2 per cent may result in crack propagation in steel, which may affect the durability and integrity of transmission and distribution pipelines and compressed natural gas steel tanks. Second, higher hydrogen volumes may have a negative effect on the efficiency and emissions of end-use appliances. Both industrial and household appliances are adjusted to operate on a particular bandwidth of gas quality parameters,

---

66 Article 1(15) of the 2009 Gas Directive defines 'linepack' as: 'the storage of gas by compression in gas transmission and distribution systems, but not including facilities reserved for transmission system operators carrying out their functions'.

67 Dries Haeseldonckx en William D'haeseleer, 'The use of the natural-gas pipeline infrastructure for hydrogen transport in a changing market structure' (2007) 32(10/11) *International Journal of Hydrogen Energy* 1381–1386.

68 See the discussion on Article 1(2) 2009 Gas Directive under section 4.2.

69 See on this issue: Rafaella Gerboni, 'Introduction to Hydrogen Transportation' in Ram B. Gupta, Angelo Basile and T. Nejat Veziroğlu, *Compendium of Hydrogen Energy Volume 2: Hydrogen Storage, Distribution and Infrastructure* (Woodhead Publishing Series in Energy, Cambridge 2016) 283–299.

70 Klaus Altfeld and Dave Pinchbeck, 'Admissible Hydrogen Concentrations in Natural Gas Systems', Gas for energy No. 3 (2013), *GERG study*, 36–47.

which historically differ from Member State to Member State. Especially gas turbines such as those found in gas-fired power plants are highly sensitive to variations in the gas quality and higher hydrogen volumes. Third, although on an energy-to-weight ratio, hydrogen contains more energy than methane (a kilogram (Kg) of hydrogen contains 2.4 times more energy than methane), hydrogen has the lowest volumetric energy density of all fuels. As a result, admixing hydrogen to the natural gas flow will lower the energy content of the gas mixture and have a downward effect on the Wobbe Index thereof.[71] As calorific value is heat, and heat is economic value, changes in the hydrogen content in natural gas networks may also require a commercial revaluation of the gas supplied to consumers. From the above it is clear that the introduction of hydrogen into the natural gas system presents potential technical and safety challenges. The next question is. then: who decides what levels of hydrogen in the natural gas system are acceptable?

5.2. SAFETY AND TECHNICAL CONDITIONS FOR INJECTION AND TRANSPORTATION OF HYDROGEN

Rules on the technically and safe injection of gas into the natural gas system can relate to either 'access' or 'connection' to the system.[72] On the difference between these two terms the European Court of Justice in the *Sabatauskas* case ruled that 'access to the system includes the right to use [electricity] systems and that connection corresponds to physical connection to the system'.[73] A crucial technical safety criteria, which is decisive as to whether or not access to, and thus the use of, the natural gas network is granted, is the issue of gas quality.

A gas quality standard prescribes the maximum and minimum acceptable limits of individual parameters and components of a gas.[74] Historically, national gas quality standards have been of a heterogeneous nature, as the parameters defined therein were based on the chemical composition of locally produced or

---

71 See, on the impact of hydrogen admixing to natural gas on the caloric value thereof: Zachariah Wolff, Tineke Egyedi and Kas Hemmes, 'From natural gas to hydrogen via the Wobbe index: The role of standardized gateways in sustainable infrastructure transitions' (2007) 32(9) *International Journal of Hydrogen Energy* 1235–1245.

72 Hannah Kruimer, *The non-discrimination obligation of energy network operators* (Intersentia, Cambridge 2013) 142–143.

73 European Court of Justice, C-239/07 *Julius Sabatauskas and Others* [2008] ECR II-7253, paragraphs 41–42. With regard to the physical connection, Article 8 of the 2009 Gas Directive determines that Member States need to ensure that objective and non-discriminatory technical rules are defined for the connection to the system of liquefied natural gas facilities, storage facilities, and networks.

74 Daisy Tempelman, 'Harmonising Gas Quality: Obstacles and Challenges in an Internal Market' in Martha Roggenkamp and Henrik Bjornebye (eds.), *European Energy Law Report X* (Intersentia, Cambridge 2014) 88–89.

supplied natural gas. As the 2009 Gas Directive does not lay out the minimum and/or maximum values for the various chemical components present in natural gas, there was no regulatory pressure on Member States to bring their gas quality specifications in conformity with a European norm.[75] This lack of a EU approach to gas quality changed when a collection of EU Commissioners collectively came to the conclusion that '[t]he interoperability of gas systems requires greater harmonization including co-ordination of the gas quality specifications at the EU entry points and within the EU to facilitate the development of a liberalized and competitive European gas market.'[76]

The European Commission acted by issuing two mandates directed to the European Committee for standardization (CEN). The first mandate which was issued in 2007, mandate M/400, requests the CEN to draw up a European standard that defines the gas quality characteristics, parameters and their limits, for gases classified as group H that are to be transmitted, injected into and withdrawn from storages, distributed and utilized.[77] As legal justification for issuing such a mandate, the Commission pointed to Article 6 of the 2003 Gas Directive (now Article 8 of the 2009 Gas Directive), which requires Member States to ensure that technical rules are defined which ensure the interoperability of transmission, distribution, LNG, and storage systems. As CEN standards are voluntary by nature, the Commission intended to elevate the status of the standard through a binding reference thereto in the Network Code on interoperability and data exchange rules (INT NC).[78]

Notably, hydrogen was explicitly excluded from the scope of the work of CEN under mandate M/400 as, according to the European Commission: 'current gas flows do not contain hydrogen and it is not an issue yet in the gas market, i.e. production, transport or appliance-use'. For this reason, the eventually adopted CEN standard EN 16726:2015 contains an Annex of a merely informative nature covering the admissible concentration of hydrogen in natural gas systems.[79] Also on the adoption of another parameter which is of influence

---

75 See, however, Tempelman, 'Harmonising Gas Quality', 105, on the effort by the 'European Association for the Streamlining of Energy Exchange – gas (EASEE-gas)' to adopt a common business practice on gas quality.

76 First Report of the High Level Group on Competitiveness, Energy and the Environment, Contributing to an integrated approach on competitiveness, energy and environment policies, 2 June 2006, http://ec.europa.eu/enterprise/environment/hlg/doc_06/first_report_02_06_06.pdf.

77 H-gases are those gases which at 15° Celsius and 1013,25 mbar have a Gross Wobbe Index between 45.7 and 54.7 MJ/m^3.

78 A 'standard' is defined under Article 2(1) of the Regulation on European Standardization (Regulation (EU) No 1025/2012) as: 'a technical specification, adopted by a recognized standardization body, for repeated or continuous application, *with which compliance is not compulsory* (...)' (emphasis added).

79 European Committee for Standardization, 'Gas Infrastructure – Quality of Gas – Group H' (2015), EN 16726:2015, available in CEN shop.

on how much hydrogen can be added to natural gas, the Wobbe Index, the representatives of the Member States in the CEN technical commission failed to reach consensus. A second mandate, M/475, presented CEN with the task to adopt a standard for the use of biomethane as a transport fuel and for injection into natural gas pipelines. As the aim of the mandate is the promotion of biomass-based gases, the Commission refers *inter alia* to Article 16 of the 2009 Renewable Energy Directive as its legal foundation. Again, the determination of a common maximum hydrogen limit was considered to be premature.[80] The adopted CEN standard EN 16723-1 only contains a reference to the informative Annex E to CEN standard EN 16726:2015.

Informative Annex E, titled 'Hydrogen – Admissible Concentrations in natural gas systems', refers to a study by the European Gas Research Group which found that the admixing of hydrogen up to 10 per cent by volume of hydrogen to natural gas is an option for certain sections of the natural gas system.[81] When determining the specific allowed percentage of hydrogen for a certain region, Member States are advised to take into account the effect of hydrogen on underground porous rock storage, steel tanks in CNG vehicles, gas turbines, and gas engines.

In conclusion, in absence of a common and binding norm on a hydrogen limit at the EU level, individual Member State regulation remains determinative of what is considered to be safe and technically possible.

5.3. DETERMINATION OF NATIONAL HYDROGEN LIMITS

In absence of a standard for hydrogen levels in natural gas at the EU level, Member States have discretion to set the hydrogen limit at the national level, including for gas interconnection points. This explains why, for example. The maximum level of hydrogen which is allowed in the natural gas stream in the Netherlands is set at 0.02 per cent mol, while in Germany this is 10 per cent mol.[82] This may result in hydrogen enriched natural gas from one Member State being rejected by a neighbouring State. In this section we will review what types of actions are open to those entities whose gas is rejected due to a difference in allowed hydrogen contents between two countries.

80 Jacques Dubost, 'Injection/Admixture of H2 to the NG system: compatibility, interoperability and safety', presentation during workshop of the Joint Research Center of the European Commission: *Putting Science into Standards: Power-to-Hydrogen and HCNG*, 22 October 2018, https://ec.europa.eu/jrc/sites/jrcsh/files/hcng-2014-s2-dubost.pdf.

81 For the report to which Annex E refers, see: Klaus Altfeld and Dave Pinchbeck, 'Admissible hydrogen concentrations in natural gas systems' (2013), Gas for Energy 03/2013.

82 Francesco Dolci and others, 'Incentives and legal barriers for power-to-hydrogen pathways: An international snapshot' (2019) 44(23) *International Journal of Hydrogen Energy* 11394–11401.

A first mechanism for resolving trade barriers arising from different quality standards between two adjacent TSOs of different countries is the Network Code on interoperability and data exchange rules (INT NC) which has been adopted as a Commission Regulation.[83] The Network Code prescribes the terms and conditions which adjacent transmission system operators need to cover in an interconnection agreement in respect of an interconnection point.[84] Although the list of issues which need to be addressed includes 'measurement principles for gas quantities and quality', the Code emphasizes that its content is without prejudice to the competence of Member States to set gas quality standards and the then still ongoing work under mandate M/400.[85] In this same spirit, Article 15, dealing with cross-border trade restrictions due to gas quality differences, points to the national system operators for finding a solution to such a restriction by way of, for example, swapping and co-mingling. Similarly, when the adjacent system operators fail to find a practical solution for overcoming the restriction caused by gas quality it is for the *national* regulatory authorities to demand action.[86] This demand requires the involved system operators to cooperate and develop a cost–benefit analysis of technically feasible options, without changing the gas quality specifications, which may include flow commitments and gas treatment. The duration of these procedures may, however, not provide much relief to the shipper of a natural gas-hydrogen blend in the short-term.

In conclusion to this section, in absence of an EU norm prescribing what levels of hydrogen Member States need to accept in their natural gas flows, these States maintain a high degree of discretion to set national limits. The differences in the allowed hydrogen levels in the natural gas system between countries could form an important barrier for the storage of hydrogen from renewable sources in the European gas system.

5.4. ACCESS TO THE SYSTEM FOR HYDROGEN AS RENEWABLE GAS

As far as access conditions to the gas system for 'green' or 'renewable' hydrogen is concerned, the 2018 successor of the 2009 Renewable Energy Directive (RED), known as REDII establishes under Article 20(2) that Member States need to require TSOs as well as DSOs to publish technical rules for network connection,

83 Commission Regulation (EU) 2015/703 of 20 April 2015 establishing a network code on interoperability and data exchange rules, OJ L 113/12 (hereafter 'INT NC').
84 Article 3 INT NC.
85 Recital 4 and 5 INT NC.
86 Article 15(2) INT NC.

including on gas quality, odorization and pressure requirements. However, the TSOs and DSOs are regulated by the Member States. The ball would, hence, be played back to the Member States. As a result, the REDII does very little for the establishment of an EU-wide standard for access conditions of green hydrogen to the gas system.

6. CONCLUSION

This chapter sketched the different ways in which electricity storage via Power-to-Gas can play a role in the EU energy law framework. But this is just one part of the picture. The other is the fact that the industry is facing several technical challenges such as advancing the availability of large-scale Power-to-Gas facilities and suitable hydrogen storages. These technical developments need to be accompanied with legal frameworks/innovations for successful implementation. At the end of the day the use of Power-to-Gas as an electricity storage option as part of a 'hydrogen economy' does not only depend on technical innovation, but also on innovative adaptions in law.

The core energy law challenges that need to be overcome alongside the technical challenges are mainly concerned with the definitions of storage and the feeding of hydrogen into the gas system. A key outcome of this contribution is the uncertainty that currently exists with regard to the applicability of natural gas legislation to hydrogen. Although the Gas Directive does not mention the term 'hydrogen' once, the wording of Article 1(2) of this Directive is sufficiently open and ambiguous to allow different views on its scope.

If Power-to-Gas plants shall be operated with the aim to store electricity, there is the issue of overlap, namely that both the Gas- and the Electricity Directives govern the storage of hydrogen created by Power-to-Gas. This can be problematic if the rules are different from each other, for instance with regard to who is allowed to operate an electricity and/or gas storage facility. By reconciling and aligning provisions of the Gas Directive and the proposed recast Electricity Directive, the EU could work towards an increased interlinkage between gas and electricity legislation.

It will be crucial to watch closely whether legislators can follow through in creating legal frameworks for cross-sectoral technologies like Power-to-Gas. The ever-increasing technical integration of different energy sources and new storage and conversion technologies is certainly creating pressure in that direction. The 'Clean Energy for All Europeans' package might be a good first step, but without a similar renovation of EU gas legislation, we're only halfway through the story.

PART II

HYDROPOWER CONCESSIONS IN THE EU

A Need for Liberalisation or Privatisation?

CHAPTER VI

EU LAW AND NORWEGIAN HYDROPOWER LEGISLATION

A Challenging Interface

Knut F. KROEPELIEN

1. INTRODUCTION

Norway is not a member of the European Union (EU), but fully integrated in the EU internal market through the rights and obligations included in the Agreement on the European Economic Area (EEA Agreement).[1] The Agreement has general provisions on free movement of goods, services, workers and capital, on the right of establishment as well as competition, non-discrimination and state aid. The Agreement covers all sectors of the economy except agriculture and fisheries.[2] The power sector, including hydropower, is included. In the annexes to the main text of the EEA Agreement, in particular in Annex IV, legislation relevant for the energy sector is included, multilaterally and dynamically following EU legislative initiatives. This is unlike the Swiss bilateral and static model for market integration based on ad hoc agreements. About 70 legal acts in the energy field have so far been included in the annexes to the EEA Agreement, including in particular the electricity market directive[3] and the regulation on cross-border trade in electricity.[4]

The EEA Agreement is based on a so-called 'two-pillar' structure whereby EU institutions and processes are 'mirrored' to ensure formal sovereignty for Iceland, Liechtenstein and Norway. This means that it is not the European Commission that controls implementation of the EEA Agreement, but the EFTA Surveillance Authority (ESA). The Court of Justice of the European

1 Agreement on the European Economic Area, OJ L1, 3.1.1994, p 3, as amended.

2 See further: 'Outside and Inside – Norway's agreements with the European Union', Official Norwegian Reports NOU 2012:2, Chapter 1; Meld. St. 5 (2012–2013) 'The EEA Agreement and Norway's other agreements with the EU'. Report to the Storting (White Paper).

3 Annex IV to the EEA Agreement, Point 22.

4 Annex IV to the EEA Agreement, Point 20.

Union (CJEU) does not hear cases regarding the EEA agreement, but instead the EFTA court.

Originally, it was assumed that the energy sector, and in particular the hydropower sector with its public ownership based on concessions and non-moveable assets, would not be much affected by the EEA Agreement.[5] As this chapter will demonstrate, this has been proven wrong.

Initially, EU energy policy consisted largely in applying competition policy to the energy sector. This was also the starting point when the EEA Agreement was negotiated in the early 1990s. At that stage, there were nine EC regulations and directives on energy, which were incorporated into the EEA Agreement. The only mention of energy in the Agreement itself is in Article 24, in Part II on the free movement of goods.

In recent years, the scope of the legislation for the EU internal energy market has been widened extensively. It has also been made more detailed, and a supranational legal framework with corresponding institutional arrangements has developed. The legislation influences Norway and its hydropower producers directly through the EEA Agreement. Further, it has a more indirect influence through its effects on the European energy market where electricity is traded physically and financially.

This chapter will try to examine two main areas of influence of EU law through the EEA Agreement. First, the national regulation of hydropower through concessions based on public ownership of hydropower (Section 3) and, second, administrative procedures to strike a balance between renewable hydropower production and aquatic biodiversity (Section 4). Before this, an overview of the key national sector regulation of hydropower with a focus on the concession system will be given as a starting point (Section 2).

This chapter will only cover the specific issue of the interface between Norwegian hydropower concessions and EU Law, and will not address other aspects of hydropower production.[6]

Finally, as concerns terminology, the word 'concession', has been chosen, not 'licence', for administrative decisions that set conditions for hydropower production, since this is the terminology most used in legal sources in the area. Further, to help the reader, the legal references to the national acts of 1917 on waterfall rights and regulation of waterways as amended in 2018 have been used, not the references used at the time of the court cases and administrative appeals. The phrase 'reverting property right' has been preferred to 'repatriation'

5 See n. 2 above, NOU 2012:2 p 546.

6 Other issues of relevance but not covered by this chapter include the application of state aid law and competition law, the EU energy market legislation in the electricity market directive and regulation, the EU infrastructure and Connecting Europe Facility, the EU renewables directive, the EU emissions trading scheme ETS, the EU state Aid rules, the EU Energy Union and governance regulation and the energy efficiency regulation.

for the particular Norwegian concept of '*hjemfall*', whereby a property right returns to the state after a set time. A good English term does not really exist as far as this author is aware. Finally, the word 'ground rent' has been used for the Norwegian word '*grunnrente*', which refers to the extraordinary profit made by certain economic activities that exploit limited natural resources.

2. OVERVIEW OF NORWEGIAN HYDROPOWER LEGISLATION

2.1. THE NORWEGIAN HYDROPOWER SYSTEM

The Norwegian power sector is quite unique in a European context. Renewable and flexible hydropower covers around 95 per cent of the electricity production.[7] Norway is in most years a net exporter of electricity. This leads to Norway having Europe's highest share of renewable energy in its gross final energy consumption with around 70 per cent, together with Iceland.[8] As a consequence, it enjoys a privileged situation with regard to climate mitigation in the power sector and energy security. Another consequence is that the resource base for electricity production depends on the precipitation in a given year. This is a significant difference from the rest of Europe where security of supply is mainly secured through thermal power plants, with fuels available in the global energy markets.

Another special feature of the Norwegian hydropower system is its high storage capacity.[9] Norway has half of Europe's reservoir storage capacity, and more than 75 per cent of Norwegian production capacity is flexible. Production can be rapidly increased and decreased as needed, at low cost. This is important because there must be a balance between production and consumption at all times in the physical power system to stabilise frequency and voltage. The growing share of intermittent production technologies, such as wind and solar power, makes it even more vital that there is another source of CO_2-free flexibility available in the rest of the system.

Renewable power plants are generally sited where there is access to resources. Hydropower installations are even more constrained in that respect.

7 Hydropower covered 95.8 per cent of electricity production in 2017 (source: Statistics Norway, SSB). Wind power, which represented 1.9 per cent of electricity production for the same year is on the increase (+ 34.9 per cent compared to 2016) and will soon change this picture.

8 European Environment Agency, based on European Commission, 'Indicative trajectories for the share of energy from renewable sources in gross final consumption of energy, from national renewable energy action plans (NREAPs)', November 2018.

9 Norway has more than 1000 hydropower storage reservoirs with a total capacity of more than 86.5 TWh. The 30 largest reservoirs provide about half the storage capacity. Total reservoir capacity corresponds to 70 per cent of annual Norwegian electricity consumption (Energy Facts, 2019).

Production capacity is therefore unequally distributed between different regions of Norway. Meanwhile, it has been a constant goal of Norwegian authorities to have a well-developed power grid for transmitting electricity to consumers in all parts of the country.

Deregulated since 1991, the Norwegian power system is closely integrated with the other Nordic systems, both in physical terms and through market integration. In turn, the Nordic market is integrated with the rest of Europe through cross-border interconnectors to the Netherlands, Germany, the Baltic states, Poland and Russia. Integration with other countries' power systems, the well-developed power grid and the characteristics of hydropower production make Norway's power supply system very flexible, reducing vulnerability to fluctuations in production between seasons and years.

Under Norwegian law, river systems have from the very beginning been subject to private ownership.[10] This principle is now laid down in the first paragraph of section 13 of Act No 82 of 24 November 2000 Relating to River Systems and Groundwater (Act on water resources)[11] which provides that: 'A river system belongs to the owner of the land it covers, unless otherwise dictated by special legal status.' The private ownership rights are, however, significantly limited by administrative law which *inter alia* subjects the exploitation and acquisition of waterfalls to concession requirements.[12]

The hydropower sector has therefore, since the beginnings and the passing of the Industrial Concession Act in 1917, been subject to extensive regulation to ensure public control and predominance of public ownership.[13] Hydropower is still regarded wholly or partly as a public good where the 'ground rent' or the extraordinary value of exploitation of a natural resource should belong to the society.

A key regulatory measure has been the adoption of a concession regime whereby the state, regional authorities and municipalities have had special rights. More recently, the concession regime has also covered common, environmental aspects to ensure a balance between the need for clean power production and preservation of the aquatic biodiversity of the waterways, typically wild trout and salmon.

The following figure provides an overview of the legal framework application to the different phases of hydropower production in Norway.

---

[10] T. Falkanger and K. Haagensen (eds.), *Norsk vassdrags- og Energirett*, Universitetsforlaget, Oslo 2002, p 31 et seq.

[11] In Norwegian: Lov 24. november 2000 nr. 82 om vassdrag og grunnvann (vannressursloven).

[12] Case E-02/06, *EFTA Surveillance Authority v The Kingdom of Norway* (Watercourses, *Hjemfall*), delivered on 26 June 2007, [2007] EFTA Court Reports 167, para 16; Falkanger and Haagensen (eds.), *Norsk vassdragsrett*, Tano, Oslo 1988, p 29 et seq.

[13] F. Arnesen, U. Hammer, P.H. Høisveen, K. Kaasen and D. Nygaard, 'Energy Law in Norway' in M. Roggenkamp, C. Redgwell, A. Rønne and I. del Guayo (eds.), *Energy Law in Europe* (3rd ed.), Oxford 2016, para 11.25.

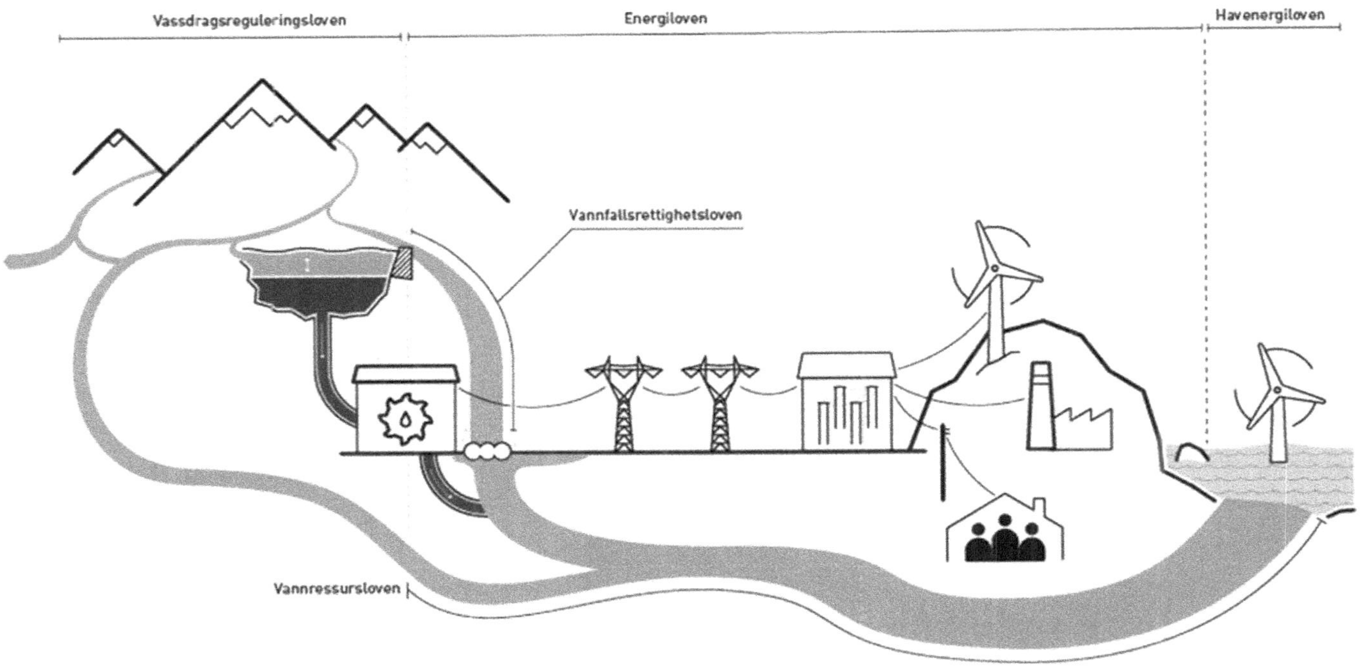

Figure 1. Hydropower production in Norway
Source: Ministry of Petroleum and Energy, Energy Facts.[14]

14 See Energy Facts website at https://energifaktanorge.no/en/.

2.2. ACT ON RIGHTS TO WATERFALLS

The key piece of legislation regarding Norwegian hydropower is the revised Act on rights to waterfalls (Waterfall Rights Act, *vannfallrettighetsloven*) from 1917, as amended.[15] The Act, in sections 2 and 5, establishes a system whereby public concessions are needed to acquire waterfalls and such concessions, with some exemptions, can only be acquired by public institutions. The Act contains provisions on revision of concessions, conditions, procedures and compliance rules. Under the current rules, concessions may only be issued to public bodies, i.e. state-owned enterprises, municipalities and regional authorities, and to companies where such bodies hold at least two-thirds of the capital and the votes in the company. This means that private actors may own up to one-third of a publicly-owned company that holds a concession, ensuring that no minority stakeholders can exercise negative control under company law. Concessions issued under the Act include conditions on concession fees and mandatory sales of power to the municipalities where waterfalls are situated (so-called *konsesjonskraft*). Historically, this approach was more or less stable from 1917 to 1992 when the interface with the right of establishment and free movement of goods and capital under the EEA agreement became an issue.[16] It culminated in the Watercourse judgment of the EFTA court of 26 June 2007[17] and amendments of the Act. This case and the subsequent law amendments are further analysed in Section 3 below.

2.3. ACT ON REGULATION OF WATERCOURSES

The Act on regulation of Watercourses from 1917 (*vassdragsreguleringsloven*) was last amended in 2017, with amendments that entered into force on 1 January 2018. Pursuant to the Act, a concession is required in order to regulate the annual variations in a waterway, typically through dams, controlling the flow in a river or transfer water between river systems for use in power generation above a certain threshold. Several provisions of the Act also apply to run-of-river hydropower plants that generate more than 40 GWh per year. Concessions set out the highest and lowest permitted water levels in reservoirs and may also require the establishment of a business development fund in the municipality where a development takes place. Concessions also include rules for reservoir

15 The last amendments, including the change of name of the act entered into force on 1 January 2018.

16 Ot.prp. nr. 61 (2007–2008) om lov om endringer i lov 14. desember 1917 nr. 16 om erverv av vannfall, bergverk og annen fast eiendom m.v (industrikonsesjonsloven) og i lov 14. desember 1917 nr. 17 om vasdragsreguleringer (vassdragsreguleringsloven), p 13 et seq.

17 See n. 12 above.

management, which may include provisions on the minimum permitted rate of flow and on the volumes of water that may be released at different times of year. In addition, concessions may include conditions relating to concession fees and mandatory sales of power.

The Act contains provisions on the balance between energy exploitation and the environment, the conditions for a concession, measures to reduce negative impacts and the revision of concessions, the relevant procedures as well as sector-specific rules on expropriation of private property. Importantly, the Act establishes a system of revision of concessions every 30 years, including the conditions with regard to reduction of negative environmental impacts. This point will be further analysed in Section 4 as this has been a key issue in several cases before the ESA.

2.4. ACT ON WATER RESOURCES

The Water Resources Act of 2000 (*Lov om vassdrag og grunnvann, vannressursloven*) establishes a system of concessions for all measures in waterways that are above a de minimis threshold with no negative consequences for public interests.[18] Measures regarding hydropower production that are not covered by the Act on regulation of watercourses from 1917 are thus covered by this Act. Importantly, the Water Resources Act also contains provisions on the balance between environment and renewable production and the amendment of concessions through changes in concessions (Section 28 (*omgjøring*)) and new consideration of old regulations without concessions (Section 66 (*innkalling*)).

2.5. ACT ON ENERGY

The Energy Act of 1990 regulates the energy system and the energy market in Norway (*Lov om produksjon, omforming, overføring, omsetning, fordeling og bruk av energi m.m.*, so-called *Energiloven*). It is the Act that covers most issues concerning the rights and obligations of market participants, including those that are selling and buying renewable power based on hydropower production. This Act is of minor relevance for this chapter although it is of course the key piece of legislation when implementing the EU acquis concerning the internal energy market.

The purpose of the 1990 Energy Act is to ensure that energy is generated, converted, transmitted, traded, distributed and used rationally and in the best

18 Section 8 and chapter 3, Water Resources Act.

interests of society. This includes taking into consideration any public and private interests that are affected. The Act provides a legal framework for competition in electricity generation and trading. The development and operation of the grid is a natural monopoly, and the Act provides the legal basis for regulating the grid companies. The Energy Act also regulates marketplaces for trade in electrical energy, cross-border interconnectors, district heating facilities, responsibility for system operation, electricity supply quality, energy planning and contingency planning for power supplies.

Developers must apply for concessions under the Energy Act to construct wind farms and high-voltage power lines. Distribution grid companies can obtain general local area concessions. This means that they do not need to apply for a concession for each separate installation within an area.

2.6. OTHER RELEVANT LEGISLATION

Norwegian hydropower is covered by the Act on electricity certificates (*Lov om elsertifikater*) adopted on 24 June 2011. The Act aims to promote production of electricity from renewable energy sources. It is an implementing measure to reach the national targets agreed under the EEA Agreement and based on the fulfilment of EU targets for renewable energy in gross final consumption of energy by 2020 in Directive 2009/28/EC. Owners of additional Norwegian hydropower production in the same way as other producers of new renewable energy like wind, bio or solar power have a right to receive certificates according to the Act, while sellers of power who cannot comply with their quota obligation can purchase certificates. Therefore, the Act establishes a national market for electricity certificates, which has been linked to the Swedish electricity certificates market since 1 January 2012, and subject to a bilateral agreement between the two countries. The electricity certificate market is a constructed market in the sense that the demand for certificates arises from a statutory obligation to purchase them. Sales of electricity certificates give power producers a supplementary income in addition to that derived from sales of electricity.[19]

Hydropower producers are also covered by general public legislation in Norway including the Planning and Building Act (*plan- og bygningsloven*)[20] and the Act on public administration (*forvaltningsloven*)[21] with its general provisions on amendments of public decisions in section 35.

19 For a description of the electricity certificates scheme in Norway, see: O. Boge, 'The Norwegian-Swedish Electricity Certificates Market' in M.M. Roggenkamp and H. Bjørnebye (eds), *European Energy Law Report X*, Intersentia, Cambridge, Antwerp/Portland 2014, Chapter IX.

20 Lov om planlegging og byggesaksbehandling (plan- og bygningsloven).

21 Lov om behandlingsmåten i forvaltningssaker (forvaltningsloven).

3. EFTA COURT CASE E-2/06 ON PUBLIC OWNERSHIP

3.1. CASE BACKGROUND

In its 2012 proposal to the Norwegian parliament (*Storting*) concerning the ratification of the EEA Agreement,[22] the Norwegian government assumed that the concession regime relating to resource management, including hydropower, would not be much affected by the EEA agreement and EU law. This was especially based on Article 125 of the Agreement which was copied from the then relevant EU Treaty which states that: 'This Agreement shall in no way prejudice the rules of the Contracting Parties governing the system of property ownership.' The parliamentary document emphasised that the role of public ownership would not be changed by the EEA Agreement and that the rules on concessions for private companies to be returned to the state after a certain number of years (reverting property rights or reversion (*hjemfall*)) would not be problematic. Some provisions on distinctions between foreign and Norwegian private parties were changed,[23] since they were obviously discriminatory, but not the distinction between private and public ownership as such.

Despite the government's assessment, some lawyers in academia and in the industry challenged this opinion and in 2001 ESA started formal investigations that led to a reasoned opinion in 2002. The problem was not the system with return of concessions to the state in itself ('reversion' or '*hjemfall*'), but the distinction between private and public owners and the relationship with EEA rules on right of establishment and free movement of capital.[24] The process became politically very difficult in Norway, and despite political initiatives to accommodate ESA's concerns by amending the concession regime, nothing happened until 2006 when ESA launched legal proceedings before the EFTA Court. The key contentious issues in the case became the conditions for concession for acquisition of hydropower resources, the scope of the EEA Agreement, free movement of capital and right of establishment, indirect discrimination, public ownership and proportionality. The judgment came in June 2007 and Norway formally lost the case.

The next Sections analyse the three main elements of the judgment: the scope of application of the EEA Agreement concerning the management of natural resources (Section 3.2); property ownership (Section 3.3); and proportionality (Section 3.4). Thereafter, the chapter continues by explaining how, despite

---

22 St. prp. nr. 100 (1991–92), Om samtykke til ratifikasjon av Avtale om Det europeiske økonomiske samarbeidsområde (EØS), undertegnet i Oporto 2. mai 1992, p 167 and 200.

23 Ministry of Petroleum and Energy, *Ot.Prp. nr. 82 (1991–1992) om endringer I energilovgivningen som følge av en EØS-avtale.*

24 EEA Agreement, Part III, Chapter 2 (Right of establishment) and Part II (Free movement of goods).

the government losing the case, the Norwegian concession system and public ownership regime was paradoxically strengthened and continued in compliance with EU and EEA law (Section 3.5). The chapter builds on previous analysis by several other authors.[25]

3.2. SCOPE OF THE EEA AGREEMENT CONCERNING MANAGEMENT OF NATURAL RESOURCES

The Norwegian Government, as Defendant, argued primarily that the issue of management of natural resources fell outside the scope of the EEA Agreement as such. It stated that the system of reversion had been introduced in order to achieve state ownership over developed waterfalls at the end of the concession period, while at the same time providing the private sector with incentives to develop natural resources in the interest of society as a whole. The rules at issue were an integral part of the 'management of natural resources' falling outside the scope of the EEA Agreement.[26] Furthermore, it was argued that it is an internal public affair how states choose to regulate and organise ownership within the public sphere, which is not subject to EEA law.[27] The Defendant, supported by the Netherlands and Poland as interveners,[28] also submitted that the application was unfounded since 'the contested rules fall outside the scope of the EEA Agreement'.[29]

The Defendant argued also that, when assessing whether the contested rules fall under the EEA Agreement, it must be taken into account that they govern the management of essential natural energy resources. The Applicant, ESA, argued that there was no legal reason why the general rules of the EEA Agreement should not apply to the exploitation of natural resources too. On that point, the Court noted that 'the interpretation of the defendant was not supported by the provisions of the EEA Agreement. No provision exempts such rules from the scope of the Agreement.'[30] The Defendant's submission that the contested rules did not fall within the scope of the EEA Agreement were therefore strongly rejected by the Court.

From this we can conclude that arguments that exploitation of natural resources like hydropower fall outside of the scope of the EEA Agreement were

[25] Thomas Chr. Poulsen, 'Article 125 – The EEA Agreement and national systems of property ownership' in F. Arnesen, H. Haukeland Fredriksen, H.P. Graver, O. Mestad and C. Vedder (eds.), *Agreement on the European Economic Area* (Universitetsforlaget, Oslo 2018), pp 942–945.

[26] Case E-02/06, see n. 12 above, paras 3 and 40.

[27] Ibid.

[28] Ibid, paras 50–51.

[29] Ibid, para 57.

[30] Ibid, para 60.

unfounded. Indeed, it seems that this line of argument was not put forward with any enthusiasm by the Defendant since it indicated a lack of understanding of the role of the basic regulation of an internal market, also in energy and hydropower, to ensure fair and open competition. Still, it is puzzling to see that the unnuanced idea that 'resource management' in general falls outside of the EEA Agreement is widely held.

3.3. PROPERTY OWNERSHIP AND RESTRICTIONS ON THE EU RIGHTS

Second, and more convincingly, the Defendant argued that the national rules were covered by Article 125 EEA which provides that: 'This Agreement shall in no way prejudice the rules of the Contracting Parties governing the system of property ownership.' The Defendant stated that this article took precedence over conflicting provisions of the EEA Agreement.[31] Norway argued that the rules at issue were part of the basic ownership structure in the hydropower sector, and as such fell under Article 125 EEA. In the Defendant's view, Article 125 EEA should be understood to the effect that a state has sovereign rights to regulate the property rights over natural resources and has the discretion to keep its undertakings nationalised or to privatise them.

The government asserted that Article 125 had to be interpreted differently than Article 295 of the Treaty establishing the European Community (EC Treaty) (at that time) and referred to EEA negotiations and subsequent parliamentary procedures.[32] It referred to the EEA Agreement's legal and political characteristics as different from those of the EU Treaties. In its view, the wording of Article 125 EEA supported the conclusion that public ownership of essential natural energy resources was a legitimate objective.[33]

The Applicant, ESA, submitted that the difference in treatment between private and public bodies neither was objectively justified, nor fell within the ambit of Article 125 EEA. ESA submitted that Article 125 EEA corresponds to Article 295 EC. It inferred from the case law of the CJEU (previously ECJ) on Article 295 EC that, although the Contracting Parties had the power under Article 125 EEA to define the rules governing the system of property ownership, the system and the exercise of the property rights remained subject to the fundamental rules of the Agreement. In that regard it was irrelevant, in the view of the Applicant, that the case at hand concerned natural resources.

31 Ibid, para 3.

32 See F. Arnesen, et al (eds.), n. 25 above, p 942; See St. prp. nr. 100 (1991–92), n. 22 above, pp 161–167 and 200–202.

33 Case E-02/06, see n. 12 above, para 43.

In the Applicant's view, a concession system, including rules on reversion, might as such be covered by Article 125 EEA.[34]

The Court found that 'the principle of homogeneity enshrined in the EEA Agreement leads to a presumption that provisions framed identically in the EEA Agreement and the EC Treaty are to be construed in the same way.'[35] The Court continued by stating that

> [t]here are certain differences in the scope and purpose of the EEA Agreement as compared to the EC Treaty which may under specific circumstances lead to a different interpretation (see Case E-3/98 *Rainford-Towning* [1998] EFTA Ct. Rep. 205, at paragraph 21) ... [but] [u]nilateral expressions of understanding of the kind claimed to have been made by Norway and Iceland could not constitute such circumstances.[36]

The Court also decided that Article 125 EEA did not exempt/exclude the national measures establishing the system of property ownership from the fundamental rules of the EEA Agreement, notably the ones on free movement.[37] Further, in the key passage in paragraph 77, the Court stated that 'the contested rules, as they exist today, cannot be said to aim at establishing a "system of property ownership", and thus were not protected by article 125.'

As Thomas Poulson has put it, 'the principle of homogeneity excludes interpretations based on preconditions that are not part of the Agreement.'[38] The manner in which Article 125 has been triggered in this case has to be put in perspective with the extensive debate and case law around it. Its interpretation has also been commented on by many scholars.[39] This is further discussed in Section 5 below.

3.4. PROPORTIONALITY

Thirdly, the Court had to consider whether the restrictions on private owners of hydropower concessions compared to public owners were proportionate to the aims to be achieved. In paragraph 70 of the judgment, this is formulated

---

34 Ibid, para 33.

35 Ibid, para 59.

36 Ibid.

37 Ibid, para 62: It argued that: 'It follows from the case law of the ECJ on Article 295 EC that Article 125 EEA is to be interpreted to the effect that, although the system of property ownership is a matter for each EEA State to decide, the said provision does not have the effect of exempting measures establishing such a system from the fundamental rules of the EEA Agreement, including the rules on free movement of capital and freedom of establishment (see for comparison Cases C-452/01 *Ospelt v Schlössle Weissenberg* [2003] ECR I-9743, at para 24; C-302/97 *Konle* [1999] ECR I-3099, at para 38 and 182/83 *Fearon* [1984] ECR 3677, at para 7).

38 See F. Arnesen, et al (eds.), n. 25 above p 943.

39 Ibid.

as a question whether 'the restrictions at issue are objectively justified.' What is meant by 'objectively' will not be discussed here, but of course the issue of proportionality is a key legal feature when considering national measures interfering with free movement, as demonstrated by the judgments in the *Åland Vindkraft* and *Essent* landmark cases of the CJEU in the energy field.[40]

The Applicant, ESA, contended that the rules at issue were directly discriminatory and therefore only justifiable under Article 33 EEA. In its view, what needs to be assessed under that article was only public security and that therefore security of energy supply was the only ground that is relevant in that respect. ESA questioned the existence of a serious threat to public security and the suitability of the reversion system as a means of meeting such a threat. Moreover, it questioned the necessity of making a distinction between Norwegian public undertakings and private undertakings. Therefore, ESA was of the opinion that the rules could not be justified with reference to Article 33 EEA.[41]

Norway argued that the aim of maintaining and acquiring public ownership over essential energy resources was a legitimate justification under the EEA Agreement, and that the contested rules were suitable and necessary to this end. The aim of maintaining and acquiring public ownership was a means of achieving other legitimate aims, such as public security, security of energy supply, and environmental protection, and that the contested rules were suitable and necessary to achieve these objectives.[42]

Norway argued that in the assessment of suitability, the combined effect of the rules on reversion, concessions and pre-emptive purchase rights, as well as the effects of the contested differentiation, must be taken into account. Accordingly, the rules consistently ensured both short and long-term control, which was suitable to maintain strong public ownership, and thereby also suitable for the achievement of the other aims.[43]

Finally, Norway expressed the view that there were no alternative regimes which would achieve this aim as effectively as the contested rules. This concerned the aim of ensuring public security (security of energy supply), environmental protection and effective collection of economic rent. The residual competence inherent in public ownership, it argued, supplemented the control that could be achieved through command and control regulation, and the combination ensured a higher degree of control than exclusive reliance on regulatory tools allowed for. Furthermore, public ownership ensured a more efficient collection of economic rent than other alternatives, e.g. taxation.

---

40 C-573/12 *Ålands vindkraft AB v Energimyndigheten* ECLI:EU:C:2014:203, and C-492/14 *Essent Belgium NV v Vlaams Gewest and Others* ECLI:EU:C:2016:732.

41 Case E-02/06, see n. 12 above, para 35.

42 Ibid, para 40.

43 Ibid, para 47.

From a methodological point of view, Norway argued that the Court should conduct a general and overall necessity review in relation to all the public interest requirements at stake, assessed as a whole.[44]

With regard to all the aims referred to by the Defendant, the ESA stressed that the core issue was not whether reversion as such was suitable and necessary to achieve these aims, but rather whether the difference in treatment with regard to reversion was necessary in order to achieve them. In the ESA's view, that was not the case.[45]

The Court found that only two aims were legitimate under the EEA Agreement, namely security of energy supply and protection of the environment. Acquiring public control and collection of economic rent could not in themselves constitute justificatory grounds. The aim of the collection of economic rent was of an economic nature and therefore could not in itself serve as justificatory ground.[46]

Thereafter, the Court went on to consider the classical elements of suitability and necessity under the proportionality principle. It recalled that the contested rules must be suitable for achieving the intended objectives and they must not go beyond what is necessary in order to attain the legitimate objectives which they pursue.[47] Importantly, the Court found that Norway 'has failed to demonstrate that ownership control is necessary in order to meet the aims of security of energy supply or environmental protection.'[48] Regarding security of supply, the Court found that under normal circumstances neither private nor public undertakings in the hydropower sector have special obligations concerning energy supply. In crisis situations, the central authorities have the power to instruct all producers, whether they are subject to concessions or not, to implement necessary contingency measures.[49] For this reason, the Court, taking also into account the ownership structure of the Norwegian hydropower market, found it difficult to see why public undertakings should be more inclined than private undertakings to act based on non-commercial environmental considerations.[50]

3.5. DECISION AND FOLLOW-UP

The Court held that Norway had infringed Articles 31 and 40 of the EEA Agreement by maintaining in force measures as laid down in the Industrial

---

44 Ibid, para 48.
45 Ibid, para 37.
46 Ibid, para 80, which refers to Case E-1/04 *Fokus Bank* [2004] EFTA Ct. Rep. 11, para 33.
47 Ibid, para 82, which refers to see Case E-10/04 *Piazza v Schurte* [2005] EFTA Ct. Rep. 76, para 39.
48 Ibid, para 84.
49 Ibid, para 85.
50 Ibid, para 87.

Licensing Act[51] which granted to private undertakings and all undertakings from other Contracting Parties to the EEA Agreement a time-limited concession for the acquisition of waterfalls for energy production, with an obligation to surrender all installations to the Norwegian State without compensation at the expiry of the concession period, whereas Norwegian public undertakings benefited from concessions for an unlimited period of time.[52]

The judgment, delivered in June 2007, gave the Norwegian authorities a choice between either: 1) abolishing reversion and liberalising ownership (fundamentally or partly through splitting of ownership and time-limited concessions for private actors, like the French model); or 2) consolidating public ownership in accordance with Article 125 by eliminating the possibilities for future private concessions. The government chose the latter option. Because it was the summer vacation, the Parliament was not assembled, and since the matter was urgent, the government adopted a provisional arrangement pursuant to section 17 of the Constitution on 10 August 2007. The new solution was called the 'consolidation model' and meant a consolidation of public ownership. This came as quite a surprise both to ESA and the Norwegian power industry, which had not discovered that the verdict provided the opportunity for such a solution and thought that instead it was facing liberalisation of ownership.[53]

After extensive debate, the provisional instrument was replaced in autumn 2008 by a permanent legislative amendment. The opportunity to give new private licenses (or extend old ones) was removed. In order to make the scheme more EEA-robust, the principle of public ownership – following a hundred years of practice – was laid down for the first time in law, in the new first section of the Industrial Consortium Act Chapter 1 paragraph 1 which now provides that: 'The country's hydropower resources belong to and will be managed to the benefit of the general public. This is to be ensured through public ownership at state, county and municipal level.' This provision is, as mentioned earlier, not contrary to the principle of a basic private ownership of the waterway as such.[54]

The case is probably the most important political and economic case for the EFTA Court so far, and it has been the subject of many analyses, although relatively few legal ones.[55] It illustrates the broad scope of the EEA Agreement

51 *Lov 14. desember 1917 nr. 16 om erverv av vannfall, bergverk og annen fast eiendom m.v. (industrikonsesjonsloven).*

52 Case E-02/06, see n. 12 above, para 90.

53 See n. 2 above, NOU 2012:2, p 561.

54 See n. 10 above, Falkanger and Haagensen, Chapter 2.

55 See notably: O. Kolstad, 'Hjemfall – to skritt frem og ett tilbake?' (2007) 9 *Lov og Rett* 513; P. Ørebech, 'EØS-avtalens artikkel 125, med særlig vekt på diskusjonen i NOU 2004:26 Hjemfall' (2006) 2 *Lov og Rett* 26; F. Arnesen, 'EØS-retten og hjemfallsretten' (2006) 4 *Lov og rett* 238; B. Akkermans and E. Ramaekers, 'Article 345 TFEU (Ex Article 295 EC), its Meanings and Interpretations: The Treaties Shall in No Way Prejudice the Rules in Member

in framing national restrictions that can only be justified within the envelope of EU/EEA law. Formally, Norway lost the trial. But at the same time, it was the premise in the judgment of the EFTA Court paragraph 77 that showed how it could be enforced in a manner that not only continued, but even strengthened the principle of public ownership of hydropower resources in Norway.[56]

In the public debate surrounding the case, it was argued that the interference with national sovereignty was so strong that Norway should retreat from the EEA Agreement as such.[57] Arguably, no other case under the EEA Agreement has been as sensitive politically and economically.

Following the decision and the follow-up by the Norwegian authorities in 2008, the issue of public ownership seems to have settled. Concerns voiced by some lawyers regarding the consolidation model, have not been followed up[58] despite the two key messages from the Court that other regulatory measures than ownership are more effective to achieve security of supply and environmental concerns. This 'circumvention' of the proportionality test is of course in line with the national political competence enshrined in Article 125.

In fact, recent debates on sovereignty and energy in the context of the implementation of the EU's third energy package and the EU Agency for the Cooperation of Energy Regulators (ACER) in the Norwegian Parliament in the Spring of 2018 confirmed – through an eight-point list drafted by the Labour Party[59] – the broad political loyalty to public ownership as the fundamental approach to ensure energy security. The main discussion over the last 10 years has been concentrating on more marginal issues like: extension of the possibility of minority positions to other models, i.e. not only shareholder companies with limited responsibility (AS), but also companies with shared and full responsibility (ANS and DA companies); different models to calculate minority positions either through accumulation of positions in a company structure (*gjennomstrømmingsprinsippet*) or a company by company assessment (*blokkprinsippet*). Renting of property rights and time limits within the concept of 'system of public ownership' in paragraph 77 of the judgment have also been discussed. Finally, the relationship between financial positions and voting rights as cumulative conditions to meet the one-third shareholding threshold have been discussed, but without a change in government policy towards the consolidation model.

We may conclude that the EFTA court decision in the *Hjemfall* case proved that the legal scholars who argued for a more differentiated approach

States Governing the System of Property Ownership' (2010) 16:3 *European Law Journal* 292, specifically p 312.

56 See n. 2, NOU 2012:2, p 561.

57 See P. Ørebech, n. 55 above.

58 See O. Kolstad, n. 55 above, p 514.

59 Political compromise by the Labour Party: Uttalelse fra Arbeiderpartiets landsstyre, 'Landsstyreuttalelse – Vannkraften er fellesskapets eie', April 2018.

to the EEA Agreement and Article 125 compared to the EU Treaties were wrong.[60] The EEA Agreement is not a full guarantee for public ownership in all shapes in Norway. The principle of homogeneity in the internal market plays a strong role in legal assessments made by the Court.

However, it may be argued, as pointed out by Arnesen, the following fundamental question still remains open for debate, even in a time of increased national security orientation: What does Norway really want to achieve by public ownership of hydropower compared to regulatory measures?[61]

4. ESA CASES ON ENVIRONMENTAL RESTRICTIONS

4.1. BACKGROUND

At the same time as the concessions regime and public ownership restrictions under the EEA agreement found their solution around 2008 with the 'consolidation model', a new contentious aspect of EU law developed in the same area of hydropower in relation to environmental protection.

The key piece of EU legislation, Council and Parliament Directive 2000/60/EC (Water Framework Directive or WFD) based on (today's) Article 192(1) TFEU (Environment), was implemented through the Norwegian Water Regulation of 15 December 2006 nr. 1446.[62] The WFD establishes a system with holistic water management plans based on environmental targets and programmes of measures, including measures limiting hydropower production. The time limit granted to the EFTA States to publish River Basin Management Plans (RBMPs) expired on 1 May 2018. Norway undertook a voluntary implementation of the WFD in selected sub-districts across the country in the period 2009–2015, the so-called 'voluntary pilot phase'. On 4 July 2016, the Norwegian Government issued approval letters adopting the remaining RBMPs for the whole country.

In parallel to this, on 10 March 2011, ESA received a complaint against Norway on behalf of the Norwegian Association of Municipalities hosting Hydropower Plants (LVK), the Liaison Committee of Nature Conservation (SRN), the Union of Outdoor Recreation Organisations (FRIFO), the Norwegian Biodiversity Network (SABIMA) and Norwegian Salmon Rivers (Norske Lakseelver). The complainants alleged that Norway had not correctly implemented the WFD, and ESA opened case 69544.[63]

---

60 See P. Ørebech, n. 55 above, p 26.

61 See F. Arnesen, n. 55 above.

62 Formal inclusion into the EEA Agreement came on 28 September 2007.

63 For a complete overview of all the complaints in the case, see Vannportalen at: <http://www.vannportalen.no/organisering/europa/klagesaker-til-esa-om-norges-gjennomforing-av-vanndirektivet/klagesaker-til-esa-om-vanndirektivet-og-vannkraft/>

According to the organisations, regulated water courses used for hydropower production, which have been generally classified as heavily modified water bodies, would not be subject to the procedures foreseen by Articles 4 and 11 of the WFD. They argued that the latter would continue to be subject to 'autonomous national procedures', which do not comply with the requirements of the WFD.

Looking at the detailed content of the relevant provisions, it must be noted that:

- Article 4 of the WFD lists the 'environmental objectives' of the Directive. It establishes a system whereby Member States, when making operational the programmes of measures specified in the RBMPs for surface waters, shall protect and enhance all artificial and heavily modified bodies of water. The aim is to achieve good ecological potential and good surface water chemical status, at the latest 15 years from the date of entry into force of the Directive. Pursuant to Article 4(4), the deadlines established may be extended for the purposes of phased achievement of the objectives for bodies of water, provided that no further deterioration occurs in the status of the affected body of water when certain conditions specified in the Directive are met.
- Article 11(1) sets out the obligation for each Member State to ensure the establishment for each river basin district, or for the part of an international river basin district within its territory, of a programme of measures, taking account of the results of the analyses required under Article 5, in order to achieve the objectives established under Article 4. Such programmes of measures may refer to measures following from legislation adopted at national level and covering the whole of the territory of a Member State.
- Article 11(5) establishes that where monitoring or other data indicate that the objectives set under Article 4 for the body of water are unlikely to be achieved, the Member State shall ensure that relevant permits and authorisations are examined and reviewed as appropriate.

The complainants argued that Norwegian legislation did not make it possible to fulfil these provisions of the Directive.

Case 69544 was first discussed at a so-called 'package meeting' between ESA and Norwegian authorities in Oslo in November 2011 and then followed up in a long correspondence and many meetings until the case was closed by a letter from ESA on 18 August 2017. On the same day however, ESA opened a new case 81034 based on a new letter received from the complainants on 30 June 2017. This case is to my knowledge still open and has involved a new letter from ESA to the Norwegian authorities on 20 September 2017 and a reply from the Norwegian authorities on 20 October 2017. A formal letter with a confirmation of the decision of ESA was sent on 15 May 2018. At the time of publication of this chapter no more recent public information had been identified.[64]

The key issue in the first case 69544 was the availability of national measures to reach the water quality targets in the WFD (Section 4.2 below). The main two issues in the new case 81034 concern (i) the use of exemptions under the WFD and the level of environmental ambition and (ii) the use of aggregated national assessments (Section 4.3 below).

4.2. NATIONAL LEGAL MEASURES TO ACHIEVE ENVIRONMENTAL TARGETS

In point 4 of the letter sent to ESA on 10 March 2011, the complainants argue that the legal basis for revision of existing concessions for large hydropower based on the Waterfall Rights Act, the Act on Water Regulation and the Water Resources Act were not flexible enough to meet the requirements of the WFD. They argued that sections 5(3) of the Waterfall Rights Act and 10(3) of the Act on Water Regulation, with the system of revision after 50 or 30 years (depending on whether the concession was given after 1992), do not fit with the cycle of the WFD and the need to address the conditions on a more frequent basis.

ESA followed up the complaint in their letter dated 22 February 2012 by asking the Norwegian authorities about the function of revision clauses in the relevant Acts and about other instruments available in national legislation.

ESA addressed in particular the following five legal aspects of Norwegian hydropower legislation:

1. The scope of revisions clauses in hydropower concessions and the question whether they give opportunities for all types of mitigation measures to reach EEA environmental targets;
2. The timing of revision based on sections 5(3) of the Waterfall Rights Act and 10(3) of the Water Resources Act compared to the deadlines of the WFD;
3. Whether the relationship between a programme of measures in a water management plan can constitute 'special circumstances' in section 28 of the Water Resources Act;
4. The application of section 66 (*innkalling*) in the Water Resources Act;
5. The availability of a legal basis for amendment according to general principles of Norwegian administrative law due to 'compelling legal interests'.

64 Decision dated 15 May 2018, document no. 901685. The complete exchange of views was summarised in the document.

Interestingly, all of these five issues go quite far into the application of national concession law, an area of administrative law which is not at the core of the EEA Agreement and an area where EU law has been very reluctant to increased harmonisation. Indeed, attempts to introduce minimum even minor requirements for 'one-stop shop' concessions and minimum time requirements in the revised directive on renewable energy have been controversial,[65] but here the issues come up through the 'back door' of assessment of the effectiveness of compliance with targets in environmental legislation.

The Norwegian authorities first replied to ESA through letters dated 31 May 2012 and 31 July 2013 in which they argued that indeed the available legal instruments were sufficient. In particular, it was argued that amendments in concessions that are necessary to comply with targets in water management plans will be regarded as 'special circumstances' (according to sections 28 and 66 of the Water Resources Act) whenever other measures (revision) or standard requirements in the concessions themselves are not available.[66] It was argued that preparatory works and previous administrative practice would not form an obstacle to such an application.

Here it might be relevant to point out that legally 'special circumstances' according to the national legislation refers to the underlying cost/benefit analysis of new conditions, not the administrative formality of political priorities. This means that for each of the environmental targets, a solid cost/benefit analysis needs to be demonstrated before section 28 and 66 can be used by the authorities. This seems to be fully in line with the logic of the WFD.

Furthermore, the Norwegian authorities in their reply also argued that although the legislation is fragmented, it is clear to stakeholders in the industry and other stakeholders.

The issue of availability of measures was on the one hand formally closed by ESA's letter dated 20 September 2017 and the decision of 15 May 2018 mentioned in Section 4.1 above, but it might on the other hand very well return as part of ESA's more general assessment of the implementation once the RMPBs adopted in July 2016 have formally been notified.

As mentioned above, the new case covers several other issues regarding the implementation, but until now it has not led to formal measures like a letter of formal notice or a reasoned opinion from ESA. These issues, in particular, concern the justification for exemptions to delay achievement of environmental targets,[67] and in what way 'a binding national assessment on acceptable power loss sits alongside individually assessing good ecological potential for each water

[65] Article 16, Directive (EU) 2018/2001 of 11 December 2018 on the promotion of the use of energy from renewable sources.

[66] Letter 310713 p 5.

[67] Article 4(4), Water Framework Directive.

body, to ensure that the objectives of the Water Framework Directive are met'.[68] Those issues are discussed separately below.

4.3. USE OF EXEMPTIONS AND AGGREGATED ASSESSMENTS

In the complaint dated 30 June 2017 that is still ongoing with ESA under case number 81034, it is argued that the statements of the Norwegian authorities in the dialogue with ESA:

> reveal that the environmental objectives were predetermined at a national level, with little regard to the regional plans and assessments. The Ministry had already 'fixed' the maximum acceptable power loss in the revision-cases and the number of plants that could be summoned for licensing, before adopting the river basin management plans. In practice, the government therefore did not perform the required balancing act, but instead set an absolute cap on environmental improvements and number of cases based on what they considered to be an acceptable loss of power production.

In the complainants' view, the downward adjustments in the nationally adopted plans in this manner could be considered problematic because no individual assessment had occurred and because calculations of acceptable loss of power production as a result of minimum water flow are based on a standard formula (Q95) and not on individual water loss. They argue that

> it seems that the extent to which proposed measures have been accepted in the national adoptions is based on the predetermined and theoretical standard amount of water called Q95, rather than an individual assessment of the amount of water required in each water body affected by power production.[69]

On this basis, they asked the authorities to clarify how national governments may use extensions under the Directive.

In the last letter with substance from Norwegian authorities in this 'saga' on the implementation of the WFD dated 20 October 2017, it is argued that most exemptions are due to the lack of 'technical feasibility' (cf. WFD Article 4(4)(a)(1)). However, the authorities continue by emphasising not only the time needed for physical construction of installation in the waterways, but also the extensive processes needed in national legislation, including public participation, assessment of safety and security of supply issues and the right

---

68 Letter from ESA to the Norwegian Ministry of Climate and Environment, 'Implementation of Directive 2000/60 in Norway', document nr. 873289, 20 September 2017.

69 Letter from LVK to ESA on 'the implementation of the Water Framework Directive and the approval of the river basin management plans', 30 June 2017.

to appeal.[70] The Norwegian government refers to increased priority for the work, in the annual letter of allocation to the Norwegian Energy Directorate (NVE) for 2017 and 2018 with particular emphasis on the environmental targets included in the plans.[71] The Norwegian authorities also reply to ESA's questions regarding environmental ambition level by emphasising that during the national process a prioritisation and national guidelines have been necessary. The complainants seem to see this process as a national 'top-down' approach that is not in line with the bottom-up process foreseen for individual waterways in the directive.

4.4. NEXT STEPS AND COMMENTS

The final formal notification of the Norwegian water management plans according to the WFD were finally submitted in December 2018, despite the plans being approved at national level in July 2016. ESA will now assess the implementation, including the issues raised in case 81034. The correspondence may take yet another couple of years during which the national plans will also be revised.

ESA's letters in these two cases concern issues of suitability and effectiveness of national administrative law, something which has been on the margins of the scope of the EEA agreement and indeed in EU Law. It remains to be seen how far the Authority will go to investigate this issue further. The upcoming formal notification of the water management plans will trigger a new discussion about progress.

In this author's opinion, there is no legal contradiction between individual and aggregated assessments to ensure a complete and balanced cost/benefit analysis that can form a basis for setting environmental targets. Individual assessments will not be able to deal with accumulated consequences for the security of supply in a region for example. The WFD approach is based on a full assessment of all relevant factors, not only benefits for the biodiversity locally, and the isolated negative effects for public interests, but also cumulative effects. It will be interesting to see how ESA considers this.

The only weak legal point in implementation that can be seen, is the delay in the process of national assessment of hydropower production that has not been subject to concessions. The WFD does not distinguish between environmental status and impacts depending on how they are regulated. Here the ongoing assessment by national authorities of unlicensed hydropower will be important. In the end however, it might be that there will be little room for environmental

70 Letter from the Norwegian Ministry of Climate and Environment, 20 October 2017, pp 2 and 3.

71 Ibid, p 3.

improvement due to negative cost/benefit in these water bodies that have been heavily modified for over 100 years to the benefit of society.

Another key issue will be use of sections 28 and 66 of the Water Resources Act. The effectiveness of these provisions is a key element of the government's approach to flexibility of national legislation and procedures.

It should of course be noted that ESA is in close contact with the European Commission regarding significant delays also in other Member States. In this respect, it should be recalled that in general water quality in Norway is excellent and abundant compared to most Member States.

Finally, it should be mentioned that neither legal commentators, nor the Norwegian government itself, seem ever to have questioned the fundamental EEA relevance of the WFD as regards protection of the physical aspects of habitats. The adaptation text for the WFD in fact refers to the fact that other biodiversity acts are not included in the EEA Agreement. In addition to the Birds Directive, the Habitats Directive and the Natura 2000 Directive, several water regulations are not included, such as the Bathing Water Directive, the Regulation on quality required for shellfish waters and the Quality of surface water rules. In NOU 2012:12, it is commented that strangely enough, biodiversity and environmental protection in waterways is included in the EEA agreement through the WFD, but not protection of terrestrial biodiversity, although both issues seem equally relevant for the internal market since they impact the level playing-field of economic operators.[72]

5. CONCLUSIONS

EU Law has had a major impact on concessions in the Norwegian hydropower sector through the consolidation of public ownership and the upcoming new environmental conditions imposed through the implementation of the Water Framework Directive. These impacts on concessions come in addition to many other impacts linked to market integration in the EU. As commented by other authors, the environmental and economic stakes and liabilities associated with the use of hydropower require in-depth public controls in granting these rights.[73] These controls often create a challenging interface with the 'level playing-field' approach of the EU internal market.

These developments have, in the same way as similar developments in other countries, improved the competition on a level playing-field between hydropower companies in Europe. Nevertheless, there are still strong differences among

---

[72] See n. 2 above, NOU 2012:12, p 585.

[73] Florence School of Regulation, Glachant et al., 'For a harmonisation of hydropower regimes in European Single Market', Issue 2016/01, January 2016.

hydropower regimes in Europe that cannot be explained by environmental or economic criteria alone. Possible competition distortion to the common European electricity market has been a key issue. It has therefore been argued that the goal of the Commission should be to deliver a harmonised regulatory regime for hydropower. The Florence School of Regulation (FSR) study of the European national regimes has analysed issues that concern the legitimate variability of national approaches. It is argued that those issues exacerbate the distortions of competition between Member States and jeopardise the achievements of the common energy market.[74] FSR argues that new and harmonised rules regarding the implementation of rights and joint obligations are an urgent matter that the Commission should treat alongside its efforts to develop and regularise the competitive processes for hydropower rights.

In the opinion of this author, such deep harmonisation of administrative law and tax law will not be possible under the current political circumstances in Europe. Member States – and indeed Norway – are not ready for competition based on further explicit harmonisation of tax law and national administrative law. The debate on ACER in Norway in the Spring of 2018 showed how sensitive the sovereignty issues are in the area. Similar tendencies play out in most European countries as a reflection of increased scepticism towards trade and international rule-based competition. We will probably see a development where the application of the general principles on free movement, competition law and state aid law will drive the development, rather than new regulatory initiatives from the Commission.

In another, ongoing, dialogue between ESA and Norway, the issue of public ownership and national prerogatives has come up more generally based exactly on the question if competition is distorted through public ownership. Norwegian municipal undertakings are involved in substantial economic activity (training centres, testing of food quality, security services) that compete in the market, but where the municipal market actors have significant prerogatives because they do not pay taxes and are not able to become bankrupt, thereby enjoying better credit conditions. This has led to a larger discussion about the need for formal separation of the companies from the municipalities and application of normal commercial terms for these activities.[75]

The final word has certainly not been said. In fact, Article 125 on public ownership has a difficult relationship with Article 61(1) on State Aid. The mixed market economy principle is designed to balance these contradictions and the hydropower sector is a prime example of how it can work.

---

74 Ibid.

75 See n. 55 above, F. Arnesen et al., p 945.

It should also be mentioned that in a recent new case that could not be included here,[76] ESA has raised fundamental questions on the implementation of the Services Directive in Norwegian law and in particular the relationship with Norwegian hydropower-regulation and public ownership. In the answer from the Norwegian authorities it is argued that the provision of hydropower is not a 'service' but goods, and that the issue of public ownership has been settled via the *Hjemfall* case discussed above. It will be interesting to follow this case in light of similar cases opened by the European Commission for EU Member States.

For Norway, the interaction of EU law and national hydropower legislation is also an illustration of a more general point on how international trade exposure and increased competition in the renewables sectors require rethinking of the basic structure of the economy. Public resources are so heavily involved in all economic activity that the issue of competitiveness problems through lack of diversity, competence and innovation quickly comes up. The Rattsø Commission on productivity of the Norwegian Economy put it this way in 2016:

> Oil and gas exploration will continue to be an important element in the Norwegian economy, but will have a declining contribution to growth going forward. Fiscal policy leeway will gradually shrink, not least due to the imminent demographic shift from a young to an aging population. Norway is therefore at a turning point. New growth deriving primarily from new industries is required – a shift from a resource-based economy to a knowledge economy.[77]
>
> The development of new, internationally competitive industries demands refinement of innovation policies [...]. The internationalisation of the business sector must continue, and more foreign competition must be permitted in Norway.[78]
>
> International comparisons and efficiency studies on public undertakings show considerable potential for improving resource use.[79]

---

76 Unpublished exchange of letters between ESA and the Norwegian Ministry of Petroleum and Energy 2019. ESA Case No. 83484 Document No. 1065981.

77 Official Norwegian Report (NOU) 2016: 3 'At a turning point: from a resource-based economy to a knowledge economy', English Summary, p 5.

78 Ibid, p 6.

79 Ibid.

CHAPTER VII

THE LEGAL REGIME OF HYDROELECTRIC LICENCES IN FRANCE

Bernard Kieffer

1. INTRODUCTION

France has the second largest hydropower park in Europe (65 to 70 TWh per year), surpassed by Norway and followed by Sweden.

The French hydropower generation park also includes a number of small, sometimes very old, low-power installations, as well as plants such as Serre-Ponçon with a capacity of 1.3 billion m^3 and an area of 28 km^2 (the largest artificial lake in Europe). The hydroelectric facility of Grand-Maison, the most powerful, is capable of providing in just a few minutes the equivalent of the production of two nuclear units.

Hydropower accounts for 10–12 per cent of the national electricity generation in France and amounts to about 80 per cent of French renewable electricity production.

Today, the French hydropower park has about 2,500 power plants (comprising 400 licences). On average, the plants are about 50 years old. Licensed hydroelectric power generation (installations with an output exceeding 4500 kW) is divided between Electricité de France (EDF in the amount of 80 per cent) and the ENGIE Group (17 per cent). Independent producers hold the remaining licences.

After a long period of handling hydropower sectorally, the juridical framework regulating hydropower is now being increasingly integrated into the global framework of water resources law with a rationale of conciliation and usage sharing; on the one hand, to preserve resources in terms of water and biodiversity, and on the other hand, to develop renewable energies.

2. THE LEGAL FRAMEWORK FOR FRENCH HYDROELECTRICITY

Under the provisions of the Act of 16 October 1919 relating to the use of hydraulic power, only the French State may grant a right to use the driving power of rivers, lakes and tides: it establishes two entirely separate juridical regimes, depending on whether the gross maximum power of the facility is greater than 4,500 kW, or equal to or less than that value. The juridical regime is based on licensing in the first case and on permits in the second.

Prior to this landmark law in 1919, legislation on the water usage was based on both the civil code and the Act of 8 April 1898 relating to water resource management.

The civil code made water a "common asset". With passage of the Water Act of 1898, the State intervened for the first time to regulate the uses of the watercourses through an authorisation system that one might today describe as "water policing". This statute initiates a progressive restriction of property rights pertaining to water. It is not yet a matter of responding to environmental imperatives, but rather of ensuring respect for public health and safety in conjunction with the vast industrial development that France is now undergoing. One of the main principles of the Water Act is that watercourses that are not State-owned belong to waterfront residents.

It is precisely this principle that would generate the phenomenon of "waterfall obstructers" and hinder the development of hydropower: on sites suitable for development, project proponents were confronted with the speculative nature of some residents who raised the bids exorbitantly at the time of negotiations on the surrender of their waterfront rights or opposed any development of the site (and thus "obstructed" the harnessing of the falls). The Act of 1898 does not make it possible to overcome such obstacles.

Hence the Act of 16 October 1919, which is the first law permitting nationalisation of the driving force of streams, lakes and tides. Its fundamental principle, aimed at allowing the development of the hydropower, is expressed already in the very first lines of the law: "No person shall possess the right to the energy of the tides, the lakes and the rivers, whatever their classification, without a licence or permit from the State". Thus, it is not the water *per se* that is nationalised, but the use of water's driving force.

The principles laid down in the 1919 Act are still in force, although the text has been adapted and amended many times thereafter, revealing the quality and modernity of this law, which was one of the first to deal with one of the specific uses of water without ignoring the others: the standard specifications of licensing and the regulation of authorised water types established by decrees, following the law of 1919, have always taken care to ensure consideration for other uses of water when developing and exploiting the energy of waterfalls. In this respect, the 1919 law proved innovative in its conception and its conciliatory approach to the uses of the water.

Since 1919 in France, to be able to exploit the energy of a watercourse, it has been necessary to obtain a permit (for power equal to or less than 4,500 kW) or a licence (for power more than 4,500 kW).

3. EVOLUTION OF THE GENERAL LEGAL FRAMEWORK

The 1919 law is based on a sectoral approach: in French law at the time, there is no single right to water, but rights for different uses of water. This sectoral approach would remain in use up until the 1960s.

The initial stage in the reorganisation and partial consolidation of water resources law in France begins with the Act of 16 December 1964 on the regime and the distribution of water and the combatting of water pollution. This 1964 law, however, preserves the autonomy of the 1919 Act.

Another important milestone for hydroelectric power is the Fisheries Act of 29 June 1984, which toughens the rules applicable to watercourse developments and increases the obligations on operators of existing developments to protect biodiversity. Hydroelectric power producers are thereby required by law to set minimum flow-through values (and make it mandatory to maintain them in watercourses to preserve biological life in them). They must also equip their waterworks to allow migratory species to cross watercourses classified by the Ministry of the Environment.

Next, the Water Act of 3 January 1992 put an end to what remained of the autonomy of the juridical regime pertaining to hydroelectric power. This law constitutes a very clear reclaiming by the French State of global water management. The fundamental objective of this law was to protect water resources in qualitative and quantitative terms.

The 1992 law reflects a globalisation of water usage: sectoral approaches are abandoned and one definitively embraces a rationale of conciliation and sharing of usage, in an increasingly commonplace legislative and regulatory framework orchestrated by the prefects. Hydropower licences are now and will be henceforth – as were permits already – subject to both the hydropower statute (the 1919 Act) and the water statute (the 1992 Act). Water is now part of the "common heritage of the Nation": the preservation of water resources necessarily requires balanced management, an organised sharing of its use, a global approach, a reconciling of water usages.

The law of 1919 has not been rescinded: it remains in force but has been "nibbled" from the inside by this new law which tends to trivialise water uses (hydroelectric usage ceases to be a "special" use treated separately), casualising the issuance of licences (which can now be provided with appended "water regulations" prescribed by the prefects and non-contractual), by requiring that the content of the permits and licences for hydropower production is compatible or made compatible when they are renewed, notably, with the priorities assigned to water management, thereby illustrating the willingness of proponents of this law to allow the rivers to speak with a single voice.

The French Act on Electricity of 10 February 2000, which opens the electricity market in France to competition, only marginally concerns hydroelectricity. It preserves the *acquis* (body of rights and obligations) without adding much to it and only moderately favours hydropower (by promoting renewable energies and national energy independence). The protection of aquatic environments is now restraining the development of hydropower.

The Act on water and the aquatic environment of 30 December 2006 marks a new and important step in taking into account the new issues related to water management (global warming, increased risks of imbalance between supply and demand, the fight against non-point source pollution, the impact on the environment of hydroelectric production, usage conflicts in the distribution of water and control of water consumption).

This 2006 law is also part of the EU's objective of returning waterbodies to "good status" by 2015 (Water Framework Directive – WDF – of 23 October 2000). It marks a further step towards even more centralised and coercive water law. In this context, hydropower is beset by somewhat heavier environmental constraints: new classifications of rivers to preserve the most emblematic sectors (on which no new waterworks can be installed), to ensure ecological continuity required by the WFD and the movement of migratory fish; measures to reduce the effects of hydroelectric structures by modifying existing permits and licences without compensation; new provisions for reserved flows and maintenance of watercourses; strengthening of the water police force and administrative and criminal penalties.

In this increasingly restrictive context, hydropower is struggling to preserve the status quo and, even more so, to continue to develop. This, despite the "National Convention for the Development of Sustainable Hydropower", which took place on 23 June 2010 between the French government and the main French hydroelectric producers, in particular with a view to achieving both the goal of developing hydropower generation by 2020 in the amount of +3 TWh net per year and to meeting the objective of a "good" state of the majority of waterbodies.

Finally, the Act of 17 August 2015 relating to the energy transition for green growth has provided some cause for hope for hydropower production in France by retaining a target of 23 per cent renewable energies in the overall gross energy consumption in 2020 and 32 per cent of this consumption in 2030, the year in which renewables will have to amount to 40 per cent of the national electricity production.

4. THE LEGAL REGIME OF THE HYDROELECTRIC LICENCE

Designed to take into account the problems that are specific to medium and large power installations, the juridical regime of the hydroelectric licence is intended to provide the contractor with a set of guarantees or benefits that justify the importance of the investment and the nature of public utility that is often attributed to it.

In French domestic law, there is no legal definition of "hydroelectric licence". The Act of 1919 was content with distinguishing between a State-issued "permit" and "licence" based on a criterion of electrical power output, without further specification.

Administrative case law does not define it precisely either. It notes the presence or absence of certain elements that characterise the licence. It was therefore scholarly doctrine that defined it as follows:

> Act of the public authority associated with a contract by which the granting authority assigns to a licensee the exercise of certain rights under conditions determined by this contract. The licensee is subject to certain obligations towards the licensor and third parties.[1]

The granting of a licence for the development and then the operation of a hydroelectric plant is an act of the public authority (which falls under the legal category of public service delegation) in the form of a prefectural order (for licences of 4.5 to 100 MW) or a decree in Council of State (licences of more than 100 MW) setting, by means of specifications, the rights and regulatory obligations of the licensee.

In addition, this order or decree confirms a binding agreement between the State and the licensee, a contractual document setting out the reciprocal commitments of both parties (the State, as licensor, and the licensee, who accepts the licence under the specified terms and conditions). If necessary, the licence is accompanied by a declaration of public utility that allows the licensee to expropriate the land necessary for the development and operation of the hydroelectric fall. The duration for initial licences is limited by law to 75 years.

Renewals are generally granted for 20 to 45 years. Upon expiration of the initial licence, the allocated assets (financed and built by the licensee) are returned free of charge to the State in a well-maintained condition.

The licence regime therefore provides a guarantee of continuity compatible with normal depreciation times for works and equipment.

---

1 Definition given by Professor Jean L'huillier in "Hydraulic forces legislation", 1936.

In return, the State defines, in the provisions of the licence, a set of obligations that the licensee must meet, as much out of necessity as of general interest (navigation, irrigation, health and public safety, civil security, ecological monitoring of the watercourse, protection of the environment and preservation of the aquatic environment …) as well as special interests that the licence may affect (water and energy reserves, restored energy, restoration of communications, sustainability of other uses …). The provisions also specify the methods of control exercised by the State over the licensed facilities which, *ipso jure*, belong to the licensor from the first day.

In principle, the hydropower licence is based on an economic and financial balance that the licensee is entitled to have preserved, unless otherwise explicitly decided by the legislator (who always has the opportunity to impose new constraints, in the name of the general interest and excluding compensation to licensees).

The components of the hydroelectric licence are therefore as follows:

- A long-term agreement (the licence agreement) of up to 75 years, one of the longest in our domestic law;
- Between two partners: the State and the licensee (there is no such thing as a regional, county or municipal hydropower licence);
- Rights, benefits and obligations for the licensee;
- An administrative operation: construction of public works (licensed hydroelectric development);
- A primarily defined activity: the exploitation of the hydraulic power and any related uses (navigation, irrigation, flood capping, lower flood peaks, maintenance of low-water flow, storage of drinking water, etc.);
- A given territory (the licensed area);
- Users (electricity consumers and potential users depending on multiple purposes);
- A contribution to public electricity service (generation of electricity delivered over public grids), unlike hydroelectric permits;
- An economic and industrial dimension: an economic aspect of the licence based on a financial balance that constitutes the essential element, whereas this does not appear in the definition of a permit.

As for the legal nature of the hydropower licence, it constitutes simultaneously both a licence of public works and of public service:

- Public works because the licensed works, built by the licensee, are public works that will be returned to the State upon expiration of the licence and owing to the fact that, by the licence, the State entrusts the licensee with a set of rights and obligations to ensure the best usage of natural assets of a watercourse for the general good of the community.[2] As a result, the works of the licensee are of a public works nature.

- Public service, because the licence does not have the individual consumption of the licensee as its sole or predominant purpose: it is a mode of delegated management of the public electricity service. In an important public notice of 28 September 1995 on this subject, the Council of State pronounced,

> In the hydropower sector, the licensed activities are of a public service nature. This solution derives, for the exploitation of hydraulic energy and inasmuch as this exploitation aims at supplying the generated electricity to the public or to public services, from all the provisions of the law of 1919. This law imposes a number of obligations on the licensee with regard to power supply, maximum rates, energy reserves (...). It confers on the licensee various prerogatives with regard to the temporary or definitive occupation of private property and the exclusion of special rights to the use of water. It ... provides for the free return of the works to the State when the licence has expired. All these elements constitute a legal system of public service. Consequently, these licences have the essential nature of public service delegations.

Hydropower licences are therefore subject to the substantive rules of public service licences: obligations of continuity, adaptation (to technical evolution in particular), and equality (in the treatment of users, for example). Disputes with the licensor are the responsibility of the administrative court. Damage to third parties or users are "public works" liabilities (administrative court and criminal courts, if applicable).

As public service delegations, the issuance and renewal of these licences is based on the principles of transparency and fairness: hence, the obligations of publicly announced calls for tender and competitive tendering, as will be seen below.

The hydroelectric licence is also a mixed, semi-regulatory, semi-contractual act.

The specification, which is deemed an administrative contract preceded by an agreement (between State and licensee), acquires its legal force only through its approval by a regulatory act (prefectural order or decree in Council of State).

In the specifications, some clauses are open to negotiation (contractual), others not at all (regulatory). Still other clauses are partially negotiable and partially imposed (mixed).

The licence produces its effects between the parties to the contract (contractual part), but also with regard to third parties, users or non-users of the licensed service (regulatory part).

---

2 Council of State, 22 February 1928, *De Sigalas*.

The contractual dimension of the licence is one of the fundamental differences from hydroelectric permits: in both cases, there is an approving regulatory act, a comparable technical-administrative document (specifications or water regulation), but only the licence contains an agreement, and therefore a contractual element.

This contractual dimension entails the consequence, as does any administrative contract, that the State has the opportunity to modify the content of the contract unilaterally: the contracting party (licensee) accepts the principle and the eventuality by signing the licence agreement of which the content is not fixed.

If the modification causes damage to the licensee (who has not requested this modification) and unless compensation has been excluded by law and the latter can quantify it indisputably, he will be entitled to compensation if the balance of the licence is called into question. The administrative court has jurisdiction in this matter.

As mentioned above, the granting French State has been striving for several years for a new balance between energy, environmental and economic interests, by changing legislation and regulation in the direction of an ever-stronger integration of the regime of hydropower licences into the common law pertaining to water.

5. COMPETITIVE TENDERING FOR HYDROELECTRIC LICENCES

Since the Act of 29 January 1993 on the prevention of corruption and the transparency of economic life and state procedures was passed, the awarding and renewal of initial licences must be publicised beforehand to encourage applications; however, this law provided for a very important derogation in favour of licences granted to public institutions, which was the case involving Électricité de France (EDF).

Moreover, the 1919 Act introduced a "right of preference" which, in the event of equivalent offers, gave priority to the incumbent licensee for the award of a renewed licence. Under these conditions, since the mid-1990s, EDF has been granted numerous hydropower licence renewals, without any competitive tendering procedure. Some of these licences were even renewed automatically for 30 years, without any administrative procedure and on the same conditions, simply because the licensing authority did not bother to reallocate the licence on the basis of the new mandates.

All this has changed under the influence of European law, which aims to make provisions for equal access and equitable participation of tenderers in the awarding of licence contracts, both at local level and at the level of the European

Union. This is in accordance with the principles of the Treaty on the Functioning of the European Union, and in particular the principles of free movement of goods, freedom of establishment and freedom to provide services, as well as the principles deriving therefrom such as equal treatment, non-discrimination and transparency.

The automatic renewals for 30 years and the right of preference have been removed by the Water Act of 1992 and the 2006 Act on water and the aquatic environment.

Pursuant to this, EDF lost the benefit of its privileged status by becoming a public limited company pursuant to the Act of 9 August 2004: as a result of this change of status, EDF can no longer avail itself of the protective provisions that made it possible to shelter the 322 hydroelectric licences it has in operation in France from being subject to tendering competition. From now on, EDF is exposed to the same rule of competition as its competitors in France have already been (the ENGIE group and the independent producers).

EDF can no longer claim to be the sole beneficiary of the licences to be renewed; however, each year hydropower licences expire and renewals are issued for periods shorter than the initial licences. Thus, we have witnessed an uninterrupted wave of successive renewals lasting several decades. Ultimately, the 400 French hydroelectric licences will be put back into play when it is time to renew them.

The French powers that be have therefore updated the texts governing the allocation and renewal of hydropower licences by transposing into French law the 2014/23/EU Directive of 26 February 2014 on the awarding of licensing contracts, and it has been made all the more urgent by the European Commission's having sent a formal notice to France in October 2015, deeming the conditions under which the French authorities awarded and maintained the bulk of the hydroelectric licences in France for EDF incompatible with Articles 102 and 106(1) of the Treaty on European Union. These conditions, according to the Commission, contribute towards keeping EDF in an ultra-dominant position in the power supply market.

Prior to this formal notice, in the spring of 2010, the French authorities had announced the launching of procedures for competitive tendering for expiring hydroelectricity licences, mainly operated by EDF and SHEM, a subsidiary of ENGIE, following a first infringement proceeding initiated by the Commission against France. The first public call for tenders had to be launched at the end of 2011–beginning of 2012 and was to cover a dozen valley licences to be renewed before the end of 2015 (for around 5,000 MW, i.e. 20 per cent of France's hydroelectric power): a string of developments granted in the Ossau valleys, Tet, Louron, Drac, Truyere, Dordogne and Beaufortain.

Nine years have passed since this announcement and not one of these licences has yet been subject to a call for tender, because of the substantive debate that has begun between the French authorities and the European Commission on the timetable, modalities and even the opportunity of these tendering procedures.

Many voices of protest have been raised in France since 2010 (local elected representatives and parliamentarians, trade unions, professionals and employees of hydropower plants) to object against a competition that purportedly would undermine social, economic and ecological foundations, as well as the maintenance of hydroelectricity and water management which, as we have seen previously, relies now on a global approach in France and no longer on sector activities.

The issue of reciprocity is also highlighted in the debate on this issue, as the majority of European countries concerned have sheltered their hydroelectric facilities' competitive tendering.

Consequently, France has undertaken to renegotiate this entire matter with the Commission, highlighting the contributions of the Law on the energy transition for green growth of 17 August 2015, which consolidated the licences regime and aimed at guaranteeing that public service stakeholders of the French hydropower industry would be respected. This law makes it possible to regroup from now on, by homogeneous valleys, "hydraulically linked" licences coming either from the same operator, or from different operators, bringing them together in the long term under a single licensing contract (which would lead to extension of some of them and the reduction of the length of other licences). It also makes it possible to extend certain current licences for new investments not provided for in the initial contract, in accordance with national and European law. It also provides for the possibility of setting up mixed hydroelectric power companies, involving interested local communities and a hydroelectric provider appointed by the State after a public notice of competitive tender.

The French authorities thus wish to be able to mitigate the effects of a fierce competition for hydroelectric licences that are also privileged instruments of water management in France: it is sufficient to note that 75 per cent of surface water reserves in France are stored in the dams managed by EDF and that many licences are multiple-purpose. In addition to electricity generation, many of them also ensure public services or serve public interests or the common good for the benefit of third parties or other users in the areas of irrigation, tourist activities, flood capping, tourist or commercial navigation, storage of drinking water, industrial water releases or cooling, feeding of snow cannons, etc. With the announced competition of hydropower licences, many in France are concerned, on the one hand, about the fate that might befall the main source of renewable energy, and on the other, with the objectives of the common good and public services that are very often associated with it.

The discussions with Brussels have reached a new step in 2019. In March of this year, the European Commission sent letters of formal notice to seven Member States (Austria, France, Germany, Poland, Portugal, Sweden and United Kingdom) and a second complementary letter of formal notice to Italy to ensure that public contracts in the hydroelectric power sector are awarded and renewed in conformity with EU law.[3] In the case of France, as for Portugal, the European Commission considers that both the legislation and the practice of the national authorities are contrary to EU law. The European Commission is of the view that the French legislation allows some hydropower concessions to be renewed or extended without the use tender procedures.

6. CONCLUSION

Over the past few years, the legal regime pertaining to hydropower licences has changed markedly in France, mainly as a result of European law, which tends to favour opening markets, in a framework of non-discrimination and transparency.

This pressure from European law has added to the evolution of the internal legal framework in France, which tends to trivialise the hydroelectric licences regime by gradually erasing its initial specificities and by applying to it a global approach to water law that tends to favour protection and conservation of aquatic environments.

It is in this complex framework, remaining fully aware of the objectives and the means of the energy transition, that the French authorities must determine, in agreement with the European Commission, satisfactory ways of conducting effective competitive bidding that will not lead to detrimental effects with regard to the fundamental issues of hydropower in France.

3 Press release, European Commission, "Hydroelectric power concessions: Commission calls on 8 Member States to comply with EU law", 7 March 2019, IP/19/1477.

CHAPTER VIII
HYDROPOWER CONCESSIONS IN ITALY

Filippo DONATI

1. INTRODUCTION

This chapter is intended to offer a brief description of the hydropower concessions system in Italy.[1] It is divided into three parts. First, it describes the evolution of the Italian legislation on hydropower concessions (Section 2). Then, it reviews the infringement procedure initiated by the European Commission and still pending against Italy (Section 3). Finally, it addresses the issue concerning the consistency of the Italian hydropower concessions regime with EU competition principles (Section 4). The chapter ends with some concluding remarks (Section 5).

2. EVOLUTION OF ITALIAN LEGISLATION ON THE DURATION OF CONCESSIONS

The Italian legislation on hydropower concessions has gradually evolved from a State monopoly to a sector subject to competition. In this regard, three main periods can be identified.

2.1. PERIOD OF STATE MONOPOLY

In the first period, from 1933 until the beginning of the 1990s, a State monopoly excluded any competition in the hydropower sector.

Initially, the exploitation of water resources for energy production was carried out by private operators. However, with the entry into force of decree n. 1775 of 1933, setting forth a consolidated text on legislation regarding water resources

---

1 This subject has been recently analysed by S.R. MASERA, *Concessioni idroelettriche. Evoluzione e prospettive*, Pisa, 2018.

(the "Water Consolidation Act"), such operators lost the possibility to have their hydropower concession renewed. According to such legislation, upon expiry of the ongoing concession, the State acquired ownership and possession of the hydropower plant. In particular, the Water Consolidation Act provided that, upon expiry of the concession, the so-called "wet works" (dams, pipes and, in general, underwater infrastructures) would be conveyed, free of charge, into State ownership (article 25, paragraph 1). The so-called "dry-works" (the infrastructures on the ground), on the other hand, would remain the property of the concessionaire, unless the State had exercised its option to buy. In such a case, the Water Consolidation Act prescribed a criterion for the calculation of the purchase price, according to which the value of the infrastructures had to be determined without considering the revenues obtainable through them (article 25, paragraph 2).

The State monopoly over the hydropower sector was later confirmed by Law n. 1643 of 1962, which nationalised the entire electricity sector and reserved to a State-owned company, ENEL, the production, transport and distribution of energy (with exceptions for local authorities and self-producers). Given such reserve, hydroelectric concessions granted to ENEL had a perpetual nature.

2.2. INTRODUCTION OF COMPETITION

The State monopoly phase lasted about 60 years. The Italian State was forced to gradually allow competition in this sector, following the European directives on competition in the energy market. In particular, Directive 96/92/EC provided common rules for the internal market in electricity, with the aim of establishing a competitive internal electricity market. Starting from the entry into force of such directive, a second phase began. In this phase, Italy tried to slow down the liberalisation process imposed by the new EU directive, by extending the duration of the concessions then in force.

A first extension was introduced by the so called "Bersani Decree" (legislative decree n. 79 of 1999) which, although formally aimed at implementing Directive 96/92/EC in Italy, tried to keep the status quo by protecting the interests of the concessionaires. As a matter of fact, article 12 of the Bersani Decree imposed competitive tenders for the award of new hydropower concessions. However, the same article provided for an extension of the concessions then in force. In particular, the concessions granted to ENEL were extended until 2029, while the concessions of other operators, expired or expiring by 31 December 2010, were extended until the latter date. Moreover, the 'beauty contest' procedure envisaged by the Bersani Decree provided a right of first refusal for the outgoing concessionaire. In practical terms, this system allowed for an extension *sine die* of the existing concessions, similarly to what happened in England for the concessions granted until 2003.

In 2004, the EC Commission launched a first infringement procedure against Italy (no. 2002/2282). The Commission challenged both the preference granted to the outgoing concessionaire and the automatic extension of the concessions in force when the Decree came into force, considering such provisions as a barrier to the entry of new players into the Italian hydropower market.

Law n. 266 of 23 December 2005 (the Budget Law for 2006) repealed the "Bersani decree". New competitive rules for granting hydropower concessions were introduced, and no right of first refusal was granted to the outgoing concessionaire. Pursuant to the new legislation, a call for tender must have been launched five years before the expiry of each relevant concession for the granting of new concessions with a 30-year duration. The procedure envisaged was based on the principles of transparency, equal treatment and open competition. At the same time, however, the Budget Law for 2006 provided for a 10-year extension of the existing hydropower concessions, provided that certain plant improvement works had been carried out by the concessionaire.

Following the entry into force of the Budget Law for 2006, the EU Commission dismissed the infringement procedure against Italy, deeming the elimination of the right of first refusal for outgoing concession-holders sufficient to restore competition; this, notwithstanding the 10-year extension of the existing concessions.

The Budget Law was later declared invalid by the Constitutional Court, with ruling n. 1 of 2008, for violation of article 117, which defines the scope of the legislative powers attributed to the State and to the Regions. The Court observed that legislation on hydropower concessions does not fall within the field of "guarantee of competition", where the State has exclusive competence, but in the field "production, transport and national distribution of energy", where the regulation is attributed to the Regions in the framework of general principles defined by the State. According to the Court, the State, by establishing a 10-year extension of the existing concessions, had breached the sphere reserved by article 117 Cost. to the competence of the regional legislators.

Despite this decision, article 7 of the so-called "Cresci Italia" decree (legislative decree n. 78 of 2010, as amended by Law n. 122 of 2010) further extended the hydropower concessions' duration by five years (12 years for stock companies with private and public shareholders). This extension was introduced in order to allow contracting authorities sufficient time to launch the new tenders, and the operators sufficient time to amortise the investments made for obtaining the 10-year extension envisaged by the Budget Law for 2006.

The EU Commission launched a second infringement procedure against Italy (proceeding n. 2011/2026), considering the five-year extension prescribed by the legislative decree n. 78 of 2010 as an unjustified advantage for existing operators and a corresponding obstacle to the freedom of establishment of other operators.

In the meanwhile, article 7 of legislative decree n. 78 of 2010 was struck down by the Constitutional Court with ruling n. 205 of 2011. In this case also, the Constitutional Court held that the State had no power to legislate with such detail on hydropower concessions, since the choice on the duration of the concession was reserved by Article 117 Cost. to each Region.

Legislative decree n. 83 of 2012 on sustainable growth opened a third phase, still in progress, with new legislation directed to launching new tenders for hydropower concessions, in order to promote competition in this sector. Under this legislation, Regions and Autonomous Provinces shall launch competitive tenders for awarding new hydropower concessions, five years prior to the expiry of the existing concession (article 37 of legislative decree n. 83 of 2012). Legislative decree n. 83 of 2012 further provides that, for those concessions which are overdue or which fall due by 31 December 2017, new tenders shall be launched within two years from entry into force of the implementing ministerial decree. It is worth noting that, pursuant to the new legislation, the winning bidder will be obliged to acquire from the outgoing concessionaire the "concession going concern" at its market value.

The maximum validity of concessions will range from 20 to 30 years and will be decided by the contracting authority (Region or Autonomous Province), depending on the project's required investments. According to the Constitutional Court, the new legislation does not violate article 117 Cost. because it sets out principles to be implemented by each Region with regard, for instance, to the duration of the new concessions (decision n. 28 of 2014).

The definition of award criteria has been reserved to a ministerial decree, not yet published, which will implement the provisions of legislative decree n. 83 of 2012.

3. THE INFRINGEMENT PROCEDURE

The European Commission has challenged the provisions of article 37 of legislative decree n. 83 of 2012 on sustainable growth, setting out new rules for granting concessions for hydropower production in Italy, in two respects.

In the first place, this legislation, by extending the duration of concessions which are overdue or which fall due by 31 December 2017, would infringe the freedom of establishment principle guaranteed by article 49 TFEU, as implemented by Directive 2006/123/EC (the "Services Directive"). In particular, such extension would infringe article 12 of the Services Directive, according to which, in the event that the number of authorisations available for a given activity is limited due to the scarcity of natural resources or technical capacity, authorisations "shall be granted for an appropriate limited period and may not be open to automatic renewal".

Secondly, the obligation for each new concessionaire to purchase the "concession going concern" at market value, even if it intends to build new plants, would result in an unjustified advantage for the outgoing concessionaire. In addition, the criteria imposed by legislative decree n. 83 of 2012 for the purchase of the concession going concern would be unreasonable and unjustified. As a matter of fact, the new concessionaire is forced to pay also for the so-called "wet works", despite the fact that these, upon expiry of the concession, would be acquired by the State, automatically and without consideration, pursuant to article 25, paragraph 1, of the Water Consolidation Act. The imposition on bid winners of such high and unjustified costs, according to the Commission, would end up guaranteeing the current concessionaires (which should not pay for the purchase of the plant) a significant competitive advantage. This would create a major obstacle to the entry of new operators into the Italian market.

It is worth noting that the Commission, while launching the new infringement procedure against Italy, did not react against other Member States which were far behind in opening the hydropower sector to competition.

As a matter of fact, the report presented by the Florence School of Regulation in 2015[2] highlighted the existence of profound differences in the regulatory framework in force in the Member States of the European Union. In particular, differences were noted with regard to the awarding procedure for hydropower concessions, the duration of the concession granted by the State and, in general, the degree of market opening to competition. In this regard, the Florence School of Regulation report indicates that, to date, various States have not yet activated a tender regime for the awarding of hydropower concessions and that probably some of them will never do so.

In such a framework, the initiation of an infringement procedure against Italy alone, notwithstanding that other Member States are far behind in opening up their hydropower sectors to competition, clearly raises some perplexities. Indeed, the Commission's behaviour seems to call into question the principle of uniform application of EU law in the Member States, in particular with respect to the freedom of establishment guaranteed by article 49 TFEU.

An uncoordinated market opening in the European Union, where some countries have guaranteed effective competition while others continue to protect national operators, would create a situation of imbalance in the European hydropower market.

The main argument used by the Commission in the infringement procedure against Italy, namely the distortion of competition deriving from the excessive

---

2 J.-M. Glanchant, M. Saguan, V. Rious, S. Douguet, *Regimes for granting the right to use hydropower in Europe*, Research Report of European University Institute, Florence School of Regulation, 2015.

duration of the Italian concessions, should also be extended to other States. Indeed, similar considerations should also apply to those countries which grant open-ended concessions (Sweden and, until 2003, the United Kingdom) or very long ones (Austria), or which grant concessions without an open and transparent tender (Germany). Why has the Commission not initiated infringement proceedings against these countries?

The Florence School of Regulation report indicates that, in light of the regulatory framework in force in Europe, the main way to ensure the application of EU law would be the harmonisation of regulatory frameworks in the Member States. The initiation of infringement procedures outside a systematic regulatory harmonisation design could, paradoxically, increase imbalances within the European Union, further favouring companies in countries that have not yet opened their hydropower sector to competition.

On 7 March 2019, the European Commission sent a complementary letter of formal notice to Italy, as it considers that the Italian authorities have failed to organize transparent and impartial selection procedures for the grant of hydropower authorisations that have expired.[3]

4. CONSISTENCY OF THE ITALIAN CONCESSIONS REGIME WITH EU COMPETITION PRINCIPLES

The new infringement procedure launched by the Commission raises some concern. As a matter of fact, the entry into force of legislative decree n. 83 of 2012, as mentioned above, opened a new phase in the Italian hydropower regulatory framework, aimed at opening up the country to competition through new tender procedures. Moreover, the objections raised by the Commission against legislative decree n. 83 of 2012 appear to be in contrast with the attitude taken in 2006, when the Commission closed the previous infringement procedure open against Italy, despite the 2006 Budget Law which provided for a 10-year extension of the then existing concessions.

In any case, contrary to what the Commission claims, article 37 of legislative decree n. 83 of 2012 does not contemplate any "automatic extension" of ongoing concessions, but rather a regulation aimed at speeding up the launching of new tenders, thus placing Italy in a more advanced position compared to that of other Member States with regard to the opening up of the hydropower sector to competition.

It is also worth noting that article 37 of legislative decree n. 83 of 2012 seeks to balance two opposing needs: the general interest in opening up the market

3 Press release, European Commission, 'Hydroelectric power concessions: Commission calls on 8 Member States to comply with EU law', 7 March 2019, IP/19/1477.

and the development of competition, on the one hand, and the protection of investment on hydropower plants, on the other side.

From this standpoint, the new legislation obliges the winning bidder to purchase the "concession going concern" at market value. According to the Commission, however, this regulation would result in an unjustified privilege for the outgoing concessionaire (mainly Italian) and an obstacle to the entry of new operators into the market. In particular, the Commission has considered as unreasonable and unjustified the obligation of the winning bidder to pay for the "wet works" which would later be acquired by the State, automatically and without consideration, pursuant to article 25, paragraph 1, of the Water Consolidation Act. According to the Commission, the new concessionaire

> has to pay to the outgoing one huge sum (...) for works belonging to the State and that, as a rule, the outgoing concessionaire has amortized totally during the concession (...). The result is a privileged position for the outgoing concessionaire, which is the only one not to be obliged to take over the plant paying a fee.

The Italian Competition Authority, in its opinion AS1137 of 4 July 2014, substantially shared the view of the Commission.

The view of the Commission appears to be only partly grounded. In particular, the Commission's interpretation of article 25 of the Water Consolidation Act might be questioned. According to the current regulatory framework, the Regions and the Autonomous Provinces may, upon expiry of hydropower concessions, decide not to grant new hydropower concessions where "they consider a prevailing public interest to exist for a different use of water, incompatible with the maintenance of hydropower use". In such a case, the "wet works" would be acquired at no cost by the Region or Autonomous Province where the hydropower plant is located. In case of a new tender, instead, the "wet works" would be part of the hydropower going concern to be transferred to the new concessionaire. In any case, article 25 of the Water Consolidation Act can be considered as repealed by article37 of legislative decree n. 83 of 2012, which, by providing that the successor pays for "wet works", clearly implies that the winning bidder acquires ownership and the right to use such works.

Overall, the approach followed by legislative decree n. 83 of 2012 seems reasonable in principle. It is based on the principle that the new concessionaire should take over ownership of the power plant, and that compensation should be paid to the outgoing concession holder for the investments made on it. Such principle guarantees the general interest in the efficient use of water resources for power-generation purposes. In any case, the purchase price to be paid for the hydropower going concern should not exceed the amount that will allow the outgoing concessionaire to recover the investment made and obtain a fair remuneration of the capital invested.

5. CONCLUDING REMARKS

In conclusion, the Commission launched an infringement procedure against a country in which, reportedly, the hydropower market is more competitive in respect to other Member States, which are not subject to infringement proceedings.

An uncoordinated market opening in the European Union might create imbalances with an adverse impact on the proper functioning of the internal market. Regulatory harmonisation, instead of launching uncoordinated infringement procedures against single Member States, would be the best way to create an internal market in the hydropower sector.

In any case, the new regime on hydropower concessions set out by legislative decree n. 83 of 2012 represents a step forward in the direction of opening up the Italian hydropower market to competition. Unfortunately, the implementation of legislative decree n. 83 of 2012 has been reserved to a ministerial decree, which has not yet been published. The reform envisaged by legislative decree n. 83 of 2012 is, therefore, not yet operational.

CHAPTER IX
HYDROELECTRIC CONCESSIONS
The Portuguese Legal Framework

Lourenço VILHENA DE FREITAS and Inês DE ABREU RÉGIO

1. INTRODUCTION

In Portugal, in 2019, renewable energy sources contribute to 51.9 per cent of the electricity generation mix. Of this 51.9 per cent, 17.5 per cent was hydroelectric power.

This chapter aims to analyse the evolution and the current legal framework applicable to the hydroelectric sector, and the impact of the process of liberalisation of the electricity market on it.

Considering that hydroelectric energy was always been an important source of energy for the Portuguese territory, some relevant measures have been adopted in the past and continue to be taken in order to ensure the sustainability of the hydroelectric sector. In view of this, this chapter also contains an analysis of the capacity mechanisms responsible for ensuring continuous hydroelectric power plant availability and, consequently, for securing the supply of hydroelectric power.

2. FROM THE EARLY DAYS TO THE MONOPOLY OF EDP

The Organisation of Postal, Telegraph, Telephone and Electricity Industries Inspection Law of 24 May 1911 was the first Portuguese official law related to the production and supply of energy – mainly hydroelectric production.[1]

More than 30 years later, the Electrification of the Country Law (Law no. 2002, 26 December 1944) created the legal framework for electrification in

---

1 SUZANA TAVARES DA SILVA, *Direito da Energia*, Coimbra Editora, 2011, p. 74.

Portugal. It established a set of private concessions related to the production and transportation of electricity which were assured by the State. In addition, the activity of electricity distribution was carried out by the municipalities.[2]

In 1975, with the nationalisation of the electric power companies, all the services facilities in the national territory were transferred to the Portuguese State, which brought to an end to the model of public service concessions. In fact, the operation companies responsible for the production, transmission and distribution of electricity were nationalised. This led to the creation of the Electricidade de Portugal ('Electricity of Portugal State Corporation – EDP' by Decree Law No. 502/756, 30 June.[3] EDP became responsible, exclusively and for an indefinite period, for the establishment and operation of the public services of electricity production, transportation and distribution in Portugal.[4]

In 1988, the electricity sector was opened to the private sector, through an amendment to the Sector Delimitation Law, approved by Decree-Law no. 449/88, 10 December.[5]

In 1991, EDP was transformed into a public limited company, which represented the first step in the process of restructuring and privatisation of EDP. In addition, EDP was split and several companies were created from the capital of EDP in order to explore the activities of the electricity sector. In this context, 'REN – National Electricity Grid' was created as the national electricity transmission grid concessionaire.[6] The same year, Decree-Law no. 99/91 revoked the 1944 Electrification of the Country Law and established the general principles applicable to electricity generation, transmission and distribution activities. This Decree-Law established the principle of free access to the electricity production activity, subject to the grant of a generation license: the issue of a bound generation license or an unbound generation license depended on whether or not the producer had the obligation to guarantee a supply of electricity for the public electricity system. Thus, Decree-Law no. 99/91, created the Public Electricity System (SEP), which comprises the National Transmission Grid (*Rede Nacional de Transporte or RNT*), operated under a public service concession regime. In practice, the RNT concessionaire (REN) is responsible for acquiring electric power from the producers and selling it to the distribution companies.

2 João Miranda, *Temas de direito da Energia*, Almedina, Lisboa, No. 3, 2008, p. 120.

3 Marisa Apolinário, *O Sector da Energia em Portugal*, Almedina, Lisboa, 2016, p. 546.

4 Marisa Apolinário, *O Sector da Energia em Portugal*, Almedina, Lisboa, 2016, p. 547.

5 João Miranda, *Temas de direito da Energia*, Almedina, Lisboa, No. 3, 2008, p. 121.

6 Later on, the evolution of the sector forced the further consolidation of the national transmission grid concessionaire position as an entity independent of other operators. Therefore, the shareholdings of EDP in the capital of REN were reduced. In 2006, REN was restructured in order to integrate regulated electricity and natural gas assets and was denominated as 'REN – Redes Energéticas Nacionais, SGPS, S.A' and was privatised in 2012.

In 1995, a package of legislation – comprising Decree-Law nos. 182/95, 183/95, 184/95, 185/95, 186/95. 187/95 and 188/95, all of 27 July – was adopted, establishing a new legal regime for the electricity sector. In particular, Decree-Law no. 182/95 established the legal scheme applicable to the National Electricity System, which comprises the Public Electric System (regulated market) and an Independent Electric System (free market). Under the SEP the production, transmission and distribution of electricity were developed as a public service in which the operators had the obligation to provide electricity according to the appropriate quality of service standards and the principle of the applying a uniform nationwide tariff.

Pursuant to article 3 of Decree-Law no. 183/95 of 27 July 1995, the integration into the SEP of new power plants was carried out in accordance with the definition of the expansion needs of the SEP's electric power system. Firstly, the Directorate General of Energy and Geology (DGEG) issued a preliminary authorisation to allocate the site chosen (without prejudice to an agreement for the use of the public water domain owned by that place), and, in accordance with a tender specification approved by the concessionaire of the national transmission grid (RNT), DGEG selected the operator of the electric power plant. Then, a bound agreement was entered into by RNT concessionaire and the producer, who also benefited from a bound generation license.[7] The terms of this license coincided with the terms of the concession agreement for the use of the water domain.[8]

Regarding production, three companies that had bounded production licenses (which had an exclusive commercial relationship with the RNT concessionary) were:

- EDP–Gestão de Produção de Energia, S.A. (an associated company which capital is wholly owned by EDP);
- Tejo Energia, S.A.;
- Turbogás–Produtora Energética, S.A. ('Turbogás').

At the end of 2005, these three companies had a combined installed capacity of 8,739 MW, of which EDP–Gestão de Produção de Energia, S.A had 7,164 MW (82 per cent of the total). In the same year, EDP, through EDP–Gestão de Produção de Energia S.A., held a market share of 63 per cent in the SEP in terms of liquid production. The EDP group also had shareholdings in the other two producers.[9]

EDP–Gestão de Produção de Energia, S.A. was responsible for hydroelectric power production. In that sector, it owned the dams and hydroelectric power

---

7 Articles 5, 8, 7, 6, 9, 18 of Decree-Law no. 183/95, 27 July 1995.

8 Article 20 of Decree-Law no. 183/95, 27 July 1995.

9 Lourenço Vilhena de Freitas, *Direito Administrativo da Energia*, AAFDL, 2013, p. 33.

facilities of Aguieira; Alqueva; Alto Lindoso; Alto Rabagão; Baixo Sabor; Belver; Bemposta; Bouçã; Bruceira; Cabril; Caldeirão; Caniçada; Caniços; Carrapatelo; Castelo do Bode; Crestuma-Lever; Desterro; Drizes; Ermal; Ermida; Foz Tua; Frades; Fratel; Fridão; Guilhofrei; Lagoa Comprida; Lindoso; Miranda; Paradela; Pateiro; Pedrogão; Picote; Pisões; Pocinho; Ponte da Esperança; Ponte de Jugais; Póvoa; Pracana; RaivaL; Régua; Rei de Moinhos; Riba Côa; Ribafeita; Ribeiradio–Ermida; Sabugueiro I; Salamonde; Santa Luzia; Senhora do Porto; Torrão; Touvedo; Valeira; Varosa; Velada; Venda Nova; Vila Cova; Vilar-Tabuaço and Vilarinho das Furnas.

In the Unbound Electricity System (*Sistema Eléctrico Não Vinculado* – SENV), comprised in the Independent Electricity System, operators were allowed to use the transportation and distribution infrastructures for the sale of electricity, by paying the applicable tariffs. The non-bound generation licenses were granted by the DGCE, at the request of the interested party, and after consulting the Planning Entity (articles 30 and 31 of Decree-Law no. 183/95, 27 July 1995).

In 2005, the EDP group had a market share of 50 per cent of the electricity supplied to the SENV. The non-bound distribution licenses were granted by the Director-General for Energy for an indefinite period.[10]

3. LIBERALISATION OF THE ELECTRICITY MARKET

The electricity sector was traditionally subject to a public monopoly extending to production, transportation and distribution activities.[11] In fact, producers included in the SEP had an exclusive commercial relationship with the RNT concessionaire based on long-term agreements. These agreements are called Energy Acquisition Agreements (*Contratos de Aquisição de Energia* or CAEs). These agreements, provided for in Decree-Law no. 182/95, were entered into by the hydroelectric power producers and the RNT concessionaire. Under the agreements, producers had the obligation to supply electricity to the RNT concessionaire and to sell all the electricity produced in the hydroelectric power plants to one single buyer. The CAE did not reflect the conditions arising from a free and competitive market. These agreements recognised the expected revenues for the producers and compensations that parties of these agreements were entitled to in case of non-compliance with, modification or termination of the agreement, for reasons not attributed to them. The fixed costs of the power plants and variable production costs were also covered by these agreements.

The European liberalisation process has completely changed this landscape. The first liberalisation package for the energy sector was published in 1991.

---

[10] Articles 37 and 39 of Decree-Law no. 183/95, 27 July 1995.

[11] Pedro Gonçalves, *Temas de direito da Energia*, Almedina, No. 3, 2008, p. 186.

As part of the package, Directive 96/92/EC aimed to address monopolistic situations and ensure third-party access (TPA) to the electricity grid. Thereafter, Directive 2003/54/EC, together with Directive 2001/55/EC for natural gas, defined the creation of an internal energy market as one of the main goals of the European energy policy.[12,13] On this internal market, consumers could freely choose their suppliers and suppliers could supply their customers without any obstacles. Therefore, it ensured free movement as foreseen in the Treaties on European Union.[14]

A series of reforms were also introduced at the regional and national levels. At regional level, in January 2004, the Portuguese Republic and the Kingdom of Spain signed the Agreement for establishing the Iberian Electricity Market (MIBEL), i.e. a single market in which all the agents would have the same rights and obligations.[15] This Agreement never came into force and, in October of the same year, the parties entered into the Santiago de Compostela Agreement, which constituted, essentially, a review of the Agreement signed in January 2004.

The reform of MIBEL came into force on 1 July 2007 and it was necessary to adopt measures to enforce the cooperation and convergence between the Portuguese and Spanish electricity systems.[16,17,18] Subsequently, at the XXIII Portuguese–Spanish Summit, that took place in Braga in January 2008, the Agreement was signed which revised the Santiago Agreement.

In Portugal, the liberalisation process started through the 'legislative package of 1995'[19] and was reinforced by Decree-Law no. 240/2004 of 27 December 2004 and further by Decree-Law no. 29/2006 of 15 February 2006 and Decree-Law no. 172/2006 of 23 August 2006.[20] Decree-Law no. 29/2006 marked a significant step in the dismantlement of monopolies, based on ownership unbundling between electricity production and supply (competitive activities) on one side, and the transportation of electricity (non-competitive activity) on the other side.[21] In this context, electricity was converted into a 'market asset'.[22]

Meanwhile, the liberalisation process was not comprehensive: it only covered the activities of production and commercialisation, but not the transportation

---

12 Please see in particular recitals 2, 4, 7, 20, article 3, paragraph 1 and articles 10, 15, 20 and 21 of Directive 2003/54/EC.

13 João Miranda, *Temas de direito da Energia*, Almedina, Lisboa, No. 3, 2008, p. 123.

14 João Miranda, *Temas de direito da Energia*, Almedina, Lisboa, No. 3, 2008, p. 123.

15 Suzana Tavares da Silva, *Temas de direito da Energia*, Almedina, Lisboa, No. 3, 2008, p. 289.

16 For more information, see the MIBEL website: https://www.mibel.com/en/home_en/.

17 Suzana Tavares da Silva, *Temas de direito da Energia*, Almedina, Lisboa, No. 3, 2008, p. 290.

18 Please see article 7 of the Santiago de Compostela Agreement.

19 Suzana Tavares da Silva, *Direito da Energia*, Coimbra Editora, 2011, p. 74.

20 Pedro Gonçalves, *Temas de direito da Energia*, Almedina, Lisboa, No. 3, 2008, p. 187.

21 Marisa Apolinário, *O Sector da Energia em Portugal*, Almedina, Lisboa, 2016, p. 554.

22 Pedro Gonçalves, *Temas de direito da Energia*, Almedina, Lisboa, No. 3, 2008, p. 187.

or distribution activities, which had been confined to concessionaires under the exclusive concession regime.

In 2009, the Third Electricity Directive 2009/72/EC, which formed part of the 'Third Energy Package', established additional common rules for the internal electricity market.

In order to comply with the EU obligations, an extensive revision of Decree-Law no. 29/2006 was carried out by Decree-Law no. 78/2011, 20 June 2011, Decree-Law no. 215-A/2012 of 8 October 2012, Decree-Law no. 178/2015 and later by Law no. 42/2016 of 28 December 2016.

These reforms concerning liberalisation impacted the hydroelectric power sector, since they determined the liberalisation of the selling of hydroelectric power and the extinction of CAEs, which we highlight below.

4. EARLY TERMINATION OF CAEs AND THE RESPECTIVE COMPENSATORY MECHANISM (CMEC)

4.1. BACKGROUND FOR THE REFORM

The liberalisation process determined the end of CAEs. In the hydroelectric power sector, the CAEs, entered into by some of the ordinary producers, were terminated and were replaced by an incentive mechanism called 'CMEC' (Costs of Maintenance of the Contractual Equilibrium). The CMEC functions as an indirect capacity payment to avoid the dismantlement of the hydroelectric power plant, in recognition of the fact that the benefit assured by the CAE will not be adequately ensured by the revenues from the sale of electricity in a liberalised market.

The ordinary regime of CAEs was terminated as a consequence of the transposition of the second Electricity Directive. This termination was also necessary in order to respect the Cooperation Protocol and the Iberian Agreement for the Building of an Iberian Electricity Market (MIBEL).

The resulting reform of the electricity system, that included the hydroelectric system, was based on three key points:

- Establish bilateral contracting relationships for commercial transactions. Thus, producers and suppliers may enter into agreements for the purchase and sale of electricity with any agent of the SEN (*Sistema Eléctrico Nacional* – National Electricity System);
- Determine the earlier termination of CAEs entered into by hydropower producers and the RNT concessionaire;
- Consequently, establish the compensatory measures designated as CMEC.

Therefore, the CMEC appeared as due compensation for the earlier termination of CAEs, ensuring an adequate economic balance for the producers and guaranteeing compensation for the investment made and the coverage of commitments underlying CAEs that are not guaranteed by expected market revenues.[23]

The details of the new regulatory regime were defined in the abovementioned Decree-Law no. 240/2004. However, it was only in July 2007 that the CAE was effectively replaced by this compensatory mechanism, in accordance with Decree-Law no. 172/2006 of 23 August 2006.

4.2. THE CMEC UNDER DECREE-LAW NO. 240/2004

Decree-Law no. 240/2004 established the provisions for the early termination of CAEs and set out compensatory measures in order to ensure a proper economic balance for the producers that held a previous CAE.

4.2.1. Early Termination of CAEs and Compensatory Measures

For the early termination of a CAE, article 9 of Decree-Law no. 240/2004 established the need for the electric producers to enter into a contract with RNT, i.e. a termination agreement for each thermal power generation plant or for each group of power plants belonging to the same applicable water production unit. The coming into effect of each termination agreements was dependent on its approval by the Ministry of Energy (responsible for the energy area) and its publication in the Portuguese Official Gazette.

Pursuant to article 14 of the Decree-Law, in its original version, the early termination of the CAE is also dependent on the grant of non-bound electricity production licenses for each power plant. In practice, with regard to the liberalisation of SEN, bound licenses are replaced by non-bound licenses.

To preserve the contractual equilibrium disrupted by the early termination of the CAE, the Decree-Law granted the parties the right to receive compensation, as from the early termination of these agreements (article 2). Thus, the CMEC, in an indirect way, functions as a capacity payment and it guarantees that hydroelectric power stations continue to operate, which is important for the reliability of the system and guarantee of production and for the modernisation of the grid. This compensation ensures the maintenance of the contractual balance and guarantees, for the producers, equivalent economic benefits to those

23 Marisa Apolinário, *O Sector da Energia em Portugal*, Almedina, Lisboa, 2016, p. 555.

provided for in CAEs, which are not adequately ensured by the anticipated free market revenues. In case of delay in the payments of this compensation, the defaulting party has the obligation to pay interest.

This framework was scrutinised by the European Commission between 2004 and 2017, which considered the CMEC mechanism as adequate and necessary.

In fact, Portugal notified the measure for compensation for stranded costs on 1 April 2004, on the basis of the Communication from the Commission relating to the methodology for analyzing State aid linked to stranded costs. The Commission approved the measure in 2004 to cover the potential losses made by three undertakings, in its Decision concerning State aid N161/2004 – Stranded costs in Portugal (Commission Decision C(2004)3468 of 22 September 2004).

Furthermore, the CMEC mechanism was also scrutinised in Commission Decision (EU) 2017/1592 of 15 May 2017 on the measure SA 35429 2017/C (ex 2013/NN).

4.2.2. *Calculation of the Compensatory Amounts and Adjustments*

The gross amount of CMEC is determined by the difference between the value of the CAE, as fixed at the time of the early termination of this agreement, and the expected revenues, in the free market, after deduction of the expected costs and charges of exploitation in the same period.[24]

The right to receive compensation for the early termination of a CAE may be granted to the producers (positive CMEC) or to the RNT concessionaire (negative CMEC). If a producer is party to more than one CAE, positive and negative CMEC are offset in order to determine the CMEC overall gross amount.

The compensation amounts may be subject to annual and final adjustments. The annual adjustments (positive or negative adjustments) take place during the activity period of each power plant, as provided for in the relevant CAE, with a maximum period of 10 years from the early termination of the CAE.[25] The final adjustment shall be carried out at the end of the activity of the power plant(s) and should not exceed a period corresponding to 10 years from the early termination of the CAE.

4.2.2.1. The impact of CMEC in the UGS Tariff

The positive CMEC, as well as the annual and final positive adjustments due to producers, constitute charges incorporated into the Underground Gas Storage

---

[24] Ibid, article 3, paragraph 1.
[25] Ibid, article 3, paragraph 5.

(UGS) Tariff. It covers costs of general economic interest by means of a fixed portion and the settlement portion and is supported by all the electricity consumers in the national territory, which are not party to a CAE.[26] In the event that negative CMEC and annual or final negative adjustments are determined, the RNT concessionaire has the right to receive corresponding compensation, paid by producers and subsequently deducted from the UGS tariff.

The fixed portion and the settlement portion are included in the UGS tariff, for each producer, from the early termination of the CAE until the originally anticipated time of termination as provided for in the CAE, applying the longest term of all the agreements held by each producer, in order to dilute these costs for the maximum period of time.[27] If at the end of this term the required compensatory amount is not fully recovered, this regime shall be extended until the amount due is fully paid.

4.2.2.2. Invoiced and Collection Operations

The invoice and collection of the fixed portion and the settlement portion from the consumers is carried out by the entities responsible for the transportation, distribution or supply of the electrical energy, and therefore each one of the entities involved in the electricity sector invoicing chain – ending in the final consumer – must have an impact on the value of the fixed portion and the settlement portion to be delivered by the RNT concessionaire to the producer or its respective assignees.

The concessionaire of the RNT is responsible for invoicing and collecting the amounts related to the fixed and settlement portions for delivery to the producer or its assignees.[28]

All entities in the electricity sector invoicing chain, up to the final consumer, pass on the amounts pertaining to the CMEC and, ultimately, the RNT concessionaire is responsible for charging the immediately subsequent entity in the invoicing chain, in order to deliver that amount to its addressees: the producers or their concessionaires.

---

26 Lourenço Vilhena de Freitas, *Direito Administrativo da Energia*, AAFDL, Lisboa, 2013, p, 43.

27 Article 5, paragraph 8, Decree-Law no. 240/2004.

28 To that end, the producers or their respective assignees shall invoice the amount corresponding to the monthly amount of the fixed portion and the settlement portion, and the concessionaire of the RNT shall, as well, on the business day following the receipt of the invoice, issue an invoice to the subsequent entity in the electricity sector invoicing chain. Subsequently, the RNT concessionaire collects the amounts related to the fixed portion and the settlement portion and delivers it to each producer or respective assignee, while also delivering the abovementioned amounts charged to the consumers with whom it has a direct relationship.

4.2.2.3. CMEC Revision Mechanism

The parameters for the determination of the CMEC amounts are determined by reference to a specific time point: the date of early termination of the CAE. However, these parameters are projected for the future because they aim to correspond to the costs of maintaining the contractual equilibrium, guaranteeing equivalent economic benefits to those that would be provided by the CAEs during the term of the contract. Therefore, in the calculation of the compensatory amount there is an element of unpredictability with regard to the value of the CAE, to expected revenues and to future variable charges. Accordingly, and in the event of a change in the operating conditions of the power stations which were considered at the time of conclusion, a mechanism for revision of the compensation must be established, which is provided for in article 11 of the Decree-Law under consideration.

The operations for determining the adjustments may lead to positive or negative results:

- In the event that positive adjustments are determined, and once they are approved, the DGEG shall report its results to the energy regulator, *Entidade Reguladora dos Serviços Energéticos* (ERSE), so that there is an impact on the UGS rate adjustment portion of the amount corresponding to the payment adjustment charge.
- In the event that negative adjustments are determined, the producer will be responsible to pay the concessionaire of the RNT the amount of the adjustment, and ERSE will reverse the UGS tariff.

4.2.3. Subsequent Developments

Decree-Law no. 240/2004 established the legal framework for the early termination of the CAE and the compensatory scheme. Since this Decree-Law came into force, the national electricity sector has changed considerably, requiring new amendments to the CMEC legal framework.

First, Decree-Law no. 199/2007 of 18 May 2007 adjusted the CMEC calculation method to the market reference price and costs, increasing the USG Tariff. This amendment was motivated by the following events:

1. The alteration of operating conditions of the electricity market at national and international levels and the approval of the new legal framework of the national electricity sector (SEN), the general legal guidelines of which are provided for in Decree-Law no. 29/2006 and later developed in Decree-Law no. 172/2006.
2. Escalation of the costs of fossil fuels in electricity production.

3. The necessary harmonisation of the prices currently practised in Portugal and Spain under MIBEL.

In the same year, Decree-Law no. 264/2007 introduced a special scheme for hydroelectric power plants according to which the exploitation licenses should remain in force for the term of the public water domain title.

In the context of the Portuguese financial and economic crisis, another important legal amendment was carried out by Decree-Law no. 32/2013, 26 February 2013, which determined the reduction of the electricity tariffs, to be executed by the Portuguese Government. The Government approved a new nominal rate applicable to the calculation of the CMEC fixed instalment annuity, allowing the reduction of said instalment by a total net present value of 120 million euros.[29]

In addition, Parliament approved, on 14 June 2017, the following recommendations to be complied with by the Portuguese Government (Resolution no. 158/2017):

- The reversal of CMEC amounts that will be determined in the final adjustment, provided for in article 170 of Law no. 42/2016 which approved the State Budget for 2017, in order to reduce the electricity tariffs for the year 2018 and beyond.
- The elimination of excessive rents in the electricity sector, specifically to reduce the CMEC amounts, by direct renegotiation or specific taxation of the producers.

The Portuguese Government has not introduced any amendment in the CMEC calculation.

5. THE CURRENT LEGAL FRAMEWORK OF HYDROELECTRIC CONCESSIONS

Decree-law no. 172/2006 established the legal framework for electricity production in the ordinary regime. According to its article 4, the activity of electricity production depends on the grant of a license to the respective producer.

However, pursuant to article 61, subparagraph (d) and article 68 of Law no. 58/2005 of 29 December 2005 (National Water Law) and article 23, paragraph 1

[29] See Order no. 85-A/2013, based on a proposal from EDP–Gestão da Produção de Energia, SA (the only producer that has accepted the early termination of CAEs).

of Decree-Law no. 226-A/2007, the capture of water for electricity production, as a private use of water resources, is subject to the previous award of the concession.[30]

The capture of public water for the production of hydroelectric energy must also be carried out in compliance with the provisions of the National Water Plan, the river basin management plans and the specific plans for water management in the energy field.

The procedure for the grant of a concession title reveals a dual concern: the protection of competition and the participation of third parties.[31]

In the event that the concession results from a public initiative, the concessionaire is chosen through a pre-contractual public tender procedure,[32] in accordance with the rules for the award of public works contracts or supply and acquisition of goods and services. The choice of procedure depends on whether or not the concession entails the execution of works. The former owner may exercise the right of preference in accordance with article 21 of this Decree-Law.

If the grant of the concession results from a request submitted by the interested party, the competent authority assesses the request and, in the absence of any cause precluding the opening of the concession procedure, this authority publicises the filing of the application for a period of 30 days in order to allow other interested parties to participate in a tender procedure.[33]

According to article 18, paragraph 8 of the National Water Law, the National Water Authority is responsible for the decisions to issue titles to use of water resources and its control and supervision.

Pursuant to article 68 of the National Water Law, the concession confers on its holder:

- The exclusive use, for the purposes and within the limits established in the respective agreement, of the objects subject to the concession;
- The right to use private land owned by third parties in order to carry out studies, surveys and polls required, by paying a compensation for any damage caused; and
- The right to claim and benefit from the necessary administrative easements and expropriations, in the event that the public utility of the use is declared.

In addition, and according to the same provision, the concession of use of water resources of the public domain is granted under the terms of a concession agreement to be entered into by the administration and the concessionaire.

---

30 Lourenço Vilhena de Freitas, *Direito Administrativo da Energia*, AAFDL, Lisboa, 2013, p. 46, fn.

31 Ana Raquel Gonçalves Moniz, *Temas de direito da Energia*, Almedina, Lisboa, No. 3, 2008, p. 41.

32 Article 24, paragraph 2 of Decree-Law no. 226-A/2007, 31 May 2007.

33 Articles 23 and 28 from Decree-Law no. 226-A/2007, 31 May and article 68, paragraph 5 of the National Water Law.

The concession agreement for the use of the public water domain establishes the terms, conditions and technical requirements of the concessionaire (provided for in Order no. 1450/2007) and sets forth all the rights and obligations of the contracting parties and the period of validity of the concession, which may not exceed 75 years.[34]

Pursuant to article 25, paragraph 4 of Decree-Law no. 226-A/2007, the conclusion of the concession agreement is subject to the provision of a financial security in order to ensure compliance with the obligations laid down in the agreement. In addition, the aforementioned Decree-Law also created the environmental restoration guarantee, due to the risks associated with the concession activities for water resources, which can be waived.[35]

The transferability of the title of use of the water domain is allowed, according to article 26 of Decree-Law no. 226-A/2007, 31 May, and the acquirer is subrogated to all rights and obligations of the assignor during the term of the respective title of use.

Pursuant to article 72 of the National Water Law, this transferability is allowed if:

- The title of use is an element of the transferred agricultural holding or of the commercial or industrial establishment or, in case of shareholdings, transfer of the company holding the title. In this case, the competent authority has to be notified at least 30 days in advance. The seller and the acquirer have to prove that the necessary requirements for the maintenance of the title are met.
- In all other cases, the transferability depends on the authorisation by the entity competent to issue the title.

In addition, according to Article 27 of Decree-Law no. 226-A/2007, the transaction and temporary assignment of the title depends on a prior notification (and not an administrative authorisation) in the event that:

- The transition or temporary assignment is related to uses at different sites within the same river basin and this possibility is provided for in their river basin management plan;
- The transition or temporary assignment does not involve the transfer of title of use relating to public supply for other uses;
- The requirements for the attribution of the title are met.

---

34 Article 68, paragraph 6 of the Water Law and also article 35, paragraph 2 and article 25, paragraph 2 of Decree-Law no. 226-A/2007.

35 Article 25, paragraphs 5 and 8 and Annex I (A) of Decree-Law no. 226-A/2007.

Lastly, it is important to note that the use of the water public domain has to comply with the environmental principles provided for in article 45 et seq. of the National Water Law and has to constitute a sustainable use of water resources, in order to guarantee their protection. Non-compliance with those principles may result in a review of the concession agreement[36]) and even the termination of the agreement.[37]

6. DIRECT CAPACITY PAYMENT MECHANISMS

6.1. BACKGROUND TO THE CHOICE OF CAPACITY MECHANISM IN PORTUGAL

The capacity markets have become a necessary feature of restructured markets, including in Portugal. They guarantee sufficient revenue and assure reliability where sole reliance on energy market revenues may not cover the long-term cost generation. Capacity mechanisms may take many forms, including payments to energy producers.[38] A capacity market pays electricity generators for having the ability to make power available, in a reliable way, regardless of how often they sell energy into the grid.

Decree-Law no. 264/2007 introduced capacity mechanisms for the first time in the ordinary regime for electric energy production in Portugal.

Article 33-A of this Decree-Law provides that the Government must define a remuneration mechanism to the available power guarantee of the power plants, which must be supported by all the electricity consumers through a feed-in-tariff remuneration scheme. The main objectives of this regime were to ensure an adequate answer to the electricity demand and adequate available capacity of the power plants in the ordinary regime. Based on this regime, Order no. 765/2010 established the regulatory framework of the power guarantee in Portugal, rewarding the availability of capacity and paying an incentive to investment for installed MW (capacity payments).

The Assistance Program entered into by and between the Portuguese Government and the European Central Bank, the European Commission and the International Monetary Fund (IMF) determined the revocation of this legal framework, according to the 'Memorandum of Understanding of Economic Policy Conditionality'. As a consequence, Order no. 139/2012 revoked

---

36 Article 28 of Decree-Law no. 226-A/2007.

37 Article 32 of Decree-Law no. 226-A/2007 and article 69, paragraph 6 of the National Water Law. See further: Ana Raquel Gonçalves Moniz, *Temas de direito da Energia*, Almedina, Lisboa, No. 3, 2008, p. 57.

38 Peter H. Griffes, 'Renewable Generation and capacity markets' (Third Quarter of 2014), (*International Association for Energy Economics*), p. 27.

Order no. 765/2010 and recommended the review and rationalisation of some of the incentives that benefited activities of the electric sector and encumbered the final electricity bill. This Order also established the principles for the review of these capacity mechanisms.

Consequently, Order no. 251/2012 reintroduced new capacity payments, limited to thermal plants and hydroelectric power facilities. Those capacity payments could only be payed after the Assistance Program to Portugal was concluded, i.e. starting in June 2014.

6.2. REQUIREMENTS FOR THE GRANTING OF INCENTIVES

According to article 2 of this Order, the capacity payments can be:

- Incentives to capacity *stricto sensu* (thermal); and
- Incentives to investment (hydroelectric power).

The incentives to capacity are payments to support the permanent availability of a certain capacity assured by thermal plants, which is needed to support the Electric National System (*Sistema Eléctrico Nacional*, SEN), and the incentive to investment is a payment to support investments in hydric technologies.

Pursuant to article 3 of Order no. 251/2012, these remuneration mechanisms are not applicable to power plants that:

- Hold a low installed liquid power; or
- Not sell the electricity in the free market scheme; or
- Hold an Energy Acquisition Agreement (*contratos de aquisição de energia*, CAE) or benefits of the compensatory mechanism introduced by Decree-Law no. 240/2004 – Costs of the Maintenance of the Contractual Equilibrium (that will be analysed below); or
- Receive or have received, directly or indirectly, any remuneration or incentive as compensation for the respective exploitation costs or that has ensured a minimum of profitability of the production activity.

In addition, incentives to investment (hydroelectric power) can only be granted to generator groups of hydroelectric power plants located in the Portuguese territory:

- If the license was issued after the entry into force of Decree Law no. 264/2007, 24 July, and prior to the entry into force of the Regulation no. 251/2012; or
- If the license is held by a party to implementation contracts of the National Program of High Hydroelectric Energetic Potential Power Plants (*Programa Nacional de Barragens de Elevado Potencial Hidroeléctrico*, PNBEPH).

The payment of those incentives is made upon request to DGEG by the producer and depends on a previous recognition of the eligibility of each generator group of power plants and a minimum availability coefficient of 70 per cent.

Even if the eligibility has been recognised, the generator group of power plants is only entitled to receive capacity payments if it proves to meet a minimum coefficient of availability, giving all the necessary information and undergoing the necessary performance availability tests.

6.3. CALCULATING THE MINIMUM COEFFICIENT OF AVAILABILITY

The entity responsible of the overall technical management of the SEN has to determine the final availability coefficient of each generator group of a power plant that benefits from the power guarantee incentives.[39] By March each year, this entity shall communicate to DGEG the final availability ratios of each group applicable to the calendar year.

The determination of the coefficients shall comply with several procedures set out in two orders: Order no. 251/2012 and Order no. 172/2013.

According to article 15 of Order no. 251/2012, the final availability coefficient applicable to each generator group shall be determined according to the values of the available active power recorded by each group in all the scheduled periods of the two calendar years immediately preceding the calendar year to which the incentive amount related, taking into account the results of the availability tests carried out in those two previous calendar years by the entity responsible for the overall technical management of the SEN. In the case of hydroelectric power plants, the power values referred to above are adjusted by the corresponding levels of reservoirs storage in order to neutralise the effect of the unavailability of water resources.

Order no. 251/2012 was developed by Order no. 172/2013. which establishes the regime for capacity verification of the power generation plants (thermal and hydroelectric), that benefit from remuneration, subsidy or co-payment mechanisms that take into account the availability of these power plants, and that are not subject to any special regime for checking availability. It sets the rules applicable to the power instructions, to be defined by the entity responsible for the overall technical management of the SEN, that must be respected during the performance of the availability tests at a particular power plant, as well as the penalties for non-compliance with those rules, which are then considered in the calculation of the final availability coefficient.

39 Article 14 of Order no. 251/2012.

Pursuant to article 2 of Order no. 172/2013, this legal framework is applicable, following certain procedures, to the power plants that:

- Have requested the recognition of the eligibility of their group of generators (paragraph (a) of article 2); and/or
- Benefit from the compensation inherent to the Costs of Maintenance of the Contractual Equilibrium (CMEC), foreseen in Decree-Law no. 240/2004 (as amended) (paragraph (b) of article 2).

For each power plant defined in the Order (i.e., power plants that have requested the recognition of the eligibility of their group of generators),[40] the entity responsible for the overall technical management of the SEN determines, once a year, the available average power according to the available power values registered in all hourly periods in the preceding two calendar years. For the power plants provided for in paragraph (b) of article 2 of Order no. 172/2013 (i.e., benefiting from the compensation inherent to the costs of maintenance of the contractual equilibrium – CMEC), the available average power is determined pursuant to Decree-Law no. 240/2004 as amended and Decree-Law no. 264/2007.

Before presenting the report with the calculation of the average available power and the final availability coefficient,[41] or the calculation elements of the average power available and the final values of the monthly availability coefficients,[42] the entity responsible for the overall technical management of the SEN shall make available to the owner of the power plants the elements used in the calculation of these values, who may, within a period of 10 days, submit a written response thereto.

6.4. THE METHOD OF CALCULATION, PAYMENT AND SUPERVISION OF CAPACITY PAYMENTS

The amounts of the capacity and investment incentives are based on different calculation methods. The amounts of the capacity incentives are determined according to a reference value applicable to all the power plants that benefit from this incentive.

The amounts of the investment incentives have adopted reference values resulting from the application of the formula provided for in the regime repealed by Order no. 139/2012, and the corresponding coverage index (CI) calculation

40 Paragraph (a) of article 2 of Order no. 172/2013.

41 Provided for in no. 3 of article 14 of Order no. 251/2012.

42 Depending on whether it is a power plant provided for in article 2 paragraph (a) or (b) of this Order.

methodology approved by the DGEG, considering the interruptibility of services contracted and the reduction, by half, of the obtained incentive value for the pumping power reinforcement.

The annual amounts of the power availability incentives must be approved by 31 July of each year by order of the member of the Government responsible for the energy sector, following a proposal by the General Director of DGEG, previously submitted to ERSE, and must be issued within 20 working days and shall be paid by the entity responsible for the overall technical management of the SEN.[43]

The attribution of these remuneration mechanisms is subject to complex and tight controls, carried out by different entities which are in constant exchange of information:

- DGEG supervises and controls the fulfilment of the conditions for the allocation of the power availability incentives;
- ERSE monitors the payments due as incentives carried out by the entity responsible for global technical management;
- DGEG shall inform the entity responsible for the overall technical management of the SEN as soon as an application for recognition of eligibility is submitted, sending the data referred to the generator group to which the request is made;
- DGEG shall also inform ERSE and the entity responsible for the overall technical management of the SEN whenever the eligibility of a generator group is recognised, sending the data concerning the conditions of the incentive, as well as informing on the circumstances for termination of the incentives granted.

7. OTHER INCENTIVES

7.1. NATIONAL PROGRAM OF DAMS WITH HIGH HYDROELECTRIC POTENTIAL

Portugal is one of the countries with the highest untapped hydric potential in the EU and a high dependence on energy from abroad. In order to ensure an increase in the current installed hydroelectric power, it is necessary to carry out a raft of investments in hydroelectric plants.

Therefore, the Portuguese Ministry of Economics, through the Directorate-General for Geology and Energy, and with the intervention of the national grid company REN and National Water Institute (*Instituto Nacional da Água*, INAG)

[43] Article 16 and 17 of Order no. 251/2012.

approved in 2007 the National Program for Dams with High Hydroelectric Potential (*Plano Nacional de Barragens de Elevado Potencial Hídrico*, PNBEPH).

This program aims to take advantage of the hydroelectric potential still to be explored, through the selection of sites for implementation or expansion of hydroelectric plants, according to the results of an environmental assessment process.[44] With the purpose of reducing the untapped hydropower potential from 54 per cent to 33 per cent by 2020, the Government has selected 10 sites in the national territory with high hydroelectric potential.

In addition, the interested parties act on their own initiative in order to construct the necessary infrastructures. Actually, they have to be submitted to tender proceedings, under the provisions of Law no. 58/2005 and Decree-Law no. 226-A/2007, in order for the grant of the respective concessions for the use of water resources.

In order to simplify these procedures, the Government approved:

- Decree Law no. 182/2008 which establishes the provisions for the implementation regime of this Program.
- Decree Law no. 301/2009 which, by use of the legislative authorisation granted by Law no. 83/2009 set out a special regime applicable to the necessary expropriations for the implementation or expansion of hydroelectric plants.

In 2017, the National Program of Dams with High Hydroelectric Potential was revised by the Portuguese Government, which decided to:

- Withdraw the hydroelectric power plants of Alvito and Girabolhos from the Program;
- Suspend the implementation of the Fridão hydroelectric power plant;
- Finish the construction of the remaining hydroelectric power plants.

7.2. MINI-HYDROELECTRIC POWER PLANTS

The promotion of the electrification of the country, through the construction of large hydroelectric power plants as well as the nationalisation of the electricity sector in 1976, has determined the extinction of several mini-hydroelectric power plants.[45]

However, Decree-Law no. 189/88, which is still in force, has established the legal framework applicable to small generators of electricity from renewable sources (Independent Electric System), including hydroelectric power plants

44 See Decree-Law no. 232/2007.

45 Cláudia Dias Soares, Suzana Tavares da Silva, *Direito das Energias Renováveis*, Almedina, 2014, p. 42.

with an injection capacity limited to 10 MW. With the objective of promoting this type of electricity production, the Decree-Law establishes a system of feed-in tariff for the sale of electricity generated by these mini-hydroelectric plants. In addition, subject to a later amendment,[46] the Decree has created an incentive for generation of electricity from renewable energy sources – an acquisition guarantee. In fact, the producers of hydroelectricity benefit from a purchase obligation, by the public grid, of the energy produced.

A later decree, Decree-law no. 35/2013, has established a new remunerative framework applicable to power plants.[47]

In 2010, the Portuguese Government designated the investment in renewable sources, mainly in small hydroelectric plants, as one of the objectives of the energy strategy for 2020 (Resolution no. 29/2010). The same year, Resolution no. 72/2010 simplified the licensing procedure and the necessary administrative authorisations for the implementation and exploitation of the mini-hydroelectric power plants. This Resolution also provided for the launch of tender proceedings, during 2010 and 2011, in order to implement licensed mini-hydroelectric power plants in the national territory. Applying this Resolution, Decree-Law no. 126/2010 established the legal regime for the implementation of hydroelectric projects with an injection capacity limited to 20 MW.

First, the open procedure regarding the operation concession of the abovementioned mini-hydroelectric power plants was intended to, simultaneously:

- Provide a title for the private use of water resources of the public domain (according to the terms provided for in Law no. 58/2005 and Decree-Law no 226-A/2007);
- Attribute a power injection capacity in the Public Service Network (RESP); and
- Identify the associated reception points for electricity generated in the hydroelectric centres.

Second, the members of the Government responsible for the areas of finance, energy and the environment were responsible for the promotion and organisation of the mentioned tender proceedings and the presidents of each hydrographic district administration (ARH) were responsible for its instruction and for the 'decision to contract'.

Third, Decree-Law no. 126/2010 fixed the concession period at 45 years and determined remuneration to the producers for the supply of electricity delivered

46 Decree-Law no. 168/99.

47 Provided for in Annex II of Decree-Law no. 189/88.

to RESP according to a specific tariff, to be in force for 25 years, with an average value of €95 per MWh.

Finally, in 2017, after reaching the conclusion that the environmental impacts created by mini-hydroelectric power plants are generally proportionately more significant than those created by the large hydroelectric power plants, the Portuguese Government has committed itself:

- To revoke Order no. 72/2010, in order to avoid a new tender procedure for the additional 100 MW; and also
- To consider reviewing the power installed (250 MW) provided for in the referred Order.

8. CONCLUSION

The hydroelectric sector has a significant participation in the energy mix, since it produces a continuous flux of energy, not subject to external meteorological factors, as is the case with other renewable energies: wind and solar energy.

The process of liberalisation of the energy market, impacted the hydroelectric sector since it determined the liberalisation of the selling of hydroelectric power and the early termination of CAEs, as exclusive and long-term agreements, entered into by the hydroelectric power producers and the RNT concessionaire, that recognised the expected revenues for the producers and compensation that parties to these agreements are entitled to in case of non-compliance with, modification or termination of the agreement, for reasons not attributed to them.

To guarantee continuous hydroelectric power plant availability and, consequently, the security of supply of hydroelectric power, capacity remuneration mechanisms have been approved and adopted by the Portuguese State.

In these terms, capacity markets have become a necessary feature of restructured markets, in order to guarantee sufficient revenue and assure reliability where sole reliance on energy market revenues may not cover the long-term costs of generation. The capacity mechanisms, introduced for the first time in Portugal by Decree-Law no. 264/2007, may take many forms including payments to energy producers.[48]

The CMEC mechanism, put in place in the context of the liberalisation of the market for the generation of electricity, aims to maintain the contractual balance between the parties to a CAE, ensuring that the energy producer shall receive an

48 Peter H. Griffes, 'Renewable Generation and capacity markets' (Third Quarter of 2014), (*International Association for Energy Economics*), p. 27.

equivalent benefit to the one it would have received under the terminated CAE, given that this benefit is not adequately ensured by the revenues obtained through the sale of electricity in a liberalised market. Therefore, the CMEC mechanism constitutes a capacity mechanism since it guarantees the sustainability of the hydroelectric sector.

Furthermore, some additional incentives have been adopted by the Portuguese State regarding the implementation and exploitation of mini-hydroelectric power plants.

PART III

INVESTMENTS AND DISINVESTMENTS IN THE ENERGY SECTOR

CHAPTER X
THE EU APPROACH TO THE REGULATION OF GUARANTEES OF ORIGIN

Dirk VAN EVERCOOREN*

1. INTRODUCTION

Consumer preferences are shifting rapidly towards products and services that are produced in a socially and ecologically sustainable way. These products and services tend to be commercialised at a (sometimes substantial) premium, reflecting the higher costs of production ensuing from observing higher standards in terms of workers' conditions and ecological impact.[1] Evidence from the 2011 Eurobarometer survey[2] has shown that the vast majority of Europeans consider environmental change to be an important issue, with the majority stating they are willing to pay more for environmentally friendly products or services. Yet, the claim that a certain product has been produced in a sustainable way is often substantiated by private labels, such as Fair Trade.[3] People buying bananas with a Fair Trade label feel/know that they are making an environmentally and socially sounder decision compared to buying ordinary bananas. There are, however also public labels, such as the EU Bio-label.[4] To seek evidence of the level of acceptance by consumers of green product claims, the European Consumers, Health and Food Executive Agency commissioned a Consumer Market Study on environmental claims for

---

* Sincere thanks go to Phil Moody, Secretary-General of the Association of Issuing Bodies, for providing insights on several topics covered within this chapter.

1 K.M.R. Taufique, A. Vocino and M.J. Polonsky, 'The influence of eco-label knowledge and trust on pro-environmental consumer behaviour in an emerging market', pp. 511–529 Published: 14 October 2016, https://www.tandfonline.com/doi/abs/10.1080/0965254X.2016.1240219?journalCode=rjsm20.

2 European Commission, Special Eurobarometer 365, http://ec.europa.eu/environment/pdf/ebs_365_en.pdf.

3 10 Principles of Fair Trade, https://wfto.com/fair-trade/10-principles-fair-trade.

4 The organic logo-website of the European Commission: https://ec.europa.eu/info/food-farming-fisheries/farming/organic-farming.

non-food products in 2014.[5] The study found that mistrust in environmental information displayed on products and in advertisements is relatively common: 44 per cent of consumers say they do not trust this type of information. However, consumers' trust in claims varies greatly depending on the specific environmental claim assessed.

Sales of electricity from renewable energy sources – often referred to as 'green electricity' – are on the rise in Europe, but this has also provoked considerable debate. A 2019 survey in the Netherlands found that about one in five Dutch people think that 'green electricity' does not exist.[6] This is probably influenced by the enduring campaigns by some Dutch non-governmental organisations (NGOs) promoting the consumption of locally produced electricity from renewable sources, which use a marketing term that leads consumers with a green electricity contract that relies on non-Dutch certification to believe that they are being duped.[7] The relatively wide-spread non-belief in a concept like electricity from renewable sources reaching the houses and companies in the form of 'green electricity' clearly demonstrates the problem of explaining abstract concepts like this to the general public. An important factor in this criticism is the lack of understanding of the basic principles of the disclosure process; the process that delivers information to electricity customers about the source of the power with which they are supplied.

For consumers to develop 'pro-environmental consumer behaviour' and change their buying decisions in favour of sustainably produced products and services, there needs to be trust in the veracity of the claims about ecological and social benefits.[8] From the customer's perspective, reliability is the key issue. How to ensure that the information about the source of the electricity supplied can be trusted by the electricity customer?

It is quite striking to see that rather early, well before public attention to issues like security of supply of energy/electricity and climate change grew to a significant level and started influencing policy, the European Union (EU) had already introduced an instrument, the Guarantee of Origin (GO), to reliably

---

5 European Commission Consumer Market Study on Environmental Claims for Non-Food Products, 2014, https://ec.europa.eu/info/sites/info/files/study_on_environmetal_claims_for_non_food_products_2014_en.pdf.

6 Een op de vijf Nederlanders gelooft niet dat groene stroom bestaat, klimaatstichting HIER, 2019, https://www.nu.nl/economie/5946804/een-op-de-vijf-nederlanders-gelooft-niet-dat-groene-stroom-bestaat.html.

7 This marketing term is 'sjoemelstroom', which is rather hard to translate. 'Fraudpower' comes close and the term is used to distinguish between what the NGO feels is 'good' (electricity proven by GOs from domestic and recently built renewables plants) and 'bad' (foreign GOs that can come from, e.g., century-old hydro plants).

8 https://www.tandfonline.com/doi/abs/10.1080/0965254X.2016.1240219?journalCode=rjsm20.

track the origin of electricity from renewable sources,[9] in order to inform the consumers of such electricity in a trustworthy manner.

This chapter starts by examining the arguments about why electricity is such a different product from others and how this influences consumer information about the origin of the electricity supplied and consumed (Section 2). It continues with a history of the GO (Section 3) and an analysis of the EU regulation of electricity disclosure (Section 4). The new provisions of the Clean Energy Package on GOs are then reviewed and commented on (Section 5). The analysis of the GOs regulation is put in perspective with the most often heard criticism on GOs (Section 6). The chapter ends with some concluding remarks (Section 7).

2. ELECTRICITY IS UNLIKE ANY OTHER PRODUCT

Producing electricity by burning coal in a power plant is not comparable to producing it with a wind turbine in many ways. The environmental impact of the two production methods is very different, notably in terms of its contribution to climate change. Even when taking into account the amount of CO_2 that was associated with building the wind turbine using lifecycle assessment (LCA) methodology, wind will be much 'cleaner' than coal when looking at the carbon (and other) emissions.

So far, an analogy can be found with the aforementioned bananas identified with a Fair Trade label. Buying electricity from a wind turbine would be the result of an ecologically motivated consumption decision, equivalent to the decision to buy the Fair Trade labelled bananas, while the decision to buy electricity from a coal plant without reference to its source would be the unmotivated consumption choice in this example.

However, once the produced electricity is injected into the grid, the metaphor no longer holds up; because once electricity has been generated and injected into the grid, it is impossible to know from what it was produced and therefore to indicate its origin (nuclear, fossil, renewable, etc). Often, when discussion turns to the purchasing of green electricity, people are sceptical. The reasons can vary: support for renewables is getting a lot of bad press in terms of cost and efficiency, but many people and companies also have difficulty understanding how buying electricity from renewable sources works, given that once electricity is generated and injected into the grid, it becomes impossible to know and to indicate the source from which it was produced. On the grid, electricity is tasteless, odourless and colourless, and has no qualities that can be used

9 And from highly efficient cogeneration plants, so-called HEC-GOs, but we will not be focusing on that type of GOs in this chapter.

to identify its source. There is no possibility to establish a link between the electricity and the technology that was used to produce it. Electrons simply do not have any qualities that can be used to identify the source of the energy they convey. This insight goes against the feelings of many people, who want to maintain the idea that there is/needs to be a physical link between the electricity from a wind turbine or other technology using a renewable energy source, and the consumption thereof. This has proven to be one of the sources of scepticism and even rejection of the concept of a 'green electricity contract' by many consumer organisations,[10] environmental NGOs[11] and therefore by many consumers.

However, we need to recognise the physical consequences of using a monopolistically-managed grid infrastructure that ensures delivery of electricity to consumers. Should one want to maintain that there should be a physical link between the electricity produced or purchased by your supplier and the power that is being delivered to end consumers, it simply becomes impossible to organise a market for electricity in general. The goal of physically ensuring that electricity produced by facilities producing electricity from renewable sources is consumed by specific end-consumers, can only be achieved by building direct lines, as defined in the European Electricity Directive, between the production facility and a specific end consumer, or by installing the production devices on the premise of consumption.

Physically speaking, a person who lives next to a coal-fired power plant operated by an electricity supplier always consumes the electricity produced by that plant, even if they enter into a contract with another electricity supplier. This would mean that electricity suppliers could only accept potential customers who are located close to the power production facilities contracted or owned by that supplier. If you maintain the need for a link between physical electricity flows and the source of the electricity, then the liberalised electricity market would not only be very different, it would not be feasible at all.

Setting up a market in electricity from renewable sources based on a physical link between electrical energy and contracts does not work either. Consumers living next to a wind turbine physically use the electricity from that wind turbine (provided the wind turbine is producing), whether they choose to do so or not. Even though they might not like the idea of wind power at all and therefore could have signed up with an electricity supplier with only

---

10 BEUC, 'Trustworthy "Green electricity" Tariffs, Policy recommendations for more transparency, better choice and environmental benefits', BEUC-W-2016-002, 6 January 2016, http://www.beuc.eu/publications/beuc-x-2016-002_jmu_trustworthy_green_electricity_tariffs.pdf.

11 See e.g. Greenpeace and other organisations Joint statement: 'Make "green electricity" markets work for consumers and energy transition', 9 March 2017, https://uploads.strikinglycdn.com/files/23778f72-b5b5-47b8-98cd-dbbea3db3eb3/beuc%20joint_statement_on_green_electricity.pdf.

nuclear and fossil plants. Similarly, consumers located next to a natural gas-fired or nuclear power plant would never be able to sign up for a 'green electricity contract' should the physical link-principle be pursued. In fact, carrying this argument to its logical conclusion means that we should get rid of transmission grids altogether and instead rely on local production and distribution grids, or direct lines in the terms of the European electricity Directives, with all of the associated disadvantages in terms of higher cost and less security of supply.

Clearly, we cannot package the 'green electrons' from a wind turbine or any other production device using renewable sources like we do with organic bananas. Yet if we want families and businesses to trust and buy green electricity, we have to be able to rely on a trustworthy instrument to prove that their electricity is truly coming from renewable sources.

Maybe another analogy would work better. Suppose I go to an ATM in Malta and withdraw some euros from my bank account. These euros are clearly not the same physical euros which I have deposited into my bank account some time ago in Belgium. Yet no one finds it strange that there is no physical pipeline to 'pump' euros from Belgium to Malta. In the financial system, we have long been accustomed to the fact that an administrative system guarantees payment, without the need to move the physical money. This analogy does not work fully either though, as it neglects the fact that there is no intrinsic difference in quality between the euros deposited and the euros withdrawn. Yet, there is an inherent and significant difference between the electrical energy produced from coal and that produced by a solar panel.

3. THE HISTORY OF THE GUARANTEE OF ORIGIN

With the goal of liberalising the electricity markets in Europe came a new challenge. How to ensure that the environmental goals of European policy, such as reducing the impact of electricity production on the environment and the climate, were pursued within the open and privatised electricity market? There was a need for new policy measures that were more in coherence with the new market.[12]

The liberalisation of the European electricity market aims at empowering the consumer.[13] The introduction of competition between different electricity suppliers provides the consumer with the option of choice. But on which criteria

---

12 M. Voogt, M.G. Boots, G.J. Schaeffer and J.W. Martens, 'Renewable Electricity in a Liberalised Market – The Concept of Green Certificates' (2000) 11(1) *Energy & Environment* pp. 65–79, https://www.jstor.org/stable/43735517?read-now=1&seq=1#page_scan_tab_contents.

13 'A Framework Strategy for a Resilient Energy Union with a Forward-Looking Climate Change Policy', Communication from the Commission to the European Parliament, the Council, the European Economic and Social Committee, the Committee of the Regions and the European Investment Bank, 25 February 2015.

could the choice between electricity suppliers be based? Reliability is a tempting, but not very convincing criterion. After all, all the electricity is delivered through the grid, which is still a monopoly, as it would make no economic sense to multiply the very expensive electricity grid infrastructure in order to foster competition. So the security of supply of a consumer's electricity depends on the quality of the grid (and therefore the distribution and transmission system grid operators), not on the supplier. Quality of service may be a criterion, as it is clear that service levels in terms of accessibility of the call centre, and the ease of understanding the bills can differ greatly between electricity suppliers. Also, the financial stability of the supply company could be a differentiator, as in several countries electricity suppliers have gone bankrupt over the past years.

But a truly significant criterion is the origin of the electricity supplied. Before liberalisation, the consumer had no choice but to accept the grid mix – the mix of sources like nuclear, hard coal, natural gas, lignite (in some European countries) and of course renewable sources such as hydro, biomass, wind (on- and off-shore), solar, etc. that was chosen by the monopolist supplying the local grid. The first Internal Energy Market Directive in 1996[14] created competition between suppliers and therefore motivated electricity suppliers to differentiate their offers in this regard. From the customer's perspective, reliability is the key issue. How to ensure that the information about the source of the electricity supplied can and will be trusted by the electricity customer?

Yet, with the rising interest of consumers in the source of their electricity, and the will of electricity suppliers (especially newcomers arriving in the liberalised European electricity market) to differentiate their offer from that of competitors, there was need for an instrument capable of 'tracking' electricity from renewable sources from the production device (wind turbine, hydro plant, solar panel array, ...) to the final consumer in a cost-efficient yet reliable way, that can be trusted by end-consumers of electricity. It is quite striking that the European legislators saw the need for a trusted information instrument regarding electricity from renewable sources at such an early stage of market liberalisation.

This instrument is generally referred to as an Energy Attribute Certificate (EAC). The European EAC is the Guarantee of Origin (GO), which labels electricity from renewable sources to provide information to electricity customers on the source of their energy. Guarantees of Origin are the only precisely-defined instruments evidencing the origin of electricity generated from renewable energy sources. In short, a GO is a 'tracker' guaranteeing that one MWh of electricity has been produced from renewable energy sources. If the customer buys the GO, they can be certain that they have purchased green electricity, as the GO is then taken out of circulation and discarded ('cancelled').

[14] Directive 96/92/EC of the European Parliament and of the Council of 19 December 1996 concerning common rules for the internal market in electricity, OJ L 27, 30.01.1997, pp. 20–29.

Therefore, GOs are the instrument for making green electricity contracts in Europe reliable.

The first legislative framework for GOs was provided by Directive 2001/77/EC,[15] but its provisions concerning GOs were vague: though recital 10 established GOs as an electricity-tracking instrument, the Directive did not state what GOs were for. The disclosure of the source of electricity to consumers was addressed by a different Directive, 2003/54/EC,[16] regulating mandatory disclosure of the source of electricity by suppliers. But strangely, this Directive did not directly link this goal to the instrument of the GO.

The uncertainties created by Directive 2001/77/EC were further reinforced by consideration of an EU-wide harmonised support scheme for renewable energy, and the contending types of scheme: feed-in tariffs and tradable green certificates.[17] Those in favour of an EU-wide support scheme saw GOs also as a flexible way of measuring target compliance, justified by efficient use of resources and fair burden sharing.

A new Commission proposal in January 2008 allowed Member States to opt out of GO trading, but the Parliamentary reading of the proposal led to increasingly negative opinion, especially concerning the use of GOs for support, disclosure and target accounting. The proposal was therefore amended to introduce transfer of renewable energy solely through separate, tradable Transfer Accounting Certificates. This proposal was rejected in June 2008 due to the perceived likely administrative burden. Finally, the role of GOs in target compliance was rejected in December 2008.

This was upheld in the newly approved Directive 2009/28/EC,[18] separating GOs and target compliance, and setting the sole function of GOs as tracking electricity generation attributes for Disclosure, as required by 2003/54/EC and later 2009/72/EC Article 3(9). This has since been supported by ECJ rulings: ECJ 1 July 2014, Case C-204/12, *Ålands vindkraft AB v Energimyndigheten* and ECJ 11 September 2014, Case C-208/12, *Essent Belgium NV v Vlaamse Reguleringsinstantie voor de Elektriciteits- en Gasmarkt.* As the debate mostly concerned the purpose of GOs, many important details regarding their use for disclosure were left for national subsidiarity by the European legislators.

---

15 Directive 2001/77/EC of the European Parliament and of the Council of 27 September 2001 on the promotion of electricity produced from renewable energy sources in the internal electricity market, OJ L 283, 27.10.2001, pp. 33–40.

16 Directive 2003/54/EC of the European Parliament and of the Council of 26 June 2003 concerning common rules for the internal market in electricity and repealing Directive 96/92/EC – Statements made with regard to decommissioning and waste management activities, OJ L 176, 15.07.2003, P. 0037–0056.

17 C. Banet, *Tradable Green Certificates Scheme under EU Law – The Influence of EU law on national support schemes for renewable electricity generation* (UniPub, Oslo 2012).

18 Directive 2009/28/EC of the European Parliament and of the Council of 23 April 2009 on the promotion of the use of energy from renewable sources and amending and subsequently repealing Directives 2001/77/EC and 2003/30/EC.

Therefore, the so-called Third Package, of which Directive 2009/28/EC is part, did bring progress in the area of GOs, but failed to create a consistent disclosure information framework at European level. The GO for electricity from renewable sources and the GO for electricity produced by high-efficiency cogeneration were defined in two different Directives (Directives 2009/28/EC and 2012/27/EC respectively), each one of which failed to state the purpose of the instrument. The purpose of the GO – making reliable the disclosure information that electricity consumers mandatorily need to receive from their electricity supplier – is defined in yet a third Directive (Directive 2009/72/EC). However, even that Directive did not explicitly mention Guarantees of Origin among the different instruments used for providing disclosure information.

4. THE REGULATION OF ELECTRICITY DISCLOSURE INFORMATION

4.1. THE PURPOSE OF CONSUMER-EMPOWERING INFORMATION

End-consumers can easily get confused by the technicalities of the electricity system. Generally, they do not show interest in such elements as frequency, voltage, short-circuit strength, reactive power and so on, simply expecting good service. This disinterest influences their attitude and, more importantly, their behaviour as electricity consumers. But in the context of the liberalised electricity market, other information can be relevant to impact consumer behaviour, e.g. the fuel source from which a certain volume of electricity was generated, the technology used to produce the electricity or the environmental impacts associated with producing the electricity. These information elements related to electricity generation are referred to as 'attributes'.

In liberalised electricity markets, consumers are able to choose not only the company that supplies them, but also a particular electricity contract. As a result, they have the possibility to choose between different offers in terms of price, but also in terms of company profile and with regard to the sources of energy and technologies used for electricity production. In order to assist consumers in making such choices, the European Union introduced a requirement for all European electricity suppliers to disclose to their clients the origins of the energy they have delivered. Such information is given to all customers through the regime that is referred to as 'disclosure information'. The goal of this provision is to enable customers to make an informed choice about the electricity they buy. This takes into account both price and criteria related to the type of electricity generation (fuel mix used, CO_2 emissions and radioactive waste production). The mandatory European disclosure scheme is an objective information scheme for the whole electricity market, providing consumers with information which they can use to realise their individual preferences. The principle of disclosure works on the premise that markets function best when participants are given adequate and reliable information.

An efficient and reliable disclosure system is key to empowering consumers to take responsibility for the consequences of their choice of electricity contract. According to the Council of European Energy Regulators (CEER), an efficient disclosure system should therefore:

- meet its objective of informing customers about the origins of the electricity they consume (and its environmental impacts, namely CO_2 emissions and nuclear waste, according to EU Directive 2009/72/EC), and
- be effective while not being too complex or costly to the suppliers and/or the issuing bodies who have to implement it. This would enhance the trust of customers towards product information.[19]

The regulation regarding disclosure information aims to provide increased transparency to consumers, allowing them the choice to purchase electricity from renewable or non-renewable sources. It enables producers, traders and suppliers to demonstrate that the electricity they sell is from renewable sources. However, the implementation of the provisions for electricity disclosure into national law has led to the development of different systems in different Member States (MS), with different methodologies for disclosure in each MS. The development of an efficient and effective green electricity market at European level was poorly supported by this situation, which makes the cross-border trade of electricity from renewable sources more difficult and disclosure systems more expensive to operate.

The result of the lack of coherence and clarity of the European legal framework is that, to this date, a vast majority of disclosed electricity is tracked using power purchase agreements or residual mix calculations. A large part is indeed tracked using so-called other 'reliable tracking systems,' which in practice seldom are as reliable as tracking by GOs. Often electricity from nuclear and fossil energy sources are tracked through bilateral contracts and are thus next to impossible to supervise. Still, the majority of electricity is not tracked at all and goes into the so-called 'residual mix'. The residual mix is the representation of the country's non-tracked generation attributes and is applied for all consumption for which no tracking instrument is used.[20] The residual mix will include almost all attributes which are not tracked with GOs, as such tracking can't be controlled and thus

---

19 CEER Advice on Customer Information on Sources of Electricity, Ref: C14-CEM-70-08, 4 March 2015, p. 13.

20 M. Klimscheffskij, T. Van Craenenbroeck, M. Lehtovaara, D. Lescot, A. Tschernutter, C. Raimundo, D. Seebach and C. Timpe, 'Residual Mix Calculation at the Heart of Reliable

accounted for. Of course, the residual mix generally is very low on renewable attributes, which might encourage some of the formerly less-environmentally-conscious consumers to more carefully consider the source of their electricity consumption and switch camp to the consumers opting for a green contract, but still the vast majority of end-users would hide behind the general mix. As the eco-minded consumer notices that his purchase has little impact on anyone else's behaviour, his motivation to pay for the desired electricity weakens.

The outcome is inefficient, with rival tracking systems. Hence, the results of this process are to a large extent unmeaningful to end-consumers, as large-scale adoption of residual mix leads to homogenous mixes and no differentiation. Even worse is the fact that contractual tracking is not transparent and therefore makes disclosure information less reliable. Finally, the current situation does not ensure a level-playing-field, as only the part of the disclosure information relating to renewable sources is regulated, and the financial and administrative burden is on those producers alone. Still GOs are responsible for the entire cost of the tracking and disclosure scheme as they are, apart from some exceptions, the only instrument regulated.

In a move to make the disclosure system more coherent, some countries have extended the instrument of the GO to all technologies for electricity generation (e.g. Austria, Switzerland). This situation is referred to as 'Full Disclosure'. In 2020, full disclosure will also become mandatory in the Netherlands.[21] Slovenia has very recently passed legislation preparing for the implementation of full disclosure in the future also.

4.2. HARMONISATION OF NATIONAL PRACTICES

There have been spontaneous harmonisation attempts on disclosure and GOs, through initiatives such as the European Energy Certificate System (EECS) developed by the Association of Issuing Bodies (AIB).[22] These initiatives were and are supported by organisations such as RECS International, the European Federation of Energy Traders, and Eurelectric.

The EECS, or 'EECS rules', is acting as a de facto standard for all AIB members, and the AIB also created an electronic data hub which allows GOs to be transferred simply, reliably and efficiently, so supporting orderly trade in GOs between EU Member States. The EECS GO has been very successful, as it was leverage for the international recognition of the GO and spurred

Electricity Disclosure in Europe – A Case Study on the Effect of the RE-DISS Project', (2015) 8(6) *Energies* pp. 4667–4696, https://www.mdpi.com/1996-1073/8/6/4667/htm.

21 Press release by *CertiQ*, 6 December 2018, http://www.certiq.nl/en/newsarticle/full-disclosure-1/.

22 Value of AIB and GOs, 2019, https://www.aib-net.org/aib/value-aib-and-gos.

continuous growth in the GO market. By facilitating reliable transparency through standardisation, consumers are empowered to make an informed choice for trusted guaranteed electricity from renewable sources. Empowered electricity customers who choose a contract that guarantees them electricity from renewable sources give a strong and clear signal to the market, via their supplier or directly. As electricity suppliers are not the end of the value chain, they pass on this signal to electricity producers, thus influencing future investments and pushing for more renewables.

European projects such as E-TRACK[23] and RE-DISS I and II[24] and the work of the Concerted Action – Renewables,[25] contributed to the harmonisation of practices with regard to disclosure information between European Member States.

4.3. THE NEED FOR A HARMONISED DISCLOSURE SYSTEM ACROSS EUROPE

The project RE-DISS II has identified a list of tasks which are relevant to be carried out on a regular (e.g. annual) basis in order to assure reliable and trustworthy tracking and disclosure systems in Europe. In general, the competent bodies for disclosure information oversight are the electricity market regulators. Several of these agencies have also been assigned as issuing body for GOs by their Member State, but this is not the case everywhere in Europe.

The tasks of calculating the residual mixes, culminating in the establishment of the European attribute mix, and providing relevant information for decisions on the recognition of foreign GOs, including the regular update of country profiles, were identified by AIB as being very close to its own tasks and very relevant to at least a large proportion of its members. In 2015, the AIB decided to take over these tasks from RE-DISS II.

It seems obvious that further integration of the different disclosure systems and a common framework for disclosure supported by a harmonised tracking system are needed. This is motivated by the need for an efficient and reliable system at European level. National solutions can be reliable, but integrating them into a European market can be very difficult and costly. Therefore, a harmonised solution is preferable from an efficiency perspective. It would be preferable that an organisation would be willing/incentivised to take over the two remaining tasks that were performed until 2015 by RE-DISS, which are of a more strategic, policy-focussed nature.

23 https://ec.europa.eu/energy/intelligent/projects/en/projects/e-track-ii.
24 https://ec.europa.eu/energy/intelligent/projects/en/projects/re-diss.
25 https://ec.europa.eu/energy/intelligent/projects/en/projects/ca-resii.

5. GUARANTEES OF ORIGIN IN THE CLEAN ENERGY PACKAGE

The conclusions from the EU Energy Council of December 2012 made an interesting reference to GOs. They read as follows:

> In relation to guarantees of origin, to further empower consumers, clarifications by the Commission would be welcomed on the best way to achieve consistent application of fuel mix disclosure at EU level which ensures that consumers are provided with accurate and complete information on all fuel mix consumption within each Member State.[26]

The question raised in the following paragraphs is to know whether the Clean Energy Package adopted in 2018/19 brings such consistency.

5.1. STRENGTHENING OF THE GUARANTEE OF ORIGIN

In the Clean Energy Package, the European Commission proposed to strengthen the GO for electricity from renewable sources, making it mandatory to use as proof of the supply of electricity from renewable sources to consumers. This should be interpreted as an improvement, as it consolidates the disclosure process on the basis of an instrument that has proven its reliability if correctly managed. The current Renewable Energy Directive (2009/28/EC) still permits the use of alternative tracking instruments as long as they are proven to be reliable and do not lead to double counting of the same produced quantity of electricity.[27] Should projects/companies use, e.g., a blockchain-based application to track production of electricity from renewable sources, but simultaneously also apply for non-blockchain-based 'regular' GOs from the government-assigned issuing body for the same production, that could lead to a blatant case of double counting. Under the revised Renewable Energy Directive (EU) 2018/2001 (RED II), this will no longer be authorised, as anyone claiming to supply or consume electricity from renewable sources will have to substantiate this claim with GOs,[28] not with e.g. Solarcoins, Blockchain certificates or any other instrument. In addition, extending the scope of GOs to include renewable

[26] Conclusions of the European Council, 28–29 June 2012, http://data.consilium.europa.eu/doc/document/ST-76-2012-INIT/en/pdf.

[27] Article 15 §7 of Directive 2009/28/EC of the European Parliament and of the Council of 23 April 2009 on the promotion of the use of energy from renewable sources.

[28] Article 19 §8 of Directive (EU) 2018/2001 of the European Parliament and of the Council of 11 December 2018 on the promotion of the use of energy from renewable sources.

gas and heating/cooling technology further consolidates the role and confirms the value of GOs.

The new legislation will bring further progress. It is now mandatory that expired GOs contribute to the residual mix.[29] This is logical, as the renewable attributes that are not claimed actively by consumers still have value and come to the advantage of all passive users. Given the growing interest in green electricity contracts, Corporate Renewable Power Purchasing Agreements (CRPPAs) and similar instruments, the number of unclaimed GOs that expire will keep decreasing, as is clearly the current trend.

The role of High Efficiency Cogeneration (HEC)-GOs is clarified, as it is now explicitly stated they should be used for disclosure. This brings them in line with renewable energy source (RES)-GOs.

The extension of GOs to renewable gases like biomethane and hydrogen produced from renewable energy sources can support the energy transition, as the successful model of electricity GOs is being used as inspiration for other energy vectors. Empowerment of consumers of gases will benefit.

Simplified information on GOs for small production devices will – if done well – contribute to further bringing down the cost of the GO systems and therefore of the disclosure systems. But it needs to be seen whether this simplified information will not deter consumer uptake of electricity produced by these small production devices. The new Directive further allows purchases of GOs directly from producers. This is also a beneficial move as, in some countries, electricity suppliers now still have a monopoly position in using GOs for claims (made in the name of their customers). This situation has been a barrier for some corporate consumers to 'green' their procurement of electricity and for setting up CRPPAs.

GOs for heating and cooling from renewable sources seem like a less likely candidate for large-scale adoption by consumers than GOs for biomethane and hydrogen, but with rising ambitions in terms of climate policy, might catch on sooner than some think. Finally, the explicit possibility for Member States to issue GOs for fossil and nuclear energy is a welcome, albeit not very ambitious step. As already stated, the introduction of 'full disclosure' on a mandatory basis would bring the disclosure system to its ultimate potential and would truly bring energy consumer empowerment on the broadest possible scale.

5.2. REMAINING CONCERNS

However, there are also a number of elements and provisions in the recast Renewable Energy Directive 2018/2001/EU that raise some questions. To start

29 Article 19 §3 of Directive (EU) 2018/2001 of the European Parliament and of the Council of 11 December 2018 on the promotion of the use of energy from renewable sources.

with the last point that was made, the fact that the European legislators did not fully exploit the potential of full disclosure, means that the GO is still solely focussed on renewable energy sources. Therefore, the residual mix will still be needed in the future. This does not automatically ensure fully consistent and reliable disclosure information for consumers.

The recast Directive introduces the possibility for a minimum capacity for GOs. This makes sense from an operational point of view, as integrating the smallest production devices into the GO-system brings about high overhead costs and yields only very limited income for producers, at least at current average price levels for GOs. But if such a minimum capacity is being introduced by Member States at different thresholds, this again becomes a factor of divergence and therefore non-harmonisation. Furthermore, new technology, specifically in IT, might bring down overhead and transaction costs for small production devices drastically. Think of blockchain-based tools where such small production devices, such as solar photovoltaic panels, could be registered and administered.

Paragraph (8) of Article 19 of the recast Renewable Energy Directive introduces another novelty, the impact of which on the European GO system cannot be easily predicted. By differentiating between the usability and the validity of a GO, this introduces the concept of a variable lifespan of a GO. As was already the case, a GO is valid for only 12 months after its production date. However, the use of a GO for disclosure purposes is extended by the process described in paragraph (8) to up to 18 months after the production date, thus introducing a different usability period than the validity period. The goal of the European legislators is not clear in this respect. It seems that different 'fuel mix'-procedures were preferred and that this outcome is actually a compromise between the disclosure models favoured by different Member States. Clearly, the input from the electricity sector, through organisations like Eurelectric,[30] has also played a role. The fear of electricity suppliers of being confronted with shorter usability of a GO due to a change in the disclosure process, leading up to the establishment of their own company and product fuel mixes, might have resonated with some negotiators.

The last but one concern to tackle is that the scope of the GO still is not fully regulated and this may negatively affect the efficiency and consistency of disclosure. The fact that a number of crucial elements of the disclosure process are left to the decisions of the Member States may result in a non-optimised European disclosure system. The rules for issuing and cancelling RES-, HEC- and Non-RES GOs should be consistent all over Europe, in order to fulfil the potential of the internal energy market to empower consumers of energy

[30] Eurelectric is the Union of the Electricity Industry – the sector association representing the common interests of the electricity industry at pan-European level, representing the electricity industry in 32 European countries.

with trustworthy information that is processed in an accurate, consistent, reliable, coherent and cost-efficient way.

But the biggest concern resulting from Article 19 of RED II relates to the newly introduced compliance obligation with the European Committee for Standardisation's CEN/CENELEC standard EN16325.

5.3. COMPLIANCE WITH EN16325 STANDARD

Standardisation is without doubt a positive thing, as it contributes to market integration at European level. The last sentence of Article 19(6) of RED II provides that: 'Member States and designated competent bodies shall ensure that the requirements they impose are compliant with the standard CEN – EN 16325.' This requirement raises particular concerns for the operation of a Europe-wide guarantee of origin system as reviewed below.

5.3.1. Inflexibility

The way that CEN/CENELEC standards are managed does not seem very adapted to the context of commodity markets, where it is essential to be able to make adjustments to the management of the market quickly and efficiently, as rules sometimes need to adapt or react to changes in the market. The process to adapt a standard within CEN/CENELEC rarely takes less than a year and can take substantially longer. This is insufficient for proactive market management.

In addition, CEN/CENELEC national teams, which do not always include competent bodies for GOs, may disagree with the competent bodies regarding specific changes. It would be undesirable that competent bodies assigned by national authorities were not able to determine collectively how they supervise the GO system, and instead would have to rely on organisations which were not considered competent in such matters by Member States. Furthermore, if there were (people representing the interests of) market participants active within the national teams, these would be far from being 'independent of production, trade and supply activities' as required of competent bodies by Article 19(5) of Directive 2019/2001/EC. The competent bodies must be independent, but those who set the rules which they must follow may not be. Resolving such differences of opinion would inevitably take time.

5.3.2. Scope of EN16325

The initial drafts of EN16325 were prepared by members of the AIB in order to provide an alternative to the EECS outside of the area covered by the activities of AIB, while still maintaining an operational compatibility with EECS. It was not intended to replace EECS or to act in combination with it within the countries covered by AIB membership. As a result, the institutional aspects which form a large part of the EECS were not included in EN16325, which contains more detail than is necessary in a formal standard.

The over-large scope of EN16325 further increases the need to develop, consider and implement changes to the standard, in order to retain the basics within EN16325, and to move all operational provisions and those provisions which are likely to require change to the EECS Rules.

5.3.3. *Compatibility with the EECS*

EN16325 was based on the EECS Rules as they were in 2010 and was adopted by CEN/CENELEC in 2012. Since 2012, there have been at least 23 substantive changes to the EECS Rules which would need to be considered for adoption within EN16325. Each of these would need to be considered by CEN/CENELEC, and any that are not adopted by EN16325 would need to be subject to detailed consideration – followed by amendment of the EECS Rules and/or EN16325 as appropriate – if harmonisation is to be achieved.

5.3.4. *Extending to Other Energy Carriers: Hydrogen, Biomethane*

CEN/CENELEC's EN16325 was initially developed as an electricity standard. However, it was always the intention to expand its scope to address other energy carriers such as hydrogen and biomethane. GOs are issued to provide evidence of the source of energy conveyed by a specific energy carrier. The energy conveyed by this energy carrier may then be used to produce energy which is conveyed by another carrier. For instance, biomass may be used to produce renewable source electricity, and this electricity could then be used by means of an electrolyser to provide hydrogen. As the original source of the energy is renewable, this means that the thus produced hydrogen is itself renewable. It is therefore important to ensure that integrating the GO systems for electricity and hydrogen does not result in double-counting or double use, and the creation of an integrated GO standard for all energy carriers will make each system more efficient and more trustworthy.

Furthermore, it costs more for a country to manage three different GO systems (and their related standards) than it does for them to manage a single system (and standard) for all energy carriers. If such a unified standard is created and deployed, then it would be beneficial for EN16325 to be restructured so that the main body addresses those issues relating to generic energy certification, while individual sections address the specific requirements of each energy carrier.

Hence, a common GO standard (provided by a revised EN16325) and an integrated system (ideally based on the EECS) for all energy carriers would lead to a more trustworthy, reliable, accurate and efficient GO system.

5.4. GO AUCTIONING

Some elements in the Clean Energy Package might work against the goal of steering the European energy system towards a low carbon, sustainable future. The RED II Directive tries to address a problem referred to as 'double compensation'[31] by taking into account the market value of GOs when determining the necessary level of public support. The Directive explicitly mentions auctioning of GOs as a way of managing the interaction of issuing GOs with support schemes.[32] But there is a risk that auctioning GOs for supported production may take away a (potential) revenue stream, and so prolong renewable producers' dependency on support. It might also delay renewable energy achieving grid parity without support. The cost of auctioning and the associated bureaucracy should be considered alongside the revenues derived from it. Auctioning may prevent suppliers (e.g. local renewable communities) from marketing locally produced energy, hindering them from acquiring the GOs from the producers and the technologies they need. The growing customer demand for specific energy products (e.g. local power) should be respected: customers should be able to exercise choice. Hence this development will introduce complexities and is potentially detrimental to the current GO market in some Member States. Furthermore, the frequency of auctions should be thought through. GOs are being continuously issued and traded, which would require frequent auctioning, and which could increase bureaucracy and costs. Finally, GO auctions should be structured in such a way as to minimise the opportunity for any market party to abuse its position.

6. CRITICISM OF GUARANTEES OF ORIGIN

6.1. THE IMPACT OF THE GUARANTEE OF ORIGIN SYSTEM

Even though the GO market has grown considerably over the past years, there are still some people who view the disclosure system as mere bureaucracy which is not having an impact on the actual development of the European electricity system. This is an often-heard criticism. So who is really making a difference in terms of achieving a transition towards as sustainable energy system?

As we have established, changes in the behaviour/decisions of electricity producers (turning down/off existing plants or building new plants) do make a

31 This term is in itself extremely misleading, as the problem that is being identified is actually 'overcompensation'.

32 Article 19 §2 of Directive (EU) 2018/2001 of the European Parliament and of the Council of 11 December 2018 on the promotion of the use of energy from renewable sources.

difference and can push the electricity market on the path toward sustainability and decarbonisation. It is less clear that electricity suppliers can influence the physical flow of the electricity, as their activity is more contractual and financial than physical in nature.

As the GO is an instrument aimed at informing electricity consumers, we need to question whether the decisions of electricity consumers can make a difference. The laws of physics imply that when households or even corporate electricity customers switch to a new electricity supplier, this has no significant impact on the physical flow of electricity that is delivered through the grid. Only in a few cases such a decision will directly impact production/investment decisions. This could be the case with the closure/opening of a plant by the consumer that has such an impact that there is need for closure/investment of an electricity production facility to supply the plant. All this might lead to the conclusion that the (green) electricity market does not have a significant impact on the European electricity market, and therefore cannot steer it in the desired direction of a decarbonised system.

As mentioned earlier, from a legal standpoint, GOs have only one direct purpose: to prove that the MWh they represent has been produced from renewable sources, allowing a consumer to claim the use of that MWh. Yet, it is hard to argue that GOs do not stimulate new investment. They are a valued revenue stream for producers of electricity from renewable sources who sell their GOs to consumers and electricity suppliers. The attempts in the RED II to avoid overcompensation might, however, work against this, as stated earlier.

Actually, it is strange to see how little faith some critics have in the power of the free market and of consumers. If more consumers demand electricity from renewable sources by buying GOs or signing GO-backed contracts, this will lead to more renewables and less fossil and nuclear. Basic economics – the law of demand and supply – indicate that if more people buy Fairtrade coffee, the area producing such coffee will grow, pushing out the coffee companies that do not treat workers well and do not respect the environment. There is no need for a direct link with new investment; the market takes care of that.

'GOs do not really help consumers to know the environmental footprint of the electricity they buy' is another point of criticism. Currently, only electricity from renewable sources is getting a GO, and in some countries,[33] it only gets a GO if the producer does not receive direct support (such as a feed-in tariff or a green certificate). As mentioned above, the AIB proposes[34] to extend the GO to track all sources of electricity and use it to provide consumers with information

33 E.g. Germany and France.

34 AIB Reflection Paper on the forthcoming RES Directive, 2015, AIB-2015-WGIA-RP01, https://www.aib-net.org/certification/eu-legislation/reflection-papers.

on the environmental impact of the associated electricity. This would truly empower consumers, by making them accountable for the environmental impact of their contract. Furthermore, it would create a level playing-field for all electricity producers, spreading system costs equally – rather than imposing them solely on the very market sector which Europe wants to stimulate.

So, do the critics have it all wrong? There is need for improvement. But critics who raise concerns about how some electricity suppliers inform their customers, or rather don't fully inform them, should not attack the instrument of the GO itself, or the system of disclosure information which relies upon the GO and which is aimed at providing information to consumers about which sources the electricity they use originated from. They should make it clear that they are merely questioning the way that GOs are being used by some market participants.

Electricity suppliers should inform their consumers much more clearly and in more detail. Many consumers would be interested in specific green products, such as a wind contract, or a local energy contract that ensures that the electricity is not only from environmentally-friendly sources, but has also been produced locally, thus supporting local employment and investments. Guarantees of Origin have the potential to empower consumers much more than is currently the case. GOs are a key instrument for Europe's internal energy market and are needed to put consumers truly in the driver's seat, so they can steer the European energy system towards a low carbon, sustainable future.

6.2. MARKET IMBALANCE

For a long period, the supply of GOs in Europe exceeded demand, which was mainly situated in countries like Germany, Switzerland, the Netherlands, Italy, Belgium and Austria. But demand has outgrown supply in recent years, thanks to different significant trends. Corporate demand is the main driver. Campaigns like the RE100[35] push global companies to join the pledge to move to 100 per cent electricity from renewable sources. The main driver here is decarbonisation, or the Paris Agreement if you will. Other drivers (to a certain extent overlapping with each other and with decarbonisation as a driver) are requirements like carbon foot-printing, Corporate Social Responsibility reporting, and commitment to Science-Based Targets.

The electrification of society and of transport is a further driving factor. The EV100 is now the equivalent of RE100 for promoting the switch to electric

[35] RE100 is a global corporate leadership initiative bringing together influential businesses committed to 100% renewable electricity, www.RE100.org.

vehicles (EVs). The EKOenergy label is already linked to charging services for EVs in Finland, making sure that the EVs are charged with green electricity.

Due to the discussion about 'double perception', awareness is growing in Norway and the other Nordic countries (the largest source of GOs) that as they export their GOs, the electricity they consume is getting increasingly 'grey' (i.e. not green, but coming from fossil or nuclear sources). That's why an increasing number of Nordic companies are now purchasing GOs, to prove that they are committed to sustainability. So there are different options: if a country that produces 100 per cent of its electricity from renewable sources – like Iceland – decides to export its GOs, the consumers in Iceland have to accept that their consumption mix is getting less green. If they do not want to accept that, they can show their commitment to electricity from renewables by buying the domestically produced GOs themselves, thus keeping the national fuel mix green, even if the production mix remained green all along. The relevant conclusion is that from a policy angle, any consumer/supplier of electricity claiming that they consume/supply electricity from renewable sources should be forced to prove this with GOs. Otherwise, the problem of double perception[36] will keep undermining the credibility of the disclosure system, as any unsubstantiated claim that electricity from renewable sources is being used raises opposition against 'greenwashing'. This requires legislation, and the support of environmental NGOs, consumer organisations and suppliers. It is vital that each of these parties is made fully aware of the benefits of a harmonised disclosure system backed by GOs, compared to other alternatives.

6.3. DEMAND FOR GREEN POWER GROWS WITH GOs

Growing demand for GOs – including in countries where many consumers assume they have green electricity based on the production mix, but that are exporting GOs and thus end up with a consumption mix that is much more grey-coloured than their production mix – has helped to bring the European GO market towards equilibrium. And if the demand for GOs grows, this is not only an important signal from the electricity consumers that they ask for more production of electricity from renewable sources, but it also will make the price of GOs go up and GOs will thus make a (greater) financial contribution to new investment in the production of electricity from renewable sources.

---

36 An example of the problem of double perception can be found in the speech given in 2015 by Icelandic President Grimsson of Iceland, stating that 100% of Iceland's energy is from renewable sources. At this time, it was already clear that a significant number of GOs were being exported by Iceland, therefore making the consumption mix far less than 100% renewable. See, e.g., https://twitter.com/Climate_Action_/status/673868368718536704.

And so, a major criticism often made by the environmental movement – the perceived lack of 'additionality' that the GO system delivers – will also be addressed.

Though here again, Iceland might be an exception. As there is indeed no cable connecting Iceland with the mainland, growing demand for green electricity in Europe will not in itself trigger new investments, adding renewable production capacity in Iceland. Moreover, the second signal that comes from growing demand for GOs, which steers investors towards renewables rather than towards traditional sources of electricity, does not work either in Iceland. After all, why would an Icelandic electricity producer even think about not using renewable sources? So from the angle of additionality, the presence of Iceland in the GO system does not seem very relevant. But then, the sole purpose of GOs as defined by the Directive is to document the origin, which it does everywhere.

6.4. LABELS OR INDEPENDENT CRITERIA SCHEMES

Environmental NGOs and consumer organisations are sometimes unwilling to endorse the potential that GOs offer, perhaps because they do not yet truly understand their nature and benefits. Also, GOs are often thought to represent average European renewable energy production, whereas they are actually information-rich and can enable very detailed product differentiation. Guarantees of Origin therefore need to be marketed more effectively. High-quality GOs could carry a 'gold' mark to simplify differentiation and enable consumer organisations to recommend only such high-quality GOs. The EECS offers the facility for tagging GOs in order to demonstrate that they qualify according to the criteria set by labels such as EKOenergy and Naturemade and TÜV SÜD Generation EE, and also sustainability criteria such as ISCC (International Sustainability and Carbon Certification) and NTA8080 (for sustainably produced biomass).

7. CONCLUSION

Starting as a purely voluntary initiative, the concept of Energy Attribute Certificates was quickly picked up by European law makers. The Guarantee of Origin has been heavily debated, but the success of the instrument cannot be denied. The growing volumes of GOs being issued, traded and – most importantly – cancelled by or for consumers to claim the consumption of electricity from renewable sources, provides a clear signal. GOs allow consumers to exercise a choice and to express their preference, not only for electricity from renewable sources, but for electricity produced by wind, solar or hydro and coming from a specific country or region. This consumer empowering quality of the GO needs to be recognised as a crucial element in the liberalisation of the European energy market.

The regulatory context of the GO system remains essentially based at national level. This continues to prove challenging in terms of establishing a European-wide market. The role of voluntary initiatives aiming at creating a harmonised system has proven to be very important. It remains to be seen how the Clean Energy Package and specifically the mandatory need to comply with the CEN standard will impact the use of the GO as an instrument. Furthermore, European coordination of disclosure practices remains important to ensure in order to empower Europe's energy consumers with trustworthy information.

CHAPTER XI

THE SCREENING OF FOREIGN DIRECT INVESTMENTS INTO THE EUROPEAN UNION

Regulation 2019/452 and its Implications for Energy Investments

Cees VERBURG*

1. INTRODUCTION

In March 2019, Regulation 2019/452 (hereinafter: the FDI-Regulation) was adopted by the European Union (EU) which shall apply from fall 2020 onwards.[1] The Regulation establishes a framework for the screening of Foreign Direct Investment (FDI) into the EU.[2] Furthermore, it creates a cooperation mechanism between the Member States, both *inter se* and with the Commission on the screening of such investments.[3] The scope of screening mechanisms, which 'may' be adopted, maintained or amended by Member States, is limited to investments 'likely to affect security or public order.'[4]

In general, the EU, and indeed most of its Member States, are known for their relative openness to FDI.[5] This is evidenced by the FDI Regulatory Restrictiveness

---

* This chapter builds on the presentation of Ms MARGARIDA AFONSO during the 30th European Energy Law Seminar in January 2019. The author would like to emphasise that the views expressed in this chapter are solely own and cannot be attributed to Ms AFONSO or her employer. Also, the author wishes to express appreciation for the valuable feedback received on earlier drafts of this chapter from DR. T. MORGANDI, C.T. NIEUWENHOUT, LLM, and PROF. M.M. ROGGENKAMP. Any errors remain the author's own.

1 Article 17, Regulation (EU) 2019/452 of the European Parliament and of the Council of 19 March 2019 establishing a framework for the screening of foreign direct investments into the Union [2019] OJ L 79 1/1.

2 Ibid. Article 1.

3 Ibid. Articles 6–11.

4 Ibid. Articles 1(1), (3) and 3(1).

5 H. ZHANG and D. VAN DEN BULCKE, 'China's Direct Investment in the European Union: A New Regulatory Regime?' (2014) 12(1)–(2) *Asia Europe Journal* 159, p. 163.

Index of the Organisation for Economic Cooperation and Development (OECD), where 22 EU Member States rank below the OECD average in relation to regulatory restrictiveness, well ahead of other large developed and developing economies such as the United States (US), India, China, Russia, Canada, and Australia.[6] Often cited benefits of FDI include economic growth, job creation, transfer of skills and technology, and increased competitiveness of domestic industries.[7]

It has been said that the FDI-Regulation is not the result of 'a genuine initiative of the Commission', but rather of a request made by certain Member States, such as Germany, France, and Italy that were concerned about growing numbers of acquisitions of EU companies in strategic sectors by investors from outside the EU.[8] Although not explicitly named in the FDI-Regulation, these concerns have primarily been sparked by Chinese (attempted) acquisitions of European companies.[9] In the context of the energy sector, one can think of the attempt by the State Grid Corporation of China to acquire 14 per cent of the shares of a Belgian gas and electricity Distribution System Operator (DSO) in 2016.[10] That same company acquired 25 per cent of the Portuguese gas and electricity Transmission System Operator (TSO) in 2012 and has more recently pursued a majority shareholding in the TSO.[11] Similarly, the Chinese company

---

6 S. Thomsen and F. Mistura, 'Is Investment Protectionism on the Rise?' (OECD, 2017). <http://www.oecd.org/investment/globalforum/2017-GFII-Background-Note-Is-investment-protectionism-on-the-rise.pdf>. This index can be found at: <https://www.oecd.org/investment/fdiindex.htm>.

7 M. Sornarajah, *The International Law on Foreign Investment*, Cambridge University Press, Cambridge, 2017, pp. 61–67. K.J. Vandevelde, 'The Economics of Bilateral Investment Treaties' (2004) 41 *Harvard International Law Journal* 469, pp. 479–480. I.A. Moosa, *Foreign Direct Investment: Theory, Evidence and Practice*, Palgrave MacMillan, New York, 2002, p. 73. S.H. SEID, *Global Regulation of Foreign Direct Investment*, Ashgate Publishing, 2002, p. 10.

8 R. Bismuth, 'Screening the Commission's Regulation Proposal Establishing a Framework for Screening FDI Into the EU' (2018) 3 *European Investment Law and Arbitration Review* 45, p. 48.

9 H. Zhang and D. Van den Bulcke, 'China's Direct Investment in the European Union: A New Regulatory Regime?' (2014) 12(1–2) *Asia Europe Journal* 159. S. Meunier, 'Divide and Conquer? China and the Cacophony of Foreign Investment Rules in the EU' (2014) 21(7) *Journal of European Public Policy* 996. A. Heinemann, 'Government Control of Cross-Border M&A: Legitimate Regulation or Protectionism?' (2012) 15(3) *Journal of International Economic Law* 843, p. 867. M. Bungenberg and A. Hazarika, 'Chinese Foreign Investment in the European Union Energy Sector: The Regulation of Security Concerns' (2019) 20(2)–(3) *Journal of World Investment and Trade* 375.

10 Enerdata, 'State Grid's acquisition of 14% in Belgian distributor Eandis blocked' (Enerdata, 2016). <https://www.enerdata.net/publications/daily-energy-news/state-grids-acquisition-14-belgian-distributor-eandis-blocked.html>. M. Bungenberg and A. Hazarika, 'Chinese Foreign Investment in the European Union Energy Sector: The Regulation of Security Concerns' (2019) 20(2)–(3) *Journal of World Investment and Trade* 375, pp. 378–381.

11 S. Morgan and S. Michalopoulos, 'China set to fully control Portugal's power grid amid Europe's inertia' (EURACTIV, 2018). <https://www.euractiv.com/section/eu-china/news/china-set-to-fully-control-portugals-power-grid-amid-europes-inertia/>. State Grid Corporation

also acquired a share in the Greek electricity TSO in 2017. Somewhat ironically, this was due to 'a spin-off scheme under Greece's latest international bailout, aimed at opening up the power market.'[12] Allegedly, Chinese interest has shifted to Europe after several attempts to acquire firms in the US encountered hostility, including the failed 2005 takeover of the mid-sized oil company Unocal by the China National Offshore Oil Corporation.[13]

In a broader context, international economic tensions have been on the rise over the last few years, both with regard to trade as well as investment. In fact, the EU is certainly not the only economy that recently (re)introduced an FDI screening mechanism.[14] Although it is perhaps difficult to establish a causal link, the United Nations (UN) observed that global FDI was down by 23 per cent in 2017 in comparison to 2016 and noted increased general hostility towards FDI.[15] Like the EU FDI-Regulation, such measures are sometimes introduced by reference to national security.[16] US President Donald Trump, for example, blocked the acquisition of semiconductor manufacturer Qualcomm by Broadcomm by executive order, while citing national security concerns.[17] The line between genuine national security concerns and protectionism is, however, a fine one.[18] This was emphasised by former EU Trade Commissioner

---

of China, 'State Grid Corporation of China Successfully Acquires a 25% Stake in REN, Portugal' (2012). <http://www.sgcc.com.cn/ywlm/mediacenter/corporatenews/02/265956.shtml>.

12 REUTERS, 'Greek Power Grid Operator Turns to China for Fresh Funding' (Reuters, 3 November 2017). <https://www.reuters.com/article/admie-china/greek-power-grid-operator-turns-to-china-for-fresh-funding-idUSL8N1N92AU>.

13 H. Zhang and D. Van den Bulcke, 'China's Direct Investment in the European Union: A New Regulatory Regime?' (2014) 12(1)–(2) *Asia Europe Journal* 159, p. 161. S. Lohr, 'The Big Tug of War Over Unocal' (*New York Times*, 6 July 2005).

14 S. Thomsen and F. Mistura, 'Is Investment Protectionism on the Rise?' (OECD, 2017). <http://www.oecd.org/investment/globalforum/2017-GFII-Background-Note-Is-investment-protectionism-on-the-rise.pdf>. United Nations Conference on Trade and Development, World Investment Report 2019, unctad/wir/2019 (Geneva: United Nations, 2019), p. 94.

15 United Nations Conference on Trade and Development, World Investment Report 2018, unctad/wir/2018 (Geneva: United Nations, 2018), pp. xi–xii. C. Verburg and J. Waverijn, 'Liberalizing the Global Supply Chain of Renewable Energy Technology: The Role of International Investment Law in Facilitating Flows of Foreign Direct Investment and Trade' [2019] 2 *Brill Open Law* 1, p. 38.

16 See for example the trade tensions between Japan and South Korea: B. Dooley, 'Japan Cites "National Security" in Free Trade Crackdown. Sound Familiar?' (*New York Times*, 15 July 2019). <https://www.nytimes.com/2019/07/15/business/japan-south-korea-trade-war-semiconductors.html>.

17 Also, Trump imposed import duties on foreign steel and aluminium while citing national security considerations. See: Proclamation 9705 of 8 March 2018, 83 FR 11625, 2018-05478. Proclamation 9704 of 8 March 2018, 83 FR 11619, 2018-05477. Presidential Order Regarding the Proposed Takeover of Qualcomm Incorporated by Broadcom Limited (White House, 12/03/2018). <https://www.whitehouse.gov/presidential-actions/presidential-order-regarding-proposed-takeover-qualcomm-incorporated-broadcom-limited/>.

18 United Nations Conference on Trade and Development & Organisation for Economic Cooperation and Development, 'Twenty-first UNCTAD-OECD Report on G20 Investment

De Gucht and this was also the reason that the proposal of certain Member States to introduce the FDI-Regulation initially divided the Commission.[19] De Gucht said 'we cannot accept – in Europe or elsewhere – that national security concerns are used as a false pretence to justify the protection of vested economic interests.'[20]

On an international level, trade and investment agreements nevertheless often contain national or essential security exceptions.[21] The General Agreement on Tariffs and Trade (GATT), for example, has included such an exception since 1947.[22] It was only recently, however, that this provision was interpreted by a Panel of the World Trade Organization (WTO) Dispute Settlement Body for the first time in a trade dispute.[23]

The purpose of this chapter is to analyse to what extent the FDI-Regulation is in line with the EU's international commitments under (recent) international investment agreements. This will be done by reference to the EU–Canada Comprehensive Economic and Trade Agreement (CETA).[24] Contrary to the EU's and its Member States' past policy, recent agreements provide for market access commitments concerning investments and, for example, extend non-discriminatory treatment to the pre-establishment phase of an investment. At first glance, introducing a general FDI screening mechanism for non-EU investors is at odds with such commitments, since a distinction is made between EU and non-EU investors.

This chapter is structured as follows. Section 2 will discuss the importance of FDI in the European energy sector and, more specifically, briefly recall certain existing measures that already restrict FDI in this sector at both the EU and Member State levels. Subsequently, section 3 will introduce the screening mechanism of the FDI-Regulation followed by an examination of its compatibility with the EU's commitments under investment and trade agreements in section 4. As said, this will be done by reference to the recent CETA which contains the

---

Measures' (25/06/2019). <https://unctad.org/en/PublicationsLibrary/unctad_oecd2019d21_en.pdf>, p. 3. United Nations Conference on Trade and Development, World Investment Report 2019, unctad/wir/2019 (Geneva: United Nations, 2019), p. 98.

19 K. De Gucht, 'EU-China Investment: A Partnership of Equals' SPEECH/12/421 07/06/2012 (European Commission). <http://europa.eu/rapid/press-release_SPEECH-12-421_en.htm?locale=en>. S. Meunier, 'Divide and Conquer? China and the Cacophony of Foreign Investment Rules in the EU' (2014) 21(7) *Journal of European Public Policy* 996, p. 1012.

20 K. De Gucht, 'EU-China Investment: A Partnership of Equals' SPEECH/12/421 07/06/2012 (European Commission). <http://europa.eu/rapid/press-release_SPEECH-12-421_en.htm?locale=en>.

21 Article 24(3), the Energy Charter Treaty (adopted 17/12/1994, entered into force 16/04/1998).

22 Article XXI(b), General Agreement on Tariffs and Trade (adopted 30/10/1947, entered into force 01/01/1948).

23 *Russia – Measures Concerning Traffic in Transit*, Report of the Panel, WT/DS512/R, 5 April 2019, para. 7.20.

24 Comprehensive Economic and Trade Agreement (European Union–Canada) (adopted 30/10/2016, entrance into force still pending).

most far-reaching market access obligations concerning FDI ever undertaken by the EU. Finally, this chapter will end with a conclusion.

2. FDI AND THE EUROPEAN ENERGY SECTOR

FDI is important to the EU, this was the outcome of a recent study conducted by the European Commission and which evaluated all economic sectors: 'While only 3 percent of European companies in the sample considered in 2016 were owned or controlled by non-EU investors, they represented more than 35 percent of total assets in the sample and around 16 million jobs.'[25] Over 80 per cent of these investments were held by investors from the US, Switzerland, Norway, Canada, Australia, and Japan.[26] In relation to the European electricity and gas sectors, US and Canadian investors are the most active non-European investors.[27] Russian investments can, unsurprisingly, primarily be found in the gas sector.[28] The same holds true for investments originating from the Gulf States.[29] Chinese investors, whose share is relatively limited, primarily hold assets in the electricity sector: both in the production and transmission segments.[30] Notably, 67 per cent of the assets in the sector labelled 'manufacture of coke and refined petroleum products' is held by foreign investors while foreign ownership in the mining and quarrying sector is just slightly lower with 56 per cent.[31] It is thus safe to say that non-EU investors play an important role in the EU energy sector.[32]

2.1. RESTRICTIONS AT THE EU LEVEL

Since energy is vital to the functioning of a contemporary society, the energy sector is often considered as being of strategic importance.[33] This explains why both at the EU and the Member State levels FDI restrictions exist. The sections

---

25 Commission Staff Working Document on Foreign Direct Investment in the EU Following up on the Commission Communication, 'Welcoming Foreign Direct Investment while Protecting Essential Interests' of 13 September 2017, SWD(2019), 13/3/2019, p. 1.

26 Ibid.

27 Ibid. pp. 40–42.

28 Ibid.

29 Ibid.

30 Ibid.

31 Ibid. p. 93.

32 See also: L. Reins, 'The European Union's Framework for FDI Screening: Towards an Ever More Growing Competence Over Energy Policy?' (2019) 128 *Energy Policy* 665, pp. 666–668.

33 A. Heinemann, 'Government Control of Cross-Border M&A: Legitimate Regulation or Protectionism?' (2012) 15(3) *Journal of International Economic Law* 843, pp. 863–864.

below will briefly introduce these, although it has to be noted that such restrictions sometimes apply to both intra-EU and extra-EU investments.

The most obvious examples of EU legislation that may affect FDI are the application of the EU Merger Regulation and European legislation directly regulating the energy sector.[34]

The EU Merger Regulation (Regulation 139/2004) is aimed at ensuring that brownfield investments (i.e. the acquisition of existing companies/assets) do not lead to situations in which companies increase their market power to such a degree that it may distort competition and 'endanger the interests of consumers, the economy and society as a whole.'[35] In the mining and quarrying, and electricity, gas, steam, and air-conditioning supply sectors, this Regulation was relevant in 655 merger cases in total.[36] On the basis of the Regulation, 'Member States may take appropriate measures to protect legitimate interests other than those taken into consideration by this Regulation and compatible with the general principles and other provisions of Community law.'[37] Public security is explicitly considered as a legitimate interest.[38]

The energy sector also plays an important role in the European programme for critical infrastructure protection, which 'might have a significant impact on the market access of foreign [...] investors.'[39] As becomes clear from the Critical Infrastructures Directive, infrastructures related to the production, transmission and supply of oil, gas, and electricity may be considered as 'European critical infrastructure.'[40] According to the Commission, '[s]pecific attention must be given to the security, integrity and ownership of these infrastructures and

[34] H. Zhang and D. Van den Bulcke, 'China's Direct Investment in the European Union: A New Regulatory Regime?' (2014) 12(1–2) *Asia Europe Journal* 159, pp. 166–171. A. Heinemann, 'Government Control of Cross-Border M&A: Legitimate Regulation or Protectionism?' (2012) 15(3) *Journal of International Economic Law* 843, pp. 859–860.

[35] H. Zhang and D. Van den Bulcke, 'China's Direct Investment in the European Union: A New Regulatory Regime?' (2014) 12(1–2) *Asia Europe Journal* 159, p. 168. Council Regulation (EC) No 139/2004 of 20 January 2004 on the Control of Concentrations between Undertakings [2004] OJ L 24/1. Communication from the Commission to the European Parliament, the European Council, the Council, the European Economic and Social Committee and the Committee of the Regions, 'Welcoming Foreign Direct Investment while Protection Essential Interests', COM(2017) 494 final, 13/9/2017, p. 8.

[36] As of 23/4/2019. This figure includes intra-EU brownfield investments.

[37] Article 21(4), Council Regulation (EC) No 139/2004 of 20 January 2004 on the Control of Concentrations between Undertakings [2004] OJ L 24/1.

[38] Ibid.

[39] H. Zhang and D. Van den Bulcke, 'China's Direct Investment in the European Union: A New Regulatory Regime?' (2014) 12(1–2) *Asia Europe Journal* 159, p. 167.

[40] Article 2(b) and Annex I, Council Directive 2008/114/EC of 8 December 2008 on the identification and designation of European critical infrastructures and the assessment of the need to improve their protection [2008] OJ L 345/75. See also: M.M. Roggenkamp, 'Protecting Energy Infrastructure in the EU: The Impact of External Damages on Supply Security' in M.M. Roggenkamp et al (eds.), *Energy Networks and the Law: Innovative Solutions in Changing Markets*, Oxford University Press, Oxford 2008, pp. 124–128.

the need to ensure their continuous operation.'[41] Furthermore, the Gas and Electricity Directives state that gas and electricity TSOs owned by third country nationals cannot operate in the EU 'unless it has been demonstrated in the process of certification that it will not put at risk the security of energy supply to the Member State in which it would operate or to the Union.'[42] In the context of prospecting, exploring for and producing of hydrocarbons, the EU Hydrocarbon Directive allows Member States to 'refuse, on grounds of national security, to allow access to and exercise of these activities to any entity which is effectively controlled by third countries or third country nationals.'[43]

It is thus apparent that foreign investors in the EU energy sector may already be confronted with various barriers, which underlines the strategic nature of activities in the sector.

2.2. RESTRICTIONS AT THE MEMBER STATE LEVEL

FDI restrictions at the Member State level are, first of all, existing FDI screening mechanisms as employed by nearly half of the EU constituency, including Austria, Denmark, Germany, Finland, France, Latvia, Lithuania, Italy, Poland, Portugal, Spain, and the United Kingdom (UK).[44] The exact scope, content, and design of such mechanisms differs and ranges from applying across the board to specified strategic sectors, which often includes the energy sector.[45] Although a comprehensive examination of the existing FDI screening mechanisms and other relevant legislation that may affect market access for non-EU investors

---

41 Communication from the Commission to the European Parliament, the European Council, the Council, the European Economic and Social Committee and the Committee of the Regions, 'Welcoming Foreign Direct Investment while Protection Essential Interests', COM(2017) 494 final, 13/9/2017, p. 8.

42 Ibid. Article 11, Directive 2009/72/EC of the European Parliament and of the Council of 13 July 2009 concerning common rules for the internal market in electricity and repealing Directive 2003/54/EC [2009] OJ L 211/55. Article 11, Directive 2009/73/EC of the European Parliament and of the Council of 13 July 2009 concerning common rules for the internal market in natural gas and repealing Directive 2003/55/EC [2009] OJ L 211/95. Article 53, Directive (EU) 2019/944 of the European Parliament and of the Council of 5 June 2019 on common rules for the internal market for electricity and amending Directive 2012/27/EU (recast) OJ L 158/125. Directive (EU) 2019/692 of the European Parliament and of the Council of 17 April 2019 amending Directive 2009/73/EC concerning common rules for the internal market in natural gas [2019] OJ L117/1.

43 Article 2(2), Directive 94/22/EC of the European Parliament and of the Council of 30 May 1994 on the conditions for granting and using authorizations for the prospection, exploration and production of hydrocarbons [1994] OJ L 164/3.

44 Communication from the Commission to the European Parliament, the European Council, the Council, the European Economic and Social Committee and the Committee of the Regions, 'Welcoming Foreign Direct Investment while Protection Essential Interests', COM(2017) 494 final, 13/9/2017, p. 7.

45 Ibid.

currently applying within the EU is beyond the scope of this chapter, examples from France, Austria, Germany, and the Netherlands will be used as illustration.

In France, for example, authorisation of the Minister of Economic Affairs may be necessary in certain strategic sectors.[46] If a proposed investment by a non-EU investor would lead to interests exceeding one third of equity or voting rights in a French resident company, prior authorisation is required. Activities concerning the supply of 'electricity, gas or other energy sources' are considered strategic and therefore require the approval of the Minister.[47] Brownfield investments that are considered to be contrary to the national interest may be prohibited.[48] It has been said that the French 'government has informally thwarted the takeover of domestic firms by foreign investors and helped to find national solutions.'[49] In the energy sector, an example of this practice was the proposed takeover of Suez by the Italian company ENEL, which was hindered and the alternative, a domestic merger with Gaz de France, resulted in GDF Suez.[50]

In Austria, investments by companies originating from outside the EU, the European Economic Area, and Switzerland engaged in 'energy supply' activities require the approval of the Minister of Economic Affairs when that company acquires 25 per cent of the shares or a controlling interest.[51] This procedure does not apply, however, if it is precluded by EU or international law.[52]

In Germany, relevant screening legislation can be found in the Foreign Trade and Payments Act and the Foreign Trade and Payments Ordinance.[53] The Ministry of Economic Affairs and Energy can investigate 'whether the acquisition of a domestic company by a non-EU resident or the direct or indirect acquisition [...] of a stake in a domestic company by a non-EU resident poses a threat to the public order or security' of Germany.[54] This may,

---

46 Article L151-3, Monetary and Financial Code, Legislative Section, consolidated version of 1 November 2010. Decree 2017-932 of 10 May 2017.

47 A. Salama, 'Simplification of French Foreign Investment Procedures' (Lexology, 20/9/2017). <https://www.lexology.com/library/detail.aspx?g=a2bcf123-cc4d-45b7-ba50-04a9a9d51de9>.

48 Article L151-3(II), Monetary and Financial Code, Legislative Section, consolidated version of 1 November 2010.

49 A. Heinemann, 'Government Control of Cross-Border M&A: Legitimate Regulation or Protectionism?' (2012) 15(3) *Journal of International Economic Law* 843, pp. 848–849.

50 Ibid.

51 Section 25a, Foreign Trade Act, 2011.

52 Ibid. Section 25a(2).

53 Sections 4 and 5, Foreign Trade and Payments Act of 6 June 2013 (Federal Law Gazette I p. 1482), as last amended by Article 4 of the Act of 20 July 2017 (Federal Law Gazette I p. 2789). Sections 55–62, Foreign Trade and Payments Ordinance of 2 August 2013 (Federal Law Gazette [BGBl.] Part I p. 2865), as last amended by Article 1 of the Ordinance of 19 December 2018 (BAnz AT 28.12.2018 V1).

54 Section 55(1), Foreign Trade and Payments Ordinance of 2 August 2013 (Federal Law Gazette [BGBl.] Part I p. 2865), as last amended by Article 1 of the Ordinance of 19 December 2018 (BAnz AT 28.12.2018 V1).

for example, be the case when an acquisition targets a 10 per cent share in a company that is engaged in developing and modifying software 'for controlling power plants, grids or the operation of facilities or systems used to supply electricity, gas, fuel, fuel oil or district heat'.[55] Otherwise, a 25 per cent threshold applies. The Ministry of Economic Affairs and Energy may prohibit or issue instructions regarding a transaction in order to safeguard public order and public security.[56] Even if the FDI screening mechanism does not apply, the German government has found ways to block undesirable transactions in the energy sector while citing 'national security' concerns. For example, when a share in the TSO 50Hertz came up for sale and the China State Grid Company was about to invest, the government used a domestic development bank to acquire the share instead, thereby preventing the Chinese investment.[57]

Beyond the applicable FDI screening mechanisms, legislation specifically regulating activities in the energy sector may also affect the ability of foreign investors to invest in the EU. Legislation in the Netherlands would be an example of this. Although the country does not screen inbound FDI, the ability of foreign investors to invest in gas and electricity grids is restricted by law. Both the Gas Act and the Electricity Act state that, in principle, the ownership of the grid rests directly or indirectly in public hands,[58] thereby excluding domestic and foreign private entities. Deviation from the general rule is only possible subject to specific conditions, including that 75 per cent of the shares in the grid operator and controlling interest therein shall remain in the hands of the State, either directly or indirectly.[59] In addition, certain required licenses in the Netherlands necessary to carry out activities – such as operating a nuclear power plant – may be personal; meaning that the acquisition of a Dutch legal entity, holding such a license, by a foreign investor is not accompanied by a transfer of the relevant license.[60] Consequently, this provides the competent authorities with the ability to review whether the acquisition complies with specified public interests.[61]

---

55 Ibid. Sections 55(1) and 56(1).

56 Ibid. Section 62.

57 Z. Bentley, 'Germany Blocks China State Grid Bid for 50Hertz, Citing "National Security" Fears' (Infrastructure Investor, 2018). <https://www.infrastructureinvestor.com/germany-blocks-china-state-grid-investment-50hertz-citing-national-security-fears/>.

58 Articles 85 and 85a, Gas Act of 22 June 2000, Stb 305, 318 and most recently amended in 2018 by Stb 488. Articles 93 and 93a, Electricity Act 1998 of 2 July 1998, Stb 427 and most recently amended in 2018 by Stb 488. Kamerstukken II, 31 350 nr. 6 (24 June 2008).

59 Article 85b, Gas Act of 22 June 2000, Stb 305, 318 and most recently amended in 2018 by Stb 488. Article 94, Electricity Act 1998 of 2 July 1998, Stb 427 and most recently amended in 2018 by Stb 488.

60 Article 70, Nuclear Energy Law of 21 February 1963, Stb 514 and most recently amended in 2018 by Stb 355.

61 Kamerstukken II, 31 350 nr. 6 (24 June 2008).

3. REGULATION 2019/452 – AN OVERVIEW

As has become apparent from the previous section, Member States' laws and regulations concerning FDI are far from uniform. This means that non-EU investors can channel investments into the EU through Member States that are very open to FDI and subsequently use those investments as 'springboards' to the rest of the EU by benefitting from the internal freedoms as created by the EU Treaties.[62] In turn, this may undermine the more restrictive policies of other Member States.[63] In addition, the Commission felt that there was a need to protect assets that have a significant 'European dimension given their links to programmes or projects of Union interest.'[64]

In light of these considerations, the Commission defined the following objectives to be achieved:

- provide a coherent framework to screen foreign direct investment in the EU on grounds of security or public order, without impinging on Member States' national prerogatives;
- facilitate close and systematic cooperation among Member States and between Member States and the Commission with regard to the screening of certain foreign direct investment when these raise security or public order concerns, including strengthened exchange of information;
- increase transparency of foreign direct investment that may have an impact on security or public order;
- effectively address cases of foreign direct investment raising security or public order concerns in relation to projects or programmes of Union interest;
- prevent circumvention of national foreign direct investment screening mechanisms.[65]

The FDI-Regulation is supposed to achieve these objectives and is summarised as establishing

> a framework for the screening by Member States of foreign direct investments into the Union on the grounds of security or public order and [...] a mechanism

62 S. Meunier, 'Divide and Conquer? China and the Cacophony of Foreign Investment Rules in the EU' (2014) 21(7) *Journal of European Public Policy* 996, p. 1001. Communication from the Commission to the European Parliament, the European Council, the Council, the European Economic and Social Committee and the Committee of the Regions, 'Welcoming Foreign Direct Investment while Protection Essential Interests', COM(2017) 494 final, 13/9/2017, p. 9.

63 S. Meunier, 'Divide and Conquer? China and the Cacophony of Foreign Investment Rules in the EU' (2014) 21(7) *Journal of European Public Policy* 996, p. 1001.

64 Communication from the Commission to the European Parliament, the European Council, the Council, the European Economic and Social Committee and the Committee of the Regions, 'Welcoming Foreign Direct Investment while Protection Essential Interests', COM(2017) 494 final, 13/9/2017, p. 9.

65 Ibid. p. 10.

> for cooperation between Member States, and between Member States and the Commission, with regard to foreign direct investments likely to affect security or public order.[66]

The Regulation states that it does not 'limit the right of each Member State to decide whether or not to screen' particular investments.[67] Nevertheless, as will be seen below, those Member States that decide not to enact a screening mechanism still have certain obligations under the Regulation. This section will first introduce the framework for FDI screening mechanisms as proposed by the Regulation followed by an explanation of the cooperation mechanism.

On the basis of Article 3(1) of the Regulation, 'Member States may maintain, amend or adopt mechanisms to screen foreign direct investments in their territory on the grounds of security or public order.' The definitions of the FDI-Regulation are quite straight forward. On the basis of Article 2(1), a FDI is

> an investment of any kind by a foreign investor aiming to establish or to maintain lasting and direct links between the foreign investor and the entrepreneur to whom or the undertaking to which the capital is made available in order to carry on an economic activity in a Member State, including investments which enable effective participation in the management or control of a company carrying out an economic activity.

A foreign investor is 'a natural person of a third country or an undertaking of a third country, intending to make or having made a foreign direct investment.' Screening is defined as 'a procedure allowing to assess, investigate, authorise, condition, prohibit or unwind foreign direct investments.'[68]

Screening mechanisms are instruments 'of general application' and accompanied by administrative requirements, implementing rules or guidelines which set out the terms, conditions and procedures for screenings.[69] These rules and procedures are to be applied transparently and may not discriminate between third countries.[70] Importantly, it must be clear what thresholds, that may trigger the screening, apply and what the grounds for screening are.[71] Importantly, foreign investors – as well as the undertakings concerned – 'shall have the possibility to seek recourse against screening decisions of the national authorities.'[72]

---

66 Article 1(1), Regulation (EU) 2019/452 of the European Parliament and of the Council of 19 March 2019 establishing a framework for the screening of foreign direct investments into the Union [2019] OJ L 79 1/1.

67 Ibid. Article 1(3).

68 Ibid. Article 2(3).

69 Ibid. Article 2(4).

70 Ibid. Article 3(2).

71 Ibid.

72 Ibid. Article 3(5). A screening decision is defined in Article 2(6) as 'a measure adopted in application of a screening mechanism.'

The most crucial terms of the regulation, namely 'security and public order' remain undefined. Nevertheless, the Regulation states several criteria that may be considered by Member States and the Commission while determining whether an investment is likely to affect security or public order, some of which relate directly to the energy sector. For example, the effects of a FDI on 'critical infrastructure, whether physical or virtual, including energy, transport [...] and real estate crucial for the use of such infrastructure' may be considered.[73] Critical technologies, including 'energy storage, quantum and nuclear technologies' may also be taken into account, as well as the 'supply of critical inputs, including energy or raw materials.'[74]

The Regulation also states certain factors that may be considered concerning the foreign investor; most importantly, whether it is 'directly or indirectly controlled by the government, including state bodies or armed forces, of a third country, including through ownership structure or significant funding.'[75]

The cooperation mechanism is laid down in Articles 6–8 of the Regulation. In relation to FDIs that undergo screening in a particular State, Article 6 obliges that Member State to notify the Commission and other Member States of the FDI undergoing screening.[76] Subsequently, other Member States may provide 'comments' if they consider that the proposed FDI is likely to affect their security or public order or if they have relevant information.[77] In a similar vein, the Commission may 'issue an opinion'.[78] These comments and opinions shall be 'duly justified' and the Member State undertaking the screening 'shall give due consideration' to them, although it still has the final say in the screening decision.[79] A very similar cooperation mechanism exists by virtue of Article 7, which concerns FDIs that are not undergoing screening, although this procedure does not apply to investments made before 10 April 2019.[80]

FDIs that are likely to affect 'projects or programmes of Union interest' are specifically addressed in Article 8, which makes the procedures of Articles 6 and 7 applicable by reference. For the purpose of this provision, projects or programmes of Union interest 'shall include those projects and programmes which involve a substantial amount or significant share of Union funding, or

73 Ibid. Article 4(1)(a).
74 Ibid. Article 4(1)(b) and (c).
75 Ibid. Article 4(2)(a). See also: A.E. Alvarado Garzón, 'From State-Controlled Enterprises to Investment Screening: Paving the Way for Stricter Rules on Foreign Investment' [2019] *Transnational Dispute Management*, forthcoming, pp. 9–19.
76 Article 6(1), Regulation (EU) 2019/452 of the European Parliament and of the Council of 19 March 2019 establishing a framework for the screening of foreign direct investments into the Union [2019] OJ L 79 1/1.
77 Ibid. Article 6(2).
78 Ibid. Article 6(3).
79 Ibid. Articles 6(5) and (9).
80 Ibid. Article 7.

which are covered by Union law regarding critical infrastructure.'[81] As said, this may include infrastructures relating to the production, transmission and supply of oil, gas, and electricity.[82] In deviation from the earlier cooperation mechanisms, opinions of the Commission issued under Article 8 shall be taken into utmost account by the Member State where the investment is proposed and an explanation to the Commission must be made if the opinion is not followed.[83]

Even for Member States that decide not to adopt a screening mechanism, the Regulation contains certain obligations. For example, each year they have to submit a report to the Commission which includes aggregated information on FDIs of the previous year.[84] In a similar vein, Member States that do not maintain a screening mechanism have the obligation to comply with information requests by the Commission and other Member States concerning proposed FDIs in that Member State.[85]

All in all, the Regulation seems – *de jure* – to be relatively free from obligations, in the sense that no FDI screening mechanism has to be established and the opinions and comments issued by the Commission and other Member States do not bind the Member State where the investment is proposed; it retains the final say in a screening decision. Nevertheless, the *de facto* consequences of the Regulation should not be underestimated, as screening mechanisms can have a 'strong preventative effect' on FDI.[86] In the US, for example, in the context of the Committee on Foreign Investment in the United States (CFIUS) the US President has the power to block transactions, and while these formal powers have rarely been used in practice, many proposed acquisitions were abandoned by the 'acquirer because of concerns raised by members of CFIUS during the review process.'[87] It has been said that '[s]ince 1990, nearly half of the transactions CFIUS investigated were terminated by the firms involved, because the firms decided to withdraw from the transactions rather than face a negative determination by CFIUS.'[88]

---

81 Ibid. Article 8(3).

82 Article 2(b) and Annex I, Council Directive 2008/114/EC of 8 December 2008 on the identification and designation of European critical infrastructures and the assessment of the need to improve their protection [2008] OJ L 345/75.

83 Article 8(2)(c), Regulation (EU) 2019/452 of the European Parliament and of the Council of 19 March 2019 establishing a framework for the screening of foreign direct investments into the Union [2019] OJ L 79 1/1.

84 Ibid. Article 5.

85 Ibid. Article 9.

86 A. Heinemann, 'Government Control of Cross-Border M&A: Legitimate Regulation or Protectionism?' (2012) 15(3) *Journal of International Economic Law* 843, p. 851.

87 R. Bismuth, 'Screening the Commission's Regulation Proposal Establishing a Framework for Screening FDI into the EU' (2018) 3 *European Investment Law and Arbitration Review* 45, p. 54. J.K. Jackson, 'The Committee on Foreign Investment in the United States (CFIUS)' (Congressional Research Service, RL33388, 3 July 2018), p. 7.

88 Ibid. p. 57.

4. COMPATIBILITY WITH THE EU'S COMMITMENTS UNDER TRADE AND INVESTMENT AGREEMENTS

4.1. INTRODUCTION

The EU and its Member States have been negotiating and concluding investment agreements for decades, including the 1994 Energy Charter Treaty (ECT).[89] In the past, these treaties primarily provided for post-establishment investment protection, although the Commission did try to include pre-establishment investment liberalisation commitments in the ECT.[90] More recent investment and trade agreements negotiated by the EU have broken with this traditional practice and foresee investment liberalisation commitments by providing for market access to foreign investors and by extending the non-discrimination regime of the treaties – as laid down in national treatment (NT) and most-favoured nation treatment (MFN) obligations – to the pre-establishment phase of an investment which covers the activities of establishment, acquisition, and expansion.[91]

At first glance, the introduction of a FDI screening mechanism would violate such commitments, in particular the NT obligation, since foreign investors are subjected to a screening that does not apply to domestic investors while the very purpose of NT is to ensure that foreign investors are treated in the same manner as domestic investors.

Both the FDI-Regulation as well as a Commission report of 2017 concerning the Regulation proposal demonstrate awareness of this potential tension.[92] According to the Commission, the FDI-Regulation scope for action – which is limited to security and public order – is framed in accordance with the relevant

---

89 Energy Charter Treaty (adopted 17/12/1994, entered into force 16/04/1998).

90 A. Joubin-Bret, 'Admission and Establishment in the Context of Investment Protection' in August Reinisch (ed.), *Standards of Investment Protection*, Oxford University Press, Oxford 2008, pp. 11–12. Article 13(2), CONF 56, Draft ECT – Second version, 1 May 1993. <http://www.energycharter.org/fileadmin/DocumentsMedia/ECT_Drafts/16_-_ECT_2__01.05.93_.pdf>.

91 Articles 8.4, 8.6 and 8.7, Comprehensive Economic and Trade Agreement (European Union–Canada) (adopted 30/10/2016, entrance into force still pending). Articles 8.4, 8.5 and 8.6, EU–Vietnam Free Trade Agreement (European Union-Vietnam) (adopted 30/06/2019, entrance into force is still pending). Articles 8.10 and 8.11, EU-Singapore Free Trade Agreement (adopted 19/10/2018, entrance into force is still pending). M.L. Marceddu, 'The Emerging Profile of the European IIAs' (2016) 13 *Transnational Dispute Management* 1, pp. 13–14.

92 Communication from the Commission to the European Parliament, the European Council, the Council, the European Economic and Social Committee and the Committee of the Regions, 'Welcoming Foreign Direct Investment while Protection Essential Interests', COM(2017) 494 final, 13/9/2017, p. 10. Recital 3, Regulation (EU) 2019/452 of the European Parliament and of the Council of 19 March 2019 establishing a framework for the screening of foreign direct investments into the Union [2019] OJ L 79 1/1.

exceptions contained in trade and investment agreements which should preclude a violation of international obligations under such treaties. The purpose of this paragraph is to analyse whether that is actually the case. The EU–Canada CETA will be analysed, since it contains the most far-reaching investment liberalisation commitments undertaken by the EU in an international agreement.

4.2. EU–CANADA CETA

The CETA was negotiated in five years and is considered to be one of the first 'mega-regional' free trade agreements (FTA) concluded that liberalises trade and investment in a comprehensive manner.[93] About the agreement, one author wrote that it 'is in all probability the most lengthy and complex FTA ever drafted.'[94] The liberalisation of FDI and the exceptions thereto are particularly technical. Investment is regulated in Chapter 8 of the agreement, called 'Investment', although relevant exceptions can also be found in other Chapters. This section will be subdivided as follows: 1) the market access and non-discrimination commitments will be explained; followed by 2) an overview of the ability to maintain non-conforming measures; and 3) an analysis of the relevant exceptions that, according to the Commission, are phrased in such a manner as to safeguard the FDI-Regulation.

4.2.1. Market Access and Non-Discrimination

In the absence of any treaty commitments under international law to the contrary, States have the sovereign right to regulate the admission of foreign investors into their economy as they see fit: they may admit such investments, prohibit them or subject them to regulations such as, for example, screening mechanisms.[95] On the basis of the CETA, the Contracting Parties have nevertheless restricted this sovereign right.[96]

Firstly, on the basis of Article 8.4 CETA, certain limitations on market access through governmental measures are prohibited.[97] These include economic needs

[93] A. De Mestral, 'When Does the Exception Become the Rule? Conserving Regulatory Space under CETA' (2015) 18(3) *Journal of International Economic Law* 641, p. 641.

[94] Ibid. In a similar vein, see: A.K. Bjorklund and L. Vanhonnaeker, 'National Treatment' in M.M. Mbengue and S. Schacherer (eds.), *Foreign Investment Under the Comprehensive Economic and Trade Agreement (CETA)*, Springer, Cham 2019, p. 60.

[95] A. Joubin-Bret, 'Admission and Establishment in the Context of Investment Protection' in A. Reinisch (ed.), *Standards of Investment Protection*, Oxford University Press, Oxford 2008, p. 2.

[96] Note, investments in certain sectors fall outside the scope of the investment chapter, see: Article 8.2(2) and (3), Comprehensive Economic and Trade Agreement (European Union-Canada) (adopted 30/10/2016, entrance into force still pending).

[97] Ibid. Article 8.4(1).

tests, foreign equity participation limitations, and quotas.[98] Nevertheless, certain market access limitations may be maintained, such as unbundling requirements in network-bound industries, including in the energy sector, zoning and planning regulations, and measures adopted under competition law.[99]

Secondly, on the basis of Articles 8.6 and 8.7 CETA, rules of non-discrimination on the ground of nationality have been extended to the pre-establishment phase of an investment. For example, Article 8.6(1) CETA states:

> Each Party shall accord to an investor of the other Party and to a covered investment, treatment no less favourable than the treatment it accords, in like situations to its own investors and to their investments with respect to the *establishment, acquisition, expansion*, conduct, operation, management, maintenance, use, enjoyment and sale or disposal of their investments in its territory (emphasis added).

This approach is often referred to as prescribing 'pre-establishment rights' and, in principle, this means that the Contracting Parties have accepted a limitation on their sovereign right to regulate the entrance of foreign investors into their economies.[100] In the context of FDI screening mechanisms this essentially entails that if such mechanisms are not applied in relation to domestic investors, they should not be applied to foreign investors from the other Contracting Party either.[101] In practice however, few – if any – States would allow unfettered market access to foreign investors. Therefore, this right is often subject to a range of exceptions and derogations.[102] It has been said that CETA contains an 'unprecedented' number of such exceptions which makes application of the agreement rather complex and technical.[103]

4.2.2. Non-Conforming Measures and the Standstill Clause

While the 2019 EU–Vietnam FTA also provides for pre-establishment rights, the technique employed in this agreement differs significantly from the CETA.

---

98 Ibid.

99 Ibid. Article 8.4(2).

100 A. Joubin-Bret, 'Admission and Establishment in the Context of Investment Protection' in A. Reinisch (ed.), *Standards of Investment Protection*, Oxford University Press, Oxford 2008, p. 13.

101 A.K. Bjorklund and L. Vanhonnaeker, 'National Treatment' in M.M. Mbengue and S. Schacherer (eds.), *Foreign Investment Under the Comprehensive Economic and Trade Agreement (CETA)*, Springer, Cham 2019, pp. 58–59.

102 A. Joubin-Bret, 'Admission and Establishment in the Context of Investment Protection' in A. Reinisch (ed.), *Standards of Investment Protection*, Oxford University Press, Oxford 2008, p. 13. A. Reinisch, 'National Treatment' in M. Bungenberg, J. Griebel, S. Hobe and A. Reinisch (eds.), *International Investment Law: A Handbook*, C.H. Beck, Baden-Baden 2015, p. 851.

103 A.K. Bjorklund and L. Vanhonnaeker, 'National Treatment' in M.M. Mbengue and S. Schacherer (eds.), *Foreign Investment Under the Comprehensive Economic and Trade Agreement (CETA)*, Springer, Cham 2019, p. 60. A. De Mestral, 'When Does the Exception

In the EU–Vietnam FTA, these pre-establishment rights only apply to economic sectors or activities indicated in an accompanying annex (positive listing, or 'opt in model') while in the case of CETA, these pre-establishment rights apply across the board subject to exceptions indicated in an annex (negative listing, or 'opt out model').[104] In the so-called schedules contained in these annexes, the CETA Contracting Parties have specified all existing non-conforming measures 'that each Party wants to maintain, notwithstanding the conclusion of CETA.'[105] All in all, these schedules are more than 800 pages long.

In practice, maintaining exceptions to the investment liberalisation commitments is done in two ways. Firstly, the EU, its Member States, and Canada are allowed to maintain 'non-conforming measures' – *i.e.* measures that in principle differentiate between foreign and domestic investors – on the basis of Article 8.15(1) CETA. These non-conforming measures are incorporated in the schedules of the Parties. Canada, for example, has negotiated an exception for its Investment Canada Act, which contains the FDI screening mechanism for non-Canadian investments into Canada.[106] This allows Canada to 'review a direct "acquisition of control", as defined in the Investment Canada Act, of a Canadian business by an investor of the European Union if the value of the Canadian business is not less than CAD 1.5 billion.'[107] France, whose FDI screening mechanism was introduced in section 2.2, has incorporated various exceptions relating to the agricultural, fishing, business services, healthcare, retail, and education sectors, but not its FDI screening mechanism of the Monetary and Financial Code.[108] Neither has Germany obtained an exception for its Foreign Trade and Payments Act and Ordinance. Since the FDI-Regulation did not exist at the time of conclusion of CETA, it is also not incorporated in the schedule of the EU. Under Articles 8.15(1)(b) and (c), non-conforming measures listed in the schedules of the Contracting Parties may be continued or renewed to the extent that they do not 'decrease the

---

Become the Rule? Conserving Regulatory Space under CETA' (2015) 18(3) *Journal of International Economic Law* 641.

104 A. Joubin-Bret, '30/06/2019, entrance into force are still Admission and Establishment in the Context of Investment Protection' in A. Reinisch (ed.), *Standards of Investment Protection*, Oxford University Press, Oxford 2008, p. 13. Compare: Articles 8.4, and 8.5, EU-Vietnam Free Trade Agreement (European Union-Vietnam) (adoption pending).

105 C.C. Daigremont, 'Most Favoured Nation Treatment' in M.M. Mbengue and S. Schacherer (eds.), *Foreign Investment Under the Comprehensive Economic and Trade Agreement (CETA)*, Springer, Cham 2019, p. 84.

106 Annex I, Schedule of Canada – Federal: Reservations applicable in Canada (applicable in all Provinces and Territories), Reservation I-C-1, Comprehensive Economic and Trade Agreement (European Union-Canada) (adopted 30/10/2016, entrance into force still pending).

107 Ibid. Investment Canada Act (R.S.C., 1985, c. 28 (1st Supp.)). N. Campbell, J. O'hara and T. Cullen, 'The Impact of New Transatlantic Trade Agreements on Commercial and Investment Transactions' (2015) 16(3) *Business Law International* 185, pp. 201–202.

108 Reservations Applicable in the European Union, Reservations Applicable in France, pp. 103–113, 2016/0206 (NLE).

conformity' of the measure with Articles 8.6 and 8.7 CETA. This is, in effect, a standstill obligation.[109] Thus, while Canada has been able to negotiate an exception for its FDI screening mechanism – albeit with an increased threshold that triggers its application – this does not seem to be the case for the EU and its Member States which, due to the standstill obligation, are also prohibited from introducing further non-conforming measures after the conclusion of the treaty.[110]

Secondly, on the basis of Article 8.15(2) CETA, Articles 8.6 and 8.7 CETA 'do not apply to a measure that a Party adopts or maintains with respect to a sector, subsector or activity as set out in its Schedule to Annex II.' While annex II of the EU and its Member States does include some exceptions relevant for the energy sector, such as the nuclear energy sector, there is – again – no mention of exceptions for FDI screening mechanisms.

In addition to these exceptions Article 8.15 further includes exceptions regarding government procurement, subsidies, and it clarifies the relationship of the CETA to certain WTO Agreements, all of which are not relevant for FDI screening mechanisms.[111]

In contrast to Canada, the EU and its Member States have thus seemingly refrained from incorporating their FDI screening mechanisms into their schedules of non-conforming measures to the extent that they were in existence at the time of conclusion of the CETA. This means that Canada is allowed to screen FDI from the EU without violating the NT obligation while this is not the case for the EU and its Member States: these exceptions are not strictly speaking reciprocal but rather represent the equilibrium reached after an extensive negotiating process. Whether the EU and its Member States would actually violate their commitments under the CETA depends on their ability to successfully invoke one of the other available exceptions under the treaty.

4.2.3. *Relevant Exceptions Concerning 'Security and Public Order'*

Besides the specific exceptions included in Chapter 8 of the agreement, CETA also contains a Chapter that is devoted to 'Exceptions'.[112] Chapter 28 contains provisions that may cover the scope of the FDI-Regulation since they address security and public order. This would ensure that the FDI-Regulation does not violate the CETA.

---

109 P. Delimatsis, 'The Evolution of the EU External Trade Policy in Services – CETA, TTIP, and TiSA after Brexit' (2017) 20 *Journal of International Economic Law* 583, p. 598.

110 N. Campbell, J. O'Hara and T. Cullen, 'The Impact of New Transatlantic Trade Agreements on Commercial and Investment Transactions' (2015) 16(3) *Business Law International* 185, pp. 201–202.

111 Article 8.15(4) and (5), Comprehensive Economic and Trade Agreement (European Union–Canada) (adopted 30/10/2016, entrance into force still pending).

112 Ibid. Chapter 28.

For example, the general exceptions clause of Article 28.3(1) CETA incorporates Article XX GATT by reference in relation to the FDI liberalisation section of Chapter 8 while Article 28.3(2) CETA contains a general exceptions clause much akin to Article XIV of the General Agreement on Trade in Services (GATS) that allows the Contracting Parties to adopt measures to 'protect public security or public morals or to maintain public order' that also applies with respect to the FDI liberalisation section of Chapter 8.[113] Furthermore, Article 28.6 CETA contains a national security exception that closely resembles the language used in Article XXI GATT. Since the relevant clauses are themselves not entirely free from difficulty, they will be analysed in turn.

4.2.3.1. The General Exceptions: Article 28.3 CETA

The general exceptions of CETA apply in relation to certain parts of the investment chapter, including its investment liberalisation sections but, interestingly, not in relation to the investment protection section.[114] In relevant part, Article 28.3 states:

> 1. [...] Article XX of the GATT 1994 is incorporated into and made part of this Agreement. The Parties understand that the measures referred to in Article XX (b) of the GATT 1994 include environmental measures necessary to protect human, animal or plant life or health. The Parties understand that Article XX(g) of the GATT 1994 applies to measures for the conservation of living and non-living exhaustible natural resources.
> 2. [...] subject to the requirement that such measures are not applied in a manner which would constitute a means of arbitrary or unjustifiable discrimination between the Parties where like conditions prevail, or a disguised restriction on trade in services, nothing in this Agreement shall be construed to prevent the adoption or enforcement by a Party of measures necessary:
>   (a) to protect public security or public morals or to maintain public order;
>   (b) to protect human, animal or plant life or health; or
>   (c) to secure compliance with laws or regulations which are not inconsistent with the provisions of this Agreement including those relating to:
>   (i) the prevention of deceptive and fraudulent practices or to deal with the effects of a default on contracts;
>   (ii) the protection of the privacy of individuals in relation to the processing and dissemination of personal data and the protection of confidentiality of individual records and accounts; or
>   (iii) safety.

---

113 Ibid. Article 28.3(2)(a). See also: Article XIV, General Agreement on Trade in Services (adopted 15/04/1994, entered into force 01/01/1995).

114 C. Titi, 'The Right to Regulate' in M.M. Mbengue and S. Schacherer (eds.), *Foreign Investment Under the Comprehensive Economic and Trade Agreement (CETA)*, Springer, Cham 2019, p. 178.

Thus, Article 28.3(1) incorporates the general exceptions of GATT by reference. Since Article 28.3(2) partially repeats Article XX GATT, the provisions largely overlap – which has been called 'awkward and unnecessary.'[115] Nevertheless, since Article XX GATT does not provide for grounds of public security or public order it does not seem properly equipped to ensure that the FDI-Regulation complies with CETA.

This may be the case under Article 28.3(2) which allows for security and public order measures as long as these are 'necessary' and 'are not applied in a manner which would constitute a means of arbitrary or unjustifiable discrimination between the Parties where like conditions prevail, or a disguised restriction on trade in services.'[116] A footnote clarifies that '[t]he public security and public order exceptions may be invoked only where a genuine and sufficiently serious threat is posed to one of the fundamental interests of society.'[117] As becomes apparent from reading the exception, and in particular from reading the sections of CETA to which it applies – namely: cross-border trade in services, temporary entry and stay of natural persons for business purposes, domestic regulation, financial services, international maritime transport services, telecommunications, electronic commerce, as well as certain parts of the investment Chapter – one can wonder whether the provision is supposed to apply to investments unrelated to rendering services through the establishment of a commercial presence.[118] After all, although supplying services through the establishment of a commercial presence in the host State by definition requires an investment, not all investments will be made with the purpose of supplying services.

Nevertheless, under the CETA, the applicable test is essentially the same as under Article XIV GATS: for a measure to be justified it must fall within the scope of a particular subparagraph and then meet the requirements of the 'chapeau'.[119]

As stated above, only 'genuine and sufficiently serious' threats posed to 'one of the fundamental interests of society' may warrant an invocation of the public security and public order exception.[120] As stated in the introduction, the line between protecting national security and disguised protectionism may be a fine one. Since the FDI-Regulation neglects to define what exactly

---

115 Ibid. p. 179.

116 Article 28.3(2), Comprehensive Economic and Trade Agreement (European Union-Canada) (adopted 30/10/2016, entrance into force still pending).

117 Ibid. Footnote 33 to Article 28.3(2)(a).

118 Ibid. Article 28.3(2).

119 *United States – Measures Affecting the Cross-Border Supply of Gambling and Betting Services*, Report of the Appellate Body, WT/DS285/AB/R, 7 April 2005, para. 292.

120 Footnote 33 to Article 28.3(2)(a), Comprehensive Economic and Trade Agreement (European Union–Canada) (adopted 30/10/2016, entrance into force still pending).

constitutes 'security or public order' one could argue that it does not even succeed in identifying the fundamental interests of society it aims to protect.

Furthermore, if the FDI-Regulation would fall within the scope of paragraph 28.3(2)(a), it still has to meet the requirements of the 'chapeau' of Article 28.3(2), namely that the measure is i) necessary and ii) not applied in a manner which would constitute a means of arbitrary or unjustifiable discrimination between the Parties where like conditions prevail, or a disguised restriction on trade in services.

Establishing the necessity 'should be determined through "a process of weighing and balancing a series of factors".'[121] For example, one should consider the 'relative importance' of the objective pursued, the 'contribution of the measure to the realization of the ends pursued by it' and the extent to which the measure has a 'restrictive impact' on international commerce.[122] Consequently, a measure is only necessary when there is no 'reasonably available' alternative that is consistent with the agreement.[123] In the context of the GATS, the Appellate Body has held that 'GATS obligations should not be deviated from lightly.'[124]

Besides establishing the necessity, the FDI-Regulation may also not be applied in a manner that is arbitrary or discriminatory, as required by the chapeau of Article 28.3(2) CETA. On the basis of WTO jurisprudence and the text of the provision itself, it becomes apparent that this test focusses on the *application* of the FDI-Regulation.[125] Concerning discriminatory treatment, the Appellate Body has held that 'mere individual instances of differential treatment' do not suffice; rather, 'patterns' of discriminatory treatment have to be established.[126] This may, in practice, be difficult to establish.

Applying these considerations to the FDI-Regulation, one can point to the alleged 'strong preventative' effect that FDI screening mechanisms can have on

---

121 *United States – Measures Affecting the Cross-Border Supply of Gambling and Betting Services*, Report of the Appellate Body, WT/DS285/AB/R, 7 April 2005, para. 305. *Korea – Measures Affecting Imports of Fresh, Chilled and Frozen Beef*, Reports of the Appellate Body, WT/DS161/AB/R, WT/DS169/AB/R, 11 December 2000, para. 164.

122 *United States – Measures Affecting the Cross-Border Supply of Gambling and Betting Services*, Report of the Appellate Body, WT/DS285/AB/R, 7 April 2005, para. 306.

123 Ibid. para. 307.

124 Ibid. para. 308.

125 *United States – Measures Affecting the Cross-Border Supply of Gambling and Betting Services*, Report of the Appellate Body, WT/DS285/AB/R, 7 April 2005, para. 339. *United States – Standards for Reformulated and Conventional Gasoline*, Report of the Appellate Body, WT/DS2/AB/R, 29 April 1996, p. 22.

126 *United States – Measures Affecting the Cross-Border Supply of Gambling and Betting Services*, Report of the Appellate Body, WT/DS285/AB/R, 7 April 2005, para. 356. M. Matsushita, T.J. Schoenbaum and P.C. Mavroidis, *The World Trade Organization – Law, Practice, and Policy*, Oxford University Press, Oxford 2006, p. 640.

proposed investments, in particular in the context of brownfield investments, which means that the restrictive impact on international commerce may be significant.[127] Also, since the FDI-Regulation does not define 'security and public order', one may wonder what the pursued objective exactly is. For example, is it politically desirable to have a legal instrument at our disposal which may prohibit foreign investors from acquiring electricity grids, even though they may be just as capable of operating such a grid as domestic investors would? Will the FDI-Regulation be applied by Member States in the pursuit of a policy of economic nationalism, thereby discriminating between foreign and domestic competitors? Earlier, it was said that France has used an FDI screening mechanism to favour the creation of national champions, even though economic nationalism may reduce economic efficiency.[128] Also, the clause seems to be written with trade in services in mind, hence the strong similarity with the GATS. However, even though certain services – in particular when supplied through the establishment of a commercial presence – may require an FDI, not all FDIs will be made with the purpose of supplying services.

Furthermore, the application of the FDI-Regulation may become discriminatory if it is often used in relation to investors from specific countries. Admittedly, one would not expect that Canadian investors would be the primary targets, but rather investors originating from Russia or China. In relation to China, it is notable that the EU and China have been negotiating a bilateral investment treaty for years, the scope of which is supposed to cover pre-establishment investment liberalisation as well as post-establishment investment protection.[129]

All in all, Article 28.3(2) CETA is probably the most important provision that could ensure that the FDI-Regulation can be justified under CETA even though a lot would depend on the exact application of the Regulation. Due to its novelty, it is currently difficult to make any meaningful comments on its application and, therefore, its conformity with the requirements of Article 28.3(2). However, as the comments made about the French FDI screening mechanism demonstrate, discrimination may be lurking in the application of such mechanisms. If that is (too) obvious, justification under Article 28.3(2) CETA may be highly questionable.

---

127 A. Heinemann, 'Government Control of Cross-Border M&A: Legitimate Regulation or Protectionism?' (2012) 15(3) *Journal of International Economic Law* 843, p. 851.

128 Ibid. pp. 848–849. C.C. Baughn and A. Yaprak, 'Economic Nationalism: Conceptual and Empirical Development' (1996) 17(4) *Political Psychology* 759, p. 760.

129 See: EU-China Comprehensive Agreement on Investment (EU–China CAI). <http://www.europarl.europa.eu/legislative-train/theme-a-balanced-and-progressive-trade-policy-to-harness-globalisation/file-eu-china-investment-agreement>.

4.2.3.2. National Security Exception: Article 28.6 CETA

Another exception that may be available is the one specifically related to national security. On the basis of Article 28.6 CETA:

> Nothing in this Agreement shall be construed:
>
> (a) to require a Party to furnish or allow access to information if that Party determines that the disclosure of this information would be contrary to its essential security interests; or
> (b) to prevent a Party from taking an action that it considers necessary to protect its essential security interests:
> (i) connected to the production of or traffic in arms, ammunition and implements of war and to such traffic and transactions in other goods and materials, services and technology undertaken, and to economic activities, carried out directly or indirectly for the purpose of supplying a military or other security establishment;
> (ii) taken in time of war or other emergency in international relations; or
> (iii) relating to fissionable and fusionable materials or the materials from which they are derived; or
> (c) prevent a Party from taking any action in order to carry out its international obligations for the purpose of maintaining international peace and security.

Paragraph (b) is most relevant and since this provision closely resembles the national security exception of the GATT, WTO jurisprudence can serve again as an appropriate benchmark for its correct interpretation and application.[130] Two important issues arise in this regard.

Firstly, paragraph (b) states that nothing in the CETA shall be construed to prevent a Party from taking action that *it* considers necessary to protect its essential security interests. As under the GATT, this may imply that the provision is self-judging in nature which may render the provision comparable to the 'get out of jail free' card of Monopoly.[131] On the basis of the first

130 Paragraph (a) relates to the exchange of information, which is not broad enough to cover the FDI-Regulation while paragraph (c) seeks to ensure that CETA Contracting Parties can impose trade sanctions in compliance with the Charter of the United Nations, although CETA – in contrast to the GATT – does not explicitly refer to the United Nations Charter.

131 M. Matsushita, T.J. Schoenbaum and P.C. Mavroidis, *The World Trade Organization – Law, Practice, and Policy*, Oxford University Press, Oxford 2006, pp. 595–597. J.W. Salacuse, *The Law of Investment Treaties*, Oxford University Press, Oxford 2010, pp. 344–345. C. Levesque and A. Newcombe, 'The Evolution of IIA Practice in Canada and the United States' in A. De Mestral *et al* (eds.), *Improving International Investment Agreements*, Routledge, Oxon 2013, p. 37. Judgment, *Military and Paramilitary Activities in and against Nicaragua (Nicaragua v. United States of America)*, Merits, Judgment, I.C.J. Reports 1986, p. 14, para. 222.

jurisprudence of Article XXI GATT this does not seem to be the case: the exception should be interpreted and applied in good faith which entails that it may not be used 'as a means to circumvent [...] obligations under the GATT'.[132] Therefore, the said exception does not grant 'unfettered discretion' to the invoking member and the exception is not entirely self-judging since dispute settlement Panels have 'the power to review whether the requirements of the enumerated subparagraphs are met.'[133]

This brings us to the second issue, namely that the three subparagraphs of paragraph (b) 'define the objective circumstances' under which a national security measure may be adopted.[134] This essentially means that as long as no national security issues arise in EU–Canadian relations as defined in the three subparagraphs of Article 28.6(b), invocation of this exception will be unsuccessful. A notable difference in this regard is that certain investment treaties, such as the ECT, refer to public order in the national security exception.[135] The CETA does not. This means that the 'self-judging' exception is narrower under CETA than the ECT and it cannot be relied upon to justify the FDI-Regulation where it concerns FDIs that raise issues regarding public order.

5. CONCLUSION

National security and public order considerations have in recent times increasingly been referred to in order to justify measures that restrict trade and investment. In that regard, the FDI-Regulation seems to fit seamlessly in the current protectionist tide. Whilst it was American investors that worried European politicians in the '70s and Japanese investors in the '80s, investments by Chinese, Russian, and Gulf State investors are currently watched vigilantly, in particular when it concerns brownfield investments made by State backed parties in critical infrastructures or high-tech sectors.[136]

Although the obligations under the FDI-Regulation may, *de jure*, not be very significant, the *de facto* effects should not be underestimated since the preventative effects of FDI screening mechanisms can be significant, as experience in the US demonstrates. This is so particularly when it is used in a manner that creates

132 *Russia – Measures Concerning Traffic in Transit*, Report of the Panel, WT/DS512/R, 5 April 2019, paras. 7.132–7.133.

133 Ibid. para. 7.102.

134 M. Matsushita, T.J. Schoenbaum and P.C. Mavroidis, *The World Trade Organization – Law, Practice, and Policy*, Oxford University Press, Oxford 2006, p. 596. *Russia – Measures Concerning Traffic in Transit*, Report of the Panel, WT/DS512/R, 5 April 2019, para. 7.101.

135 Article 24(3)(c), the Energy Charter Treaty (adopted 17/12/1994, entered into force 16/04/1998).

136 United Nations Conference on Trade and Development, World Investment Report 2019, unctad/wir/2019 (Geneva: United Nations, 2019), p. 96.

national or European champions, a practice that may be desirable in the eyes of politicians but which does not necessarily lead to most (consumer) welfare and economic efficiency. In the increasingly globalised economy, FDI is the lubricant that makes trade in goods – through the existence of global value chains – and services – through the establishment of foreign subsidiaries – function, and the energy sector is no exception.

While the existence of a legal instrument that may keep undesirable foreign investors out is currently politically opportune in an atmosphere where the anti-globalisation movement is gaining strength, it is not necessarily in compliance with recently concluded FTAs; the CETA being the prime example. While the Canadians have negotiated an exception for their FDI screening mechanism, this is not the case for the EU and its Member States. Depending on how the FDI-Regulation will be applied in practice, it may – or may not – be justified under Article 28.3(2) CETA. If the Regulation cannot be justified, Canadian investors may find themselves in an awkward situation if they are adversely affected by the Regulation: the pre-establishment rights of CETA are excluded from the investor-State dispute settlement mechanism of Chapter 8 and the obligations under CETA cannot be enforced through the domestic courts of the Contracting Parties.[137] All the adversely affected investors can do is complain to the relevant Contracting Parties. In light of this uncertainty, the EU and its Member States would be well advised to include the FDI-Regulation, as well as any national FDI screening mechanism, in the list of non-conforming measures in future FTA negotiations in the same way as Canada did in the context of CETA.

Of course, a way in which the EU and its Member States could avoid committing an internationally wrongful act under CETA is by exempting Canadian investors from the screening procedure. This is, however, easier said than done since the FDI-Regulation itself prohibits this.[138] Also, some recent FTAs concluded by the EU provide for MFN treatment in the establishment phase of an investment.[139] This means that if the EU and its Member States accord more favourable treatment to Canadian investors, investors from countries like Mexico and Japan should be accorded the same treatment. This demonstrates that regulating international economic affairs is becoming a complicated affair: the application of a specific measure in light of one FTA may well have consequences for the relationship with third countries and their investors.

---

[137] Articles 8.2(4) and 30.6, Comprehensive Economic and Trade Agreement (European Union-Canada) (adopted 30/10/2016, entrance into force still pending).

[138] Article 3(2), Regulation (EU) 2019/452 of the European Parliament and of the Council of 19 March 2019 establishing a framework for the screening of foreign direct investments into the Union [2019] OJ L 79 1/1.

[139] Article 8, Investment Chapter, EU-Mexico Trade Agreement (European Union-Canada) (adoption and entrance into force still pending). Article 8.9(1), EU-Japan Economic Partnership Agreement (European Union-Japan) (adopted 17/07/2018, entered into force 01/02/2019).

CHAPTER XII

CLOSURE OF NUCLEAR POWER PLANTS IN GERMANY, SWEDEN AND FRANCE

Different Strategies for Different Results

Romain MAUGER

1. INTRODUCTION

Among the European Union Member States, three of the countries with the highest levels of electricity produced from nuclear energy in the past decades[1] have either decided to completely phase out this form of electricity generation (Germany and Sweden) or at least to reduce it significantly (France).

One decisive factor motivated these decisions: nuclear accidents, with Three Mile Island and Chernobyl pushing for the phase-out in Sweden and Germany, and Fukushima later reinforcing the German commitment and prompting the decision to reduce the share of nuclear electricity in the electricity mix from 75 to 50 per cent in France by 2025.

These three countries have had different timelines towards their nuclear energy phase-out or reduction, with Sweden embarking on this pathway since the 1980s, Germany taking this decision in the late 1990s, while France took this stance in the early 2010s. These three countries have also adopted different legal mechanisms to reach their targets, with varying results. Sweden had set a phase-out target for 2010 but failed to comply with it due to a lack of political action to use the available legal tools. Since then, Sweden has remained in a limbo

---

1 Over 70% for France, over 50% for Sweden in the early 2000s and around a quarter for Germany until the 2010s. See for France: 'Nuclear Power in France' (2019) *World nuclear association*, available at <https://www.world-nuclear.org/information-library/country-profiles/countries-a-f/france.aspx>; for Sweden: 'Nuclear industry development – Nuclear Power in Sweden' (2019) *World nuclear association*, available at <https://www.world-nuclear.org/information-library/country-profiles/countries-o-s/sweden.aspx>; and for Germany: 'Nuclear Power in Germany' (2019) *World nuclear association*, available at <https://www.world-nuclear.org/information-library/country-profiles/countries-g-n/germany.aspx>.

concerning nuclear energy, with no set phase-out target but nuclear reactors still shutting down rapidly for economic reasons. Germany had decided on its phase-out to be completed by the early 2020s, before the Merkel Government extended this date, only to come back to the original system six months later, following the Fukushima disaster. It is now progressing swiftly towards its targets thanks to an adapted legal framework which does not require political action once launched. In contrast, France recently postponed its 75–50 per cent by 2025 objective to 2035 due to its lack of action. It also failed to adopt adequate planning tools to schedule the shutdowns and to create an effective legal framework for energy policy-backed closures. As a result, no nuclear reactor has been shut down since the adoption of the 2015 Energy Transition Act setting this target and the government has had to commit to massive compensation for taking the first two reactors offline by 2020.

This chapter describes and compares the nuclear phase-out or significant reduction of the nuclear industry as planned in Germany, Sweden and France. It identifies the main characteristics of each national policy and related legal framework in this regard, their changes over time and their effectiveness up until mid-2019.

2. STRATEGIES FOR PLANNING NUCLEAR REACTORS SHUTDOWN

This section will present the strategies adopted in Germany, Sweden and France – some more than 20 years old – to plan and organise the forced shutdown of nuclear energy reactors for policy reasons. In each country, the extent of the involvement of the State and of the reactors' operators varies, as do the legal mechanisms which have been created. This can be considered as the 'phase one' of the nuclear reactors shutdown policy for each country, while the 'phase two' will be presented in section 3.

2.1. GERMANY: A SELF-UNFOLDING, LONG-TERM POLITICAL AGREEMENT BECOME LAW

In 2000, the newly-elected German Federal Government reached an agreement with the national nuclear power industry after six months of negotiations. In essence, the 'Agreement [on the future role of nuclear energy] provides for the application of a residual electricity volume', calculated per reactor 'on the basis of a standard operating life of 32 calendar years.'[2]

2 Agreement on the future role of nuclear energy (2000), General Legislation, Germany, National Legislative and Regulatory Activities (2000) 66 *Nucl Law Bull (Nuclear Law Bulletin)*, p. 40.

The major feature of this agreement is its automaticity, as 'the right to operate a nuclear power plant will cease when the residual electricity volume, or that volume revised as a result of transfer from another installation, has been generated.'[3] The nuclear reactors must go offline without any exterior decision from a minister or other authority, shielding the State against possible litigation over administrative acts which would otherwise have to be taken for the shutdown and against potential political changes. This non-binding political agreement was eventually made law in 2002.[4] Here the legislature is side-lined and only provides legal status to an agreement it has not participated in drafting. The *modus operandi* of this legislation questioned the very constitutional principle of parliamentary democracy, especially as the *Kalkar* decision taken by the Federal Constitutional Court (*Bundesverfassungsgericht*/BVerfG) in 1978 established that 'the fundamental decision for or against the use of nuclear power is incumbent on the legislator',[5] but still allowed a very effective mechanism that enabled the swift shutdown of nuclear reactors.

The average standard operating life of 32 calendar years in the Agreement was not randomly chosen. It was calculated to ensure its constitutionality with regard to the 'limitation on business activity' the nuclear reactors' operators will suffer. Indeed, in 2000 the Federal Ministry of Environment calculated that

> the average amortization of a nuclear power plant is reached after approximately 19 years [while] after 27 years of operation, at the latest, investments in nuclear power plants have yielded a profit that corresponds to the running yield of government bonds.[6]

In other words, after 32 years of operation, it is believed that the invested capital will have had time to be amortised. In addition, as the Agreement leaves an 'average residual operating period for German nuclear power plants of about 11.5 years',[7] this gives operators ample time to plan their maintenance investments on this basis, in order to maximise their revenues while respecting a 'high standard of safety'.[8] The significant amount of time available before the required shutdown of a reactor also plays a role in establishing the constitutionality of

3 *Ibid.*

4 A. Vorwerk, 'The 2002 Amendment to the German Atomic Energy Act Concerning the Phase-out of Nuclear Power' (2002) 69 *Nucl Law Bull*, p. 8.

5 *Ibid.*, pp. 7–8, in reference to the decision 49, 89 of 31 January 1978 taken by the *Bundesverfassungsgericht* (BVerfG) *Kalkar*.

6 A. Rossnagel and A. Hentschel, 'The legalities of a nuclear shutdown' (2012) *Bulletin of the Atomic Scientists*, p. 61.

7 A. Vorwerk, 'The 2002 Amendment to the German Atomic Energy Act Concerning the Phase-out of Nuclear Power' (2002) 69 *Nucl Law Bull*, p. 10.

8 *Ibid.*, p. 8.

the Agreement. Indeed, as the operation rights 'are not abolished immediately or within a very short space of time, and ... instead a pay-back period for their investments and a suitable profit is possible within an appropriate transitional period', the German Government considers that this mechanism constitutes 'permissible stipulation of the terms and limits of property rights according to Constitutional law' instead of an expropriation.[9]

The 2000 Agreement hence created a self-applying long-term mechanism for the nuclear phase-out which allowed for high foreseeability and legal certainty for nuclear reactor operators while shielding the State against current or future litigation and exempting it from paying compensation for expropriation.

2.2. SWEDEN: A LONG-TERM TARGET BECOME LAW BUT REQUIRING POLITICAL ACTION

In 1980, a referendum was held in Sweden and resulted in the majority voting for the prohibition on building new nuclear power facilities and for the gradual phase-out of existing ones.[10] Seven years later, Parliament amended the Act on Nuclear Activities to enforce the first part of the referendum, by prohibiting the issuance of new construction licences.[11] These dates are likely connected to the two worst nuclear energy accidents of the twentieth century: the Three Mile Island accident of 1979 in the USA, and the Chernobyl accident of 1986 in the former USSR. Finally, in 1995, 'an inter-party agreement was made between the political parties forming the majority in the Parliament on guidelines for a new Swedish energy policy' that resulted in the 1997 Act on the Phasing-out of Nuclear Power.[12] This Act allowed the Government 'to revoke a permit to operate a nuclear power reactor' on a date it would decide, in order to roll out 'the transformation of the energy system' as decided by Parliament (based on energy security, price stability, and environmental impact) and with the final goal of a nuclear energy phase-out by 2010. To justify its decision to revoke a permit, the Government must base it on a set of criteria including: location, age, design and importance to the national energy supply of the reactor. In addition, the Act requires that compensation should be given to the operator, calculated on an estimated lifespan of 40 years.[13]

On 5 February 1998, only one month after the 1997 Act entered into force, the Swedish Government used this mechanism to order the shutdown of the Barsebäck 1 reactor by July of that year, due to its proximity to Denmark and

9 *Ibid.*, p. 10.

10 *Nuclear Legislation in OECD and NEA Countries – Sweden*, OECD, NEA, 2008, p. 5.

11 *Ibid.*

12 *Ibid.*, p. 6.

13 'Sweden – General Legislation' (1998) 61 *Nucl Law Bull*, p. 86.

the fact that over three million people lived within a few dozen kilometres.[14] However, the fast and unpredictable decision to shut down this reactor, without prior negotiations with the operator (Sydkraft) or any established compensation, resulted in a case brought by the company to the Swedish Supreme Administrative Court, which suspended the Government's decision.[15] On 16 June 1999, the Supreme Administrative Court ruled that the 1997 Act was compatible with the Swedish Constitution and with the European Convention for the Protection of Human Rights and Fundamental Freedoms (ECHR), thereby validating the mechanism itself and the reasoning behind the first shutdown on the grounds of its geographical location.[16] Meanwhile, the Government and Sydkraft negotiated on the compensation to be provided, agreeing on a package in the same year. Under this agreement, Sydkraft would obtain a 25.8 per cent share in a new company, merging Barsebäck's two reactors with Ringhal's four nuclear reactors. This other plant is operated by Vattenfall, the publicly-owned company. In addition, the State agreed to provide financial compensation to Sydkraft, but primarily to Vattenfall. When the Barsebäck 2 reactor would be shut down, Sydkraft's share in the joint-venture would increase to 30.2 per cent.[17] Ultimately, Barsebäck 1 was shut down on 30 November 1999 while Barsebäck 2 did so on 31 May 2005, the latter doing so without a court case, since legal certainty, timely information and reasonable compensation were provided to the operator.

Despite its proven legality and positive experience when properly implemented, this shutdown mechanism was not used in the following years and was even abolished in 2010.[18] In addition, since 1 January 2011 the ban on new nuclear reactors construction has been lifted, but only for the replacement of the then 10 remaining running reactors.[19] The goal to completely phase out nuclear energy in Sweden has been officially abandoned, arguably because of a mechanism relying on regular political decisions instead of having implemented a self-unfolding one.

2.3. FRANCE: A CHANGING AND UNCERTAIN TARGET WITHOUT ADAPTED LEGAL TOOLS

France has been a latecomer to the group of countries wishing to reduce (or end) their dependency on nuclear energy. The sheer size of its reactor fleet explains

14 O. Torp and O.J. Klakegg, 'Challenges in Cost Estimation under Uncertainty – A Case Study of the Decommissioning of Barsebäck Nuclear Power Plant' (2016) 6 *Admin Sci (Administrative Sciences)*, p. 9.

15 'Sweden – Case Law' (1998) 62 *Nucl Law Bull*, p. 52.

16 'Sweden – Case Law' (1999) 64 *Nucl Law Bull*, p. 44.

17 'Sweden – Administrative decisions' (2000) 65 *Nucl Law Bull*, p. 27.

18 'Sweden – General legislation' (2010) 86 *Nucl Law Bull*, p. 84.

19 *Ibid.*

this reluctance, as nuclear energy in France is a significant industry[20] just as it is an expression of its historically-centralised State model.[21] It has progressively locked France on this pathway with 58 reactors operating as of 2019, accounting for a total installed capacity of 63.2 GW. In 2017, this accounted for '71.6 percent of the country's electricity, the lowest share since 1988, on the decline for the fourth year in a row.'[22] The commitment to reduce the share of nuclear energy in the electricity production from approximately 75 per cent to 50 per cent by 2025 was made in 2012 during the presidential election campaign by François Hollande.[23] Once in power, he struggled to implement this commitment during the course of his term. The commitment was made law in August 2015 with the Energy Transition towards Green Growth Act (Energy Transition Act).[24] However, the lack of planning and enforcement mechanisms has led to not a single reactor being shut down in the four subsequent years, despite the commitment to ceasing operations in the oldest plant (Fessenheim, with its two reactors),[25] leaving no clear perspective on how to reach the 2025 goal.[26]

The French legal framework for a nuclear reactor's shutdown authorises only two options: either the reactor is shut down for safety reasons under the control of the nuclear safety authority (ASN),[27] or it is the reactor's operator which voluntarily requests authorisation from the Government to take this decision, based on the ASN's opinion.[28] This was the rule before the 2015 Energy Transition Act and has remained such, as this legal development was not used to elaborate an automated shutdown mechanism such as in Germany or to provide the Government with the power to decide on a shutdown for policy

---

20 A 2011 study indicates 410,000 direct, indirect and induced employees, although this is a debated figure which, according to the International Atomic Energy Agency itself, likely contains double counting. See 'Measuring Employment Generated by the Nuclear Power Sector' (2018) *NEA-IAEA*, pp. 42–43.

21 Labelled as 'jacobinism'. See R. Mauger, 'Forced nuclear energy reactors shutdown in France: the Energy Transition Act's mechanisms' (2018) 11(3) *JWELB (Journal of World Energy Law & Business)*, p. 270.

22 M. Schneider *et al*, 'The World Nuclear Industry Status Report 2018' (2018), p. 53 <https://www.worldnuclearreport.org/IMG/pdf/20180902wnisr2018-lr.pdf>.

23 A. Senecat, 'La baisse du nucléaire à 50% en 2025, une promesse jamais suivie de moyens' (8 November 2017) *Le Monde*, available at <https://www.lemonde.fr/les-decodeurs/article/2017/11/08/la-baisse-du-nucleaire-a-50-en-2025-une-promesse-jamais-suivie-de-moyens_5212107_4355770.html>.

24 R. Mauger, 'Forced nuclear energy reactors shutdown in France: the Energy Transition Act's mechanisms' (2018) 11(3) *JWELB*, p. 271.

25 'Hollande: "Une centrale fermée en 5 ans"' (2 May 2012) *Le Figaro*, available at <http://elections.lefigaro.fr/flash-presidentielle/2012/05/02/97006-20120502FILWWW00700-hollande-je-ne-fermerai-que-fessenheim.php>.

26 R. Mauger, 'Forced nuclear energy reactors shutdown in France: the Energy Transition Act's mechanisms' (2018) 11(3) *JWELB*, p. 281.

27 *Ibid.*, p. 272.

28 *Ibid.*, pp. 272–273.

reasons, such as in Sweden.[29] The tools provided by the 2015 Act to reach the target of 50 per cent of nuclear electricity by 2025 are explained in the following lines. Firstly, an installed nuclear capacity cap has been fixed at the total capacity at that time: 63.2 GW. This means that to commission the new EPR reactor being built in Flamanville, Électricité de France (EDF) will have to shut down an equivalent installed capacity (1650 MW). But this measure can at best merely stabilise the share of nuclear energy in the electricity mix, as the total electricity consumption is forecasted to diminish in the coming years.[30] Secondly, a strategic plan must be elaborated by EDF (which operates all of France's nuclear reactors) in order to detail how the utility will respect the energy policy, elaborated in the multi-annual energy plan (MEP in English, PPE – *programmation pluriannuelle de l'énergie* – in French). In this plan, EDF must specify which nuclear reactors are to be shut down and when, and the document has to be validated by the Minister in charge of energy. However, the first version submitted in April 2017 was rejected by the then Minister and no new plan had been submitted as of October 2019. The problems with this plan are twofold: although it since recently has to be published, this obligation excludes business confidentiality,[31] which is a wide exemption; in addition, it constitutes a pure 'delegation by the Government to EDF of the responsibility to plan and organize the shutdown of numerous nuclear reactors.'[32] This can be considered an indirect recognition that this part of the French energy policy is not in the hands of the Government. Thirdly, the 2015 Act created a Government commissioner to be placed within EDF's decision-making structure to oppose investment decisions which would be 'incompatible with the goals of the strategic plan or, if it does not exist, with the MEP.'[33] This negative power seems unlikely to be sufficient to mean that the French Government has control over the nuclear reactors' shutdown organisation and process.

In addition to this weak legal framework for nuclear reactors' closure, France experienced difficulties over the past few years in publishing energy planning documents on-time and of sufficient quality, especially the MEP. The first MEP for the period 2016–2018 was already adopted with a significant delay and was particularly blurry on the rolling out of nuclear shutdowns.[34] The new MEP for 2019–2023 is being finalised as of October 2019 but is already delayed, as it should have been published at the end of 2018. However, a draft version was published in January 2019 which plans to shut two reactors down in 2020

---

29 *Ibid.*, pp. 273 and 276–277.

30 *Ibid.*, p. 274.

31 Loi n° 2019-1147 du 8 novembre 2019 relative à l'énergie et au climat, art. 6 (4).

32 R. Mauger, 'Forced nuclear energy reactors shutdown in France: the Energy Transition Act's mechanisms' (2018) 11(3) *JWELB*, pp. 275–276.

33 *Ibid.*, p. 276.

34 *Ibid.*, p. 275.

(in Fessenheim) irrespective of whether Flamanville will be commissioned or not,[35] as this has already been postponed several times.[36] In addition, 12 other reactors will be shut down from 2027 to 2035 which will supposedly allow the 50 per cent target of nuclear energy in the electricity mix to be reached.[37] Nevertheless, it appears that this plan to diversify the electricity mix is built on dubious, hidden scenarios foreseeing a steep increase in electricity consumption in France in the coming decades to justify the extension of the nuclear reactors' lifetime to 50 years and over, while adding dozens of GW of renewable energy sources instead of gradually replacing the former with the latter.[38] If this increase in internal consumption does not happen, then the only solution is a strong increase in electricity exports to France's neighbours. Independent experts estimate the level of electricity exports will have to triple in size compared to the average historical levels in the past four decades.[39] If this planned increase does not take place, then France will be in a situation of massive overcapacity, mechanically lowering electricity market prices and weakening the profitability of all French electricity producers, thereby threatening the very transition to harder-to-finance renewable energy sources.[40] As a result, the new MEP for 2019–2023 seems to follow the steps of the previous version by being of no help to the proper organisation of an ordered and coherent reduction of nuclear energy in the electricity mix. The only positive point is that the Government states that the shutdown of the reactors at their 50th year will not lead to the payment of compensation.[41] This is the result of planning providing between 10 and 16 more years to the utility to rationalise its investments in these reactors.

A direct consequence of this new energy planning document in the making is that a new act is needed to legally postpone the 75–50 per cent by 2025 goal to 2035. This has been done by Article 1 of the Energy and Climate Act, adopted

---

35 'Programmation pluriannuelle de l'énergie 2019-2023 2024-2028 – Projet pour consultation' (2019) *Ministère de la Transition Ecologique et Solidaire*, p. 142, available at <https://www.ecologique-solidaire.gouv.fr/sites/default/files/Projet%20PPE%20pour%20consultation.pdf>.

36 M. Schneider *et al*, 'The World Nuclear Industry Status Report 2018' (2018), p. 53 <https://www.worldnuclearreport.org/IMG/pdf/20180902wnisr2018-lr.pdf>.

37 'Programmation pluriannuelle de l'énergie 2019-2023 2024-2028 – Projet pour consultation' (2019) *Ministère de la Transition Ecologique et Solidaire*, p. 144, available at <https://www.ecologique-solidaire.gouv.fr/sites/default/files/Projet%20PPE%20pour%20consultation.pdf>.

38 Y. Marignac, 'Trajectoire du parc nucléaire et transformation du système électrique: l'attentisme coupable de la Programmation pluriannuelle de l'énergie (PPE)' (25 January 2019) *Wise Paris*, pp. 28–29.

39 *Ibid.*, pp. 29–30.

40 *Ibid.*, pp. 30–35.

41 'Programmation pluriannuelle de l'énergie 2019-2023 2024-2028 – Projet pour consultation' (2019) *Ministère de la Transition Ecologique et Solidaire*, p. 144, available at <https://www.ecologique-solidaire.gouv.fr/sites/default/files/Projet%20PPE%20pour%20consultation.pdf>.

on 8 November 2019.[42] Despite this new opportunity to use this act to modify French Energy Law, no provision has been included to provide the State with efficient and appropriate legal mechanisms to shut nuclear reactors down for policy reasons.

3. ORGANISATIONAL AND FINANCIAL CONSEQUENCES OF THESE STRATEGIES

This section presents what can be considered as 'phase two' of the nuclear reactor shutdown policy for Germany, Sweden and France. It focuses mainly on the (mostly financial) consequences of unplanned policy changes, of its failure to reach target, or of the simple implementation of a poor legal mechanism.

3.1. GERMANY: THE COST OF SUDDEN POLICY CHANGES

Although the German nuclear energy phase-out mechanism was working well without the need for any intervention, in December 2010 the Merkel Government decided to extend the production quotas for nuclear energy 'from eight to 14 years per power plant, with an average of 12 years'.[43] However, the Government could not have foreseen that on 11 March 2011, only three months after its decision, the Fukushima Daiichi nuclear disaster would strike Japan. As a consequence, the newly-attributed electricity production quotas were cancelled, the final date for total phase out was set to 31 December 2022 and the eight oldest reactors were permanently shut down.[44]

Following this rapid policy reversal, three of the four nuclear operators in Germany (E.ON, RWE and Vattenfall) took the State to the Constitutional Court (BVerfG) to obtain compensation for their investments made between the end of 2010 and mid-2011 and for the direct shutdown of some of their reactors. For this alleged violation of the right to property, the three companies demanded €15 billion.[45] On 6 December 2016, the BVerfG issued a landmark decision for the nuclear phase-out process in Germany. Firstly, it decided that

42 Loi n° 2019-1147 du 8 novembre 2019 relative à l'énergie et au climat.

43 C. Glinski, 'Regulatory Expropriation' Under German Constitutional Law and in International Investment Law – The Case of Vattenfall' in B. Hoops *et al* (eds), *Rethinking Expropriation Law: Context, Criteria and Consequences of Expropriation Law, vol. II*, Eleven International Publishing, 2015, p. 194.

44 G. Winter, 'L'ascension et la chute de l'utilisation de l'énergie nucléaire en Allemagne : les processus, les explications et le rôle du droit' (2014) 2 *Revue Juridique de l'Environnement*, pp. 237–238.

45 M. Ludwigs, 'Germany's Nuclear Phase-Out and the Right to Property' (2016) 4 *ENLR (European Networks Law & Regulation Quarterly)*, p. 43.

the 2011 amendment to the Atomic Energy Act (the post-Fukushima act) 'is for the most part compatible with the Basic Law.'[46] Secondly, it stated that the electricity production quotas allocated in 2002 and 2010 'do not constitute, in and of themselves, stand-alone property rights enjoying protection of property', but as they are so important to the operation of a nuclear plant, they 'benefit from protection of ownership of the power plants.'[47] The Court continued with its line of reasoning and rejected the qualification of 'expropriation' for the 2011 U-turn,[48] asserting that Parliament was justified in using the Fukushima accident 'as an opportunity to accelerate the nuclear phase-out for the protection of the health of the people and the environment.'[49] However, it ultimately decided that it constituted an unreasonable 'determination of the contents and limits of property [...] as it hinders two of the complainants from using up substantial parts of the residual electricity volumes of 2002'.[50] As a result, 'the legislature must [...] provide adequate compensation, a prolongation of operational lifetimes, or some other form of settlement'.[51] This applied more specifically to Vattenfall and RWE as they owned nuclear reactors which had been immediately shut down after the accident and remained so. Of the available options for compensation, the German Federal Government chose a financial agreement and agreed to pay up to €1 billion to the two companies. Although the figure may ultimately be a lesser amount, it will only be made public in 2023.[52]

The 2010–2011 double policy change constituted a loss of legal certainty which cost time and money to the German State but resulted in obtaining judicial confirmation that the Agreement, reached 10 years earlier, was constitutional. However, in parallel to this proceedings, Vattenfall lodged another claim with an arbitrary tribunal, the International Centre for Settlement of Investment Disputes (ICSID), on the basis of the Energy Charter Treaty. Indeed, in 2011 Vattenfall was not sure its claim would be accepted by the BverfG, since the literature underlined that 'State-owned companies are not subjects of fundamental rights.'[53] Despite this, the BverfG accepted Vattenfall as a party to the case with the following reasoning:

> A legal person governed by private law, which is operated domestically for profit and entirely owned by a Member State of the European Union, can, by reason of the Basic

---

46 BVerfG, Judgment of the First Senate of 6 December 2016 – 1 BvR 2821/11 – para. 1.

47 *Ibid.*, para. 3 a).

48 *Ibid.*, para. 4.

49 *Ibid.*, para. 6.

50 *Ibid.*, para. 7.

51 *Ibid.*, para. 374.

52 'Germany to compensate utilities for nuclear phaseout losses' (24 May 2018) *World Nuclear News*, available at <https://www.world-nuclear-news.org/Articles/Germany-to-compensate-utilities-for-nuclear-phaseo>.

53 M. Ludwigs, 'Germany's Nuclear Phase-Out and the Right to Property' (2016) 4 *ENLR*, p. 44. This is also the reason Vattenfall is publicly providing on its website: Questions and

Law's openness toward European law, as an exception, invoke freedom of property and file a constitutional complaint.[54]

Hence, Vattenfall was a party to both the Constitutional Court case and the arbitration case. The outcome of the constitutional case is known but the arbitration (named *Vattenfall II*) is still pending. While it was expected to be resolved by 2017, the case has been delayed firstly by a parallel judicial event: the 2018 *Achmea* judgment of the Court of Justice of the European Union (CJEU) on intra-EU bilateral investment treaties.[55] Later that year, the ICSID tribunal cleared the potential obstacle to the continuation of its process formed by the *Achmea* judgment in a widely-commented decision.[56] Between the end of 2018 and early 2019, the process was stalled once again after Germany asked for the suspension of the judges of the arbitrary tribunal.[57] This request was rejected by the ICSID on 6 March 2019,[58] and the final decision is cautiously expected by the end of 2019.

This judicial development will provide a very interesting case in which both a Constitutional court and an international arbitration tribunal will take a position following a change in legislation. This might allow the highlighting of the different perceptions held by these two, very different, institutions on a similar case and provide an interesting comparison for future legislation on energy transition worldwide.[59]

---

answers – Vattenfall – ICSID, The lawsuit, 1. Available at <https://group.vattenfall.com/who-we-are/about-us/vattenfall-icsid/questions-and-answers-vattenfall-icsid>.

54 BVerfG, Judgment of the First Senate of 6 December 2016 – 1 BvR 2821/11 – para. 2.

55 CJEU, case C-284/16, *Achmea*, ECLI:EU:C:2018:158. For a description of this case's impact on EU law and on the Vattenfall case itself, see: C. Glinski, '*Achmea* and its Implications for Investor Dispute Settlement' (2018) 3 *CEVIA Working Paper Series*, p. 13.

56 A. Lang, 'Regime Collision between EU Law and Investment Law: New Developments in the Vattenfall Case' (12 September 2018) *Verfassungsblog*, available at <https://verfassungsblog.de/regime-collision-between-eu-law-and-investment-law-new-developments-in-the-vattenfall-case/>; Q. Decleve, 'Vattenfall v. Germany: Tribunal Subtly Avoids Applying Achmea Judgment and Finds that Article 26(6) ECT Does Not Apply to Jurisdiction Issues' (4 October 2018) *International-litigation-blog*, available at <http://international-litigation-blog.com/vattenfall-germany-tribunal-subtly-avoids-applying-achmea-judgment/>; K. Schwedt and H. Ingwersen, 'Intra-EU ECT Claims Post-Achmea: Vattenfall Decision Paves the Way' (13 December 2018) *Arbitrationblog*, available at <http://arbitrationblog.kluwerarbitration.com/2018/12/13/intra eu ect claims-post-achmea-vattenfall-decision-paves-the-way/>.

57 'Germany stalls Vattenfall nuclear case in World Bank court' (16 November 2018) *Reuters*, available at <https://www.reuters.com/article/vattenfall-arbitration-nuclear/germany-stalls-vattenfall-nuclear-case-in-world-bank-court-idUSL8N1XR10E>.

58 The Decision of the Acting Chairman of the Administrative Council can be found on the ICSID's website: <https://icsid.worldbank.org/en/Pages/cases/casedetail.aspx?CaseNo=ARB/12/12>.

59 Especially towards the notion of Legitimate expectations in a time of massive policy change impulse by the climate crisis. See e.g. V. Vadi, 'Energy Security v. Public Health: Nuclear Energy in International Investment Law and Arbitration' (2016) 47 *Geo J Int'l L (Georgetown Journal of International Law)*, p. 1069.

3.2. SWEDEN: FISCAL TOOLS AND MARKET MECHANISMS ARE EFFICIENT BUT OUT-OF-CONTROL

In the late 1990s, the Swedish Government submitted the nuclear energy sector to a so-called capacity tax on electricity generation. This tax was increased on various occasions by the different governments until 2014 and already seemed to represent 'about one-quarter of the operating cost of nuclear power in Sweden' by 2008 before being gradually abolished between 2017 and 2019.[60] This element, added to new safety rules after the Fukushima disaster, entailing heavy investments,[61] low regional electricity prices,[62] and the competition from renewable energy sources with very low marginal costs,[63] resulted in the shutdown of reactors Oskarshamn 1 and 2 in 2013 and 2017, and Ringhals 1 and 2, scheduled for 2019 and 2020.[64] If these shutdowns are realised, fiscal policy will have been more efficient and less costly for the Swedish State in terms of nuclear phase-out than others piloted by the Government and Parliament in the previous decade. However, this comes at the cost of a lack of planning for the electricity system. According to Tangerås and Lundin, these rapid shutdowns might cause a lack of electricity supply in Sweden, resulting in rising electricity prices, especially if the new nuclear energy reactor being built in neighbouring Finland (Olkiluoto) is not running well.[65] The costs to be supported by Sweden could then end up much higher than when using a State-led policy following proper planning.

It should be noted that, in addition to the above, a new inter-party energy agreement was reached in 2016, where Sweden pledged to reach 100 per cent of its electricity production from renewable energy sources by 2040, but without prohibiting nuclear energy. Nuclear energy will not be subsidised but reactors will not be shut down for policy reasons either.[66] This agreement is to some extent

60 'Nuclear capacity tax – Nuclear Power in Sweden' (2019) *World nuclear association*, available at <https://www.world-nuclear.org/information-library/country-profiles/countries-o-s/sweden.aspx>.

61 *Ibid.*, 'Boosting nuclear capacity and operational life' and 'Oskarshamn'.

62 *Ibid.*, 'Oskarshamn'.

63 J. Blazquez *et al*, 'The renewable energy policy Paradox' (2018) 82 *Renewable and Sustainable Energy Reviews*, pp. 2–3.

64 'Oskarshamn' and 'Ringhals' – 'Nuclear Power in Sweden' (2019) *World nuclear association*, available at <https://www.world-nuclear.org/information-library/country-profiles/countries-o-s/sweden.aspx>.

65 T. Tangerås and E. Lundin, 'Vad händer om kärnkraften läggs ned?' / 'What happens if nuclear power is shut down?' (18 March 2016) *Kvartal* <https://kvartal.se/artiklar/vad-hander-om-karnkraften-laggs-ned/>.

66 'Ramöverenskommelse mellan Socialdemokraterna, Moderaterna, Miljöpartiet de gröna, Centerpartiet ochKristdemokraterna'/'Framework agreement between the Social Democrats, The Moderates, the Green Party the Green, the Center Party and The Christian Democrats' (2016) *Regeringen*, available at <https://www.regeringen.se/49cc5b/contentassets/b88f0d28eb0e48e39eb4411de2aabe76/energioverenskommelse-20160610.pdf>.

contradictory as nuclear energy is not a renewable energy source and should therefore automatically be banned from the 2040 electricity generation mix. The fact this was not done at the time was, and remains, confusing.[67] Nevertheless, in the meantime, the agreement has accompanied a movement to extend the remaining reactors' operating lifetime to 50 years, such as in Forsmark.[68] The future of nuclear energy in Sweden is therefore particularly uncertain, as its policy over the last 10 years has been quite unstable and the one for the coming 10 years does not seem to be any clearer or more enduring.

3.3. FRANCE: A VOLUNTARILY POWERLESS GOVERNMENT FORCED TO NEGOTIATE COSTLY COMPENSATION

The Fessenheim nuclear power plant shutdown process is the most interesting nuclear reactor closure case to analyse in modern France for several reasons: firstly, because it is the only one being currently prepared; secondly because Fessenheim is the oldest nuclear power plant still running in France and hence somehow shows the possible way to deal with the other reactors in the future. Finally, the Fessenheim shutdown turned into a political issue in 2012 due to its location in an earthquake-prone zone and below the level of the Grand Canal of Alsace while being very close to Germany and Switzerland.[69]

The plan of the Government in 2015 was to force EDF, the operator of the reactor, to shut it down when the new Flamanville reactor was commissioned, due to take place in 2017 at the latest.[70] With the nuclear capacity cap introduced by the 2015 Energy Transition Act, EDF would then have had to shut down an equivalent installed capacity elsewhere. The two 900 MW reactors at Fessenheim were first in line because of their age and location. However, due to the cumulated delays for Flamanville's reactor commissioning, now scheduled for 2022,[71] and the hostility of EDF, this plan backfired. This situation has had two

67 'Kristersson: Utan nytt kärnkraftsmål lämnar vi energiöverenskommelsen'/'Kristersson: Without a new nuclear target, we leave the energy agreement' (2 April 2019) *Di*, available at <https://www.di.se/debatt/kristersson-utan-nytt-karnkraftsmal-lamnar-vi-energioverenskommelsen/>.

68 L. Karagiannopoulos, 'Sweden says two aging nuclear reactors safe to run til 2028' (24 June 2019) *Reuters*, available at <https://www.reuters.com/article/us-sweden-nuclear-vattenfall/sweden-says-two-aging-nuclear-reactors-safe-to-run-till-2028-idUSKCN1TP1FC>.

69 R. Mauger, 'Forced nuclear energy reactors shutdown in France: the Energy Transition Act's mechanisms' (2018) 11(3) *JWELB*, p. 278.

70 Décret n° 2007-534 du 10 avril 2007 autorisant la création de l'installation nucléaire de base dénommée Flamanville 3, comportant un réacteur nucléaire de type EPR, sur le site de Flamanville (Manche), art. 3, II.

71 'Résultats semestriels 2019' (26 July 2019) *EDF*, p. 12, available at <https://www.edf.fr/sites/default/files/contrib/groupe-edf/espaces-dedies/espace-finance-fr/informations-financieres/informations-reglementees/resultats-financiers---semestriel/2019/20190726-s1-2019-cp-fr.pdf>.

consequences: the need to negotiate with EDF and the impossibility to decree Fessenheim's reactors to shut down at the Government's will.

In 2017, the *Conseil Constitutionnel* stated that an 'authorization to operate an electricity production facility cannot be considered an asset subject to property rights by its holder',[72] thereby excluding any expropriation claim. However, in a similar move to that made by the German BverfG in 2016,[73] the judge also took into account the importance of such authorisations and especially under the principle of legitimate expectation or a 'legally established situation based on the guarantee of the rights proclaimed in article 16 DDH' in French law.[74] As a result, although the nuclear capacity cap does not breach this principle due to it being based on general interest objectives (the 'diversification of the energy mix' goal) and leaves, theoretically, the choice of which reactor to shut down and when to the operator, EDF can still request compensation.[75] It is the Government's combined lack of efficient legal tools for pursuing enhanced nuclear policy and its will to see EDF execute a political commitment (to shut down Fessenheim by 2017 at the latest), that the latter was not invited to discuss, which led to the need for compensation. Consequently, the agreement reached requires the State to pay €490 million by 2021 to EDF, in addition to complementary payments until 2041, calculated on the electricity market price and the average production of other reactors similar to the ones in Fessenheim.[76] The outcome of the new legal regime for nuclear reactor shutdowns in France is therefore much more expensive than the German one[77] and closer to the Swedish outcome,[78] but without the proper energy policy tools themselves. Above all, the French Government validates the view 'that a nuclear reactor can be operated for 60 years or more by accepting compensation until 2041',[79] in spite of no nuclear reactor in France having reached this age and the ASN not having provided its agreement to such a perspective. Nevertheless, the current Government validated the principle of commercial exploitation until the 50th year of operation for the 12 reactors to be shut down by 2035 (in addition to Fessenheim's two reactors) and probably until the 60th for the others as it appears in the latest draft of the MPE.[80]

---

72 R. Mauger, 'Forced nuclear energy reactors shutdown in France: the Energy Transition Act's mechanisms' (2018) 11(3) *JWELB*, p. 278.

73 See section 3.1 of this chapter.

74 R. Mauger, 'Forced nuclear energy reactors shutdown in France: the Energy Transition Act's mechanisms' (2018) 11(3) *JWELB*, pp. 278–279.

75 *Ibid.*, p 279.

76 *Ibid.*, p 280. In addition to a couple of non-financial side clauses.

77 See section 3.1 of this chapter.

78 See section 2.2 of this chapter.

79 R. Mauger, 'Forced nuclear energy reactors shutdown in France: the Energy Transition Act's mechanisms' (2018) 11(3) *JWELB*, p. 280.

80 'Programmation pluriannuelle de l'énergie 2019–2023 2024–2028 – Projet pour consultation' (2019) *Ministère de la Transition Ecologique et Solidaire*, p. 144, available at <https://www.ecologique-solidaire.gouv.fr/sites/default/files/Projet%20PPE%20pour%20consultation.pdf>.

However, the Fessenheim reactors are still running.

On 8 April 2017, the minister in charge of energy adopted a decree stating in Article 1 that the operating authorization of Fessenheim's reactors was abrogated, before adding in Article 2 that this abrogation will take place when EDF's last conditions are met.[81]

Still, as was expected by many legal scholars due to the poor quality of this decree,[82] on 25 October 2018 the *Conseil d'Etat*, the supreme administrative court in France, repealed it.[83] Indeed, the decree was illegal, as it disrespected the Energy Code, since EDF had not requested a repeal of the operating authorisation of Fessenheim's reactors. This would have been the only way by which to proceed in this case due to the lack of an effective legal framework adopted two years earlier by the same Government. At the date of writing, this request had still not been submitted by EDF although it should happen soon, as the utility announced it would shut the reactors down in the spring of 2020 at the latest.[84]

In the long term, the lack of an appropriate legal mechanism for organising the required nuclear reactor shutdowns to reach the goal of diversification of the electricity mix in France might lead to other such unclear and costly situations. For example, in the MEP the Government wants EDF to spread out the shutdown of the reactors both time- and location-wise. The rationale behind this smoothened-out transition is to facilitate the adaptation of the electricity system (generation, transportation and distribution) and to reduce the societal impact, in terms of unemployment for the local areas, by requesting EDF to avoid completely decommissioning a power plant (hence maintaining at least one reactor running per site). The problem is that the more the Government is willing to control the date, order and location of the reactors to shut down – in other words, to force EDF to adapt to its energy policy (including social concerns) – the more it might have to pay for it.

4. CONCLUSION

This chapter has presented the different strategies developed by Germany, Sweden and France for organising the closure of nuclear reactors. These

81 R. Mauger, 'Forced nuclear energy reactors shutdown in France: the Energy Transition Act's mechanisms' (2018) 11(3) *JWELB*, p. 280.

82 *Ibid.*

83 CE, 25 October 2018, *Commune de Fessenheim et autres*, n° 410109 and following, para. 4.

84 'Programmation pluriannuelle de l'énergie 2019–2023 2024–2028 – Projet pour consultation' (2019) *Ministère de la Transition Ecologique et Solidaire*, p. 142, available at <https://www.ecologique-solidaire.gouv.fr/sites/default/files/Projet%20PPE%20pour%20consultation.pdf>.

strategies have had different consequences in terms of democratic oversight, compensation costs, and target-reaching. The table below provides a summary of the characteristics of each mechanism but does not constitute a thorough analysis of the full legal framework for nuclear energy (e.g. setting out all the conditions permitting shutdown of a reactor). It also allows less nuanced statements than in the body of the text of this chapter.

Table 1. Characteristics of national nuclear energy reactors closure mechanisms

Country	Germany	Sweden (1997–2010)	Sweden (2010–2017)	France
Negotiation with nuclear industry companies beforehand to create the shutdown mechanism	Yes	No	Not relevant	No
Involvement of Parliament in the creation of the mechanism	No	Yes	Not relevant	Yes
Self-unfolding mechanism	Yes	No	No	No
The Government can order a shutdown for policy reasons	No	Yes	No	No
The Government can organise the order of shutdowns	No	Yes	No	No
Court cases launched by companies against the mechanism	Not for the first version. Yes following the rapid policy change	Yes against the first, not for the second	No	No
Compensation provided to operators	Not for the first version. Yes following the rapid policy change	Yes for both reactors (significantly more for the first)	No	Yes (significantly more expensive than in Germany)

As a conclusion, it is clear that the key factors for a stable and fiscal revenue-saving nuclear shutdown mechanism are foreseeability and legal certainty. Mechanisms such as the German one or the first Swedish one, when implemented with enough foreseeability and without sudden policy changes, lead to limited or no compensation liability. Other mechanisms based on taxes and markets or insufficiently clear and prescriptive legal frameworks can have extremely variable direct compensation costs (from virtually zero to hundreds of millions), but deprive policy-makers of any control over nuclear reactor shutdowns and can therefore endanger security of supply.

CHAPTER XIII

PHASING OUT COAL-FIRED POWER PLANTS IN THE EUROPEAN UNION

Examples from the Netherlands and Germany

Lolke BRAAKSMA and Ruven FLEMING

1. INTRODUCTION

The European Union (EU) is committed to ambitious climate targets.[1] Member States of the EU (hereinafter: Member States) are required to meet legally binding targets by 2020, 2030 and 2050, aiming to progressively reduce the emissions of greenhouse gas. Three targets are particularly relevant in the EU. For 2020, the 20-20-20 targets of the climate and energy package of 20 per cent greenhouse gas emissions reduction, 20 per cent of energy consumed coming from renewables, and a 20 per cent increase in energy efficiency. For 2030, the targets of the climate and energy framework,[2] which require the EU as a whole to reduce greenhouse gas emissions by 40 per cent by 2030 compared to 1990 levels[3]

1 E.g. the United Nations Climate Pact of 1992, which has been transposed into clear targets in the Kyoto Protocol of 1997 (COP 3). The Kyoto Protocol is still relevant since it consists of two phases – the first was relevant for the period up to 2012 and the second covering the period 2013–2020. Under the second phase of the Kyoto Protocol, the EU as a whole needs to reach a reduction of greenhouse gas emissions of 20 per cent by 2020, compared to 1990 levels. This goal has been included in the EU's 'Climate and Energy package'. Another example is the Paris Agreement of 2015 (COP 22), ratified by 181 parties, which contains objectives to halt global warming to 2°C, and preferably 1.5°C in 2100 compared to pre-industrial levels. To reach this goal every party has to develop Nationally Determined Contributions (NDCs) every five years (article 4, paragraph 2 of the Agreement).

2 Communication of the Commission, 'A Clean Planet for all – A European strategic long-term vision for a prosperous, modern, competitive and climate neutral economy' COM/2018/773 final.

3 43 per cent greenhouse gas emissions reduction in sectors covered by the EU Emission Trading Scheme (hereinafter: EU ETS) and 30 per cent greenhouse gas emissions reduction in the non-EU ETS sector.

and the long-term strategic vision of the EU to achieve at least 80 per cent greenhouse gas emissions reduction by 2050.[4]

Realising these objectives, however, turns out to be challenging. Many Member States are in the process of (partially) phasing out electricity production from coal as a measure to cut their CO_2 emissions.[5] Nevertheless, a comprehensive EU coal exit strategy is not provided in current legal frameworks and/or packages. Coal-fired power plants still account for nearly a quarter of electricity generation in the EU, offering jobs to an estimated 240,000 people, whilst serving the security of energy supply.[6]

In this context, the societal and legal debates regarding the phase-out processes of coal-fired electricity production will be analysed in two Member States: the Netherlands and Germany. These countries have long but different relationships with coal-fired power plants as a means for electricity production. We focus on identifying and discussing the (legal) implications, bottlenecks and safeguards, both at EU level and the national level, that are relevant when phasing out coal for electricity production in these countries.[7] To this end, we start by analysing the legal framework relevant to the phase-out of coal-fired power plants at the EU level (Section 2). After that, we describe the examples of the Netherlands (Section 3) and Germany (Section 4). Finally, general observations and conclusions are made (Section 5).

2. PHASING OUT COAL-FIRED POWER PLANTS FROM A EUROPEAN UNION PERSPECTIVE

2.1. INTRODUCTION

In this section, we are exploring to what extent the EU has competence – according to EU primary legislation – to decide whether Member States can use coal for electricity production and whether they can decide about a coal phase-out (para. 2.2). After that, an overview of how the emissions of coal-fired power plants are regulated under secondary EU law is provided and the relevance

4 Council Conclusions on EU position for the Copenhagen Climate Conference (7–18 December 2009) 2968th ENVIRONMENT Council meeting Luxembourg, 21 October 2009: https://www.consilium.europa.eu/uedocs/cms_data/docs/pressdata/en/envir/110634.pdf: II 8.

5 For a comprehensive overview on the status of the phase-out of coal-fired power plants in the Member States in September 2018 see: https://beyond-coal.eu/wp-content/uploads/2018/09/Overview-of-national-coal-phase-out-announcements-Europe-Beyond-Coal-September-2018.pdf.

6 See: https://ec.europa.eu/clima/citizens/eu_en.

7 Issues of competition law when closing coal-fired power plants will not be addressed in this chapter.

of these regulations for Member States that want to phase out electricity production with coal as the primary source is shown (para. 2.3). We conclude the section by analysing whether financial compensation should be provided to owners and/or investors if a coal-fired power plant is closed down (para. 2.4).

2.2. THE PRIMARY LAW COMPETENCE OF THE EUROPEAN UNION

Due to the division of powers between the EU and its Member States,[8] it is necessary for the EU to have competence to act on a certain issue.[9] A competence that shall provide the EU with regulatory powers in a particular area[10] must have been conferred upon it[11] via an article in the European Treaties.[12]

The phasing out of coal usage for the production of electricity strikes at the core of two vital interests, environmental protection and energy security. Both interests are included as potential areas of EU competence in the Treaty on the Functioning of the European Union (TFEU) (article 194 TFEU for energy and article 192 TFEU for the environment). The treaty also regulates the relationship between these competences on the one hand and the permanent sovereignty of states over their natural resources on the other hand.[13]

It is settled case law of the European Court of Justice (ECJ) that the legal basis of an EU measure must be selected by the legislator on the grounds of objective reasons that can be subject to judicial review.[14] The European legislator may, thus, not pick a legal basis as he sees fit. Instead, he shall look for the "centre of gravity" of a measure, which determines its legal basis.[15] The "centre of gravity"

8 Paul Craig and Grainne de Burca, *EU Law Texts Cases and Materials*, 5th edition (Oxford University Press, Oxford 2011), pp. 75–78 (hereinafter: Craig/De Burca).

9 Ibid, p. 74.

10 Ibid, p. 75.

11 Article 5(2) Treaty on European Union (hereinafter: TEU); Jan H Jans and Hans HB Vedder, *European Environmental Law*, 3rd edition (Europa Law Publishing, Groningen 2008), p. 10 (hereinafter: Jans/Vedder).

12 Craig/De Burca, above n. 8, pp. 75–76.

13 The permanent sovereignty over natural resources is a rule of international law, originating from United Nations Assembly Resolution 1803 (XVII), as adopted on 14 December 1962.

14 Case C-45/86 *Commission of the European Communities v Council of the European Communities* [1987] ECR I-1493 paragraph 11; Case C-300/89 *Commission of the European Communities v Council of the European Communities* [1991] ECR I-2867 paragraph 10; Case C-155/91 *Commission of the European Communities v Council of the European Communities* [1993] ECR I-939 paragraphs 10–15; Case C-187/93 *European Parliament v Council of the European Union* [1994] ECR I-2857 paragraphs 22–23; Case C-268/94 *Portuguese Republic v Council of the European Union* [1996] ECR I-6177 paragraph 22; C-176/03 *Commission of the European Communities v Council of the European Union* [2005] ECR I-7879 paragraph 45.

15 Jans/Vedder, above n. 11, p. 68; Mathew L Schemmel and Bas de Regt, 'The European Court of Justice and the Environmental Protection Policy of the European Community' (1994) 17(1)

is the area on which the anticipated measure has most bearing.[16] If the "centre of gravity" is protection of the environment measures should be brought under article 192 TFEU.[17] If the measure is mainly dealing with energy, article 194 TFEU is the applicable legal basis.[18]

Energy regulation has been traditionally singled out by the legal literature as an area of minimum harmonisation, where Member States might establish their own legislation within the framework provided by the EU.[19] Several decisions of the ECJ assert that Member States indeed have the right to legislate in the field of energy if the EU has not, not yet, or not comprehensively exercised its right to do so.[20]

The literature commonly agrees that today article 194 TFEU provides the central EU competence in energy matters.[21] Coal, after all, is a form of energy that may be produced in individual Member States. While article 194(1) TFEU is providing the EU with a general competence to regulate matters in the area of energy, this competence is curtailed in article 194(2) TFEU, which says: "measures shall not affect a Member State's right to determine the conditions for exploiting its energy resources, its choice between different energy sources and the general structure of its energy supply, without prejudice to Article 192(2)(c)."[22] This paragraph is the so-called sovereignty clause, which says that decisions concerning the national energy mix remain the prerogative of Member States. In other words: the Member States are in charge when it comes to the decision whether or not coal shall be exploited and/or used for electricity generation, but equally if coal should be phased out as a source of electricity production.

This picture does not substantially change when looking at the environmental competence of the EU in article 192 TFEU. Article 192(1) TFEU is essentially giving the EU institutions the right to take action to serve environmental protection objectives that are laid down in article 191 TFEU. While the EU has taken several measures that might have an indirect bearing on the phase-out of the use of coal for electricity production (see section 2.3 on

Boston College International and Comparative Law Review 53; Ronald van Ooik, 'Cross-Pillar Litigation Before the ECJ: Demarcation of Community and Union Competences' (2008) 4(3) *European Constitutional Law Review* 399.

16 Ibid.

17 Ibid.

18 Angus Johnston and Guy Block, *EU Energy Law* (Oxford University Press, 2012) paragraph 1.05 (hereinafter: Johnston/Block).

19 Ibid, paragraph 15.03.

20 Such as Case 6/64 *Flaminio Costa v E.N.E.L.* [1964] ECR I-585 at 593; for a discussion of this and further cases see Christian Calliess and Matthias Ruffert, *EUV/AEUV Kommentar*, 4th edition (Beck, München 2011) article 194 AEUV, paragraph 23 (hereinafter: Calliess/ Ruffert); Carl-Otto Lenz and Klaus Dieter Borchardt, *EU Verträge Kommentar*, 5th edition (Bundesanzeiger Verlag, Köln 2010) Vorbemerkungen zu Artikel 191–193 AEUV paragraph 3.

21 Johnston/Block, above n.18, paragraphs 1.05/1.08.

22 Article 194(2) TFEU.

secondary law below), it has not issued an act that is explicitly prescribing all Member States to phase out coal for electricity production in power plants. The theoretical discussion on whether or not such an act of the EU might in the future be based on article 192 TFEU falls outside the scope of this chapter and is, thus, not pursued.

What emerges from this brief observation is that the Member States, not the EU, would be allowed to decide whether or not coal can be used for electricity production. Nevertheless, the EU has the power to issue environmental legislation that may have indirect impacts on the phasing out of coal-fired power plants for electricity production. As the next section will show, the EU has, in fact, put into place a comprehensive secondary law framework that affects the use of coal as a primary energy source for electricity generation.

2.3. THE LEGAL FRAMEWORK IN THE EUROPEAN UNION

Since the EU initiated its policy to create an internal energy market in the early 1990s, the energy sector has been regulated by an extensive set of EU laws. In this context, three directives are particularly relevant when regulating the use of coal as a primary energy source for electricity production, namely the Electricity Directive,[23] the Industrial Emissions Directive (hereinafter: IE Directive)[24] and the EU Emission Trading Scheme Directive (hereinafter: the ETS Directive), which we will discuss below.

The Electricity Directive from 1996 and the subsequent Electricity Directives, provide that Member States have to adopt an authorisation procedure – in accordance with objective, transparent and non-discriminatory criteria – when new electricity-generating capacity is constructed.[25] When authorising new generating facilities, the public authorities have to consider, for example, the protection of the environment, energy efficiency, emissions and the nature of the primary energy sources, such as the use of wind, coal or gas.[26]

23 Directive 96/92/EC of the European Parliament and of the Council of 19 December 1996 concerning common rules for the internal market in electricity. On 5 June 2019 the new Electricity Directive came into force (Directive (EU) 2019/944 of the European Parliament and of the Council of 5 June 2019 on common rules for the internal market for electricity), recasting Directive 2009/72/EC of the European Parliament and of the Council of 13 July 2009 concerning common rules for the internal market. Directive 2009/72/EC, in turn, repealed Directive 2003/54/EC of the European Parliament and of the Council of 26 June 2003 concerning common rules for the internal market in electricity. In the following, Directive 2019/944 will be used as point of reference and called the "Electricity Directive".

24 Directive 2010/75/EU of the European Parliament and of the Council of 24 November 2010 on industrial emissions.

25 See article 8 of the Electricity Directive.

26 See article 8(2) of the Electricity Directive. This list of criteria has been expanded with the introduction of the EU ETS Directive (Directive 2003/87/EC of the European Parliament

Member States have transposed this obligation differently in their national legal orders. Some imposed an electricity permit for building (large) coal-fired power plants, such as the United Kingdom and Denmark, whilst others, such as the Netherlands, did not (see section 3).[27]

The emissions of coal-fired power plants, which consist of carbon dioxide (CO_2), sulfur dioxide (SO_2), carbon monoxide (CO), but also fine particles (PM_{10}) emissions, are primarily regulated on the EU level by the IE Directive and the ETS Directive.

The IE Directive – which is based on article 192(1) TFEU – prescribes an integrated approach on combating industrial emissions, aiming to achieve effective protection of the environment as a whole, resulting in an obligatory environmental permit for activities listed in Annex I IE Directive, such as coal-fired power plants.[28] This permit contains conditions and specific emission limit values, based on best available techniques (BAT), which should be achieved by the installation.[29] BATs are, in short, the most effective and advanced techniques that are economically and technically viable.[30] According to the latest BAT conclusions,[31] Member States can impose an energy efficiency rate of 32.5 per cent to 44 per cent for large combustion plants, such as coal-fired power plants.[32] Setting stricter conditions than those achievable by the use of BAT can be required in order to achieve environmental quality standards. In that case, additional measures shall be included in the permit.[33]

---

and of the Council of 13 October 2003 establishing a scheme for greenhouse gas emission allowance trading within the Community) and the Energy Efficiency Directive (Directive 2012/27/EU of the European Parliament and of the Council of 25 October 2012 on energy efficiency).

27 For the United Kingdom, this permit is the Development Consent Order (DCO) on the basis of the Planning Act 2008, see: http://www.legislation.gov.uk. See for Denmark: ens.dk. More information about both regimes can be found in: Martha M Roggenkamp, Catherine Redgwell, Anita Rønne and Iñigo del Guayo (eds.), *Energy Law in Europe – National, EU and International Regulations* (Oxford University Press, Oxford 2016), (hereinafter: Roggenkamp, Redgwell, Rønne and del Guayo), Chapters 6 and 14.

28 See for a critical appraisal on the procedure on how BAT conclusions are set: Lolke Braaksma and Hanna Tolsma, 'Integrated Pollution Prevention and Control – A critical legal perspective on all-inclusive integration' in Marjan Peeters, Mariolina Eliantonio, *Research Handbook on EU environmental law* (Edward Elgar, Cheltenham 2020) (to be published, reference is to final draft chapter).

29 See article 3(5) of the IE Directive for the definition of Installation used in this Directive and for an overview of the relevant procedures: Suzanne Kingston, Veerle Heyvaert and Aleksandra Čavoški, *European Environmental Law* (Cambridge University Press, Cambridge 2017), Chapter 9.

30 Article 3(10) of the IE Directive.

31 BAT conclusions are adopted by the Commission as Implementing Decisions in accordance with the examination procedure and function as the reference for setting the permit conditions procedure, see article 13 of the IE Directive.

32 Best Available Technique Reference Document for Large Combustion Plants (BREF LCP), available at: http://eippcb.jrc.ec.europa.eu/reference/BREF/LCP/JRC_107769_LCPBref_2017.pdf.

33 See article 18 IE Directive.

The ETS Directive is based on article 192(1) TFEU and covers around 45 per cent of the EU's greenhouse gas emissions, such as CO_2.[34] The scheme is primarily based on a cap and trade system which, in short means that: (a) greenhouse gas emissions of large emitters are capped by allocating emission allowances; and (b) the trading of those allowances is made possible to create an incentive to reduce greenhouse gas emissions in a cost-effective manner.[35] To achieve the 2030 targets, the ETS Directive was revised, to increase the pace of emission cuts in the period 2021–2030 by reducing the overall number of emission allowances.[36]

To clarify the relationships between the ETS Directive and the IE Directive, article 26 ETS Directive stipulates that the environmental permit cannot contain emission limit values for CO_2, clarifying the relationships with the IE Directive.[37] The rationale behind this rule is to prevent a duplication of regulation, as stricter emission limit values in environmental permits would interfere with the market-based cap and trade system of the EU emission trading scheme leading to less cost-effective CO_2 emission reduction.[38] Multiple authors have pointed to the debate on whether Member States can still impose more stringent protective measures on the basis of article 193 TFEU, which encompasses a legal basis for Member States to pursue more ambitious environmental goals than measures based on article 192 TFEU to achieve the objectives under article 191 TFEU, for example by limiting CO_2 emissions in environmental permits which are regulated by the IE Directive.[39] This could be relevant when trying to close coal-fired power plants, as only the EU can alter the cap in the ETS Directive. Nevertheless, it seems difficult to reconcile imposing (strict) CO_2 emission limitations under the IE Directive on the bases of article 193 TFEU with the system from the EU ETS and the aim to be cost-effective.

The above shows that (secondary) EU law also does not provide for a direct legal basis to ban coal-fired power plants for Member States. Member States do have the possibility to prescribe an energy efficiency rate of 32.5 per cent to 44 per cent for coal-fired power plants. Prescribing more stringent CO_2 emission

---

34 See: https://ec.europa.eu/clima/policies/ets_en.

35 Edwin Woerdman, Martha Roggenkamp and Marijn Holwerda, *Essential EU Climate Law* (Cheltenham: Edward Elgar 2015), Chapter 3.

36 Directive 2018/410 of the European Parliament and of the Council of 14 March 2018 amending Directive 2003/87/EC to enhance cost-effective emission reductions and low-carbon investments, and Decision (EU) 2015/1814. See: https://ec.europa.eu/clima/policies/ets/revision_en.

37 See also article 9(1) IE Directive.

38 Frans Oosterhuis and Marjan Peeters, "Limits to integration in pollution prevention and control" in Marjan Peeters and Rosa Uylenburg (eds), *EU Environmental Legislation. Legal Perspectives on Regulatory Strategies* (Edward Elgar, Cheltenham 2014) p. 100.

39 See for a comprehensive overview e.g.: Lorenzo Squintani, *Beyond Minimum Harmonisation. Gold-Plating and Green-Plating of European Environmental Law* (Cambridge University Press, Cambridge 2019), paragraph 1.3.

limitations in the environmental permit than necessary on the basis of the EU ETS is more than likely not possible as a result of the relationship between the IE Directive and the ETS Directive, and the cap and trade system prescribed in the latter directive.

2.4. A NEED FOR FINANCIAL COMPENSATION?

A highly relevant question for Member States and for any owner of a coal-fired power plant (hereinafter: the owner) is whether, and if so, the extent to which, financial compensation is required from a EU perspective when a coal-fired power plant is closed ex officio. In this regard, two articles come to mind that provide safeguards for the rights of the owners: article 1 First Protocol of the Convention for the Protection of Human Rights and Fundamental Freedoms (hereinafter: Article 1 First Protocol) in which the protection of property is regulated, and article 13(1) Energy Charter Treaty (hereinafter: ECT), which aims to improve (international) collaboration between authorities and companies regarding energy by protecting investments in the energy sector.[40]

Article 1 First Protocol stipulates that:

> Every natural or legal person is entitled to the peaceful enjoyment of his possessions. No one shall be deprived of his possessions except in the public interest and subject to the conditions provided for by law and by the general principles of international law.
>
> The preceding provisions shall not, however, in any way impair the right of a State to enforce such laws as it deems necessary to control the use of property in accordance with the general interest or to secure the payment of taxes or other contributions or penalties.

Closing down a coal-fired power plant will most likely be considered as an interference with the property of owners. Such a decision needs to have a proper legal basis and needs to be taken in the general interest. Furthermore, a fair balance needs to be struck between the general interest involved in closing coal-fired power plants, and the property rights of the owners of the plant. Member States do have a margin of appreciation when assessing whether a fair balance has been struck. Relevant in this regard are the foreseeability of the measure, the transitional time that has been given to earn back investments, but also whether a transition towards electricity production from biomass or Carbon Capture and Storage (CCS) is subsidised.[41]

---

40 The Energy Charter Treaty is a multilateral trade and investment agreement.

41 CCS is the process of capturing CO_2 emissions from (usually large) point sources, such as a coal-fired power plant or a biomass power plant, transporting it to a storage site, and depositing it in a place where it will not enter the atmosphere, normally underground.

Article 13(1) of the ECT stipulates that:

> Investments of Investors of a Contracting Party in the Area of any other Contracting Party shall not be nationalized, expropriated or subjected to a measure or measures having effect equivalent to nationalization or expropriation (hereinafter referred to as 'Expropriation') except where such Expropriation is:
>
> (a) for a purpose which is in the public interest;
> (b) not discriminatory;
> (c) carried out under due process of law; and
> (d) accompanied by the payment of prompt, adequate and effective compensation (...).

This article could be relevant for investors from non-EU countries investing in Dutch and/or German power plants and for investors from certain EU countries. The possibility to bring a claim on this basis depends on the country of origin of the investor. For non-EU investors in Dutch and/or German coal-fired power plants coming from countries that are parties to the ECT this could theoretically be a possibility.

There are also investors from other EU countries (German RWE invested in the Netherlands; Swedish Vattenfall in Germany). For these cases 22 Member States signed an agreement to make the ECT inapplicable intra-EU.[42] Nevertheless, investors from Sweden, Hungary and other Member States that did not sign the agreement, might still be able to use this basis in the ECT to get compensation when closing a coal-fired power plant, but this will depend on the circumstances of each individual case.[43] We will now turn to two Member States to illustrate the issue.

3. THE EXAMPLE OF THE NETHERLANDS[44]

3.1. INTRODUCTION

The Dutch Parliament agreed to a motion in 2015 to phase out all coal-fired power plants in the Netherlands.[45] Coincidentally, this was the same year that

---

42 See for this agreement: https://ec.europa.eu/info/sites/info/files/business_economy_euro/banking_and_finance/documents/190117-bilateral-investment-treaties_en.pdf, which was proposed after Case C-284/16 *Slovak Republic v Achmea* 6 March 2018.

43 In Sweden, the *Novenergia II* case is pending by the Svea Court of Appeal in which the applicability of the ECT is discussed, see: www.italaw.com/cases/6613.

44 This section is partly based on Lolke Braaksma, Kars de Graaf and Martha Roggenkamp, "Afscheid van kolen(centrales): waar een wil is, is een wet?", *Ars Aequi* 2019/68, 6, pp. 449–458.

45 With the passing of the motion Van Veldhoven and Van Weyenberg (*Parliamentary Papers II* 2016/17, 34627, No. 15, p. 12), the Dutch government committed to shut down all coal-fired power plants. This obligation is – however – not bound to a specific date.

the share of electricity produced with coal as the primary fuel was the highest it had ever been, totalling 35.3 per cent of actual production.[46] At that time, 10 coal-fired power plants were relevant in the Netherlands. Five plants were built in the 1970s and 80s, and would be closed soon,[47] two dated from the 1990s and three plants were permitted in 2007 and only became fully operational in 2015/2016. These last five coal-fired power plants currently provide almost 1500 jobs and account for a large part of the Dutch electricity production, but will all be closed before 2030 when the Bill "Prohibiting the Use of Coal in Electricity Production" is adopted.[48] This Bill was proposed in order to follow up on the Paris Agreement and in that light, to achieve a 49 per cent CO_2 emission reduction by 2030 compared to 1990 levels.[49]

3.2. BACKGROUND

The Netherlands has a long history of using coal as an important domestic energy source.[50] Not only that, the Netherlands had vast coal mining production in its most southern province, Limburg, which lasted until 1974.[51] By that time, fundamental changes had taken place, such as the discovery of the largest natural gas field in Europe, the Groningen gas field in 1959 and international shifts in demand for coal and petroleum resources. After the oil and energy crises in 1973 and 1979, the Dutch government decided to reduce its dependency on gas and oil – which accounted for around 80 per cent of the total share of electricity production then – and to diversify its energy production by investing in electricity generation with coal and other fuels.[52]

By the year 2000, the electricity production sector was fully liberalised and also predominantly privatised. As a result, there were few possibilities for government interventions in this sector.[53] After power outages in Northeastern America and Ontario, the Netherlands and other Member States of the

---

46 Available at: https://opendata.cbs.nl/statline/#/CBS/nl/dataset/80030ned/table?fromstatweb.

47 The Amer-8, the Gelderland-13 and the Borssele-12 plants were closed in 2015 as a result of the Agreement on Energy for Sustainable Growth (het Energieakkoord) in 2013, see section 3.3 below.

48 *Parliamentary Papers II* 2018/19, 35 167, No. 2.

49 Ibid, pp. 1–3. The Dutch government set a higher target than the EU target of 40% CO_2 emission reduction by 2030 and strives to achieve a 55% CO_2 emission reduction by 2030. The Bill is also important to achieve the 2020 goals, see paragraph 3.4.

50 Roggenkamp, Redgwell, Rønne and del Guayo, p. 726. The base-load of electricity in the Netherlands is primarily supplied by a mixture of coal-, nuclear- and gas power plants.

51 *Parliamentary Papers II* 1965/66, 8424, No. 2; *Parliamentary Papers II* 1969/70, 10312, No. 2.

52 See: *Parliamentary Papers II* 1979/1980, 15 802 No. 8, p. 2; *Parliamentary Papers II* 1979/1980, 15 802 No. 11 and 12, pp. 44/45.

53 Roggenkamp, Redgwell, Rønne and del Guayo, pp. 731–733.

EU in 2003,[54] the Dutch government wanted to know whether the security of supply in the Netherlands was sufficiently guaranteed in the future. In 2003, the then Minister of Economic Affairs (L.J. Brinkorst) sent a letter to the House of Representatives concerning the Security of Energy Supply.[55] In this letter, the Minister mentioned the possibility that there could be an increasing structural shortage of domestic means of production relative to domestic demand after 2007. Taking into account the rising demand for electricity (around 2 per cent per year at that time), the limited growth of Dutch production capacity and the expected supply and demand developments elsewhere in the EU, the Minister concluded that large investments in the electricity production sector were needed to secure future security of supply. A new policy implementing this strategy was laid down in the Energy Reports of 2005 and 2008.[56]

Both Energy Reports concluded that the construction of new power plants, including coal-fired power plants, is inevitable. In addition, the Dutch government pointed out that realising new coal-fired power plants would not conflict with existing environmental and climate policies, as these power plants would be accompanied by the capture and permanent geological storage of CO_2 (CCS), thus neutralising their environmental impact in the near future.[57]

The policy in the Energy Reports to invest more in the electricity production sector has been successful to construct new power plants, including coal-fired power plants. A number of the planned coal-fired power plants would be required to invest in CCS or participate in demonstration projects for CCS. In the end, the decision-making processes for three new coal-fired power plants were completed in 2007, two on the Maasvlakte Rotterdam (Engie and Uniper) and one at the Eemshaven in Groningen (RWE).[58] These plants became operational in 2015/2016 and are capable of co-firing biomass, but were met with continuous opposition. The decision-making processes were met with continuous opposition.[59] However, given the absence of an electricity production license

---

54 See for example: http://edition.cnn.com/2003/US/08/14/power.outage/.

55 In Dutch: "Voorzienings- en leveringszekerheid van Energie"; *Parliamentary Papers* 2002/03, 29 023, No. 1, p. 4. This position is reiterated by the Minister in a letter to the House of Representatives, see: *Parliamentary Papers II* 2003/04, 29 023, No. 4, p. 5.

56 *Parliamentary Papers II* 2004/05, 29 023, No. 14 (Attached file); *Parliamentary Papers II* 2007/08, 31 510, No. 1.

57 *Parliamentary Papers II* 2007/08, 31 510, No. 1 (Attached file), pp. 11–13.

58 *Parliamentary Papers II* 2006/07, 28 240 and 29023, No. 77.

59 See for example: https://www.nrc.nl/nieuws/2007/07/04/die-kolencentrales-zijn-niet-nodig-11352350-a624911. And several procedures at the court, see for example: The Administrative Jurisdiction Department of the Council of State (*Afdeling Bestuursrecht van de Raad van State*), 30 November 2011, ECLI:NL:RVS:2011:BU6363.

in Dutch legislation, or any other legal basis to directly influence the primary energy source used, a legal basis to deny the request to develop a coal-fired power plant was, and still is (largely) missing in the Netherlands.[60]

The idea of combining the new coal-fired power plants with CCS (onshore) was later abandoned because of the cost of CCS in relation to the price of CO_2 emission allowances under the EU ETS and because underground storage of CO_2 on land has become virtually impossible because of societal and political opposition.[61]

3.3. PHASING OUT COAL-FIRED POWER PLANTS: SOCIETAL AND LEGAL DEBATE

In order to reach the EU 2020 targets, the Dutch government together with 47 organisations, concluded the Agreement on Energy for Sustainable Growth (*het Energieakkoord*) in 2013,[62] resulting in a variety of measures to reduce CO_2 emissions and increase the share of renewable energy sources and also energy efficiency.[63] At that moment, the share of renewable energy was just 4.5 per cent of total energy consumption, lagging behind most other Member States.[64] Closing the (older) coal-fired power plants which dated from the 1970s and 1980s was included as one of the measures mentioned in the Energieakkoord.[65] The agreement also included ambitions to create 15,000 new jobs and to provide education- and work-to-work facilities for employees who lost their jobs as a result of the closure.[66]

The legal basis for the closure of these power plants was found in the Dutch Environmental Protection Act (*Wet milieubeheer*). The Dutch government imposed stricter efficiency requirements for industrial power plants running on coal or a combination of coal and other fuels, leading to a shutdown of these "older" coal-fired power plants, which could not achieve an energy efficiency rate of 40 per cent.[67]

---

60 It can be questioned whether the Electricity Directive has been transposed correctly in the Netherlands by not including a legal basis to deny a permit requested for building a coal-fired plant (see section 2.2 above).

61 See also chapter 20 in this book.

62 The Agreement on Energy for Sustainable Growth can be found on: www.energieakkoordser.nl.

63 Ibid, p. 29.

64 Ibid, p. 2.

65 Ibid, pillar 6.

66 Ibid, pillar 8.

67 See Article 5.12a(3) and Article 5.14(1) of the Activities Decree (*Activiteitenbesluit*). This rate was first upped to 38 per cent by 1 July 2017, and became 40 per cent after that date.

Despite the Energy Agreement, the process to implement measures to reach the climate goals was still deemed insufficient by many, including the non-governmental organisation (NGO) Urgenda, which filed a lawsuit against the Dutch government. The result is the world-renowned *Urgenda* case, in which the District Court in The Hague ordered the Netherlands to reduce CO_2 emissions by 25 per cent by the end of 2020 compared to emission levels in 1990.[68] This decision was upheld by the Appeal Court in The Hague in 2018 and is cause for concern for the Dutch government. The Environmental Assessment Agency (*Planbureau voor de Leefomgeving*) projected that binding energy and climate targets, including the decision in the *Urgenda* case to reduce CO_2 emission by 25 per cent by the end of 2020, were not going to be met.[69] In order to comply with the *Urgenda* verdict, the Dutch government announced it would take additional measures for the short term, including a 28 million Euros subsidy to accelerate CO_2 emission reductions in industry.[70]

On 28 May 2019, the Dutch Climate Act (*Klimaatwet*)[71] was approved by the Dutch Senate which sets a dot on the horizon: a binding obligation to reduce greenhouse gas emissions by 95 per cent in 2050 in comparison with 1990 levels, with an intermediate target in 2030 of 49 per cent reduction (article 2(1) and article 2(2) Climate Act).[72] On 28 June 2019, the Dutch government has presented its definitive national Climate Agreement (*Klimaatakkoord*) to parliament. This agreement functions as the Dutch strategy to achieve the intermediate target of 2030 set in the Climate Act.[73]

In order to achieve the new and intensified climate goals, the Dutch government has agreed to phase out all remaining coal-fired power plants by 2030.[74] Although this closure is not a part of the Climate Agreement, it does (also) contribute to the 2030 targets.[75]

In contrast to the five older coal-fired power plants, the decision to close the new coal-fired power plants cannot be based on stricter energy efficiency requirements, as this would be at odds with EU regulations. As discussed above,

---

68 Court of The Hague (*Rb. Den Haag*) 24 June 2015, ECLI:NL:RBDHA:2015:7145; see for a comprehensive overview of this case: Roy Suryapratim, 'Distributive Choices in Urgenda and EU Climate Law' in Martha M Roggenkamp and Catherine Banet (eds), *European Energy Law Report XI* (Cambridge, Intersentia 2017), pp. 47–68.

69 The Hague Court of Appeal (*Gerechtshof Den Haag*) 9 October 2018, ECLI:NL:GHDHA:2018:2591; *Parliamentary Papers II* 2018/19, 32 813, No. 267.

70 *Parliamentary Papers II* 2018/19, 32 813, No. 341; *Governmental Gazette* 2019, 37 424.

71 *Governmental Gazette* 2019, 253.

72 These obligations cannot be enforced before a court, but are binding for the Dutch government.

73 See the Climate Agreement, to be found at: www.klimaatakkoord.nl, p. 4.

74 This is stipulated in the latest government agreement 2017–2021 "Vertrouwen in de toekomst", literally translated as: "trust in the future", to be found at: www.kabinetsformatie2017.nl, p. 38.

75 See the Climate Agreement, to be found at: www.klimaatakkoord.nl, p. 149.

the IE Directive requires that emission limit values in the environmental permit are based on the application of the BATs, which must be technically and economically feasible. Imposing stricter energy efficiency rates than the 44 per cent mentioned in the BREF LCP (see section 2.3 above) is therefore not an option.[76] These newest plants are the most efficient coal-fired power plants ever constructed.[77] The Dutch government thus had to find another route to phase out the remaining five coal-fired power plants, which will be discussed below.

3.4. THE BILL "PROHIBITING THE USE OF COAL IN ELECTRICITY PRODUCTION"

The Dutch government issued a draft legislative proposal on the "Prohibition on the Use of Coal in Electricity Production" (hereinafter: the Bill), which was published online for public consultation in May 2018.[78] On 4 July 2019, a new version of the Bill was approved by the House of Representatives, which is currently under debate in the Dutch Senate.[79] This Bill bans the use of coal as a primary fuel for electricity production and will not only apply to coal-fired power plants that make use of coal but also to power plants that use coal in combination with biomass and plants that use coal in combination with CCS.[80]

The prohibition will become immediately effective once the Act comes into force in 2020.[81] Nevertheless, the Bill does provide for transitional periods based on the electrical efficiency rates of the coal plants.[82] In total, three categories can be identified. The first category consists of coal-fired power plants, which have an electrical efficiency rate of less than 44 per cent. These plants need to be closed before 1 January 2025.[83] Coal-fired power plants with an electrical efficiency rate of over 44 per cent fall into the second category and need to be closed before 1 January 2030.[84] The last (third) category is specifically

---

76 With the exception of article 18 of the IE Directive, see section 2.2 above.

77 Prescribing stricter emission limit values in the environmental permit would be at odds with the system in the ETS Directive (see section 2.2 above).

78 In Dutch the: "Wet verbod op kolen bij elektriciteitsproductie". To be found at: www.internetconsultatie.nl/kolencentrales. *Parliamentary Papers* II 2017/18, 32 813, No. 600. A (non-official) translation of the Act can be found at: ec.europa.eu.

79 See: https://www.eerstekamer.nl/wetsvoorstel/35167_wet_verbod_op_kolen_bij for the current state of affairs.

80 Article 2 of the Bill.

81 Ibid.

82 Electrical efficiency is the ratio between the net electricity revenue and the energy input of a specific fuel/raw material, in this case coal. See the decision dated 31 July 2017 of the European Commission, No. 2017/1442, table 2. The energy efficiency is calculated when the coal plant is operated at maximum capacity, which is often not the case, and the efficiency is less when operated at sub maximum capacity.

83 Article 3(1)(a) of the Bill.

84 Article 3(1)(b) of the Bill.

designed for the older Hemwegcentrale and requires this plant to shut down by 1 January 2020 in an effort by the Dutch government to comply with the *Urgenda* verdict.[85] The Dutch Emission Authority (*Nederlandse Emissieautoriteit*) has to monitor whether the plants will comply with the scheduled phase-out, which is supplemented with a legal basis for the Minister of Economic Affairs and Climate to enforce the prohibition by issuing penalty payments.[86]

Article 4 of the Bill provides a possibility for the Minister to award financial compensation to the owner of a coal-fired power plant when it can demonstrate that it is affected disproportionally by the prohibition compared to the other owners. Whether this article complies with article 1 First Protocol and article 13(1) ECT, is not yet clear.[87] According to the Dutch government, there is no need to compensate the owners on the basis of article 1 First Protocol, as there is no disproportionality between the general interest in closing the coal-fired power plants and the interest of the owners in operating their coal-fired power plants.[88] In the Explanatory Memorandum of the Bill, the government substantiates this claim by arguing that this interference in the property rights falls within the margin of appreciation of Member States to determine whether a fair balance is struck.[89] This is the case according to the government, as the premature closure has been foreseeable since 2005 when the Energy Report stated that further CO_2 reduction measures would be implemented within 10 years.[90] Next to that, a transitional period has been granted, to allow the owners of the three recently built coal-fired power plants to earn back part of their investment, as well as the possibility to switch to other fuels – such as biomass – that are supported by the SDE+ subsidy.[91] This again, is different for the Hemwegcentrale. The government is currently in discussion with the owner of this plant to agree on the amount of compensation as the transitional period of this plant is significantly shorter than that of other plants.[92]

This Bill is – not entirely surprisingly – met with resistance from the owners[93] and employees of the plants involved.[94] In the Climate Agreement, the government states that a "coherent and future-oriented approach" is required

---

85 *Parliamentary Papers II* 2018/19, 35 167, No. 3, p. 13.

86 Article 5 and article 6 of the Bill; *Parliamentary Papers II* 2018/19, 35 167, No. 3, para 9.

87 See the advice of the Advisory Division of the Council of State, *Parliamentary Papers II* 2018/19, No. 4; See also: J.A.M.A. Sluysmans, "Compensatie voor kolencentrales" (2019) 119, *Tijdschrift voor Bouwrecht*.

88 *Parliamentary Papers II* 2018/19, 35 167, No. 3, p. 13.

89 Ibid.

90 Ibid, p. 19.

91 Switching to other fuels, such as gas or hydrogen is also possible. See section 3.3 above.

92 *Parliamentary Papers II* 2018/19, 32 813, No. 303.

93 These reactions can be found at: www.internetconsultatie.nl/kolencentrales/reacties.

94 See for example: https://nos.nl/artikel/2168068-eigenaar-kolencentrale-wil-stoppen-met-steenkool.html.

to enable employees working in the fossil fuel sector to transition to other economic sectors.[95] A special committee has been assigned by the Dutch Socio-Economic Council (*Sociaal-Economische Raad*) to investigate and advise on the possibilities and risks for such a transition. Alongside that, the Government announced that 22 million Euros will be made available for work-to-work guidance and education of people who might lose their jobs in the fossil fuels sectors.[96]

3.5. CONCLUSION ON THE NETHERLANDS

Not so long ago, the Dutch government pursued a policy aimed at obtaining new investments in electricity production capacity and diversification of primary energy sources. This policy resulted in the realisation of three new coal-fired power plants. Since then, social and political ideas have shifted quickly leading to the Bill "Prohibiting the Use of Coal in Electricity Production" to end the use of coal as a primary fuel for electricity production in the Netherlands before 2030. Questions remain. Is, for example, the closure of the ultra-modern coal-fired power plants that became operational in 2015/16 a good idea from an EU point of view? National CO_2 emission reductions as a result of this measure might be emitted elsewhere in the EU by less clean and efficient power plants under the EU ETS cap and trade system. Decommissioning the Dutch coal-fired power plants would be a purely nationally oriented measure in this regard. It is known that gas-fired power plants will help to secure the future Dutch security of energy supply, but where will this primary fuel come from when the gas extractions from the Groningen fields are expected to be halted in 2022?[97] Another question is whether the owners of, and investors in, the coal-fired power plants will receive financial compensation when the Bill is passed.[98] As can be seen, a lot is still unknown. One thing, however, remains

95 This letter can be found at: https://www.rijksoverheid.nl/ministeries/ministerie-van-economische-zaken-en-klimaat/documenten/kamerstukken/2019/06/28/kamerbrief-voorstel-voor-een-klimaatakkoord, p. 20.

96 To be found at: https://www.rijksoverheid.nl/actueel/nieuws/2019/06/13/kabinet-trekt-ruim-20-miljoen-uit-voor-werkgelegenheidseffecten-energietransitie.

97 To be found at: https://www.rijksoverheid.nl/documenten/kamerstukken/2019/09/10/kamerbrief---gaswinningsniveau-groningen-in-2019-2020. See: https://www.reuters.com/article/us-netherlands-gas/netherlands-to-halt-groningen-gas-production-by-2022-idUSKCN1VV1KE.

98 Solutions in this regard are to smarten the grid and promote more storage options, see e.g. Lea Diestelmeier, *Unlocking Flexibility with Law: developing a Legal Framework for Smart Electricity Systems*, Thesis, Rijksuniversiteit Groningen 2019. See on the role of gas-power plants in the Netherlands: Martha M Roggenkamp, 'Reducing Gas Production from the Groningen Field: The Need to Balance Safe Production with Supply Security' in Martha M Roggenkamp and Catherine Banet (eds), *European Energy Law Report Volume XI* (Intersentia, Cambridge 2017), pp. 301–316.

clear: the days of the last five coal-fired power plants in the Netherlands are numbered once the Bill is adopted.

4. THE EXAMPLE OF GERMANY

4.1. INTRODUCTION

It might come as a surprise to some that Germany, well-known for its energy transition, has been (and still is) a coal country, with respect to both production and usage of coal. In 2018, more than one-third of electricity generation in Germany was still based on coal.[99] Some 146 terawatt-hours of that came from lignite, the most polluting form of coal. At the same time 20,800 people were working in the lignite industry alone and more than 50 per cent of employees are 50 years and older, making them very vulnerable in case of redundancies.[100]

However, redundancies are very likely in the German coal sector in the near future. Germany is obliged to achieve the climate goals at international and European level that have been discussed earlier in this chapter. But in addition, Germany also fixed targets at the national level for the time-horizons 2020, 2030 and 2050 that are even more ambitious than those of the EU or the international community. Germany set itself the goal to achieve 40 per cent emission reduction compared to 1990 levels by 2020.[101] Germany also has specific 2030 aims, that are designed for sectors not currently covered by the EU ETS (so called non-EU ETS sectors) and that come on top of EU commitments. In particular, Germany needs to reduce greenhouse gas emissions by 55 per cent by 2030 compared to 2005 levels under this policy.[102] Finally, Germany unilaterally decided on certain reductions by 2050 in its "Klimaschutzplan 2050" of 2016: until 2050 80–95 per cent of greenhouse gas emissions, compared to 1990 levels, need to be reduced nationally.[103]

---

99 Bundesministerium für Wirtschaft und Energie, "Rahmen und nächste Schritte für die Kohleausstiegsgesetzgebung", available at: https://www.bmwi.de/Redaktion/DE/Downloads/P-R/rahmen-und-naechste-schritte-kohleausstiegsgesetzgebung.pdf?__blob=publicationFile&v=10 (hereinafter: Next Steps).

100 Umweltbundesamt, "Beschäftigungs-entwicklung in der Braunkohleindustrie: Status quo und Projektion", available at: https://www.umweltbundesamt.de/sites/default/files/medien/3521/publikationen/2018-07-25_climate-change_18-2018_beschaeftigte-braunkohleindustrie.pdf, p. 11.

101 Energiekonzept für eine umweltschonende, zuverlässige und bezahlbare Energieversorgung, 28 September 2010, p. 4, available at: https://archiv.bundesregierung.de/resource/blob/656922/779770/794fd0c40425acd7f46afacbe62600f6/energiekonzept-final-data.pdf?download=1.

102 Bundesministerium für Umwelt, Naturschutz und nukleare Sicherheit, "Klimaschutzplan 2050", p. 7, available at: https://www.bmu.de/fileadmin/Daten_BMU/Download_PDF/Klimaschutz/klimaschutzplan_2050_bf.pdf.

103 Ibid.

4.2. BACKGROUND

Coal mining is not simply relevant for German electricity production. It is deeply entrenched in German culture, society and politics. "*Glück Auf*", the traditional greeting of coal miners, is used as a way to say hello or wishing success in some parts of Germany. "*Der Steiger kommt*", a traditional coal-miners song, is used by (amongst others) Schalke 04 and Erzgebirge Aue, two major football clubs from West and East Germany, as club anthem.[104] This epitomises how coal mining culture can unite an otherwise often still separated country. But it does not stop at football: even one of the two parties that are forming the current German government is using the song in its party gatherings to create a sense of community. Two crossed hammers, the symbol of coal mining in Germany, are used to sell beer, as an emblem for music bands and even (in gold) on wedding rings.

In a country that features very little domestic gas reserves and even less oil, coal was the only energy source that could be produced domestically for two centuries, enabling a country that is otherwise scarce of natural resources to get a glimpse of what energy security means. During the peak of the "Cold War" (1962–1979), coal was used to reassure the German population that, in case of extreme crisis, energy independence might be possible.

4.3. SOCIETAL DEBATE

Coal has always been the number one source of base-load electricity in Germany. It also served as the backbone of West German industry, which settled in the *Ruhrgebiet* precisely because of its vast coal reserves. The *Ruhrgebiet* also forms the most prominent part of the biggest of the 16 German *Länder*, North-Rhine Westphalia. This meant that coal always played a central role in West German politics. However, this was by no means restricted to the West. In the former DDR[105] (East Germany) coal was also produced in bulk and viewed as a vital "enabler" of the creation of industrial production in East Germany. The fact that several *Länder* both in East and West Germany have traditionally been "coal producing areas" makes them key players and movers/shakers in the current legal set-up concerning the German coal phase-out, as will be discussed throughout this part of the chapter.

---

104 Emotional accounts of what this is looking like can be obtained for Erzgebirge Aue at: https://www.youtube.com/watch?v=08eCUENnePM and Schalke 04 at: https://www.youtube.com/watch?v=zrxUOnDyHjc.

105 Deutsche Demokratische Republik, the official name of East Germany until 1989.

Other than nuclear power, which has been controversial for its environmental impacts in Germany since the 1980s,[106] coal has mainly been controversial because of its economics and costs, not (at least not until very recently) because of its environmental footprint. The "war" about domestic coal production that raged in the late 1980s and early 1990s in many European countries, like the UK also reached Germany. However, unlike the Thatcher-government in the 1980s that embarked on a confrontational course with the aim of ending domestic coal production in the UK,[107] Germany opted for a smoother transition. It decided to heavily subsidise the domestic German coal industry and stretch the phase-out of uneconomic domestic hard coal production over 30 years, from 1989 to the end of 2018. On 21 December 2018 the German President, Frank-Walter Steinmeier was present when the coal mine "*Prosper Haniel*" produced the last German hard coal.[108] This approach of gradually lowering production over decades has nevertheless been seen as a success, setting the traditional coal-producing country Germany apart from other traditional coal-producing countries such as the UK, where the phasing out of domestic coal production let to societal unrest and protests.[109]

4.4. LEGAL DEBATE

While the debate over the final phase-out of coal-fired power plants and lignite coal has been present in some areas of society for a decade now, no government dared to touch the toxic issue until very recently, in order not to anger German voters that are proud of their remaining pieces of coal industry. However, in the run-up to the last German general elections, the pan-European movement towards a final coal phase-out also reached Germany and politicians were no longer able to simply ignore this. After the troubled elections of September 2017, it took almost half a year for German parties to create a new government. When the new government was finally installed, the coalition agreement postponed or circumvented some of the most contentious issues, such as the coal phase-out. The government "outsourced" the decision about coal to an expert

106 Christian Joppke, *Mobilizing Against Nuclear Energy: A Comparison of Germany and the United States* (University of California Press, Berkeley 1993), pp. 91 et seq.

107 Earl A. Reitan, *The Thatcher Revolution* (Rowman & Littlefield Publishers, Oxford 2003), p. 61 et seq (hereinafter: Reitan).

108 Bundespräsidialamt, "Zentrale Abschiedsveranstaltung für den deutschen Steinkohlenbergbau", available at: https://www.bundespraesident.de/SharedDocs/Reden/DE/Frank-Walter-Steinmeier/Reden/2018/12/181221-Abschied-Steinkohlebergbau.html%22.

109 Reitan, above n. 107, pp. 61 et seq.

commission, the government's commission on "growth, structural transformation and employment", colloquially referred to as the "Coal Commission". It consisted of all relevant societal stakeholders, from environmental NGOs and Trade Unions to the energy industry,[110] and was asked to come up with a suggestion for Germany's coal phase-out. The idea behind it was to organise the phase-out of domestic lignite coal production and coal-fired power plants along the lines of the successful earlier phase-out of hard coal. It would be organised in one big societal effort where all stakeholders, from industry to environmental activists, from coal miners to Prime-Ministers of the *Länder*, agree to one big compromise.[111]

Importantly, the *Länder* also participated in the coal commission. While their formal role was similar to that of other stakeholders, they were at the very least *primus inter pares*. This specific role is anchored in German law, or more specifically in the German constitution (*Grundgesetz*). Article 74 No. 11 of the German constitution includes the right to regulate the mining sector and energy activities. This right is shared (or as it is more aptly called in the German jurisdiction: "competing") between the federal government (*Bund*) and the *Länder*. The general rule is that *Länder* have the general right to regulate these areas, according to article 72(1) German constitution. This right is subject to the condition that the federal government has not used its law-making competence in the respective area. The competence of the federal government, however, is curtailed by article 72(2) German constitution, which prescribes that the federal government can only act if and to the extent that similar living conditions in all parts of the country or the preservation of legal and economic unity of the country requires a federal act. A substantial part of public law education at German universities is dedicated to the correct interpretation of these conditions. For this chapter, however, it suffices to say that the *Länder* are in a strong position when it comes to mining law and a coal phase-out would not be possible without their place.

The Coal Commission started working on 6 June 2018 and published its final report and recommendations in January 2019.[112] While these recommendations are not legally binding, the German government issued a document on 3 July 2019 in which it pledged to act accordingly.[113] According to this information,

---

110 "Kommission, Wachstum, Strukturwandel und Beschäftigung – Abschlussbericht" (Bundesministerium für Wirtschaft und Energie, Berlin 2019), pp. 6–7, available at: https://www.bmwi.de/Redaktion/DE/Downloads/A/abschlussbericht-kommission-wachstum-strukturwandel-und-beschaeftigung.pdf?__blob=publicationFile (hereinafter: Final Report).

111 Ibid, pp. 6–7.

112 Ibid.

113 Bundesministerium für Wirtschaft und Energie "Rahmen und nächste Schritte für die Kohleausstiegsgesetzgebung", available at: https://www.bmwi.de/Redaktion/DE/Downloads/P-R/rahmen-und-naechste-schritte-kohleausstiegsgesetzgebung.pdf?__blob=publicationFile&v=10 (hereinafter: Next Steps).

the German government is currently translating the recommendations into a Bill that will be presented to the German parliament by the end of 2019/beginning of 2020.[114]

Very broadly speaking, the measures are twofold. One part is dealing with the technicalities of actually ending electricity production from coal-fired power plants, while other measures are concerned with structural, monetary support for those *Länder* where the coal-fired power plants are located (again, showing the important leverage of the *Länder* in this process). The latter part is, to some extent, also a political decision to ease resistance amongst coal-producing regions, because their approval will be required in the second chamber of parliament (*Bundesrat*), due to the competing legislative competence for mining, as discussed earlier. It is the aim of the Coal Commission to create a broad societal consent, also including the energy companies, to avoid expropriation claims.[115] Below is a list of the most important recommendations.

4.4.1. *Final End Date 2038*

The main recommendation of the Coal Commission is to phase out electricity production from coal in Germany by 2038 at the latest.[116] However, the Commission also considers 2035 as the possible end date, subject to technological and economic developments. The developments and the exact end date will be reassessed in 2032.[117]

4.4.2. *Gigawatts Count, not Power Plants*

The Coal Commission is suggesting a quick start of the phase-out. In 2017, a total of 42 gigawatts of electricity produced from coal-fired power plants were made available to the market (20 gigawatts from lignite-fired plants and 22 gigawatts from hard-coal-fired plants.[118] In addition there was the German electricity capacity reserve that consisted of 4.3 gigawatts of electricity, produced from coal, that were not made available to the market.[119]

114 Ibid.

115 Ibid, p. 2.

116 Final Report, p. 65.

117 Ibid.

118 Kraftwerksliste Bundesnetzagentur (bundesweit; alle Netz- und Umspannebenen), Stand: 19.11.2018; Anlagen "in Betrieb zzgl. Endgültig stillgelegt 2018".

119 The capacity reserve has been installed by an ordinance of the German government of 28 January 2019 (*Kapazitätsreserveverordnung*), available at: https://www.bgbl.de/xaver/bgbl/start.xav#__bgbl__%2F%2F*%5B%40attr_id%3D%27bgbl119s0058.pdf%27%5D__1568192101617.

In 2022 coal-fired power plants with a capacity of 12.7 gigawatts will be switched off.[120] Until 2030, only those with a 17 gigawatts capacity shall remain in production; by 2038 this number must come down to 0.[121] However, the recommendations leave it to politicians to negotiate with the plant owners which plants have to go first and which last. In theory Germany's climate goals for 2030 could be met with this compromise, but because there is no detailed road map for the period between 2022 and 2030, a situation could occur where a significant number of power plants are switched off "at the last minute" by 2029 to meet the 17 gigawatts obligation in 2030. This practice, however, would likely result in a situation where Germany misses its 2030 climate goals, as such "last minute" decisions might not result in a timely phase-out.

4.4.3. *Electricity Price shall be Stabilised*

The Coal Commission recommends that end consumers should not be burdened with the cost of the coal phase-out. Taking coal-fired power plants off the electricity markets is anticipated to shorten the supply of electricity and wholesale electricity prices could soar as a result.[122] This shall be countered by an increase in electricity production from renewable energy sources. However, this production is associated with additional, different costs, for instance concerning grid-extension.[123] These increasing costs would need to be borne by transmission and distribution system operators, who, however, could pass these costs on to the final consumer (industry but also household consumers) in the form of increasing transmission/distribution grid charges. To prevent burdening end consumers of electricity with these costs, the Coal Commission recommends a subsidy. From 2023 onwards private and industrial end consumers shall receive a subsidy from the government to ease the increase in grid charges. The Commission suggests that 2 billion Euros per year will be necessary.[124]

This raises the issue whether such a subsidy could be classified as state aid, and if the answer is yes, then the next question would be whether such state aid is allowed or illegal under EU and German law. This would heavily depend on the concrete guise of the subsidy. The Commission appears to be very aware of this issue and remains vague on what exactly is planned. The Final Report of the Coal Commission advocates a government subsidy or an "alternative measure of equal effect".[125] Parliament, when translating this into a law, will face substantial challenges not to infringe state aid rules.

---

120 Final Report, p. 62.
121 Ibid, pp. 63–64.
122 Ibid, p.66.
123 Ibid.
124 Ibid.
125 Ibid.

4.4.4. *Structural Transformation*

One of the burning issues for those *Länder* with considerable coal reserves is what comes after coal? A contract between the national and *Länder* governments is envisaged by the Coal Commission, in which the federal government pledges to give a total of 40 billion Euros to the *Länder* in addition to current subsidies to keep workers going (1.3 billion Euros every year – for a period of 20 years).[126] This money shall be used to realise measures that are listed in a chapter in the Final Report.[127] Measures are specific and tailor-made for the respective coal-mining districts and include mobility and digitalisation projects to improve physical and digital infrastructure with the aim to get new investors into the region.[128]

4.4.5. *Avoid Expropriation Claims*

The (largely) successful approach of the hard coal and nuclear phase-outs, to create a consensus with companies to avoid expropriation claims, shall be replicated.[129] The Commission, thus, recommends coming to a negotiated solution with the power plant owners. During these negotiations compensation is one of the options on the table, but legal challenges afterwards should be avoided as much as possible. The government and parliament now have to make up their mind on how exactly this is supposed to take place, as the Commission did not provide further details.

4.5. CONCLUSION ON GERMANY

While the Coal Commission finished its work, the government and parliament will have to put this compromise into a legally binding document and execute it. However, signs are emerging that pushing the compromise through in its current form could be difficult. The debate on whether 2038 as an end date is too late is rife in Germany. The Fridays for Future movement is creating a lot of pressure to fast-forward the end date for the phase-out of electricity produced from coal in Germany. Increasingly, politicians from the entire political spectrum are

126 Bundesregierung, "Der Einstieg in den Kohleausstieg", available at: https://www.bundesregierung.de/breg-de/aktuelles/der-einstieg-in-den-kohleausstieg-1574264.

127 Final Report, chapter 5.

128 Ibid, pp. 73–81.

129 One exception is Vattenfall, which launched expropriation claims in the context of the German nuclear phase out, both before the German Constitutional Court and in international arbitration fora, see BVerfGE 1 BvR 2821/ 11, 1 BvR 1456/12, 1 BvR 321/12; ICSID Case No. ARB/12/12.

trying to tap into these sentiments, demanding an earlier end date for the coal phase-out in Germany.[130] All in all, the debate in Germany is slowly progressing and legally binding decisions are expected by the end of 2019 or the beginning of 2020.

5. CONCLUSION

The phase-out of coal as a primary fuel for electricity production purposes is starting in some countries. The assessment of the process in two EU Member States, the Netherlands and Germany, flagged up four broader legal observations.

First, Member States and not the EU are in charge of deciding on a coal phase-out. While it might be tempting for proponents of such a coal-phase out to demand a "European solution", we found that the EU likely lacks the competence to directly impose a coal phase-out upon Member States. In secondary EU law, there are a number of instruments touching upon certain aspects of coal-usage for the production of electricity, but there is also no EU Directive or Regulation (the two most important, legally binding EU law instruments for energy regulation) that would address a coal phase-out directly. As a consequence, the Member States are in charge when it comes to the use of coal and a potential phase-out of coal to reach the EU climate targets.

Second, the regulation of coal as a primary energy source for electricity production is strongly dependent on political trends – which might be reversed at very short intervals. The Netherlands has taken a kind of "flip-flop" approach towards coal. While coal was seen as a great opportunity around the millennium, only a couple of years later sentiment changed and with it its regulation, which is now very much against the use of coal in the Netherlands. Germany's approach to regulation was less erratic, but the downside is a protracted and more cumbersome process.

Third, when engaging in a phase-out of coal, Member States try to avoid expropriation claims. We looked at two Member States and found similar efforts in both to design the phase-out process in an all-encompassing manner that takes all relevant societal stakeholders "on board", including the owners of coal-fired power plants. However, the litmus test will now be the design of concrete laws in both countries and the concrete measures that shall give effect to the aim of avoiding expropriation claims.

---

130 Unexpected, for instance, was the current intervention of the strictly-conservative Prime-Minister of Bavaria, Markus Söder, who demanded 2030 as an end date, see *Tagesschau* "Söder will Kohleausstieg schon 2030", available at: https://www.tagesschau.de/inland/soeder-kohleausstieg-101.html.

Fourth and finally, the phase-out of coal needs to be seconded by (legal) measures that enable successful transitions in those regions that rely on coal sector-related employment. Those regions tend to be neglected regions, especially in Germany, that have a long history of suffering from economic downturns. Law-makers seem to have understood the power of distributive justice instruments to organise and retain social cohesion by allocating monetary and other benefits to the people that are going to be "hit hard" by a coal phase-out.

PART IV

OFFSHORE DECOMMISSIONING IN THE NORTH SEA

CHAPTER XIV

THE REGULATION OF DECOMMISSIONING IN THE NETHERLANDS

From Removal to Re-Use

Dinand DRANKIER and Martha M. ROGGENKAMP*

1. INTRODUCTION

Decommissioning is traditionally the last step in the lifetime of an energy asset.[1] After the planning, construction and operation of the asset, decommissioning entails restoring an energy site to its original state or as close to that state as is desirable given the merits of the various options for dealing with the energy asset.[2] The term 'decommissioning', however, lacks a codified legal definition.[3] Generally, the term is interpreted as encompassing the entire process dealing with the removal or re-use of an asset, the disposal of the removed asset or parts thereof and the restoration of the energy site.[4] In terms of terminology,

---

* This chapter builds on the presentation of Roderick Verstegen, EBN (now Taqa), at the 29th European Energy Law Seminar in The Hague. The authors appreciate the feedback provided by him when preparing the chapter.

1 Examples of energy assets include installations and structures such as oil and gas platforms, wind turbines, mining works other than offshore platforms, nuclear reactors, power plants, electricity cables and gas or oil pipelines.

2 R.J. HEFFRON, 'Energy Law for Decommissioning in the Energy Sector in the 21st Century' (2018) 11 *The Journal of World Energy Law & Business* 189, p. 190.

3 B.A. HAMZAH, 'International Rules on Decommissioning of Offshore Installations: Some Observations' (2003) 27 *Marine Policy* 339, pp. 339–340. All relevant international legal instruments concerning decommissioning, including the United Nations Convention on the Law of the Sea, the International Maritime Organization Guidelines and Standards for the Removal of Offshore Installations and Structures on the Continental Shelf and in the Exclusive Economic Zone, and the OSPAR Convention for the Protection of the Marine Environment of the North-East Atlantic, do not mention the term *decommissioning*. Only OSPAR Decision 98/3 on the Disposal of Disused Offshore Installations mentions the term but does not define it.

4 HAMZAH (n 3), pp. 339–340; A.D.M. FORTE, 'Legal Aspects of Decommissioning Offshore Structures' in D.G. GORMAN ET AL, *Decommissioning Offshore Structures*, Springer-Verlag,

it is, moreover, important to note that instead of 'decommissioning' the terms 'abandonment' and 'abandonment and removal' are used in academic literature and by the industry.[5] In more recent years, however, decommissioning has become the preferred term.

From a regulatory perspective, the rules in place for decommissioning differ per type of energy asset, per location and per jurisdiction. The focus of this chapter will be on the assets used for the production of hydrocarbons, such as platforms, wells, cables and pipelines, in the offshore areas of the Netherlands. This issue is currently highly topical. Given the fact that the oil and gas reservoirs located in the Netherlands are maturing, most of the hydrocarbon production assets are foreseen to reach the end of their economic lifetime in the upcoming two decades.[6] Projections show that this may lead to the decommissioning of approximately 150 platforms, over 3,000 km of pipeline and more than 600 wells located on the Dutch Continental Shelf.[7] Given the financial and environmental implications of decommissioning, these projections warrant a closer analysis of the Dutch legal framework for decommissioning offshore.[8]

This chapter will evolve in three steps. The first part will briefly elaborate on the international legal regime in place with regard to decommissioning. Subsequently, part two will elaborate on the Dutch legal regime for decommissioning. Finally, the last part of the chapter will briefly look at re-use as a form of decommissioning as this concept is gaining momentum in the Netherlands.

2. DECOMMISSIONING OFFSHORE

2.1. THE ROLE OF INTERNATIONAL LAW

Decommissioning installations offshore differs from the situation onshore as states have limited jurisdiction offshore.[9] Offshore the extent to which

London, 1998, p. 126. OSPAR Decision 98/3 seems to take the same approach by explicitly mentioning re-use, recycling and final disposal as options for decommissioning.

5 Hamzah (n 3), pp. 339–340; Forte (n 4 above), p. 126; M.J.J. van Beuge, 'De Verwijdering van Energie-installaties (Deel 1): Offshore Installaties' *Nederlands Tijdschrift voor Energierecht* 194, p. 194; J. Paterson, 'Decommissioning of Offshore Oil and Gas Installations' in G. Gordon, J. Paterson and E. Üşenmez, *Oil and Gas Law: Current Practice and Emerging Trends*, Dundee University Press, Dundee, 2011, p. 285.

6 EBN, *Netherlands Masterplan for Decommissioning and Re-use* (2016), p. 11.

7 Nexstep, *Offshore Re-use & Decommissioning Inventory* (2007 as updated in 2019).

8 It should be noted that in contrast to other North Sea states, the Netherlands will also be facing large-scale decommissioning onshore. The legal arrangements for onshore decommissioning fall outside the scope of this chapter.

9 Jurisdiction consists of the right of a state to legislate and enforce this legislation within a territory or over particular subjects. Jurisdiction always needs to have an implicit or explicit basis. The most common forms of jurisdiction are territorial jurisdiction, where a state enjoys

states may regulate energy activities, such as the construction, operation and decommissioning of energy assets, depends on the maritime zone where the activity takes place. These maritime zones are determined by international law, in particular the law of the sea. For decommissioning in the North Sea, two maritime zones are of specific importance: the territorial sea and the continental shelf. These zones are governed by the United Nations Conventions on the Law of the Sea of 1958 and in particular, the Convention of the Territorial Sea and the Contiguous Zone and the Convention on the Continental Shelf, and its successor, the United Nations Convention on the Law of the Sea of 1982 (UNCLOS).[10]

Historically, the sea was considered international territory so that all nations were free to use it for seafaring trade.[11] This freedom has gradually been limited. To start with, coastal states claimed a territorial sea in order to protect themselves. Whereas the territorial sea originally was three nautical miles, it currently entails the water column, the seabed and subsoil up to 12 nautical miles (22.2 kilometers) from shore.[12] The territorial sea is considered to be part of the land territory and coastal states thus have full jurisdiction and, consequently, all national laws apply in this area.[13] With the need and the available technique to develop offshore oil reservoirs, the 1958 Convention on the Continental Shelf identified the concept of a 'continental shelf'. Geologically, a continental shelf is a relatively shallow submarine area adjacent to the coast. Under international law the continental shelf zone is limited to that part of the geological continental shelf that is located beyond the territorial sea and extends up to a maximum of 200 nautical miles (370.4 kilometers) from shore.[14] In case of a continental shelf, coastal states may exercise *sovereign rights* for the purpose of exploring and exploiting natural resources.[15] This entails that coastal states, in contrast to the territorial sea, only have a functional jurisdiction, i.e. jurisdiction that is limited to the regulation and enforcement of the exploration and exploitation of natural

jurisdiction over its territory, and treaty-based jurisdiction, where a state enjoys jurisdiction by virtue of an international treaty that allocates this jurisdiction to it.

10 This treaty entered into force in 1994 and is ratified by 168 countries, including the Netherlands. For an elaborate analysis of the international law of the sea, see D.R. Rothwell and T. Stephens, *The International Law of the Sea*, Hart Publishing, Oxford, 2016.

11 Hugo Grotius, *Mare Liberum* (or *The Freedom of the Seas*), 1609.

12 United Nations Convention on the Law of the Sea (UNCLOS), Montego Bay, 1982 (hereinafter UNCLOS), article 3.

13 UNCLOS, article 2.

14 UNCLOS, article 76(1); hereinafter the term *continental shelf* will be used to refer to the continental shelf as defined by UNCLOS, the geological phenomenon continental shelf will be referred to as *geological continental shelf*.

15 UNCLOS, articles 76 (1) and 77 and article 2(1) Convention on the Continental Shelf.

resources and thus to the construction and operation of any installations necessary for the execution of these activities.[16] The North Sea is one continental shelf. In order to delimit the borders of the coastal states bordering the North Sea, several delimitation agreements have been concluded.[17]

UNCLOS also introduced a third zone: an exclusive economic zone (EEZ). The EEZ can extend up to 200 nautical miles from shore but also takes into account the waters superjacent to the seabed.[18] By contrast to the continental shelf, an EEZ needs to be explicitly proclaimed by the coastal state. All North Sea states have proclaimed an EEZ.[19] In their EEZs, they hold sovereign rights for the purpose of exploring, exploiting, conserving and managing natural resources, the production of energy from the water, currents and winds and other activities for the economic exploitation and exploration of the EEZ.[20] The latter can be of specific importance when designing potential re-use of installations for carbon dioxide injection and/or offshore hydrogen production.[21]

The above shows that the freedom of all nations to use the sea has progressively been reduced since the 1950s. This is partly due to technical developments and increasing energy demand. Therefore a balance needs to be struck between the right of coastal states to explore and exploit the sea/seabed and the rights of other users of the sea for shipping and navigation. As the use of fixed installations for exploiting energy resources has the most impact on other users of the sea, international law also provides further guidance on the use of such offshore assets. Apart from the need to establish safety zones around installations and installing permanent means for giving warning of their presence, international law also provides that offshore installations need to be removed if they are no longer in use. Below we will discuss the main provisions governing removal of installations as provided by UNCLOS and the International Maritime Organization, as well as the dumping provisions in the London Convention and the OSPAR Convention.

---

16 UNCLOS, articles 80 and 60.

17 See for these agreements C. Redgwell, 'International Regulation of Energy Activities' in *Energy Law in Europe – National, EU and International Regulation*, 3rd edition, Oxford University Press, Oxford, 2016, p. 58.

18 UNCLOS, article 57.

19 The Netherlands proclaimed an EEZ by Act of 27 May 1999 establishing an Exclusive Economic Zone of the Kingdom (*Rijkswet van 27 mei 1999 tot instelling van een exclusieve economische zone van het Koninkrijk*), *staatsblad* 27 May 1999, number 281, which entered into force on 28 April 2000.

20 UNCLOS, article 56(1)(a).

21 For a deeper analysis of whether carbon dioxide storage is an economic exploitation activity, see M. Brus, 'Challenging Complexities of CCS in Public International Law' in M.M. Roggenkamp and E. Woerdman, *Legal Design of Carbon Capture and Storage: Developments in the Netherlands from an International and EU Perspective*, Intersentia, Antwerp, 2009. See also Chapter XX of this volume by M.M. Roggenkamp.

2.2. REMOVAL OBLIGATIONS

2.2.1. Law of the Sea

Both the 1958 Convention on the Continental Shelf and UNCLOS provide that abandoned or disused installations need to be removed. However, there is an important distinction between both conventions, as article 5(5) of the 1958 Convention on the Continental Shelf explicitly stated that abandoned or disused installations should be *entirely* removed, whereas article 60(3) of UNCLOS tones down the obligation by stating that:

> Any installations or structures which are abandoned or disused shall be removed to ensure safety of navigation, taking into account any generally accepted international standards established in this regard by the competent international organization. Such removal shall also have due regard to fishing, the protection of the marine environment and the rights and duties of other States. Appropriate publicity shall be given to the depth, position and dimensions of any installations or structures not entirely removed.[22]

In other words, whereas the rules on removal are more relaxed and facilitate a partial removal, UNCLOS also identifies some general criteria – safety of navigation, marine environment and rights and duties of other states – that need to be taken into account in case of a removal. Apart from this, UNCLOS refers to 'generally accepted international standards' established by a competent international organisation. Such standards have been developed by the International Maritime Organization (IMO), which is a specialized agency of the United Nations and acts as the global standard-setting authority for the safety, security and environmental performance of international shipping.

2.2.2. IMO Guidelines

In 1989 the International Maritime Organization produced a set of non-binding guidelines and standards on the decommissioning of offshore installations and structures. Although these guidelines are non-binding, UNCLOS signatories have an obligation to take into consideration their content in accordance with article 60 of UNCLOS.

The IMO guidelines distinguish between three options, i.e. that an installation and/or structure needs to be entirely removed, partially removed or can remain in place. Installations and/or structures installed before 1 January 1998 need to be removed entirely if they are standing in less than 75 meters of water and weigh less than 4,000 tonnes, excluding deck and superstructure. For installations

22 UNCLOS, article 60(3).

and/or structures put in place after January 1 of 1998, the obligation to remove entirely applies if they are standing in less than 100 meters of water and weigh less than 4,000 tonnes.[23] Nevertheless, if such entire removal is not feasible or would involve extreme costs, or unacceptable risk to personnel or the marine environment, the coastal state may still opt for partial removal.[24] However, no exception applies to installations or structures located in or near selected routes for international navigation.[25]

Heavier installations and structures positioned in deeper waters can be partially removed as long as the remaining parts will not cause unjustifiable interference with other uses of the sea. This entails that an unobstructed water column sufficient to ensure safety of navigation, but not less than 55 meters, should be provided above any partially removed installation or structure which does not project above the surface of the sea.[26]

Last but not least, the guidelines provide for non-removal but only if the installation or structure will serve a new use and is not causing unjustifiable interference with other uses of the sea.[27] This option is becoming of increasing relevance as oil and gas fields are getting depleted and new uses of the sea and the seabed are being explored.

Except for those situations where complete removal is required, a decision to partially or not remove an abandoned or unused installation or structure should be based on a case-by-case assessment of the navigational and potential environmental effects, the feasibility as well as the costs and risks of removal and any justifications for leaving in place the infrastructure.[28]

2.2.3. *Installations and Structures*

The removal obligations discussed above refer to abandoned and disused *installations* and *structures*. However, neither the Geneva Conventions and UNCLOS nor the IMO Guidelines define these terms. Given the explicit reference to safety of navigation and the fact that safety zones usually are established around platforms and not around subsea pipelines and cables, it is assumed that the term installations and structures refers to fixed objects arising above sea level such as oil and gas production platforms, but not to subsea cables and pipelines.[29] The removal obligations will therefore basically not apply to submarine pipelines

[23] IMO Guidelines, articles 3.1. and 3.2.
[24] IMO Guidelines, article 3.5.
[25] IMO Guidelines, article 3.7.
[26] IMO Guidelines, article 3.6.
[27] IMO Guidelines, articles 3.4. and 3.5.
[28] IMO Guidelines, article 2.1.
[29] M.M. Roggenkamp, 'Petroleum Pipelines in the North Sea: Question of Jurisdiction and Practical Solutions', *Journal of Energy and Natural Resources Law*, 1998, pp. 92–109.

and cables, although a distinction needs to be made between types of pipelines and cables, i.e. those which are part of the production installations, and others.

2.3. DUMPING

2.3.1. *London Convention*

Whereas the Law of the Sea Conventions and the IMO Guidelines govern the (partial or entire) removal of abandoned or disused installations and structures, they do not provide any further insight about the status of (parts of) the installations which *have not* been removed and how to deal with installations that *have* been removed. Are these activities allowed or are they to be considered as dumping? On the international level, the London Convention for the Prevention of Marine Pollution by Dumping of Wastes and Other Matters is the central legal instrument dealing with dumping.[30] In 1996 the London Convention was amended by the Protocol to the Convention on the Prevention of Marine Pollution by Dumping of Wastes and Other Matter (London Protocol), which entered into force in 2006.[31]

The London Convention defines *dumping* as the deliberate disposal at sea of wastes, vessels, aircraft, platforms or other man-made structures.[32] It distinguishes between wastes of which dumping is prohibited and waste of which dumping is possible pursuant to a special or general permit.[33] Since the entry into force of the London Protocol, authorised dumping is limited to materials listed in Annex I of the Protocol and subject to the award of a permit.[34] Vessels, platforms and other man-made structures are listed in Annex I and consequently dumping of these assets is subject to the award of a permit by the national competent authority.

2.3.2. *OSPAR Convention*

As regards the North Sea area, dumping is also governed by the OSPAR Convention for the Protection of the Marine Environment of the North-East Atlantic of 1992. The OSPAR Convention is ratified by 15 states, including all North Sea states and the European Union, and entered into force in 1998. Its primary aim is to protect the maritime environment in the North-East Atlantic,

30 Convention on the Prevention of Marine Pollution by Dumping of Wastes and Other Matter, London, 1972 (hereinafter: London Convention).

31 1996 Protocol to the Convention on the Prevention of Marine Pollution by Dumping of Wastes and Other Matter, London, 1996 (hereinafter: London Protocol), article 23.

32 London Convention, article III(1)(a).

33 London Convention, article IV(1).

34 London Protocol, article 4 and Annex I.

which includes the North Sea. Given the potential environmentally disturbing effects emanating from abandoning disused installations or structures, the Convention also provides rules on the removal and dumping of abandoned and/or disused installations and pipelines, whereby *dumping* is defined as the deliberate disposal in the maritime area of, inter alia, offshore installations and pipelines.[35] Article 5 of Annex III of the Convention stipulates that:

> No disused offshore installation or disused offshore pipeline shall be dumped and no disused offshore installation shall be left wholly or partly in place in the maritime area without a permit issued by the competent authority of the relevant Contracting Party on a case-by-case basis. The Contracting Parties shall ensure that their authorities, when granting such permits, shall implement the relevant applicable decisions, recommendations and all other agreements adopted under the Convention.[36]

Decisions regarding dumping are taken on the basis of a case-by-case approach and require a marine environmental quality assessment. The placement of disused offshore installations or pipelines in the North-East Atlantic for other purposes than those for which they were designed and constructed is also only possible after authorization by the competent authority of the contracting party.[37] If remains of an installation or pipeline remain in situ or are placed elsewhere, contracting parties need to take appropriate measures to prevent or eliminate pollution caused by accidents.

Whereas Annex III of OSPAR requires a permit to dump or leave in place a disused installation or pipeline, contracting parties also need to take into account OSPAR Decision 98/3 on the Disposal of Disused Offshore Installations. This binding Decision goes a step further than the Convention as it in principle prohibits the dumping or the leaving in place of disused offshore installations[38] and limits the exceptions for which a permit can be awarded. A permit is only possible for 1) all or part of the footings of a steel installation weighing more than 10,000 tonnes in air, placed in the maritime area before 9 February 1999, 2) a gravity-based or floating concrete installation or a concrete installation constituting a concrete anchor base, 3) any other disused offshore installation, when exceptional and unforeseen circumstances resulting from structural damage or deterioration, or from some other cause presenting equivalent difficulties, can be demonstrated.[39] Since the OSPAR decisions

35 Convention for the Protection of the Marine Environment in the North-East Atlantic, Paris, 1992 (Hereinafter OSPAR Convention), article 1(f)(ii)(2).

36 OSPAR Convention, Annex III, article 5(1).

37 OSPAR Convention, Annex III, articles 8 and 10(d).

38 OSPAR Decision 98/3 on the Disposal of Disused Offshore Installations, Sintra, 22–23 July 1998 (hereinafter OSPAR Decision 98/3), point 2.

39 OSPAR Decision 98/3, point 3 and Annex I.

only apply to offshore installations, the more general rules of Annex III of the OSPAR Convention remain in place for disused submarine pipelines.

2.4. THE NORTH SEA

The seabed of the North Sea qualifies as a continental shelf. The delimitation of the shelf between the states bordering the North Sea is based on a number of bilateral agreements.[40] As all North Sea states also are party to UNCLOS, the above rules on offshore decommissioning of installations and structures apply to them. However, in practice the extent to which disused installations and structures will be removed may differ, as the continental shelves of the Netherlands and Denmark have relatively shallow waters and the continental shelves of the United Kingdom and Norway are situated much deeper. As oil and gas production in the North Sea area started in the early 1970s, the question of decommissioning is now becoming more and more relevant. Experience with decommissioning is gradually being developed. The assessments involve not only an assessment of complete or partial removal but also of the extent to which the removal obligations apply to disused pipelines and cables, and more recently, the question whether or not the installations and pipelines can be re-used. So far these assessments are solely based on provisions of international law as EU law only relates to exploration and production of offshore hydrocarbons and offshore safety. A common approach with regard to decommissioning and re-use is missing.

3. OFFSHORE DECOMMISSIONING IN THE NETHERLANDS

3.1. INTRODUCTION

The discovery of the Groningen (onshore) gas field in 1959, amongst others, led to an increased interest in exploration activities offshore. The discovery of the first offshore gas field in 1970 (Block L 10) was followed by several other, relatively small, gas fields and the construction of three main gas transportation systems: NGT or Noordgastransport (from L10 to Uithuizen), WGT or Westgastransport (from K10 to Den Helder) and NOGAT (F15 also to Den Helder), which also is connected to the Danish continental shelf. Oil discoveries have been less. After the find of the first offshore oil field in 1980 (block Q1) only a few other smaller oil fields were found in that area.

[40] See n 17 above.

In 2019 the oil and gas infrastructure on the Dutch Continental Shelf consists of some 600 wells at a depth of 2,000–4,000 meters, 156 platforms (of which 151 are steel jackets and monopiles, two are steel gravity-based structures and two are concrete gravity-based structures), and about 3,000 kilometers of pipelines. The first offshore decommissioning started around the 1990s and is expected to peak around 2023. Total decommissioning costs offshore are estimated at approximately €5 billion.[41]

3.2. EXPLORATION AND PRODUCTION OF HYDROCARBONS

The use of the sea and the seabed requires a specific authorization, depending on the activity involved. For the purpose of this chapter, we need to distinguish between the exploration, production and storage of hydrocarbons, which are governed by the Mining Act and other (non-energy) activities requiring a permit on the basis of the Water Act (*Waterwet*).[42]

3.2.1. Licensing Regime

The exploration and production of hydrocarbons are governed by the Mining Act (*Mijnbouwwet*).[43] This Act has applied since 2003 and replaces, amongst others, the Continental Shelf Mining Act of 1965 (CS Mining Act). It governs exploration and production of minerals (including oil and gas) onshore and offshore as long as these minerals are located at a depth of at least 100 meters.[44] The Act is supplemented by secondary legislation, i.e. a Royal Decree (*Mijnbouwbesluit*) and a Ministerial Decree (*Mijnbouwregeling*).

The Mining Act provides for a licensing regime based on the principles of the EU Hydrocarbons Licensing Directive (Directive 94/22/EC). Whereas

---

41 See draft explanatory note to a Bill amending the Mining Act (p. 1), https://www.internetconsultatie.nl/mijnbouwwerken. According to R. Verstegen at the 29th European Energy Law Seminar at The Hague in 2019, decommissioning costs in 2015 amounted to €0.1 billion in 2015 and are expected to amount to €5 billion.

42 Act of 29 January 2009, regarding regulation concerning the management and use of water systems (*Wet van 29 januari 2009, houdende regels met betrekking tot het beheer en gebruik van Watersystemen), Staatsblad* 29 January 2009, number 107 (hereinafter Water Act). Please note that since 24 June 2015 a special regime has applied for the development of wind energy offshore, see *Wet van 24 juni 2015, houdende regels omtrent windenergie op zee (Wet windenergie op zee)*, Staatsblad 30 June 2015, 261.

43 Act of 31 October 2002, regarding regulations concerning the exploration for and the production of minerals and concerning mining related activities (*Wet van 31 oktober 2002, houdende regels met betrekking tot het onderzoek naar en het winnen van delfstoffen en met betrekking tot met de mijnbouw verwante activiteiten), Staatsblad* 14 November 2002, number 542 (hereinafter Mining Act). The Mining Act uses the term minerals (*delfstoffen*) to delimitate its working sphere.

44 Mining Act, article 2(1)–(2).

the CS Mining Act provided for an exclusive exploration and production license, the new Mining Act also introduced a separate storage license.[45] Since the Environmental Management Act does not apply on the Dutch Continental Shelf, the Mining Act also provides for a separate environmental permit.[46] Surprisingly the Mining Act does not provide for a license for offshore pipelines and cables. However, article 94 of the Mining Decree requires a permit for the construction of offshore cables and pipelines, i.e. cables and pipelines connecting two mining installations or a mining installation and another installation for, respectively, the transport of electricity or electronic signals, or the transport of substances.[47] Although its legal basis is unclear, this permit governs the construction of pipelines and cables between mining installations and/or the shore but only as far as necessary to ensure its technical integrity and to limit the risk of damage. Consequently, it does not govern the exploitation of these pipelines or provide any rules with regard to its owners and/or applicants.

Exploration and production of hydrocarbons require two separate licenses. An exploration license is usually awarded following a process of competitive bidding and if an 'economically exploitable quantity of hydrocarbons' has been discovered, the holder of the exploration license will usually be awarded a production license. A prerequisite for the award of both licenses is that the applicant is technically and financially capable to carry out the proposed activities.[48] Licenses are usually awarded to a consortium of several oil companies.[49] By contrast to other North Sea states, the Dutch competent authority (Minister of Economic Affairs and Climate) is not involved in establishing the consortium or in drafting the Joint Operating Agreement.

3.2.2. *State Participation*

Since the development of the Groningen field the Dutch state has always participated in hydrocarbons production. In order to stimulate exploration, state participation applies to exploration activities since 2000. In practice the state participates via a limited liability company called BV Energie Beheer Nederland or EBN. The shares in EBN are held by the Dutch state, represented by the Ministry of Economic Affairs and Climate. EBN is, however, not a licensee but a non-operating partner on the basis of an Agreement of Cooperation. Depending on the year in which a license was awarded its participating share can vary from

---

45 Mining Act, article 6 for the exploration and production of minerals and article 25 for the storage of substances.

46 Mining Act, article 40.

47 Mining Decree, article 94.

48 It goes beyond the scope of this chapter to elaborate on the Mining Act's licensing system. For an analysis, see M.M. Roggenkamp, 'Energy Law in the Netherlands' in M.M. Roggenkamp et al, *Energy Law in Europe*, Oxford University Press, Oxford, 2016.

49 Mining Act, article 22.

40 per cent to 50 per cent. However, as of the 2003 Mining Act their share is set at 40 per cent.[50] When participating in exploration and/or production, EBN will pay its share of 40 per cent or 50 per cent of the activities and receive an equal part of the profit. It should be noted that in practice EBN also participates in offshore pipeline companies (e.g. WGT and NOGAT) with a share varying between 40 per cent and 50 per cent, either on a contractual basis or as a shareholder.

3.2.3. *Mining Installations*

The Mining Act makes a distinction between so-called *mining works* and *mining installations*. Whereas the former term denotes all works necessary for the exploration, production and storage of minerals, the term installation applies to all equipment that needs to be anchored on or is situated above surface waters. All offshore oil and gas installations necessary for the exploration and production of hydrocarbons thus qualify as mining installations, including accommodation platforms for offshore workers.[51] The holder of an exploration and/or production license is entitled to construct and operate mining installations as long as it takes into account all safety and labor provisions and the earlier-mentioned environmental permits. Pipelines and cables between mining installations and between mining installations and facilities onshore do not fall qualify as a mining installation.

3.3. DECOMMISSIONING

The distinction that is made in international law between installations and pipelines and cables can also be found in the Dutch Mining Act. Below we will first discuss the rules governing the removal of mining installations and then we will examine the situation with regard to disused offshore pipelines and cables.

3.3.1. *Mining Installations*

The Dutch Continental Shelf consists of shallow waters with depths of less than 50–60 meters. In addition, the offshore reservoirs are relatively small. Consequently, Dutch offshore platforms are also rather small and lightweight. Approximately 50 per cent of all platforms on the continental shelf weigh less than 1,500 tonnes and 75 per cent weigh less than 2,500 tonnes.[52] According to UNCLOS and the IMO Guidelines all platforms should be totally removed.

---

50 Chapter 5.2.1 and 5.2.2 Mining Act.

51 Mining Act, article 1 (m)–(n).

52 EBN, *Focus on Dutch Oil & Gas* (2015), p. 42.

The Mining Act acknowledges this principle and requires a complete removal of disused mining installations as well as materials near the facility.[53] The term *disused* is not defined in the Act, but it appears from the explanatory memorandum of the Act that the removal provision aims at assuring that installations that no longer are in use for, inter alia, the exploration or production of minerals, should be removed.[54] The term *disused* can thus be interpreted as referring to a situation where a platform is no longer used for a mining activity. The removal obligation is not limited to the platform itself but pertains to the wells, since they are part of the mining installation.[55] Wells that are permanently abandoned need to be sealed by using cement or an equivalent alternative and the casing needs to be removed down to six meters below the seabed.[56]

The removal obligation rests with the operator in case of a joint venture or with the last license holder in case of a single license holder.[57] When the license has lapsed, the obligation rests with the last operator or license holder.[58] The fact that the removal obligation always rests on one party, either the single license holder or the operator, streamlines communication, since the Ministry will only have to interact with one interlocutor on the issue of decommissioning. Given the significant costs involved in the removal of installations, there is always a risk that the operator or licensees are no longer willing or capable to pay for the removal costs once production has ceased. In order to prevent such situation, the Minister may require some sort of financial security such as a bank guarantee or any equivalent from the operator or licensee to cover the future decommissioning costs. It is up to the Minister to decide when such financial guarantee is needed, the kind of guarantee and the amount of the financial security.[59] To date, however, the Minister has not made use of this instrument.[60] Given the participation of EBN and tax allowances it is estimated that tax payers carry 73 per cent of the total cost of decommissioning.

The removal of a mining installation is subject to a removal plan.[61] The removal plan specifies: 1) the way in which the mining installation will be removed as well as any scrap metal and other material in its vicinity; 2) the way the mining installation and related materials will be transported after they have been removed; 3) the final destination of the installation, all related materials and the waste from the platform; and 4) a timeline within which these activities will

53 Mining Act, article 44(1).

54 *Kamerstukken II* 29 September 1998, 26219, nr. 3, p. 26.

55 Mining Decree, article 2.

56 Mining Regulation, article 8.5.3.2.

57 Mining Act, articles 44(5) and 41(4).

58 Ibid.

59 Mining Act, articles 47(2) and 46(3).

60 Changes to the regime as suggested in a draft Bill amending the Mining Act. See: https://www.internetconsultatie.nl/mijnbouwwerken.

61 Mining Decree, article 60(1).

be performed.[62] A removal plan has to be submitted for approval to the Minister eight weeks prior to the planned removal date.[63] By contrast to decommissioning onshore, where a removal plan needs to be submitted within one year after production has ceased,[64] the Mining Act does not provide such detailed guidance for decommissioning offshore as it merely states that the Minister may set a time limit for decommissioning.[65] According to the explanatory memorandum of the Act this provision is meant as a means to force unwilling operators into fulfilling their removal obligation, but also as a mechanism to allow for a postponement of the removal obligation in case a mining installation continues to be used as a part of the offshore gas transport infrastructure.[66]

3.3.2. Decommissioning Pipelines and Cables

Similarly to UNCLOS and the IMO Guidelines, the Mining Act does not contain a removal obligation for disused pipelines and cables but leaves it to the discretion of the Minister whether or not to require a complete or partial removal.[67] However, a distinction needs to be made between types of pipelines and cables. Those which are part of the mining installation need to be removed in conjunction with the installation. The extent to which other disused pipelines and cables need to removed, will be based on an assessment of the costs and benefits of removal, especially in relation to the freedom of navigation and the environmental consequences caused by removal and non-removal respectively. Pipelines constructed after 2016 have to be removed, unless the assessment shows that the social costs of removal do not outweigh the social benefits.[68] In case of removal, the obligation lies with the pipeline or cable manager (*beheerder*) or the last pipeline or cable manager.[69] In contrast to the provisions pertaining to mining installations, the Minister cannot set a deadline for removal of a pipeline or cable.

However, so far disused pipelines usually are left in place as long as they are 'clean and safe'.[70] In that case, the pipeline or cable manager has to inform the Minister of its intention.[71] The Minister can instruct the manager on how to leave the pipeline or cable behind. In addition he can oblige the pipeline

---

62 Mining Decree, article 61(2).

63 Mining Decree, article 60(2).

64 Mining Decree, article 39(1).

65 Mining Act, article 44(4).

66 *Kamerstukken II* 29 September 1998, 26219, nr. 3, p. 27.

67 Mining Act, article 45(1).

68 Beleidsnote Noorzee 2016–2012, p. 49. See: https://www.rijksoverheid.nl/documenten/beleidsnota-s/2015/12/14/beleidsnota-noordzee-2016-2021.

69 *Kamerstukken II* 29 September 1998, 26219, nr. 3, pp. 27–28.

70 This is especially the case since pipelines and cables are usually located under the seafloor rather than on the seafloor.

71 Mining Decree, article 104(1).

manager to periodically check the pipeline and stipulate remedial actions.[72] In practice, this may be difficult to enforce as there is no guarantee that the pipeline manager will still exist in future. In this regard it may be relevant that the Minister, as in case of mining installations, may request a financial guarantee from the pipeline or cable manager to cover the costs of removal.[73]

3.4. CURRENT PRACTICE

Since the 1990s around 1.000 production locations have been abandoned and this has resulted in the decommissioning of 717 wells, 7 subsea facilities and 31 surface installations (top sides), of which 14 have been re-used.[74] In addition, about 39 pipelines have been removed but also more than 10 pipelines have been abandoned but not been removed. In the coming years more reservoirs will be depleted and wells as well installations be abandoned. In addition, other energy activities of the North Sea are being investigated. This has led to a new focus on the potential re-use of installations and pipelines. By re-using these facilities a decision on removal can be postponed.

4. RE-USE AS A NEW PARADIGM

4.1. INTRODUCTION

Installations can be re-used for several reasons and purposes, which vary from re-using (parts of) the installations as an artificial reef, re-using installations, wells and reservoirs for the permanent storage of carbon dioxide or re-using platforms for 'power-to-x' technologies, which involve the conversion of offshore-produced electricity into alternative energy carriers such as hydrogen and ammonia. Although the IMO Guidelines and the OSPAR Convention facilitate a re-use of installations, their focus was primarily usage as artificial reefs.[75] Only in more recent times, have other re-use options than merely rigs-to-reefs been considered as a viable alternative. Consequently, the Minister of Economic Affairs and Climate is preparing an amendment to the Mining Act to promote the re-use of offshore assets.[76] When considering re-use of installations,

---

72 Mining Decree, article 104(2)–(3).

73 Mining Act, article 48.

74 Figures provided by Nexstep October 2019. See also: https://www.nexstep.nl/re-use/past-projects/.

75 IMO Guidelines, article 3.4.1. even explicitly mentions the enhancement of living resources as a potential re-use option.

76 A draft Bill to amend the Mining Act and enable, inter alia, the re-use of installations has been published for consultation during spring 2019. See: *Kamerstukken II*, 13 December 2017 (*Duurzame ontwikkeling en beleid*), 30196, nr. G, p.2.

two prime issues need to be addressed. First, does the intended re-use involve the entire installation and how is the new use of the installation regulated? Secondly, what does any re-use mean for any decommissioning in the long term?

4.2. LEGAL ISSUES

Although the IMO Guidelines and OSPAR Decision 98/3 explicitly allow for the re-use of offshore platforms, the OSPAR Decision 98/3 prohibits leaving installations in place unless these installations have found a new purpose regulated by the national authorities. When considering the earlier mentioned re-use options, it is important to identify whether these alternatives are being regulated. So far, this is only the case for the permanent storage of carbon dioxide offshore. Following the need to transpose Directive 2009/31/EC on the geological storage of carbon dioxide into national law, the Mining Act has been amended and chapter 3 of the Mining Act now provides for a licensing regime for carbon storage. Although a hydrocarbons production license and a carbon storage license are two different licenses, both licenses (and installations) fall under the scope of the Mining Act. However, when (part of) a disused installation is transformed into an artificial reef or used for converting electricity into another gas than natural gas, the installation can no longer be considered as a 'mining installation' and thus falls outside the scope of the Mining Act. It therefore needs to be assessed whether these activities and installations can be governed by another legal or regulatory framework.

The issue of re-using an installation or part of it as an artificial reef has been discussed for several decades. Will such re-use promote biodiversity or should it be considered as some sort of waste and thus be prohibited? The OSPAR Guidelines on Artificial Reefs in relation to Living Marine resources of 2012 provide clear guidance on the issue, as they state that 'no materials should be used for the construction of artificial reefs which constitute wastes or other matter whose disposal at sea is otherwise prohibited.'[77] However, these guidelines are non-binding and still leave some room for re-using a disused platform as an artificial reef. In order to enable such a re-use on the Dutch Continental Shelf and to circumvent the situation that a disused mining installation has to be entirely removed, it would be necessary to find another legal basis. The only alternative would be a permit under the Water Act, since this Act regulates all activities taking place in onshore and offshore waters unless these activities are governed by specific sectoral laws such as the Mining Act. Does the Water Act permit the re-use of a disused installation as an artificial reef? A permit under

77 OSPAR Guidelines on Artificial Reefs in relation to Living Marine Resources, Bonn, 2012 (hereinafter OSPAR Guidelines on Artificial Reefs), point 13.

the Water Act also requires a new use and an assessment whether the artificial reef can be considered as an installation. To the extent that an artificial reef is an installation, a water permit can be awarded on the basis of article 6.13 of the Water Decree. Such a permit can be awarded under certain conditions, such as the need to compensate for any negative environmental impact and, if necessary, cease the permitted activity.[78] In theory, the permit could also include a removal obligation and the possibility to require a financial guarantee.[79] Whether it is feasible to remove an artificial reef remains to be seen.

Like artificial reefs, the re-use of installations for the production of hydrogen and/or ammonia is not governed by the Mining Act.[80] This means that the installations needed for these activities have to be permitted under the Water Act. By contrast to artificial reefs, the situation is rather straightforward, as these installations still can be considered as an installation and therefore a water permit can be awarded for the installation in place, although for another purpose then originally intended.[81] The same may apply to offshore pipelines which no longer will be used to transport hydrocarbons. A pipeline transporting hydrogen or any other chemical substance from an offshore installation to shore will not qualify as a pipeline under the Mining Decree and will thus need a permit on the basis of the Water Decree. As a consequence, not only does a new permit need to be applied for but in addition the re-used installations and pipelines would no longer be subject to the operational rules of the Mining Act and/or Mining Decree. However, at the moment the Water Act does not provide for such operational and safety rules. This could thus result in a regulatory gap, which needs to be addressed.

Re-use of installations can serve many purposes and the extent to which it is feasible is not only a matter of analyzing the economic, legal and technical challenges. However, with regard to the issue of decommissioning it will merely postpone the decision to decommission the installation, as a re-used installation may also become disused, maybe except for a re-use as an artificial reef. In order to deal with such postponed disuse, the parties involved and the legislator are confronted with several issues. Is the original licensee exempted from all decommissioning obligations if an installation is re-used or is the original licensee still responsible for some of the decommissioning obligations? Is it sufficient to include a decommissioning obligation in the new water permit or should the Water Act be amended so as to address the decommissioning obligations?

---

78 Water Act, article 6.20(1).

79 Water Act, article 6.20(1).

80 An interesting observation in this respect is that the production of molecules in 'power-to-x' activities is not covered by the Mining Act, but that the storage of molecules in the subsoil *would* be covered by the Mining Act. This is the case since the Mining Act regulates all subsoil storage of substances.

81 Water Decree, article 6.13(1)(c).

4.3. A NEW APPROACH REQUIRED?

The current regulatory framework for offshore energy activities does not provide any standardized and streamlined procedure for re-using mining installations. Although the Water Act could facilitate re-use for other purposes than those provided for by the Mining Act, the provisions in the Water Act are limited and provide for a rather ad hoc solution. Given the fact that it is envisaged that many other energy activities will be developed offshore and these activities require a stable regulatory framework instead of ad hoc decisions, it could be argued that the entire legal framework should be amended so that the construction and exploitation of offshore installations are governed by one single Act instead of several independent but related sectoral laws.

5. CONCLUSIONS

Decommissioning of oil and gas installations on the Dutch Continental Shelf is based on the main principle of international law that disused installations in shallow waters need to be entirely removed. Although some experience has been gained with the removal of disused installations and pipelines, large-scale decommissioning is expected around 2023. Given new technologies and climate-change mitigation concerns, several re-use options are emerging, which may result in the award of new permits for other uses of existing installations and an extension of some decommissioning strategies. Despite the advantages of re-using installations, this option should not be used as a loophole to circumvent existing removal obligations. Although the current legal framework does not seem to prohibit the re-use of installations and pipelines, all three re-use options briefly discussed in this chapter suffer from ambiguities, uncertainties and barriers in the regulatory framework that may hinder their offshore operationalization. To facilitate re-use and the emerging new energy activities offshore, a thorough revision of the current legal framework governing decommissioning and offshore permitting is necessary. This should be done for the Dutch Continental Shelf but preferably for the entire North Sea area.

CHAPTER XV

DECOMMISSIONING OF OFFSHORE INSTALLATIONS UPON THE UK CONTINENTAL SHELF

Greg Gordon and John Paterson

1. INTRODUCTION

The decommissioning of an offshore installation is a complex and multi-faceted process encompassing cessation of production, the plugging and abandonment of wells, cleaning operations (which may involve the release of hydrocarbons and the use of chemicals), and the cutting, dismantling, lifting and transportation of a range of materials, some of which are potentially hazardous, for eventual re-use, recycling or disposal. All of this frequently takes place against a background of imperfect knowledge as to the state of the facilities being dismantled and in sometimes challenging offshore conditions. It is a process that is attended by significant commercial and physical risks and which involves both detailed legal regulation and an often-complex web of contractual relations between the operator of the installation and a host of service providers.

Some statistics may help to provide a sense of the scale of the task of decommissioning the infrastructure upon the United Kingdom Continental Shelf ("UKCS"). In excess of 500 installations have been emplaced on the UKCS since 1967, varying in type from small-scale subsea installations to truly monolithic gravity-based concrete structures;[1] it is anticipated that between 2018 and 2027, 71 of those will have been decommissioned.[2] Some 5,000 wells have been drilled and some 3,000 pipelines laid, with a cumulative length of 15,000 kilometres.[3]

---

1 Oil and Gas Authority ("OGA"), *Decommissioning Strategy* (London, 2016), available for download at: www.https://www.ogauthority.co.uk/media/1020/oga_decomm_strategy.pdf, p. 5. All websites referred to in this chapter were last accessed on 2 September 2019.

2 OGUK, *Decommissioning Insight 2018* (London, March 2019), available at: https://oilandgasuk.co.uk/wp-content/uploads/2019/03/OGUK-Decommissioning-Insight-Report-2018.pdf, p. 36.

3 OGA, n. 1 above.

The UK Government estimates that around 10 per cent of the UK's offshore infrastructure has been decommissioned to date.[4] Estimates of the total cost of this decommissioning activity (past and future) have varied significantly. Around 2010, £20 billion was a commonly-given figure.[5] More recently, cost estimates have risen, with the Wood Review suggesting a range of between £35 and £50 billion.[6] In 2017, the Oil and Gas Authority ("OGA")[7] estimated a cost of £59.7 billion, whilst setting £39 billion as an aspirational target of what could be achieved if the industry were to be able to unlock cost savings through a combination of experiential learning and improved efficiencies.[8] The 2019 estimate from the OGA has adjusted the projected total down to £49 billion.[9] While it is too early to state with confidence that cost estimates have peaked,[10] there are some signs that the efficiencies to which the OGA referred are starting to take effect. For instance, the closeout report for the Rose field reveals a significant saving as a result of the decommissioning work being undertaken as part of a larger campaign alongside the neighbouring Stamford field.[11] Similarly, the OGA's 2018 Cost Estimate Report highlights significant savings made in other projects as a result of simplified methodologies and technical innovation.[12] The OGA is in the process of undertaking work intended to guide contracting methodologies so as to reduce costs. Irrespective of such innovation, decommissioning costs upon the UKCS remain high compared to many other jurisdictions, due to a combination of the sheer scale of some of the first-generation installations, deep

---

4 Department for Business, Energy and Industrial Strategy ("BEIS"), Strengthening the UK's Offshore Oil and Gas Industry, (London, March 2019), available at: https://assets.publishing.service.gov.uk/government/uploads/system/uploads/attachment_data/file/785544/strengthening-uk-offshore-oil-gas-decommissioning-industry-cfe.pdf, p. 9.

5 See, e.g., Oil & Gas UK, *2010 Oil & Gas UK Activity Survey*, p. 17, available at: http://oilandgasuk.co.uk/wp-content/uploads/2015/05/EC020.pdf.

6 Sir I. Wood, *UKCS Maximising Recovery Review: Final Report*, available at: www.gov.uk/government/uploads/system/uploads/attachment_data/file/471452/UKCS_Maximising_Recovery_Review_FINAL_72pp_locked.pdf, p. 50.

7 The Oil and Gas Authority is discussed in greater detail in section 3, below.

8 OGA, *UKCS Decommissioning: 2017 Cost Estimate Report* (London, 2017), available at: https://www.ogauthority.co.uk/media/4742/ukcs-decommissioning-cost-report-v2.pdf, p. 16.

9 OGA, *UKCS Decommissioning: 2019 Cost Estimate Report* (London, 2018), available at: https://www.ogauthority.co.uk/media/5906/decommissioning-estimate-cost-report-2019.pdf, p. 4.

10 For more information on the OGA's estimating methodology see *2019 Cost Estimate Report*, pp. 30–32.

11 Spirit Energy, *Rose Decommissioning Close-Out Report*, 2018, available at: https://assets.publishing.service.gov.uk/government/uploads/system/uploads/attachment_data/file/745345/Rose_Close_Out_Report.pdf, pp. 11, 13 and 29.

12 OGA, *UKCS Decommissioning: 2018 Cost Estimate Report* (London, 2018), available at: https://www.ogauthority.co.uk/media/4999/decommissioning-a5-2018-pdf-version.pdf. See the brief case-studies relating to flowline recovery using Anchor Handling Vessel (p. 6) and plugging and abandonment practice (p. 17), each of which effected budgetary savings of around 30% compared to the established methodology.

water, technically-demanding subsea wells[13] and the particular demands of the UK regulatory regime which ranks, alongside others in the North East Atlantic area, as one of the most demanding in the world.

Following this introductory section, this chapter shall be divided into three main parts. It will commence by outlining the relevant international law standards, focusing in particular upon the regime under the OSPAR Convention,[14] which is especially relevant as it contains a more rigid and exacting set of requirements than are to be found in other international law instruments bearing on the topic. It will then go on to consider the UK's domestic decommissioning regime before considering the contractual practices which are beginning to emerge in decommissioning projects.

2. INTERNATIONAL LAW

Outside of the territorial sea, the decommissioning of offshore installations involves a consideration of the law relating to the continental shelf. Issues of international law therefore arise, at both a global and regional level. Each shall be considered in turn.

2.1. THE LAW OF THE SEA

At a global level, the international law relating to the removal of offshore installations is comprised of one article in UNCLOS,[15] supplemented by the non-binding IMO Guidelines.[16] The provisions of the London Convention on Dumping[17] and its 1996 Protocol[18] are relevant to the question of how an offshore installation may be disposed of.[19]

---

13 Ibid., p. 11.

14 See n. 37 below.

15 Art 60(3).

16 International Maritime Organization, "Guidelines and Standards for the Removal of Offshore Installations and Structures on the Continental Shelf and in the Exclusive Economic Zone" (1989).

17 Convention on the Prevention of Marine Pollution by Dumping of Wastes and Other Matter (signed 29 December 1972, entered into force 30 August 1975) (1972) 11 *International Legal Materials* 1294.

18 Protocol to the Convention on the Prevention of Marine Pollution by Dumping of Wastes and Other Matter (signed 11 June 1996, entered into force 24 March 2006) (1997) 36 *International Legal Materials* 1.

19 UNCLOS Art 210(6), provides, "National laws, regulations and measures shall be no less effective in preventing, reducing and controlling such pollution than the global rules and standards". Beckman argues that this is in effect a reference to the London Convention, and arguably also to the Protocol. R. Beckman, "Decommissioning of Offshore Installations and Structures" in H.M. Nordquist et al (eds) *Regulation of Continental Shelf Development: Rethinking International Standards* (Brill 2014) pp. 259–280 at p. 270.

Taking these provisions together, global international law provides for a legal regime possessing the following features:

- The law relating to the removal of offshore installations is concerned principally with ensuring safety of navigation, not environmental protection.[20] The law relating to the disposal of waste offshore, by contrast, is significantly concerned with environmental protection.[21]
- The law does not universally mandate the complete removal of offshore installations. Although UNCLOS speaks of the "removal" of redundant offshore installations, it is plain from the fact that it also adverts to the need to provide "appropriate publicity ... to the depth, position and dimensions of any installations or structures not entirely removed" that this is a qualified obligation.[22] Moreover, the IMO Guidelines offer only qualified support for the principle of complete removal. While those Guidelines envisage that installations weighing less than 4,000 tonnes in air and standing in shallow water[23] will ordinarily be removed in their entirety, outside of the specific context of installations which intrude upon shipping lanes[24] there is no absolute requirement for complete removal. Such removal is not required where this is "not technically feasible or would involve extreme cost, or an unacceptable risk to personnel or the marine environment."[25]
- Moving on from the topic of removal of offshore installations and turning to the topic of their disposal at sea, international law presently follows a bifurcated path, with some nations being bound only by the relatively permissive provisions of the London Dumping Convention, as originally adopted,[26] and others having subscribed to the more restrictive provisions of the London Convention Protocol.[27] However, in the specific context of the disposal of offshore installations, the difference is not as dramatic as might first appear. The London Dumping Convention divides wastes into three categories, in accordance with three Annexes to the Convention.

---

20 See UNCLOS Art 60(3); Art 3.7, IMO Guidelines (1989).

21 See e.g. UNCLOS Art 210.

22 UNCLOS Art 60(3).

23 I.e., water of less than 75m depth, or 100m if the installation was emplaced before 1 January 1998: IMO Guidelines, paras. 3.1 and 3.2.

24 As noted above, the IMO Guidelines provide that such installations must be removed in their entirety: para. 3.7.

25 IMO Guidelines para. 3.5.

26 The Convention on the Prevention of Marine Pollution by Dumping of Wastes and Other Matter 1972.

27 1996 Protocol to the Convention on Prevention of Marine Pollution by Dumping of Wastes and Other Matter 1972.

> Only Annex I materials are prohibited from being dumped; Annex II materials can only be dumped after a special permit has been obtained, while the dumping of Annex III materials can be authorised by the issue of a general permit. The London Convention Protocol begins from the premise that dumping at sea is prohibited.[28] This is, however, subject to the proviso that the dumping of some specified forms of wastes[29] is acceptable, upon receipt of a permit which may only be granted if certain limited conditions are met.[30] The abandonment or toppling at site of platforms or other man-made structures at sea, for the sole purpose of deliberate disposal is expressly included in the definition of dumping;[31] however "vessels and platforms or other man-made structures at sea"[32] are listed among the Annex I list of wastes that may be considered for dumping. The Protocol further stipulates that "[p]articular attention shall be paid to opportunities to avoid dumping in favour of environmentally preferable alternatives".[33] This, together with the Protocol's adoption of the precautionary principle[34] as well as the "polluter pays" principle,[35] means that anyone proposing to dump an installation or structure would have to demonstrate that there were no environmentally preferable options and that appropriate preventive measures were being taken "when there is reason to believe that wastes or other matter introduced into the marine environment are likely to cause harm even when there is no conclusive evidence to prove a causal relation between inputs and their effects".[36] However, where these provisions can be satisfied, a permit to dump could be obtained.

It would, therefore, seem to be fair to characterise the globally-applicable international legal obligations – even after the advent of the 1996 Protocol – as somewhat open-textured and quite nuanced in nature: generally antagonistic to dumping as a matter of principle but admitting of exceptions that require the balancing of risks and benefits and permitting a relatively broad range of outcomes, and driven in large measure by the facts and circumstances of the individual case.

---

28 1996 Protocol, Article 4(1.1).

29 1996 Protocol, Annex 1(1.1)–(1.8).

30 The assessment procedure for determining the grant of a permit is set out in Annex 2 to the 1996 Protocol.

31 1996 Protocol, Article 1(4.2).

32 1996 Protocol, Annex 1(1.4).

33 1996 Protocol, Article 4(1.2).

34 1996 Protocol, Article 3 (1).

35 1996 Protocol, Article 3(2).

36 1996 Protocol, Article 3(1).

2.2. OSPAR: THE POSITION IN THE NORTH EAST ATLANTIC AREA

Upon the UKCS, however, OSPAR,[37] the regional convention relevant to North East Atlantic Area, is of greater immediate relevance than global international law. This regime has, through amendment, come to be more rigid, prescriptive and exacting than the provisions contained in general international law. In discussing international law, this chapter shall therefore focus in particular upon the provisions of OSPAR.[38]

2.2.1. OSPAR 1992

When first promulgated, OSPAR's provisions relative to the decommissioning of offshore installations were broadly similar to those imposed by general international law. It defines dumping as including specifically "any deliberate disposal in the maritime area of ... (2) offshore installations and offshore pipelines",[39] but not "the leaving wholly or partly in place of a disused offshore installation or disused offshore pipeline, provided that any such operation takes place in accordance with any relevant provision of the Convention and with other relevant international law".[40] Thereafter, the Convention goes on to set out a position that is similar in all important respects to that discussed above in relation to UNCLOS 1982 and the London Dumping Convention. Article 5(1), for example, provides that

> [n]o disused offshore installation or disused offshore pipeline shall be dumped and no disused offshore installation shall be left wholly or partly in place in the maritime area without a permit issued by the competent authority of the relevant Contracting Party on a case-by-case basis.

Similarly, Articles 8 and 10 of Annex III are open to the possibility of leaving installations in place or emplacing them on the seabed for purposes other than

37 The Convention for the Protection of the Marine Environment of the North-East Atlantic of 1992. The Convention is generally known as OSPAR as it is the successor to the Oslo Convention for the Prevention of Marine Pollution by Dumping from Ships and Aircraft 1972 and Paris Convention for the Prevention of Marine Pollution from Land-based Sources 1974.

38 For a fuller account of the international law regime, see e.g. R. Beckman, "Decommissioning of Offshore Installations and Structures" in H.M. Nordquist et al (eds), *Regulation of Continental Shelf Development: Rethinking International Standards* (BRILL 2014) 259–280; L. Moller, "UN Law on Decommissioning Offshore Installations" in M. Hammerson and N. Antonas (eds), *Oil and Gas Decommissioning: Law, Policy and Comparative Practice* (2nd edition, Globe Law and Business 2016) 21–43C.

39 OSPAR 1992, Article 1(f).

40 OSPAR 1992, Article 1(g).

those for which they were originally intended – in other words, their re-use as artificial reefs. This will only be possible, however, where it is specifically authorised by the competent authority of the Contracting Party[41] and in accordance with guidelines to be drawn up by the OSPAR Commission.[42]

Thus, OSPAR was initially an essentially process-driven instrument which required due regard to be had to high-level principles while providing Member States with significant room for manoeuvre in their implementation. It was not a highly prescriptive instrument. This, however, was to change as a result of the Brent Spar incident.[43]

The Brent Spar was a 14,500-tonne floating steel structure intended as an oil storage and tanker-loading facility to be used on an interim basis until a pipeline could be built to transport hydrocarbons from the Brent field to the UK mainland. Once the pipeline became operational, the installation fell redundant and preparations were made for its decommissioning and disposal. After an extended period of discussion between Shell and the UK Government involving the consideration of a range of disposal options, and in compliance with the provisions of international and domestic law, Shell's plan for deep-water disposal was approved by the Government on the basis that it constituted the Best Practicable Environmental Option (BPEO).[44] However, Greenpeace, the environmental NGO, strongly objected to this outcome, occupied the installation and mounted a high-profile campaign to have the decision reversed. Under significant consumer pressure, in particular to its downstream operations in continental Europe,[45] and to the displeasure of the UK Government,[46] Shell agreed to re-open the question of how Brent Spar was to be disposed of.[47] As well as developing new in-house ideas for disposal it held an open call for proposals and organised a structured stakeholder dialogue process in order to enhance the transparency of the decision-making procedure. Using this process, a list of proposals was eventually narrowed down to two options: the original deep-water disposal plan and the re-use of sections of the Brent Spar in a quay expansion project in Mekjarvik, Norway.

41 OSPAR 1992, Annex III, Article 8.

42 OSPAR 1992, Annex III, Article 10(d).

43 For a full account of the Brent Spar incident, see G. Brownless and J. Paterson, "Complex and contentious risk-based decision making in the field of health, safety and the environment: Comparative analysis of two UK examples", Health and Safety Executive, Research Report 448 (2006).

44 J. Paterson, "Decommissioning of Offshore Oil and Gas Installations" in G. Gordon, J. Paterson and E. Usenmez, *UK Oil and Gas Law: Current Practice and Emerging Trends Volume I:Resource Management and Regulatory Law* (Edinburgh University Press, Edinburgh 2018) ("Gordon, Paterson and Usenmez Volume I"), para. I-12.23.

45 S.C. Zyglidopoulos, "The Social and Environmental Responsibilities of Multinationals: Evidence from the Brent Spar Case" (2002) 36 *Journal of Business Ethics* 141.

46 J. Paterson, n. 44 above, para. I-12.29.

47 Ibid., paras. I-12.27–28.

The latter was ultimately chosen through the application of a set of criteria (taking account of the net energy balance, the waste hierarchy and the safety risks involved in each option) and the UK regulator authorised it on the basis that it was as least as good as the originally selected BPEO.

2.2.2. OSPAR Decision 98/3

Albeit that it was the original Oslo Convention that was in force at the relevant times during the Brent Spar case, it was clear that insofar the new OSPAR Convention simply repeated the terms of the earlier instrument, it now appeared to allow disposal options that did not enjoy public support. As such, the 1992 Convention was quickly was amended, by Decision 98/3 on the Disposal of Disused Offshore Installations,[48] ("Decision 98/3"). Echoes of Shell's Brent Spar process abound. The preamble to the Decision emphasises the significance of the waste hierarchy and intimates a strong policy preference against dumping at sea, stating that "re-use, recycling or final disposal on land will generally be the preferred option for the decommissioning of disused offshore installations in the maritime area".[49] These sentiments permeate the binding elements of the Decision. Paragraph 2 effects a general prohibition on the "dumping, and the leaving wholly or partly in place, of disused offshore installations within the maritime area." Derogation from that general prohibition is permitted, but only in certain tightly-defined circumstances. Paragraph 3 provides that derogations, involving leaving all or part of an installation in place or dumping as appropriate, may be permitted, but only if the derogation relates to:

(a) all or part of the footings of a steel installation weighing more than 10,000 tonnes[50] in air emplaced before 9 February 1999;[51]

---

48 Adopted by Ministerial Meeting in July 1998; available for download from https://www.ospar.org/documents?d=32703.

49 Preamble to Decision 98/3, Fifth recital.

50 Such derogations have been granted for NW Hutton, Miller, Murchison installations and has been sought in relation to Brent Alpha, Ninian North, Brae Alpha and Bravo and East Brae installations.

51 This differs from the equivalent provision in the IMO Guidelines in two significant respects. Firstly, it imposes a significantly stricter threshold than the IMO Guidelines, which set the limit at 4,000 tonnes. Thus under OSPAR, fewer installations will qualify to be left wholly or partly in place than would be envisaged by the IMO Guidelines. On the other hand, the cut-off date of 9 February 1999 is more than a year later than the date specified by the IMO Guidelines, which provide at para. 3.13 that no installation or structure should be emplaced on or after *1 January 1998* unless its "design and construction … is such that entire removal … would be feasible". This raises the possibility of an installation having been placed on the UKCS after 1 January 1998 but before 9 February 1999 and being allowed under OSPAR to have its footings left in place at decommissioning despite the wording of the IMO Guidelines. The crucial issue here, of course, is that while Decision 98/3 is binding, the IMO Guidelines are not.

(b) a concrete installation (including a gravity-based concrete installation, a floating installation and any concrete anchor base which results, or is likely to result, in interference with other legitimate uses of the sea);[52]
(c) any other disused offshore installation when exceptional or unforeseen circumstances resulting from structural damage or deterioration, or from some other cause presenting equivalent difficulties, can be demonstrated.[53]

A derogation may only be issued after consultation with the other Contracting Parties after the competent authority has concluded that there are "significant reasons why an alternative disposal … is preferable to re-use, recycling or final disposal on land."[54] There is no possibility for those other parties to veto the decision of the competent authority, but it may be supposed that, were significant concerns to be expressed, then a re-examination of the decision would be likely, given the likelihood of a broader public reaction.

2.3. THE PROSPECTS FOR ARTIFICIAL REEFS UPON THE UKCS

As restrictive as these derogation cases appear to be, a question increasingly asked regarding the UKCS is whether it would be possible to leave an installation in place or otherwise locate it on the seabed as an artificial reef. Generally, this would require consideration of the London Convention; in the North-East Atlantic region it would require consideration of the OSPAR Convention. In this regard, it is necessary to consider the terms of the Guidelines relating to artificial reefs that both organisations have drawn up. Despite the apparent openness of both conventions to the possibility, the Guidelines in each case appear considerably more restrictive. In the case of the London Convention, the lengthy guidance document opens with the statement that one of the objectives is "to ensure that placement of artificial reefs is not used as a mechanism to circumvent the provisions of the London Convention on the 'dumping' of waste".[55] On the other hand, a review of the Guidelines suggests that provided there is otherwise compliance with the London Convention, the option of re-using such installations as artificial reefs is not actually ruled out. For example, in discussing the materials that may be used in the construction of artificial reefs, it is provided that these can be "natural, recycled, or prefabricated".[56]

---

52 Such derogations have been granted for Frigg, MCP-01 and sought for Brent Bravo, Charlie and Delta and Dunlin Alpha installations.

53 OSPAR Decision 98/3, para. 3 and Annex 1. After being severely damaged in the catastrophic fire that killed 167 workers, Piper Alpha received such a derogation and was toppled in situ.

54 Ibid., para. 3.

55 London Convention and Protocol/UNEP, *Guidelines for the Placement of Artificial Reefs*, UNEP Regional Seas Reports and Studies No. 187, 2009, p. 1.

56 Ibid., para. 3.2.2.

Whilst a preference is stated for natural materials, the guidance is also explicit that reefs "in exposed, high energy area[s] should be built of heavy materials such as rocks, concrete and steel".[57] Nevertheless, in the section dealing specifically with platforms, it is once again made clear that: "When applying these Guidelines under the London Convention 1972, they should not be viewed as a tool for the reconsideration of dumping of wastes or other matter in contravention of Annex I to the London Convention 1972."[58]

In view of the focus of the London Convention Guidelines on the materials that may legitimately be used in the construction of an artificial reef, it is instructive to note that the OSPAR Convention itself states that: "No placement of matter in the maritime area for a purpose other than that for which it was originally designed or constructed shall take place without authorisation or regulation by the competent authority of the relevant Contracting Party."[59] The possibility that the issue will be subject to further specification is then raised: "Such authorisation or regulation shall be in accordance with the relevant applicable criteria, guidelines and procedures adopted by the Commission".[60] In terms familiar from the discussion of the London Convention Guidelines, the OSPAR Convention goes on to state that: "This provision shall not be taken to permit the dumping of wastes or other matter otherwise prohibited under this Annex."[61]

As regards further specification, the Contracting Parties to the OSPAR Convention approved the "OSPAR Guidelines on Artificial Reefs in relation to Living Marine Resources" in 1999.[62] The original Guidelines were replaced in 2012,[63] but the key wording remains unchanged. Thus, while on the face of it redundant oil and gas installations look as if they would be prime candidates for such re-use insofar as the Guidelines mention that "Materials used for the construction of permanent artificial reefs will of necessity be bulky in nature, for example geological material (i.e. rock), concrete or steel", this option appears immediately to be closed off to the extent that the Guidelines also provide that "No materials should be used for the construction of artificial reefs which constitute wastes or other matter whose disposal at sea is otherwise prohibited."[64]

---

57 Ibid.

58 Ibid., Annex 6, para. 1.2.

59 Ibid., Annex 2, Article 5.

60 Ibid.

61 Ibid.

62 For an insightful discussion of the 1999 Guidelines and the debates preceding their adoption, see Dolly Jørgensen, "OSPAR's exclusion of rigs-to-reefs in the North Sea", (2011) *Ocean and Coastal Management*, doi: 10.1016/j.ocecoaman.2011.12.012.

63 *OSPAR Guidelines on Artificial Reefs in relation to Living Marine Resources*, Reference number: 2012-3.

64 Ibid., para. 11.

2.4. CONCLUSION ON INTERNATIONAL LAW

It may thus be concluded that, in international law, the possibility certainly exists for redundant offshore oil and gas installations to be left wholly or partly in place or, indeed, to be moved from their original location and dumped elsewhere. Under the London Convention, despite the strict reminders about not attempting to bypass the provisions prohibiting dumping, it also appears to be the case that such installations could also be used to form artificial reefs. At the regional level in the area covered by the OSPAR Convention, however, the position is apparently much more restrictive. Despite many aspects of the OSPAR Guidelines seemingly echoing their earlier London Convention counterparts, the prohibition on constructing artificial reefs out of material otherwise regarded as waste appears to rule out this form of re-use. It might be contended that where permission was granted to leave an installation in place as an artificial reef, it would thereby, by definition, not constitute waste, but it appears as if this is a chicken and egg situation which OSPAR itself is keen to resolve in favour of the more restrictive alternative. In view of the political sensitivities in the region following Brent Spar, this position is easy to understand.

3. DOMESTIC LAW AND PRACTICE

3.1. REGULATORY RESPONSIBILITY

Although most of the responsibility for the regulation of the UK's oil and gas industry has now passed from the Secretary of State to the Oil and Gas Authority,[65] the Secretary of State has retained responsibility for the decommissioning of offshore installations. In this area, the OGA's role is limited to acting as a consultant and to encouraging efficient practice and cost reductions.[66] Importantly, however, the OGA, and not BEIS, is charged with the task of regulating well-plugging and abandonment operations. Thus a bifurcated approach has been taken to offshore decommissioning upon the UKCS.

65 The Oil and Gas Authority ("OGA") was created in 2015 in order to implement the recommendations of the Wood Review on Maximising Economic Recovery. For more on Maximising Economic Recovery ("MER"), see J. Chandler, *Petroleum Resource Management: How Governments Manage Their Offshore Petroleum Resources*, Edward Elgar, Cheltenham 2018; G. Gordon, J. Paterson and U. Vass, "Maximising Economic Recovery" in Gordon, Paterson and Usenmez, n. 91 below, Vol I, Chapter I-5.

66 See further the discussion in Section 3.2, below.

3.2. THE UK'S STATUTORY FRAMEWORK

The UK's domestic law on decommissioning is contained primarily in the Petroleum Act 1998 (as amended), supplemented by detailed guidance on how the Minister's discretion is to be applied.[67] Central to the Petroleum Act 1998's approach is the abandonment plan.[68] No one may commence or continue decommissioning without an approved abandonment plan.[69] The Secretary of State is empowered to serve a notice requiring the submission of a detailed abandonment programme relative to an offshore installation[70] or submarine pipeline.[71] The notice will either specify the date by which the abandonment programme is to be submitted to the Secretary of State or, as is more usual in practice, provide for it to be submitted on or before a date to be specified in future.[72] Failure to comply with such a notice without reasonable excuse is a criminal offence.[73] The recipient of the notice must consult with the OGA prior to submitting their plan to the Secretary of State, must carry out such other consultation as the Secretary of State may specify, and must, so far as is reasonably practicable, design their programme so as to minimise cost.[74] The categories of persons upon whom a notice may be served differ depending upon whether the notice relates to an installation or a pipeline. In the case of an installation, the notice may be served upon:

(a) the operator of the installation;
(b) the licensee;
(ba) a person who has transferred his interest under a licence without the consent of the Secretary of State;
(c) a person party to a joint operating agreement or similar agreement;
(d) a person falling outside the above categories who owns any interest in the installation otherwise than as security for a loan;
(e) a body corporate outside the above categories but which is associated with a body corporate within any of those categories.

67 BEIS, *Guidance Notes: Decommissioning of Offshore Oil and Gas Installations and Pipelines*, (November 2018), available for download from: https://assets.publishing.service.gov.uk/government/uploads/system/uploads/attachment_data/file/760560/Decom_Guidance_Notes_November_2018.pdf ("BEIS, *Guidance Notes*").

68 The term "abandonment" is used instead of "decommissioning" throughout the legislation.

69 Persons who do so are guilty of an offence: Petroleum Act 1998, s. 28A.

70 As defined by s. 44.

71 As defined by ss. 26 and 45.

72 Section 29(2).

73 Section 29(3).

74 Section 29(2A). For further discussion of the interaction of the decommissioning regime with the Maximising Economic Recovery regime, see Chapter I-5. Note in general, however, that the OGA is required to "consider and advise on ... alternatives to abandonment or decommissioning" and how to ensure that costs are minimised. See s. 29(2B).

This is a broad range of persons, and the provision is designed in order to maximise the likelihood that the Secretary of State will at all times be able to identify a party upon whom a notice may be served.[75] The scope of these provisions is further extended by the fact that a section 29 notice may be served upon parties who fall into one of the above categories and who intend to become engaged in relevant activities on an offshore installation.[76] This means that a notice may be served upon e.g. the prospective purchaser of an interest in an oil field and associated installations, even before the deal has been completed.[77]

In the case of pipelines, ownership is of the essence. The Secretary of State may serve a notice upon either the person who has been statutorily designated as owner, or a person who has not been so designated but who nevertheless owns an interest in the pipeline, or upon associated bodies corporate.[78] The current BEIS Guidance states that the obligation is also imposed upon "parties to a JOA or similar agreement".[79] This statement, however, has no statutory foundation and would therefore seem to be incorrect.

The abandonment programme produced in response to the section 29 notice may be rejected or approved, and if approved, this may be subject to modification or the imposition of conditions. These can include the requirement that the party collaborate with other parties engaged in decommissioning activities, although only if such collaboration will not add to the cost of implementing the programme.[80] Prior to approval, the Secretary of State must consult with the OGA[81] who will advise in particular on the potential for using an alternative methodology or whether the programme's cost could be reduced. In the event that the abandonment plan is deemed unsatisfactory and is rejected, or if a party fails to comply with the section 29 requirement to produce a programme, the Secretary of State may prepare an abandonment programme. There is a duty to ensure that the works stipulated in an approved abandonment programme are undertaken, and that all conditions are complied with, and this duty is imposed jointly and severally upon each of the persons who submitted the plan.[82] Where there is default in undertaking the programme or failure to

---

75 Parties in categories (d) and (e) have the comfort that a notice will only be served upon them if the Secretary of State is satisfied that parties in categories (a) to (c) have made "adequate arrangements, including financial arrangements ... to ensure that a satisfactory abandonment programme" is undertaken.

76 Section 30(5)(b) as amended by s. 72(4) of the 2008 Act.

77 As s. 29 notices are revocable, such a prospective purchaser would have strong grounds to call for the revocation of the notice in the event that the proposed transaction did not proceed.

78 Petroleum Act 1998 s. 30(2).

79 BEIS, *Guidance Notes*, n. 67 above, para. 3.12.

80 Petroleum Act 1998 s. 32(2A)(a).

81 Petroleum Act 1998 s. 28A.

82 Section 36.

comply with a condition, the Secretary of State may issue a remediation notice, stipulating actions that must be undertaken within a specified time. Breaching a remediation notice is a criminal offence.[83] In addition, the Secretary of State is empowered to undertake the remedial work and charge the defaulting party for the work undertaken,[84] although in practical terms serious questions may of course arise as to a party's ability to pay if it has found itself in a position of default.

Section 29 notices may be withdrawn;[85] parties who are divesting themselves of assets frequently request and obtain a withdrawal of the notice.[86] However this provides the divesting party with only limited comfort, as the Secretary of State has the right to recall such parties,[87] or to serve a further notice at a future date.[88]

Approved abandonment programmes may be revised, either at the request of the party who submitted the plan or at the instance of the Secretary of State. Alterations can arise as a result of a need to make technical changes to the programme[89] or for other reasons, including the identification of a new approach, perhaps involving cooperation with other parties also decommissioning assets in the same area, which may serve to reduce costs. Importantly, either the Secretary of State or the persons who submitted the abandonment programme may propose that any person who has a duty to carry out the programme may be relieved of that duty or that another person may have the duty imposed upon them.[90] This is the legal foundation for the Secretary of State's ability to recall a party who has had a section 29 notice withdrawn and who has no current interest in the licence or the installation.

---

83 Section 37(2). There is a statutory defence in the event that the defaulter can demonstrate that it exercised due diligence.

84 Section 37(3).

85 Section 31(5).

86 The Government is willing to withdraw the notice if satisfied that the party acquiring the assets has the technical and financial capability to meet the decommissioning responsibilities. However as incoming parties are frequently significantly smaller corporations than those divesting themselves of the assets, questions can arise as to the financial capability of the purchaser and where this is so the Secretary of State will require the parties to enter into a financial security agreement. For a fuller discussion, see J. Aldersey-Williams, "Decommissioning Security" in Gordon, Paterson and Usenmez, n. 91 below, Vol I, Chapter I-13.

87 Section 34(1)(b) and (2).

88 Section 31(5).

89 This is an entirely sensible provision as it can be that, once decommissioning work has begun in earnest, it is discovered either that the installation "as built" does not wholly match the design documentation, or that its condition has deteriorated over time, necessitating a change to the proposed decommissioning programme.

90 Section 34(1)(b) and (2).

4. COMMERCIAL AND CONTRACTUAL ISSUES

As the UKCS becomes a progressively mature province and the level of decommissioning activity ramps up, commercial and contractual issues become increasingly important. The regulatory context in which decommissioning works are undertaken, the fiscal regime and the practical difficulties in undertaking decommissioning work all have an impact upon contracting practice within the industry. These issues are relevant both to contracts as between oil companies themselves (principally Joint Operating Agreements and Decommissioning Security Agreements) and those entered into between the operator and the contractors employed to undertake the task of decommissioning. Each category of contracts shall be considered in turn.

4.1. JOINT OPERATING AGREEMENTS AND DECOMMISSIONING SECURITY AGREEMENTS

As has been noted above, section 38 of the Petroleum Act 1998 gives the Secretary of State the right, in certain limited circumstances, to demand security against the cost of decommissioning activities. However, this power is seldom used:[91] Aldersey-Williams notes that "the assumption is that owners will pay the costs of decommissioning out of cash flow from other producing assets".[92] In the long term, this assumption is plainly illogical[93] and even in the shorter term it might be thought to be a questionable way in which to proceed.[94] In practice,

---

91 Aldersey-Williams suggests that there are "around a dozen such securities in existence": J. Aldersey Williams, "Decommissioning Security" in G. Gordon, J. Paterson and E. Usenmez, *UK Oil and Gas Law, Volume I: Resource Management and Regulatory Law*, 3rd edition, Edinburgh University Press ("Aldersey-Williams, 'Decommissioning Security'"), para. I-13.11.

92 Aldersey-Williams, "Decommissioning Security", para. I-13.2.

93 This is so for two reasons: oil and gas is a diminishing asset and will eventually run out. Thus, at the very least, the cost of the decommissioning of the final tranche of installations to be decommissioned cannot be met out of cash-flow from other producing assets as no such assets will remain. Moreover, oil and (to a lesser extent) gas are carbon-intensive fuel sources. Assuming that we continue on the current trend towards decarbonisation of the energy sector, then – unless swift and significant progress is made with the rolling out Carbon Capture and Storage programmes – oil and gas may (along with coal) become effectively unproducible long before the resource has been exhausted. This may hasten the point at which there ceases to be a cash-flow from other producing oil and gas assets.

94 The price of oil is volatile, and in times of low oil price, oil companies are liable to fall into insolvency. In the absence of adequate security arrangements, and given the prevalence of joint and several liability, there is at least the theoretical possibility that an initial wave of defaults could lead to knock-on effects throughout the sector. In a worst-case scenario, and despite the breadth of the categories of persons against whom the Government can serve s. 29 notices, this could lead to situations where on some fields no solvent party remains to whom the Government could look to undertake the necessary decommissioning activities.

requests for decommissioning security are much more likely to be sought either as between parties to a Joint Operating Agreement ("JOA")[95] or in the context of mergers and acquisitions activity;[96] and it may be that the economic self-interest of these companies will serve to protect the UK Government from the worst of the potential consequences of its decision not to routinely demand the provision of decommissioning security.

There being no regulatory requirement, outside of the context of a section 38 demand, to enter into a Decommissioning Security Agreement ("DSA"), the parties to a JOA are generally free to deal with the matter of decommissioning security as they see fit. While most modern JOAs will contain a clear obligation to enter into a DSA once the field enters into development, many older JOAs do not. Where this is so, the question of whether to enter into a DSA at any given time becomes a matter for agreement between the parties.

Oil and Gas UK has developed a style of Decommissioning Security Agreement.[97] The Agreement was designed specifically for use as between JOA co-venturers and has been in broad use within that context for around a decade.[98] The precise form of security required will vary from agreement to agreement, with parent company guarantees, banker's letters of credit and insurance bonds all in use[99] and other more bespoke methods, such as the use of trusts to allow the accumulation of a fund from ongoing revenue streams, also being occasionally seen.[100] The level of security given is based upon the operator or security-provider's estimate of decommissioning costs, multiplied up by a contingency and then discounted to a net present value.[101] Depending

---

95 Because the parties to a JOA are jointly and severally liable to undertake the work described in an abandonment programme, it is prudent for them to have security in place to ensure that no one party ends up paying a disproportionate share of the cost of the decommissioning activity.

96 Here, security from the purchaser is desirable for the seller because, as we have seen, even if the seller is released the from a s. 29 notice, it still faces the prospect of recall, and therefore has an interest in ensuring that the purchaser will not default upon its decommissioning obligation.

97 This is available for purchase from OGUK's website, at: https://oilandgasuk.co.uk/product/op021/.

98 It is sometimes also used as a starting point when security is required in the mergers and acquisitions context.

99 As always, it is important for parties to consider the covenant of the party responsible for making payment in the event that the security needs to be called upon. A properly drafted DSA will provide stipulations in this regard relating to e.g. the credit rating of the provider of the financial instrument.

100 See further Aldersey-Williams, "Decommissioning Security", para. I-13.18.

101 The contingency is applied because of the difficulty in accurately pre-estimating the cost of decommissioning activities. It may be that as the market for the provision of these services becomes more established the percentage applied by way of contingency – which currently varies quite widely in accordance with a range of factors, including the bargaining power of the parties – will both reduce and become more stable.

on the circumstances,[102] the net present value of the remaining reserves may also be deducted. Security is then granted in accordance with the granter's participating interest in the JOA.[103] The level of security required is reviewed annually. Formerly, due to uncertainty as to whether the then-current tax reliefs would still be available at the future point when the decommissioning activity was to be undertaken, the level of security sought was gross of tax relief.[104] Given the very high level of tax reliefs upon the UKCS,[105] however, this meant that significantly more security was being demanded than would ever truly be required, always assuming that the government did not intend to disturb the tax relief arrangements.[106] This was an economically inefficient situation which had the effect of diminishing the amount of capital and/or credit available for investment in the UKCS, which in turn impacted upon the liquidity of the asset transfer market upon the UKCS.[107] This situation was addressed by the introduction in 2013 of Decommissioning Security Deeds. These Deeds are entered into between the UK Government and oil companies and are intended to have the effect of committing the Government to maintaining the level of tax relief current at the time of entering into the agreement. Although the legal effectiveness of these instruments remains untested and there is at least a theoretical risk that they could be rendered unenforceable by the passage of primary legislation, the industry has taken significant comfort from them and DSAs are now entered into on a net basis. As at 27 March 2018,[108] 86 Decommissioning Security Deeds had been entered into between the Government and oil companies,[109] and Oil and Gas UK estimated that these had unlocked more than £5.7 billion which would otherwise have been fruitlessly tied up in DSAs.

---

102 This deduction is more common in the context of a DSA between JOA co-venturers, where it is usually seen as justifiable because, in the event that one of the parties defaults, the others will, as a result of the JOA's default provisions, become entitled to the defaulter's interest in the field. It is less common outside of that context.

103 So if the granter has a 40% interest of the relevant JOA, it will provide 40% of the security.

104 HM Treasury, *Decommissioning Relief Deeds: increasing tax certainty for oil and gas investment in the UK Continental Shelf* (July 2012), para. 2.17.

105 In fields which historically paid Petroleum Revenue Tax, these reliefs could in some circumstances amount to 75%: HM Treasury, *Decommissioning Relief Deeds*, para. 2.8.

106 In the case of fields to which PRT had been applied, a security granted without reference to tax reliefs would have to be four times larger than it would in reality need to be, assuming the tax reliefs continued to be available at the time of decommissioning. In non-PRT fields, the level of security was likely to be twice as large as necessary: Aldersey-Williams, "Decommissioning Security", para. I-13.35.

107 HM Treasury, *Decommissioning Relief Deeds*, n. 104 above, para, 3.2.

108 Robert Jerwick (Exchequer Secretary to the Treasury), *Decommissioning Relief Deeds: Written statement HCWS590*, 27 March 2018.

109 Of these Deeds, 83 continued to be in force.

4.2. THE LOGIC DECOMMISSIONING CONTRACT

Since the mid-1990s, a set of standard contracts – initially developed as part of the CRINE initiative, and now administered by LOGIC – has been available for use for various activities undertaken upon the UKCS.[110] Use of these contracts is not statutorily mandated or otherwise insisted upon by the UK regulatory agencies; the contracts are simply made available as a resource to be used if and how parties see fit. Nevertheless, their convenience and the fact that the LOGIC contracts are developed by a committee of industry experts mean that they remain highly influential upon the UKCS. It has taken some considerable time for a standard form Decommissioning contract to emerge, but LOGIC's General Conditions of Contract for Offshore Decommissioning was published in December 2018.[111] Although, for the reasons given above, it cannot be guaranteed that this contract will be universally used, its emergence is a very significant and welcome development that requires some comment.

The LOGIC Decommissioning contract is designed to deal only with the relationship between the operator and the contractor who has been hired to effect the decommissioning of a piece of infrastructure, from the cessation of production to the delivery to shore.[112] It does not deal with the relationship between the joint owners of the installation (discussed in section 4.1, above) and neither is it relevant to the expensive and environmentally-sensitive operations which will govern the plugging and abandonment of wells,[113] or to the relationship between the operator and the contractor ultimately responsible for onshore disposal.[114]

Broadly speaking, the contract is modelled on LOGIC's Offshore Construction standard,[115] but some notable differences become apparent when the contracts are compared. These arise both as a result of the need to consider the special

---

110 L. Dawson, "The LOGIC Contracts" in G. Gordon, J. Paterson and E. Usenmez, *UK Oil and Gas Law: Current Practice and Emerging Trends, Volume II: Commercial and Contract Law Issues* (3rd edition, Edinburgh University Press, Edinburgh 2018), para. II-5.01–03.

111 LOGIC, General Conditions of Contract (including Guidance Notes) for Offshore Decommissioning, December 2018, available for download from: https://www.logic-oil.com/content/standard-contracts0, ("LOGIC, *Decommissioning Contract*").

112 LOGIC, *Decommissioning Contract*, Guidance Notes, p. 47. The guidance notes also indicate that it is appropriate for individual phases of the above-mentioned scope of work.

113 Plugging and abandonment typically accounts for around half of the expenditure in a decommissioning project. LOGIC, *Decommissioning Contract, Guidance Notes*, p. 47 states that LOGIC's *General Conditions for Well Operations* should be used for this phase of decommissioning activity. While that contract is a useful starting point, the plugging and abandonment contractor should give careful thought to whether the principle risks inherent in the work that is being undertaken are all properly addressed by that contract.

114 Ibid.

115 LOGIC, *General Conditions of Contract (including Guidance Notes) for Offshore Construction*, 3rd edition, November 2018, available for download from: https://www.logic-oil.com/content/standard-contracts0.

risks which arise as a result of the complexities of decommissioning operations and as a result of the regulatory law applicable to decommissioning activities.

The contract contains an Ownership and Disposal of Material clause, which provides clarity on the circumstances in which ownership of the decommissioned facility passes,[116] and also detailed Indemnity and Hold Harmless provisions.[117] The Ownership and Disposal of Material clause is necessary as ownership is relevant to the question of who has responsibility for ensuring the appropriate disposal of waste material. The effect of the Environmental Protection Act 1990 is that the owner of material which is to be disposed of will remain responsible even after it has passed into the hands of a sub-contractor to the extent that he has a duty of care, for example, to ensure that "the transfer is only to an authorised person or to a person for authorised transport purposes".[118] In other words, the originator of waste cannot wash his hands of responsibility for its ultimate disposal simply because he has passed the material to another; he needs to take all reasonable steps to ensure that the waste is managed and disposed of "correctly and legally".[119] The Indemnity and Hold Harmless clause is more complex than that found in many LOGIC contracts. In addition to providing the standard cross-indemnity in relation to the parties' own personnel and property,[120] it also contains provisions relating to loss or damage to third-party oil and gas production faculties[121] and allocating the responsibility for pollution liability[122] and obligation to recover, remove or mark wrecks and debris.[123]

Perhaps the most significant of the special features in the Decommissioning Contract, however, is the Technical Information and Assumptions clause.[124] This, when read together with the Contractor to Inform Itself clause[125] and

---

116 LOGIC, *Decommissioning Contract*, Clause 19.

117 In addition to the standard indemnities found in routine oil and gas contracts, the operator (by clause 22.2(d)) indemnifies the contractor against loss or damage to third-party oil and gas production faculties, and also (by clause 22.2(d)) against the majority of pollution claims.

118 Section 34(1)(c)(i).

119 Natural Scotland, *Duty of Care: A Code of Practice*, Scottish Government, October 2012, p. 24.

120 LOGIC, *Decommissioning Contract*, Guidance Notes, p. 47, Clauses 22.1(a)–(b) and 22.2(a)–(b).

121 Clause 22.2(d), which places this responsibility upon the operator.

122 Clause 22.3, which generally places this responsibility upon the operator.

123 Clauses 22.5 and 22.6. This responsibility is divided up between the parties depending upon the circumstances in which the obligation has arisen.

124 Clause 12.

125 Clause 6. In other LOGIC contracts this contains a provision whereby the Contractor is deemed to have satisfied itself as to the extent and nature of the work involved; in the Decommissioning Contract, this provision is heavily qualified, giving the Contractor additional protection. The Contractor warrants only that it has sufficient skill and resources to undertake the work, always assuming that the technical information provided by the operator is materially accurate and subject to the proviso that the assumptions contained in the contract are correct. "Technical information" and "assumptions" are discussed further below.

Variation procedure,[126] provides a sophisticated solution to the problem of indeterminacy of work-scope arising as a result of uncertainty as to the physical condition and characteristics of the facilities that are to be decommissioned. The contract envisages that the operator will provide technical information to the contractor and will also make a number of assumptions about the status and condition of the installation. It then provides what is to happen if that information or those assumptions turn out to be incorrect or incomplete. The contract stops short of warranting that the Technical Information is correct, providing instead that, to the "best knowledge" of the operator, the information "gives a reasonable representation of the facility".[127] It then expressly acknowledges that the scope of work, programme and contract price have all been based upon the technical information and assumptions being correct.[128] This means that in the event of technical information or assumptions proving to be inaccurate, the contractor cannot pursue the operator for a breach of warranty, but will instead be able to seek a variation in the contract to reflect the alteration to the scope of work.

It is understood that this has proved to be somewhat controversial, with some within the operating community being of the view that this approach may lead to price uncertainty or that contractors may make speculative or unwarranted variation claims. However, the present authors consider the mechanism provided in the LOGIC Decommissioning Contract to be an appropriate means of dealing with the uncertainty inherent in works of this nature. It is not obvious that the contractor should bear the risk of an increase in work-scope if that arises due to an imperfect state of knowledge on the part on the part of the operator as to the condition of the operator's own property.[129] The approach undertaken would therefore seem to be fair to the contractor. Perhaps less obviously, but just as importantly, it also has the potential to be beneficial to the operator, as it should allow the contractor to have the confidence to price the job based on the presumptive work-scope only, without having to build in the contingency that a prudent contractor would otherwise have to build

126 Clause 14.

127 Clause 12.1.

128 The operator is obliged to inform the contractor of any relevant non-disclosures or errors promptly upon those coming to light.

129 This is not to say that the operator is necessarily to blame or at fault if some of its working assumptions about the installation turn out to be wrong. There are many reasons why matters might turn out to be different from how the operator expected. Across the long life of the installation, drawings may have been destroyed or misplaced, particularly if (as is common) ownership of the installation has changed hands; there may have been unauthorised or undocumented changes to the design during the construction, installation or alteration of the installation, or the installation may turn out to be in worse physical condition than was anticipated. The point is simply that the risk needs to lie somewhere, and would seem to be unfair for the operator – who has had the longer association with the property and bears the statutory responsibility to decommission it – to allocate that risk to the contractor.

in if it were on risk for unexpected change in the work-scope. An imprudent contractor, of course, might not build in such a contingency. Such an approach might save some money in individual projects where there happened to be no material increase in work-scope, but a contractor who systematically adopted such a strategy would run significant risk of being driven into insolvency if even a small number of projects did not proceed as anticipated. Overall, the provisions of the LOGIC Decommissioning Contract would seem to provide a sustainable and economically efficient means of contracting and have the potential to make a positive contribution to the OGA's policy of reducing decommissioning costs.

5. CONCLUSION

As decommissioning of offshore oil and gas infrastructure on the UKCS has gathered pace, attention has passed from a focus on the extent to which international obligations appropriately reflect public expectations about the actions of the industry when production has ceased, to a more detailed consideration of how multiple large-scale projects should proceed either simultaneously or potentially in quick succession. This refocusing has occurred in no small measure as a result of the establishment in the relatively recent past of the Oil and Gas Authority, whose mandate is principally to implement the Maximising Economic Recovery Strategy, which in turn includes consideration of the balance to be struck between efficient and timely decommissioning, on the one hand, and the ongoing availability of infrastructure to avoid the risk of stranded reserves, on the other. Beyond that, the OGA has a role to play in assisting the industry in reducing the cost of decommissioning – largely because a substantial proportion of those costs will fall upon the taxpayer as a consequence of the operation of decommissioning allowances. The ability to deliver these efficiencies will, of course, depend to some extent upon technological advances, but the role to be played in this regard by innovative contractual arrangements should not be underestimated. Whether those costs might be further reduced by public opinion going full circle and calling for installations to be left in place to the extent that they have become part of the marine ecosystem is beyond the scope of this chapter, but would appear to be an issue of growing importance.[130]

---

[130] Henry, Lea-Anne and G. Mayorga-Adame, Claudia & Fox, Alan & Polton, Jeff & Ferris, Joseph & McLellan, Faron & Mccabe, Christopher & Kutti, Tina & Roberts, J. (2018). Ocean sprawl facilitates dispersal and connectivity of protected species. Scientific Reports. 8. 10.1038/s41598-018-29575-4.

CHAPTER XVI

REGULATION OF INFRASTRUCTURE DECOMMISSIONING IN THE DANISH OFFSHORE OIL AND GAS SECTOR

The Final Chapter in the Danish Oil Adventure

Clara Greve Brett

1. INTRODUCTION

Compared with other Western European countries, the Danish oil adventure began rather late in 1972 when production started from the Dan Field. Gas production did not commence until 1984, also from the Dan Field.[1] Since production commenced offshore, 48 steel platforms and five subsea installations have been placed on the seabed. The steel platform topsides facilities weigh between 7,000 and 15,000 tonnes, with a jacket weight of up to 3,500 tonnes. All installations are made of steel except for the South Arne Platform which has a concrete gravity-based storage (GBS) that is used to store oil before transporting this via the SAL system.[2] In addition, approximately 1,700 km of pipelines have been installed ranging from 1" to 42" in diameter. Currently many of the facilities on the continental shelf are ageing and some of the early platforms are standing idle or only process water, having exhausted the oil and gas reservoirs in their original field.[3] Although the Danish Continental Shelf is considered to be a "mature province", no meaningful decommissioning

---

1 Miljø-, og Energiministeriet, Danmarks Geologiske Undersøgelse Olie og Gas i Danmark (*Kort fortalt nr. 4*), pp. 7–8.

2 For further details see: https://www.offshore-technology.com/projects/arne/. Methods for marine removal of even a concrete gravity-based storage (GBS) have been developed which may make it possible to de-ballast and refloat the GBS if necessary.

3 The Dagmar and Rolf fields have not produced for years and Ragnar has technically been "shut down" for a number of years.

activities have been carried out to date. However, this is set to change in the coming years. The Danish Energy Agency has estimated that decommissioning of existing facilities, including the plugging and abandonment[4] of wells and related activities will cost approximately DKK 41 billion (€5.5 billion).[5]

The Kingdom of Denmark consists of continental Denmark, the Faroe Islands and Greenland. The Danish Constitution applies to all areas of the Danish Kingdom, although the Faroe Islands and Greenland have their own home rule arrangements and have established independent hydrocarbon regulatory regimes.[6] So far, hydrocarbons have only been produced in continental Denmark and only in the Danish sector of the North Sea. From 1993 until 2014 Denmark has been a self-sufficient oil-producing nation. In fact in 1993 Denmark was the only country in the EU which was self-sufficient in both oil and gas.[7] Although no longer fully self-sufficient, Denmark is still an exporter of oil and gas.[8] Denmark is presently the third-largest oil producer in Western Europe[9] after Norway and the United Kingdom, and the fifth-largest gas producer in Western Europe after Norway, the United Kingdom, the Netherlands and Germany.[10]

This chapter will examine the regulation of decommissioning in continental Denmark by first presenting a general background to oil and gas exploration and development in Denmark as well as the main principles of the legal framework. Thereafter the issues related to liability and securities during the decommissioning phase will be examined. Finally, the chapter will explore the regulation of pipelines compared with other offshore installations on the Danish Continental Shelf.

---

4 The term "abandonment" is typically said to include demolition and removal together with any necessary site restoration. The terms "decommissioning" and "abandonment" can be used interchangeably, but during the past few years there has been a move towards the use of the term decommissioning, as it better conveys the idea that the licensees are not abandoning their obligation or carelessly leaving anything to remain after cessation of production. See, J. Paterson, 'Decommissioning of offshore installations' in G. Gordon and J. Paterson (eds), *Oil and Gas Law – Current Practice and Emerging Trends*, Dundee University Press, 2007, p. 149.

5 *Travaux préparatoires* to the Danish Subsoil Act proposed Act No. 116 of 28 January 2015 – specific commentary no. 22.

6 The Greenlandic and Faroe Island hydrocarbon legislation regulating each system is Greenland Parliament Act No. 7 of 7 December 2009, on mineral resources and mineral resource activities with subsequent amendments in 2014 and Faroe Islands Act 1998 No. 31 on Hydrocarbon activity on the Faroe Islands.

7 For further information see Statistics Denmark's report at: https://www.dst.dk/extranet/flipping/65aar/files/assets/basic-html/page34.html, or Oil and Gas Production in Denmark 2006, p. 50.

8 First 50 – Oil Gas Denmark 2016, p. 20.

9 Eurostat's report: https://ec.europa.eu/eurostat/statistics-explained/index.php?title=File:Crude-Oil-Production-Europe-MTOE-1990-2014.png&oldid=310070.

10 Statista's 2018 statistic: https://www.statista.com/statistics/264101/world-natural-gas-production-by-country/.

2. OIL AND GAS EXPLORATION AND PRODUCTION IN DENMARK

2.1. REGULATORY AUTHORITIES

The main regulatory authority for offshore activities in Denmark is the Ministry of Energy, Utilities and Climate. However, in accordance with section 37 of the Danish Subsoil Act, much of the Ministry's authority has been subrogated to the Danish Energy Agency. In terms of Health, Safety and Environment (HSE) issues, health and safety activities are primarily handled by the Danish Working Environment Authority's offshore group, while most environmental issues are handled by the Danish Environmental Protection Agency, acting under the auspices of the Ministry of Environment and Food. Using the words of the Offshore Safety Directive,[11] the Danish Energy Agency is the "licensing authority" while the Danish Working Environment Authority is the "competent authority".

2.2. THE SOLE CONCESSION

In 1932 the first Danish Subsoil Act came into force.[12] Thereafter the first Danish license was issued in 1935 to Frederick F. Ravlin. This license is known as the Sole Concession. The concession covered the entire onshore area of Denmark and was extended to the offshore territory in 1963 following the ratification of the Geneva Convention on the Continental Shelf (see below Section 3.1). The concession was transferred a number of times subsequent to 1935, without any commercial discoveries being made, before finally being relinquished in 1959 by Frederick F. Ravlin. In 1962, after negotiations with the government, AP Møller was awarded the Sole Concession against payment of 40 DKK (approximately $7 USD). In order to ensure that the license-holder had sufficient experience to carry out the exploration activities, the Danish Underground Consortium (DUC) was founded. The DUC originally consisted of AP Møller, Shell and Gulf Oil. Gulf acted as operator until 1974 at which point Gulf Oil withdrew from the concession and the operatorship was transferred to AP Møller. In 2018 Total E&P took over as operator from AP Møller as part of a transaction whereby Total E&P acquired AP Møller's worldwide oil and gas business known as Maersk Oil.

---

11 Directive 2013/30/EU of the European Parliament and of the Council of 12 June 2013 on safety of offshore oil and gas operations and amending Directive 2004/35/EC.

12 The Act has been amended several times since. The most current version of the act is Consolidated Act No. 1190 of 21 September 2018 on the use of the Danish subsoil.

2.3. LICENSING REGIME

In 1981 the terms of the Sole Concession were renegotiated and, after significant political pressure, the DUC parties were required to relinquish parts of the concession area. The relinquished areas were subsequently made available for licensing in accordance with the licensing regime introduced in the Danish Subsoil Act.[13]

Following the agreement with the DUC parties, the first public licensing round was held in 1984 and 15 licenses were awarded in this round.[14] As a result of the implementation of the EC Hydrocarbons Directive,[15] an Open Door procedure was introduced in 1997. Although in general Danish offshore production has been characterized by a comparatively low but stable number of participants, recent years have seen a great deal of transactional activity with regard to the participants on the Danish Continental Shelf. Not only did the recent 7th licensing round show there was much interest in bidding for acreage, but many changes have also happened to the key participating companies.[16] By the middle of 2017 the producing operators on the Danish Continental Shelf were Maersk Oil (AP Møller), DONG E&P, Hess Denmark and Wintershall Noordzee BV. By the end of 2017 Total E&P was in the process of acquiring Maersk Oil, INEOS E&P had taken over DONG E&P, Hess announced that it would sell Hess Denmark[17] and Wintershall merged with Deutsche Erdöl AG (DEA). Presently 20 licenses are in force in Denmark, not including any licenses which may be awarded in the current 8th licensing round.[18]

Unlike some jurisdictions, Denmark does not operate with separate exploration and production licenses. Instead the Danish licensing system (based on the requirements in the Offshore Safety Directive article 4) in 2015 introduced a division of phases at certain points in the life of the license. Pursuant to section 24b of the Danish Subsoil Act, these phases include:

1) when the license is granted and initial phase;
2) transitioning to a new work obligation;

---

13 B. Sandroos, *Undergrundsloven med kommentarer*, Jurist- og Økonomforbundets Forlag, København 2012, p. 39.

14 For an overview of the Danish licensing history see: http://www.nordsoefonden.dk/en/danish-oil-and-gas-history.

15 Directive 94/22/EC of the European Parliament and of the Council of 30 May 1994 on the conditions for granting and using authorizations for the prospection, exploration and production of hydrocarbons.

16 Energistyrelsen, 17 December 2015, *Danmarks Olie- og Gasproduktion 2014*, p. 4.

17 Hess Denmark has since announced that no sale will be completed at this present time.

18 For further information on licenses currently in place on the Danish Continental Shelf, see: https://ens.dk/en/our-responsibilities/oil-gas/licences-oil-and-gas/danish-licences-and-licensees.

3) drilling an exploration or appraisal well;
4) moving into the development phase;
5) approval of the production plan and production phase; and, finally,
6) the decommissioning phase.

All licenses used on the Danish Continental Shelf are based on a model form of license agreement. Over the years the model license provided by the Danish authorities has been subject to some changes. Most of these changes are minor. The latest version of the model license available from the Danish Energy Agency is from the 8th Licensing Round of 2018.[19] All Danish licenses are awarded to joint ventures and the parties to these joint ventures operate on the basis of a Joint Operating Agreement (JOA). Similarly to the licenses, all JOAs used on the Danish Continental Shelf are based on a model. Minor variations to the model can be negotiated between the parties but are subject to approval by the Danish Energy Agency. Furthermore, over the years the model JOAs provided by the Danish authorities have developed, but most of the model JOA provisions have remained unchanged. The latest version of the model JOA available from the Danish Energy Agency is from 2019.[20]

As all licenses are awarded by the Danish Energy Agency, any direct or indirect assignment of license interests must, similarly, first be approved by the Danish Energy Agency in accordance with section 29 of the Danish Subsoil Act, section 33 of the model license and section 9(1)(f) of the model JOA. The Danish Energy Agency not only has to approve the transfer itself but also the terms and conditions related to this.[21] In addition, any assignment also is required to be approved by the co-licensees in accordance with section 9(1)(d) of the JOA, although such consent must not be unreasonably withheld. Furthermore, the co-licensees have the right of first refusal in accordance with section 9(2) of the JOA. A party assigning all or part of its interests still remains liable to the other licensees for obligations attached to its interest which are incurred prior to the effective date of assignment in accordance with section 9(1)(g) of the JOA. The assignee also becomes liable for such obligations.

In addition to this *inter partes* liability obligation, secondary liability towards the Danish state was introduced in Denmark in 2015 with the addition of section 29a to the Danish Subsoil Act.

The JOA contains additional general provisions which are of importance for decommissioning such as assigning liability for financial obligations (section 2.2), agreement of decommissioning programmes and budgets (sections 3.18.3 and 5.6), liability related to the removal of installations (section 10.2.7) and

---

19 https://ens.dk/en/our-responsibilities/oil-gas/legislation-and-guidelines.

20 Ibid.

21 B. Sandroos, *Undergrundsloven med kommentarer*, Jurist- og Økonomforbundets Forlag, 2012, p. 245.

default in payments (section 11). Section 3.18.3 of the model JOA specifies that prior to submitting a development plan to the Danish Energy Agency the licensees must agree the terms of a decommissioning plan.

2.4. GUIDELINES

In order to provide additional clarification and guidance to the industry, the Danish Energy Agency has issued Guidelines for drilling in 2009[22] and a number of new guidelines in 2018, including:

- *Guidelines on Security and Insurances* for companies holding an Exploration and Production License pursuant to the provisions of the Danish Subsoil Act;
- *Guidelines on Technical Capacity* concerning the use and exploitation of the Danish subsoil; and
- *Guidelines on Decommissioning Plans* for Offshore Oil and Gas Facilities or Installations.[23]

These guidelines are meant to ensure that the offshore activities are carried out properly. The Guidelines on Technical Capacity, for example, re-state in further detail the requirements of the Danish Subsoil Act section 24b that the licensees have sufficient technical capacity to carry out each phase of the life of the license, including the decommissioning phase.[24] The Guidelines on Security and Insurance provide additional information on the security. The licensee must be able to demonstrate that the obligations of each phase can be met by way of the company's equity capital, earnings, insurances and the security provided by the company in favor of the Danish state. The purpose of these guidelines is to facilitate use of more flexible security while not increasing the risk to the Danish state.[25]

3. LEGAL FRAMEWORK GOVERNING DECOMMISSIONING

3.1. INTERNATIONAL LAW

Legal regulation of decommissioning of offshore installations and structures on the continental shelf outside the Danish territorial waters is first of all

22 Energistyrelsen, Guidelines for Drilling 1988 (2009).

23 The guidelines are available at: www.ens.dk.

24 Guidelines on Technical Capacity, p. 3.

25 Guidelines on Security and Insurances, p. 2.

determined by international law. Denmark has ratified the main international conventions which govern decommissioning of offshore installations, namely: the Geneva Convention on the Continental Shelf (ratified on 31 May 1963),[26] the United Nations Convention on the Law of the Seas, UNCLOS (ratified with effect on 16 November 2004), the OSPAR Convention (ratified in 1995) and the London Convention on Marine Pollution and Dumping (ratified on 29 December 1972).[27]

UNCLOS article 60(3), which deals with decommissioning of offshore installations, makes specific reference to "accepted international standards established in this regard by the competent international organisation."

The International Maritime Organization (IMO) carries out the role of the "competent international organisation".[28] In 1989 the IMO adopted IMO Resolution A.672, also referred to as the 1989 Guidelines and Standards. The IMO Guidelines have been implemented into Danish law by the Danish Subsoil Act.

Furthermore, as a party to the OSPAR Convention, Denmark considers itself obligated to implement relevant decisions and recommendations, such as OSPAR Decision 98/3 on the Disposal of Disused Offshore Installations which is of relevance to decommissioning.[29]

3.2. NATIONAL LAW

3.2.1. *Danish Subsoil Act*

The Danish Subsoil Act governs the licensing regime for exploration and production of hydrocarbons and construction of pipelines in relation thereto. This includes the statutory requirements which apply to the cessation of production. When the first licenses where granted in Denmark in the 1980s focus was placed mostly on the exploration and production phases of the licensed activities and less attention was given to the decommissioning phase of the projects. The main focal point when dealing with decommissioning in legislation and licenses was to ensure the Danish state's right to take over any facilities if a license was terminated.

---

26 The Convention was ratified by Royal Order No. 259 of 7 June 1963.

27 Ratified by Executive Order No. 552 of 29 December 1972 and Implemented by Act on the Protection of Marine Environment, most current Consolidated Act No. 1033 of 4 September 2017.

28 IMO Guidelines and Standards, paragraph 3, and M. Hammerson and N. Anthonas, *Oil and Gas Decommissioning Law, Policy and Comparative Practice*, Globe Law and Business, 2016, p. 36.

29 Section 32a: Guidelines on decommissioning plans for offshore oil and gas facilities or installations, 7 August 2018: https://ens.dk/sites/ens.dk/files/OlieGas/20180808_afviklingsvejledning_ss32_a_english.pdf, p. 2.

According to section 33 of the Danish Subsoil Act the licenses shall provide detailed provisions on the actions to be taken in respect of installations established by the licensee when the license expires. In accordance with section 37 of the license, the Danish state is without qualification entitled to take over all or part of any facility, equipment or installations if a license terminates due to its expiry, relinquishment, lapsing or revocation. Furthermore, the Danish Energy Agency may require the licensee to remove all or part of any facilities etc. that the state does not wish to take over. This corresponds to the fact that the Danish Continental Shelf is relatively shallow, with water depths generally cited to be less than 70 meters for the producing fields and, subject to the IMO Guidelines, Denmark is thus bound to ensure a complete removal of unused installations.

Each licensee must, in accordance with sections 24a–24c of the Danish Subsoil Act, demonstrate to have sufficient technical and financial capacity to carry out activities related to the next phase of the license, including the removal of installations once production has been discontinued. Furthermore, in accordance with section 24f of the Danish Subsoil Act, the licenses granted under the Act may require that the licensees provide security for the fulfillment of their license obligations. The abovementioned guidelines provide details for how these requirements are fulfilled.

The Danish Subsoil Act was amended in 2015 to include section 32a. In accordance with this provision the applicants must include a plan for the decommissioning of the installations related to their application under sections 10 (approval of production and development plan), 17 (use of pipeline), 23 (storage or other use) or 28 (additional work related to such licenses) of the Danish Subsoil Act. All installations which currently exist on the Danish Continental Shelf were established and approved prior to 19 July 2015 and, consequently, the operators, pursuant to section 32a(4), had to submit decommissioning plans in July 2018. The further requirements of the content of the decommissioning plan will be discussed in Section 3.3 below.

3.2.2. Danish Offshore Safety Act

The Offshore Safety Act entered into force in 2006 in order to implement the EU Offshore Safety Directive. It resulted in some changes to the Danish decommissioning regime. The Offshore Safety Act uses a slightly different wording than the Danish Subsoil Act, as the Offshore Safety Act follows the directive's wording and deals with the operator's obligations more so than the license group as a whole. The term "operator" is used to refer to the operator that conducts the license activities on behalf of the licensees, including operating or managing and controlling the functions of a production installation. The term "owner" is used to refer to an entity legally entitled to control the operation of a non-production installation. The *travaux préparatoires* show that "non-production installations", for example, could be pipelines from field-to-field and pipelines from field-to-coast.

Pursuant to section 31 of the Danish Offshore Safety Act[30] the operator and owner shall ensure that a permit from the *supervisory authority* is obtained before a fixed installation, possibly with connected infrastructure, or a pipeline is decommissioned. The supervisory authority in relation to the Danish Offshore Safety Act is the Danish Work Environment Authority.

Furthermore, decommissioning of a fixed offshore installation, connected infrastructure or a pipeline shall be planned and carried out in a way that ensures the health and safety risks as well as any major environmental incidents that could be connected with the work are identified, assessed and reduced to a level "as low as is reasonably practicable" (ALARP) – cf. section 56 of the Offshore Safety Act.[31]

In addition to the Offshore Safety Act the Executive Order on Management of Health and Safety in Connection with Offshore Oil and Gas Operation provides further regulation of the health and safety aspects of the decommissioning process.[32]

3.2.3. *Danish Act on the Marine Environment*

Generally environmental regulation of offshore installations etc. is implemented into Danish law by the Danish Subsoil Act with regard to approval of construction, changes and decommissioning of installations and pipelines.[33] However, handling of pollution stemming from, e.g. decommissioning or other discharges, is regulated by the Danish Marine Environment Act.

The Danish Act on the Marine Environment[34] contains a general provision against dumping in section 25: "Discharges of substances or materials shall not take place, apart from the dumping of seabed material included". Emergency dumping is allowed in cases where human life or safety is at risk, or the safety of a platform, in accordance with section 58 of the Act.

3.3. DECOMMISSIONING PLAN

As mentioned in Section 3.2.1 above, applicants seeking an approval of their plan for development and operation ("PDO") – cf section 10 of the Danish Subsoil

---

30 Consolidated Act No. 125 of 6 February 2018 on Offshore Safety.

31 This principle was previously only codified in Executive Order No. 729 of 3 July 2009 on management of safety and health on offshore installations etc.

32 Executive Order No. 835 of 15 June 2018 on management of health and safety in connection with Offshore Oil and Gas Operations.

33 B. Sandroos, *Undergrundsloven med kommentarer*, Jurist- og Økonomforbundets Forlag, 2012, p. 50.

34 Consolidated Act No. 1033 of 4 September 2017 on Protection of the Danish Marine Environment.

Act or an approval to use a pipeline in accordance with section 17 must submit a plan for the decommissioning of the installations included in the application in accordance with section 32a of the Danish Subsoil Act. These so-called decommissioning plans have undergone quite some additional regulation in recent years.

Before 2019 all Danish JOAs contained an obligation for licensees to prepare an "abandonment agreement". The purpose of the agreement was to deal with *inter partes* liabilities and ensure that sufficient security would be placed by each party for its share of the decommissioning costs owed towards the other licensees. The abandonment agreement had to be agreed before a PDO was submitted to the Danish Energy Agency. In addition to the abandonment agreement, the licensees also had to prepare a decommissioning plan in accordance with section 37 of the license. The decommissioning plan had to include information about the removal of facilities, environmental assessment, a statement of expected costs and a description of their procedure for ensuring that the financial resources required for implementation of the decommissioning plan are available. A decommissioning plan only had to be submitted two years before the license was to terminate, or an installation was expected to have served its purpose. One challenge with this approach is that it was practically very difficult to determine the point in time two years prior to termination of a license or decommissioning of the field due to variable factors such as oil prices and production levels.

Section 32a of the Danish Subsoil Act was added in 2015 and, as a consequence, applicants now need to submit an early decommissioning plan together with the PDO, thus protecting the Danish Government's interests better by adequately dealing with the issues at the point of PDO approval. As a consequence, the 2019 model JOAs no longer contain an obligation for the parties to agree an abandonment agreement, but rather a decommissioning plan. Going forward the licensees will therefore not necessarily enter into separate abandonment agreements. It should, however, be kept in mind that all current producing licenses on the Danish Continental Shelf were granted before these changes occurred and consequently the parties already have abandonment agreements in place.

In 2018 the Danish Energy Agency published Guidelines for Decommissioning Plans, which describe in more detail the requirements for the content of the decommissioning plans. Although the guidelines are significantly more detailed than the previous regulation, they are not exhaustive.

As much of the information which is necessary to prepare a full decommissioning plan is not available at the beginning of a development, additional assessments may need to be made during the production phase, particularly in the period of time as cessation of production approaches. The guidelines therefore make a distinction between *early* decommissioning plans and *final* decommissioning plans. The decommissioning plans are expected to be finalized five years before the expected commencement of decommissioning.[35] The early decommissioning plans do not need to contain quite the same content as the final plans. For example there is no requirement for an early plan to include an assessment of impact on other installations, a Comparative Assessment or an Environmental Impact Assessment.[36] Also, the level of assessments provided is expected to change from the early to the final decommissioning plan. For example, early plans are expected to describe decommissioning *options* in as much detail as possible whereas the final decommissioning plans are expected to determine the *actual* decommissioning methods selected on the basis of completed technology, cost assessments, Environmental Assessments and consents from licensees. This allows for decommissioning obligations to change over time as new technology and methodologies become available.

Decommissioning plans need to be updated annually with regard to financial conditions and the Danish Energy Agency can require that a decommissioning plan is updated every five years with regard to any changes to the choice of decommissioning methods.

Overall the decommissioning plan must contain a description of the installations which are to be decommissioned, the way in which the decommissioning should be carried out, as well as any economic aspects. The economic aspects include calculations of decommissioning cost estimates, estimates of remaining production, an account of the trigger mechanism[37] and a description of how and when the funds necessary for carrying out the decommissioning plans will be made available.

The costs of decommissioning need to be borne by the licensees. It was for this reason that licensees concluded abandonment agreements in the past. Since 2015, the decommissioning plans must contain provisions for security which aim to ensure that each licensee provides adequate security for the benefit of the other licensees with regard to decommissioning costs. The security must be proportional to the licensees' share of interest in the license. Neither the abandonment agreements, nor the decommissioning plans are based on a public model, and although they must be approved by the Danish Energy Agency, they are a negotiated document between the parties and based on the specific circumstances of each development. Therefore variations can and do occur between the different decommissioning plans currently in place.

In accordance with most of the abandonment agreements of the past, the operator is responsible for annually providing the licensees with estimates of the decommissioning costs and requesting them to adjust their security if necessary.

---

35 Decommissioning Guidelines, p. 4.

36 For full overview of the requirement of the content see Table 2, p. 8, of the Decommissioning Guidelines.

37 This mechanism provides the trigger point indicating how to determine the point at which provision of security is to commence.

The types of security which each licensee must provide are agreed between the licensees in the operating committee. This *inter partes* security can generally be provided in the form of a trust fund, an irrevocable guarantee of performance, a bond or a letter of credit. It can be expected that licensees will continue to request a similar form of *inter partes* security to ensure that all licensees will be able to meet their share of the decommissioning costs. Failure to maintain adequate security in accordance with the abandonment agreement was considered a default under the JOAs – cf. section 3.18 of the "old" JOAs – and, similarly, failure to maintain adequate security in accordance with the decommissioning plan is considered a default under the 2019 model JOA section 3.18.3.

When the *final* decommissioning plans have been approved, the decommissioning project can move into the actual decommissioning work consisting of: well closure, termination of operations, decommissioning of offshore and subsea installations as well as pipelines. When the dismantling or demolition work has been carried out, the remediation work can be finalized. After a period of environmental monitoring, the decommissioning project can be completed.

The decommissioning plans must to be approved by the Danish Energy Agency, but the agency will consult other relevant Danish authorities including the Danish Maritime Authority, the Danish Environmental Protection Agency and the Danish Working Environment Authority as part of the approval process.

4. LIABILITY AND DECOMMISSIONING

4.1. PARTIES LIABLE FOR CARRYING OUT THE DECOMMISSIONING

In accordance with section 33 of the Danish Subsoil Act the license must lay down the actions to be taken regarding the offshore installations. As the provision refers to the license it indirectly places the liability on the licensees. However, the provision does not explicitly determine who is liable for carrying out the decommissioning of offshore installations. Sections 24a, 24b and 32a of the Danish Subsoil Act place the responsibility for proving sufficient technical and financial competency as well as preparation of the decommissioning plan on the licensees. Similarly, the wording of the model license, section 37(6), and the Guidelines on Decommissioning Plans place the liability for decommissioning solely on the licensees, regardless of whether the installation is owned by the licensee or another party.[38]

---

[38] G. Tuesen, Olieeventyrets problembørn – regulering og fjernelse af installationer til havs, *UfR.1996B.235*.

Presently, most installations and facilities on the Danish Continental Shelf are owned by the licensees, however a few are not and in the future there could be other installations or facilities used where ownership is separated from the licensees such as in case of a leased FPSO.[39,40] In cases where the licensees are not also the owners of the installation, it would therefore be beneficial to clarify if the owner of an installation is intended to carry any decommissioning liability as is the case in other North Sea countries. However, presently the full liability remains with the licensees under the Danish Subsoil Act and licenses and with the operator or owner as defined in section 31 of the Danish Offshore Safety Act.

4.2. LIABILITY FOR ACCIDENTS DURING DECOMMISSIONING

Decommissioning of an offshore installation is a highly time-consuming and complicated process that requires a balance of protection of the environment as well as other users of the sea. There are considerable differences between fields in terms of size, complexity and the number of installations.[41] In accordance with the IMO guidelines, "costs, technical feasibility and risks of injury to personnel associated with removal should be taken into account when considering the disposal options".

Licensees carry a strict liability in accordance with section 35 of the Danish Subsoil Act:

> 35(1) A licensee shall be liable to pay damages for any loss, damage or injury caused by the activities carried on under the licence, even though such loss, damage or injury was caused accidentally.
>
> (2) In the event that the injured party contributed to the loss, damage or injury, either intentionally or through gross negligence, the damages payable may be reduced or lapse.

Decommissioning generally takes place after the license has terminated, lapsed or been relinquished, and it could be argued that decommissioning activities are outside the license and, therefore, the strict liability provision of section 35 does not apply. However, decommissioning takes place as a natural

39 Floating production storage and offloading vessels. In many cases the FPSO's ownership remains with the FPSO owning contractor that may also man and operate the vessel which is leased by the licensees.

40 *Travaux préparatoires* LFF 2015-01-28 No. 116 Danish Subsoil Act, Special Comments to No. 22.

41 Fornyelsesfonden, "A Danish Field Platforms and Pipelines Decommissioning programmes": https://www.scribd.com/document/410055848/A-danish-field-platforms-and-pipelines-decommissioning-programmes-pdf, p. 29.

continuation of the exclusive rights conferred on the licensee and is an obligation placed on the licensee by the license as well. On that basis, decommissioning should be considered part of the license and would consequently also be covered by section 35.[42]

In order to cover potential liability, licensees are obligated in accordance with Section 24e of the Danish Subsoil Act, section 30 of the model license and section 3.12 of the model JOA, to obtain and maintain adequate insurance to cover damage to installations, pollution and environmental damage, site restoration and liability towards third parties amongst other things.

The group of licensees can, in accordance with section 31 of the license, become liable on a joint and several basis for loss, damage or injury that happens during decommissioning.

The actual decommissioning work consists of a wide variety of work-scopes. It is likely that a number of different contractors will be carrying out the various aspects of decommissioning works such as removing and transporting installations, plugging and permanently abandoning wells etc. As the contractors will be conducting the work, some form of risk allocation will be agreed between the licensees and the contractors. There are no standard contracts available on the Danish market and companies may rely on their own contracts or use, for example, LOGIC's standards for offshore construction work or the international standard contract DISMANTLECON that was developed by BIMCO[43] in May 2019. Whichever form of contracting is used, it is certain that liability clauses will be intensely scrutinized. The future will tell whether liability caps, time-limits on the contractors' liability and other forms of liability limitation will be accepted by licensees.

4.3. SECURITY FOR DECOMMISSIONING LIABILITIES

All licensees must have sufficient financial and technical capability to carry out license activities including decommissioning activities (cf section 24a of the Danish Subsoil Act). The Danish Energy Agency carries out a specific assessment of the financial capacity of licensees in each individual case. Furthermore the Danish Energy Agency will assess whether the security is sufficient prior to entering into each new phase of the license activities in accordance with

---

42 M. Jespersen, "Fjernelse af Anlæg fra Den Danske Kontinentalsokkel", *Marius No 196*, Sjørettsfondet, 1993. Similar approach is found in the Norwegian Petroleum Activities Act. M. Hammerson and N. Anthonas, *Oil and Gas Decommissioning Law, Policy and Comparative Practice*, Globe Law and Business, 2016, p. 308.

43 BIMCO is the world's largest international shipping association. BIMCO produces standard contracts for the shipping and offshore industry.

section 24b of the Danish Subsoil Act. As mentioned above the licensees must provide the Danish Energy Agency with adequate security for the completion of their license obligations (cf section 32 of the license and 24f of the Danish Subsoil Act).

The security must be made in favor of the Danish state for all public law and private law obligations and for all liabilities related to loss, damage or injury caused by the license activities. The security required is an unconditional and irrevocable guarantee as a surety with primary liability (*selvskylderkaution*), without any limitation in time for, "the due satisfaction of all existing and future obligations and liabilities incurred".[44]

The security is usually provided by way of a parent company guarantee, but only if the parent company's financial position is acceptable as demonstrated by a satisfactory rating from a recognized rating agency such as Standard & Poor's, Moody's or Fitch Ratings. In cases where a parent company is not accepted, the security can be provided by way of bank guarantee or an escrow account.[45] Failure to provide adequate security will result in the party not being awarded the license.

As possible claims for damages may arise years after the activities have been carried out, a guarantee is not generally limited in time and is therefore not usually returnable. However, if the guarantor requests it, the Danish Energy Agency may carry out a specific assessment to determine if the guarantee can be returned. The guarantee is more likely to be returned in the case where it is replaced by a new guarantee, when for example a licensee assigns its license interest. The Danish Energy Agency has stated that it is unlikely that a guarantee will be returned when a well is involved in the license activities, irrespective of whether the well is plugged and abandoned.[46]

Based on the model Parent Company Guarantee section 3, the guarantee relates to liabilities incurred by the licensee in relation to activities carried out under the license regardless of whether such obligations and liabilities are incumbent on the licensee "solely or jointly and severally with any Co-licensees and/or other parties". However, pursuant to section 5, the individual license-holder's guarantee is capped at twice the respective guaranteed entity's share of the relevant liability.

---

[44] A model Parent Company Guarantee can be found at: https://ens.dk/en/our-responsibilities/oil-gas/legislation-and-guidelines. It should be noted that only guarantees in Danish wording will be accepted by the Danish Energy Agency.

[45] The bank or financial institution must hold an internationally recognized credit rating corresponding to "upper medium grade" or better, corresponding to A3 (Moody's), A- (S&P), A- (Fitch) or a similar rating from another internationally recognized credit rating institution.

[46] Guidelines on security and insurances, p. 4.

4.4. SECONDARY FINANCIAL LIABILITY FOR DECOMMISSIONING

In 2015 secondary financial liability was introduced in Denmark with section 29a of the Danish Subsoil Act in order to mitigate the risk of future licensees being less financially stable and defaulting on their decommissioning obligations. In accordance with section 29a, a party assigning its share of interest in a license remains secondarily liable for decommissioning costs related to any installations that existed at the time of assignment (this includes installations on which work had begun – cf section 32a). Secondary financial liability applies both in cases of direct and indirect assignment.

Secondary liability relates to all parties who have been granted a license in accordance with section 5 of the Danish Subsoil Act (exploration and production of hydrocarbons), section 17 (establishing and operating pipelines) or section 23 (exploration and use of the subsoil for storage or purposes other than production).

The assignor only retains secondary financial liability for installations which existed at the time of transfer. Pursuant to the *travaux préparatoires* and the guidelines, these installations are defined as facilities and installations such as platforms, subsea installations, pipelines etc. which existed physically and were placed at the site of their use at the time of assignment. Installations also include initiated installations, including drill rigs being used within the licensed area, and pipelines in the process of being positioned in the approved position.

The assignor cannot become liable for decommissioning costs of facilities which were installed after the time of the transfer. The time of transfer is determined as the point in time from which the Danish Energy Agency has approved that the transfer will take place. The specific "time of transfer" will usually be found in the assignment agreement between the assignor and assignee.

The assignor's financial liability is limited pursuant to section 29a(3) to a pro rata share of the expenses for carrying out the decommissioning attributable to the assigned interest.

The assignor's liability is further limited by the fact that it is secondary. Consequently, the assignor only becomes liable if the assignee has defaulted. All legal rights and options provided in the JOA must have been exhausted before any secondary liability is activated.

If the assignee ("Original Assignee") subsequently assigns all or part of its license interest to a new assignee ("New Assignee"), the liability of the Original Assignee remains. However, the New Assignee will become secondarily liable for future decommissioning costs while the original assignor moves down and becomes "tertiarily" liable and so forth with every new assignment. The remaining licensees must first direct any claim towards the last assignor and, in accordance with the Danish Subsoil Act, it can only be directed towards a previous assignor if the later assignor defaults on its payment.

In accordance with section 29a(1), the assignor is liable to both the remaining licensees as well as state-owned companies and the Danish state if the state has been compelled to take over the decommissioning on behalf of the assignee.

The assigning party must enter into an assignment agreement with the remaining licensees dealing specifically with the question of secondary liability. The *travaux préparatoires* state that this agreement should be made in accordance with the same principles as the decommissioning plans which the licensees must prepare pursuant to section 32a(6). The Guidelines on Decommissioning Plans specifically state that, as part of the economic aspects of the decommissioning plans, the licensees are obligated to inform previous licensees about updated information on decommissioning costs and the estimated trigger point for decommissioning as soon as information is available.[47] It must be expected that the assignment security agreement will provide additional details on this right to receive future information.

In June 2018 the Danish Energy Agency developed a standard declaration on secondary liability which the assigning licensee must provide to both the Danish state and the at-any-time-remaining licensees.

It should be noted that, at this stage, financial liability for decommissioning under the Danish Subsoil Act does not extend to contractors who may own and lease facilities to the licensees at a field. This differs from similar arrangements under, for instance, the UK Petroleum Act 1998,[48] which allows the relevant authority to issue "Section 29 notices" for decommissioning to owners and managers of installations on a field even where they are not licensees in the field.[49]

4.5. DURATION OF LIABILITY

The question of duration of liability related to decommissioning is of utmost relevance for the licensees, especially for abandoned wells or when a permit is granted to leave all or any part of installations or facilities in place. The international regulations allow for derogation from the total removal requirement in cases where the installation is, for example, made of concrete. The expected deterioration time for concrete installations in water is between 500 and 1,000 years, which effectively means that if liability is not limited in time the licensees carry the liability in perpetuity.

---

47 Section 32a: Guidelines on decommissioning plans for offshore oil and gas facilities or installations, p. 6.

48 See section 30(1) of the UK Petroleum Act 1998, which outlines who the Secretary of State can issue notices to requiring them to submit a decommissioning plan.

49 J. Paterson, 'Decommissioning of offshore installations' in G. Gordon and J. Paterson (eds), *Oil and Gas Law – Current Practice and Emerging Trends*, Dundee University Press, 2007, p. 168.

Neither the Danish Subsoil Act nor the Danish Continental Shelf Act contain provisions on the length of the liability for installations or facilities left *in situ*. Consequently, the liability is not limited in time and may remain with licensees as long as any part of the installation is not removed, which is also supported by the Danish Energy Agency's statement that parent company guarantees will not be returned in cases where a well is involved in the license activities.[50] This question has led to very difficult negotiations in other North Sea jurisdictions where environmental considerations may make the most favored decommissioning method unacceptable to licensees. For example, leaving a pipeline *in situ* may be the best environmental solution but licensees may not be willing to accept the unlimited time liability that would come with that. The liability will naturally be extra burdensome for the licensees if they would retain a *strict liability* beyond the time when decommissioning has been completed. As this question has not been specifically addressed in Danish legislation, the starting point must be that the strict liability is not time limited. However, should strict liability end when the decommissioning phase is completed, then licensees would only remain liable for any installations left *in situ* in accordance with general Danish regulation of liability.[51]

5. DECOMMISSIONING OF PIPELINES

5.1. INTERNATIONAL VIEW ON PIPELINES

As various types of pipelines are used in relation to exploration and production of oil and gas it should first be clarified which "type" of pipeline is being discussed in order to determine which legal regime applies to the pipeline in question. For the legal discussion it is most practical to make this distinction based on the use: i) the intra- or inter-field pipelines; and ii) the field-to-coast pipelines (Transit pipelines fall outside the scope of this chapter). Intra-field pipelines connect two or more installations or structures within a license area, whereas inter-field pipelines connect installations or structures across license areas. The field-to-coast pipelines transport the hydrocarbons from the fields to an onshore facility or pipeline system.

As described above in Section 3.1, the coastal state has the exclusive right to authorize and to regulate "the construction, operation and use of installations

50 Danish regulation on CCS allows for the responsibility of a storage site to be transferred to the competent authority under certain provisions and upon payment of financial contribution. A similar approach may be accepted and taken by the authorities in the future with regards to oil and gas installations which, for whatever reason, have wholly or partly been left *in situ*.

51 G. Tuesen, Olieeventyrets problembørn – regulering og fjernelse af installationer til havs, *UfR.1996B.235*.

and structures" in accordance with UNCLOS article 60. IMO's 1989 guidelines similarly apply to the removal of "installations and structures". However, neither "installations" nor "structures" are defined terms and the question is whether a pipeline used in relation to exploration and production of hydrocarbons should be considered an installation or a structure.

Unlike the field-to-coast pipelines which cross into territorial waters, the intra- and inter-field pipelines are purely located on the Danish Continental Shelf. It is generally agreed in the legal literature that production platforms are installations.[52] Intra-field pipelines are generally viewed as part of the production installation[53] and are consequently subject to the functional jurisdiction of the coastal state – cf. article 60 of UNCLOS. Inter-field pipelines are more difficult to categorize as they can be part of the production installation in the case of, for example, a tie-in or can function more as a transportation pipeline bringing e.g. the produced oil to a field-to-coast pipeline. In either case these pipelines are, regardless of the classification, connected to the production facilities and are subject to Danish functional jurisdiction – cf. article 60.[54]

The field-to-coast pipelines are generally accepted to fall under UNCLOS article 79(4). They go from the Exclusive Economic Zone of the continental shelf through the territorial waters and onshore, and are subject to the jurisdiction of the coastal state.[55]

5.2. DANISH VIEW ON PIPELINES

5.2.1. *Pipelines and Terminology in Danish Legislation*

Similarly to UNCLOS, the Danish Subsoil Act does not contain a definition of installations or structure in general. Indeed the Act never even uses the term "structure". It refers to pipelines interchangeably as either a "pipeline" or a "rørledningsanlæg". This term is translated as a "pipeline facility" in the unofficial translation of the Danish Subsoil Act. The term "anlæg" is also used to refer to production platforms, for example, and the term is in fact translated both as "installation" and "facility" in the unofficial translation. Furthermore, pipelines are indirectly referred to as both an installation and facility in the Act.

---

52 M.M. Roggenkamp, "Petroleum Pipelines in the North Sea: Questions of Jurisdiction and Practical Status", *Journal of Energy and Natural Resources Law*, 1998, p. 94.

53 C. Redgwell 'International Regulation of Energy Activities' in M.M. Roggenkamp, C. Redgwell, A. Rønne and I. Del Guayo (eds), *Energy Law in Europe*, Oxford University Press, 2016, p. 64.

54 Ibid.

55 Ibid.

Some clarity was provided in 2018 when the Guidelines on decommissioning plans included a definition of "installations" which included: i) pipelines internally in fields, between several fields, and to the shore; ii) pipelines for use for production of hydrocarbons from Danish territory; and iii) pipelines and preparation plant on the Danish Continental Shelf for use for production from foreign fields.

The starting point is consequently that Danish decommissioning regulation pursuant to the Danish Subsoil Act applies equally to pipelines and production platforms.

The Danish Offshore Safety Act applies to oil and gas operations as defined in section 3(1)(16), which include

> all activities related to exploration and production and pipeline transport of oil and gas as well as other substances and materials between the offshore installation and onshore installation, or between several offshore installations, including design, planning, construction, installation offshore, as well as the operation, modification and decommissioning of installations, connected infrastructure and pipelines.

Unlike the Danish Subsoil Act, there is a clear definition of "installations" in the Offshore Safety Act in section 3(1)(1), based on the Offshore Safety Directive. Pipelines are not included in the definition of installations.[56] In line with the directive, the Danish Offshore Safety Act also makes a distinction between the operator who, among other things, controls the function of a production installation and the owner, who e.g. controls the operation of a pipeline.

As can be seen there is an inconsistent use of the terms installations and facilities between these two Acts and it can cause some confusion over terminology.

5.2.2. *Regulation of Pipelines in Denmark*

Pipelines on the Danish Continental Shelf are regulated by different Danish Acts depending on the intended use and ownership. The Danish Subsoil Act regulates pipelines used in offshore oil and gas production – the so-called intra- and inter-field pipelines. The Danish Subsoil Act refers to intra-field pipelines as "local pipelines". The Pipeline Act[57] regulates the government-owned oil pipeline going from the offshore fields to the onshore terminal at Fredericia. Finally, the Danish Continental Shelf Act[58] regulates all other pipelines on the Danish Continental Shelf.

56 See *travaux préparatoires* No. 49 of 30 October 2014, Special comments to section 3.

57 Consolidated Danish Act No. 277 of 25 March 2014 on the Establishment and Utilisation of a Pipeline for Transportation of Crude Oil and Condensate.

58 Executive Order No. 361 of 18 November 2006 on certain pipeline installations for transport of hydrocarbons on the territorial sea and continental shelf provides a more detailed regulation than what is found in the Continental Shelf Act.

Uniquely for Denmark compared with other North Sea countries, all field-to-shore pipelines have been constructed and owned by a state-owned company.

A license must be obtained in accordance with section 17 of the Danish Subsoil Act in order to establish a pipeline on the Danish Continental Shelf related to offshore oil and gas production. Similarly to licenses used for oil and gas production, the licenses used for pipelines lay down high-level regulations for what should be done with the pipeline after it becomes disused or when the license expires or is relinquished without imposing any general removal obligation.

The Danish Energy Agency has not developed a model license for the construction or operation of pipelines. Over the years a few licenses have been made publicly available; however, only one of these licenses was related to construction of a pipeline under the Danish Subsoil Act.[59] Of those licenses made publicly available, all appeared to have similar wording notwithstanding that they were governed by different Acts. The licenses simply state that when the pipeline will be taken out of use the method of disposal will be determined by the legislation in place at the time as well as the internationally recognized standards. The licenses generally state that the Danish Energy Agency may require the pipeline to be wholly or partially removed.[60]

As seen, despite the inconsistent terminology used, pipelines are subject to the same decommissioning scheme as other offshore "installations" under Danish legislation. However, the final decision on the decommissioning method may vary, as removal of a pipeline can cause significant disturbance to the seabed.

The Danish government has previously stated that all installations on the Danish Continental Shelf should be removed. However, these general remarks do not seem to have been aimed at pipelines, and indeed the few pipelines which have been taken out of use have been cleaned, plugged and left *in situ*.[61] It is not yet clear whether this is because a decision as to the final decommissioning method of these pipelines has been postponed, or whether it is an indication of how pipelines generally will be dealt with in Denmark going forward.

6. CONCLUSION

By contrast to other North Sea states, decommissioning of unused installations has not yet taken place on the Danish Continental Shelf. However, as major

59 Other licenses related to the construction of the pipeline between the Harald and Trym fields and the Nord Stream pipeline.

60 C.G. Brett and L.S. Christensen, "Denmark" in M. Hammerson and N. Anthonas (eds), *Oil and Gas Decommissioning Law, Policy and Comparative Practice*, Globe Law and Business, 2016, p. 308.

61 See eg, Permit for replacing a pipeline between Halfdan A and Dan FG, 11 June 2009 and Miljø og Klima, *Danmarks Olie og Gas Produktion 2008*, Chapter 4.

redevelopment will take place in the Tyra field and as production is rapidly declining in other fields, decommissioning has become a topic of increased focus from both industry and the Danish authorities in recent years. Both parties have worked closely together to ensure clarity in the regulatory framework and guidelines in order to ensure safe decommissioning that complies with Denmark's international obligations.

Recognizing international regulations, the Danish Energy Agency has previously stated that as a starting point, all installations on the continental shelf must be removed, although it may be appropriate to retain some installations for future import and offshore storage. In case of decommissioning, it is necessary in each decommissioning case to strike the right balance between environmental risks, health and safety challenges, as well as technical challenges both in the situations where a derogation from the removal obligation can be granted, but also when determining the actual removal method.

As in other North Sea states, the possibility of re-use of installations has been investigated. The Offshore Center Denmark[62] conducted a study on decommissioning of the Danish platforms and pipelines in 2011. This study of decommissioning possibilities considered all options for re-use *in situ* of the existing facilities, including conversion into a renewable energy hub, a fish farm, a prison, military application, a navigation beacon, a communication hub, or for CO_2 sequestration or gas storage. All possibilities were found to be too uncertain and opportunity-driven, while also leaving too many uncertainties regarding ownership and future decommissioning liabilities unresolved. Therefore, the possibility for re-use was rejected.[63]

The study also evaluated all potential options for re-use of pipelines in their current or other positions. It was found that the re-use of pipelines was technically and economically unfeasible.[64]

If indeed the Danish state sees a potential for re-use of some installations for other purposes then many uncertainties concerning ownership, liability and maintenance will have to first be resolved.[65] It is certain that the last word has not been written in this final chapter of hydrocarbon production in Denmark and additional regulatory clarification will need to be provided along the way.

---

62 This study was carried out with the Fornyelsesfonden: a foundation under the Danish Business Authority, and also in cooperation with Semco Maritime, Offshore Energy, Rambøll, Blue Water Shipping and Stena Innovative Recycling.

63 Fornyelsesfonden, A Danish Field, Platforms and Pipelines Decommissioning Programmes, p. 70.

64 Fornyelsesfonden, Danish Sustainable Offshore Decommissioning project, p. 18.

65 Denmark's Oil and Gas Production 2009, report published by the Danish Energy Agency, 2010, p. 41.

CHAPTER XVII
DECOMMISSIONING PRACTICE IN NORWAY

Dag Erlend HENRIKSEN

1. INTRODUCTION

This chapter aims to put decommissioning on the Norwegian Continental Shelf (NCS) into a historic and factual perspective. In addition it intends to present the basic regulatory framework governing decommissioning and to provide some comments on the future of decommissioning on the NCS. It is thus not its purpose to present and review the *details* of Norwegian decommissioning law.

The chapter is structured as follows: section 2 starts with a brief overview of the history of oil and gas exploration and production on the NCS and also provides some facts and figures with regard to decommissioning. This is followed in section 3 by an introduction to Norwegian decommissioning law, which includes public law and the contractual regime between licensees. Finally, section 4 will provide some thoughts on the future of decommissioning on the NCS.

2. DECOMMISSIONING ON THE NCS: BRIEF HISTORIC AND FACTUAL BACKGROUND

Petroleum activities started on the NCS in 1965 with the award of the first production licences. The first discovery was made early in 1967, but it was not until the end of 1969 that the first commercial discovery was made. This was the Ekofisk-field, which started producing in 1972 and which is still producing. Since then more than 1000 production licences have been awarded, of which approximately 600 are still active today.[1] There are 41 companies holding licence interests in these licences.[2]

---

1 Figures from September 2019.

2 An important part of Norwegian petroleum policy is to award production licences to a group of companies qualified on the basis of their exploration and production capabilities.

Even if less than half the expected recoverable resources on the NCS have been produced, the NCS is a mature petroleum province. Currently there are around 85 fields producing, as well as some 8000 km of gas export pipelines. There are close to 500 installations on the NCS, and among these are 12 concrete installations, 23 steel floating installations and 59 steel installations resting on the seabed. In addition, there are close to 400 subsea installations. The 12 concrete installations represent approximately 70 per cent of the total weight of all installations on the NCS. Many of these installations are approaching the end of their expected lifetime. However, production and installation lifetime has in many cases been extended substantially due to the tie-in of satellite fields and improved recovery. These factors have prolonged the economic viability of installations, and pushed back the expected deadline for a final disposal decision. It should be expected that this trend will be strengthened in the future.[3]

All petroleum installations are subject to the decommissioning requirements of the Petroleum Act. The same set of rules applies to concrete gravity base structures weighing more than 1 million tonnes, floating vessels such as FPSOs, subsea structures placed on the seabed, pipelines, cables and wells. The term 'decommissioning' is not defined in the Petroleum Act, but is generally understood as the phase in the lifetime of an installation where it goes from production to permanent shutdown and subsequently to final disposal. Thus, the term decommissioning comprises shutting down production permanently, cleaning the installation and removing any hazardous substances, abandonment, removal and scrapping of an installation.

The first decommissioning projects on the NCS were carried out as early as 1996 and 1997 and followed the shutdown of North East Frigg and the Odin field in 1993 and 1994, respectively. The most recent decommissioning project involves the successful single-lift removal of the 13,000 tonnes Yme platform topside in August 2016.[4] It is expected that in the period up to 2025 that installations of a total weight of close to 200,000 tonnes need to decommissioned – all of which are situated in the North Sea, i.e. the southern parts of the NCS.

From 1995 when the first decommissioning plan was approved and until November 2018 around 20 decommissioning plans have been processed and approved by the authorities. A total number of 20 decommissioning plans have been approved so far, of which six have been approved in the last two years.

Consequently, production licences are never awarded to a single company. The word 'licensees' in this chapter thus refers to a licence group.

3 Ref. Proposition 80 S (2017–2018) on development and operation of the Johan Castberg-field including status for the oil and gas business proposal to the Storting (parliament), section 2.2.5 on p. 33.

4 Interestingly enough, all these three fields are under re-development and will be producing again under newly awarded production licences with new licensees.

In the coming five-year period about 25 per cent of the fields producing today may be closed. Although this seems a major increase, the situation is not as dramatic as it may look. This is due to the fact that production from these fields is marginal compared to total production.

3. NORWEGIAN DECOMMISSIONING LAW

3.1. INTRODUCTION

It is customary to describe the relevant legal framework as comprising three main components: the international legal instruments such as treaties and conventions, the applicable domestic legislation and the contractual regime between licensees and between licensees and contractors. In this section, I will only briefly describe the international legal instruments and the contractual regime, and rather concentrate on the most relevant parts of domestic legislation.

Norwegian petroleum legislation is structured along the different phases of petroleum activities: from the opening of areas, exploration, development, production, to cessation of production and decommissioning. Decommissioning has been addressed in the legislation from as early as 1965, when the first Petroleum Regulation was enacted. This was continued into the updated Regulation of 1972 and was further developed in Norway's first Petroleum Act of 1985. With the revised Petroleum Act of 1996, we saw a comprehensive set of rules on decommissioning in Chapter 5 of the Act, which was further detailed in Chapter 6 of the applicable Petroleum Regulation. See section 3.3 below where these provisions are explained in more detail.

3.2. RELEVANT INTERNATIONAL LEGAL INSTRUMENTS

Albeit that the Norwegian petroleum legislation provides authorities wide discretionary powers to make decisions on decommissioning and final disposal, these powers are limited by international treaties and conventions to which Norway is a party, most notably the following:

- The Geneva Convention on the Continental Shelf of 1958[5]
- The UN Convention on the Law of the Sea of 1982 (UNCLOS)[6]

---

5 https://treaties.un.org/doc/Treaties/1964/06/19640610%2002-10%20AM/Ch_XXI_01_2_3_4_5p.pdf.

6 https://treaties.un.org/Pages/ViewDetailsIII.aspx?src=TREATY&mtdsg_no=XXI-6&chapter=21&Temp=mtdsg3&clang=_en.

- The Convention for the Protection of the Marine Environment of the North-East Atlantic of 1992[7] (OSPAR)
- The IMO Guidelines and Standards for the Removal of Offshore Installations and Structures on the Continental Shelf and in the Exclusive Economic Zone (IMO Resolution A.672) of 1989[8]

The Norwegian legal system is based on a principle of incorporation, which entails that neither of these treaties is directly applicable under Norwegian law. Nevertheless, under the principle of assumption of compliance, whereby interpretation of Norwegian law is to be based on an assumption that it complies with international law,[9] these treaties are still relevant to the interpretation and application of Norwegian law. This implies that the provisions of the Petroleum Act will be interpreted and applied within the boundaries stipulated by these treaties. Thus, when applying the powers under the Act to make decisions on decommissioning, abandonment and final disposal of installations, Norwegian authorities will comply with the existing restrictions set out by, in particular, the OSPAR convention.

In general, this implies that dumping or abandonment as a starting point will not be allowed under Norwegian law unless specifically permitted by competent authorities in compliance with recommendations and decisions adopted under the OSPAR convention. OSPAR decision 98/3 addresses disposal of disused offshore installations, and states that abandonment as an option for final disposal is only allowed for concrete installations and the bottom frame of steel installations weighing more than 10,000 tonnes which were put in place before 9 February 1999.

3.3. DOMESTIC LEGISLATION[10]

3.3.1. *Introduction*

The obligation to carry out decommissioning arises as a consequence of a field development, meaning that any installation used in petroleum activities under a licence according to Sections 3-3 or 4-3 of the Petroleum Act must be subject

7 https://www.ospar.org/site/assets/files/1290/ospar_convention_e_updated_text_in_2007_no_revs.pdf.

8 https://cil.nus.edu.sg/wp-content/uploads/formidable/18/1989-Guidelines-and-Standards-for-the-Removal-of-Offshore-Installations-and-Structures-on-the-Continental-Shelf-and-in-the-Exclusive-Economic-Zone.pdf.

9 Jan E. Helgesen, *Teorier om 'folkerettens stilling i norsk rett'* (Oslo 1982).

10 Norwegian domestic legislation on decommissioning has been the subject of numerous articles and lectures, e.g. Bakken, Kristensen and Navestad in 'Oil and Gas Decommissioning: Law, Policy and Comparative Practice' (2013). See also the white paper Meld. St. 28 (2010–2011) – An industry for the future – Norway's petroleum activities.

to a decommissioning plan, which is to be submitted as set out in the detailed provisions of Chapter 5 of the Petroleum Act – see section 3.3.2 below where a detailed review of these provisions is included.

The obligation to prepare and submit a decommissioning plan rests with the licensees: either the licensees to a production licence[11] where the installations are placed, or the licensees to a so-called 'pipeline licence'.[12] The decommissioning plan forms the basis for the authorities' decision with respect to the decommissioning activities; upon approval of the decommissioning plan, the authorities will make a decision on final disposal. The licensees will then be obliged to carry out the actual decommissioning according to such decision.

Specific decommissioning requirements are to be determined on a case-by-case basis, as is the solution for final disposal. Within the limits of international obligations, a decision on final disposal may be complete or partial abandonment or removal, dumping, scrapping onshore or reuse.

3.3.2. *Overview of the Relevant Provisions of the Petroleum Act*

As mentioned above, decommissioning is addressed in Chapter 5 of the Petroleum Act, which provides a comprehensive framework regarding decommissioning:

- Section 5-1 sets out the obligation of the licensees to submit a decommissioning plan.
- Section 5-2 states that the licensees must notify the Ministry of Petroleum and Energy (MPE) of the time of termination if the use of an installation is expected to terminate permanently prior to the expiry of the licence.
- Section 5-3 provides both the powers for the MPE to make a decision with respect to disposal and the legal obligation for licensees to carry out the decision. In addition, this section provides a legal basis for the secondary liability of a former licensee.
- Section 5-4 regulates the liability for damages and abandonment, and provides for a possibility for the licensees and the State to agree on a take-over by the State of future liabilities against an agreed financial compensation.
- Section 5-5 stipulates that encumbrances on an installation which is required to be removed, will lapse.
- Section 5-6 provides for a right of the Norwegian State to take over fixed installations if a licence expires, is surrendered or revoked, or when the use of such a fixed installation has been terminated permanently, and sets out more detailed provisions in case this right is exercised.[13]

---

[11] Section 3-3 of the Petroleum Act.

[12] Section 4-2 of the Petroleum Act.

[13] The take-over right for the State in Section 5-6 has never been used.

The details of these provisions will be discussed in more detail in the following paragraphs.

3.3.3. *The Decommissioning Plan*

The decommissioning plan is the key tool for authorities when making a decision on the disposal of installations. The decommissioning plan shall be submitted to both the MPE and the Ministry of Labour and Social Affairs.[14]

According to Section 5-1 of the Petroleum Act a decommissioning plan shall be submitted between five and two years prior to the expiry of the production licence or the permanent cessation of the use of the installation. However, the MPE may decide upon or consent to a different timescale for submitting the decommissioning plan. Licensees are required to prepare and submit a decommissioning plan during the mentioned time period regardless of whether the most probable solution for an installation is further use. The reason for this is to ensure that the decision on disposal is taken on the basis of a holistic approach where all possible solutions are considered.

Thus, the decommissioning plan shall include the licensees' proposal for either continued production or cessation of production and disposal of installations. Section 5-1 lists some alternatives for disposal, but others may also be relevant; further use related to petroleum activities, other use, complete or partial removal or abandonment. Further use related to petroleum activities may comprise continued production from the licence area or providing processing services to other fields, and other uses may e.g. be related to transport or storage of CO_2.

The decommissioning plan shall consist of two parts; a part dealing with disposal and a part on impact assessment.[15] There are few specific requirements regarding the content of the plan; Section 5-1 of the Petroleum Act merely states that the plan shall include all information and assessments deemed necessary to make a decision on disposal according to Section 5-3.

With respect to the disposal part of the decommissioning plan, some more information on the required content is provided in the two first paragraphs of Section 44 of the Regulation to the Petroleum Act:[16]

> The disposal part of the decommissioning plan shall contain a description of:
>
> a) The field history;
> b) The facility, including location, depth, type of material etc.;

---

14 Regulation 27.06.1997 no 653 section 43 last paragraph (http://www.npd.no/en/Regulations/Regulations/Petroleum-activities/#Section 43).

15 Regulation 27.06.1997 no 653 section 43 first paragraph (http://www.npd.no/en/Regulations/Regulations/Petroleum-activities/#Section 43).

16 Regulation 27.06.1997 no 653 section 44 (http://www.npd.no/en/Regulations/Regulations/Petroleum-activities/#Section 44).

> c) Deposit and production;
> d) The possibility for continued production;
> e) Relevant disposal alternatives;
> f) Other aspects of importance to the choice of disposal solution;
> g) Recommended disposal solution, including a time schedule for implementation of the disposal;
> h) Other information required pursuant to the safety regulations applicable at any time.
>
> For each of the relevant disposal alternatives the following shall be dealt with:
>
> a) Technical, safety related, environmental and economic aspects;
> b) Relationship to other users of the sea, including information and evaluations on the impact on fisheries and shipping.

The requirements regarding the content of the impact assessment follow from the first paragraph of Section 45 of the Regulation:[17]

> The impact assessment shall contain a description of the effect that each of the relevant disposal alternatives may have on commercial and environmental aspects, and what can be done to reduce discharges and emissions in connection with disposal, and to remedy any damage or inconvenience.

According to Section 5-1 third paragraph of the Petroleum Act the Ministry may exempt the licensees from the obligation to submit a decommissioning plan.

3.3.4. *The Decision on Disposal*

As mentioned above, the decommissioning plan is the key tool for the authorities when making a decision on disposal of the installations, cf. Section 5-3 of the Petroleum Act. The decision is made by the MPE, in close co-operation with the Ministry of Labour and Social Affairs as the superior body to the Petroleum Safety Authority. When making the disposal decision and stipulating conditions, the Ministry is not bound by the decommissioning plan and the licensee's proposals.

Albeit that the provision itself does not prescribe a specific solution and thus provides the MPE with discretionary powers, the first paragraph of Section 5-3 states that the Ministry shall base its decision on evaluations of technical, safety, environmental and economic concerns as well as consideration of other users of the sea. The reason for limiting the discretion of the MPE in this manner is to ensure that a disposal solution is not solely

---

17 Regulation 27.06.1997 no 653 section 45 (http://www.npd.no/en/Regulations/Regulations/Petroleum-activities/#Section 45).

based upon economic concerns, but also upon securing that other concerns, such as environmental considerations and considerations concerning other users of the sea, are taken into account.

Both parts of the decommissioning plan, the disposal part and the impact assessment part, are made subject to a public consultation process. The purpose of this process is twofold: to inform the public and affected interests, and to receive comments on the licensees' proposal for disposal.

On the basis of this public consultation process and its own review of the received decommissioning plan, the Ministry may require further information and evaluations.

Before making its decision, the Ministry may also, in the event that the factual circumstances or the assumptions that formed the basis for the submitted decommissioning plan have changed significantly, require a new or amended plan to be submitted. The Ministry may also stipulate specific conditions in connection with the decision, typically to protect affected interests such as other users of the sea, or to require the use of specific technology or methods when carrying out the decommissioning activities.

When making its decision, the Ministry shall set a time limit for the licensees' implementation of the decision.

3.3.5. *The Obligation to Implement the Disposal Decision*

The decision and the conditions stipulated in the disposal decision are legally binding upon the licensees, who are obliged to carry out the necessary decommissioning activities to comply with the decision. This obligation is unaffected of the possible expiry of the licence prior to the completion of the decommissioning activities; see Section 5-3 second paragraph last sentence, which says that the 'obligation to carry out the decision relating to disposal is applicable even if this decision is made or is to be implemented after the expiry of the licence.'

Section 5-3 also addresses the situation where the installation is not owned by the licensees, as would typically be the case with FPSOs or similar installations; see Section 5-3 second paragraph, which says that the 'licensee and *the owner* are under obligation to make sure that a decision relating to disposal is carried out, unless otherwise decided by the Ministry.' (emphasis added).

Should the licensees fail to carry out the decision on disposal within the specified time limit, the Ministry 'may take necessary measures on behalf of the licensees or other responsible parties, and for their account and risk' (see Section 5-3 sixth paragraph). Such measures could in the extreme case be to engage a contractor to carry out the decommissioning activities, or to effectuate contracts already entered into. Necessary measures may also be directed toward securing the integrity of the installation in order to ensure that removal is feasible, or to maintain navigational aids such as lights. This provision should be read in conjunction with Section 10-16, which provides the Ministry with powers to issue coercive fines in case the licensees should fail to meet a time limit specified in a decision.

Licensees or owners responsible for carrying out decommissioning are liable to third parties who suffer damages or inconveniences caused wilfully or negligently during the execution of such activities (see Section 5-4 first paragraph). This applies even if the damage or inconvenience is caused by a contractor engaged to carry out decommissioning activities on behalf of the licensees or the owner, in which case the contractor may be subject to a recourse claim.[18] Liability on the basis of Section 5-4 first paragraph could, according to the wording of the provision, arise from any activity carried out in relation to 'disposal of the facility or other implementation of the decision.' This implies that liability could be based upon Section 5-4 until the disposal decision has been completely fulfilled, regardless of whether the activity resulting in damage or inconvenience takes place offshore or onshore at a scrapping yard.

If it has been decided that the installation shall be abandoned, liability may be based on Section 5-4 second paragraph, which states that 'the licensee or owner shall be liable for damage or inconvenience caused willfully or inadvertently in connection with the abandoned facility, unless otherwise decided by the Ministry.'

Under the standard joint venture agreement applied in practically all production licences on the NCS, the licensees in the joint venture are jointly and severally liable for any obligations arising as a result of the activities of the joint venture. However, when an installation has been abandoned in accordance with a disposal decision, damage and inconvenience could occur after the expiry of the licence. Section 5-4 third paragraph aims at rectifying this and provides that when more than one party is liable according to the first or second paragraph, these parties are jointly and severally liable for financial obligations. Thus, this provision ensures that the licensees previously operating the installation will still be jointly and severally liable for damage and inconvenience caused in connection with the abandoned installations. According to Section 5-4 third paragraph, the Ministry may, however, decide otherwise. If a disposal decision directs that the installation shall be abandoned, the licensees and the State may agree that the responsibility for future maintenance and liability shall be transferred from the licensees to the State against an agreed financial compensation.

---

18 It should be noted that if the damage in question is caused by pollution resulting from decommissioning activities, the liability of the licensee is strict and regardless of fault, and that, in such a situation, any recourse against the contractor is limited. See: Section 7-4 of the Petroleum Act.

3.3.6. *Liability of Assignors – Secondary Liability*

3.3.6.1. Background

Section 5-3 third paragraph of the Petroleum Act states that if

> a licence or a participating interest in a licence has been transferred pursuant to Section 10-12 first paragraph, the assignor shall be alternatively liable for financial obligations towards the remaining licensees for the cost of carrying out the decision relating to disposal.

The purpose of this provision is to contribute to securing that there are sufficient means available to carry out the disposal decision. The effect of the provision is that a licensee will not be free from financial liability related to disposal of installations even if he assigns his participating interest in a licence to a new licensee towards the end of the production phase. If the buyer (the new licensee) fails to meet his obligations under the joint and several liability provisions of the joint operating agreement, the other licensees in the licence group may direct the claim against the seller (the previous licensee); the seller's liability is alternative – or secondary – to the buyer's liability.

This provision was introduced in 2009 and should be viewed against the development in stakeholder participation on the NCS during the 2000s.[19] Prior to 2000 the NCS was dominated by some 15–20 financially strong players, but in particular from 2001 onward new players emerged, some of which had substantially less financial capacity than the supermajors who dominated earlier. On the NCS today, the variety between licensees is greater than before with respect to financial capacity, technical competence, business strategies and objectives. Some of the newcomers were in particular targeting opportunities in late-life licences, and in combination with thin balance sheets, questions were raised as to whether the newcomers had the required financial strength to meet the financial commitments related to decommissioning. Due to the joint and several liability between licensees, this was perceived as creating higher financial risks for the other licensees. The secondary liability was introduced to reduce this risk.

3.3.6.2. Details of the Secondary Liability

The secondary liability of the previous licensee set forth in Section 5-3 third paragraph is merely a financial liability for the decommissioning costs. In case

---

19 See the preparatory works to this provision – Ot.pr. nr. 48 Om lov om endringer i lov 29. November 1996 nr. 72 om petroleumsvirksomhet, which can be found here: https://www.regjeringen.no/no/dokumenter/otprp-nr-48-2008-2009-/id550876/.

of a default by the new licensee, the assignor will not become responsible for implementing the disposal decision and for carrying out the decommissioning activities.

In practice, the secondary liability will be directed against the assignor through a claim for recourse from the non-defaulting licensees who, in accordance with the joint and several liability of the joint operating agreement, have been obliged to cover the buyer's share of decommissioning costs.

There is no statute of limitations for the secondary liability as such; an assignor may become liable regardless of when the transfer of the licence interest took place. If the licence interest has been subject to subsequent transfers, the claim should be directed against the latest assignor: see Section 5-3 third paragraph fourth sentence which states that the

> assignor's obligations will exist through subsequent transfers of the licence or a participating interest in the licence, but to the effect that claims shall initially be directed to the company being the previous assignor of the participating interest.

According to Section 5-3 third paragraph third sentence, the secondary liability is calculated on the basis of the size of the licence interest assigned. This serves to limit the assignor's liability to a share of the decommissioning costs proportionate to the licence interest he has sold.

Further, the third sentence of Section 5-3 third paragraph states that the secondary liability shall be stipulated after deduction of the tax value of the decommissioning costs, i.e. the liability is calculated on an after-tax basis. As the combined tax rate of the applicable corporate tax and the petroleum tax amounts to 78 per cent, the claim against the assignor will therefore only represent 22 per cent of the incurred decommissioning costs defaulted on by the buyer. The effect of this after-tax calculation of the liability is that the payment by the seller of a recourse claim for defaulted decommissioning costs is not deductible from its taxable income, and for the receiving parties, this payment is not treated as taxable income.

The secondary liability is limited to those installations that existed[20] at the time of the transfer.[21] This implies that the seller will only be liable for

---

20 This expression is defined in the first paragraph of Section 45a of the Regulations to the Petroleum Act as 'facilities, including wells, that existed physically at the time of the transfer and that are located at their destination.' This provision further states that the 'liability also comprises facilities commenced, including wells, in the process of being located within the area for the production licence.' See: http://www.npd.no/en/Regulations/Regulations/Petroleum-activities/#Section 45a.

21 According to the second paragraph of Section 45a of the Regulations to the Petroleum Act, the time of transfer is defined as the day the transfer is registered in the Petroleum Register. See: http://www.npd.no/en/Regulations/Regulations/Petroleum-activities/#Section 45a.

decommissioning costs related to the installations operating during the time he was a licensee.

3.3.6.3. Licence Transactions v Share Transactions

The secondary liability set out in Section 5-3 and described above applies only to licence transactions (asset deals), and not to transactions relating to the shares of a licensee or the parent company of a licensee (corporate transactions). This follows from the expression 'a licence or a participating interest in a licence' at the start of the provision. However, also corporate transactions which directly or indirectly relate to a licensee, are subject to the same consent requirement as asset deals provided that the shareholding in question 'may provide decisive control of a licensee possessing a participating interest in a licence' (see Section 10-12 first paragraph). In light of the fact that some players have withdrawn from the oil and gas business and some have sold their Norwegian oil and gas subsidiaries, the Ministry of Petroleum and Energy introduced in 2017 a condition for providing its consent to corporate transactions, that a seller of shares directly or indirectly in a licensee will also be liable on a secondary basis for any future default of the licensee of its share of decommissioning costs. Due to the fact that this liability does not follow directly from the Petroleum Act, but is merely a condition of the consent to the share transaction, the Ministry of Petroleum and Energy has issued a standard guarantee declaration that must be signed by the selling company.

3.3.6.4. Tax Issues Relating to Secondary Liability Settlement in Share Transactions

In contrast to the asset deals, the legislation does not offer an after-tax solution for the settlement based on the secondary liability of the seller of shares in a licensee. Due to the fact that sellers in this situation typically are domiciled in other countries, the tax treatment of a payment by the seller will not be subject to Norwegian tax legislation. However, the receipt of the payment by the non-defaulting licensees on the NCS will most likely be treated as taxable income. The Norwegian Oil and Gas Association has brought attention to this issue and asked the Ministry of Finance for amendments to the tax legislation, but so far the situation remains as set out above.

3.3.6.5. A Clean Exit is not Possible

This secondary liability for the seller, both in asset deals and in corporate transactions, implies that it is not possible to obtain a clean exit from the NCS. To limit the financial exposure for sellers, so-called decommissioning security agreements are more often than not required from the buyer or its parent company. The Norwegian Oil and Gas Association has prepared two alternative models for decommissioning security agreements: one based on the provision of a letter of credit and one based on a parent company guarantee.[22] The latter model is more comprehensive and includes the definition of a threshold below which the parent company's credit rating must not fall, and if it does, this model requires the buyer to provide a letter of credit. Both models apply a trigger date mechanism related to the net-present value of future decommissioning costs. In some transactions, the parties have agreed on alternatives to these decommissioning security agreements, such as adding a negotiated share of estimated future decommissioning costs to the purchase price (which will be reimbursed to the buyer if the secondary liability does not arise).

3.3.6.6. Decommissioning Security Agreements

The financial settlement under the decommissioning security agreements will, according to the Ministry of Finance, not be similar to the after-tax settlement between the seller as former licensee and the non-defaulting licensee, and will thus be calculated on a before-tax basis. The receipt of such a guarantee payment will then treated as taxable income. The stipulation of the guarantee amount must take this into account, implying that it will normally be for 100 per cent of the buyer's share of decommissioning costs, as the secondarily liable seller otherwise would not be able to honour his obligations of paying 22 per cent of the costs to the non-defaulting licensees.[23] According to industry, this results in higher costs related to procuring and maintaining guarantees under the decommissioning security agreements, than would have been necessary had the settlement under these agreements – similarly to the settlement between the seller and the non-defaulting licensees – also been on an after-tax basis. As these costs are deductible under the 78 per cent petroleum tax regime, this could result in reduced tax revenues.

3.4. THE CONTRACTUAL REGIME BETWEEN LICENSEES

As mentioned, practically all production licences apply a standard joint operating agreement (JOA) drafted by the Ministry of Petroleum and Energy, setting out detailed provisions of the licensees' rights and obligations *inter partes*. The entering into of this JOA is a condition for receiving the production licence.

---

22 https://www.norskoljeoggass.no/globalassets/dokumenter/naringspolitikk/skatt-og-fiskalt/modellavtaler/norog-5--decomssioning-security-agreement-for-removal-obligations-engelsk-150517.pdf.

23 He receives 100% of the defaulted costs from the guarantor, and is left with 22% net after having paid tax.

With respect to decommissioning, the JOA reflects and supplies the provisions of the Petroleum Act – see Article 30.1 where the operator is obliged to propose to the management committee that a decommissioning plan is prepared in accordance with the time limits of the Petroleum Act. If the management committee decides that a decommissioning plan shall be prepared, the operator shall carry this out in close co-operation with the other licensees.

Article 30.3 of the JOA reflects Section 5-1 of the Petroleum Act, as it states that the decommissioning plan shall comprise proposals for continued production or the shutdown of production and disposal of installations, i.e. further use of the installation in petroleum activities, other use, complete or partial removal or abandonment. Similarly to the Petroleum Act, this provision also states that the decommissioning plan shall address technical matters, matters concerning safety and matters relating to protection of the environment and economic issues as well as give due consideration of other users of the ocean for each of the relevant disposal alternatives.

Article 32 of the JOA regulates the internal process within the joint venture with respect to the execution of the decommissioning plan once it has been approved by the Ministry of Petroleum and Energy, but it is a very general regulation. According to Article 32.1 the operator shall submit a proposal to the management committee on how the disposal decision may be carried out. Assumingly, this proposal will need to address issues such as timing, estimated costs, procurement strategies and major contracts. The management committee may change, adopt or reject the proposal. Article 32.2 states that unless the management committee makes a decision concerning the proposal made by the operator within three months, the proposal shall be deemed approved.

4. THE FUTURE OF NCS DECOMMISSIONING

The specific decommissioning requirements are to be determined on a case-by-case basis. Although removal of installations is not an invariable rule, and the Norwegian legislation provides the authorities with wide discretionary powers, the trend is that most installations are fully removed. This is based upon both international legislation and environmental concerns. However, the large gravity-based concrete production platforms have not yet reached a point of time where a decommissioning plan must be submitted. It is expected that for some of these installations, weighing more than 1 million tonnes with a height of well over 300 metres, at least partial abandonment may be the most appropriate decision after the installation has been cleaned from all hazardous substances and stripped of all production equipment.

As many of the close to 500 installations on the NCS are nearing the end of their economic life, it is expected that decommissioning activities on the NCS will increase substantially in the near future. Industry estimates[24] suggest that around 240,000 tonnes of offshore infrastructure will be decommissioned and brought ashore from the NCS over the next eight year, of which around 123,000 tonnes are topside weights and around 115,000 tonnes are substructure weights. All this relates to fields and installations located in the Norwegian North Sea, as no decommissioning is expected in the relatively less mature Norwegian Sea and Barents Sea. Total decommissioning costs from now and until 2025 are estimated at close to 5.2 billion euros.[25]

On the other hand, industry is working hard to prolong the economic lifetime of both producing fields and installations on the NCS, and has in many cases been able to prolong the economic viability of installations and pushed back the expected deadline for a final disposal decision. Part of this has been helped by the introduction of third-party use of the installations as a result of neighbouring fields tying into existing installations. It is expected that this trend will be strengthened in the future.

---

24 See Decommissioning Insight 2017 – published by the UK Oil and Gas Industry Association.

25 See the Market Report related to cessation and disposal prepared by Dr. Tedchn. Olav Olsen for the Norwegian Petroleum Directorate: http://www.npd.no/Global/Norsk/3-Publikasjoner/Rapporter/Markedsrapport/Rapport-R04-20180302.pdf.

PART V

CCS AS A CLIMATE TOOL

North Sea Practice

CHAPTER XVIII
CCS LEGISLATION IN NORWAY
The EU CCS Directive and its Implementation into Norwegian Law

Sofie Fogstad Vold

1. INTRODUCTION

Since 1996, carbon dioxide (CO_2) has been captured and stored geologically offshore on the Norwegian continental shelf. The first project was at the Sleipner field. Decades of experience from management of hydrocarbons on the continental shelf, combined with the introduction of a high tax on CO_2 emissions and sales specifications for gas, incentivized this first carbon capture and storage (CCS) project in Norway, as well as in Europe. Back in 1996, there was no CCS-specific legislation in Norway. The CCS part of the activities on the Sleipner field was regulated through existing pollution and resource management legislation. These regulations do to some extent still apply for CCS activities today. CCS-specific regulations first came into place when Norway implemented in 2014 the European Union Directive 2009/31/EC on the geological storage of carbon dioxide (the CCS Directive).

The chapter starts by presenting the main components of the Norwegian CCS policy, including its objectives and main projects (Section 2).Thereafter, the chapter makes an in-depth descriptive analysis of the content of the CCS Directive (Section 3). The chapter then moves the focus towards the process of implementation of the CCS Directive into Norwegian law and provides an overview of the main pieces of CCS legislation in Norway (Section 4), before ending with some concluding remarks (Section 5).

2. BACKGROUND ON NORWEGIAN CCS POLICY

2.1. CCS AND CCUS

Carbon dioxide capture and geological storage is a range of various technologies allowing capture of carbon dioxide from industrial processes or electricity generation from fossil sources and storing it safely and permanently in geological formations. This prevents the carbon dioxide from entering into the atmosphere. Further, where CCS is applied to an industrial process or electricity/heat generation based on biological material, one can actually achieve a net out-take of carbon dioxide from the atmosphere, so-called "negative emissions". This is often referred to as BECCS or Bio-CCS, and is one of few known technologies today that can provide negative emissions.

Another common abbreviation is CC*US*. Here, potential *use* of the captured carbon is included, either as an alternative to permanent storage or as a step towards permanent storage. From a climate mitigation perspective, use of the carbon dioxide that does not lead to permanent out-take of the CO_2 from the atmosphere but only functions as a postponement could have a positive effect depending on the timeframe of the postponement. Where the carbon dioxide re-enters the atmosphere after short time, CCU does not have any climate mitigation effect.

2.2. ON THE NEED FOR CCS

Through the Paris agreement to the UN Framework Convention on Climate Change (UNFCCC), the global community committed itself to "strengthen the global response to the threat of climate change", through

> [h]olding the increase in the global average temperature well below 2 degrees above pre-industrial levels and pursue efforts to limit the temperature increase to 1.5 degrees above pre-industrial levels, recognizing that this would significantly reduce the risks and impacts of climate change.[1]

Norway signed the UNFCCC on 4 June 1992 and ratified the Convention nationally by a royal decree on 11 June 1993. The UNFCCC entered into force formally on 21 March 1994, in accordance with its Article 23.[2] Norway ratified the Kyoto Protocol in May 2002, and became party to the Protocol when it entered into force on 16 February 2005. The Paris agreement was signed by Norway on 22 April 2016, and ratified on 20 June the same year.

To meet the ambitious aims of the Paris agreement, a wide range of climate mitigation technologies will need to be applied across all sectors. Various reports by both the Intergovernmental Panel on Climate Change (IPCC) and the International Energy Agency (IEA) have underscored that CCS is one of many necessary technologies. The latest report from IPCC, the special report

---

1 Article 2, Paris Agreement.

2 UNFCCC full text: https://unfccc.int/resource/docs/convkp/conveng.pdf.

on the consequences of 1.5 degrees Celcius warming, yet again showed that CCS has a role to play in the most realistic scenarios and pathways.[3] Previous estimates presented in the IPCC in its Fifth Assessment Report in 2014 showed that keeping within the 2 degrees Celcius pathways would be 138 per cent more expensive if carbon capture and storage was not applied. In the IEA's Sustainable Development Scenario, CCUS accounts for 7 per cent of the cumulative emissions reductions needed globally to 2040. This implies a rapid deployment of CCUS, increasing today's 30+ million tonnes of CO_2 captured each year to 2,300 million tonnes of CO_2 per year by 2040.[4]

In Norway, CCS has been part of climate policies for many years. The current Solberg Government identified CCS as one of five areas of enhanced national climate policy efforts in a White Paper to the Parliament in 2014.[5] The other four areas of efforts are: i) reduced emissions from the transport sector, ii) development of low emission technologies in industry, iii) renewable energy, and iiii) environmentally-friendly shipping. These five areas of enhanced national climate policy efforts are also pointed at in Norway's Intended Nationally Determined Contribution, delivered as input to the Paris Agreement negotiations in 2015.[6]

Following up on this, the Government published its CCS policy in a white paper to the Parliament in 2014,[7] often referred to as the Governments "CCS Strategy". The main aim for the efforts within CCS was formulated as "identify measures that can contribute to technology development and cost reductions" (author's translation). To date, the essence of this is still the main aim with the Government's efforts on CCS, recently repeated in the Government's political platform released in January this year, as an ambition to

> contribute to the development of technologies for capture, transport and storage of CO_2 and having an ambition to realise a cost effective solution for full scale CCS in Norway, provided this incites technology development in an international perspective (author's translation).[8]

---

3 IPCC, Special report on the impacts of global warming of 1.5 °C above pre-industrial levels and related global greenhouse gas emission pathways, 2018. Available at: <https://www.ipcc.ch/sr15/>.

4 IEA on CCUS: https://www.iea.org/topics/carbon-capture-and-storage/.

5 White paper Meld. St. 13 (2014–2015): https://www.regjeringen.no/no/dokumenter/meld.-st.-13-2014-2015/id2394579/.

6 Norway's INDC, 2015, p. 5: https://www4.unfccc.int/sites/submissions/INDC/Published%20Documents/Norway/1/Norway%20INDC%2026MAR2015.pdf, press release: https://www.regjeringen.no/en/aktuelt/innsending-av-norges-klimamal-til-fn/id2403782/.

7 Norwegian Government's CCS strategy, Prop. 1 S (2014–2015): https://www.regjeringen.no/no/dokumenter/Prop-1-S-20142015/id2005418/.

8 Granavolden-plattformen, Chapter 13 "Klima og miljø"; https://www.regjeringen.no/no/dokumenter/politisk-plattform/id2626036/.

2.3. STATUS OF CCS IN NORWAY

Today, there are 18 large-scale CCS facilities in commercial operation in the world, five under construction and 20 in various stages of development. The first CCS facilities came in the US during the 1970s and 1980s, driven by the potential for enhanced oil recovery (EOR) through injection of CO_2 into oil reserves to increase oil extraction. This resulted in storage of a large share of the injected carbon dioxide in the pores that previously held the oil. From 1990 and onwards, several projects have come into operation in Norway, Canada, Brazil, Saudi Arabia and the United Arab Emirates. Most of these project are connected to EOR. Only Quest, in Canada, and Sleipner and Snøhvit, in Norway, have dedicated geological storage for the carbon dioxide. Projects in the pipeline are situated in, amongst others, China and Australia.[9]

As mentioned above, the first CCS project in Norway started operations in 1996 at the Sleipner gas field. It was the first offshore CO_2 storage project in Europe. The project was incentivized by a combination of sales specifications for the gas, making separation of the CO_2 from the gas stream necessary in the first place, and a newly introduced high tax on carbon dioxide emissions from the Norwegian Continental Shelf. These two factors made a good case for capturing and storing the carbon dioxide from the gas stream instead of releasing it into the atmosphere. Since 1996, around 1 million tonnes of carbon dioxide have been captured and stored yearly at Sleipner, in a dedicated, geological storage, a porous sandstone rock formation 800–1000 meters below the seabed surface. As a first of its kind, Sleipner has been a showcase for CCS with an extensive monitoring program which allows for research and external verification of the CO_2 plume behavior. To this day, none of the monitoring programs have shown any indication of seepage.

The second CCS project in Norway came into operation in 2007 at the Snøhvit liquefied natural gas (LNG) production site. The LNG process requires CO_2 to be removed from the natural gas prior to liquefaction to prevent dry-ice formation. Similarly as for the Sleipner CCS project, the requirement to remove the CO_2 as part of the commercialization of the gas, combined with a high tax on CO_2 emissions, gave the right incentives for capturing and storing the CO_2 permanently. Around 700,000 tonnes of carbon dioxide have been stored yearly at Snøhvit since the beginning of operations.

In total, the CCS projects at Sleipner and Snøhvit mitigate 3–4 per cent of Norway's yearly emissions. Both projects came into operation before the EU CCS Directive was implemented into Norwegian law. At the beginning, they

---

9 Global CCS Institute (GCCSI) The Global Status of CCS 2018. Available at: https://www.globalccsinstitute.com/resources/global-status-report/.

were therefore sanctioned under the petroleum and environmental regulations in Norway. When the CCS Directive was implemented, both projects needed to update their environmental permits accordingly. This has not resulted in any necessary changes to monitoring plans or structural changes to the projects.

On the basis of the experience with CCS on the Norwegian Continental Shelf and the acknowledgement of the necessity of CCS in a future climate-neutral world, Norway has an ambitious policy aimed at developing CCS technologies. The Norwegian CCS strategy[10] covers the whole development chain, from research and innovation through the CLIMIT program, to industrial demonstration of carbon capture at the Technology Centre Mongstad (TCM), to large-scale demonstration projects. It is the state-owned CCS enterprise Gassnova[11] that is operating the demonstration part of the CLIMIT program, representing the Government's interests at TCM and handling the overview of the technical parts of the large-scale demonstration project currently in planning.

The full-scale demonstration project currently in planning consists of carbon capture from existing industrial sites, transport by ship and geological storage below the seabed off the West coast of Norway. On the basis of competitive tenders, industrial actors have been chosen to participate in their concepts. Norcem, a cement plant owned by HeidelbergCement, studies CO_2 capture from their production plant in Brevik, Porsgrunn. Fortum Oslo Varme (FOV) studies CO_2 capture from their waste incineration plant in Oslo. Both Norcem and FOV are looking to capture around 400,000 tonnes of carbon dioxide per year. Equinor, Shell and Total are working together on a solution for storage and transport of carbon dioxide. They are studying a ship-based transport solution from the capture plants on the East coast of Norway, to an onshore interim storage facility on the West coast which will be connected to the offshore geological storage by a pipeline. The partners, Equinor, Shell and Total are using "Northern Lights" as their working name on the transport and storage scope of the demonstration project. The Government's aim with the project is to "develop technology for capture, transport and storage of CO_2, having an ambition to realize a cost effective solution for full scale CCS in Norway, provided that this results in technology transfer in an international perspective"[12] (author's translation). Hence, for the project to be successful, it is necessary to see subsequent projects benefitting from the technology developments achieved through this project, in combination with cost reductions.

---

10 Norwegian Government's CCS strategy, Prop. 1 S (2014–2015): https://www.regjeringen.no/en/topics/energy/carbon-capture-and-storage/id86982/.

11 Gassnova: https://www.gassnova.no/en/about-us.

12 Granavolden platform, January 2019, political platform of the Solberg Government, Chapter 12 on Climate (only in Norwegian): https://www.regjeringen.no/no/dokumenter/politisk-plattform/id2626036/#klima.

To achieve technology dissemination, the industrial participants in the project have agreed to share the larger part of both their learnings and technology developments. This has been a prerequisite for the Government in the competitions and agreements on state aid for the studies, and it will continue to be an important part of the agreements for investment and operations. In summer 2019, Gassnova launched a website containing information on the full-scale demonstration project, including the industrial participants' study reports and other relevant information.[13]

Cost reductions can be achieved through transfer of knowhow and technology development. Another way to achieve cost reductions for subsequent projects is to establish an infrastructure that may be used by those subsequent projects. The design of the demonstration project currently in planning has taken this into consideration. Transport of carbon dioxide by ship is flexible and would allow further capture projects to connect quite easily to the storage infrastructure. The storage site that Equinor, Shell and Total are studying has a much larger capacity than what is needed for the capturing plants in the project. When dimensioning the pipelines from the interim storage facility on the West coast, the potential for further capture projects to connect is of great importance. Currently, the project is planning for a pipeline capacity of 1.5 million tonnes of CO_2 per year, meaning there will be capacity for potentially another 700,000 tonnes of CO_2 in addition to the two capture sites in the project. Further, upsizing the pipelines to a capacity of 5 million tonnes of CO_2 per year can be done at a reasonable cost when necessary. This means that for subsequent carbon capture projects, the infrastructure investments will be tied to the capture plant, not transport and storage. From the storage and transport operators' view, further volumes of CO_2 are also beneficial, as this would drive down the costs per carbon dioxide unit stored.

The industrial partners in the full-scale demonstration project are working to finalize the last study phase in an industrial project development process, the FEED-phase (front and end engineering design phase). These studies will be finalized by the end of 2019, and will form the technical background upon which a potential investment decision may be taken. If everything goes according to plan, the Government may take its investment decision by 2020/2021. Provided that there is a positive investment decision, this will be the first Norwegian CCS project following the permitting process provided for in the CCS Directive. Hence, even though hard to value, the project may also provide some legal experience with a framework that has been in place

13 CCS Norway, website operated by Gassnova, launched summer 2019: https://ccsnorway.com/experiences.

for almost a decade, but which has never been applied from the beginning to the end of a project.

3. THE CCS DIRECTIVE: A DESCRIPTIVE ANALYSIS

Before addressing the Norwegian national regulation of CCS, a presentation of the EU Directive on transport and storage of carbon dioxide is necessary, as it forms the basis for the current Norwegian regulation on CCS.

The CCS Directive was adopted on 23 April 2009. The Directive contains a preamble, which is followed by eight chapters; 1) Subject matter, scope and definitions, 2) selection of storage sites and exploration permits, 3) storage permits, 4) operation, closure and post-closure obligations, 5) third-party access, 6) general provisions, 7) amendments, and 8) final provisions. The Directive was adopted with two annexes, specifying in annex I the "Criteria for the characterisation and assessment of the potential storage complex and surrounding area referred to in article 4(3)" and in annex II the "Criteria for establishing and updating the monitoring plan referred to in article 13(2) and for post closure monitoring". Further, in 2011, the European Commission adopted four Guidance documents to "provide an overall methodological approach for implementing the key provisions of the CCS Directive and help ensure environmentally safe geological storage of CO_2 across the EU".[14]

Guidance documents made by the European Commission have no legal standing as such. In the case of the CCS Directive, it is the Directive in itself that gives the authority to the Commission to make these guidance documents. That gives the Guidance documents some sort of authority. And, needless to say, they do of course give an indication of how the European Commission interprets the Directive and what the Commission requires from Member States' national regulations in order to be in compliance with the aims of the Directive.

3.1. PREAMBLE

From the Directive's preamble, Article 1 and the European Commission's Guidance documents, it is clear that this directive is supposed to serve the European Union's environment and climate ambitions. Article 1 states that "This Directive establishes a legal framework for the environmentally safe geological storage of carbon dioxide (CO_2) to contribute to fight against climate change." Through the first parts of the preamble, the necessity of

[14] Guidance Documents adopted by the European Commission in 2011: https://ec.europa.eu/clima/policies/innovation-fund/ccs/implementation_en.

CCS as a climate mitigation technology is repeated with a focus of CCS technologies place in bridging the gap to reaching the climate targets (preamble, recitals (1)–(5)). Further, the next few recitals outline the assessments that were done in advance of the Directive, mapping out the necessity for a regulatory framework for CCS. After considering that there are already a number of legislative instruments in place to manage some of the environmental risks of CCS, "in particular regarding capture and transport of CO_2", the preamble and the rest of the Directive is first and foremost devoted to the storage part of CCS activities.

The preamble then moves on to a quite important starting point in recital (19), reminding of the fact that each Member State retains the right to determine the areas within its territory from which storage sites may be selected. "This includes [of course] the right *not to* allow any storage in parts or on the whole of their territory" (emphasis added). From this starting point, it is only logical that carbon dioxide storage activities must be based on licenses or permits issued by national authorities. This is the clear system of the CCS Directive; all carbon dioxide storage activities, including activities in advance of the actual storage activity, have to be based on a permit or license issued by national authorities.

From recital (30) of the preamble and onwards, liability provisions are discussed. There are several "phases" of responsibility for the operator of the storage site. Firstly, before and throughout operations, liability for damage to the local environment and climate resulting from any failure of permanent containment of CO_2 is regulated by the EU Directive on environmental liability,[15] and by the EU ETS Directive[16] with regard to emission allowances. Further, the CCS Directive in itself establishes the obligation for the operator to take corrective measures in case of leakages or significant irregularities, as well as having a financial security in place already before injection starts that can cover any requirements in line with the Directive, including post-closure obligations. Once the storage site is closed, the operator continues to hold certain responsibilities according to the CCS Directive in terms of monitoring, taking corrective measures and upholding the financial security. After the transfer of responsibility, only a few liabilities remain on the hands of the operator – (preamble, recitals (30)–(37)).

Last, but not least, the preamble discusses third-party access to CO_2 transport networks and storage sites in recital (38). This underscores the internal marked dimension of CCS activities and follows the regular principles for non-discriminatory access.

---

15 Directive 2004/35/EC of the European Parliament and of the Council of 21 April 2004 on environmental liability with regard to the prevention and remedying of environmental damage.

16 Directive 2003/87/EC, n. 20 below.

3.2. PARAGRAPHS

As mentioned above, Article 1 in chapter 1 of the Directive, *Subject matter and purpose*, states that the directive "establishes a legal framework for the environmentally safe geological storage of carbon dioxide (CO_2) to contribute to the fight against climate change". Article 2 specifies the scope of application of the Directive as "geological storage of CO_2 in the territory of the Member States, their exclusive economic zones and on their continental shelves [...]", before it moves on to clearly prohibit any activity beyond this geographical scope and also any "storage of CO_2 in the water column".

In chapter two, *selection of storage sites and exploration permits*, the Directive first lays out the national authority's right to decide upon areas for exploration. Then, the Directive sets out the provisions for an exploration permit, necessary to hold for any actor wanting to explore the possibility for carbon dioxide storage, upon the government's decision to allow for such activity. In practice, it will almost always be necessary to do some exploration of a site before the government is ensured that the requirements for a storage site are fulfilled[17] and before an operator will be willing to invest in the necessary infrastructure for the actual storage activity. Another important point to the exploration permit is that it gives the holder of the permit exclusive rights to explore the potential CO_2 storage complex (Article 5(4)).

Once a suitable storage site has been selected, chapter three of the CCS Directive, *storage permits* makes it clear that no storage activity can take place without a storage permit. Articles 6 to 11 go through the necessity of holding a storage permit, what information an application for a storage permit must include, the conditions for a storage permit, the contents of the storage permit, the Commission's role as a reviewer of the draft storage permit and how to handle changes, reviews, updates and withdrawal of a storage permit.

The requirements to the contents of the storage permit in chapter three, Article 9, anticipate several of the obligations pursuant to chapter four of the Directive. Chapter four describes the obligations throughout *operations, closure and post-closure*. These include, amongst others, monitoring and reporting, measurements and liability provisions. The requirements in this chapter have a clear practical impact on securing an "environmentally safe geological storage of carbon dioxide (CO_2) to contribute to the fight against climate change" (Article 1). The storage operator is, through Article 9, obliged to describe how they plan to monitor and report, which corrective measures they foresee applying, on what conditions they will close the storage site and how they have established a financial security mechanism at the time of applying for a storage permit.

[17] CCS Directive Article 4 and annex I.

Further, Article 12 of chapter four requires that the CO_2 stream consists "overwhelmingly of carbon dioxide". In this lies an environmental security mechanism, as no operator holding a storage permit may store a CO_2 stream to which waste or other matters have been added for the purpose of disposal (Article 12(1)). Article 12(1)(a)–(b) of the CCS Directive specifies where the threshold for any "incidental associated substances" lies, before paragraph 2 gives the Commission a mandate to "adopt guidelines to help identify the conditions applicable on a case by case basis for respecting the criteria laid down in paragraph 1", if appropriate. These guidelines can be found in the Commission Guidance Document 2 from 2011 on *Characterisation of the Storage Complex, CO_2 Stream Composition, Monitoring and Corrective Measures.* The wording on the CO_2 stream composition in the CCS Directive is the same as the one found in another legal framework bearing on CO_2 sequestration in geological formation below the seabed, namely the London Protocol.[18] The London Protocol prohibits "dumping of any wastes or other matter" in order to prevent marine pollution. The exemptions from the ban on dumping of wastes or other matters at sea, include a carbon dioxide stream from carbon dioxide capture processes for sequestration, provided it is meant to be disposed of into a sub-seabed geological formation and that it consists "overwhelmingly of carbon dioxide".[19] The specifications in the London Protocol coincide with those of the EU CCS Directive.

Articles 13 and 14 set out the monitoring and reporting obligations. It is the Member States' obligation to ensure that the operator carries out monitoring in line with Article 13 and reports according to Article 14. Article 16 states the obligation of the operator to take corrective measures in case of leakages or significant irregularities, and the competent authority's right to intervene if the operator fails to take the necessary corrective measures. The competent authority shall recover the costs of this from the operator, including drawing on the financial security (article 16(5)). Article 17 sets the conditions and obligations for closing the storage and the post closure period.

The last three articles of chapter four, 18, 19 and 20, concern the transfer of responsibility for the storage site and financial obligations on the operator throughout operations, closure and post-closure, as well as for a period of time after the transfer of liability.

In terms of timeline, it makes most sense to start with the article in the middle first, Article 19 on the financial security. The financial security must be presented as a part of the application for a storage permit. Article 19 also requires the financial mechanism to be "valid and effective before commencement of injection". The mechanism is hence in place from the beginning of injection,

---

18 1996 Protocol to the Convention on the Prevention of Marine Pollution by Dumping of Wastes and Other Matter, 1972 (London Protocol). Article 4 bans the dumping of wastes or other matter and Article 5 prohibits incineration at sea of wastes or other matter.

19 London Protocol, annex 1.

and it is meant to ensure that "all obligations arising under the permit issued pursuant to this Directive, including closure and post-closure requirements, as well as any obligations arising from inclusion of the storage site under Directive 2003/87/EC,[20] can be met". The financial security shall remain valid and effective until the responsibility for the storage site has been transferred in line with Article 18 (Article 19(3)).

As mentioned, it is Article 18 and the transfer of responsibility that marks the "end" of the financial security according to Article 19(3). For a transfer of responsibility from the operator to the competent authority to happen, several criteria must be fulfilled according to Article 18. In addition to the other obligations the operator has under the CCS Directive, and the obligation to surrender emission allowances in the event of a leakage according to Directive 2003/87/EC, Article 18(1) paragraphs (a)–(d) of the CCS Directive set conditions for the transfer of responsibility in itself. Firstly, all available evidence must indicate that the stored CO_2 will be completely and permanently contained (Article 18(1) paragraph (a)). Secondly, a minimum period of time following the closure of the storage site must have elapsed. This period of time shall be no shorter than 20 years, unless the competent authority is convinced that the criterion referred to in paragraph (a) is complied with before the end of that period (Article 18(1) paragraph (b)). Thirdly, the financial obligation according to Article 20 must be fulfilled and fourthly the site has been sealed and the injection facilities have been removed (Article 18(1) paragraphs (c) and (d)). Also for these provisions, the Commission may adopt guidelines. The Commission has adopted a Guidance document on this from 2011, named *Criteria for Transfer of Responsibility to the Competent Authority*. Article 18(3) to (5) go through the formalities of adopting a final decision on transfer of responsibility. Article 18(6) lays out the requirements for monitoring after the transfer of responsibility and (7) states the responsibility of the operator for any fault on his part.

The last remaining responsibility on the operator's shoulders is the financial mechanism according to Article 20. The operator must make a "financial contribution available to the competent authority before the transfer of responsibility pursuant to Article 18". The financial mechanism shall cover "at least the anticipated cost of monitoring for a period of 30 years". It may be used to "cover the costs borne by the competent authority after the transfer of responsibility to ensure that the CO_2 is completely and permanently contained in geological storage sites". Here as well, the Commission may according to Article 20(2) adopt guidelines for the estimation of the costs. These guidelines

20 Directive 2003/87/EC of the European Parliament and of the Council of 13 October 2003 establishing a scheme for greenhouse gas emission allowance trading within the Community. (EU ETS).

are found in the Guidance Document 4 from 2011 together with guidance on the financial security pursuant to Articles 19–20: *Financial Security (Art. 19) and Financial Mechanism (Art. 20)*. One question of interest to both a potential operator and the competent authority is what form the financial security may take. The Guidance documents underline that it is up to the national competent authority to make the final decision on form. It remains to be seen what mechanisms will be deemed the most appropriate.

Chapter five of the Directive, *third-party access*, is the chapter that makes the internal market and competition side of CO_2 transport and storage activities clear. Access to infrastructure put in place shall be provided in a "transparent and non-discriminatory manner determined", while considering, amongst other things, the storage capacity, proportion of CO_2 reduction obligations, technical specifications and other aspects based on duly substantiated reasonable needs of the operator (Article 21(2) paragraphs (a)–(d)).

Chapter six lays out the *general provisions* on competent authority, transboundary cooperation, registry, information to the public, reporting by the Member States on the implementation of the Directive, amendment of annexes etc. And finally, chapters seven and eight go through the *amendments* necessary to other regulations due to the CCS Directive and the *final provisions* on review and entry into force.

4. THE IMPLEMENTATION PROCESS IN NORWAY AND OVERVIEW OF THE LEGISLATION

On the basis of being considered EEA relevant, according to the EEA Agreement Articles 1 and 2,[21] Norway implemented the CCS Directive into Norwegian law by a royal decree in 2014.[22]

4.1. IMPLEMENTATION TECHNIQUE

The Directive was implemented through one new legal act, the Storage Regulation[23] and through additions and amendments to two existing regulations,

21 EEA Agreement full text: https://www.efta.int/media/documents/legal-texts/eea/the-eea-agreement/Main%20Text%20of%20the%20Agreement/EEAagreement.pdf.

22 PRE-2014-12-05-1517, PRE-2014-12-05-1518 Gjennomføring av EUs lagringsdirektiv: Forskrift om utnyttelse av undersjøiske reservoarer på kontinentalsokkelen til lagring av CO2 og om transport av CO2 på kontinentalsokkelen, og Forskrift om endring av forskrift 27 juni 1997 nr. 653 om petroleumsvirksomhet Kongelig resolusjon. Statsråd Tord Lien.

23 Forskrift om utnyttelse av undersjøiske reservoarer på kontientalsokkelen til lagring av CO2 og om transport av CO2 på kontientalsokkelen, forskrift 5 desember 2014 nr. 1517 (Lagringsforskriften).

namely the Petroleum Regulation[24] and the Pollution Regulation.[25] The new storage regulation covers all carbon capture, transport and storage activities that are not happening in relation to petroleum activities. The new chapter in the Petroleum Regulation covers carbon capture, transport and storage activities in relation to petroleum activities. The new chapter in the Pollution Regulation safeguards the environmental requirements of the CCS Directive and applies to all carbon capture, transport and storage activities, regardless of whether it is in relation to petroleum activities or not.

Why the implementation of the CCS Directive ended up in two sets of regulations from a resource management perspective is a timely question. When looking at the different main considerations behind the regulations, it does to some extent make sense to separate at least the Pollution Regulations requirements from the Storage Regulations and Petroleum Regulations, as they are set out to safeguard quite different considerations. The new Storage Regulation and the Petroleum Regulation are based on resource management considerations, whilst environmental considerations are at the forefront throughout the new chapter in the Pollution Regulation. However, this does not entirely explain the regulatory division between CCS activities in relation to petroleum and not. The royal decree states that the starting point was only one regulation. Throughout the parliamentary hearing of the regulation, feedback was given in several instances on possible challenges following from making CCS activities in relation to petroleum activities subject to a different legal framework from the one regulating the petroleum activity. With a view not to create two sets of framework with inequalities in relation to liability subjects, financial matters and taxation, it made more sense to separate the regulation of CCS in relation to petroleum activities and frame that within the already existing regulations for petroleum activity. This would also allow continuation of the well-functioning cooperation between the environmental authorities, the security authorities and the resource management authorities already in place for the petroleum activity.

4.2. RESOURCE MANAGEMENT PRINCIPLES

Further, the resource management principles that come across the CCS Directive do, to a large extent, coincide with the principles upon which the Norwegian Petroleum Regulations are based; comprehensive assessments, considerations of necessary resource management issues and security issues as well as a good co-existence with other users of the areas with the resources. To get an optimal

---

24 Forskrift 27 juni 1997 nr. 653 (Petroleumsforskriften).

25 Forskrift 1 juni 2004 nr. 931 (Forurensninsforskriften).

application of these principles, close collaboration between several national governing and regulatory bodies is necessary. Building on the experiences from the petroleum sector, Norway has developed a good model for collaboration and involvement of the various different actors on the Governments side. These include, amongst others, three ministries; the Ministry of Petroleum and Energy, the Ministry of Climate and Environment, the Ministry of Labour and Social Affairs and several directorates, like the Environmental Directorate and the Petroleum Directorate.

4.3. SCOPE OF APPLICATION

In relation to preamble recital (19) and to chapter two, Article 4(1) of the CCS Directive, laying out the national authority's right to decide upon areas for exploration, only offshore geological storage below the seabed is considered within Norwegian law. This is set out in the Storage Regulation §1–3, in the Petroleum Regulation §1, referring to the Petroleum Act §1–4 and in the Pollution Regulation §1–3. Hence, Norwegian authorities have limited the geographical scope to a greater degree than what is required by the Directive itself. The reasoning behind this limitation is based on geological assessments of suitable areas.

4.4. A PERMITTING SYSTEM

As mentioned above, through the implementation of the CCS Directive in Norway only exploration and storage of CO_2 on the continental shelf is allowed. This is based on geological circumstances. The experience from the petroleum activity on the continental shelf did also play a great role when forming the Storage Regulation. It is a permit-based system, with the same starting point as the CCS Directive: the resources belong to the state; hence, any exploration and exploitation requires a permit. In order to make the permitting system for CCS as similar and familiar to the operators on the Norwegian Continental Shelf as possible, the same progress in terms of permits and names is used in the Storage Regulation, Petroleum Regulation and Pollution Regulation. Any CCS activity requires an exploration permit, an exploitation permit and finally an injection permit before any CO_2 may be stored. The name "Storage permit" used by the CCS Directive is not used as a stand-alone permit in the Norwegian CCS legislation, but the requirements of the storage permit are covered by the requirements to the exploitation permit following the Storage Regulation and the Petroleum Regulation, in combination with the injection and storage permit required by the Pollution Regulation.

4.5. REVIEW OF THE NORWEGIAN CCS LEGISLATION

There are currently several regulations pertaining to CCS activities in Norway. As presented in Section 4.1 above, the CCS Directive has been implemented into Norwegian law through one new regulation and through changes in two existing regulations; The Storage Regulation, the Petroleum Regulation and the Pollution Regulation. It follows from the form of a directive that there is some room of manoeuvre for the Member States when implementing it into national law. The main aim of a directive is to reach a common target or a common baseline; how each country chooses to uphold this common ground is left to the national states to decide upon.[26]

In addition to the regulations put in place to fulfil the criteria of the CCS Directive, several others come into play when regulating CCS activities like building acts and regulations and other climate regulations like, for instance, the EU ETS.[27] These will only be touched upon briefly where relevant.

4.6. THE NEW STORAGE REGULATION

The new Storage Regulation establishes a permitting system for exploration and exploitation of subsea reservoirs for the purpose of permanent geological storage of CO_2 in line with the CCS Directive and inspired by the existing Petroleum Regulation in Norway. Most of the provisions resembles the provisions of the Petroleum Regulation. This was done intentionally, as the regulation is thereby familiar to the operators on the Norwegian Continental shelf. Chapter 5 of the Storage Regulation includes some new provisions reflecting directly the provisions of the CCS Directive chapters three, four and five. These include the provisions on the storage permit, obligations and liabilities throughout operations, closure and post-closure and third-party access to the infrastructure.

4.7. CHANGES TO THE PETROLEUM REGULATION

The additions made in the Petroleum Regulation consist of reflecting the rules of the CCS Directive that relate to resource management, and which were not covered by the existing provisions of the Petroleum Regulation. In addition to

26 Treaty on the functioning of the European Union – Part 6, Title I, chapter 2 – Legal acts of the Union: https://eur-lex.europa.eu/legal-content/EN/TXT/PDF/?uri=CELEX:12012E/TXT&from=EN.

27 Directive 2003/87/EC, n. 20 above.

some minor changes in other provisions, like the inclusion of definitions of "CO_2 stream", "storage complex" and "storage site" in §2, the provisions included in chapter 4A are the same provisions included in the new Storage Regulation that reflect the provisions of the CCS Directive. This means to a large extent the totality of chapter 5 of the Storage Regulation, reflecting chapter three, four and five of the CCS Directive, makes up the new chapter 4A of the Petroleum Regulation.

4.8. CHANGES TO THE POLLUTION REGULATION

This is where the environmental requirements of the CCS Directive are set out. The provisions of this chapter mirror the provisions of chapter five in the Storage Regulation that have an environmental aspect. This means that the provisions from chapter three, four and five of the CCS Directive related to environmental considerations and standards are included here. When assessing whether an application for an injection permit under the Pollution Regulation is acceptable, the main concern is the environmental aspect. This permit is an "additional" prerequisite for the operator to have in hand before injection of CO_2 into a storage site may commence, as it comes in addition to the storage permit. This may seem like a double permitting system on paper; however, through several decades of close cooperation between the environmental authorities, the security authorities and the resource management authorities, these permits and assessments are considered in cooperation with one another in order to find the solutions that safeguard both the resource management considerations and the environmental considerations in the best way.

In addition to the injection permit covering environmental requirements, there is the obligation to account for emission allowances according to Directive 2003/87/EC for any leakages from the transport network and storage site. Norway participates fully in the EU ETS. One of the requirements to the application for an injection and storage permit under the Pollution Regulation §35-5 is that the application contains a program for calculation and measurement of emissions covered by the EU ETS, in line with the requirements of the legal act[28] through which Directive 2003/87/EC is implemented into Norwegian law. Installations covered by the EU ETS must each year surrender a number of emission allowances that are equal to the total emissions from that installation during the preceding calendar year (Article 12(3)). According to Article 12(3a), the obligation to surrender allowances "shall not rise in respect of emissions verified as captured and transported for permanent storage to a facility

[28] Klimakvoteforskriften, FOR-2004-12-23-1851.

for which a permit is in force in accordance with Directive 2009/31/EC" (the EU ETS as amended by Directive 2009/29/EC). Dependant on the price of the emission allowances of the EU ETS, this mechanism does provide a more or less functioning incentive for capture and permanent storage of CO_2 for operators of installations with emissions covered by the EU ETS (provided someone offers the service of transport and storage). Today, the CCS provisions in the EU ETS cover capture of non-biogenic CO_2, transport by pipeline and permanent geological storage of CO_2. There are therefore several questions that need assessment and clarification moving forward, for instance the question of how to organize transport by any other means than by pipeline.

5. FINAL REMARKS

When the CCS Directive was implemented into Norwegian law, the two CCS projects in relation to petroleum activities needed to update their permits accordingly. This was done without major complications and the projects are now permitted under the provisions of the Petroleum Regulation chapter 4A, in line with the CCS Directive.

Even though this gave a preliminary use of the national regulations that were implemented as a consequence of the CCS Directive, there is, to date, no complete experience with the application of the CCS Directive provisions on CCS projects that are not initiated in relation to petroleum activity in Norway. Outside of Norway there is not a lot of experience to draw on either. The European Commission's considerations of the content of a storage permit may be found in the European Commission's Opinion after their review of the draft storage permit in the Peterhead CCS project from 2016.[29] It gives some insights as to what the European Commission puts emphasis on, but the document is quite short and the project was unfortunately shut down right after the issuance of the permit. Further projects are needed to get a better picture of the functioning of the regulations and the content of the requirements therein.

This is, to some extent a "chicken and egg" situation. The Global CCS Institute (GCCSI) points towards the necessity for policies, legislation and financial models to get the necessary development and deployment of CCS in a climate mitigation context. Because of the capital-intensive nature of CCS facilities, GCCSI underscores the importance of policy confidence and regulatory certainty for investments. However, regulatory certainty in this case, where there are

29 Commission opinion of 20 January 2016 on a draft permit for the permanent storage of carbon dioxide in the depleted Goldeneye gas condensate field: https://ec.europa.eu/clima/sites/clima/files/lowcarbon/ccs/implementation/docs/c_2016_152_en.pdf.

a lot of regulations in place already, will only be gained through application of these regulations. And only upon application and experience from real projects, one might argue, would it make sense to review the legislation if deemed necessary.

With the new full-scale demonstration project currently in planning in Norway, learnings in terms of the application of the regulatory framework are expected. In January 2019, Equinor were awarded an exploitation permit for the storage area that they, together with Shell and Total, are considering for permanent geological storage of CO_2.[30] Step by step throughout the project, experience will be gained with regard to the legislation and challenges uncovered that may not yet have been discovered.

30 Press release from the Norwegian Petroleum Directorate, dated 15 January 2019: https://www.npd.no/en/facts/news/general-news/2019/Award-of-exploitation-permit-for-CO2-storage/.

CHAPTER XIX

DEVELOPMENTS IN UK CARBON CAPTURE AND STORAGE

John Paterson

1. INTRODUCTION

CO_2 has been transformed in recent years in both scientific and popular understanding from an inert gas of limited significance beyond certain industrial processes to a substance whose presence in increased quantities in the atmosphere is now known to pose considerable risks in the shape of global warming and climate change. In this context, a wide array of international, regional and domestic initiatives have been undertaken with a view to reducing its emission into the atmosphere.[1] Recognising that ultimately the required level of reduction will depend upon a substantial shift from dependence on fossil fuels to renewable sources of energy, but also that this shift is unlikely to occur quickly enough to prevent problems – given political, economic and technological constraints[2] – interest has grown in the possibility of capturing CO_2 as it is produced in the burning of fossil fuels or in other industrial processes, and then sequestering it permanently in geological formations (such as saline aquifers or depleted hydrocarbon reservoirs) – a process known as carbon capture and storage (CCS). Deploying the technology would thus allow governments to meet the dual objectives of emissions reduction and energy security.

---

1 See, for example, the UN Framework Convention on Climate Change 1992, the 1998 Kyoto Protocol to that Convention and the range of initiatives that they have given rise to, not least the EU's ambitious, but initially flawed, Emissions Trading System (Directive 2003/87/EC (as amended by Directive 2009/29/EC)) and more recently the Paris Agreement of 2015.

2 For example, the UK Government noted that balancing supply and demand and dealing with the increased intermittency in supply resulting from more and more renewable generation meant that fossil fuels would remain as significant factors in the energy mix for some time to come. See Department for Energy & Climate Change (DECC), *CCS Roadmap: Supporting Deployment of Carbon Capture and Storage in the UK* (April 2012) p. 4 (Ministerial Foreword). https://assets.publishing.service.gov.uk/government/uploads/system/uploads/attachment_data/file/48317/4899-the-ccs-roadmap.pdf.

This response to the problem of CO_2 raises both technological and legal challenges. Within the EU there is a desire to see the required technology developed and demonstrated in order that CCS may become part of the overall solution to the problem of greenhouse gases (GHGs). To this end, the Carbon Capture and Storage Directive[3] establishes a framework within which commercial actors may be reassured about the extent of the liability they are taking on and the point at which they may transfer long-term liability for sequestered CO_2 to the state. In parallel, of course, the Directive also seeks to reassure *states* that they are only taking on long-term liability for sequestered CO_2 at the point at which they may be satisfied that it will indeed remain where it has been put. In this last regard, there are encouraging data from the Intergovernmental Panel on Climate Change, which reports that

> Observations from engineered and natural analogues as well as models suggest that the fraction retained in appropriately selected and managed geological reservoirs is very likely to exceed 99% over 100 years and is likely to exceed 99% over 1,000 years.[4]

The question is, then, to what extent does the CCS Directive provide the reassurance that the various stakeholders – governmental, commercial and public – require? In attempting to answer it, the Commission expresses general confidence in the Directive, concluding that it "is fit-for-purpose and sets up the necessary regulatory framework to ensure the safe capture, transport and storage of carbon dioxide while allowing the Member States sufficient flexibility."[5] On the other hand, it has been candid about the chicken-and-egg situation it faces: "the lack of practical experience of projects going through the regulatory process precludes a robust judgement of the performance of the Directive."[6] It is clear, nevertheless, that, whatever else is required, it is essential that the necessary practical experience be gained as quickly as possible. To that end, the Commission stresses that "[i]t is important to maintain support for commercial-scale demonstration projects both in the power and industry sectors, as this is essential to gain experience, bring down costs and demonstrate

---

3 Directive 2009/31/EC.

4 IPCC Special Report, *Carbon Dioxide Capture and Storage – Summary for Policymakers – A Special Report of Working Group III of the Intergovernmental Panel on Climate Change*, para. 25; available online at: https://www.ipcc.ch/site/assets/uploads/2018/03/srccs_summaryforpolicymakers-1.pdf.

5 REPORT FROM THE COMMISSION TO THE EUROPEAN PARLIAMENT AND THE COUNCIL Climate action progress report, including the report on the functioning of the European carbon market and the report on the review of Directive 2009/31/EC on the geological storage of carbon dioxide, Brussels, 18.11.2015 COM(2015) 576 final, para. 4.3.5.

6 Ibid., Annex 2, para. 5.1.

safe and reliable underground storage of CO_2." It points to the substantial support provided by the EU under the Innovation Fund,[7] but emphasises that "[i]t is essential for successful demonstration projects that Member States match the EU's financial support, as well as involving the private sector."[8] Much, then, depends upon the Member States' willingness not only to transpose the Directive, but to take the further steps necessary to make CCS a practical reality.

This chapter traces the recent evolution of the UK's approach to CCS, with particular attention to the transposition of the CCS Directive and the development of the regulatory framework required to encourage demonstration and ultimately commercial-scale implementation. It might at first glance appear an odd time to be considering these issues; the UK is, after all, on the cusp of leaving the EU and, at the time of writing (in the summer of 2019), the prospect of that happening without a Withdrawal Agreement appears significantly increased.[9] It is nevertheless the case that the UK's approach to its departure is premised on things staying very much as they are in relation to environmental law, at least in the short term, whilst even the new Prime Minister (Boris Johnson) appears fully committed to the more-ambitious-than-the-EU target of net-zero emissions by 2050.[10] In short, paradoxically, it is not inconceivable on the face of it that the UK might be seeking to take a leadership role in relation to CCS.

The next section considers the legislative and regulatory framework the UK has developed over the past decade or so in relation to CCS, including discussion of the interaction between the licensing and leasing regimes. This is followed in Section 3 by a review of the sometimes problematical efforts to translate the potential established by that framework into practical

---

7 The latest report indicates the extent to which promised EU funding has been forthcoming: "NER 300 is one of the world's largest funding programmes for innovative low-carbon energy demonstration projects. Some 39 projects in renewable energy and carbon capture and storage in 20 different Member States have been awarded EUR 2.1 billion in funding from the auction of 300 million ETS allowances." REPORT FROM THE COMMISSION TO THE EUROPEAN PARLIAMENT AND THE COUNCIL, EU and the Paris Climate Agreement: Taking stock of progress at Katowice COP, Brussels, 26.10.2018 COM(2018) 716 final. Notwithstanding this positive assessment, the relatively low price of carbon achieved so far has negative consequences not only for the fund but more broadly for the extent to which there is a clear economic incentive to effect necessary industrial change. For a discussion, see: Corjan Brink, Herman R.J. Vollebergh, Edwin van der Werf, "Carbon pricing in the EU: Evaluation of different EU ETS reform options" (2016) 97 *Energy Policy* 603–617.

8 Note 5 above, Annex 2, para. 5.2.

9 Silke Goldberg, 'Brexit and Its Impact on the Energy Sector: Pulling the Plug?', *European Energy Law Report XII*, Cambridge: Intersentia, 2018, pp. 13–41.

10 See the Climate Change Act 2008 (2050 Target Amendment) Order 2019, SI 2019/1056.

CCS projects, before Section 4 considers the latest developments in the shape of the 2018 Action Plan. Conclusions are then drawn.

2. THE LEGISLATIVE AND REGULATORY FRAMEWORK IN THE UK

2.1. ENERGY ACT 2008

It is important to note from the outset that the legislative foundation for CCS in the UK actually pre-dates the EU Directive. CCS having been identified as important by the Stern Review published in 2006,[11] the UK Government launched an initial competition for demonstration projects in 2007.[12] The Energy Act 2008 accordingly included provisions relating to CCS, designed to allow those demonstration projects to proceed. As the Explanatory Notes to this Act indicate, whereas

> most of the activities involved in CCS are standard industrial processes and can be readily regulated by established legislation ... permanent storage of carbon dioxide is a novel activity, and existing legislation to control depositions below the surface of the land and seabed is not well suited to licensing the storage of carbon dioxide.[13]

Thus, the 2008 Act, insofar as it relates to CCS, is focused on the storage element and deals specifically with the licensing of sites for storage and with the decommissioning of infrastructure used for CCS purposes. The UK's approach envisages storage taking place offshore rather than under the land. At the time of the passage of the 2008 Act, this emphasis was driven by the expectation that developers would only be interested in offshore storage in the short term (given the ready availability of depleted oil and gas reservoirs there) and by the recognition that onshore storage would require amendment of the then draft EU Directive. Given the Government's desire to ensure an efficient demonstration competition which envisaged operation by 2014, there was no enthusiasm to wait until relevant changes had been effected at the EU level.[14]

---

11 "'Carbon capture and storage' technology is important, as it would allow some continued use of fossil fuels and help guard against the risk of fossil-fuel prices falling in response to global climate-change policy, undermining its effectiveness." Nicolas Stern, *The Economics of Climate Change: The Stern Review*, Cambridge: Cambridge University Press, 2006, p. 186.

12 Energy Act 2008, Explanatory Notes, para. 49. These projects are discussed further in Section 3 below.

13 Energy Act 2008, Explanatory Notes, para. 49.

14 Ibid, para. 50.

2.2. REGULATORY INSTRUMENTS

2.2.1. Licensing

The basic legal instrument by which the UK controls storage of CO_2 takes the form of a licence. Section 1 of the 2008 Act asserts the UK's rights under Part V of the UN Convention on the Law of the Sea (relating to the Exclusive Economic Zone) to utilise the area beyond the territorial sea for certain specified purposes including the storage of gas, as well as the unloading of gas to pipelines or installations and the exploration of this area with a view to such exploitation.[15] On this basis, the section originally continued by asserting that "Her Majesty may by Order in Council designate an area as an area within which the rights to which this section applies are exercisable" and defined such an area as a "Gas Importation and Storage Zone".[16] This was amended by the Marine and Coastal Access Act 2009 so as to ensure that the Gas Importation and Storage Zone is consistent with any declared Exclusive Economic Zone.[17] Section 17 of the 2008 Act prohibits certain activities within a "controlled place" without a licence.[18] A controlled place is defined offshore as the territorial sea or the waters in a Gas Importation and Storage Zone.[19] Since the passage of the 2009 CCS Directive,[20] the UK is now required to ensure that CCS activities are either prohibited or licensed both onshore and offshore. Appropriate amendments to the definition of a controlled place have been effected by secondary legislation applying to England, Wales and Northern Ireland[21] and to Scotland.[22] The activities which require a licence are: "use of a controlled place for storage" of CO_2; "the conversion of any natural feature in a controlled place for the purpose of storing" CO_2;

---

15 Note that this section covers both the storage of CO_2 on a permanent basis as well as that of natural gas with a view to its being recovered for use.

16 Section 1(5).

17 Marine and Coastal Access Act 2009, Sched. 4, Part 1, s. 5.

18 Section 26 permits the licensing authority to seek an injunction (interdict in Scotland) to "restrain any actual or apprehended breach of section 17". This section has been amended in relation to Wales and Northern Ireland by The Storage of Carbon Dioxide (Amendment of the Energy Act 2008 etc.) Regulations 2011, reg. 8.

19 Section 17(3). It may be wondered whether the definition of a controlled place is sufficient given that it focuses on the water column, whereas storage will involve the use of the subsurface. There is no doubt that the Crown does possess the rights required in relation to the subsurface of the continental shelf, insofar as section 1(1) of the Continental Shelf Act 1964 is drafted broadly to include "Any rights ... with respect to the sea bed and subsoil". But the question remains whether the 2008 Act is drafted broadly enough so as to allow a licence to be granted in relation to the specific activity of storing CO_2 in the subsoil.

20 Directive 2009/31/EC of the European Parliament and of the Council of 23 April 2009 on the geological storage of carbon dioxide and amending Council Directive 85/337/EEC, European Parliament and Council Directives 2000/60/EC, 2001/80/EC, 2004/35/EC, 2006/12/EC, 2008/1/EC and Regulation (EC) No. 1013/2006.

21 The Storage of Carbon Dioxide (Amendment of the Energy Act 2008 etc.) Regulations 2011.

22 The Energy Act 2008 (Storage of Carbon Dioxide) (Scotland) Regulations 2011, reg. 2.

exploration of a controlled place in connection with the previous uses; and establishment of an installation for these purposes.[23] Section 22 provides that anyone carrying out an unlicensed activity will be guilty of an offence and subject to the penalties specified. Section 18[24] permits the licensing authority to grant licences in respect of one or more of the activities listed in section 17(2) and also specifies the circumstances in which the licensing authority will be either the Oil and Gas Authority[25] or one of the devolved authorities.

2.2.2. Crown Lease

So far the conceptual approach to the control of storage of CO_2 offshore will be familiar to anyone acquainted with the UK's approach to the control of exploration for and production of hydrocarbons offshore. At this point, however, the 2008 Act includes an innovation in the shape of the Crown lease. The first mention in the context of CCS comes in section 18(3) where it is stated that the controlled place (previously defined as the territorial sea or the waters in a Gas Importation and Storage Zone) "in respect of which a licence is granted may be determined by reference to the provisions of a Crown lease which has been or may be granted." Such a lease is further defined as "a lease of property forming part of the Crown Estate, or an authorisation to exercise rights forming part of that Estate".[26] The Explanatory Notes to the 2008 Act point out that, notwithstanding the authorisation contained in the licence,

> in order to make use of the sea, the seabed or spaces under the seabed for the purpose of these activities, an operator would in addition have to obtain a lease or authorisation from The Crown Estate, who administer the relevant rights to the offshore area.[27]

Insofar as this is true, however, it may be wondered how hydrocarbon activities have taken place on the UKCS for more than five decades without any such lease ever having been granted. Be that as it may, this document is now clearly an essential component of any CCS project and the terms of the more familiar licence from the Secretary of State or the devolved authorities will need to be read in conjunction with those of the Crown lease. The situation is complexified

23 Section 17(2). Note that s. 33 sets out the circumstances in which the use of CO_2 for enhanced oil recovery may be treated as an activity within the meaning of s. 17(2).

24 As amended by The Storage of Carbon Dioxide (Amendment of the Energy Act 2008 etc.) Regulations 2011, reg. 3, and The Energy Act 2008 (Storage of Carbon Dioxide) (Scotland) Regulations 2011, reg. 2.

25 The licensing authority was previously the relevant government department. Since the Energy Act 2016, however, this function has been transferred to the OGA. Policy in relation to carbon capture, utilisation and storage remains a matter for the department, currently the Department for Business, Energy and Industrial Strategy.

26 Energy Act 2008, s. 18(4).

27 Energy Act 2008, Explanatory Notes, para. 55.

further by the transfer in 2017 of the Crown Estate's "Scottish assets" to Scottish Ministers as part of the further devolution of power following the independence referendum in 2014.[28] Thus, a lease in the Scottish zone[29] would have to be obtained from the body so designated by the Scottish Ministers, namely Crown Estate Scotland.[30]

2.3. TRANSPOSITION OF EU DIRECTIVE

Dealing first with the licence, the initial regime under the 2008 Act has had to be developed to implement the requirements of the 2009 Directive. Power to make regulations in respect of the licensing requirements is conferred on each licensing authority by section 19 of the Act,[31] while section 20 sets out the terms and conditions upon which a licence may be granted. Note that section 20(4) provides that the "provisions of a licence may be expressed by reference to provision made in a Crown lease". Beyond that, it is possible that a licence "may provide … for the commencement of the licence to be conditional upon the commencement of a Crown lease which has been or may be granted" and "for the period of the licence to be determined by reference to the period of such a Crown lease."[32] The question of the interaction of the licence and the lease will be discussed further below. Regulations under section 19 have so far been made by the Secretary of State for Energy and Climate Change (thus, those relevant to storage beyond the territorial sea) in the shape of The Carbon Dioxide (Licensing etc.) Regulations 2010.[33] These regulations stipulate at the outset that a licence may not be granted for the purpose of storing CO_2 in the water column.[34] The applicant must either specify a period during which exploration will be permitted or state why exploration is not required.[35] Grant of the licence will then constitute the "exploration permit" required by Article 5 of the 2009 Directive.[36] Regulation 4 then envisages an appraisal period sufficient to select

---

28 The Crown Estate Transfer Scheme 2017, SI 2017/524.

29 That part of the UK's Exclusive Economic Zone where Scottish Ministers have responsibilities for devolved functions. See the Scottish Adjacent Waters Boundaries Order 1999, SI 1999/1126, the Exclusive Economic Zone Order 2013, SI 2013/3161; and the Gas Importation and Storage Zone (Designation of Area) Order 2009, SI 2009/223.

30 Established by the Crown Estate Scotland (Interim Management) Order 2017 (SSI 2017/36) and nominated by the Scottish Ministers under the Scotland Act 1998 s. 90B(1) as the transferee for the purposes of the Crown Estate Transfer Scheme (n. 28 above).

31 See also Energy Act 2008, ss. 21, 29(1) and (7), and 104(2).

32 Energy Act 2008, s. 20(4)(a) and (b).

33 SI 2010/2221.

34 Regulation 2. See 2009 Directive Art. 2(4), consistent with OSPAR Decision 2007/1 to prohibit the storage of carbon dioxide streams in the water column or on the sea-bed.

35 Regulation 3.

36 For the content of the licence, see The Storage of Carbon Dioxide (Amendment of the Energy Act 2008 etc.) Regulations 2011, reg. 5 and sched. 1.

a storage site and to prepare the documentation required for the application for a storage permit under Regulation 6 (as required by Article 6 of the 2009 Directive). Regulation 7 then transposes Article 8 of the Directive, specifying the conditions upon which a storage permit will be granted, while Regulation 8 does the same for Article 7 in respect of the information that must be included in a storage permit.[37] Section 23 of the 2008 Act provides for offences relating to licences, for example, carrying out an activity under a licence for which a prior consent was required without first obtaining that consent. Where a licensee fails to comply with the provisions of a licence, the licensing authority may direct them to do what it considers necessary so as to comply, and specify a period of time for such compliance. The licensing authority has a duty to consult the licensee in such circumstances, but also has the right to take action on behalf of the licensee or make arrangements for others to do so where the latter fails to comply with the direction.[38] Where such action is required, the licensing authority may recover reasonable costs (and interest) from the licensee.[39] Section 25 provides that it is an offence to fail to comply with a direction under section 24 and specifies the penalties. Regulation 10 provides the licensing authority with additional powers in relation to corrective measures that may be undertaken where "a significant irregularity or a leakage has been detected", while regulation 11 confers powers in relation to the review, modification and revocation of a storage permit. Revocation is a possibility under this regulation where, for example, the licensing authority becomes aware of "any (or any risk of) leakages or significant irregularities" and "it decides that modification of the permit would be insufficient in the light of" these matters.[40] Where a storage permit is revoked, the consequences in terms of closure or of consideration of a new licence application are laid out in regulation 12. Insofar as the CCS model envisages that at a certain point the reservoir or other geological formation into which CO_2 will be injected will be considered to be full and require closure, with a view to indefinite sequestration, it is appropriate that before an application for a storage permit is made the applicant considers what will happen after such closure. Regulation 13 of the 2011 Regulations requires the drawing up of such a plan before application for a storage permit and also the approval of such a plan before a permit can be granted. The licensing authority has the power to require modifications to the plan prior to approval.[41] The fact

---

37 See also sched. 2 to the 2011 Regulations covering acceptance and injection of CO_2; monitoring; reporting, and notification of leakages and significant irregularities; notification and implementation of changes; review, and modification or revocation of the permit; corrective measures; financial security.

38 See s. 24(1)–(4). See also The Storage of Carbon Dioxide (Amendment of the Energy Act 2008 etc.) Regulations 2011, reg. 10.

39 Section 24(5)–(7).

40 See reg. 11(5) and (7).

41 Regulation 13(3)(b).

that a site has been closed does not affect any obligations that the licensee may have as a consequence of legislation implementing the Environmental Licensing Directive[42] or the Emissions Trading Scheme.[43]

Article 25 of the 2009 Directive requires Member States to set up registers of storage permits granted and of all closed storage sites. This is implemented by section 29 of the 2008 Act, while regulation 9 of the 2010 Regulations specifies the information that must be included in the register. Note that despite the transfer of the licensing function to the OGA, the register is maintained by the Secretary of State, whilst the OGA is obliged to provide to him or her such information as it may hold which the latter requires in order to comply with the duties related to the register.[44]

In light of the transparency implied by the public register, it is also noteworthy that the Government's approach has sought to ensure that "local communities and other stakeholders are effectively engaged throughout the process of design, construction, operation and decommissioning".[45] To this end, the Scottish Government established a Regulatory Group in 2009 with a view to considering the permits required along the CCS chain and testing the extent to which existing regulations were sufficient for the task of meeting the expectations of the range of interested parties. The output from this exercise includes a CCS Regulatory Test Toolkit, which identifies stakeholder engagement as a key component in the establishment of the regulatory framework itself and not just of the implementation of regulation once it is established.[46]

2.4. INTERACTION BETWEEN THE LICENCE AND THE CROWN LEASE?

As noted above, the licence (and associated storage permit) is not the only instrument that an operator will need to consider. Since the Energy Act 2008, the Crown Estate, which had previously exercised the Crown's property rights

42 Articles 5 to 8 dealing with necessary preventive measures and remedial action. See reg. 14(a) of the 2011 Regulations. Note also that sched. 2 to The Environmental Damage (Prevention and Remediation) Regulations 2009, which lists activities causing damage for which liability exists, is specifically amended by reg. 15 of the 2011 Regulations to add the operation of CO_2 storage sites.

43 Even though CCS is now included within the ETS, permits will require to be surrendered in the event of any leakage to the atmosphere. See reg. 14(b) of the 2011 Regulations.

44 Energy Act 2008, s. 29(8). Interestingly, on its website, the OGA reads this section as imposing the duty on the Authority: "Section 29 of the Energy Act provides that the OGA must maintain a register containing prescribed information relating to licences"; see: https://www.ogauthority.co.uk/licensing-consents/carbon-storage/.

45 DECC, *CCS Roadmap: The Regulatory Framework* (April 2012) p. 3, para. 1.1. https://assets.publishing.service.gov.uk/government/uploads/system/uploads/attachment_data/file/48319/4902-ccs-roadmap--regulatory-framework.pdf.

46 Global CCS Institute, Scottish Government, and Scottish Carbon Capture and Storage, *Carbon Capture and Storage Regulatory Test Toolkit* (undated).

in the seabed out to the limit of the territorial sea (12 nautical miles from the baseline as established under the UN Convention on the Law of the Sea) is now empowered to issue leases constituting "an authorisation to exercise rights forming part of" its Estate,[47] which Estate now includes the Exclusive Economic Zone declared by the UK[48] and which rights include the storage of gas.[49] As discussed above, in relation to the Scottish zone, these powers are now exercised by Crown Estate Scotland.[50] The precise way in which the Crown Estate and Crown Estate Scotland exercise this power is via three documents: an Agreement for Lease (AfL), a lease and, if required, a pipeline lease. The AfL provides the holder with a time-limited exclusive option to progress to a full lease upon satisfaction of certain conditions, including obtaining a storage licence from the OGA. The situation is thus arrived at where, as noted above, the grant of the licence by OGA may, under section 20(4) of the 2008 Act, be contingent upon the grant of a Crown lease, whilst the progress from the AfL to the full lease, as determined by the Crown Estate/Crown Estate Scotland, may be contingent upon the grant of a storage permit by the OGA. This could be read as a multiple-lock mechanism to ensure that the state and the environment are protected to the fullest possible extent. Given that complex hydrocarbon operations have successfully proceeded for over five decades on the basis only of a licence from the Secretary of State, it could equally be read as the imposition of unnecessary bureaucracy in a process where it is the Government's stated aim to "remove barriers and obstacles to deployment" of CCS.[51]

There is perhaps another justification for the involvement of the Crown Estate beyond the 12 nautical mile limit, namely the likelihood that in the years ahead there will be increasing competition among different users of the EEZ, not least among the hydrocarbon, renewable and CCS sectors of the energy industry. As such, the Crown Estate and Crown Estate Scotland can play an important role in relation to spatial planning. On the other hand, this does again raise the problem that it has no function in relation to hydrocarbon developments and as such there will need to be careful cooperation with the OGA – which of course raises the question of whether the whole matter would have been better left to the sole agency which has inherited and built upon long departmental experience of the continental shelf. Be that as it may, the system appears now to be well-established in the sense that there is a statutory basis for the Crown lease.[52]

---

47 Section 18(4).

48 Section 1(5) as amended by the Marine and Coastal Access Act 2009, Sched. 4, Part 1, s. 5.

49 Section 1(3)(b).

50 See n. 29 above and associated text.

51 See DECC, *CCS Roadmap: Supporting Deployment of Carbon Capture and Storage in the UK*, April 2012, p. 5, (Ministerial Foreword by Secretary of State for Energy and Climate Change, Edward Davey).

52 It was previously the case that model agreements were available on the Crown Estate website, but as at the end of July 2019, these appear no longer to be available either from the Crown

It is also interesting to note that whatever the concerns expressed above, the first grant of an AfL by Crown Estate Scotland[53] was followed swiftly by the first grant by the OGA of a carbon storage licence.[54]

2.5. TRANSPORTATION OF CO_2

While, as was suggested previously, the general view of the Government has been that it is really only *storage* of CO_2 that raises new challenges requiring specific legislation and regulation, it is nevertheless the case that *transportation* has also required legal change, albeit to a much more limited extent. The right already exists under section 12 of the Pipe-lines Act 1962 for a person seeking to construct a pipeline to apply to the Secretary of State for an order for the compulsory acquisition of rights over land for that purpose. In the case of CCS, however, in the same way that it is envisaged that storage could involve the re-use of depleted reservoirs,[55] so could transportation involve the re-use of existing pipelines previously used for the transportation of natural gas. Insofar as these pipelines cross private land they may be subject to servitudes or easements which are expressed in terms of a specific substance being transported in a specific direction. A proposal to change the substance (CO_2 instead of natural gas) and the direction of transportation (to the reservoir instead of from the reservoir) could be subject to a series of hold-up problems along the length of the pipeline while individual negotiations are conducted. Section 108 of the Energy Act 2011 thus amends the Pipe-lines Act 1962 by inserting a new section 12A, which provides the owner of an existing pipeline with the right to seek an order from the Secretary of State for the compulsory acquisition of rights over land where it is intended that the pipeline be converted in order to convey CO_2.

3. TRANSLATING THE LEGISLATIVE POTENTIAL INTO PRACTICAL PROJECTS

From the foregoing, there is certainly no evidence that the UK has been anything other than fully committed to the development of CCS as a key part of its response to the challenge of climate change in the context of the need

Estate or Crown Estate Scotland. This is in stark contrast to the approach of the OGA, which provides full details of the licensing process as well as copies of issued licences: https://www.ogauthority.co.uk/licensing-consents/carbon-storage/.

[53] https://www.crownestatescotland.com/media-and-notices/news-media-releases-opinion/crown-estate-scotland-issues-first-agreement-for-critical-co2-storage-infrastructure.

[54] https://www.ogauthority.co.uk/news-publications/news/2018/carbon-capture-storage-licence-awarded/.

[55] See also Chapter XV in this volume on "Decommissioning of Offshore Installations upon the UK Continental Shelf" (G. Gordon and J. Paterson).

simultaneously to take care of energy security; the UK was actively putting in place the legal and regulatory framework even before the coming into force of the EU CCS Directive. It has taken more than a decade, however, for that enthusiasm to bear fruit in the shape of the award of a lease and a licence in a situation where there is a genuine prospect of successful implementation. After a false start with the failure of the initial demonstration competition and the abandonment of plans for the retrofit of capture technology at Longannet and for a new-build power station at Kingsnorth,[56] the Coalition Government coming to power in 2010 set about ensuring that the technology would be competitive with other low carbon options and allow the industry "to take investment decisions to build CCS equipped fossil fuel power stations in the early 2020s".[57] The extent of this support was considerable and included, *inter alia*, the provision of £1 billion in capital support to launch a commercialisation programme, creating a CCS Cost Reduction Task Force, and, of particular importance in the present context, developing regulation in relation to both deployment and long-term storage.[58]

A new commercialisation competition opened in April 2012. Of the four so-called "full-chain" projects (that is, projects which involve capture, transport, and storage) shortlisted, two preferred bidders were announced in March 2013. The first of these would involve retrofitting capture technology to the existing gas-fired power station at Peterhead in north-east Scotland. Captured CO_2 would then be transported to a depleted offshore gas field for storage. The second shortlisted project, named the White Rose Project, would see the construction of a new coal-fired power station at the existing Drax site in Yorkshire in England. CO_2 captured there would also be transported offshore, but in this case injected into a saline aquifer. Each of these projects envisaged that 90 per cent of CO_2 produced during electricity generation would be captured and stored permanently. Each project was the subject of detailed discussions between its promoters and the Government department then responsible (the Department for Energy and Climate Change or DECC) in relation to the terms for Front End Engineering and Design (FEED) studies aimed at 'de-risking' proposals before final decisions on investment and construction were taken. The DECC awarded contracts and funding for FEED studies in relation to both the White Rose and Peterhead projects.[59] In July 2014, the White Rose Project was among successful

56 See National Audit Office, Carbon capture and storage: lessons from the competition for the first UK demonstration, Report by the Comptroller and Auditor General, HC 1829, Session 2010–12, 16 March 2012.

57 DECC, *CCS Roadmap*, above n. 51, p. 5.

58 Ibid.

59 See Guidance: UK carbon capture and storage: https://www.gov.uk/uk-carbon-capture-and-storage-government-funding-and-support. For further details, see also Greg Gordon, Aileen McHarg and John Paterson, "Energy Law in the United Kingdom" in Martha Roggenkamp, Catherine Redgwell, Anita Rønne and Iñigo del Guayo (eds.), *Energy Law in Europe: National, EU and International Regulation* (3rd edn.) Oxford: Oxford University Press, para. 14.258.

bidders for support from the European Commission's NER300 funding, with €300 million awarded.[60]

At that point, then, the problems of the initial competition appeared to have been laid to rest and the UK was on course to deliver a functioning CCS project. Even the withdrawal of a key investor in the White Rose Project[61] was not seen as fatal and could indeed have been read as an acceptance on the part of that project that the competition was most likely to be won by the Peterhead rival. Ongoing economic problems at that time, however, meant that the Government was actively looking for ways to save money. In the context of the UK economy, £1 billion is not a very significant sum of money and, given the acknowledged importance of CCS for both emissions reduction and energy security, removing that support would look like the ultimate false economy. That, however, is exactly what happened. The 2015 Spending Review and Autumn Statement saw the quiet removal of the capital support scheme. The manner of its removal is noteworthy and would appear to indicate the Government was well aware that this was a contentious – not to say embarrassing – decision. The announcement was not made in Parliament, nor did the details appear in the Spending Review documentation. Rather, the news came in a notification to the Stock Exchange.[62]

As such, it is now a question whether the concern with creating the right regulatory environment, which involves balancing the needs and expectations of developers with the protection of workers, the public, and the environment, will have any practical significance.[63]

4. LATEST DEVELOPMENTS

4.1. FROM CCS TO CCUS

One could be forgiven for assuming that the UK Government has been entirely preoccupied with Brexit since the referendum on leaving the EU in 2016.[64] While that is substantially true, it is significant that some of the

---

60 Available at: http://europa.eu/rapid/press-release_MEMO-14-465_en.htm.

61 https://www.drax.com/press_release/drax-announces-plan-end-investment white rose carbon-capture-storage-project/.

62 The announcement was originally available at: http://www.londonstockexchange.com/exchange/news/market-news/market-news-detail/other/12597443.html, but as at 1 August 2019 was not at that address and a search within the London Stock Exchange website did not reveal a new location. It is interesting to note in parallel that whilst there was also the factor of public opposition to CCS to consider in some jurisdictions (as in the Netherlands), this was not the case in the UK. One may speculate that the fact that all carbon sequestration in the UK is planned for the offshore area means that this issue does not have the immediacy of, say, shale gas exploration and development (so-called "fracking"), which has, of course, encountered very considerable public hostility in the UK.

63 DECC, *CCS Roadmap: The Regulatory Framework* (April 2012) p. 3.

64 See S. Goldberg, "Brexit and Its Impact on the Energy Sector", n. 9 above.

most important non-Brexit initiatives that have been announced during that period relate to the issues discussed in this chapter. Thus, in October 2017 the UK Government published its Clean Growth Strategy.[65] This included the promise to "[d]emonstrate international leadership in carbon capture usage and storage (CCUS), by collaborating with our global partners and investing up to £100 million in leading edge CCUS and industrial innovation to drive down costs".[66] Then, in November 2018, the UK Government published an action plan focused specifically on CCUS in which three key roles are identified for the technology: flexible gas power generation; industrial processes; and heat, especially in the development of a hydrogen economy.[67] The Action Plan is certainly ambitious insofar as it aims to "develop and test commercial and regulatory concepts incrementally during the 2020s", then deploy "at scale during the 2030s" to the extent justified, all with a view to gaining cost advantages and meeting carbon emission targets set for 2050.[68] Much significant detail, nevertheless, remains to be filled in, but there is a stated aim of doing much of this during 2019 – for example, commencing "detailed engagement with industry on the critical challenges to delivering CCUS in the UK, in particular the cost structures, risk sharing arrangements and the necessary market-based frameworks"[69] – and it is also the case that the UK has both considerable expertise and opportunity to be successful.[70]

4.2. THE CCUS ACTION PLAN

Some key indications of the Government's thinking may be discerned from the Action Plan. Thus, the Government believes that a "staged approach will enable … all parties to learn by doing."[71] Whilst it intends to "examine and report, during 2019, on the opportunity of maximising economies of scale

65 HM Government, The Clean Growth Strategy: Leading the Way to a Low Carbon Future, October 2017. This was presented to Parliament pursuant to ss. 12 and 14 of the Energy Act 2008 and updated in April 2018. Available online at: https://assets.publishing.service.gov.uk/government/uploads/system/uploads/attachment_data/file/700496/clean-growth-strategy-correction-april-2018.pdf.

66 Ibid., p. 12.

67 Clean Growth: The UK Carbon Capture Usage and Storage deployment pathway – an action plan, November 2018: https://assets.publishing.service.gov.uk/government/uploads/system/uploads/attachment_data/file/759637/beis-ccus-action-plan.pdf.

68 Ibid., p. 15.

69 Ibid., p. 18.

70 See the institutions, actors and sites listed at ibid., pp. 16–17. For an indication of the considerable capacity that the UK possesses (in excess of 78 billion tonnes of CO_2, sufficient for more than a century's worth of UK and European emissions) see the database at: http://www.co2stored.co.uk/home/index.

71 Ibid., p. 15.

by developing shared carbon dioxide infrastructure network in an industrial centre, and the potential for cost effective deployment that provides value for money",[72] is also clear that "the role of Government is not to pick winners and subsidise or protect them".[73] To the contrary, it sees that a

> successful proposition will be one that is supported by local and regional communities, authorities and businesses. It will need to be consistent with the market based framework set out by Government and include the wider industrial and economic benefits of establishing CCUS in the place.[74]

And lest there be any doubt in that regard, it stresses that it is "keen to see CCUS facilities brought forward through market mechanisms which take full advantage of innovation and competition".[75] None of that, on the face of it, looks particularly contentious, especially from a Conservative Government, but it is questionable whether this approach is entirely consistent with the principles the Government has set out for the future strategy of the power sector as a whole, which include "*wherever possible*, use market mechanisms that take full advantage of innovation and competition", but also suggest that the "Government must be prepared to *intervene* to provide insurance and preserve optionality" (emphasis added).[76] So, is the insistence on the market and a rejection of "picking winners" in the case of CCUS wholly consistent with the Government's overall principles for the power sector? Or does CCUS have to cross a higher threshold? This is an issue to be considered as further detail emerges following engagement with industry and other stakeholders.

4.3. TRANSPORT AND STORAGE INFRASTRUCTURE

The Action Plan also offers an insight into the Government's latest thinking in relation to transport and storage infrastructure. In this regard, it is influenced by experience in the offshore oil and gas industry meaning that it assumes that initial projects will be "full-chain", where a single developer builds and operates carbon capture, transport and storage infrastructure, with later projects then able to link into that infrastructure.[77] It is recognised, given this approach, that the initial investment will require incentivisation and the Government is now

72 Ibid., p. 29.
73 Ibid., p. 15.
74 Ibid., p. 30.
75 Ibid., p. 31.
76 Ibid., p. 35.
77 Ibid., p. 38.

reviewing options for "development of a commercial model to enable investment in, and deployment of carbon dioxide transport and storage infrastructure in the UK".[78]

It is also notable that re-using existing oil and gas infrastructure is seen as a way of reducing CCUS costs. To this end, the Government "will coordinate a process, in collaboration with project developers, owners of existing assets, and relevant regulators, to identify assets with potential for re-use".[79] This will require a high degree of coordination and collaboration, and the Government is clear that it "expects that regulators, developers and owners of existing assets will work closely together, where assets are identified with potential for re-use, in order to maximise the potential economic life of those assets".[80] In support of this the Government is working in the near term with the licensing and leasing authorities to develop "a policy on re-use of infrastructure for the purposes of transporting and/or storing carbon dioxide."[81] As ambitious as all of this appears, it must be acknowledged that it is entirely consistent with the emerging approach to the regulation of the offshore oil and gas industry in the context of the establishment of the OGA and the development of the Maximising Economic Recovery UK Strategy.[82]

4.4. ENHANCED OIL RECOVERY

Whilst there is only a passing mention in the Action Plan,[83] it is also appropriate at this point to mention a possible use of captured CO_2 in the context of enhanced oil recovery (EOR). This is clearly of interest in the context of the UKCS as a mature hydrocarbon basin and has received considerably greater attention in earlier Government publications.[84] CCS and EOR are easily mentioned in the same breath, especially when, as in the Action Plan, the reference is not simply to Carbon Capture and Storage, but to Carbon Capture *Utilisation* and Storage. Whilst both carbon sequestration and CO_2 for EOR involve the injection of the gas into geological structures and both result in its permanent placement in those

---

78 Ibid.

79 Ibid., p. 40.

80 Ibid.

81 Ibid.

82 For a discussion see, Greg Gordon, John Paterson and Uisdean Vass, "The Wood Review and Maximising Economic Recovery upon the UKCS" in Greg Gordon, John Paterson and Emre Usenmez (eds.), *UK Oil and Gas Law: Current Practice and Emerging Trends (Vol. 1 Resource Management and Regulatory Law)*, Edinburgh: Edinburgh University Press, pp. 132–169. See also Chapter XV of this volume by Greg Gordon and John Paterson on "Decommissioning of Offshore Installations upon the UK Continental Shelf".

83 Above n. 65, p. 24.

84 See, for example, DECC, *Next Steps in CCS: Scoping Document*, August 2014, esp. chapter 8 "Enhanced oil recovery (EOR)".

structures, the different intention in each case results in their being subject to different regulatory regimes. Thus, whilst, as we have seen, carbon sequestration is subject to the regime involving licensing and leasing based on the provisions of the Energy Act 2008, using CO_2 for EOR is not; instead it is a matter for the OGA under the Petroleum Act 1998[85] and, in particular, does not involve the Crown Estate or Crown Estate Scotland.[86] This might appear to be an interesting anomaly, but not one necessarily to trouble any of the actors involved. From the point of view of future liabilities, however, it is interesting that the regime under the Energy Act 2008 takes such an interest in checking that CO_2 injected for purposes of storage is behaving as expected before liability transfers to the state, the same is not the case where CO_2 is injected for purposes of EOR. Were there to be any adverse event involving CO_2 following plugging and abandonment of the wells associated with a previously producing reservoir, would the liability lie with the companies responsible for decommissioning under the Petroleum Act 1998? Or would the fact that the Crown Estate and Crown Estate Scotland appear to be exercising property rights when they issue leases for carbon storage indicate that ownership of CO_2 in strata lies with them however it got there and thus that liability in the case of an adverse event would equally lie with them? The fact that the law applicable to the various uses of the seabed and subsoil has developed piecemeal over several decades without, it would appear, any overall plan means that it is not easy to answer these questions. It could be objected, of course, that the amounts of CO_2 involved in EOR are relatively small compared to a storage site and equally that, as the IPCC reported, there is relatively high confidence that injected CO_2 will not escape. But it is a question whether these are convenient *ex post* justifications rather than an indication of a well-thought-out overall legislative and regulatory regime. Insofar as the latter is true, it would be important to bear in mind that there might well be other issues that have perhaps not been considered. It will be important as the Action Plan proceeds to ensure that all are alert to unintended conflicts – or indeed gaps – between the various normative orders in play in the offshore area.

5. CONCLUSIONS

Despite some false starts, and the frustration of time lost, the UK at present appears to be in a relatively strong position in relation to the development of CCS. The legislative and regulatory regime (subject to the points raised in

85 See, for example, the various consents required under a petroleum production licence. Petroleum Licensing (Production) (Seaward Areas) Regulations 2008, SI 2008/225.

86 The uncertainty apparent here may be traced back to the CCS Directive, which is not clear on this issue. It would appear, therefore, that the legal treatment of CO_2 for EOR is a matter for individual Member States.

the previous section) appears to be well bedded in. Any conceptual worries about the interaction of the Crown lease and the carbon storage licence have hopefully been dispelled by the successful grants by Crown Estate Scotland and the OGA respectively in late 2018. Equally, if one considers the concerns expressed by the European Commission in relation to the need to "maintain support for commercial-scale demonstration projects both in the power and industry sectors, as this is essential to gain experience, bring down costs and demonstrate safe and reliable underground storage of CO_2",[87] the Action Plan surely meets all of the European Commission's concerns. As with so much in the UK at the moment, however, it is impossible to reach any conclusion with any degree of certainty when practically everything is in a state of wholly unprecedented uncertainty.

---

87 Above n. 5, Annex 2, para. 5.2.

CHAPTER XX

CARBON CAPTURE AND STORAGE IN THE NETHERLANDS

A Long and Winding Process

Martha M. Roggenkamp

1. INTRODUCTION

Carbon capture and storage (CCS) has been a policy of the Dutch government for almost two decades, although the interest in developing CCS has faced many ups and downs. The interest in CCS started as an important instrument in the process of energy transition, i.e. a policy aiming to transition away from a fossil fuel economy and to limit the level of CO_2 emissions.

The policy of energy transition was developed by several ministries[1] in early 2000 and led to the establishment of the Energy Transition Task Force (ETTF) in January 2005, which consisted of representatives from industry, government, research organizations, financial institutions and non-governmental organizations (NGOs). In the Transition Action Plan 'More with Energy' that was presented in May 2006, the task force set some ambitious goals for 2050, i.e. energy savings of 1.5 to 2 per cent each year, a substantial use of renewable energy sources and a reduction of CO_2 emissions by half (compared to 1990) and at the same time strengthening the position of Dutch industry. In order to make the gas industry more sustainable, the task force considered the need for projects involving CO_2 capture and (underground) storage. As part of a Working Programme 'Clean and Efficient'[2] of 2007 the Dutch government aimed at examining the possibility of CCS and to develop and subsidise three

1 These ministries were at that time: the Ministry of Economic Affairs, the Ministry of Housing, Spatial Planning and the Environment, the Ministry of Transport, Public Works and Water Management, the Ministry of Agriculture, Nature Management and Food Quality, the Ministry of Foreign Affairs, and the Ministry of Finance.

2 TK 1998–1999, 26 219, No 7, p. 20 and TK 2009–2010, 32 343, No 3, p. 4.

demonstration projects in the Netherlands.[3] The task force even presented the ambitious idea that the Netherlands could be turned into an EU CO_2 hub due to the expected large number of (soon to be) depleted oil and gas fields.[4] It thus focused on developing CO_2 storage locations *onshore* as suitable reservoirs would (soon) become available and it was the least costly option. Despite a serious attempt to set up a pilot phase in Barendrecht where Shell was involved both as the capturer at a refinery near Rotterdam and as the holder of a gas production licence (and potential storage licence), the project failed due to major public opposition. As a result, no storage licence was award for this project.[5] Consequently, the focus shifted to storage in depleted gas reservoirs *offshore*. In its 2017 Coalition Agreement, the Dutch government again highlighted carbon capture and storage as one of the central pillars of its climate policy and an important interim tool to reduce carbon dioxide emissions.[6] According to the 2019 Climate Agreement, the Netherlands need to reduce by 2030 its greenhouse emissions by 49 per cent compared to 1990 levels, and 95 per cent by 2050.[7] CCS, although on a limited scale, is included as one of the proposed instruments to reach this goal.[8] Given the *de facto* ban on onshore storage of carbon dioxide, the focus is on the storage of CO_2 offshore.

Some of the first pilot projects primarily considered means to capture CO_2 but others also looked primarily at the final part of the CCS chain, i.e. subsoil storage. The new Mining Act, which entered into force in 2003,[9] already facilitated such storage as it introduced a separate licence for subsoil storage. Article 25 of the Mining Act required a person to obtain a licence in order to store 'substances'. The term 'substances' was not defined but was generally understood to include CO_2.[10] However, this regime has in practice never been applied to storage of CO_2 as a more stringent regime was introduced in 2009

---

3 TK 1998–1999, 26 219, No 7, p. 20. These projects included: (1) the Zero Emission Power Plant (ZEPP) project in Drachten, involving the capture of CO_2 from a gas-fired power plant and injecting the CO_2 into the nearby Akkrum gas field for enhanced recovery; (2) developing a 840 MW gas-fired power plant in the Rotterdam area and capturing CO_2, by using the cryogene principle (freezing CO_2); and (3) testing CO_2 capture at the Buggenum (coal-fired and biomass) plant.

4 See Advice of working group CO_2 storage of Platform New Gas (Nieuw Gas) to the Task Force on Energy Transition, March 2006, pp. 11 and 25.

5 See TK 2010–11, 28982 No. 113.

6 Coalition Agreement 2017–2021 Confidence in the Future (*Regeerakkoord 2017–2021 Vertrouwen in de toekomst*), 2017, p. 38. The Dutch government aims at a reduction of carbon dioxide emissions by 18 megatons in 2030 through carbon dioxide storage.

7 See, for the Dutch Climate Agreement, also Chapter XIII of this volume by L. Braaksma and R. Fleming, as well as Chapter XXIII of this volume by G. van der Veen and K. de Graaf.

8 See letter from the Minister of Economic Affairs and Climate to Parliament of 28 June 2019 at: www.klimaatakkoord.nl.

9 Staatsblad 2002, 542. The Mining Decree and the Mining Regulations entered into force at the same time (Staatsblad 2002, 604 and 245).

10 See preparatory works to the Act, TK 1998–1999, 26219, no. 7, p. 20.

following the need to transpose Directive 2009/31/EC on geological storage of CO_2 into national law.

2. LEGAL FRAMEWORK

2.1. INTRODUCTION

Directive 2009/31/EC on geological storage of CO_2 was implemented in Dutch law on 6 June 2010.[11] The Dutch legislature transposed the Directive (almost to the letter) as a separate chapter in the Mining Act governing storage (of substances and carbon dioxide) as it wanted to avoid any major delays in the implementation process.[12] The Mining Act was also considered as the proper legal basis, as it already provided for a regime on the storage of substances (including the storage of CO_2).[13] The Mining Act, nevertheless, needed some particular amendments because the Directive included additional requirements regarding exploration, monitoring and closure. Similarly to the Directive, the Mining Act primarily governs the final part of the CCS chain; the capture of CO_2 and to some extent also the transport of CO_2 is regulated by other laws.

2.2. LICENSING REGIME

As provided by the Directive, geological storage of CO_2 may involve two licences: one licence for exploring suitable sites and another licence for subsoil storage. Both types of licence are exclusive in the sense that only one licence can be awarded per area/reservoir.[14] These licences are basically available to all entities possessing the necessary technical and financial capacities and are issued on the basis of objective, published criteria. With regard to carbon dioxide storage licences some additional assessment criteria exist, such as the risks of carbon dioxide leakage and the risk of significant health and environmental effects.[15]

Following the CCS Directive and general practice in the hydrocarbons sector, licences need to be awarded in competition. This entails that the Minister will be calling for alternative bids once a licence application has been made.[16] If no use is made of an exploration licence, competitive bidding will take place when awarding a storage licence. If use is to be made of a (almost) depleted

[11] Act of 6 June 2010, Staatsblad 2010, 381.
[12] Articles 25–32 Mining Act.
[13] Article 25 Mining Act.
[14] Article 26(6) Mining Act.
[15] Article 27(3) Mining Act.
[16] Article 26b Mining Act.

oil or gas reservoir, account needs to be taken of the fact that a hydrocarbons production licence may already apply. In that case, the Mining Act allows for the additional award of an exploration licence or a carbon dioxide storage licence.[17] Given the requirement of competitive bidding, the person holding the hydrocarbons exploration or production licence does not hold a privileged position in the award procedure for a carbon dioxide storage licence and will not automatically be rewarded the licence. The holder of the hydrocarbons licence thus needs to compete with all other applicants and does not have a priority right. This situation may result in a situation where holders of a hydrocarbons licence will be less interested in applying for a licence to (re)use the reservoir for CO_2 storage. On the other hand, the holder of a hydrocarbons licence will have an advantage when applying for such storage licences as it is familiar with the reservoir and has all relevant technical and geological knowledge of the field.

The provisions in the Mining Act regarding carbon dioxide exploration permits are less detailed than the Directive,[18] probably because the Netherlands anticipated making use of depleted oil and gas fields and, consequently, sufficient knowledge of the subsoil should be available for granting storage licences.[19] A storage licence is required, with or without an exploration permit, if a site has found to be suitable for the storage of CO_2. The CO_2 storage provisions in the Mining Act are identical to those in the Directive.[20] By contrast to other licences, however, a CO_2 storage permit also needs to be assessed by the Commission.[21] If awarded, a storage licence should provide information about the total quantity of CO_2 to be stored, the maximum injection rates, an approved monitoring plan, an approved provisional post-closure plan, and the type of financial security that ensures that all obligations arising under the permit can be met.[22]

2.3. TRANSPORT AND STORAGE

2.3.1. The Mining Act

The provisions in the Mining Act applying to carbon dioxide storage are more or less similar to the Directive. Although not explicitly stated, it may be assumed that in parallel to the Directive any injection of carbon dioxide for the purpose of enhanced hydrocarbon recovery (EHR) is not to be considered as storage unless such injection is combined with, or will result in, geological storage of CO_2.[23]

---

17 Article 26(7) Mining Act.
18 In case of exploration, the general licensing principles of the Mining Act will apply.
19 TK 2009–2010, 32 343, No. 3, p. 5.
20 Articles 25–31d Mining Act and Arts 6–9 CCS Directive.
21 Cf Art 10, CCS Directive.
22 Article 31b Mining Act.
23 Recital (20) Directive 2009/31/EC.

The holder of a carbon dioxide storage licence is bound by a large number of requirements dealing with the need to provide information on the quantity and quality of the carbon dioxide and the execution of risk management, to monitor the site on the basis of a monitoring plan and to report any irregularities or leakages, as well as the need to make any necessary corrective measures and to provide financial securities.[24] The holder of the carbon dioxide storage licence is, moreover, obliged to keep a register of the delivered, stored and leaked quantities of carbon dioxide and to inform the Minister on a yearly basis about the monitoring outcomes. The State Supervisor of Mines is required to regularly inspect the storage sites.[25] Moreover, the licensee is required to hold an emission permit in order to compensate for potential leakages by way of purchasing and submitting an equal number of emissions allowances.[26]

As regards of the transport of CO_2, the Mining Act provides little guidance. If a dedicated pipeline needs to be constructed to transport carbon dioxide to a subsoil storage facility, the developer will need a pipeline permit as provided for by the Mining Decree. This permit only governs the construction but not the operation of the pipeline. Moreover, this construction permit does not in any way specify the substance for which the pipeline will be used or has to be used. In principle, this seems to imply that once a pipeline is constructed, it can be used to transport any substance under the condition that the pipeline is operated in accordance with the operational rules found in the Mining Decree. These rules in turn primarily pertain to regular inspections of the strength and integrity of the pipelines and the need to prevent and limit any damage stemming from leakages.[27] This entails that in accordance with the Directive, the development of a CO_2 pipeline will need to be based on an environmental impact assessment and that the pipeline operator also needs a CO_2 emissions permit in case of any leakage.[28] Consequently rules applying to pipelines transporting CO_2 as part of the CCS chain differ from those that apply to pipelines transporting CO_2 to carbon users like greenhouse growers. The latter pipelines do not require an environmental impact assessment or a CO_2 emissions permit.

CO_2 storage reservoirs and pipelines may be considered as a natural monopoly and/or an essential facility and therefore the Directive provides for a regime of non-discriminatory third-party access.[29] When granting access the operator of the facility may take into account the following: (i) the available capacity, (ii) the incompatibility of technical specifications, (iii) any duly

---

24 Articles 31b–31h Mining Act and Art 4, Mining Decree implementing Art 13, CCS Directive.

25 Articles 126–130, MiningAct and Arts 14–15, CCS Directive.

26 See also Martha M. Roggenkamp, 'Transportation of CO2 in the EU' in I. Havercroft, R. Macrory, R. Stewart, *Carbon Capture and Storage – Emerging Legal and Regulatory Issues*, 2nd edn., Hart Publishing, Oxford 2018, p. 251.

27 Articles 99 and 100 Mining Decree.

28 These requirements have been transposed into the Environmental Management Act.

29 Article 21 of the CCS Directive.

substantiated reasonable needs of the owner, and (iv) CO_2 reduction obligations to be met through CCS.[30] An almost similar provision can be found in the Mining Act.[31] Such approach is also in line with the regime governing third-party access to upstream pipelines as provided for in the Gas Act.

2.3.2. *Offshore Transport and Storage: Some Specific Provisions under International Law*

When assessing the geological storage of carbon dioxide offshore, it also needs to be assessed whether such activity can be considered as dumping of waste under international law. Although the London Protocol originally listed carbon dioxide as a substance that could be considered dumping at sea,[32] the Protocol was amended in 2006 as a result of which the injection of carbon dioxide streams in subsea reservoirs is possible if the following three conditions are met: (i) the disposal is into a sub-seabed geological formation, (ii) the carbon dioxide streams consist *overwhelmingly* of carbon dioxide, and (iii) no wastes or other matter are added for the purpose of disposing of those wastes or other matter.[33] The same situation more or less applies under the 1992 OSPAR Convention for the Protection of the Marine Environment of the North-East Atlantic. This Convention also allows for the sub-sea storage of carbon dioxide. This storage is allowed under the same conditions as under the London Protocol, but adds a fourth criterion in that the carbon dioxide is intended to be retained in the sub-sea formations permanently and will not lead to significant adverse consequences for the marine environment, human health and other legitimate uses of the maritime area.[34] On the issue of dumping, it can thus be concluded that both the London Protocol and the OSPAR Convention do not hamper the permanent geological storage of carbon dioxide offshore.

As regards transport, the situation is slightly different, as article 6 of the London Protocol prohibits the export of waste to other countries for dumping at sea. This prohibition prevents any transboundary transport of CO_2 for geological storage. In 2009 a proposal was made to amend the Protocol by adding a provision making such transboundary disposal possible, dependent on prior agreement or arrangement concluded between the countries concerned.[35] This

30 See also Martha M. Roggenkamp, 'Transportation of CO2 in the EU' in I. Havercroft, R. Macrory, R. Stewart (eds), *Carbon Capture and Storage – Emerging Legal and Regulatory Issues*, 2nd edn., Hart Publishing, Oxford 2018, p. 253.

31 Article 32 Mining Act.

32 London Protocol, Annex I.

33 Ibid.

34 OSPAR Convention, Annex II, article 3.

35 Resolution LP.3(4) on the amendment to article 6 of the London Protocol adopted on 30 October 2009. See: http://www.imo.org/en/KnowledgeCentre/IndexofIMOResolutions/London-Convention-London-Protocol-(LDC-LC-LP)/Documents/LP.3(4).pdf.

amendment to the London Protocol is essential for developing transboundary CCS and is of specific relevance for the North Sea area where several states border one another. However, the amendment needs to be ratified by 33 contracting parties and in 2018 only five parties (Norway, the UK, the Netherlands, Finland and Iran) have done so. In order to allow for a provisional application of this amendment, the parties to the London Convention adopted a resolution at their annual meeting on 14 October 2019. This resolution provides for an interim solution pending sufficient ratifications. Parties who wish to make use of this possibility need to deposit a declaration of provisional application and provide notification of any agreements or arrangements with the Secretary-General of the IMO.[36]

2.3.3. Re-Use of Offshore Reservoirs and Installations

As the Netherlands in particular is considering carbon dioxide storage in (almost) depleted oil and gas fields, it is necessary to consider how such re-use relates to the re-use of existing wells and installations. This may also depend on the fact whether a production licence already has lapsed before a CO_2 storage licence is awarded.

In general disused offshore installations need to be removed entirely. However, as both the production of hydrocarbons and the storage of carbon dioxide are governed by the Mining Act, they are considered as a mining activity. Since the removal clause from the Mining Act is not limited to a particular type of mining activity, the Minister of Economic Affairs and Climate has taken the position that a platform will only have to be removed after all mining activities have been ceased. As a consequence of this, the removal obligation does not apply to mining installations that will be re-used for storage once hydrocarbons production has ceased.[37] The last holder of a licence pursuant to the Mining Act or the last operator of the platform will be responsible for the decommissioning of the asset.[38] In the case of a re-used platform for carbon dioxide injection, this will be the licence-holder or operator of the carbon dioxide activities. However, the question remains how to deal with the costs of removal. Does it mean that the holder of the production licence will be exempted from the payment of all removal costs? This will become of special relevance if different parties hold the CO_2 storage licence.

A slightly different situation may appear if the hydrocarbons production has ceased and the carbon dioxide storage is contemplated as an option for the longer term. In that case, the assessment as to the disuse of the installation

---

36 http://www.imo.org/en/MediaCentre/PressBriefings/Pages/22-CCS-LP-resolution-.aspx.

37 *Kamerstukken II* 6 May 2011, 32343, nr. C, p. 3.

38 Ibid.

might be different. Can the Minister request the operators to leave their assets in place for longer periods of time in order to keep them 'mothballed' for potential re-use? Or should another party be appointed to maintain the installation in the period in between the end of the production (and possibly the licence has lapsed) and the award of a carbon dioxide storage licence? Who will then be responsible for the maintenance costs and liability for damage caused by or from the installation? Further governmental guidance will be necessary to identify which reservoirs and installations may play a role in large-scale offshore storage of carbon dioxide in the future and to provide for a transitional regime on the basis of which wells and installations are kept in place whilst future use and decommissioning is considered. Currently, the Mining Act does not provide any guidance to facilitate such re-use.

2.4. CLOSURE AND POST-CLOSURE

A crucial phase in the process of creating permanent geological storage of CO_2 is the closure of the storage site after completion of the injection. The Mining Act applies the same conditions for closure and the post-closure plan as the CCS Directive.[39] Consequently, the licensee or operator needs to close the well in accordance with a closure plan that has been approved by the competent authority and, as a general rule, the licensee or operator remains responsible for monitoring the well after it has been closed and has to take all necessary corrective measure when leakages occur.[40] This liability only ends when the licence is cancelled and the competent authority (Ministry of Economic Affairs and Climate) takes over responsibility for the licence area. The responsibility can be transferred to the authorities after a period of at least 20 years if and when (i) all available evidence indicates that the carbon dioxide is permanently stored, (ii) the storage site is permanently closed and the injection facilities have been removed, and (iii) the licence-holder provides a financial contribution sufficient to cover the anticipated monitoring costs for at least 30 years.[41] After the transfer of responsibility to the Dutch state, in principle, the (former) operator will be absolved from liability from any costs incurred after the transfer of responsibility, unless there has been fault on the part of the operator.[42]

Given the absence of any carbon dioxide storage licences, it is too early to assess how this regime will work in practice. However, industry has already identified a number of obstacles. One of the obstacles is the absence of any criteria for assessing when carbon dioxide is permanently stored, especially in combination

---

39 Article 31j Mining Act and Art 17, CCS Directive.

40 Articles 29d–29f Mining Decree.

41 Article 31j Mining Act.

42 Article 31k, para 5, Mining Act and Art 18, para 7, CCS Directive.

with the 20-year period before a licensee can transfer its responsibility to the authorities. Secondly, there is considerable financial uncertainty. What are the anticipated costs of monitoring and any potential corrective measures? In case of any leakage the licensee/operator needs to purchase as many ETS allowances as are necessary to cover the volume of leaked carbon dioxide. However, currently it is impossible to assess the costs for such allowances in the longer term. This creates considerable uncertainty that may need to be addressed in order to stimulate carbon storage.

3. DEVELOPING CO_2 STORAGE PROJECTS OFFSHORE

Following the public opposition to carbon storage onshore and the switch to offshore storage, several attempts have been made to develop such projects. However, this first attempt to develop carbon storage offshore has not been very successful, partly due to financial constraints but also due to changes in the energy market. More recently, another offshore CCS project is being developed. Below, these projects will be discussed.

3.1. FIRST DEMONSTRATION PROJECTS

3.1.1. The 'Green Hydrogen' Project

The 'Green Hydrogen' was meant to be a cross-border CCS project in which capture would take place at Air Liquide near Rotterdam (and possibly later from the Antwerp facility) and the captured CO_2 would be shipped during a period of 10 years by ship to the Danish Continental Shelf where it would be injected into an almost depleted oil field operated by Maersk.[43] The injection of carbon dioxide was intended for enhanced oil recovery. The project was planned to start in 2016 but this did not happen due to funding problems as the NER 300 funds were withdrawn late 2012. The problem lies not only in the absence of EU and national funding but also in the low allowance price on the EU Emissions Trading System (ETS), which does not cover operational costs.

By contrast to other CCS projects, this project did not aim to transport CO_2 from the emitter to the storage reservoir by pipeline but by ship. Moreover, it involved a cross-border shipment and this is basically not permitted by Article 6 of the London Protocol (see above). However, in the case of the Green Hydrogen project the cross-border shipment did not aim at the disposal of CO_2 but at the

---

[43] The ROAD project is undertaken by EON Benelux, Electrabel and GdF Suez. See further: http://www.globalccsinstitute.com/projects/12706 ('Green Hydrogen') and http://www.road2020.nl/en/ ('ROAD').

injection of CO_2 for the purpose of enhanced oil recovery. If so, the export of CO_2 would be in line with international law but, on the other hand, could also imply that this project, basically, cannot not be considered as a CCS project.

3.1.2. *The ROAD Project*

In the same period, the ROAD[44] project was developed. ROAD involved a joint venture (Maasvlakte CCS Project C.V.) consisting of Uniper (previously E.ON Benelux), GDF SUEZ Energie Nederland and TAQA Energy. Uniper and GDF Suez Energie aimed at CO_2 capture at Uniper's MPP3 power plant near Rotterdam (Maasvlakte) and subsequent transport through a 25 kilometres (20 kilometres offshore) pipeline to reservoirs operated by TAQA Energy in P15 and P18 some 20–40 kilometres from Rotterdam. The original aim was to start injecting in 2015.

By contrast to 'Green Hydrogen', this project managed to organise all necessary permits. Whereas in 2012 all emissions and capture permits had been awarded and became irrevocable,[45] the licence for the permanent storage of carbon dioxide in block P18 was awarded to TAQA in 2013[46] and all necessary transport permits were issued early 2015. However, this project also was faced with an issue regarding financing as the price of ETS allowances at that time was very low and caused a financing gap compared to plan of more than €100 million. However, the main reason for the lack of success was the fact that parties withdrew from the project in September 2017[47] due to the possible early closure of coal-fired power plants (see Chapter XIII of this volume by Braaksma and Fleming). This illustrates that future CCS projects no longer will benefit the electricity sector as the number of generators using fossil fuels as their primary resources will decline but will rather be relevant for other CO_2 emitting industries.

3.2. THE PORTHOS PROJECT

In 2019 the Porthos project was launched. Porthos is an acronym for Port of Rotterdam CO_2 Transport Hub & Offshore Storage, and is a joint initiative of the Port of Rotterdam, the gas infrastructure company 'Gasunie', and the company EBN, which is representing the Dutch state in oil and gas exploration and production. This project differs from the two projects discussed above as it

---

44 ROAD is an acronym for 'Rotterdam Opslag en Afvang Demonstratieproject'.

45 See for an overview of all permits, the 'Guidance on CCS permitting, including description of Permitting Guidance Tool' prepared under the CATO-2 programme at: www.co2-cato.org.

46 Stc No 21233 of 29 July 2013. The European Commission issued its Opinion on the draft permit on 28 February 2012, C(2012)1236 final.

47 See Letter to Parliament of 20 October 2017 at: www.overheid.nl.

involves the transport and storage of carbon dioxide only and does not engage any capturers. Moreover, it also aims at transporting carbon dioxide for other purposes than geological storage. In other words, the project involves Carbon Capture Use and Storage (CCUS). The 'usage' part is primarily focussing on the use by greenhouse growers in the province of South Holland. Although such use does not result in permanent storage of captured CO_2, it may be an important element in the process of energy transition, i.e. energy savings, as it allows greenhouse growers to make use of captured CO_2 for growing their products instead of purchasing and burning natural gas.[48]

It follows from the above that the project is designed as an open access pipeline starting in the Rotterdam port area and terminating at a geological offshore storage facility or being connected to the existing OCAP pipeline that transports CO_2 to greenhouse growers. The pipeline will have a length of approximately 30–33 kilometres and run through the Rotterdam port area where it can serve several industries emitting CO_2. Most of the CO_2 will be transported to an empty gas field (P18 operated by TAQA[49]) situated about 20–25 kilometres off the coast and where it can store approximately between 2 and 5 million tonnes of CO_2 per year until the reservoir has been filled. Other reservoirs can be connected to the pipeline at a later stage and, if successful, the pipeline could, in the longer term, also accommodate CO_2 suppliers from Belgium and Germany.[50]

The pipeline and storage facility are intended to operate as open access facilities, which means that third parties can request non-discriminatory access to the transport and storage facilities, probably on the basis of a negotiated tariff (see above). In order to assess the interest of industrial parties in such access, Porthos investigated such interest ('open season') during the spring of 2019. As a result, Porthos is now focussing on concluding a Joint Development Agreement (JDA) with the companies that have shown interest. Companies that have signed such a JDA before 14 October 2019 will be granted priority access in case of scarce capacity. Moreover, by concluding a JDA the companies also agree to jointly conclude a transport and storage agreement and to commit themselves to prepare the capture process and to organise all necessary capture permits.

Currently the route of the pipeline is being investigated. This means that an environmental impact assessment was initiated in May 2019, which involves

48 See also Martha M. Roggenkamp, 'Carbon Capture Storage and Reuse of CO_2 – Law and Policy in the Netherlands' in *European Energy Law Report V*, Intersentia, Cambridge 2008, pp. 109–208 and 'Transportation of Carbon Dioxide in the European Union' – Some Legal Issues' in I. Havercroft, R. Macrory and R, Stewart (eds), *Carbon Capture and Storage – Emerging Legal and Regulatory Issues*, Hart Publishing, Oxford 2018, Chapter 13.

49 Use is made of the platform situated at P18-A, and from there the carbon dioxide will be injected in the P18-2 and P18-4 fields.

50 See: www.rotterdamccus.nl.

an assessment of two possible routes. As regards the storage permit, it can be noted that this project aims at injection in P18-4 just like the ROAD project. In order to be able to use this storage for the Porthos project, the Minister of Economic Affairs and Climate has agreed to an extension of the permit as a result of which the permanent storage of carbon dioxide needs to start no later than 1 January 2021.[51] It is therefore most likely that use can be made of the existing storage permit. As before, financing will be one of the key issues for the project's success. In this regard it is relevant that the price of ETS allowances has increased since 2015 and the project may rely on some EU funding, as it was selected as a Project of Common Interest in 2018.[52] In July 2018 also the Dutch government awarded Porthos some funding.[53] Finally, the parties involved may also benefit from the national support scheme 'SDE++'. Although this support scheme initially was intended to provide support to renewable energy projects, the support scheme has been changed so that, as of 2020, support may also be granted to other climate-friendly techniques such as CCS and CCUS. However, the funds will be limited and will not be awarded to CCS projects starting after 2035.[54] Together this may result in a situation that Porthos may be successful and the first CCS project in the Netherlands may get started in 2020.

4. CONCLUSION

The Netherlands is facing severe challenges in order to meet its climate goals. This was clearly illustrated by the *Urgenda* case, and a large number of policy instruments have been included in the 2019 Climate Agreement. CCS and CCUS are listed as possible means to assist in reaching these climate goals. It is interesting to note that CCUS was already included in the Working Programme of 2007, which amongst other things promoted the use of carbon dioxide in the Dutch greenhouse agriculture sector. One of the major disadvantages of using CO_2 for other uses is the possibility that the CO_2 will still be emitted, which may be problematic if the user (like a greenhouse grower) is not required to hold an emissions permit. So it remains to be seen how effective CCUS will be in reaching the climate goals.

As regards CCS, the Netherlands is now focussing on the possibilities offshore. Some earlier demonstration projects have not been successful, as they have not materialised. Lack of finances and/or public support has played an important role. This may change in the future as the price of emissions allowances

51 Amendment to the storage permit awarded on 29 July 2019, Stc. 2016, no. 4809.
52 https://ec.europa.eu/energy/en/topics/infrastructure/projects-common-interest.
53 See: www.rotterdamccus.nl and https://projecten.topsectorenergie.nl › projecten › porthos.
54 See Letter to Parliament of 28 June 2019 on the Climate Agreement, p. 15.

is gradually increasing. Apart from this, it is interesting to note that it is no longer the electricity sector that needs to apply CCS, given the increased use of renewable energy sources, but rather other industrial sectors like refineries and the cement industry. This may also explain why the Porthos project has a different approach. Instead of developing a point-to-point CCS chain (from capturer to storage), this project is being developed as an open access infrastructure project. It offers pipeline and storage capacity to all interested parties who wish to permanently store CO_2. This obviously brings with it some other risks such as a lack of interest. However, applying an open season and subsequently concluding with all interested parties a joint development agreement, may limit that risk. Although other risks remain, it may be that this project possibly could be successful.

PART VI

FROM EU CLIMATE GOALS TO NATIONAL CLIMATE LAWS

CHAPTER XXI

A STOCKTAKE OF LEGAL RESEARCH ON THE UNITED KINGDOM'S CLIMATE CHANGE ACT

Present Understandings, Future Opportunities

Thomas L. MUINZER and Gavin McLeod LITTLE

1. INTRODUCTION

When the UK Parliament's Climate Change Act 2008 (CCA) was passed into law it was the first time a country employed national framework legislation to impose economy-wide legally binding long-term emissions reduction targets upon itself in the interest of combatting climate change. One should not oversimplify the drivers behind the CCA's creation by reducing them purely to a response to challenges posed by anthropogenic climate change. Geopolitical concerns pertaining to the issue of UK energy security also acted as a substantial regime driver.[1] Nevertheless, the contribution of this pioneering framework has been widely – and deservedly – recognised.[2] Despite its imperfections,[3] it is 'one of the most important items of legislation passed by any national Parliament in the world in modern times.'[4]

This chapter starts by reviewing the background to the adoption of the CCA (Section 2). It continues by outlining the Act's main features (Section 3). It then

1 See further T.L. MUINZER, *Climate and Energy Governance for the UK Low Carbon Transition: The Climate Change Act 2008*, Palgrave MacMillan, UK, 2018, p. 2.

2 See, e.g., Hill on the 'clear symbolic and practical value for the UK' and the 'positive institutional impact in terms of how government manages responsibility', in K. HILL, *The UK Climate Change Act 2008 – Lessons for National Climate Laws*, ClientEarth, London, 2009, p. 6; H. TOWNSEND, 'The Climate Change Act 2008: Something to be Proud of After All?' (2009) 7(8) *Journal of Planning and Environmental Law* 842.

3 See further the discussion below.

4 Interview with MHARI MACDONALD, 'Meet our Academic', University of Dundee, published (online) 15/3/19: https://www.dundee.ac.uk/cepmlp/news/2019/article/meet-our-academic-dr-thomas-muinzer.php.

provides evaluative reflection and comment on the legal research analysing it (Section 4). In doing so, it also addresses and comments on ways forward for the literature. Finally, it ends with some concluding remarks (Section 5).

2. BACKGROUND TO THE ADOPTION OF THE CLIMATE CHANGE ACT

The CCA was passed by the UK Parliament on 26 November 2008. In implementing the framework legislation, the UK supplanted a soft policy-oriented regime with a more substantial and robust statutory one.[5] The socio-political background and internal conditions that generated the emergence of the framework were complex.[6] It should also be noted that this particular type of legislative scheme was relatively novel and radical in the context of conventional UK law-making at the time,[7] and that it remains so today.

Reduced to its major essentials, the Act's emergence was driven by a culmination of the following factors:

- substantial campaigning by Non-Governmental Organisations (NGOs), in particular by *Friends of the Earth UK*;[8]
- an increased emphasis placed on political 'green' credentials by the UK's two main political parties (Labour and Conservative), arising in that period for a range of complex political reasons;[9]
- publication of the influential *Stern Report* (October 2006), providing an economic analysis of the impacts of climate change that, in the words of that report, led 'to a simple conclusion: the benefits of strong and early action [in the sphere of climate change] far outweigh the economic costs of not acting';[10]

---

5 See further: DETR, Climate Change: The UK Programme (HM Government, 2000); DEFRA, Climate Change: The UK Programme 2006 (HM Government, 2006).

6 See Muinzer, pp. 1–39, 'Background to the Climate Change Framework', in n. 1 above *Climate and Energy Governance for the UK Low Carbon Transition*; N. Carter, 'Combating Climate Change in the UK: Challenges and Obstacles' (2008) 79(2) *The Political Quarterly* 194.

7 C.T. Reid, 'A New Sort of Duty? The Significance of "outcome" Duties in the Climate Change and Child Poverty Acts' (2012) 4 *Public Law* 749; S. Turner, 'Northern Ireland's Consent to the Climate Change Act 2008: Symbol or Illusion?' (2013) 25(1) *Journal of Environmental Law* 63.

8 N. Carter and M. Childs, 'Friends of the Earth as a policy entrepreneur: "The Big Ask" campaign for a UK Climate Change Act' (2018) 27.6 *Environmental Politics*, pp. 994–1013.

9 Carter and Childs, ibid., pp. 1002–1003.

10 N. Stern, et al., *Stern Review: The Economics of Climate Change* (HM Government, 2006), p. vi.

- some degree of genuine cross-party political concern attaching increasingly to the problem of anthropogenic climate change, driven in part by scientific publications from the Intergovernmental Panel on Climate Change (IPCC), which served to highlight the severity of the climate problem;[11]
- an increased desire from elements of the business and investor community for greater long-term market clarity, coupled with the understanding that the long-term nature of a CCA-form regime could substantially improve market predictability and investor certainty.[12]

The development of an emerging cross-party political concern was highlighted in April 2005 when three Members of Parliament (MPs) from the Conservative, Labour and Liberal Democrat parties together brought a model Climate Bill before the UK Parliament. That particular Bill was not passed, but it was significant symbolically as an indication of what was possible.[13]

3. MAIN FEATURES OF THE CLIMATE CHANGE ACT

3.1. STRUCTURE OF THE CCA

The CCA is a long and complex legal text, running to 101 sections and 8 schedules. The sections are grouped into six Parts. The substance of Parts 1–4 is particularly important. The titles to those Parts, which read as follows, indicate the main thrust of their subject-matter:

- 'Carbon Target and Budgeting' (Part 1);
- 'The Committee on Climate Change' (Part 2);
- 'Trading Schemes' (Part 3);
- 'Impact of and Adaptation to Climate Change' (Part 4).

The remaining two Parts are also important, but they engage or involve certain relatively narrow or technical matters, such as technical adjustments to existing items of UK law, lawyerly aids to interpretation including definitions of technical terms, clarifications pertaining to the jurisdictional reach of various sections of the Act, and similar. These Parts are entitled:

- 'Other Provisions' (Part 5); and
- 'General Supplementary Provisions' (Part 6).

---

11 IPCC, *AR4 Climate Change 2007: Synthesis Report* (IPCC, 2007).
12 Carter, above n. 6.
13 See Muinzer, above n. 1, pp. 9–10.

3.2. SCOPE AND TARGETS

The CCA applies a 34 per cent greenhouse gas (GHG) emissions reduction target to the UK for 2020, with the emissions reduction percentage based on 1990 emissions levels.[14] It also applies an 80 per cent GHG emissions reduction target based on 1990 levels for 2050.[15] As we write, the UK Government has just legislated to have a 'Net Zero' 2050 target, which means the 2050 target has increased from 80 to 100 per cent.[16] Muinzer has characterised these two reduction markers as the regime's 'milestone' targets[17] The targets are economy-wide, and cover emissions arising in the UK. This latter point calls for a very particular method of emissions calculation, which is in keeping with pre-established international emissions reporting practices, as the Committee on Climate Change (CCC) has summarised:

> [t]he internationally agreed standard for reporting greenhouse gas emissions to the UN covers emissions from activities within the UK. *This approach does not include emissions embedded in the goods and services the UK imports*, nor exclude those in exports ... [emphasis added].[18]

The 2020/2050 34 per cent/100 per cent milestone targets benchmark an emissions reduction trajectory for a carbon budgeting scheme that is constructed around these dates by Part 1 of the CCA.[19] This carbon budgeting scheme covers all major socio-economic sectors and activities within the UK, including *inter alia* energy, transport, heating and agriculture, and is divided into successive five-year periods that continually roll on, one after another.[20] Each five-year budget establishes an economy-wide cap on UK GHG emissions. Specific budget levels are recommended by the CCC; however the Secretary of State is ultimately responsible for selecting the level and is therefore at liberty to depart from the CCC's advice if he so chooses. The Secretary of State issues the budget level in a statutory instrument that is laid before Parliament, and this requires parliamentary approval before it enters into law.[21] The CCA targets exceed the EU's climate targets and therefore allow the UK to contribute to meeting its EU objectives while going beyond them.[22]

---

14 CCA, s. 5(1)(a).

15 CCA, s. 1(1).

16 Climate Change Act 2008 (2050 Target Amendment) Order 2019, amending CCA, s. 1.

17 Muinzer, above. n. 1, pp. 21, 103, 113.

18 CCC, *Reducing UK Emissions: 2018 Progress Report to Parliament* (CCC, June 2018), p. 32.

19 CCA, ss. 4–10.

20 CCA, ss. 4.

21 CCA, ss. 4 and 5; see also CCA, s. 5(3); 'affirmative resolution procedure' refers to the approval of UK Parliament.

22 The EU is discussed further below.

3.3. THE CARBON BUDGET SYSTEM

The carbon budget system incorporates a net UK carbon account framework[23] that involves carbon units, with a carbon unit representing a quantity of GHG.[24] Therefore, where a five-year carbon budget cap is in place, quantities of carbon units can be credited/debited to the UK account in accordance with the limit cap. The UK's 'removals' of targeted GHGs are incorporated into the system so that they can be reflected in the budget, with removals accruing through land use, land-use change or forestry activities.[25] This permits a net UK emissions level to be calculated by deducting these sorts of removals from the UK's GHG releases over a particular period of time.[26] Bearing in mind the fixed reduction percentages pegged to the 2020 and 2050 milestone dates, present and desirable forthcoming net UK emissions levels can be sketched out into the future over the projected five-year budgetary cycles. Each consecutive five-year budget is reduced, driving economy-wide emissions levels progressively downward over time.

The first carbon budget ran from 2008–2012, and the GHG reduction figure was set at 25 per cent below 1990 levels. The second carbon budget increased this to 31 per cent for the next five-year cycle (2013–2017). The CCA requires a given budget to be set at least 12 years in advance,[27] such that at the time of writing the fifth carbon budget (2028–2032) has already been decided and passed, set at a 57 per cent reduction on 1990 levels.[28] Although the overall scheme is rather convoluted, it has proven successful to date in practice. For example, the UK met its 34 per cent milestone target considerably in advance of the 2020 deadline.[29] Researchers have highlighted various in-built merits underlying the five-year budgeting cycles, which:

> provid[e] the flexibility to accommodate short-term fluctuations in annual carbon emissions, which can occur for economic reasons (such as business cycle fluctuations), technical reasons (such as the temporary closure of a power station), and climate reasons (such as a severe winter). The carbon budgets concern overall emissions from all sectors.[30]

---

23 CCA, ss. 26–28, s. 1(1), s. 4(1)(a).

24 See CCA, s. 26(1).

25 CCA, s. 29(1)(b).

26 CCA, s. 29(1)(a)–(c).

27 CCA, s. 4(2)(a)–(b).

28 Carbon Budget Order 2016 (SI 2006 No. 785).

29 See further discussions below.

30 S. Fankhauser, A. Averchenkova and J.J. Finnegan, *10 Years of the UK Climate Change Act*, Policy Report, Grantham Research Institute on Climate Change and the Environment & LSE, 2018, p. 2. N.B., the broad range of the UK's socio-economic sectors and activities which are subject to the carbon budget system is outlined in section 3.2 of this chapter.

The CCA asserts that this reduction regime applies to a specific group of 'targeted greenhouse gases',[31] as follows: carbon dioxide (CO_2); methane (CH_4); nitrous oxide (N_2O); hydrofluorocarbons (HFCs); perfluorocarbons (PFCs); sulphur hexafluoride (SF_6).[32] The gases treated by the UK are driven by the United Nations Framework Convention on Climate Change (UNFCCC) climate governance tradition,[33] as absorbed through the regional circumstances of Europe.[34] The CCA permits the Secretary of State to increase the number of gases included within the targeted GHG definition if international developments indicate that another gas should be added.[35] The 1990 baseline level that the reductions are measured from takes account of the UK's carbon dioxide, methane and nitrous oxide emissions levels for 1990. However, the CCA also asserts that the hydrofluorocarbon, perfluorocarbon and sulphur hexafluoride quantities – which are far less substantial than the other gases but far from insignificant – are to be measured from 1995 levels.[36] This means that the CCA is employing the '1990 baseline' as a technical legal term that provides for rhetorical convenience but that incorporates two distinct baseline dates within its legal meaning (1990 and 1995).

In principle, a degree of banking and borrowing of carbon can occur under the carbon budgeting scheme, meaning that there is some capacity to carry amounts from one carbon budget to another.[37] This can permit, in certain circumstances, as much as one per cent of a later carbon budget period to be 'carried back' to an earlier period. In doing so, the earlier period can bear the additional burden and the later period can have its level reduced a little.[38] Conversely, if a carbon budget is overshot then the Secretary of State must report to Parliament promptly on the means by which the carbon debt will be rebalanced in the forthcoming periods.[39] To date this circumstance has

31 CCA, s. 24(1).

32 CCA, s. 24(1)(a)–(f).

33 For further discussion of the UNFCCC governance tradition, which derives from the background and lead up to the 1992 UNFCCC, the substance of the Convention itself, and the developments flowing from it, including Kyoto 1 and Kyoto 2, see Muinzer, 'Multilevel Drivers: The International Level and the Devolved Level (Northern Ireland, Scotland and Wales)' in n. 1 above, *Climate and Energy Governance for the UK Low Carbon Transition*, pp. 82–121.

34 Muinzer, ibid.

35 CCA, s. 92(3). Due to their complex nature, which includes inter-state and international travel that poses challenges for emissions regulation, emissions from international aviation and shipping are not included in the carbon account at present. They are, however, incorporated into the 2050 milestone target itself, and so monitoring of these emissions is undertaken, including where the work of the CCC is concerned, which tracks these emissions in the broader context of its carbon budgeting advice.

36 CCA, s. 25(1).

37 CCA, s. 17.

38 CCA, s. 17(1)–(2).

39 CCA, s. 19(1). N.B., the issues of compliance and enforcement are discussed in more detail in section 4.2 of this chapter. See also section 3.5 for further detail on the Secretary of State.

not arisen, and the UK has met its carbon budget requirements in reasonably comfortable fashion.[40] Given the seriousness of anthropogenic climate change, this success is a very positive achievement. In our view, the relative comfort with which the UK has been meeting its objectives serves as an indicator that the CCA's obligations should be *strengthened*, including its short-term carbon budget levels and indeed the 2050 milestone target as well.[41]

3.4. THE FUTURE OF THE SYSTEM

While the positive results of the carbon budget must be acknowledged, the future is substantially more uncertain than the present. The CCC and indeed the UK Government itself have made clear that the UK is not on course to meet its fourth and fifth carbon budgets as things stand.[42] This is cause for serious concern, and it indicates that the UK is moving from a more relaxed condition where much of the 'low-hanging fruit' of the low carbon transition has been picked, to a more challenging and intense period. Moreover, it is arguable that in recent years the UK Government's policy objectives have (despite the ostensibly ambitious goals of its 2017 *Clean Growth Strategy*) shifted from proactive support for an ambitious, world-leading low carbon transition to what is, in effect, a more modest and reactive 'least cost' transition.[43] Since the collapse of the Conservative/Liberal Democrat Coalition Government in 2015, there have been a number of Treasury-led reforms which have had a significant impact on the funding mechanisms for low carbon energy. For example, the Control for Low Carbon Levies has imposed a moratorium on new low-carbon energy subsidies until at least 2025;[44] the scope of the Renewable Heat Incentive has been restricted;[45] the Feed in Tariff scheme has been closed to most

---

40 See further BEIS, *2018 Provisional UK Greenhouse Gas Emissions* (BEIS, 2018).

41 As noted above, as we write UK Government has legislated to increase the 2050 milestone target to 'Net Zero', which serves to vindicate our position here.

42 CCC, *An Independent Assessment of the UK's Clean Growth Strategy* (CCC, 2018); BEIS, *Updated Energy and Emissions Projections 2017* (BEIS, 2018).

43 R. Gillard and K. Lock, 'Blowing policy bubbles: re-thinking emissions targets and low-carbon energy policies in the U.K' (2017) 19(6) *Journal of Environmental Policy and Planning* pp. 638–653. See also UK Government, October 2017, *The Clean Growth Strategy. Leading the way to a low carbon future*, pp. 93–112, available at: https://assets.publishing.service.gov.uk/government/uploads/system/uploads/attachment_data/file/700496/clean-growth-strategy-correction-april-2018.pdf.

44 D. Hirst, *Control for low carbon levies*, House of Commons Briefing Number 8187, 20 December 2017.

45 See National Audit Office, HC 779 Session 2017–2019, 23 February 2018, *Low-carbon heating of homes and businesses and the Renewable Heat Incentive*, available at: https://www.nao.org.uk/wp-content/uploads/2018/02/Low-carbon-heating-of-homes-and-businesses-and-the-Renewable-Heat-Incentive.pdf.

new applicants;[46] the Green Investment Bank has been sold in controversial circumstances;[47] and a taxpayer-backed subsidy to support the purchase of ultra-low emission vehicles has been restricted.[48]

We therefore argue that achieving the objectives of the CCA in this difficult and changing policy context will require a much greater effort than before, involving yet more substantial policy change and broader innovation in regulation and governance. This must include developments that have been characterised as a *deepening* of the decarbonisation regime; that is to say, the application of a 'greater socio-economic depth of reach' that includes much stronger recognition of the fact that the generation of heat and electricity must 'no longer be treated as the low-hanging fruit that can bear the lion's share of emissions reductions'.[49] In other words, in addition to intensifying efforts in the sphere of heat and electricity, the CCA decarbonisation drive must be pressed much more broadly and proactively across all of the UK's socio-economic sectors, including transport, in order to offset serious projected medium- and long-term problems.

3.5. THE INSTITUTIONAL FRAMEWORK AND ITS FUTURE

It is to be noted that the primary duties and obligations under the terms of the CCA are generally borne by the Secretary of State, who has been mentioned above. These include the legally binding duties to secure the 2020 and 2050 milestone targets.[50] The Secretary of State is a lead Minister who is a member of the UK Government. In addition to bearing the CCA's primary duties, the Secretary of State is given certain powers that permit him to work towards these obligations in practice, as in the case of determining the carbon budget levels that are brought before UK Parliament for approval.[51] The UK Government's Department for Business, Energy and Industrial Strategy (BEIS) leads on energy and climate change mitigation in the UK, and so the appearance of 'Secretary of State' in the CCA normally indicates the Minister at the head of this Department,

46 Ofgem, *About the FIT scheme*, available at: https://www.ofgem.gov.uk/environmental-programmes/fit/about-fit-scheme.

47 House of Commons Committee of Public Accounts, Twenty-Fifth Report of Session 2017–19, HC 468, 14 March 2018, *The sale of the Green Investment Bank*, pp. 8–11, available at: https://publications.parliament.uk/pa/cm201719/cmselect/cmpubacc/468/468.pdf.

48 Office for Low Emission Vehicles, 2 November 2018, 21 November 2018 (accessed), *Changes to the plug-in car grant*, available at: https://www.gov.uk/government/publications/plug-in-car-grant-changes-to-grant-level-november-2018/upcoming-changes-to-the-plug-in-car-grant.

49 Muinzer, above n. 1, p. 124.

50 CCA, s. 1(1); s. 4(1) and s. 5(1)(a).

51 As discussed above in section 3.3.

fully titled the Secretary of State for Business, Energy and Industrial Strategy. It should be borne in mind, however, that the Department for Environment, Food and Rural Affairs takes a lead role on climate change adaptation, and so 'Secretary of State' can indicate the Minister at the head of this Department where adaptation rather than mitigation is at issue. The generalised nature of this designation in the legislation helps to guard against numerous tedious legislative amendments where a government department might be closed or re-organised, as happens fairly frequently in the UK.[52]

A further key actor imbued with an important role under the terms of the CCA is particularly interesting because, unlike the Secretary of State, it was created by the framework itself: the CCC.[53] The CCC was established by the Act as an expert advisory and reporting body designed to sit at an independent remove from the UK Government. Most importantly, it advises and reports on the CCA transition to the UK Parliament, the Secretary of State, and the UK's devolved Governments of Northern Ireland, Scotland and Wales. Examples of principal advisory and reporting functions include advising the Secretary of State on the setting of carbon budgets,[54] and providing major annual reports on the progress being made under the terms of the CCA to the UK Parliament.[55] The CCC is a highly respected body, and its independence from UK Government in terms of how the legislation lays its functions and processes out is of real significance.[56] To date, the CCC has carried out its functions with a substantial, self-evident degree of independence and excellence, and remains highly valued.[57] It is notable that the CCC is well-resourced,[58] and we would highlight that the UK Government holds the power to constrict (or indeed expand) its funding, such that in the view of some this could provide an indirect

---

52 BEIS itself was only created in 2016.

53 That is, the Committee on Climate Change, as abbreviated earlier. Note that shortly before the passage of the CCA, a 'shadow' version of the CCC was established prior to the CCC-proper being 'formally constituted' in order to provide advice on the 2050 target (see Hill, above n. 2; quoting p. 34 fn. 14). In this novel case the shadow CCC's advice helped to contribute usefully to the setting of the 2050 milestone target; however, in our view the general practice of a body being established in shadow form to advise on (other) elements of a Parliamentary Bill that will also create that body's outcome design must be avoided on constitutional grounds, as it creates a conflict of interest that provides for an inappropriate channel to influence the wider form of the final outcome legislation, including (potentially) with regard to the ultimate outcome design of the shadow body itself.

54 CCA, s. 34.

55 CCA, s. 36.

56 See generally CCA, ss. 32–43 and Schedule 1.

57 A. Averchenkova, S. Fankhauser and J.J. Finnegan, *The Role and Influence of the UK's Committee on Climate Change*, Policy Brief, Grantham Research Institute on Climate Change and the Environment & LSE, October 2018.

58 The CCC has a significant budget, and sitting members of the Committee are supported by 'a Chief Executive and a Secretariat of approximately 30 staff, on a full time equivalent basis': CCC, *Corporate and Business Plan 2016–2019* (CCC, October 2016), p. 12.

means of exerting a degree of control over the institution. There is no evidence that this channel of influence has ever been exerted in practice, and it would be unlawful for the UK Government to employ it as leverage, given that the CCA's legislative design preserves the CCC's position as an independent body.[59] Nonetheless, the framework could be improved if control over the CCC's finances was determined instead by the UK Parliament at regular intervals.

While the autonomous CCC is not prevented from creating other sub-committees within its own structure, it includes an important Adaptation Sub-Committee (ASC) that was mandatorily created by the CCA.[60] This provides the Secretary of State and other key governance actors with specialist advice and analysis specific to the issue of climate change *adaptation* (as opposed to *mitigation*).[61] The creation of the ASC speaks to the broader theme of Part 4 of the CCA, which is given over to the problem of adaptation. Here, the CCA establishes a scheme that provides for the creation of an *adaptation report*; this report assesses and summarises the adaptation problems and risks faced in the UK.[62] Within a maximum of every five years, another report of this kind is to be produced,[63] and in this manner the current condition of understanding in the UK is able to continually update itself. In addition to these reports, bespoke *adaptation programmes* must also be produced: these set out adaptation objectives and elaborate on proposals and policies intended to assist in securing the objectives.[64] The *programmes* have an inter-connected relationship with the risk assessment *reports* that have just been noted: firstly, because each individual programme must follow on naturally from the risk assessment report preceding it in an ongoing cycle;[65] and secondly, because a given adaptation programme must endeavour to tackle the problems flagged up in the risk report that has preceded it.[66]

---

59 The CCC is a public body that 'may do anything that appears to it necessary or appropriate for the purpose of, or in connection with, the carrying out of its functions' (CCA, s. 39(1)), and although it receives certain directions from the UK Government and national authorities under CCA, s.42 over the course of its advisory and reporting work, the 'power to give directions under this section does not include power to direct the Committee as to the content of any advice or report' (CCA, s. 42(4)). For more on the CCC's independent design, see further CCA, Schedule 1, which contains substantial detail on the Committee's constitution.

60 See CCA, Schedule 1, para 16, 'The Adaptation Sub-Committee'.

61 CCA, Schedule 1, para 16.10.

62 CCA, s. 56.

63 CCA, s. 56(3). If a delay in publishing a report arises the Secretary of State must explain why and state when the report will be provided to Parliament (CCA, s. 56(4)).

64 CCA, s. 58(1)(a)–(c). The risk reports have a UK-wide orientation, and although they are followed by 'national' adaptation programmes, an onus also falls in practice to the Devolved Administrations of Northern Ireland, Scotland and Wales to produce strategy programmes of their own that cover their devolved areas of competence.

65 CCA, s. 58(3).

66 CCA, s. 58(1).

The CCA has also made certain modest adjustments to pre-existing areas of UK law, e.g., Waste Reduction Schemes,[67] and given the Secretary of State various distinct narrow powers to do particular things, e.g., to introduce mandatory emissions reporting by companies.[68] More broadly, Muinzer has described the regime as establishing a *skeleton framework* that in turn creates capacities for action, regulation and innovation that serve to put substantive *flesh on the bones*.[69] The significant capacities opened up by the framework to enable the creation of trading schemes provide an example. These schemes can be created via secondary legislation,[70] with the main powers to issue them falling to the Secretary of State.[71] The CCA sketches out the capacities for action in an abstract, general way, and places its emphasis on enabling their deployment rather than on asserting that such schemes 'must' be deployed. Here then, the skeleton framework provides for powers that can be employed in order to issue trading schemes, while the substance of the matters that they are to be applied to (i.e. the regulatory/normative 'flesh on the bones') remains undetermined by the central provisions of the Act. The types of trading schemes that are enabled include both schemes that limit/encourage the limitation of activities that emit, cause or contribute to the emissions of GHGs directly or indirectly, and schemes that involve activities that consist of, cause or contribute to reductions or removals of GHG from the atmosphere, again either directly or indirectly.[72]

4. EVALUATING THE LEGAL RESEARCH BASE FOR THE CLIMATE CHANGE ACT

Bearing in mind the importance of the issues to hand – anthropogenic climate change – and the pioneering nature of the CCA's design, academic analysis of this legal framework has been relatively slow in coming forward.[73]

---

67 CCA, ss. 71–75 and Schedule 5 as originally enacted.

68 CCA, s. 85. On these and other more modest components of the framework, see Muinzer, pp. 41–81, 'The Content of the Act', in n.1 above, *Climate and Energy Governance for the UK Low Carbon Transition* (particularly pp. 43–48 and pp. 76–81).

69 See e.g., Muinzer above n.1 pp. 3–4.

70 CCA, s. 44(1).

71 CCA, s. 47. The devolved governments can also employ roughly equivalent powers in their areas of competence.

72 CCA, s. 44(2)(a)–(b). See further CCA, Schedules 2–4.

73 Initial legalistic commentaries tended to be light and descriptive, see e.g., (Anon.) 'Climate Change Act 2008' (2008) (45) 7 *Criminal Law Week*; B. Farmer, 'The Climate Change Act 2008,' (2009) 32(22) *Company Secretary's Review* 174; M. Grekos, 'Climate Change Act 2008' (2009) 4 *Journal of Planning and Environment Law* 454; 'Energy Legislation: the Climate Change Act 2008' (2008) December, 1 *Environmental Law Monthly* (legislative comment). Some went a little deeper, e.g., P.G.G. Davies, 'Carbon Targets, Carbon Budgeting and the

Nevertheless, over a decade after its passage by Parliament, it has been receiving more attention from legal researchers. A reasonably well-developed body of critical discussion and analytical knowledge on the framework has now emerged.[74] These academic discussions reveal a series of fundamental questions surrounding the design of climate change legislation.

4.1. THE CCA'S INTERACTION WITH THE UK'S MULTILEVEL GOVERNANCE SYSTEM

One matter that has received significant consideration from researchers concerns the CCA's interaction with different levels of governance structures and processes: the CCA's nation state-level positioning in the context of the UK's multilevel governance system. Indeed, the CCA exists and operates in a broader constitutional setting involving both external international/supranational and internal substate levels of governance. At first sight, the CCA may be thought of as a 'national/UK-wide' framework, since it is both fundamentally driven by and locked in at the nation state level, spanning the UK as a whole. Interestingly, however, analysis also suggests that the Act initially functioned at least in part as a response to supranational EU politico-legal drivers.[75]

It must be noted that the UK was an EU Member State at the time of the CCA's creation.[76] Even though the CCA was an internal invention of the UK Parliament, meaning that it did not directly transpose or apply EU law within the UK, EU membership means that a relationship to EU-level governance exists insofar as the Act was required to take account of significant EU-level drivers. For example, it was designed with a measure of flexibility in order to accommodate the EU's Emissions Trading Scheme within the CCA decarbonisation process.[77] International-level developments have also exerted a profound formative influence, notably the UNFCCC, and the crucial agreements

Committee on Climate Change: the 2008 UK Climate Change Act and the 2050 Vision' (2009) 17(1) *Environmental Liability* 3; H. Townsend, 'Climate Change Act 2008: Will it do the Trick?' (2009) 11(2) *Environmental Law Review* 116; P. McMaster, 'Climate Change – Statutory Duty or Pious Hope?' (2008) 20(1) *Journal of Environmental Law* 115.

[74] See, eg, the studies discussed below (and those raised elsewhere in this paper); see also R.B. Macrory, 'The UK Climate Change Act – Towards a Brave New Legal World?', pp. 306–322, in I. Backer, O. Fauchald and C. Voigt (eds), *Pro Natura* Universitetsforlaget, Oslo 2012; see further C.T. Reid, 'Climate Law in the United Kingdom' in E.J. Hollo, K. Kulovesi and M. Mehling (eds), *Climate Change and the Law*, Springer, 2012.

[75] T.L. Muinzer, 'Does the Climate Change Act 2008 Adequately Account for the UK's Devolved Jurisdictions?' (2016) 25(3) *European Energy and Environmental Law Review*, pp. 87–100.

[76] See further the detailed analysis of EU-UK governance dynamics in this area in T.L. Muinzer, 'An Evaluation of the Implications of EU Climate and Energy Governance for the UK in light of Brexit' (2017) 23(2) *European Journal of Current Legal Issues* (online).

[77] See further Muinzer above n. 75.

that have flowed from it, most particularly the Kyoto Protocol and the Paris Agreement and their attendant implications.[78]

It has also been demonstrated that the CCA cannot be construed simply as a centralised 'nation state' endeavour. Doing so would fail to recognise and take account of the devolution of substantial law and policy-making powers to the 'substate' nations and regions of the UK, ie Northern Ireland, Scotland and Wales. There have been important studies of the CCA's significance at the substate level, notably by Turner and Reid.[79] This has led to enhanced understanding of the substate (sometimes called 'subnational'[80]) level's explicit and implicit impact on nation state level framework processes and intended outcomes, and the capacities for climate change action and constraint existing in Northern Ireland, Scotland and Wales. Indeed, it has become evident that the UK's devolved nations and regions have a major role to play in determining whether the UK as a whole will continue to achieve the substantive targets and procedural obligations it has at state level.[81]

Much of this work was galvanised by the emerging realisation that the substate elements and dimensions of the CCA have tended more often than not to be somewhat hidden or eclipsed by the nation state/UK orientation of the framework. While research has helped to close this gap in knowledge, it is arguably the case that it has also served to leave the largest and most populous of the UK's substate regions – England – behind. The focus of substate analysis has been on Northern Ireland, Scotland and Wales due to the fact that they have powerful devolved governments and legislatures. England, however, does not,[82] and as a partial consequence has received much less attention. This has arguably created a knowledge-gap in the literature, such that targeted analysis of England's role, influence, capacities, constraints and performance would be an important research project.

These considerations suggest that in drafting national climate legislation it is advisable to carefully and prudently account for substate and localised levels of governance, even where the primary legislative focus may be on crafting a

78 Muinzer, above n. 33.

79 Turner, above n. 7; S. Turner, 'Committing to Effective Climate Governance in Northern Ireland: A Defining Test of Devolution' (2013) 25(2) *Journal of Environmental Law* 203; Reid, above n. 7; C. Reid, 'Scotland: Constraints and Opportunities in a Devolved System' in M. Peeters, M. Stallworthy and J. de Cendra de Larragan (eds), *Climate Law in EU Member States: Towards National Legislation for Climate Protection*, Edward Elgar, Cheltenham 2012.

80 Multilevel governance theory tends to conceptualise a 'national' and 'subnational' level, but given that members of some territories below national levels will tend to consider themselves as members of a distinct nation in their own right (e.g., the Scottish/Scotland in the UK), the term 'subnational' can be unhelpful. 'Substate' seems preferable.

81 See Turner, above n. 79 ('Committing to Effective Climate Governance in Northern Ireland') and Reid, above n. 79 ('Scotland: Constraints and Opportunities in a Devolved System').

82 UK Parliament is the legislative body for English law.

'national' Act. This is due to the fact that substate scales of governance may likely impact the national decarbonisation agenda in complex and substantial ways in spite of the legislation's national-level orientation. Internationally, the legislation's relationship to, and interaction with, the UNFCCC and its associated agreements, notably the Paris Agreement, should also be a primary consideration. Pertinent supranational agreements may also be relevant to the design, as highlighted by the manner in which the CCA utilises a flexibly-designed emissions reduction regime that permits UK participation in the EU's important Emissions Trading Scheme mechanism to contribute to reductions in the UK carbon account.

4.2. COMPLIANCE REGIME, ENFORCEABILITY AND JUDICIAL REVIEW

Another outstanding issue concerns how the CCA explicitly establishes a variety of substantive and procedural duties but does not stipulate *sanctions* that are to be applied where major duties are breached.[83] This raises concerns in relation to *enforceability* and *accountability* under the terms of the Act. When establishing the background to these concerns, scholars have considered the innovative nature of the regime's headline 2020/2050 milestones, where the CCA can be seen to apply emissions reduction targets that go beyond the specific legal duties normally imposed on public bodies in the UK.[84] For example, Reid has emphasised the novel nature of these sorts of duties, pointing out that they resemble in some ways the sorts of goal-led duties that tend to characterise some aspects of EU environmental law and policy, namely EU Directives.[85] These tend to be applied downwards from the EU level to Member States in a form where obligations to secure goals and outcomes are placed on Member States, but with the approaches underpinning how the goals are reached being left up to the Member States themselves in large part. Thus, for instance, the EU's Ambient Air Quality Directive[86] applies limits and target values to major air pollutants within Member States, and the Member States take a primary role in determining the ways in which they will meet the targets.

Reducing matters to their essentials, it can be seen that these sorts of legally binding duties mean that a particular outcome is to be attained, such that failure to secure the outcome constitutes a breach of the legal duty by the Secretary of State, who bears the legal obligation (in the case of the 2020/2050

83 Reid, above n. 7.
84 Reid, ibid; see also Reid, above n. 79.
85 Reid, above n. 7, pp. 752–753.
86 Directive 2008/50/EC.

milestone targets).[87] Yet the 'outcome' orientation of this type of duty goes beyond asserting in law that something must be done in conventional, direct terms, to insist instead that a result or outcome must be attained even though a broad range of other actors not directly subject to the duty will have to do significant things if it is to be achieved. This type of scenario places demands on public authorities that differ from conventional duties that typically predominate in the context of UK law.[88]

Complexities surrounding the enforceability of the CCA duties have been flagged by legal scholars, notably Stallworthy[89] and Townsend.[90] The framework has drawn criticism for failing to incorporate explicit sanctions for the breach of its major duties,[91] in particular where the milestone targets for 2020 and 2050 are concerned.

Nevertheless, judicial review provides the UK courts with a facility to ensure that duties imposed by Parliament on public actors are appropriately abided by.[92] This means that the inappropriate exercise of public authority under the terms of the CCA can be judicially reviewed in the courts, including a failure on the part of the Secretary of State to achieve a CCA milestone target. A *prima facie* assumption that sanctions and remedies are unavailable where a breach of a CCA duty has occurred merely because they are not incorporated formally into the legislation is therefore incorrect, insofar as the mechanism of judicial review creates a channel for this in the courts.[93]

Here, the scholarship reveals an additional problem. Where the breach of a major substantive duty under the Act has unquestionably occurred, UK courts will probably award 'declaratory relief', meaning that there has been a breach of the particular legal obligation.[94] This raises the question of whether it would be possible to claim compensation for a breach of these substantive obligations under the CCA. In practice, it is very unlikely that individuals could claim compensation even where the court has declared a breach, for two main reasons: first, because the headline substantive duties are owed to the UK public in general rather than to specific individuals or sections of the public; and secondly, due to the difficulty in attributing specific losses arising as a consequence of the Secretary of State's breach of the duty to specific sections

87 Reid, above n. 7, p. 753.

88 Reid, above n. 7, p. 749.

89 M. Stallworthy, 'Legislating Against *Climate* Change: A UK Perspective on a Sisyphean Challenge' (2009) 72(3) *Modern Law Review* p. 412.

90 Townsend, above n. 2, p. 842.

91 McMaster, above n. 73.

92 See M. Elliott and R. Thomas, *Public Law*, OUP, Oxford, 2011, Part 4 ('Judicial Review') in M. Fordham (ed.), *Judicial Review Handbook*, 6th edition, Hart, Oxford, 2012.

93 See also Reid, above n. 7, p. 757.

94 A. McHarg, 'Climate Change Constitutionalism? Lessons from the United Kingdom' (2011) 2(4) *Climate Law* 469, p. 477.

of the public or individuals as a consequence of climate change. Yet, in terms of general principle, this latter circumstance is presumably how it should be: the purpose of judicial review here is to ensure that the UK Government is abiding by its climate change obligations, which are owed to all. It is not intended to facilitate a narrow 'cash-grab' for private individuals who may know how to work the legal system.

Furthermore, and for better or worse, the omission in the legislation of sanctions for breach of the substantive duties did not arise through thoughtlessness,[95] but rather reflects the overall legislative intention, where the regime has been constructed in a manner that prevents individuals from raising explicit causes of action in the courts that will open up streams to accrue damages. The milestone targets are aspirational goals that the UK Government is obligated to achieve, and it is binding on the Government to strive to do so. Challenges engaging the breach of *procedural* duties will likely be more successful in terms of concrete outcomes. If a reporting or consulting procedural duty has been ignored or breached, a court may likely order that the obligation is carried out. At a point in time where the Paris Agreement is placing a high importance on countries preparing and reporting on the Nationally Determined Contributions that they intend to achieve in order to mitigate climate change,[96] these sorts of safeguards could become increasingly significant. Nonetheless, in overall terms, Stallworthy neatly captures the general picture when he comments that 'the role of the courts is likely to be limited, and certainly not one that could realistically be expected to apply constraints on the major issues.'[97]

4.3. ACCOUNTABILITY

The issue of *accountability* has also been flagged up as a prominent concern in the literature. It has been established that if a public authority is doing all it

---

95 See UK Government, 'Taking Forward the UK Climate Change Bill: The Government Response to Pre-Legislative Scrutiny and Public Consultation', Cm 7225 (HM Government, 2007) at pp. 23 and 52–54. Note especially: 'We do not consider that other compliance mechanisms which have been proposed would, in reality, strengthen the framework introduced by the Bill … Furthermore, attempting to set out specific sanctions within the Bill itself carries a risk that whatever sanction was specified might be less stringent than one which could be prescribed by a court of law. The revised Bill therefore reflects our strongly-held view that the duties in the Bill are legally enforceable and that the threat of judicial review is an appropriate sanction to ensure the obligations in the Bill are adhered to.' Ibid., p. 23, paras 1.58–1.59.

96 See Paris Agreement, Article 4, paragraph 2.

97 M. Stallworthy, 'New Forms of Carbon Accounting: the Significance of a Climate Change Act for economic Activity in the UK' (2007) 331 *International Company & Commercial Law Review*, p. 340.

reasonably can to put a failure right, including where the public authority has not accomplished a target duty and is therefore in breach of it, the UK courts will be unlikely to interfere.[98] It has also been established that '[c]ourts will ... take general practicalities into account, including budgetary constraints, scarcity of necessary resources, the lack of a governmental actor's room to manoeuver due to the permitted political behaviour of other governmental institutions, and so on.'[99] This set of circumstances means that concerns arise around the extent to which blame and responsibility for failures to meet substantive duties under the CCA can be apportioned directly and actively to appropriate actors.

In essence, although the Secretary of State has a primary responsibility under the CCA to ensure that the milestone target reductions and other important substantive duties are achieved, if a failure to meet a given duty is substantially driven to some extent by the decisions of other governmental actors that are beyond the immediate control of the Secretary of State, the courts will make some allowance for this. This might occur, for instance, where the Treasury has applied budgetary constraints that negatively impact on financial supports for energy decarbonisation.[100] Carter has drawn out the position of the Treasury as 'arguably the most powerful institution within Whitehall', and has highlighted this power in the context of climate governance.[101] The act of merely placing a legal *duty* on the Secretary of State does not equate to radically displacing extant power away from powerful actors like the Treasury. In other words, although the Secretary of State is accountable for a breach of the primary substantive duties under the terms of the legislation, the legal duty placed on the Secretary of State is not equivalent to the power required to secure that duty in practice, and the courts will make allowance for this. An accountability deficit is seen to arise.

4.4. THE FUTURE FOR RESEARCH ON THE CCA: TOWARDS AN INTERDISCIPLINARY RESEARCH AGENDA

Thus far, this section has provided an evaluation of the legal research base in relation to the CCA. Given that the CCA is a complex, pioneering legislative regime, it is unsurprising that legal scholarship has been at the

98 C. Callaghan, 'What is a "Target Duty"?' (2002) 5(3) *Judicial Review*, pp. 185–186.

99 Muinzer, above n. 1, p. 27.

100 For example, Lockwood (writing in 2013) has emphasised that 'the Treasury ... retains decision making over taxation and subsidy, including the Levy Control Framework for climate policies paid for on energy bills'; M. Lockwood, 'The political sustainability of climate policy: The case of the UK Climate Change Act' (2013) 23(5) *Global Environmental Change* 1339, p. 1343.

101 Carter, above n. 6, p. 201.

forefront of understanding. It should be emphasised, however, that where a pervasive, economy-wide framework like the CCA is at issue, it is particularly inappropriate for members of the academic community to become overly entrenched within their narrow disciplines, as often occurs. Reaching out more broadly amounts to a substantial intellectual challenge for lawyers and non-lawyers alike, and may result in varying degrees of success, but nevertheless, the broad intention should be to place a meaningful emphasis on knowledge-sharing and exchange, geared always towards pressing on to the attainment of a greater cumulative interdisciplinary understanding.

In this context, it should be appreciated that much legal scholarship on the CCA is intellectually cognate with the social sciences.[102] As such, it can be linked to interesting and useful effect with work in the social sciences (and beyond). Space precludes substantial elaboration: the primary purpose here is to draw the general methodological point, rather than to elaborate on the literature. To take an example, the legal treatment of the issue of *accountability* has concluded that a latent 'accountability deficit is seen to arise' under the terms of the Act on certain grounds.[103] This insight can be usefully linked to the theme of systemic accountability that arises in the political sciences.[104]

In terms of the very limited pool of work engaging the CCA specifically in that area, the most developed treatment is perhaps the work of Bache et al. Their investigation of the CCA's top-down target drivers and multilevel and devolved systems of implementation, undertaken by political scientists with specialist skills in the application of multilevel governance theory, has produced interesting results.[105] Taking the CCA's carbon reduction targets and the attainment of associated transport-related carbon reduction objectives as the primary material of analysis, this work has suggested that a system characterised by 'fuzzy governance' structures is resulting in turn in a form of 'fuzzy accountability', with one consequence being 'the absence of a clear, explicit or integrated accountability system for the governance of transport or carbon emissions'.[106] The authors contend that this serves to feed into undermining the national decarbonisation drive in a complex systemic manner.[107] These sorts of insights can be usefully combined with the legal

102 In the UK, socio-legal studies in particular tend to be incorporated within the social sciences. See further G. Samuel, 'Is Law Really a Social Science? A View from Comparative Law' (2008) 67 *Cambridge Law Journal*, pp. 288–321.

103 Quoting from the discussion of *accountability*, above.

104 See further Part III ('Accountable Governance') of M. Bovens, R.E. Goodin and T. Schillemans (eds), *The Oxford handbook of Public Accountability*, OUP, Oxford, 2014.

105 I. Bache, I. Bartle, M. Flinders, and G. Marsden, 'Blame games and climate change: Accountability, multi-level governance and carbon management' (2015) 17(1) *The British Journal of Politics and International Relations*, pp. 64–88.

106 Bache et al., ibid., p. 67.

107 See above n. 105 generally, and in particular Section 3, 'Carbon Emissions Management and Transport Governance' (ibid., pp. 74–77).

insights on the 'accountability deficit' noted above. Doing so frames a more complete picture of the extent to which systemic governance regimes and legislative determinants can undermine an accountability continuum that might otherwise deceptively appear to be stable and robust.

These points flag up a positive way ahead for CCA research, insofar as they serve to emphasise that the scholarship on it can be enriched by efforts on the part of lawyers to reach across traditional intellectual disciplinary divides.[108] Additionally, however, and less optimistically, the foundations of the significant successes and contributions to knowledge reflected in the emergent body of work on the CCA are threatened and partially undermined by problems in the literature.

For example, some expert commentary is overly critical of the Act, such as Pielke's analysis of the CCA, which has been widely cited by others.[109] Written in 2009, it incorrectly concludes that the CCA's substantive targets are not realistically achievable. The targets are certainly attainable with an adequate level of commitment from the UK Government, and it was relatively unsurprising that the 2020 target was secured far in advance of then, during the Act's second carbon budget.[110] At any rate, the analysis misunderstands the 2020 milestone target, believing it to be 2022 (the date of the closure of the third carbon budget),[111] which, had that been the case, would have afforded even *more* time to achieve the reduction percentage. As to the 2050 target, the international consensus on this, most particularly in light of the Paris Agreement, is that it has been *too weak*.[112] Indeed, it has been noted above that at the time of writing the UK Government has legislated for a Net Zero target for 2050, adjusting the 80 per cent reduction figure up to 100 per cent, duly emphasising the achievability of the initial 80 per cent figure. The increased Net Zero figure itself is certainly not unachievable as it stands, if the UK Government and other key actors – notably the UK's devolved governments – display the will to see it through.

108 Interdisciplinarity has been crucial in developing a coherent *scientific* understanding of climate change and its projected impacts to date; see: S. Weart, 'Rise of Interdisciplinary Research on Climate' (2013) 110(1) *Proceedings of the National Aacademy of Science*, pp. 3657–3664. Lawyerly knowledge pertaining to the CCA (and to wider climate change law and policy issues) has an important role to play in going forward in contributing more broadly to interdisciplinary knowledge in the social sciences.

109 R.A. Pielke, 'The British Climate Change Act: A Critical Evaluation and Proposed Alternative Approach' (2009) 4(2) *Environmental Research Letters* 1.

110 See *2017 Provisional UK Greenhouse Gas Emissions Statistical Summary* (BEIS, March 2018).

111 Pielke, above n. 109, pp. 2 and 6.

112 In January 2019 the IPCC reported as follows: 'Estimates of the global emissions outcome of current nationally stated mitigation ambitions as submitted under the Paris Agreement would lead to global greenhouse gas emissions in 2030' indicative of '[p]athways' that 'would not limit global warming to 1.5°C, even if supplemented by very challenging increases … after 2030': *Global Warming of 1.5°C: Summary for Policymakers* (IPCC, 2019), p. 20.

Undue negativity about the framework of this sort would be of relatively little consequence if it stood alone, but it has been amplified substantially due to the manner in which it has been internalised relatively uncritically into the wider literature.[113] This points to the broader and perennial academic problem of the research community acting as a negative echo chamber.[114] Here, misunderstandings or unsupported arguments can enter in a relatively uncritical way into an emerging body of academic commentary, receive multiple citations, and become so embedded in the discourse that ongoing citations are rolled out exponentially across the field as it develops. As they enter the fabric of the scholarship, they can transmute into something that is cited as a matter of course without thoughtful critical judgement being applied.[115]

Moreover, flawed analyses of the CCA can generate distortion if they are read in concert with critiques that acknowledge the necessity of getting to grips with climate change to some extent but undermine pioneering CCA-style action by advocating a relaxation in current frameworks for various reasons. Those reasons tend to involve an assumption that the problem of climate change will be solved in the future by new technology (e.g., next-generation renewables), or/and that future market adjustments can resolve it.[116] Thus, Moselle and Moore state that:

> Current UK and EU policies favour renewable energy over other means of emissions reduction to an extent that is not justified by objective economic analysis. Moreover, the rigid 2020 targets lead to an excessive emphasis on rapid deployment of technologies rather than promoting long term innovation … [C]limate policy should therefore abandon the 2020 renewable energy target.[117]

We would argue that commentaries of this sort lack awareness of the key role of renewable energy as part of a range of measures to reduce emissions, and, from a more specifically legal perspective, of the now proven capacity of effective

---

113 Examples are too numerous to mention. The most recent incorporation of Pielke's work at the time of writing seems to be the (otherwise) excellent study M.A. Sait, U.E. Chigbu, I. Haniduddin and W.T. De Vires, 'Renewable Energy as an Underutilised Resource in Cities: Germany's "Energiewende" and Lessons for Post-Brexit Cities in the United Kingdom' (2019) 8(1) *Resources* 7.

114 This is the authors' expression.

115 i.e. so-called 'hat tipping', where prominent sources are cited out of respect for the author or from habit rather than because of the quality of the source: see for discussion of citation analysis, K. Campbell, D.W. Vick, A.D. Murray and G. Little, 'Journal Publishing, Journal Reputation and the United Kingdom's Research Assessment Exercise' (1999) 26(4) *Journal of Law and Society* 470, pp. 473–474.

116 This type of thinking is part of the thrust in, e.g., P. Lilley, '£300 Billion, The Cost of the Climate Change Act', Global Warming Policy Foundation, UK, 11 December 2016.

117 B. Moselle and S. Moore, *Climate Change Policy: Time for Plan B*, Policy Exchange, UK, 2011, p. 10.

legislative target-setting to focus minds and maintain a sense of urgency about tackling climate change. That is, they exemplify the sort of conservative thinking – and in some instances unhelpful complacency – that the UK Parliament intended the CCA and CCC to challenge directly. What is certainly the case, however, is that given the existential importance of reducing emissions, all future interdisciplinary research and academic debate on the CCA must be robust, rigorous and searching.

5. CONCLUDING REMARKS

Sections 2 and 3 of the discussion above have highlighted the novel, pioneering nature of the CCA. They have emphasised the importance of the CCA in one of the most crucial and urgent areas of governance in contemporary times, i.e. combating climate change. They have also offered an outline of its form, character, and central features. Section 4 has provided an evaluation of legal research on the CCA. It has addressed the general condition of the legal research, while at the same time seeking to provide a meaningful sense of the key issues and findings arising from it.

The discussion above has necessarily been a selective exercise. Emphasis has been put on the CCA's relationship to its international, supranational and substate setting, the complex implications of the framework's duties, the reach and role of the courts, and the perceived 'accountability deficit'. Other issues could have been addressed in this chapter to complete the picture. Those include the CCA's relationship to the UK's constitution and broader issues of constitutionality, as explored in detail by McHarg[118] and Muinzer.[119] Some initial efforts have also been made to contextualise the CCA in the wider setting of national climate legislation arising in other countries,[120] though this thread of scholarship is underdeveloped at present.

Significant comparative legal research has also arisen, as in the case of Taylor and Scanlen's treatment of the UK/New Zealand climate legislation experience,[121] although this strand of research is also underdeveloped at the present time. The CCA is also beginning to interact with conceptual characterisations of law in the UK, and within environmental law in particular.

---

118 McHarg, above n.94.

119 T. Muinzer, 'Is the Climate Change Act 2008 a Constitutional Statute?' (2018) 24(4) *European Public Law*, pp. 733–754.

120 See further E. Scotford and S. Minas, 'Probing the Hidden Depths of Climate Law: Analysing National Climate Change Legislation' (2018) 28(1) *Review of European, Comparative & International Environmental Law* 67.

121 P. Taylor and K. Scanlen, 'The UK Climate Change Act – An Act to Follow?' (2018) 14(3) *Policy Quarterly* 66.

This is perhaps most colourfully represented by the work of Professor Liz Fisher. Fisher draws on the thinking of Richard J. Lazarus, Michal Callon and others to depict certain aspects of environmental law as amounting to 'hot law';[122] she emphasises that UK climate law is engaging with an issue that has been construed as a 'super-wicked problem',[123] and classifies the climate change challenge as 'legally disruptive'.[124]

Both the existing legal research base and the new approaches of Professor Liz Fisher and others can be built upon and developed to enhance understanding of the CCA as a radical and crucial legislative regime to address climate change. The nature of the legal research on the CCA is such that there are significant opportunities for interdisciplinary collaboration, particularly with the social sciences. Problems in the research have also been flagged-up, including misinterpretation of the CCA, which have been internalised into the literature. If the research opportunities on the CCA are to be realised, therefore, legal and other scholars must guard against this, and exercise careful critical judgement as the field develops.

---

122 See generally E. Fisher, 'Environmental Law as "Hot" Law' (2013) 25(3) *Journal of Environmental Law*, pp. 347–358.

123 E. Fisher, E. Scotford and E. Barritt, 'The legally disruptive nature of climate change' (2017) 80.2 *The Modern Law Review*, pp. 173–201.

124 Ibid.

CHAPTER XXII

THE SWEDISH CLIMATE POLICY FRAMEWORK AND THE CLIMATE ACT

Kristina FORSBACKA

1. INTRODUCTION

As a general point of departure, Sweden wants to take a leading role in the global work to realise the ambitious targets in the Paris Agreement. The ambition is to be an international role model through the country's national climate work and by contributing to the financing of emissions reductions and adaptation measures in developing countries. The Government also finds it important to demonstrate that it is possible to combine a transformation to a low-carbon society with welfare and international competitiveness. Sweden has successfully implemented climate policies to mitigate greenhouse gas (GHG) emissions, such as carbon taxes on fossil fuel and strict energy efficiency standards in housing and incentives to increase renewable energy, while at the same time furthering economic growth.

In June 2017, the Swedish Parliament (*Riksdag*) adopted a 'Climate Policy Framework' which includes very ambitious climate targets, as well as a Climate Act.[1] The Climate Policy Framework is the most important climate reform in Swedish history, and a key component in fulfilling Sweden's obligations under the Paris Agreement.[2]

The Climate Policy Framework was prepared by the Cross-Party Committee on Environmental Objectives,[3] a committee consisting of representatives of

1 The background and reasoning for the Climate Policy Framework is explained in the preparatory works, Regeringens proposition 2016/17:146 Ett klimatpolitisk ramverk för Sverige (the Preparatory Works).

2 The Preparatory Works, p. 44 f.

3 This committee, including representative from all political parties at the time represented in the Parliament, was established by the Government in 2010 to achieve broad agreement as regards important environmental issues.

all political parties,[4] and was backed by a broad political majority. The British Climate Change Act from 2008 was an inspiration.

Adopting legislation, the Climate Act, which regulates a structured process for the Government's climate change work and defines climate targets, is new in Swedish politics, as there has been a long-standing tradition of regulating climate policy in Orientational Bills (*Swedish: inriktningsproposition*) adopted by Parliament.[5] The model with a Climate Policy Framework was chosen because climate policy shows many similarities with economic policy, where Sweden has introduced a Fiscal Policy Framework, similar to the Climate Policy Framework.[6] The framework consists of three parts: (i) a Climate Act; (ii) new, ambitious, interim and long-term climate targets; and (iii) a Climate Policy Council. The purpose of the Climate Act is to ensure that the climate policy is carried out in a long-term and continuous manner that grants stability to consumers and industry. Regulating parts of the climate policy in legislation clarifies the Government's responsibility in relation to its citizens, and describing the procedure of the Government's climate work ensures that the forms for the work become known and accessible to everyone.[7]

This chapter analyses the new legal framework established by the 2017 Climate Act in Sweden. It starts by providing a general background to national climate change policy (Section 2). Then, it reviews in a systematic manner the three main components of the Swedish Climate Policy Framework which are: the new ambitious long-term climate targets (Section 3), the Climate Act (Section 4), and the Climate Policy Council (Section 5). The chapter ends with some concluding remarks and observations on possible consequences of the Climate Act (Section 6).

2. GENERAL BACKGROUND

2.1. SWEDISH GREENHOUSE GAS EMISSIONS AND PRIORITY AREAS

Sweden has made considerable GHG emissions reductions, while at the same time managed decoupling emissions from economic growth. The GHG

---

4 With the exception of the Sweden Democrats which did not have representation in Parliament at that time.

5 Orientational Bills are bills adopted by Parliament – and thus binding until changed – that include the direction of future policies but are not legislative acts. Such bills have been commonly used when it comes to Swedish climate policy issues such as climate targets.

6 The Preparatory Works, p. 42.

7 The Preparatory Works, p. 44 f.

emissions have decreased by 25 per cent between 1990 and 2015,[8] and Sweden wants to continue to be a role model in this area.

The main sources of GHG emissions in Sweden are transport, industry and the agricultural sector.[9] In the European Union (EU), GHG emissions can mainly be divided into those that are part of the EU Emissions Trading Scheme (EU ETS) and those that are included in the EU Effort Sharing Regulation (ESR), also referred to as non-ETS sectors.[10] In Sweden, more than 80 per cent of the emissions from industry, as well as more than 90 per cent of the emissions from electricity and district heating production are included in the EU ETS. As Swedish energy production in large part consists of hydropower and nuclear,[11] the main challenge in Sweden is to reduce emissions in the transport sector, agriculture and energy-intensive industries.[12]

The new ambitious target by 2045 requires that all policy areas take a larger and more integrated responsibility for the climate policy. The framework shall work cross-sector, and the Climate Policy Council, an interdisciplinary expert body, shall make independent assessments of whether the actions within the various relevant policy areas proposed by the Government are in alignment with the climate targets.[13]

2.2. POLITICAL CONSENSUS ON CLIMATE POLICY PRIORITIES

Sweden has a long tradition of political agreements when it comes to questions of great and fundamental importance to society. It has been considered important to uphold this tradition also when it comes to climate change policy, which includes a societal transformation, which concerns issues of a profound character and great importance for the whole of society.

In 2010, the Swedish Government appointed a Cross-Party parliamentary Committee, with the task of proposing how the Swedish environmental quality objectives and generational goal were to be achieved. The Committee included

---

8 The Preparatory Works, p. 14 f.

9 The Preparatory Works, p. 14 f.

10 See Regulation (EU) 2018/842 of the European Parliament and of the Council of 30 May 2018 on binding annual greenhouse gas emission reductions by Member States from 2021 to 2030 contributing to climate action to meet commitments under the Paris Agreement and amending Regulation (EU) No 525/2013 (The ESR Regulation): https://eur-lex.europa.eu/legal-content/EN/TXT/PDF/?uri=CELEX:32018R0842&from=EN.

11 Hydropower and nuclear amounted to a total of 80 per cent of Swedish electricity production in 2017 (about 40 per cent each), see: https://www.energiforetagen.se/sa-fungerar-det/elsystemet/produktion/.

12 The Preparatory Works, p. 14 f.

13 The Preparatory Works, p. 41 f.

representatives from all political parties represented in the Swedish Parliament at the time. The work of the Cross-Party Committee was to be carried out in close cooperation with trade and industry, non-profit organizations, municipalities and governmental agencies. In 2014, the Government tasked the Cross-Party Committee with proposing a climate policy framework and a strategy for an overall long-term climate policy.[14] Key persons from environmental non-profit organizations, business organisations, science and public administration acted as experts to assist the committee.

According to the Paris Agreement, all countries need to raise their climate ambitions. All states, local governments, enterprises and the civil society need to act so that emissions decrease as required under the agreement.[15] One prerequisite for the new ambitious Swedish goals is that the rest of the world also acts so that the emissions are reduced in accordance with the Paris Agreement.[16] Sweden intends to take action, on the international level, within the EU and through its national climate policy in a manner that furthers such a development. The Swedish Government intends to follow the climate commitments made by other countries, and how these contribute to the global climate transformation, but also how these affect the competition situation of Swedish enterprises. It is also the intention of the Government to contribute to decreasing emissions on the global level through export of renewable energy and climate efficient products and services (technology transfer commitments), while at the same time strengthening the competitive edge of the Swedish enterprises (industrial policy objectives). The Swedish long-term climate goal also requires that the ambition in the EU ETS is increased.[17]

3. NEW CLIMATE TARGETS

In order for the world to achieve the ambitious targets set by the Paris Agreement, all countries need to increase their climate ambitions and undertake stricter targets. As a consequence, the first part of the Swedish Climate Policy Framework includes new stricter national climate targets. In terms of trajectory, the Swedish Climate Policy Framework includes a long-term target for 2045, and the interim targets for 2030 and 2040 in the ESR sector, including a target for the transportation sector.

The long-term target is included in the Climate Act, while interim targets are to be decided by the Government, or if there are special reasons,

14 The Preparatory Works, p. 7: https://www.government.se/495f60/contentassets/883ae8e123bc4e42aa8d59296ebe0478/the-swedish-climate-policy-framework.pdf.

15 The Preparatory Works, p. 27.

16 The Preparatory Works, p. 25 f. and p. 27.

17 The Preparatory Works, p. 28 f.

by Parliament.[18] In order to ensure a long-term climate policy across party lines and terms of office of Parliament, both the long-term target for 2045 as well as the interim targets for 2030 and 2040 have been be adopted by Parliament.[19] The following paragraphs describe the different climate targets set in Sweden.

3.1. A LONG-TERM ZERO NET EMISSIONS TARGET BY 2045

The Climate Policy Framework introduces an ambitious long-term target: by 2045, Sweden shall have zero net emissions of greenhouse gases into the atmosphere, and shall thereafter achieve negative emissions.[20]

Negative emissions mean that Sweden overall will help reduce the amount of GHG emissions into the atmosphere. That is, the amount of greenhouse gases emitted by Sweden shall be less than the amount of greenhouse gases reduced through the natural eco-cycle, or through climate projects pursued by Sweden abroad. The emissions from operations in Sweden shall be at least 85 per cent lower than in 1990. In order to reach the long-term target, carbon capture and storage (CCS) can be used, where no other reasonable alternatives are available.[21]

Based on current population forecasts, the new target would mean that annual emissions in Sweden would be less than one tonne per person in 2045.[22]

As explained above, the target also assumes that the rest of the world acts so that the emissions are reduced in accordance with the Paris Agreement, and that the EU adopts an increased ambition in the EU ETS. The Government intends to follow the climate commitments and climate measures taken by other countries, and how these contribute to the global climate transformation and affect the competition situation for Swedish corporations.[23]

3.2. INTERIM EMISSIONS TARGETS

The Climate Policy Framework also includes the following interim targets for 2030 and 2040:

- By 2030, emissions from domestic transport, excluding domestic aviation, shall be reduced by at least 70 per cent compared to 2010;

---

18 The Preparatory Works, p. 27 f. and p. 47.
19 The Preparatory Works, p. 28.
20 The Preparatory Works, p. 1 and p. 25.
21 The Preparatory Works, p. 27 f.
22 'The Swedish climate policy framework', Government Offices of Sweden, Ministry of the Environment and Energy: https://www.government.se/495f60/contentassets/883ae8e123bc4e42aa8d59296ebe0478/the-swedish-climate-policy-framework.pdf, p. 3.
23 The Preparatory Works, p. 25 f.

- By 2030, emissions in Sweden in the sectors covered by the EU ESR (greenhouse gas emissions outside the EU ETS) shall be at least 63 per cent lower than in 1990;
- By 2040, emissions in Sweden in the sectors that will be covered by the EU ESR shall be at least 75 per cent lower than in 1990.

As regards the targets to be met by 2030 and 2040, these can in part be achieved through supplementary measures, such as the increased uptake of carbon dioxide by forests, or investments in climate projects abroad. Such measures may be used to achieve a maximum of eight and two percentage points, respectively, of the emission reduction targets for 2030 and 2040. This means that by 2030 emissions from activities in Sweden should be at least 55 per cent lower than in 1990, and by 2040 at least 73 per cent lower than in 1990.[24]

The above targets reflect the international leadership role that Sweden intends to take, and demonstrate that Sweden itself will undertake to achieve emission reductions which by far exceed Sweden's required emission reductions under the coming EU ESR.

4. THE CLIMATE ACT

4.1. BACKGROUND TO THE CLIMATE ACT

According to the Climate Policy Framework, part of the Government's climate policy work shall be regulated in law. The reasoning for this is further explained in the Preparatory Works. According to Chapter 1 Section 2 in the Swedish Constitution (Swedish: *Regeringsformen*), the public authorities have an obligation to promote sustainable development, which leads to a good environment for present and future generations. The Government also refers to Sweden's obligations under the UN Framework Convention on Climate Change to reduce GHG emissions. Based on these undertakings, there is an obligation for the public authorities in Sweden to act in a manner that ensures that the climate system is not changed in a harmful manner, and to protect its citizens from dangerous changes in the climate system. The Government has a responsibility to ensure that the climate policy is carried out in accordance with these obligations.[25]

The introduction of a legal Act which describes how the Government's climate work shall be structured, means that the form of the climate work will

---

24 The Preparatory Works, p. 1 and p. 29 f.

25 The Preparatory Works, p. 43 f.

be accessible to everyone. The possibility to be informed of the legal regulations and understand how the work develops, and what measures need to be taken in the next step, increases. Legal regulation will also make it more difficult for the Government to act in a manner which would counteract, or not sufficiently promote, the possibility of reaching the national climate targets. A regulation in a Climate Act is, as opposed to a political agreement, legally binding and increases the possibility that future climate work can also be carried out in a long-term and continuous manner, while the work also becomes clearer and more transparent. By adopting the Climate Act, Parliament and Government also send an important signal to the citizens and industry, and to other states, that Sweden is committed to undertaking the climate work in a serious manner.[26] However, it can be noted that the Climate Act does not grant any rights to individuals, nor does it include enforcement provisions.

4.2. REGULATORY/COMPLIANCE APPROACH PURSUED BY THE CLIMATE ACT

The Swedish Climate Act entered into force in January 2018. The Act includes instructions to the Government and establishes that each successive Government has an obligation to pursue a climate policy based on the climate targets adopted by Parliament. The Climate Act contains generally kept provisions on how the Swedish Government shall plan and monitor its climate work. The Government shall provide reports on the progress of the work to achieve the targets set by Parliament.

The Climate Act establishes that the Government's climate policy shall be based on the climate targets set by Parliament. The Act also describes how the Government's work is to be carried out: the Government is required to present a *climate report* every year in the Budget Bill, and to draw up a *climate policy action plan* describing how the climate targets are to be achieved every four years. Climate policy targets and budget policy targets shall be carried out so that the respective targets interact.

The Climate Act regulates the procedure for the Government's work. It does not include policies such as subsidies, incentives and taxes that are adopted to *reach* the climate targets. These are to be set out in separate legislation, as has been done. Furthermore, the Act focuses on measures to mitigate future climate change, and does not include provisions on adaptation to existing climate change. This does not mean that adaptation is seen as unimportant, but rather that adaptation is considered to be more connected to water management and overall environmental protection. As the Act focuses on domestic measures,

26 The Preparatory Works, p. 44 f.

it does not include provision on capacity building and climate investments in developing countries. It can be noted that Sweden has taken an active role in financing climate investments in developing countries. The Swedish Government has supported projects under the Clean Development Mechanism and capacity-building projects in developing countries, and supported and contributed to World Bank Climate Funds. However, these measures are decided in the Budget Bill and carried out by the Government and its agencies, and not regulated in the Climate Act.

As in the UK Climate Change Act, the Swedish Climate Act does not include enforcement provisions, but leaves that to the system of parliamentary review and public accountability.[27] Parliament has an obligation to control the work of the Government, according to Chapter 13 in the Constitution. This control function is carried out by the Committee on the Constitution (*konstitutionsutskottet*), which shall review the Government's work. The Committee on the Constitution shall review the Ministers' service and their handling of governmental matters, and there is also a possibility for Parliament to file a motion of no confidence against a Minister.[28]

The Climate Act is a new and innovative piece of legislation, when compared to the Swedish legal tradition. As described above, Swedish climate policy has so far been regulated in Orientational Bills. The Council on Legislation, which reviews proposed legislation, expressed doubts whether the Act will fulfil the purpose expressed in the Preparatory Works, in its opinion on the draft Climate Act. The Council, *inter alia*, referred to the fact that the Act does not include enforcement provisions, nor any other specific legal effects, and that the provisions of the Climate Act are quite general in nature. However, in response to this, the Government pointed at Parliament's obligation to control the work of the Government described above and argued that introducing a legal Act adds to transparency and sends a strong signal to the citizens and industry that the Government takes climate issues seriously.[29]

An independent Climate Policy Council will review how well the Government's overall policy meets the climate targets. The work of the Climate Policy Council is not regulated in the Climate Act, but in a separate Ordinance issued by the Government, as further described in Section 5 below.

As the Swedish Climate Act is general in nature and not very extensive, it only includes five sections. Each section is reviewed individually in the next few paragraphs.

---

27 See the *Urgenda* case (Rechtbank Den Haag, case no. C/09/456689/HA ZA 13-1396), it seems like such legal review could take place even though there are no such specific legal regulations.

28 The Preparatory Works, p. 45 f.

29 The Preparatory Works, p. 45 f.

4.3. DETAILED ANALYSIS OF THE CLIMATE ACT PROVISIONS

The five sections of the Climate Act are organised around three main themes: content and purpose; long-term targets; and planning, monitoring and reporting.

4.3.1. The Content and Purpose of the Climate Act

4.3.1.1. Section 1

The first section of the Climate Act describes the content and purpose of the Act, and clarifies that the Act is addressing the Government's obligations as regards its climate work. Furthermore, it establishes that the Government as a collective – and ultimately the Prime Minister – is responsible for compliance with the Act.

4.3.1.2. Section 2

The second section includes provisions describing the purpose of the climate work to be carried out by the Government, and how the work shall be carried out.

The Government shall implement a climate policy with the aim to prevent dangerous interference with the climate system. According to the Preparatory Works, the starting points of the policy provisions are (i) the UN Convention on Climate Change, and (ii) Chapter 1 Section 2 in the Constitution, which includes the obligation on public authorities to promote sustainable development, which will ensure a good environment for present and future generations. In order to reach the climate targets, a radical adaptation of society will be required.[30]

Furthermore, it is stated that the climate policy work of the Government shall also contribute to the protection of ecosystems and of present and future generations against harmful effects of climate change. The Government shall focus on reducing carbon dioxide and other greenhouse gas emissions, and maintaining and restoring environmental functions that mitigate climate change and its harmful effects. This includes the use of natural functions in the ecosystem.

Importantly, it is also established in this section that the climate work shall be *based on scientific research* and on relevant technical, social, economic and environmental considerations.[31]

---

30 The Preparatory Works, p. 51 f.

31 The Preparatory Works, p. 51 f.

4.3.2. *A Long-Term Target*

4.3.2.1. Section 3

In order to create the prerequisites for a long-term and stable climate policy, the Climate Act establishes that the Government's climate policy shall be based on the long-term, time-bound emission target adopted by Parliament (after proposal by the Government). In addition to this long-term target established by Parliament (see section 3.2 above), the Government shall set any other emission reduction targets needed to achieve the long-term target.

Importantly, it is established in this section that the climate policy shall be implemented in such a manner that enables climate *targets and budgetary targets* to *interact*. It is emphasised in the Preparatory Works that it is a prerequisite for a sustainable climate policy that conflicting goals between budget policy and climate policy are avoided.[32]

According to the Preparatory Works, the Government shall decide in each specific case whether these targets shall be decided by Government or submitted to Parliament for decision.[33] The long-term target of net zero emissions by 2045 has been adopted by Parliament, as have the interim emissions targets in the ESR for 2030 and 2040, as described above. The Swedish interim target for 2020, a 40 per cent reduction, has also been decided by Parliament.[34]

It should be noted, however, that the Swedish emissions reduction targets depend on other countries and the EU taking additional action.

4.3.3. *Planning, Monitoring and Reporting*

Planning, monitoring and reporting to Parliament on a regular basis can contribute to clarity, continuity and long-termism of the climate policy. The Climate Policy Framework is therefore complemented with a planning and monitoring system, which takes the emission targets adopted by Parliament as its starting point.[35]

Based on this reasoning, it is established that a yearly climate report, as well as a climate action plan for each Government's term of office, shall be submitted to Parliament. The climate plan shall include a description of the development of the emissions in the ESR sector, the EU ETS and of total emissions. In order to achieve the ambitious climate targets set out, an efficient, credible and long-term policy is required. Regular action plans can contribute to creating

32 The Preparatory Works, p. 37.
33 The Preparatory Works, p. 47.
34 The Preparatory Works, p. 27.
35 The Preparatory Works, p. 39 f.

continuity and predictability. The purpose of the action plan, is, according to the Preparatory Works, to show how the Government's collected policy, within all relevant cost areas and over all, contributes to reaching the interim targets and the long-term emission target. The basic parts of this system are regulated in the Climate Act.[36]

4.3.3.1. Section 4

Section 4 in the Climate Act states that the Government each year shall include a *climate report* to Parliament in the Budget Bill. The climate report shall contain information on how the results of the policy carried out have impacted on the possibility of reaching the agreed climate targets, and assess whether there is need of additional measures and, if so, when and how such additional measures shall be decided. The purpose of the provision is continuity in the ongoing climate work. As the information is made public in this manner, the need for and importance of taking measures within all policy areas is made visible, while at the same time Parliament and the public are given access to information on how the climate work is carried out on a regular basis.[37]

4.3.3.2. Section 5

Section 5 establishes that the Government, every fourth year (at the start of its term of office) shall draw up a *climate policy action plan*, which shall be presented to Parliament the year following a general election. The action plan shall include Sweden's commitments within the EU framework and internationally, historical greenhouse gas emissions data, including the most recent emissions inventory, and emissions reduction projections. Furthermore, the Government shall assess the effect of the policies decided, and other measures, and report on the contribution these have had in reaching the climate targets. The Government shall report the measures planned and the impact of these. All measures which can have an impact on reaching the national and global targets shall be reported on. This includes also measures taken or planned in relation to Sweden's international engagements, such as aid, technology transfer and international investments. The Government shall also report on how certain decided or planned measures other than those with the direct aim to reduce emissions or further the protection of the environment, can affect the ability to reach the climate targets. Finally, any additional measures, in addition to measures already decided or planned, which can be required in the long term in order to reach the national and global targets shall be described.[38]

---

36 The Preparatory Works, p. 39 f.

37 The Preparatory Works, p. 53.

38 The Preparatory Works, p. 53.

As the climate policy action plans must be worked out every four years, it will be the task of every Government to draw up or revise an existing action plan for how the climate targets will be achieved. The action plan shall be submitted to Parliament the year after a general election, and thus ensure that the work to reach the interim targets and the long-term emission target is integrated in the Government's other policy areas from start.[39]

5. THE CLIMATE POLICY COUNCIL

The third pillar of the Climate Policy Framework is the establishment of a Climate Policy Council. The Climate Policy Council is an interdisciplinary expert body, which shall support the Government by providing an independent assessment of how the overall policy presented by the Government is compatible with the climate targets. The Council shall evaluate whether the direction of various policy areas will increase or reduce the likelihood of achieving the climate targets. It can be noted that, though the Climate Policy Council must be independent from the Government, it is established under the Government, and not the Parliament. Comparison is made to the model regarding the existing Swedish Financial Policy Council, which was introduced in 2007, and which has a similar role to review the Government's financial policy.[40]

The work of the Climate Policy Council is not regulated in the Climate Act, but in a Government Ordinance with Instructions to the Climate Policy Council (*Förordning (2017:1268) med instruction för Klimatpolitiska rådet*) (the Ordinance). The Council is led by a committee, which shall consist of a chairman, a deputy chairman and no more than six other delegates. The delegates are appointed by the Government after proposal from the Climate Policy Council. The Council shall make proposals that ensure the committee includes delegates with high scientific competence within climate, climate policy, political economics, social science and behavioural science and that there is an even allocation of competence.[41]

The Swedish Climate Policy Council shall:

- Evaluate if the present policy in different policy areas contributes or counteracts the climate targets;
- Review the effects of both existing and planned policies from a broad societal perspective;
- Identify policy areas where additional measures need to be taken if the climate goals are to be achieved.

---

39 The Preparatory Works, p. 40.
40 The Preparatory Works, p. 41 f.
41 Section 11 in the Ordinance.

Besides evaluating the Government's policy, the Climate Policy Council is also tasked with evaluating the analytical methods and models which are the basis for the policy, as well as contributing to the debate regarding climate policy.[42]

The Climate Policy Council must by the end of March each year report to the Government, including an assessment of the climate work and mitigation of the emissions achieved, how the Government's policy complies with the climate targets, any other analyses and assessments that the Council has made. The Council must also, within three months from the Government's submission of its climate policy action plan, submit a report with an assessment of the Government's plan.[43]

The Climate Policy Council has its office at the Swedish Research Council for Sustainable Development, Formas.

The Climate Policy Council submitted its first report to the Government in March 2019, following the Government's first report in November 2018. In its report, the Council concluded that the mitigation of GHG emissions reductions achieved is too slow, and that the reductions have slowed down when they need to accelerate to between five and eight per cent per year. Additional policy measures are needed if the targets are to be achieved. The Council pointed out transport (especially domestic transport) and the EU ETS as critical sectors. The Council noted that Swedish GHG emissions have decreased quite significantly from an international perspective, but assesses that the current climate policy is not strict enough to reach the targets set.

6. CONCLUDING REMARKS

Though the content may seem to be quite general, the signal that the legislator sends through the adoption of a Climate Act is an important step.

As the policy instruments that will realise the mitigation action required must be adopted in other legislation, additional legislative measures are crucial. The intention is that the Swedish climate policy will work cross-sector and involve all actors. However, through the Climate Act, the Government has a tool and a regulated process for carrying out its climate work, which includes monitoring and reporting on the climate work. The Government also has the assistance of the Climate Policy Council, the interdisciplinary expert body, which includes delegates with broad expert competence. The Climate Act is an important step towards a transparent long-term stable climate policy, but further measures are required. The results achieved thorough the Act will to a large extent depend on the measures taken by the Government and the Climate Policy Council.

---

42 Section 2 in the Ordinance: https://www.klimatpolitiskaradet.se/summary-in-english/.

43 Section 5 in the Ordinance.

Furthermore, though the Climate Act mainly regulates the Government's climate policy work and does not grant rights to individuals, reference is made to the Act in various different contexts. One example is the licensing process for the enlargement of the Preem oil refinery in Lysekil on the Swedish West coast. Preem applied for an environmental permit to increase its refinery operations in the plant, which is included in the EU ETS. As the Swedish long-term climate target includes also emissions from industries in the EU ETS, a significant increase from the operations of Preem refinery would affect the ability to achieve the Swedish climate targets. The Swedish Environmental Protection Agency (EPA) notified the Government under Chapter 17 Sections 1 and 3 the Environmental Code, that the Preem application for an increased permit for its refinery operations is a matter of such great importance that the permissibility should be decided by Government, and not by the courts. In its notification the EPA referred also the adoption of a Swedish Climate Act. Preem argues that its plant in Lysekil is one of the world's most efficient refineries, and that the production increase applied for would make it possible to produce additional, more environmentally friendly products at the plant. Production increase in another plant instead of the Lysekil plant would, according to Preem, result in increased global GHG emissions. In August 2019, the Government decided that it will decide the permit matter. The matter will now be prepared by the Land and Environment Court of Appeal, which will then submit the matter to the Government for decision. The decision of the Government is expected in 2020.

CHAPTER XXIII

CLIMATE LITIGATION, CLIMATE ACT AND CLIMATE AGREEMENT IN THE NETHERLANDS

Gerrit VAN DER VEEN and Kars DE GRAAF

1. INTRODUCTION

In 2015, a Dutch court case attracted worldwide media attention. For the first time, a court of law had ordered a State to adopt measures to tackle climate change. The Hague District Court ruled that the State must take more action to reduce greenhouse gas emissions in the Netherlands. It ordered the State to ensure that Dutch greenhouse gas emissions in the year 2020 would be at least 25 per cent lower than the 1990 levels. The Urgenda Foundation had requested the court for a ruling.[1]

Late 2018, the Hague Court of Appeal confirmed the District Court's judgment, albeit on different grounds.[2] In the meantime, all branches of Dutch government have been actively involved in climate mitigation efforts. In addition to the judiciary, the legislative and administrative branches within the Dutch system of separation of powers (*Trias Politica*) are now more intensively involved than in 2015.

Dutch Parliament continued working towards the introduction of a Climate Act. The Act of 2 July 2019, setting up a framework for the development of policy aimed at the irreversible and phased reduction of Dutch greenhouse gas emissions in order to reduce global warming and climate change (*Klimaatwet*,

1 The Hague District Court, 24-06-2015, ECLI:NL:RBDHA:2015:7145, AB 2015/336 note Ch.W. Backes, O&A 2015/58 note T.G. Oztürk and G.A. van der Veen, ECLI:NL:RBDHA:2015:7196 (English translation).

2 The Hague Court of Appeal 09-10-2018, ECLI:NL:GHDHA:2018:2591, AB 2018/417 note Ch.W. Backes and G.A. van der Veen, O&A 2018/51 note T.G. Oztürk and G.A. van der Veen, ECLI:NL:GHDHA:2018:2610 (English translation).

or Climate Act), entered into force on 1 September 2019, with the exception of Section 7, which will enter into force on 1 January 2020.

A further development was that the administration, in close cooperation with industry and societal parties, worked towards an agreement on voluntary measures to reduce the emissions of greenhouse gases in the Netherlands (*Klimaatakkoord*, or Climate Agreement) and succeeded in June 2019. The Climate Agreement is an agreement between a multitude of Dutch stakeholders with the aim of devising measures to reduce global warming as a result of greenhouse gas emissions, allowing the Netherlands to meet the European and international targets for 2030 and 2050. Covering 600 measures to reduce greenhouse gas emissions, the Agreement is one of the instruments used to execute the order contained in the judgments of the District Court and the Court of Appeal, although it also refers to the year 2020. The Climate Agreement also complements the Climate Act in the sense that the Climate Act itself does not incorporate any measures to reduce the emission of greenhouse gases but does impose upon the government the obligation to draft a document incorporating such measures for the purpose of achieving the climate targets laid down in the Act.

In this chapter, we will examine the three trends outlined above. A pivotal question we will address in the process is the extent to which climate targets are enforceable in a court of law. The two lower courts were clear on this question, but the *Urgenda* action has not finished yet. An appeal from the 2018 ruling has been brought by the Dutch State to the Dutch Supreme Court, which aimed to hand down its decision before the end of 2019 and has done so at the brink of publishing this chapter. Besides, do the Climate Act and the Climate Agreement offer citizens and civic organisations sufficient arguments to bring legal action to enforce specific international, European and national targets?

2. THE *URGENDA* CASE

The *Urgenda* case revolves around at least two questions. The first question is whether there are any legal grounds that can result in a court ruling ordering the State to adopt (drastic) climate measures. The second question is whether a court of law, when delivering a judgment against the State in this case, would effectively take the place of the legislator.

2.1. DISTRICT COURT JUDGMENT

The District Court started its reasoning by acknowledging that, based on the State's current climate policy, the Netherlands will achieve a reduction of at the most 17 per cent in 2020, which is below the norm of 25 to 40 per cent for developed countries deemed necessary in climate science and international climate policy, such as Report IPCC 4 (see below).

Urgenda based its assertion that the State was acting unlawfully towards it on Book 6 Section 162 of the Dutch Civil Code (DCC) and Articles 2 and 8 of the European Convention on Human Rights (ECHR). Urgenda argued that the State did not meet its duty of care to its citizens and therefore acted unlawfully towards them. The District Court ruled that Urgenda did not meet the requirements to invoke Articles 2 and 8 ECHR, but it accepted the Civil Code as a valid basis for State liability. According to the District Court, the State must do more to avert the imminent danger caused by climate change, also in view of its duty of care to protect and improve the living environment as laid down in the Dutch Constitution. The State's duty of care is further influenced by the international obligations the State has taken on vis-à-vis other States by adopting international treaties. The State is responsible for effectively controlling the Dutch emission levels. Moreover, the costs of the measures ordered by the Court are not unacceptably high. Therefore, the State should not hide behind the argument that the solution to the global climate problem does not depend solely on Dutch efforts. Any reduction of emissions contributes to the prevention of dangerous climate change and as a developed country, the Netherlands should take the lead in this, according to the District Court. The District Court held that the judiciary does not enter the domain of politics when ordering that the Dutch State must make sure Dutch greenhouse gas emissions are reduced by at least 25 per cent in 2020 compared to 1990.[3] The Court considered that its duty is to provide legal protection, also in cases against the government, whilst respecting the government's scope for policymaking. For these reasons, the Court exercised appropriate restraint and therefore limited the reduction order to 25 per cent: the lowest limit of the 25–40 per cent norm that follows from climate science, most notably the IPCC's Fourth Assessment Report 2007.

2.2. COURT OF APPEAL RULING

As stated before, the Court of Appeal upheld the judgment.[4] This time, though, Urgenda's reliance on Articles 2 and 8 ECHR was successful. In short, the

---

3 See Eleanor Stein and Alex Geert Castermans, 'Case Comment – Urgenda v. the State of the Netherlands: The "Reflex Effect" – Climate Change, Human Rights, and the Expanding Definitions of the Duty of Care' (2017) 13(2) *McGill Journal of Sustainable Development Law*, pp. 305–324; Surapratim Roy and Edwin Woerdman, 'Situating Urgenda v the Netherlands within comparative climate change litigation' (2016) 34(2) *Journal of Energy and Natural Resources Law*, pp. 165–189; K.J. de Graaf and J.H. Jans, 'The Urgenda Decision: Netherlands Liable for Role in Causing Dangerous Climate Change' (2015) 27(3) *Journal of Environmental Law*, pp. 517–527.

4 See Suryapratim Roy, 'Urgenda II and its Discontents' (2019) 13(2) *Carbon & Climate Law Review*, pp. 1–12; Laura Burgers and Tim Staal, 'Climate action as positive human rights

Court of Appeal ruled that the State has a positive obligation to protect the lives of citizens within its jurisdiction under Article 2 ECHR, while Article 8 ECHR creates the obligation to protect the right to home and private life. This obligation applies to all activities, public and non-public, which could endanger the rights protected in these articles, and certainly in the face of industrial activities which are dangerous by their very nature. If the State knows of the existence of a real and imminent threat, it must take precautionary measures to prevent infringement of the right to life to the extent possible. According to the Court of Appeal, this required the Court to assess the asserted (imminent) dangerous climate change. Having heard the arguments, the Court believed that it is appropriate to consider dangerous climate change a real threat, resulting in the serious risk that the current generation of citizens will be confronted with loss of life and/or a disruption of family life. Thus, it follows from Articles 2 and 8 ECHR that the State has a duty to protect against this real threat.

The Court of Appeal ruled that the reduction in emissions of at least 25 per cent by end 2020, as ordered by the District Court, was in line with the State's positive obligation under Articles 2 and 8 ECHR to put in place an appropriate legislative and administrative framework to provide effective deterrence against threats to the right to life. The Court of Appeal also addressed the argument that it would enter the domain of politics. The State had argued that limiting the cumulated volume of Dutch greenhouse gas emissions, as ordered by the District Court, could only be achieved by adopting new legislation and regulations, either by Parliament or lower governmental bodies. This would mean that from a substantive point of view the District Court's order constituted an obligation to create legislation and that the District Court was not in the position to impose such an order on the State. In fact, such order would be at odds with Dutch ideas on the separation of powers. However, according to the Court of Appeal the District Court correctly considered that Urgenda's claim was not intended to create legislation, either by Parliament or lower government bodies, and that the State retained complete freedom to determine how it would comply with the order. Even if it were correct to hold that compliance with the order can only be achieved through creating legislation by Parliament or lower governmental bodies, the order in no way prescribed the content of such legislation. For this reason alone, the order was not an 'order to create legislation', according to the Court. The Court of Appeal added that it is obliged to apply provisions with direct effect of treaties to which the Netherlands is party, including Articles 2 and 8 ECHR. After all, such provisions form part of the Dutch jurisdiction and, according to the Dutch Constitution, even take precedence over Dutch laws where the latter deviate.

---

obligation: The appeals judgment in Urgenda v the Netherlands' in R.A. Wessel, W. Werner, B. Boutin (eds.), *Netherlands Yearbook of International Law 2018*, T.M.C. Asser Press, 2019.

2.3. EXPECTATIONS ABOUT THE UPCOMING SUPREME COURT DECISION

Both the District Court judgment and the Court of Appeal ruling have captured considerable attention, though also drawing a great deal of criticism. When writing this chapter, our wait was for the Supreme Court's decision. While we waited, we pondered the question whether the Supreme Court will hand down a decision of its own or essentially pass off the case to the highest court concerned with the interpretation of the human rights laid down in the ECHR: the European Court of Human Rights (ECtHR). The Supreme Court, after all, recently gained the authority to request the ECtHR to give advisory opinions on questions of principle relating to the interpretation or application of the rights and freedoms defined in the ECHR. This option is laid down in Protocol no. 16 to the ECHR,[5] which entered into force in the Netherlands on 19 January 2019.[6]

The Supreme Court did not pass the case on so that the ECtHR did not have to focus on the interpretation of Articles 2 and 8 ECHR. The Supreme Court decided to review the case and therefore it had to contemplate those articles itself.

This was not a first. Two prominent decisions, handed down on 19 July 2019, serve as notable examples. In the first decision, the Supreme Court addressed the action brought against the State by relatives of the victims of the Srebrenica massacre on the basis that in 1995 the State acted wrongfully in the period before and after the fall of the town of Srebrenica, when Dutch UN peacekeepers in the region did too little to stop the advance of the Bosnian Serbs and protect the Bosnian Muslim population. The action was based in part on Articles 2 and 3 ECHR. In relation to Article 2, the Supreme Court considered that a State has a positive obligation to take appropriate action in order to protect the right to life of citizens within its jurisdiction. This positive obligation is to be interpreted

> in a way which does not impose an impossible or disproportionate burden on the authorities, bearing in mind the difficulties involved in policing modern societies, the unpredictability of human conduct and the operational choices which must be made in terms of priorities and resources.[7]

---

5 Protocol No. 16 to the Convention for the Protection of Human Rights and Fundamental Freedoms, Explanatory Report.

6 Staatsblad 2019/8.

7 Referring to ECtHR 20 December 2011, Application no. 18299/03 (*Finogenov e.a. v Russia*), §209.

If the argument is made that a State failed to fulfil its positive obligation arising from Article 2 ECHR, the ECtHR holds that the question that needs to be reviewed is whether

> the authorities knew or ought to have known at the time of the existence of a real and immediate risk to the life of an identified individual or individuals from the criminal acts of a third party and that they failed to take measures within the scope of their powers which, judged reasonably, might have been expected to avoid that risk.[8]

As comes across from the decision, the ECtHR emphasises that the question whether a State took all such measures it could reasonably be expected to take needs to be answered by considering all relevant circumstances of the case. For this reason, the Supreme Court will examine whether the military command at the time knew or, judged reasonably, ought to have known of the existence of a real risk that the rights afforded to the Bosnian refugees under Article 2 (and Article 3) ECHR would be violated and, if so, whether the peacekeepers failed to take measures which, judged reasonably and with due observance of all circumstances, might have been expected to avoid that risk.[9]

The second decision handed down on 19 July 2019 concerned the extraction of natural gas in the Dutch province of Groningen. About 15 to 20 years ago, the area started experiencing earth tremors caused by the gas extraction since 1963. The damage from these tremors was reason enough for the Dutch authorities to scale down and, eventually, they plan to stop extraction altogether. The Supreme Court was asked to review whether the gas extraction could be deemed unlawful. It held that the State is liable in tort within the meaning of Section 6:162 DCC if it knows or ought to know (i) that the Groningen gas extraction presents a danger in view of the seismic movement, (ii) that there is a real risk of such danger materialising, and (iii) that the materialisation of such danger can result in severe or widespread damage, yet nonetheless fails to take such timely and appropriate measures as the State, in view of the circumstances, might reasonably be expected to take in order to avoid that damage. The Supreme Court made reference to articles from the ECHR, including Articles 2 and 8. According to the Supreme Court, the inevitable conclusion was that the State knows or ought to have known, at least from 1 January 2005 onwards, (i) the dangers associated with the Groningen gas extraction, (ii) the real risk of these dangers materialising,

---

8 Referring to ECtHR 28 October 1998, Application no. 23452/94 (*Osman v United Kingdom*), §116; ECtHR 28 March 2000, Application no. 22492/93 (*Kiliç v Turkey*), §63.

9 Supreme Court, 19 July 2019, ECLI:NL:HR:2019:1223.

and (iii) the circumstance that materialisation of these dangers can lead to serious or widespread damage.

In both decisions, the Supreme Court attached much weight to the State's awareness of direct, serious dangers to human life. We had doubts as to whether the Supreme Court would be willing to take the step of classifying long-term dangers such as the risk of (dangerous) climate change as a risk within the meaning of Articles 2 and/or 8 ECHR.

The Supreme Court considered the case itself and arrived at the verdict that Articles 2 and/or 8 ECHR were violated. Next, it reviewed the question whether the Court of Appeal entered the domain that is the legislator's prerogative. After all, if the order is to be considered an order to create legislation, it might constitute an inroad on the judicial tasks of the judiciary.[10] This applies likewise to the violation of human rights referred to by the Supreme Court.[11] It is the – tentative – view of these authors that several options are available to the State to comply with the judicial orders, but that it nonetheless tends to be necessary to introduce legislation to force society to reduce emissions. In the appellate proceedings, the State had failed to make a sufficiently plausible argument that the only useful action would be to create legislation. In that case, the choice to create legislation after all amounts to nothing but the legislator's own choice rather than an obligation on the part of the State as a consequence of the order contained in the ruling. It follows that this interpretation does not imply the judiciary's infringement on the legislator's domain. The decision of the Supreme Court will gain at least as much attention as the two decisions before did.[12]

3. THE DUTCH CLIMATE ACT

The Dutch legislator has now chimed in as well. After a long run-up and several readings, the Dutch Climate Act came finally into operation on 1 September 2019. The Climate Act sets targets and provides for a number of instruments to ensure that these targets can be achieved. An important question in light of the above would be to what extent the targets set by the legislator can be enforced, in a court of law, for instance.

---

10 Supreme Court, 21 March 2003, ECLI:NL:HR:2003: AE8462 39, with commentary from Ch.W. Backes, NJ 2003/691, with commentary from T. Koopmans (*Waterpakt*).

11 Supreme Court, 09 April 2010, ECLI:NL:HR:2010: BK4549 190, with commentary from F.J. van Ommeren, NJ 2010/388, with commentary from E.A. Alkema (*Staat en SGP v Clara Wichmann c.s.*).

12 Supreme Court, 20 December 2019, ECLI:NL:HR:2019:2006.

3.1. TARGETS OF THE CLIMATE ACT

Section 2 of the Climate Act sets out the main objective of the Act, which is to reduce greenhouse gas emission levels by 95 per cent by 2050 (compared with 1990). The Act provides 'a framework for developing policy aimed at an irreversible and gradual reduction of Dutch greenhouse gas emissions' by the aforesaid 95 per cent.

It also sets two other targets. Pursuant to Section 2(2), the relevant ministers aim to reduce the greenhouse gas emissions by 49 per cent by 2030 and to make energy production carbon-neutral and fully reliant on renewables by 2050. The purpose of these two targets is to make it easier to achieve the overarching objective. Strikingly, though, the 2030 target is nothing more than a goal to strive for; in fact, it is the only intermediate target in the Act. The ambition to have Dutch energy production fully carbon-neutral by 2050 is not beyond reproach either. For example, there is no obligation for Dutch energy consumption to be carbon-neutral. In addition, the Act allows for Carbon Capture and Storage by power plants, meaning that CO_2 is produced after all.

In summary, the Act establishes one key binding objective: the 95 per cent emissions reduction by 2050. The other two aims are mere targets.

3.2. INSTRUMENTS PROVIDED BY THE CLIMATE ACT

Section 3 of the Act obliges the government to formulate, for the first time in 2019 and then every five years, a climate plan setting out the policy aimed at achieving the climate targets for the following 10 years. Section 3(2) lists some of the required elements of these climate plans. They include the measures to be taken in order to achieve the objectives of Section 2, the projected share of renewables, the projected primary energy consumption savings, the measures to be taken to stimulate the share of renewables and primary energy consumption savings, an analysis of the most recent scientific insights into climate change reduction, and a number of analyses of a different nature.

Pursuant to Section 4, the first climate plan is due to be adopted in 2019, after which it will be reviewed at least once every five years.[13] Progress reports are scheduled to be delivered every two years after adoption and subsequent reviews. If so warranted by the reports in view of the objectives of the Act, measures will be taken. The first climate plan relates to the 2021–2030 period.

The climate plan offers an important opportunity to frame the European and international obligations the Dutch State has to comply with. When drafting the

---

13 A draft climate plan on the basis of the Climate Act has been published online (www.internetconsultatie.nl/klimaatplan) on 24 August 2019.

climate plan, the legislator sought to align with the substance and procedures of the integrated National Energy and Climate Plan (NECP), which all EU Member States are required to prepare pursuant to EU Regulation on the Governance of the Energy Union.[14] Each Member State's NECP must set out action plans implementing the Energy Union's energy and climate objectives. NECPs have time horizons of 10 years and may be updated after five years. Member States are required to submit progress reports every two years, which may give rise to policy adjustments, nationally and EU-wide. The first draft NECP relates to the 2021–2030 period, offering a glance towards 2040. The NECP cycle dovetails with the ambition cycle of the Paris Agreement, the signatories to which agreed to raise their ambition levels – also known as Nationally Determined Contributions, or NDCs – every five years. Translated to the Dutch situation, the climate plan will help define the terms of the NECP and the NDCs. The better part of the Climate Plan is likely to incorporate the agreements made as part of the Climate Agreement (Section 4).

The Act also provides for a climate and energy outlook. Once a year, the PBL Netherlands Environmental Assessment Agency (*Planbureau voor de Leefomgeving*) will present the responsible minister with a climate and energy outlook. A scientific report, this document charts the consequences of the climate policy conducted in the previous year. For that year, the outlook maps at least the greenhouse gas emissions, including a sector-by-sector overview, as well as the developments and measures impacting the emissions. The *Planbureau voor de Leefomgeving* is an autonomous research agency advising the Dutch government. Essentially, the idea is for this agency to map the past, but it is not entirely clear whether they are also expected to provide forward-looking analyses. It is likely that 'the consequences of the climate policy conducted in the previous year' include a calculation of the effects of said policy for a subsequent period and, more particularly, an assessment as to whether this policy moves us closer to or in fact away from achieving the objectives. The minister is obliged to present the outlook to Parliament in a policy document. This document will provide an overall picture of the realisation of the climate policy as set out in the climate plan, represent the key aspects of this realisation broken down by ministry, represent the consequences of each ministry's budget for climate policy, as well as the financial consequences for households, companies and government bodies resulting from significant climate policy developments that are not in line with the climate plan. The purpose of the climate policy document and the climate and energy outlook is to enable Parliament to check the executive's implementation of its climate policy and demand changes to it if necessary.

---

14 See Regulation (EU) 2018/1999 of the European Parliament and of the Council of 11 December 2018 on the Governance of the Energy Union and Climate Action.

3.3. ENFORCEABILITY OF THE CLIMATE ACT

It is obvious that the legislator does not want the Climate Act to be enforceable in a court of law. This is illustrated by a quote from a 22 November 2018 memorandum to the Lower House of Parliament:

> The difference between the 2050 objective and the 2030 target is relevant in that it determines the way in which Parliament can compel the government to adhere to the targets. Neither target constitutes an obligation that can be enforced in a court of law. The texts of the bill and the explanatory notes are so abundantly clear that the persons introducing the bill regard the odds of a court ruling differently to be low. This does not alter the fact that courts have their own responsibility to judge on the scope and substance of acts and treaties.[15]

A similar text can be found in the Memorandum of Amendment of 27 June 2018:

> The target will be implemented according to the advice provided by the Council of State, as a policy objective with the aim of reducing legal liability. This stresses the policy's aim of being a political mandate for the government rather than a limit value which can be enforced in a court of law.[16]

These two passages demonstrate that the legislator had the express aim of keeping the courts out of the picture. It follows that the Climate Act is a purely political document. The explanatory memorandum thus explains that the hard binding target provides a clear signal to industry on the one hand but will not be legally enforceable in a court of law on the other. In other words, the target is meant to be binding on government, while accountability must be discussed in the political arena only, not in court. That leaves the legally relevant fact that according to the explanatory documents the Act does not preclude such legal actions as *Urgenda*. The Climate Act, it follows, leaves intact the option to bring legal action, in the sense that it does not include any provision ruling them out. Apart from that, the Climate Act establishes a policy framework, no more, no less. It is impossible to argue, therefore, that the legislator has drafted a watertight text regulating the reduction of greenhouse gas emissions and that the court would 'consequently' enter the legislator's domain if – in the wake of the Hague District Court and Court of Appeal – it ordered the State to take measures.

Then again, it is not difficult to imagine the State referring to the Climate Act in a future action involving climate issues and invoking the *legislative and administrative framework* it introduced for the very purpose of tackling climate change and eliminating threats to human life. As a result, it might be that

15 Lower House, session year 2018–2019, 34 534, no. 13, p. 2.
16 Lower House, session year 2017–2018, 34 534, no. 10, p. 7.

the options to hold the State liable are slightly more limited by the introduction of the Climate Act after all.

4. THE CLIMATE AGREEMENT

The Climate Agreement aims to commit the Dutch State and a multitude of interest groups to climate objectives. It makes concrete the measures necessary to achieve one of the targets of the Climate Act. That target is the objective from Section 2 of the Climate Act: reducing the country's greenhouse gas emissions by 2030 by 49 per cent in comparison with 1990.

This being an agreement, there needs to be *consensus ad idem*, which has been reached. The negotiations were conducted at five so-called 'sector tables', representing the following five sectors: Industry, Electricity, Mobility, Built Environment and Agriculture. Each sector discussed possible measures and delivered a statement on how their sector would achieve the number of megatonnes of greenhouse gases emissions reduction necessary for that sector by 2030 in order to reach the joint 49 per cent reduction target. The measures presented and their consequences for greenhouse gas emissions are indicative. Consequently, the parties at the table only reached agreement on the basis of indicative figures.

The Climate Agreement provides for an immense number of – proposed – measures to be taken by the five sectors. Industry, for example, proposes the introduction of a CO_2 tax for large companies. Large companies that are subject to the EU Emissions Trading System (EU ETS) will be charged with a CO_2 tax from 2021 if they emit CO_2 in excess of the 2030 emission reduction goal. Furthermore, a limitation of carbon capture and storage (CCS) subsidies is anticipated. CCS subsidies will therefore be reduced to a maximum of 7.2 megatonnes of CO_2 and will be subject to strict requirements. In addition, the energy tax on natural gas will go up.

To further illustrate the scope of the agreements, we will provide here a sample of agreements that might affect urban and regional planning. The spatial impact of proposed measures from the Climate Agreement, as far as the classical spatial planning is concerned, will be enshrined in the environmental and spatial planning policy. Nonetheless, the developments within the Agriculture and Land Use sector – the green sector, which tends to fall outside the purview of urban and regional planning in the classical sense – require attention. When it comes to claiming space, Agriculture and Land Use and other 'Built Environment' themes are fierce competitors. The Climate Agreement also provides:

> The parties have agreed as follows: The different, increasing and partly conflicting claims for green space arising from the climate and broader sustainability agenda are classified in the National Environmental Strategy (*Nationale Omgevingsvisie*, or NOVI)

> under the priority: Future-proof development of rural areas. Closer consideration of such claims and spatial planning will be integrated into regional and local area processes, including the RESes. As part of the NOVI Monitor, the Planbureau voor de Leefomgeving will issue periodic reports on the safeguarding of the national interests and priorities and monitor progress of the area-specific approach. The trend thus diagnosed may cause parties to confer on the implementation of certain – new – activities and instruments in order to safeguard collective and public interests.[17]

The message that comes across from the Climate Agreement is that the objectives agreed upon need to be turned into other instruments, subject to consultation and perhaps parliamentary approval. It cannot be stressed enough that the Climate Agreement is an initial setting to frame policy for the purpose of implementing other legal instruments, which may have mandatory effect. They need not be so, but the possibility is expressly referenced. For example, the Climate Agreement provides for the dairy and feed sectors to make agreements on optimising feed in order to reduce methane emissions, one such agreement being to improve the feed conversion by developing feed that reduces methane emissions. It is noted in the text of the agreement that for any wish to enforce collective measures a consideration must be made about the appropriateness of a covenant or whether in fact declaring agreements to be universally applicable may be a better option.[18]

The Climate Agreement is silent on its own enforceability. It states that the details and implementation of the agreement will be entrusted to the participating parties, including central government, to the extent possible. In this way, the parties themselves will bear primary responsibility for the effective implementation of the Climate Agreement. Sector-specific implementing committees will be set up under the supervision of the relevant ministers. The Minister of Economic Affairs and Climate Policy will set up an overarching progress committee.

The idea, it follows, is for the implementation of the agreements to remain in the hands of the participating parties, who will bear responsibility for the effective execution of the Climate Agreement, with each sector being responsible for executing their own specific set of agreements.[19] It is clear from the text of the Climate Agreement itself that it is but a first step, with many aspects still requiring consultation among the parties involved. If necessary, the government will wield a 'big stick' in the form of legislation. Neither the Climate Agreement nor the many measures announced can be enforced in law *per se*.

---

[17] Climate Agreement, pp. 126–127. 'RESes' stands for Regional Energy Strategies.

[18] Climate Agreement, p. 130.

[19] Climate Agreement, p. 14.

5. CONCLUSION

Ever since the Hague District Court handed down its landmark *Urgenda* judgment in 2015, all elements of the Dutch *trias politica* have upped their involvement with mitigating climate change. Although the Dutch government repeatedly expressed its intention to comply with the judgment, it still lodged an appeal. On 9 October 2018, the Hague Court of Appeal upheld the District Court's judgment, although it advanced other grounds for doing so. The Supreme Court confirmed the judgment of The Hague Court of Appeal on 20 December 2019. Not just for reasons of principle, but also because as late as August 2019 the government admitted that it has taken insufficient action to achieve the targets set in the court orders. Measures still need to be taken to ensure that the Dutch emissions of CO_2 are reduced by 9 Megatonnes more before 2021. There is, consequently, a relevant material reason for the parties to continue the case. Although the legislative and executive powers have also chimed in when it comes to climate change mitigation measures, the only actually enforceable measures have thus far been imposed by the judiciary. It is unlikely that this situation will change before long. While the Climate Act has set reduction targets for 2030 and 2050, it is clear from the explanatory notes to the Act that these targets are not enforceable in law. The same applies to the measures proposed in the Climate Agreement. These are the result of consultations with interest groupings and still need to be fleshed out. It is quite possible, though as yet uncertain, that part of these measures will precipitate into legislation or otherwise prove mandatory. Be that as it may, the Climate Act and the Climate Agreement demonstrate, on the one hand, that climate change is now at the centre of the political arena and of the debate in society and, on the other, that there is still a long way to go and that legal enforceability of reduction targets is anything but a done deal.

Lightning Source UK Ltd.
Milton Keynes UK
UKHW050209030621
384393UK00037B/477

9 781780 689500